International Trade in East Asia

NBER–East Asia Seminar on Economics
Volume 14

National Bureau of Economic Research
Tokyo Center for Economic Research
Chung-Hua Institution for Economic Research and
 Academia Sinica
Korea Development Institute
Hong Kong University of Science and Technology
Productivity Commission, Australia

International Trade in East Asia

Edited by **Takatoshi Ito and Andrew K. Rose**

The University of Chicago Press

Chicago and London

TAKATOSHI ITO is professor at the Research Center for Advanced Science and Technology, University of Tokyo, and a research associate of the NBER. ANDREW K. ROSE is the Bernard T. Rocca Jr. Professor of International Trade at the Haas School of Business, University of California, Berkeley, director of its Clausen Center for International Business and Policy, and a research associate of the NBER.

The University of Chicago Press, Chicago 60637
The University of Chicago Press, Ltd., London
© 2005 by the National Bureau of Economic Research
All rights reserved. Published 2005
Printed in the United States of America
14 13 12 11 10 09 08 07 06 05   1 2 3 4 5
ISBN: 0-226-37896-9 (cloth)

Library of Congress Cataloging-in-Publication Data

NBER–East Asia Seminar on Economics (14th : 2003 : Taipei, Taiwan)
    International trade in East Asia / edited by Takatoshi Ito and
Andrew K. Rose.
        p.   cm. — (NBER–East Asia seminar on economics ; v. 14)
    "This volume contains edited versions of papers at the NBER's East
Asia Seminar on Economics 14th annual conference, held in Taipei,
Taiwan, on September 5–7, 2003"—Ackn.
    Includes bibliographical references and index.
    ISBN 0-226-37896-9 (cloth : alk. paper)
    1. East Asia—Commerce—Congresses. 2. East Asia—Commer-
cial policy—Congresses. 3. Technological innovations—Economic
aspects—East Asia—Congresses. 4. Technology transfer—Eco-
nomic aspects—East Asia. 5. Investments, Foreign—East Asia—
Congresses. 6. Trade blocs—East Asia—Congresses. 7. Protectionism—East Asia—Congresses. 8. International trade—Congresses.
I. Ito, Takatoshi, 1950– II. Rose, Andrew, 1959– III. Title.
IV. NBER–East Asia seminar on economics (Series) ; v. 14.

HF3820.5 .A46N34 2003
382′.095—dc22
                                                              2004063696

Relation of the Directors to the
Work and Publications of the
National Bureau of Economic Research

1. The object of the NBER is to ascertain and present to the economics profession, and to the public more generally, important economic facts and their interpretation in a scientific manner without policy recommendations. The Board of Directors is charged with the responsibility of ensuring that the work of the NBER is carried on in strict conformity with this object.

2. The President shall establish an internal review process to ensure that book manuscripts proposed for publication DO NOT contain policy recommendations. This shall apply both to the proceedings of conferences and to manuscripts by a single author or by one or more co-authors but shall not apply to authors of comments at NBER conferences who are not NBER affiliates.

3. No book manuscript reporting research shall be published by the NBER until the President has sent to each member of the Board a notice that a manuscript is recommended for publication and that in the President's opinion it is suitable for publication in accordance with the above principles of the NBER. Such notification will include a table of contents and an abstract or summary of the manuscript's content, a list of contributors if applicable, and a response form for use by Directors who desire a copy of the manuscript for review. Each manuscript shall contain a summary drawing attention to the nature and treatment of the problem studied and the main conclusions reached.

4. No volume shall be published until forty-five days have elapsed from the above notification of intention to publish it. During this period a copy shall be sent to any Director requesting it, and if any Director objects to publication on the grounds that the manuscript contains policy recommendations, the objection will be presented to the author(s) or editor(s). In case of dispute, all members of the Board shall be notified, and the President shall appoint an ad hoc committee of the Board to decide the matter; thirty days additional shall be granted for this purpose.

5. The President shall present annually to the Board a report describing the internal manuscript review process, any objections made by Directors before publication or by anyone after publication, any disputes about such matters, and how they were handled.

6. Publications of the NBER issued for informational purposes concerning the work of the Bureau, or issued to inform the public of the activities at the Bureau, including but not limited to the NBER Digest and Reporter, shall be consistent with the object stated in paragraph 1. They shall contain a specific disclaimer noting that they have not passed through the review procedures required in this resolution. The Executive Committee of the Board is charged with the review of all such publications from time to time.

7. NBER working papers and manuscripts distributed on the Bureau's web site are not deemed to be publications for the purpose of this resolution, but they shall be consistent with the object stated in paragraph 1. Working papers shall contain a specific disclaimer noting that they have not passed through the review procedures required in this resolution. The NBER's web site shall contain a similar disclaimer. The President shall establish an internal review process to ensure that the working papers and the web site do not contain policy recommendations, and shall report annually to the Board on this process and any concerns raised in connection with it.

8. Unless otherwise determined by the Board or exempted by the terms of paragraphs 6 and 7, a copy of this resolution shall be printed in each NBER publication as described in paragraph 2 above.

Contents

Acknowledgments

This volume contains edited versions of papers presented at the fourteenth annual conference of the NBER's East Asia Seminar on Economics, held in Taipei, Taiwan, on September 5–7, 2003. The meeting was originally planned for June 2003, but was delayed because of the Severe Acute Respiratory Syndrome (SARS) scare.

The East Asia Seminar on Economics (EASE) series has been organized by the National Bureau of Economic Research (NBER) in Cambridge, MA, with the Tokyo Center for Economic Research (TCER); the Korea Development Institute (KDI) in Seoul; the Chung-Hua Institution for Economic Research (CIER) in Taipei; the Hong Kong University of Science and Technology (HKUST); and the Productivity Commission, Australia.

We are indebted to members of the program committee who organized the conference. The Chung-Hua Institution for Economic Research (CIER) was the local host. Participants were all grateful to the local organizing members at CIER, led by Dr. Tain-jy Chen and Dr. Shin-Horng Chen, for their superb hospitality during the conference. The NBER provided logistical support. We are greatly indebted to CIER and NBER, not only for managing the conference with great skill, but also for handling the sudden change in the conference schedule because of SARS.

Introduction

Takatoshi Ito and Andrew K. Rose

This volume contains papers from the fourteenth annual NBER–East Asia Seminar on Economics (EASE-14), held in Taipei, China on September 5–7, 2003 (after a delay of almost three months due to the SARS epidemic during the winter and spring of 2002–2003). The local sponsors were the Chung-Hua Institution for Economic Research and Academia Sinica.

The fourteenth annual NBER–East Asia Seminar on Economics was concerned with the topic of international trade, one of the most prominent fields of economics, which has attracted scholars since at least the time of Adam Smith and David Ricardo. This topic is of special concern to East Asian countries for a few reasons. A number of countries achieved high rates of economic growth since World War II, at least in part due to their export performances. This includes Japan in the 1950s and 1960s, the newly industrialized economies (NIEs) in the 1970s and 1980s, and other Southeast Asian countries in the 1980s and 1990s. All these countries have benefited from a global trend toward trade liberalization. Some of the NIEs and Southeast Asian countries accelerated their growth by accepting foreign direct investment. The high economic growth rates sometimes caused trade tensions. Often exporters (Japan and Korea in the past, China more recently) have been targeted by advanced economies for dumping or some other violations of fair trading practices, though some of the charges have been disputed by exporters. Before the World Trade Organization

Takatoshi Ito is a professor at the Research Center for Advanced Science and Technology, University of Tokyo, and a research associate of the National Bureau of Economic Research. Andrew K. Rose is the Bernard T. Rocca Jr. Professor of International Trade at the Haas School of Business, University of California-Berkeley, director of its Clausen Center for International Business and Policy, and a research associate of the National Bureau of Economic Research.

(WTO) was created, disputes were often settled bilaterally with import quotas or export restraints. These disputes are now typically taken to the recently created WTO dispute settlement mechanism.

In the 1990s, there have been an increasing number of regional trade agreements in the world. The North American Free Trade Agreement (NAFTA) has been quite prominent, but the Southern Common Market (MERCOSUR) and the European Community/European Union (EC/EU) have also prompted much debate, especially concerning the consistency between these regional agreements and the WTO. The sixth annual East Asia Seminar on Economics, "Regionalism versus Multilateral Trade Arrangements," in 1997 dealt with many of these issues. Until recently, the Asian region has been slow to adopt regional trading arrangements. If any, Asians tended to favor open regionalism in that a most-favored-nation clause was activated so that any regional concessions were also applicable to others. However, in the last few years, great interest in regional trade arrangement has been observed in Asia. The ASEAN Free Trade Agreement (AFTA) is making progress in eliminating tariffs among ten Southeast Asian countries. Japan has concluded an economic partnership agreement (a free trade agreement plus) with Singapore and is now negotiating with Korea, the Philippines, and Thailand. China has entered negotiations with Association of Southeast Asian Nations (ASEAN) for a free trade agreement. The Asian countries appear to have entered a new stage of their trade relationship among themselves and between them and the rest of the world.

The participants of EASE-14 were particularly interested in empirical aspects of international trade of relevance to East Asia. Topics of interest included the existence of regional trading blocks, strategies for improving productivity and facilitating technological change through trade, barriers to international trade, and the determinants of international integration.

International trade is by its very nature a general equilibrium phenomenon. For instance, production patterns are both important determinants of trade patterns and are also importantly determined by trade. Naturally enough, a number of the papers in the volume are concerned with either the determinants of trade patterns (such as productivity or R&D) or their consequences (e.g., employment). Again, the nature of man-made trade barriers is an important cause of trade flows, but protectionism is, in turn, importantly affected by trade patterns. Accordingly, a number of the papers are thus concerned with either the effects or causes of protectionism (or both); these can be either regional or multilateral and either conventional (e.g., the Multifiber Agreement [MFA] or antidumping procedures) or unusual (e.g., border delays).

The feedback between the causes and consequents of international trade means that it is not easy to group papers together into easily identifiable clusters or, rather, that there are many alternative ways to think about how the pieces of EASE-14 fit together. But certainly one major theme of EASE-14 was the relationship between productivity and trade. In "Physical and Human Capital Deepening and New Trade Patterns in Japan," Keiko Ito and Kyoji Fukao seek to explain the rising capital-labor ratios experienced in Japan during the last couple of decades (a phenomenon common to a number of Organization for Economic Cooperation and Development [OECD] countries). As has long been recognized, a primary suspect for trend changes in factor intensities is growing international openness, as trade naturally leads to specialization in industries of comparative advantage as dictated by factor abundance. Does a growing international division of labor explain changing Japanese factor intensities? No. Ito and Fukao use a massive disaggregated empirical data set to document the fact that Japanese trade (especially with China) has changed the factor content of net exports of Japanese labor. This naturally leads one to suspect that Japanese firms outsourcing production to China to take advantage of abundant cheap Chinese labor are the primary culprits. Nevertheless, it turns out that the changes take place across all industries, while the trend differences between industries are relatively small. Thus the within-industry changes swamp the differences between sectors. The mystery remains, though Ito and Fukao have provided a service to the profession by ruling out trade as an important determinant of trending Japanese factor intensities.

The Ito and Fukao work is implicitly based on the fundamental importance of factor proportions in driving trade patterns, an idea with a long and honorable heritage in the field stemming back at least to the work of Heckscher and Ohlin. An even older approach stretching back to Ricardo emphasizes the role of labor productivity. Of late, researchers have stopped taking productivity as given and have started to focus on the determinants of technological productivity to ask simple questions like "What drives exports?" More particularly, what are the forces that drive firms and industries to be able to sell not only at home but also abroad? Are exporter firms that have been proven in a "trial by fire" domestically then able to compete successfully abroad through some sort of Darwinian process? Or does exporting lead a firm to acquire new skills and knowledge, which then enables them to be more productive at home and abroad? Chin Hee Hahn uses a disaggregated Korean data set to answer this fundamental question and finds evidence for both lines of causality; exporting improves productivity, while it is also true that more productive firms tend to export.

In "International R&D Deployment and Locational Advantage: A Case Study of Taiwan," Meng-chun Liu and Shin-Horng Chen focus on another key determinant of export success, namely research and development. This can be thought of as another way to go inside the black box of productivity to understand the determinants of technological productivity. Multinationals can perform R&D in a variety of different locales. The choice of

R&D location can have important implications for the local economy yet remains an issue that is underresearched. Liu and Chen seem to fill that void by studying how R&D decisions by multinationals are made using a unique data set on corporate R&D in Taiwan. They find a large local bias toward R&D activities that are export oriented and are able to characterize the reasons why multinationals choose to disperse their R&D activities to foreign affiliates.

A different take on the effects of foreign investment is provided by Tain-Jy Chen and Ying-Hua Ku, who are interested in the implications for domestic employment rather than the importance of multinational activity for trade and production. In "The Effects of Overseas Investment on Domestic Employment," they focus on the Taiwanese manufacturing industry. Because there are both income and substitution effects possible, it is not clear ex ante what the effects of foreign investment will be for domestic labor. It turns out, in fact, to be heterogeneous, typically being positive for labor but differing across occupations.

While there are many natural determinants of trade patterns (such as factor abundance, labor productivity, proximity, comparative advantage, etc.), man-made "artificial" trade barriers are also important. Among the most controversial policy issue of late are preferential trading agreements, typically enacted by regional groupings of countries. It has long been recognized that these regional arrangements can lead both to (welfare-enhancing) trade creation as well as (harmful) trade diversion, and there is every reason to believe that there might be analogous effects on international investment flows. Philippa Dee and Jyothi Gali investigate these matters in "The Trade and Investment Effects of Preferential Trading Arrangements." They use a massive bilateral data set involving trade and investment flows between many pairs of countries and controls for a host of exogenous determinants of international activity, including geographical proximity and the size of the economies (the so-called gravity regression). Their verdict is negative net trade creation by preferential trade agreements, and their work leads us to reflect on the value of further regional integration.

The relationship between integration and trade is explored further in "The Formation of International Production and Distribution Networks in East Asia." In this paper, Mitsuyo Ando and Fukunari Kimura exploit a disaggregated data set of the activities of Japanese firms to explore international networks of production and distribution. East Asia is unusually integrated in terms of production, with high levels of trade in intermediates. In addition, integration in the region has experienced an enormous change with the reemergence of China, which plays an increasingly important role. Ando and Kimura are able to quantify a number of trends from their Japanese data set and are able to tease out a rich tapestry of details concerning firm size, industrial differences, the use of affiliates and local firms, and the role of multinationals.

Shujiro Urata and Kozo Kiyota are interested in similar questions but focus more precisely on formal East Asian trade arrangements. Rather than use a gravity model with its absence of relative prices, they employ a different methodological framework. In particular, they use a computational general equilibrium model with a number of sectors and countries (the Global Trade Analysis Project model). They find similar results in that the effects of regional arrangements are positive for members but can adversely affect outsiders *even though the actual effects on trade patterns may be small in practice.*

Most papers in EASE-14 concentrated on the traditional economic determinants of trade patterns—underlying sources of comparative advantage, whether natural or artificial, such as protectionism. An atypical set of trade determinants that is of considerable interest is financial crises, such as the one that rocked East Asia in late 1997. In "The Effects of Financial Crises on International Trade," Zihui Ma and Leonard K. Cheng compare the roles of banking and currency crises on exports and imports. They use a traditional gravity model of bilateral trade flows and find relatively strong results, especially for the role of currency crises in export stimulation.

The WTO came into existence in 1995, supplanting its predecessor the General Agreement on Tariffs and Trade (GATT) as the premier international organization in charge of policing and liberalizing international trade. One of the most visible new parts of the WTO is the dispute settlement system, a mechanism for quickly allowing the judicial resolution of disputes involving international trade practices. In his paper "WTO Dispute Settlements in East Asia" Dukgeun Ahn analyzes the incidence of disputes by country and industry and notes the striking international differences in the use of the system, with Korea and Thailand being prominent users. He concludes with a noteworthy plea for a better alignment between private-sector interests and access to the system.

One of the most important types of protectionism in practice currently is antidumping (AD) policy. In "The Growing Problem of Antidumping Protection," Thomas Prusa shows that AD policy is growing quickly, primarily because new users of the legislation are filing at much faster rates than traditional users. Industries that are losing comparative advantage use AD policy, but there are a large number of other users as well; countries that have experienced large exchange rate and other macroeconomic shocks also employ it disproportionately. Prusa provides a fine summary and urges both researchers and policymakers to pay more attention to this growing but subtle protectionism.

While the most egregious protectionism is concentrated in agriculture, the textiles industry has long received particularly striking protection under the MFA. In "Tight Clothing: How the MFA Affects Asian Apparel Exports," Carolyn L. Evans and James Harrigan engage in a fascinating study of the MFA, with a particular emphasis on apparel imports into the United States. Above and beyond analyzing the effects of quotas and tariffs, they find that East Asia exporters have suffered a natural loss in comparative advantage to producers in Mexico and the Caribbean as fashion patterns speed up. That is, as fashions begin to change more rapidly, timeliness plays an increasingly important role in production, and production naturally shifts to importers in greater proximity.

Another interesting but unconventional type of protectionism is analyzed by Edgar Cudmore and John Whalley. In "Border Delays and Trade Liberalization," they analyze the effects of government-induced border delays on trade. In developing countries (especially poor and/or corrupt ones), customs clearance delays are widespread and extremely costly. The resulting queuing costs can be considerable and may be exacerbated if queuing rises because of, for example, tariff liberalization. In a partial equilibrium sense, bribes can alleviate border delays and improve welfare. They show that the magnitude of these costs and effects can be large through an illustration of Russian trade data.

1
Physical and Human Capital Deepening and New Trade Patterns in Japan

Keiko Ito and Kyoji Fukao

1.1 Introduction

Until the beginning of the 1990s, Japan accomplished comparatively high economic growth through an exceptionally rapid accumulation of physical and human capital. Table 1.1 compares growth accounting results for the U.S. economy (Jorgenson, Ho, and Stiroh 2002) with those for the Japanese economy (Fukao, Inui, Kawai, and Miyagawa 2004). We can see that, compared with the United States, Japan's economic growth until 1990 was relatively more dependent on labor quality growth and increases in physical capital per capita. However, as is well known, high economic growth based on rapid capital accumulation is not sustainable in the long run because of the diminishing rate of return to physical and human capital.

Evidence suggests that Japan is caught in this trap of diminishing rates of return. Figure 1.1 shows that as the physical capital-output ratio increased over the past three decades in Japan, the rate of return to physical capital steadily declined. Comparing South Korea and Japan with other Organization for Economic Cooperation and Development (OECD) economies, Pyo and Nam (1999) showed that the two countries both enjoyed a more rapid rise in their capital-output ratios but also suffered a faster decline in the rate of return to capital. Looking at human capital, Katz and

Keiko Ito is a lecturer of economics at Senshu University. Kyoji Fukao is a professor in the Institute of Economic Research, Hitotsubashi University, and a fellow of the Research Institute of Economy, Trade and Industry (RIETI).

The authors would like to thank the editors of this volume, the discussants, Chin Hee Hahn and Ji Chou, participants of the fourteenth annual NBER–East Asia Seminar on Economics, and two anonymous referees for their helpful comments. The authors are also grateful to Yoshimasa Yoshiike and Tangjun Yuan for undertaking meticulous data calculations.

Table 1.1 Sources of economic growth: U.S.–Japan comparison (annual rate, %)

	Real GDP growth (a)	Man-hour growth (b)	Labor productivity (GDP/man-hour) growth (c) = (a) − (b)	TFP growth (d) = (c) − (e) − (f)	Contribution of labor quality growth (e)	Contribution of capital services/man-hour growth		
						Subtotal (f) = (g) + (h)	Contribution of IT capital (g)	Contribution of non-IT capital (h)
A. The result of growth accounting for the U.S. economy: 1973–2000[a]								
1973–95	2.78	1.44	1.33	0.26	0.27	0.80	0.37	0.43
1995–2000	4.07	1.99	2.07	0.62	0.21	1.24	0.87	0.37
B. The result of growth accounting for the Japanese economy: 1973–98[b]								
1973–83	3.56	1.53	2.03	−0.30	0.65	1.68	0.16	1.52
1983–91	3.94	1.79	2.15	0.40	0.46	1.29	0.37	0.92
1991–98	1.25	−0.08	1.34	0.03	0.21	1.10	0.33	0.76
1995–98							0.52	0.63

[a] Jorgenson et al. (2002).

[b] Fukao et al. (2004), table 6.2.

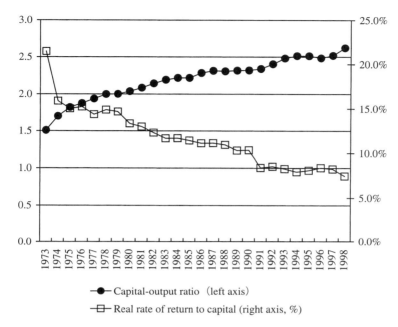

Fig. 1.1   Japan's capital-output ratio and rate of return to capital: 1973–1998
Source: JIP database.
Note: The numerator of the rate of return to capital is the surplus of the national accounts deflated by the gross domestic product (GDP) deflator.

Revenga (1989) found that while educational earning differentials expanded drastically in the United States in the 1980s, the college wage premium in Japan increased only slightly. As Genda (1998) showed, the underlying reason is that the employment of skilled workers, such as older male college graduates, expanded rapidly in Japan, resulting in an excess supply of skilled workers relative to the number of available management positions that contributed to the stagnation of earnings for older college graduates. Probably partly as a result of this decline in the rates of return, the accumulation of physical and human capital has slowed down over the past decade (table 1.1).[1]

We should note that according to standard trade theory, rapid growth based on capital accumulation is sustainable if the economy gradually specializes in physical and human capital intensive products. Under such a specialization process, the factor price equalization mechanism will work to offset the effect of diminishing rates of return to physical and human capital.

1. Godo (2001) found that the speed of catch-up of Japan's average schooling years to the U.S. level slowed down during the 1980s because of the decline in the Japan-U.S. ratio in average schooling years for tertiary education.

For Japan, the 1990s were an age of "globalization" marked by a deepening of the international division of labor, especially with other East Asian countries: not only did international trade and direct investment flourish, there has also been a marked change in the commodity composition of both imports and exports, and East Asia has overtaken North America as the most important origin and destination of Japan's trade. Trade theory suggests that this deepening of the international division of labor would lead Japan to further specialize in physical and human capital–intensive products and to outsource unskilled labor–intensive products to other East Asian countries, and these changes in trade patterns should affect the ratio of wages to the rental prices of capital and the ratio of skilled labor wages to unskilled labor wages. The purpose of this paper is to examine this deepening of the international division of labor since the 1980s and to evaluate how much of the diminishing rate-of-return effect was cancelled out by the international division of labor.

Several recent studies, such as Feenstra and Hanson (1996b, 1999, 2001), Kimura (2001), and Fukao, Ishido, and Ito (2003), have shown that the fragmentation of the production process and vertical intraindustry trade (i.e., intraindustry trade where goods are differentiated by quality) between developed and developing economies may have boosted the vertical division of labor within industries. This type of international division of labor would cause a deepening of the physical and human capital within each industry in developed economies. However, as the resulting capital deepening will occur within each industry, we cannot correctly analyze this type of division of labor by using interindustry trade data. Consequently, we study the international division of labor by looking at both interindustry trade and intraindustry trade.

The remainder of the paper is organized as follows. In section 1.2, we examine physical and human capital deepening in Japan. In section 1.3, we take a broad look at Japan's interindustry trade and factor contents in order to measure to what extent Japan's capital deepening is offset by international trade. In section 1.4, after providing an overview of the changes in Japan's intraindustry trade and vertical division of labor, we conduct econometric analyses to investigate the determinants of the changes in factor intensities using industry-level data. Section 1.5 presents our conclusions.

1.2   Physical and Human Capital Deepening in the Japanese Economy

In this section, we look at the trends of physical and human capital deepening in Japan and examine the macroeconomic change in the capital-labor ratio and the change in the skilled-labor ratio (the percentage of skilled labor in total labor) by decomposing these changes into the contribution of the increase in the capital-labor ratio or the share of nonproduction workers within each industry (the within effect) and the contribution of the reallocation between industries (the between effect).

First, we consider the increase in the capital-labor ratio and the share of nonproduction (or skilled) workers in the manufacturing sector and the Japanese economy as a whole. As figure 1.2 shows, the capital-labor ratio measured as real capital stock (in 1990 prices) divided by the number of workers has increased considerably over the last three decades: the capital-labor ratio for both the economy as a whole and manufacturing industry grew fivefold from three million yen per person in 1970 to 15 million yen per person in 1998.

In order to examine human capital deepening in Japan, we compiled data on the number of nonproduction or skilled workers using the data of the *Population Census*. "Skilled workers" are persons whose profession is classified either as "professional and technical" or as "managerial and administrative." We define "nonproduction workers" here as persons whose profession falls into one of the following categories: professional and technical occupations; managers and administrators; clerical and secretarial occupations; sales occupations; service occupations; protective occupa-

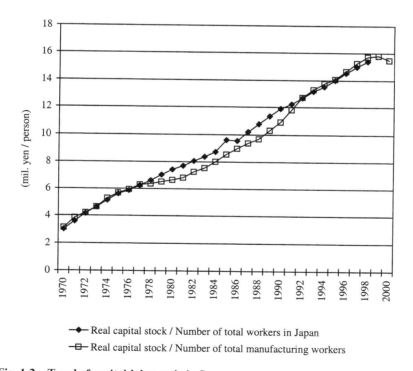

Fig. 1.2   **Trend of capital-labor ratio in Japan**
Source: Authors' calculation based on the JIP database.

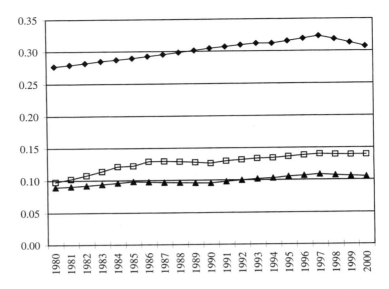

Fig. 1.3   **Share of skilled and nonproduction workers in total workers**
Source: Authors' calculation based on *Population Census* data.

tions; occupations in agriculture, forestry, and fishing; occupations in transportation and telecommunications; and other occupations. The definition of nonproduction workers is much broader than the definition of "skilled workers" and includes not highly educated workers. The share of nonproduction (or skilled) workers in the total number of workers has been increasing, as shown in figure 1.3, though the growth rate is much more moderate than that of the capital-labor ratio. In the period from 1980 to 2000, the share of nonproduction workers in manufacturing increased from 27.7 percent in 1980 to 30.7 percent in 2000.[2] The share of skilled workers also grew during 1980–2000: in the manufacturing sector, it rose from 9.0 percent to 10.5 percent, while in the economy as a whole it expanded from 9.8 percent to 13.9 percent.[3]

The increase in the capital-labor ratio and in the share of nonproduction (or skilled) workers can be decomposed into the contribution of the increase within each industry (within effect) and the contribution of the re-

2. This latter value, though, is substantially below the peak of 32.3 percent reached in 1997. The decline in the share of nonproduction workers since 1998 is most likely the result of firms' restructuring efforts—the dismissal of managers, sales personnel, and so on—following the further deterioration of the Japanese economy.
3. For details on the compilation of the skilled/nonproduction workers data, see appendix.

allocation between industries (between effect) using the following decomposition formula:

$$\Delta P = \sum_{i=1}^{n} \overline{S}_i \Delta P_i + \sum_{i=1}^{n} \overline{P}_i \Delta S_i$$

$$i: \text{industry } (i = 1, 2, \ldots, n)$$

$$P = \frac{\sum_{i=1}^{n} K_i}{\sum_{i=1}^{n} L_i} \text{ or } \frac{\sum_{i=1}^{n} L_{s,i}}{\sum_{i=1}^{n} L_i}$$

$P_i = \dfrac{K_i}{L_i}$: capital-labor ratio in industry i, or

$\quad = \dfrac{L_{si}}{L_i}$: share of nonproduction (or skilled) workers in total number of workers in industry i

$S_i = \dfrac{L_i}{L}$: share of workers in industry i in total number of workers in the economy as a whole or in the manufacturing sector.

Variables with an upper bar denote the average value of the period. Δ denotes the change in the variable over time. The first term of the right-hand side represents the increase in the factor intensity within each industry (within effect), while the second term represents the reallocation between industries (between effect).

Ideally, we should use highly disaggregated cross-industry data available for our decomposition analysis. Unfortunately, such data were unavailable, so we had to use the relatively aggregated data of the JIP database.[4] We should note that our estimates of the within effect might suffer from upward biases as a consequence of this aggregation problem.

The results of our decomposition analysis are reported in tables 1.2 and 1.3. As for the growth in the capital-labor ratio, the decomposition provided in table 1.2 shows that there was a negative between effect in most periods between 1970 and 1998, thus providing evidence for the decline of the capital-intensive sectors of the economy. Moreover, the magnitude of the between effect is very small throughout the entire period, and most of the growth in the capital-labor ratio is attributable to the within effect. In contrast, the decomposition of the growth of the share of skilled or nonproduction workers presented in table 1.3 shows that here the between effect was positive in all cases, indicating that the share of human capital–intensive industries has increased steadily both in the manufacturing sector and in the economy as a whole. The within effect was also positive with the ex-

---

4. In the following decomposition, we used data of thirty-five manufacturing industries and forty-three nonmanufacturing industries.

Table 1.2   **Decomposition of capital-labor ratio growth (annual rate, %)**

	1970–80	1980–90	1990–2000	1980–2000
A. Decomposition of capital-labor ratio growth: Manufacturing sector				
Growth rate of K-L ratio	11.24	6.43	4.18	6.65
Between effect	−0.45	−1.01	−0.05	−0.90
Within effect	11.69	7.44	4.24	7.55
	1970–80	1980–90	1990–98	1980–98
B. Decomposition of capital-labor ratio growth: The whole economy				
Growth rate of K-L ratio	14.65	6.01	3.70	5.97
Between effect	0.13	−0.81	−0.45	−0.92
Within effect	14.52	6.82	4.15	6.89

Source: Authors' calculation based on the JIP database.
Note: The capital-labor ratio is defined as the real capital stock (in 1990 prices) divided by the number of workers.

Table 1.3   **Decomposition of the growth of the share of skilled or nonproduction workers (annual rate, %)**

	1980–90	1990–2000	1980–2000
A. Decomposition of the growth of the share of nonproduction workers: Manufacturing sector			
Growth rate of the share	1.00	0.08	0.55
Between effect	0.12	0.16	0.14
Within effect	0.88	−0.07	0.41
B. Decomposition of the growth of the share of skilled workers: Manufacturing sector			
Growth rate of the share	0.65	0.97	0.84
Between effect	0.29	0.25	0.27
Within effect	0.36	0.71	0.57
C. Decomposition of the growth of the share of skilled workers: The whole economy			
Growth rate of the share	2.88	1.03	2.10
Between effect	1.02	1.06	1.02
Within effect	1.86	−0.02	1.08

Source: Authors' calculation based on *Population Census* data and the JIP database.

ception of two cases in the period of 1990–2000, and it was always greater than the between effect except for these two cases.

The most important implication of these results is that the within effect is very large. Some part of this within effect may have been caused by the international division of labor within each industry. We analyze this issue in section 1.4.

Our decomposition analysis thus suggests that physical and human capital deepening in the Japanese economy is mostly attributable to the within-industry shift, not to the between-industry shift, though we could see a negative within effect during the period 1990–2000 for the share of nonproduction workers in the manufacturing sector and the share of skilled workers in the whole economy. In the last two decades, and particularly in the 1990s—the age of globalization—both the within-industry capital deepening and the between-industry allocation may have been caused by expanding international trade. The between-industry shift may be partly explained by the change in patterns of interindustry trade, which affects the size of each industry in Japan, while the within-industry shift may be explained by the change in patterns of intraindustry trade, which affects the mixes of factor inputs in each industry. In the following sections, we will examine the change in Japan's trade patterns and analyze the determinants of the changes in factor intensities in Japan.

1.3   Japan's Interindustry Trade and Factor Contents

In this section, we take a general look at the pattern of Japan's interindustry trade in the last two decades and then estimate how factor contents in Japan's international trade changed during this period.

1.3.1   Overview of Japan's International Trade

Although Japan's overall import–gross domestic product (GDP) ratio has gradually declined over the last two decades, imports of manufactured products have actually grown faster than the economy as a whole (see table 1.4). According to Japan's trade statistics, the increase in imports mainly concentrated on electrical machinery and labor intensive goods, such as apparel and wooden products. Because the share of the manufacturing sector in GDP declined during this period, the ratio of imports of manufactured products to gross value added in the manufacturing sector increased rapidly, by 11.5 percentage points from 15.2 percent in 1985 to 26.7 percent in 2000 (table 1.4).[5]

The commodity composition of Japan's exports at the two-digit level has remained relatively stable over the last fifteen years. Nevertheless, looking at trade patterns at a more detailed commodity classification level, it becomes clear that Japan's specialization has changed: the country is increasingly specializing in the export of capital goods and key parts and components in the automobile and electrical machinery sector, while it has become a net importer of many household electrical goods.[6]

What is more, along with the change in the commodity composition,

5. The United States experienced a similar trend during the 1980s, when this ratio jumped by 12.4 percentage points from 18.3 percent in 1978 to 30.7 percent in 1990 (Sachs and Shatz 1994). Comparing export shares and import penetration in the United States, Canada, the United Kingdom, and Japan during the period 1974–1993, Campa and Goldberg (1997) found import penetration to be extremely stable and significantly lower in Japan than in the other countries. However, if we were to conduct a similar analysis today using more recent data, we would probably reach a different conclusion.

6. The share of machine parts in Japan's total exports to East Asia increased from 31.7 percent in 1990 to 40.2 percent in 1998, while the share of capital goods, which include some machine parts, increased from 53.2 percent to 56.8 percent during the same period (MITI 1999).

Table 1.4   Japan's share of imports and the manufacturing sector in GDP, employment, and gross value added (%)

	Imports of goods and services/GDP	Imports of manufactured products (c.i.f.)/GDP	Imports of services/GDP	Share of manufacturing sector in total GDP	Share of manufacturing sector in total employed persons	Imports of manufactured products (c.i.f.)/gross value added by manufacturing sector
1980	15.1	5.1	1.7	29.2	26.2	17.4
1985	11.3	4.5	1.6	29.5	26.5	15.2
1990	9.4	5.3	1.6	28.2	26.2	18.7
1995	7.8	5.0	1.3	24.7	24.7	20.3
2000	9.5	6.3	1.3	23.4	22.3	26.7

Sources: Economic and Social Research Institute, Cabinet Office, Government of Japan, *Annual Report on National Accounts 2002*, Economic Planning Agency, Government of Japan, *Annual Report on National Accounts 2000*.

Notes: Official SNA statistics for the year 2000 are based on 1993 SNA. For years before 1989, only statistics based on 1968 SNA are available. In order to make long-term comparisons we derived values for 2000 by an extrapolation based on values of 1995 and the 1995–2000 growth rate of each variable reported in SNA statistics based on 1993 SNA. c.i.f. = cost plus insurance and freight.

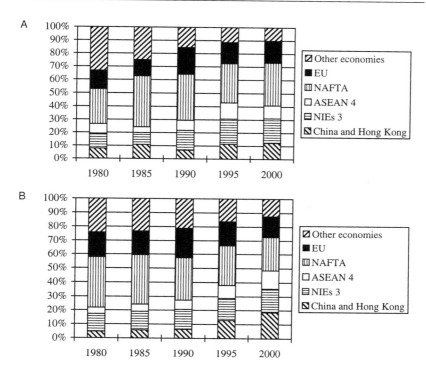

Fig. 1.4   Japan's major trade partners: Manufacturing products, 1980–2000:
A, **Share of major trade partners in Japan's exports of manufactured products;**
B, **Share of major trade partners in Japan's imports of manufactured products**
Source: Ministry of Finance, *Trade Statistics.*

there has been a shift in the regional composition of Japan's trade, with East Asia replacing North America as the most important region for the country's exports and imports. As figure 1.4 shows, trade with nine East Asian economies (China, Hong Kong, Taiwan, Korea, Singapore, Indonesia, Thailand, the Philippines, and Malaysia) accounted for 48.5 percent of Japan's total manufactured imports and 41.0 percent of total manufactured exports in 2000.

The increase in the nine East Asian economies' share in Japan's exports and imports extends across almost all manufacturing industries, suggesting that there has been a significant rise in two-way trade between Japan and the East Asian economies (see figure 1.5). Particularly conspicuous is the jump of these economies' share in Japan's electrical machinery imports between 1990 and 2000. A large rise can also be observed in many labor intensive products, which in this figure are classified as "other manufactured products" or "pottery." As a result, by 2000, the nine East Asian economies provided 64.2 percent of Japan's electrical machinery imports and 49.2

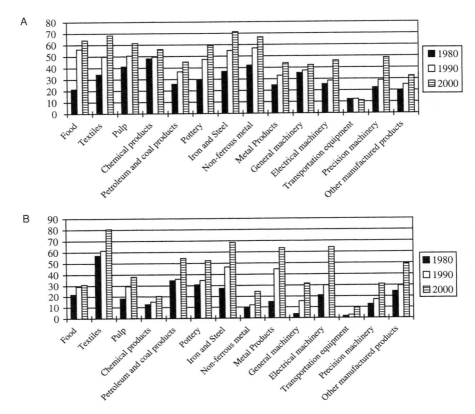

Fig. 1.5   Share of the nine East Asian economies in Japan's trade in manufacturing products: 1980–2000, by commodity: *A,* Share of the nine East Asian economies in Japan's exports; *B,* Share of the nine East Asian economies in Japan's imports

Source: Ministry of Finance, *Trade Statistics.*

Note: The nine East Asian economies are China, Hong Kong, Taiwan, Korea, Singapore, Indonesia, Thailand, the Philippines, and Malaysia.

percent of Japan's imports of "other manufacturing products." The East Asian economies' share in Japan's total imports of machinery and intermediate products such as metal products and chemical products also increased rapidly. On the export side, the increase in the East Asian economies' share in the 1990s was particularly pronounced in the electrical machinery and precision machinery sectors.

This rise in Japan's imports of labor-intensive products and exports of capital- and technology-intensive products (such as machinery and advanced intermediate products) can be easily recognized as a deepening of the international division of labor with the relatively unskilled labor abundant East Asian economies. However, how can we interpret the rapid expansion in the two-way trade within many industries? As an illustration, let us look at Japan's bilateral trade in electrical machinery (at the three-digit level) with China and Hong Kong in 1999. This is where the conspicuous increase in two-way trade in recent years has been concentrated, and the patterns that can be observed provide a clue to answering the preceding question.

These patterns are shown in table 1.5 and point at two important facts. First, they suggest a division of labor within the electrical machinery industry: vis-à-vis China and Hong Kong, Japan is a net importer of relatively labor-intensive products (such as television and radio-broadcast receivers and electrical household goods) but a net exporter of other, more technology-intensive products. This means that in order to correctly understand the division of labor and factor contents in trade between Japan and East Asia, we need to analyze trade patterns at the detailed commodity level; otherwise, the analysis will suffer from aggregation bias problems (Feenstra and Hanson 2000).

The second important fact this table shows is the existence of huge intraindustry trade between Japan and China plus Hong Kong. For example, in the case of television receivers, the total trade value is thirty-seven times greater than the trade balance. It seems that we need to analyze intraindustry trade in order to correctly evaluate the impact of trade on the Japanese economy. We do this in section 1.4.

1.3.2   Factor Contents in Japan's Trade in Manufacturing Products

In this subsection, we analyze the changes in factor contents in Japan's trade. In order to avoid aggregation bias, we should calculate factor contents at the most disaggregated level possible.[7] The most disaggregated data on direct factor requirements are those available in the *Report on Industrial Statistics* of the Ministry of International Trade and Industry, which is based on the *Census of Manufacturers*. The data are classified by the four-digit Standard Industrial Classification for Japan, which listed 540 manufacturing industries in 1990.

There is no direct converter between this industry classification and the nine-digit Harmonized Commodity Description and Coding System (HS) classification used by the Ministry of Finance for the compilation of Japan's international trade statistics. In order to link the two data sets—on factor requirements and on international trade—we used the basic industry classification of the *Japan Input-Output Tables 1990* by the Management and Coordination Agency, which lists 341 manufacturing industries, as our benchmark classification. Using the supplementary converter tables

---

7. Using the Management and Coordination Agency of the Japanese Government's "1980-85-90 Linked Input-Output Tables," Sakurai (2004) estimated factor contents in Japan's trade for the years 1980, 1985, and 1990.

Table 1.5   Japan's trade in electrical machinery and office machines with China and Hong Kong in 1999 (billion yen)

Commodity classification, SITC R3	Japan's exports to China and Hong Kong (f.o.b. base)	Japan's imports from China and Hong Kong (f.o.b. base)	Japan's net exports to China and Hong Kong
75 Office machines and automatic data processing machines	275.3	231.0	44.2
751 Office machines	173.5	117.2	56.3
752 Automatic data processing machines and units	59.0	83.7	−24.8
759 Parts of and accessories suitable for 751–752	42.8	30.1	12.7
76 Telecommunications and sound recording apparatus	316.7	302.5	14.1
761 Television receivers	37.5	39.5	−2.1
762 Radio-broadcast receivers	6.8	41.2	−34.4
763 Gramophones, dictating, sound recorders, etc.	n.a.	n.a.	n.a.
764 Telecommunications equipment and parts	272.4	221.8	50.6
77 Electrical machinery, apparatus, and appliances	1,377.9	454.2	923.7
771 Electric power machinery and parts thereof	65.7	122.7	−57.0
772 Elect. app. such as switches, relays, fuses, plugs	235.2	65.9	169.4
773 Equipment for distributing electricity	48.7	63.9	−15.2
774 Electric apparatus for medical purposes	12.9	1.2	11.7
775 Household type, elect. and nonelectrical equipment	14.1	52.3	−38.3
776 Thermionic, cold and photo-cathode valves, tubes	724.0	85.7	638.3
778 Electrical machinery and apparatus, n.e.s.	277.3	62.6	214.8
Total	1,969.8	987.7	982.1

Source: Statistics Canada, *World Trade Analyzer 2001.*
Notes: n.a. = not available. n.e.s. = not elsewhere specified.

of the input-output (I-O) statistics, we converted both the factor requirement data and the international trade data into the basic I-O classification. As a result, we obtain factor requirement and international trade data for 246 manufacturing industries.[8] However, because inverse matrix coefficients were available for only 103 manufacturing industries, we reclassified the data for 246 manufacturing industries into 103 manufacturing industries. Then we estimated direct and indirect factor requirements using the corresponding I-O table.

Ideally, we would use up-to-date factor requirement data and I-O tables in order to take changes in production technologies into account. Unfortunately, data on the factor requirements for production and nonproduction workers are available only until 1990 because the *Census of Manufacturers* after that year does not cover headquarter activities. Because of this constraint, we used constant-factor requirement and I-O data of 1990 for our analysis of the entire 1980–2000 period.[9]

Factor content in Japan's trade in year t (t = 1980, 1990, 2000) is calculated by

$$X_t = D(I - A)^{-1}T_t,$$

where ($K \times 1$) vector $X_t = [x_{k,t}]$ denotes the total contents of factor k in Japan's trade of year t. ($K \times J$) matrix $D = [d_{k,j}]$ denotes the quantity of primary factor k directly used per unit of output in industry j in year 1990. ($J \times J$) matrix A is the input-output matrix of year 1990.[10] ($J \times 1$) vector T_t is the net-export vector of year t in 1990 prices. In order to derive trade data in 1990 prices, we used the deflators of the Management and Coordination Agency's *Japan Linked Input-Output Tables* and the *Wholesale Price Index* of the Bank of Japan at the three-digit level.[11]

We analyzed factor content in terms of the following four primary factors: physical capital (book value), production labor (number of workers),

8. The factor requirement data of the *Census of Manufacturers* are on an establishment basis, and each establishment is classified by its most important product. Because many establishments produce various commodities simultaneously, this classification method is problematic. The I-O converter from the *Census of Manufacturers* to the basic I-O classification takes account of this problem and converts establishment-based data into activity-based data. We used the I-O converter in order to construct the factor requirement data for each I-O classification-based industry. Therefore, our factor requirement data were also transformed into the activity-based data.

9. Because of this methodology, there is a risk of overestimating factor contents in trade in recent years in the case of industries where total factor productivity has grown rapidly.

10. The I-O matrix here covers only manufacturing industries. Therefore, our analysis does not include indirect factor requirements through changes in production in nonmanufacturing industries.

11. The conversion of trade statistics at the HS nine-digit level into trade data classified at the basic industry level of the I-O tables in 1990 price was conducted by H. Nosaka, T. Inui, K. Ito, and K. Fukao as part of the Japan Industrial Productivity (JIP) database project. The result is included in the JIP database. For more detail on this database, see Fukao, Inui, Kawai, and Miyagawa (2004).

nonproduction labor (number of workers), and land (book value).[12] In order to analyze how the increase in Japan's trade with the East Asian economies affected Japan's factor markets, we subdivided Japan's total net exports in each industry into gross exports and gross imports by six regions, namely (a) China and Hong Kong; (b) the newly industrialized economies (NIEs)-3 (Taiwan, South Korea, and Singapore); (c) the Association of Southeast Asian Nations (ASEAN)-4 (Indonesia, Thailand, Malaysia, and the Philippines); (d) the United States; (e) the European Union (EU); and (f) all other economies.

The results of the factor content analysis for the years 1980, 1990, and 2000 are reported in table 1.6. Reflecting Japan's huge trade surplus, Japan is a net exporter of all the four primary factors. For example, according to our calculations, in the year 2000, Japan recorded factor content net exports of 363,000 production workers, which represents 4.7 percent of the total of production workers (7,717,000) in manufacturing in 1990. Compared with the trade pattern observed in 1990, the 2000 figure for factor content net exports of production labor represents a decline of 42 percent. This decline was almost entirely caused by Japan's trade with China and Hong Kong (see table 1.7). In the year 2000, about one-third of factor content gross imports of production workers came from China and Hong Kong (table 1.6).

In the case of nonproduction workers, there were factor content net exports of 378,000 nonproduction workers in the year 2000, which represents 10.9 percent of the total of nonproduction workers (3,456,000) in manufacturing in 1990. Compared with trade patterns in 1980, net exports of nonproduction workers have increased by 89,000, which is equivalent to 2.6 percent of the total of nonproduction workers in 1990. The major increase in this factor content occurred in Japan's trade with the United States (table 1.7).

In the case of land, factor content net exports in 2000 amounted to 1.36 trillion yen (in 1990 prices), which is equivalent to 10.5 percent of the total land value (12.9 trillion yen) used in manufacturing in 1990. Net exports of land have gradually declined over the last twenty years (table 1.7).

Capital stock factor content net exports in 2000, meanwhile, stood at 9.12 trillion yen (in 1990 prices), which represents 16.5 percent of the total capital stock (55.4 trillion yen) in manufacturing in 1990. Compared with 1980, this represents an increase in net exports of capital stock by 1.1 trillion yen or 2.0 percent of the total capital stock in 1990 (table 1.7).

---

12. Ideally we would use the real values of physical capital and land stocks instead of the book values. However, we chose to use the book values because it is difficult to obtain capital stock and land stock deflators at such a detailed industry level. While it would be possible to roughly estimate the ratio of real value to book value of physical capital stock by utilizing various survey data on capital stocks, it would be extremely difficult to estimate the real value of land due to data constraints and the volatility of land prices.

Table 1.6   Factor contents (direct plus indirect) of trade for Japan's manufacturing sector: 1980–2000, by region

	Gross exports			Gross imports			Net exports		
	1980	1990	2000	1980	1990	2000	1980	1990	2000
Production labor									
World total	923,474	1,388,633	1,941,421	306,751	761,507	1,578,368	616,723	627,125	363,053
China and Hong Kong	73,317	97,278	242,423	22,976	87,209	513,402	50,341	10,070	−270,979
NIEs 3	99,132	198,831	353,213	54,302	138,387	218,617	44,830	60,444	134,596
ASEAN 4	61,937	103,502	189,007	10,060	51,945	177,053	51,877	51,557	11,953
U.S.	223,380	440,972	583,364	90,578	178,069	273,127	132,801	262,903	310,237
EU	133,426	286,382	324,457	61,872	174,314	208,738	71,554	112,068	115,719
Other economies	332,281	261,667	248,957	66,963	131,583	187,430	265,318	130,084	61,527
Nonproduction labor									
World total	408,313	675,630	985,796	118,829	291,902	607,572	289,484	383,728	378,224
China and Hong Kong	31,756	44,161	119,781	5,861	21,364	127,705	25,895	22,797	−7,924
NIEs 3	46,089	100,185	186,061	15,805	44,569	106,804	30,285	55,617	79,257
ASEAN 4	28,616	50,583	96,495	3,679	16,693	79,591	24,937	33,890	16,904
U.S.	96,813	215,813	294,537	42,276	87,408	136,926	54,537	128,405	157,610
EU	60,203	141,939	169,484	26,359	70,748	90,007	33,844	71,191	79,477
Other economies	144,836	122,948	119,439	24,850	51,119	66,540	119,986	71,829	52,900

(*continued*)

Table 1.6 (continued)

	Gross exports			Gross imports			Net exports		
	1980	1990	2000	1980	1990	2000	1980	1990	2000
Land (million yen, in 1990 prices)									
World total	2,367,285	3,154,935	4,251,546	782,374	1,777,449	2,895,281	1,584,911	1,377,486	1,356,265
China and Hong Kong	202,601	223,700	557,028	39,703	128,046	621,391	162,899	95,654	−64,362
NIEs 3	282,507	502,354	807,407	107,479	275,660	437,886	175,028	226,694	369,521
ASEAN 4	183,807	271,144	428,155	34,754	124,603	337,695	149,052	146,541	90,460
U.S.	522,355	931,945	1,195,965	228,689	418,488	565,778	293,666	513,457	630,186
EU	297,871	591,223	655,089	149,588	397,799	457,527	148,284	193,424	197,562
Other economies	878,144	634,570	607,902	222,161	432,854	475,004	655,982	201,716	132,898
Capital stock (million yen, in 1990 prices)									
World total	11,087,602	15,378,504	21,701,611	3,068,328	7,169,480	12,586,585	8,019,274	8,209,024	9,115,026
China and Hong Kong	944,937	1,111,021	2,901,756	145,135	469,155	2,313,326	799,802	641,866	588,430
NIEs 3	1,327,911	2,442,986	4,195,098	403,842	1,113,916	2,263,765	924,069	1,329,070	1,931,333
ASEAN 4	878,622	1,312,625	2,286,969	114,037	401,754	1,552,102	764,585	910,871	734,867
U.S.	2,479,216	4,629,732	6,052,100	975,571	1,879,475	2,710,964	1,503,645	2,750,257	3,341,137
EU	1,372,409	2,903,521	3,353,937	629,500	1,691,120	2,012,755	742,909	1,212,401	1,341,182
Other economies	4,084,507	2,978,619	2,911,750	800,244	1,614,061	1,733,673	3,284,263	1,364,559	1,178,077

Source: Authors' calculation.

Table 1.7 **Changes in factor contents (direct plus indirect) of net exports for Japan's manufacturing sector: 1980–2000, by region**

	Net exports		
	1980–90	1990–2000	1980–2000
	Production labor		
World total	10,403 (0.1)	–264,073 (–3.4)	–253,670 (–3.3)
China and Hong Kong	–40,272 (–0.5)	–281,049 (–3.6)	–321,321 (–4.2)
NIEs 3	15,614 (0.2)	74,152 (1.0)	89,766 (1.2)
ASEAN 4	–320 (–0.0)	–39,603 (–0.5)	–39,924 (–0.5)
U.S.	130,101 (1.7)	47,335 (0.6)	177,436 (2.3)
EU	40,513 (0.5)	3,651 (0.0)	44,164 (0.6)
Other economies	–135,234 (–1.8)	–68,557 (–0.9)	–203,792 (–2.6)
	Nonproduction labor		
World total	94,244 (2.7)	–5,505 (–0.2)	88,739 (2.6)
China and Hong Kong	–3,098 (–0.1)	–30,721 (–0.9)	–33,819 (–1.0)
NIEs 3	25,332 (0.7)	23,641 (0.7)	48,973 (1.4)
ASEAN 4	8,953 (0.3)	–16,986 (–0.5)	–8,033 (–0.2)
U.S.	73,868 (2.1)	29,205 (0.8)	103,073 (3.0)
EU	37,347 (1.1)	8,286 (0.2)	45,632 (1.3)
Other economies	–48,157 (–1.4)	–18,929 (–0.5)	–67,087 (–1.9)
	Land (million yen, in 1990 prices)		
World total	–207,425 (–1.6)	–21,221 (–0.2)	–228,646 (–1.8)
China and Hong Kong	–67,244 (–0.5)	–160,017 (–1.2)	–227,261 (–1.8)
NIEs 3	51,666 (0.4)	142,826 (1.1)	194,492 (1.5)
ASEAN 4	–2,512 (–0.0)	–56,080 (–0.4)	–58,592 (–0.5)
U.S.	219,791 (1.7)	116,729 (0.9)	336,521 (2.6)
EU	45,140 (0.3)	4,138 (0.0)	49,278 (0.4)
Other economies	–454,267 (–3.5)	–68,818 (–0.5)	–523,085 (–4.1)
	Capital stock (million yen, in 1990 prices)		
World total	189,751 (0.3)	906,001 (1.6)	1,095,752 (2.0)
China and Hong Kong	–157,936 (–0.3)	–53,436 (–0.1)	–211,372 (–0.4)
NIEs 3	405,001 (0.7)	602,262 (1.1)	1,007,263 (1.8)
ASEAN 4	146,286 (0.3)	–176,004 (–0.3)	–29,718 (–0.1)
U.S.	1,246,611 (2.2)	590,880 (1.1)	1,837,492 (3.3)
EU	469,492 (0.8)	128,781 (0.2)	598,273 (1.1)
Other economies	–1,919,705 (–3.5)	–186,482 (–0.3)	–2,106,186 (–3.8)

Source: Authors' calculation.

Notes: Data in parentheses (percentages) denote the ratio of factor contents to total input in Japan's manufacturing sector in 1990. The data on total input are taken from the Ministry of International Trade and Industry, *Census of Manufacturers 1990.*

Relative to the total amount of each of the four primary input factors used in manufacturing, Japan exported a large amount of capital and nonproduction labor but only a small amount of production labor in 2000. Because nonproduction workers, on average, are more educated than production workers and Japan is a country abundant in physical and human capital, the preceding results are consistent with the Heckscher-Ohlin theory.

As table 1.7 shows, in the period from 1980 to 2000, Japan's factor content net exports of production workers fell by 3.3 percent, while net exports of nonproduction workers rose by 2.6 percent. This change in trade patterns has the effect of increasing the implied supply ratio of production/nonproduction workers available to the manufacturing sector for other use by about 5.9 percent. More than one-half of this change (3.2 percent) was caused by Japan's trade with China and Hong Kong.

During 1980–2000, Japan's factor content net exports of capital stock grew by 2.0 percent, while net exports of workers overall (production and nonproduction) decreased by 1.5 percent. This change in the trade pattern has the effect of reducing the implied supply of capital stock per worker available to the manufacturing sector for other use by 3.5 percent. Thus, compared with the impact on the implied supply ratio of production/nonproduction workers, the effect of recent changes in trade patterns on the implied supply of capital stock per worker has been small.

By a similar calculation using the results of the factor content analysis at the four-digit level carried out by Feenstra and Hanson (2000), we can evaluate the impact of U.S. trade on its factor markets. This shows that in the period of 1982–1994, changes in U.S. trade patterns had the effect of increasing the implied supply ratio of production/nonproduction workers available to the manufacturing sector for other use by 1.0 percent, while the implied supply of capital stock per worker available to the manufacturing sector for other use fell by 2.3 percent.[13] Thus, compared with the United States, Japan experienced a much more drastic change in factor content net exports over the last two decades in terms of its implied supply ratio of production/nonproduction workers available to the manufacturing sector for other use.

The trends shown here mean that Japan's factor content net exports have changed in a direction that offsets the effect of the accumulation of physical and human capital per capita. Japan has come to export more physical and human capital–intensive products over the past two decades. However, compared with the rapid deepening of physical and human capital in the macroeconomy described in section 1.2, the offsetting effect of international trade seems to be small. Table 1.8 compares overall physical or human capital deepening in the Japanese manufacturing sector with that purely attributable to changes in factor contents of trade. Although the average annual growth rate of the capital-labor ratio for the manufacturing

13. In the period 1982–1994, the United States saw an increase in its factor content net imports of production (nonproduction) workers in manufacturing of 8.2 percent (7.2 percent). It also experienced a rise in factor content net imports of capital stock in manufacturing of 5.5 percent and a decline in net exports of (production plus nonproduction) workers of 7.8 percent of total workers in manufacturing.

Table 1.8	Physical and human capital deepening in the Japanese manufacturing sector (annual rate, %)			
	1970–80	1980–90	1990–2000	1980–2000
Growth rate of capital-labor ratio				
Manufacturing sector total	11.24	6.43	5.51[a]	7.60[b]
Changes in factor contents of trade	n.a.	–0.06	0.41[a]	0.18[b]
Growth rate of the share of nonproduction workers				
Manufacturing sector total	n.a.	1.00	0.08	0.55
Changes in factor contents of trade	n.a.	0.18	0.23	0.21

Source: Authors' calculation based on the results of tables 1.2, 1.3, and 1.7.

Note: n.a. = not available.

[a]The growth rate of the capital-labor ratio denotes the average annual growth rate from 1990 to 1998.

[b]The growth rate of the capital-labor ratio denotes the average annual growth rate from 1980 to 1998.

sector total is 7.60 percent for the 1980–1998 period, the growth rate becomes very small at 0.18 percent when we only take account of the change in the factor contents of trade. As for the growth rate of the share of nonproduction workers, the offsetting effect of international trade is also small for the 1980–1990 period and throughout the 1980–2000 period. However, in the 1990s, the contribution of international trade to the growth of the share of nonproduction workers in the Japanese manufacturing sector is much larger, which implies a significant effect of international trade on Japan's human capital deepening.

1.4   Japan's Intraindustry Trade and the Determinants of Factor Intensity within Industry

So far, we have found that the macro-level capital-labor ratio has been increasing over the last two decades and that most of the increase is attributable to the within-industry shift and not the between-industry shift. Moreover, most of the macro-level increase in the skilled or nonproduction labor share in the total number of workers has also been induced by the within-industry shift. As has been argued in previous studies, the international division of labor through the fragmentation of production processes and the import of unskilled labor–intensive intermediate inputs may have contributed to an increase in the relative demand for skilled labor in each industry. That is, if firms fragment their production into discrete activities and move nonskill-intensive activities abroad, then trade will lead to a shift in employment toward skilled workers within those industries. This type of international division of labor has been referred to as "outsourcing" in the recent literature. Feenstra and Hanson (1996a,b, 1999) and Hijzen, Görg, and Hine (2003), for example, provide econometric evidence of a positive relationship between outsourcing and the demand for skilled labor. Although the international fragmentation of production has been increasing rapidly in Japan in recent years, too, contributing to changes in trade patterns, there are few studies analyzing the impact of fragmentation on labor and capital.[14]

Moreover, vertical intraindustry trade (VIIT), i.e., intraindustry trade where goods are differentiated by quality, may have a large impact on factor demands within each manufacturing industry in Japan. As Falvey (1981) pointed out in his seminal theoretical paper, commodities of the same statistical group but of different quality may be produced using different mixes of factor inputs. Therefore, developed economies like Japan may export physical and human capital–intensive products of high quality and import unskilled labor–intensive products of low quality from developing economies. As a result, an increase in VIIT may also raise the physical and human capital intensity in Japan.

In the following subsections, we briefly outline the changes in outsourcing and VIIT patterns by industry in Japan for the period from 1988 to 2000.[15] We also discuss the relationship between changes in factor demand and trade patterns by industry. Using industry-level data, we conduct econometric analyses to investigate the determinants of the observed growth in the skilled labor share in total workers and in the capital-labor ratio. We should note that due to data constraints, the following analysis is limited to the manufacturing sector.

1.4.1 Industry-Level Overview of Fragmentation and Factor Intensity

Figure 1.6 shows the share of VIIT, a broad outsourcing measure, and a narrow outsourcing measure by industry for the year 2000, while figure 1.7 presents the average annual growth rates of these values from 1988 to 2000 by industry.[16] Following major preceding studies such as Greenaway, Hine, and Milner (1995) and Fontagné, Freudenberg, and Péridy (1997), our VIIT measure is calculated based on the assumption that the gap between the unit value of imports and the unit value of exports for each commodity reveals the qualitative differences of the products exported and imported between the two countries. Our measures of broad and narrow outsourcing are constructed following Feenstra and Hanson (1999). The broad outsourcing measure expresses imported intermediate inputs rela-

14. An exception is Sakurai (2000), who conducts a similar analysis for Japan. See section 1.4.2 for details.
15. As for the capital-labor ratio, due to data constraints, our analysis focuses only on the period from 1988 to 1998.
16. For the definition of VIIT and broad and narrow outsourcing measures, see appendix. For a more detailed analysis of VIIT in Japan and East Asia, see Fukao, Ishido, and Ito (2003).

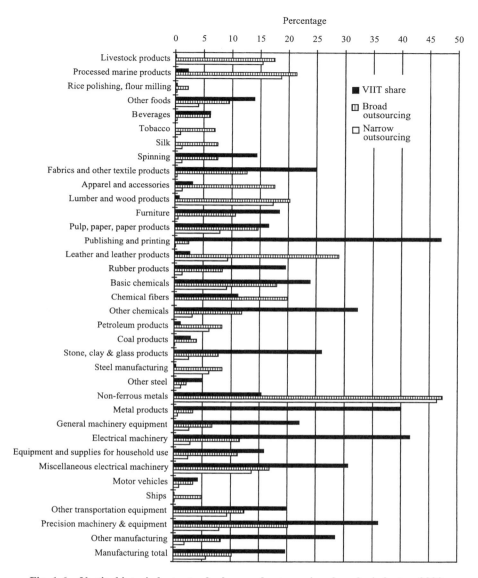

Fig. 1.6   Vertical intraindustry trade share and outsourcing share by industry: 2000
Source: Authors' calculation.

tive to total expenditure on nonenergy intermediate inputs in each industry. The narrow outsourcing measure expresses the imported intermediate inputs purchased from the same Japan Industry Productivity Database (JIP) industry as the good being produced divided by the total expenditure on nonenergy intermediate inputs in each industry. Figure 1.6 shows that

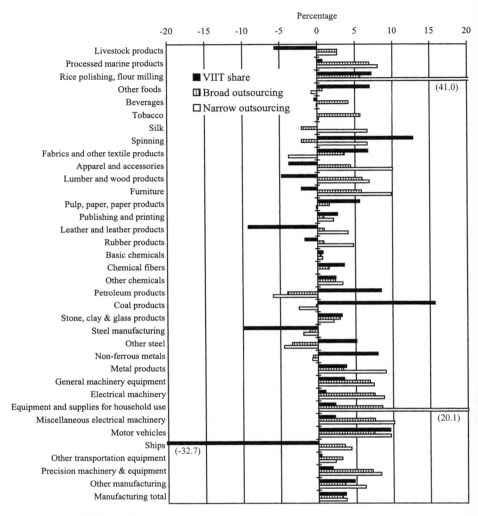

Growth rate of VIIT share: Δ ln (VIIT/Total trade)
Growth rate of broad outsourcing share: Δ ln (Broad outsourcing/Total intermediate inputs)
Growth rate of narrow outsourcing share: Δ ln (Narrow outsourcing/Total intermediate inputs)

Fig. 1.7   Annual growth rate of vertical intraindustry trade share and outsourcing share by industry: 1988–2000

the VIIT share in the year 2000 was relatively high (more than 30 percent) in publishing and printing, other chemicals, metal products, electrical machinery, miscellaneous electrical machinery, and precision machinery and equipment.

On the other hand, the broad outsourcing measure was high (more than

15 percent) in food products (livestock products and processed marine products), apparel and accessories, lumber and wood products, leather and leather products, basic chemicals, chemical fibers, nonferrous metals, other electrical machinery, and precision machinery and equipment. The narrow outsourcing measure was high (more than 5 percent) in food products (livestock products and processed marine products), lumber and wood products, pulp, paper and paper products, leather and leather products, basic chemicals, petroleum products, steel manufacturing, nonferrous metals, other electrical machinery, other transportation equipment, and precision machinery and equipment. Figure 1.7 shows that the VIIT share and outsourcing measures increased in most manufacturing sectors during the period from 1988 to 2000. In particular, we find that the outsourcing measures increased relatively more in food products, textile products, and machineries, while the VIIT share increased relatively more in food products, textile products, petroleum and coal products, nonferrous metals, and motor vehicles.

Next, let us look at the correlations between changes in factor intensities, the VIIT share, and the outsourcing measures. Table 1.9 summarizes the correlation coefficients between the annual growth rates of the shares of skilled workers, nonproduction workers, the VIIT share, and the broad and narrow outsourcing measures for the period from 1988 to 2000. Although we can see a positive correlation between skilled workers' share and the VIIT share, the correlation coefficient is not statistically significant. Moreover, the correlation coefficients between the capital-labor ratio and the VIIT share and between nonproduction workers' share and the VIIT share are negative, though not significant. As for changes in the outsourcing measures and factor intensities, a significantly positive correlation can be seen only in the case of skilled workers' share. Therefore, the simple correlation coefficient analysis does not provide strong support for the con-

Table 1.9   **Correlation coefficient matrix**

	Capital-labor ratio (a)	Skilled worker share (b)	Nonproduction worker share (c)	VIIT share (d)	Broad outsourcing (e)	Narrow outsourcing (f)
(a)	1					
(b)	0.435***	1				
(c)	0.471***	0.592***	1			
(d)	−0.059	0.262	−0.050	1		
(e)	−0.017	0.292*	0.210	−0.147	1	
(f)	0.146	0.299*	0.203	0.009	0.554***	1

Source: Authors' calculation.

Note: Each variable denotes the average annual growth rate for the period from 1988 to 2000.

***Significant at the 1 percent level.

*Significant at the 10 percent level.

jecture that outsourcing or VIIT may have contributed to physical and human capital deepening in each industry.

1.4.2   Econometric Analysis

In this section, we conduct a statistical analysis of the determinants of factor intensities using the industry-level data from 1988 to 2000. Several previous studies have analyzed the impact of fragmentation on skill upgrading (human capital deepening). Using detailed industry-level data for the United States, Feenstra and Hanson (1996a,b, 1999) estimate the effect of international outsourcing on wage inequality. Hijzen, Görg, and Hine (2003) conduct a similar analysis using U.K. data for fifty-three manufacturing industries for the period from 1982 to 1997. As for Japan, Sakurai (2000) analyzes this issue using data for thirty-nine manufacturing industries for the period from 1987 to 1990. While the studies on the United States and the United Kingdom found a strong positive relationship between outsourcing and wage inequality, Sakurai's (2000) study on Japan did not produce such clear-cut evidence. Sakurai explains that his ambiguous result might be due to the short estimation period. The present paper aims at applying and extending the Feenstra and Hanson approach by using JIP industry-level data (thirty-five manufacturing industries) for the period from 1988 to 2000. In addition, we take account of the role of skill-biased technological change (SBTC) in the increase in skilled (nonproduction) worker intensity, utilizing the JIP IT (information technology) database.[17] As Hijzen, Görg, and Hine (2003) point out, the inclusion of the 1990s in the analysis is likely to be crucial as international fragmentation and information technology progressed rapidly during the decade. However, one drawback of our analysis is that we cannot calculate wage bills for skilled (nonproduction) and unskilled (production) workers due to data constraints. Therefore, we assume that the relative wage rates of skilled (nonproduction) and unskilled (production) workers have not changed over time, and we use the ratio of the number of skilled (nonproduction) workers to the total number of workers as a proxy for the share of skilled (nonproduction) workers' wage bill in the total wage bill.

A translog cost function approach, based on the work of Berman, Bound, and Griliches (1994) and Feenstra and Hanson (1996b), is usually employed in the literature to estimate skill upgrading, and we follow this

17. According to the argument put forward by Feenstra and Hanson (1999), both SBTC and outsourcing can be considered to be associated with within-industry changes in skill intensity as a result of their effect on the relative productivity of different skill groups. That is, as fragmentation or outsourcing take the form of moving unskilled labor–intensive processes from a developed country to a developing country, they have a similar effect as technological change.

approach here. Similarly, following previous studies, we consider capital as a fixed input in the short run, while skilled and unskilled (nonproduction and production) workers are variable factors of production. Therefore, the short-run translog cost function can be presented as:

$$
(1) \quad \ln C_i = \alpha_0 + \sum_{j=1}^{J} \alpha_j \ln w_{ij} + \sum_{k=1}^{K} \beta_k \ln x_{ik} + \frac{1}{2} \sum_{j=1}^{J} \sum_{s=1}^{J} \gamma_{js} \ln w_{ij} \ln w_{is}
$$

$$
+ \frac{1}{2} \sum_{k=1}^{K} \sum_{l=1}^{K} \delta_{kl} \ln x_{ik} \ln x_{il} + \sum_{j=1}^{J} \sum_{k=1}^{K} \varphi_{jk} \ln w_{ij} \ln x_{ik}
$$

where C_i is the variable cost for industry i, w_{ij} denotes the wages of workers in skill group j, and x_{ik} denotes the fixed inputs or outputs k. Differentiating the translog cost function with respect to wages yields the factor payments to skill group j over the total wage bill.

$$
(2) \quad\quad\quad S_{ij} = \alpha_j + \sum_{s=1}^{J} \gamma_{js} \ln w_{ij} + \sum_{k=1}^{K} \varphi_{jk} \ln x_{ik}
$$

Assuming that quality-adjusted wages will be identical across industries, the wage terms can be dropped from the right-hand side of equation (2). We consider technological change, VIIT, and outsourcing as structural variables and assume there are three kinds of capital, namely IT hardware, IT software, and non-IT capital. A full set of year dummies is included in order to capture economywide skill upgrading as well as year-to-year changes in the wage levels faced by all industries. Therefore, we estimate the following equation:

$$
(3) \quad S_{ijt} = \varphi_{j0} + \varphi_{j1} \ln\left(\frac{\text{IThard}}{\text{VA}}\right)_{it} + \varphi_{j2} \ln\left(\frac{\text{ITsoft}}{\text{VA}}\right)_{it} + \varphi_{j3} + \ln\left(\frac{\text{NonIT}}{\text{VA}}\right)_{it}
$$

$$
+ \varphi_{j4} + \ln\text{VA}_{it} + \varphi_{j5}\left(\frac{\text{RDexp}}{\text{VA}}\right)_{it} + \varphi_{j6}\text{VIIT}_{it} + \varphi_{j7}\text{Outsourcing}_{it}
$$

$$
+ \varphi_{j8} D_t
$$

where IThard, ITsoft, and NonIT denote the IT hardware stock, IT software stock, and non-IT capital stock, respectively; VA is the value added in industry i, RDexp/VA is a proxy for technological change calculated as expenditure on research and development over value added, VIIT represents the VIIT value over industry i's shipments, Outsourcing reflects either broad or narrow outsourcing, and D is a full set of year dummies. Subscript t represents time. In order to examine potential differences in the effects of VIIT with Asian countries and with other countries on factor demands in Japan, we prepare three variables representing VIIT: first, Japan's VIIT with all countries in the world divided by the industry's shipments; second, Japan's VIIT with the nine Asian economies divided by the industry's shipments; and third, Japan's VIIT with all the countries except for the nine Asian economies divided by the industry's shipments.[18]

In addition, using the industry-level data, we examine whether the international division of labor contributed to physical capital deepening in Japan. We use the capital-labor ratio (physical capital stock divided by the number of workers, KL) as the dependent variable and regress it on the logarithm of the wage rate relative to the rental price of capital (ln[wage/rental price]) and variables representing the degree of the international division of labor.

The results of the generalized least squares (GLS) estimation are presented in table 1.10. This shows that the estimated coefficients on ln(IThard/VA), ln(VA), and RDexp/VA are significantly positive in all cases where skilled workers' share (SKILLED) or nonproduction workers' share (NONPROD) in the total number of workers is used as the dependent variable (columns [1] to [4]). The results imply that (a) IT hardware intensity has a positive impact on skill upgrading, and SBTC may have increased the share of skilled (nonproduction) workers; (b) the scale effect is positive and greater value added is associated with a higher skilled (nonproduction) workers' share; and (c) R&D intensity, which is a proxy for technological change, has a positive impact on skill upgrading. On the other hand, a significantly negative coefficient is obtained for ln(NonIT/VA) in all cases but one in columns (1) to (4), which suggests that increases in non-IT capital intensity favor unskilled (production workers) in Japan. As for IT software intensity, the estimated coefficients are positive in columns (1) and (2) but negative in columns (3) and (4), though they are not statistically significant in any of the cases.

As for the VIIT share, the estimated coefficients are significantly positive in columns (1) and (2) but statistically insignificant in columns (3) and (4), suggesting that VIIT raises the skill intensity calculated as the share of workers whose occupation is classified as professional and technical or managerial and administrative. Moreover, looking at the magnitude of the coefficients in column (2), VIITasia9/shipments has a much larger coefficient than VIITnon-asia9/shipments. This may reflect the fact that vertical foreign direct investment (FDI) in the Asian economies tends to consist of the transfer of low-skilled production work to these countries while high-skilled employees remain at home. We can confirm that Japanese manufacturing industries realized skill upgrading as a result of the international division of labor with the nine Asian economies. When the skill intensity is calculated as the share of nonproduction workers, however, VIIT does not have a significant impact on skill upgrading, though the estimated coefficient on VIIT is positive in columns (3) and (4). This result might be a reflection of the fact that Japanese firms reduced the share of nonproduction

---

18. For more details on the definition of the variables and data sources, see appendix.

Table 1.10   **GLS estimation results**

	SKILLED (1)	SKILLED (2)	NONPROD (3)	NONPROD (4)	KL (5)
ln(IThard/VA)	1.4988***	1.3981***	1.7536***	2.0452***	
	(7.30)	(7.07)	(5.49)	(6.32)	
ln(ITsoft/VA)	0.0364	0.0348	−0.0509	−0.0401	
	(0.43)	(0.45)	(−0.46)	(−0.33)	
ln(NonIT/VA)	−0.7162**	−0.5542**	−0.5864	−0.9365**	
	(−2.58)	(−2.02)	(−1.26)	(−2.02)	
ln VA	1.0596***	1.0844***	1.4477***	1.4978***	
	(7.20)	(6.92)	(5.17)	(6.04)	
RDexp/VA	3.0787**	2.4287*	3.8564*	5.5175**	
	(2.18)	(1.85)	(1.79)	(2.38)	
ln(wage/rental price)					−0.2732
					(−0.29)
VIITworld/shipments	0.1521***		0.0351		0.2435*
	(3.68)		(0.84)		(1.73)
VIITasia9/shipments		0.2241***		0.0370	
		(3.10)		(0.24)	
VIITnon-asia9/shipments		0.0009*		0.0005	
		(1.78)		(0.92)	
outsourcing (narrow)	0.0061	0.0033	0.0075	0.0099	−0.0018
	(0.73)	(0.44)	(0.68)	(0.83)	(−0.10)
outsourcing (difference)	−0.0320	−0.0189	−0.0315	−0.0718	−0.0196
	(−1.14)	(−0.72)	(−0.70)	(−1.45)	(−0.35)
_cons	−1.6644	−2.4111	14.4863***	14.8355***	−2.4111
	(−0.67)	(−0.94)	(3.22)	(3.61)	(−0.94)
N	439	439	439	439	385
Wald	325.60***	271.41***	187.69***	221.39***	17.51

Source: Authors' calculations.

Notes: The presence of AR(1) autocorrelation within panels and heteroskedasticity across panels is assumed. The numbers in parentheses are z-statistics. All equations include year dummies which are suppressed here. The estimation period for equations (1) to (4) is 1988–2000, while the estimation period for equation (5) is 1988–1998. Dependent variables: SKILLED indicates skilled workers' share in total number of workers; NONPROD indicates nonproduction workers' share in total number of workers; KL indicates capital-labor ratio.

***Significant at the 1 percent level.

**Significant at the 5 percent level.

*Significant at the 10 percent level.

and nonprofessional workers (such as sales persons) in the course of the restructuring efforts during the 1990s.

Although narrow outsourcing has a positive coefficient and the difference between broad and narrow outsourcing has a negative coefficient in columns (1) to (4), none of the coefficients are significant. We could not find strong evidence that outsourcing to foreign countries contributed to skill upgrading in Japan, which is not consistent with the results of studies on the United States and the United Kingdom.

As for the capital-labor ratio (column [5]), none of the explanatory variables except for the VIIT variable have statistically significant coefficients. Although VIITworld/shipments has a significantly positive coefficient, the small value of the Wald statistic indicates the weak explanatory power of the equation. Again, we could not obtain strong evidence that VIIT and outsourcing contributed to physical capital deepening in Japan, suggesting that capital deepening was caused by other factors.

1.5 Conclusion

Our aim in this paper was to investigate changing trade patterns and their effect on factor intensities in Japan, mainly focusing on the manufacturing sector. We had expected that the increasing division of labor between Japan and its East Asian neighbors during the last two decades would have affected factor prices in Japan and consequently offset the diminishing rate of return to physical and human capital. However, our results suggest that the far-reaching change in trade patterns has not substantially altered the long-term trend of diminishing rates of return to capital.

Starting from the observation that the capital-labor ratio and the share of skilled workers in the total number of workers have been growing over the last couple of decades, we first conducted decomposition analyses and found that most of the macroeconomic change in the capital-labor ratio and the change in the skilled-labor ratio were attributable to a within-industry shift rather than a between-industry shift. The between-industry shift can be partly explained by the change in patterns of interindustry trade that affects the size of each industry. However, the large within-industry effect led us to suspect that the division of labor and intraindustry trade between Japan and Asian countries may have contributed to the within-industry increase in capital intensity and skilled labor intensity. Therefore, in addition to examining the factor contents of trade from the aspect of interindustry trade, we also analyzed whether the deepening of the international division of labor and vertical intraindustry trade contributed to the within-industry change in factor intensities in Japan.

The factor content analysis showed that Japan's factor content net exports of capital and nonproduction labor have grown rapidly, while net exports of production workers have fallen by a large amount. Interestingly, the analysis also showed that the decline in the production worker content of net exports was almost entirely caused by Japan's trade with China and Hong Kong. Although international trade to a considerable extent contributed to the growth in the share of nonproduction workers in the Japanese manufacturing sector as a whole, hardly any of the macro-level accumulation of physical capital was offset by the growth in factor content net exports of physical capital.

Moreover, our empirical analysis provided only weak evidence that the deepening international division of labor contributed to the change in factor intensities in Japan. We did not find a significant and robust positive relationship between fragmentation and capital-labor ratios. As for skill intensity, we found that VIIT had a strong positive effect on the increase in the share of skilled workers when these were defined as those holding professional and technical or managerial and administrative occupations. However, we did not find such a relationship when the skill intensity was calculated as the share of nonproduction workers. We should note that the skilled (professional, technical, managerial, and administrative) labor share in the total number of workers is only around 10 percent and is much lower than the share of nonproduction workers, which is around 30 percent.

According to our results, specialization in the export of skilled labor–intensive products may have partly contributed to the increase in the relative demand for skilled (professional, technical, managerial, and administrative) labor within industry. However, at the same time, our results could also imply that changes in trade patterns (specialization in capital-intensive production) did not offset the excess supply of capital in Japan. Probably one plausible explanation for this small offsetting effect might be that VIIT or fragmentation patterns are not determined by the abundance of capital endowments but by other factors such as endowments with skilled labor, the agglomeration of industries, highly developed supporting industries, and so on. Davis and Weinstein (2003), who empirically tested the determinants of firm-level trade patterns, conclude that after controlling for national factor accumulation, firm-level export decisions seem to have little correlation with the capital intensity of their production process. We do not know yet whether this story applies to the case of industry-level trade patterns and which factors matter for trade patterns. This, however, is an issue that deserves closer scrutiny in future investigations.

Appendix

Definition of Variables Used in the Econometric Analysis and Data Sources

Labor Data

Data on skilled and unskilled labor were constructed mainly using the *Population Census of Japan,* published by the Statistics Bureau, Ministry of Public Management, Home Affairs, Posts, and Telecommunications. The *Population Census* is the most fundamental and reliable survey and is conducted every five years, covering all permanent and temporary residents in Japan. The survey report provides data on employment by detailed occupational classification (three-digit level) and by industry. We used the 1980, 1985, 1990, and 1995 employment data as benchmarks and interpolated the data for years between the benchmarks. As for the years after 1995, we utilized the *Employment Status Survey* data, published by the Statistics Bureau, Ministry of Public Management, Home Affairs, Posts, and Telecommunications, because the results of the 2000 *Population Census* were not yet available. The *Employment Status Survey* is based on a series of surveys that cover approximately 1 percent of the working population. We first calculated the skilled labor share for 1992, 1997, and 2002 based on the *Employment Status Survey*. Then, for the 1996 and 1997 data on skilled labor, we extended the 1995 employment data by occupation and industry using the growth rate of the skilled labor share from 1992 to 1997. For the 1998, 1999, and 2000 data, we extended the 1997 data using the growth rate of the skilled labor share from 1997 to 2002. The *Population Census* and the *Employment Status Survey* allow us to construct a measure of skill that is more accurate than the one based on production and nonproduction labor generally used in preceding studies. In the *Population Census* and the *Employment Status Survey,* workers are basically classified according to ten major groups as shown in table 1A.1. We distinguished two skill groups (skilled or unskilled) as well as production/nonproduction classifications. Skilled workers are those classified in major groups 1 (professional and technical occupations) and 2 (managers and administrators). Otherwise, workers are classified as unskilled. Moreover, production workers are those classified in major group 9 (plant and machine occupations, craft and related occupations, and occupations in mining and construction). Workers classified in all the other major groups are categorized as nonproduction workers.

Table 1A.1   Occupational classification in the *Population Census*

Major groups
1 Professional and technical occupations
2 Managers and administrators
3 Clerical and secretarial occupations
4 Sales occupations
5 Services occupations
6 Protective service occupations
7 Occupations in agriculture, forestry, and fishing
8 Occupations in transportation and telecommunication
9 Plant and machine occupations, craft and related occupations, and occupations in mining and construction
10 Other occupations

Notes: Skilled workers: groups 1 and 2. Production workers: group 9.

Measurement Method and Data Source for Vertical Intraindustry Trade

In order to identify vertical and horizontal intraindustry trade (IIT) we adopt the methodology used by major preceding studies on vertical IIT such as Greenaway, Hine, and Milner (1995) and Fontagné, Freudenberg, and Péridy (1997). The methodology is based on the assumption that the gap between the unit value of imports and the unit value of exports for each commodity reveals the qualitative differences in the products traded between the two economies.

We break down the bilateral trade flows of each detailed commodity category into the following three patterns: (a) interindustry trade (one-way trade), (b) intraindustry trade (IIT) in horizontally differentiated products (products differentiated by attributes), and (c) IIT in vertically differentiated products (products differentiated by quality). Then the share of each trade type is defined as:

$$\frac{\sum_j (M^Z_{kk'j} + M^Z_{k'kj})}{\sum_j (M_{kk'j} + M_{k'kj})}$$

where the variables are defined as

$M_{kk'j}$: value of economy k's imports of product j from economy k';

$M_{k'kj}$: value of economy k''s imports of product j from economy k;

$UV_{kk'j}$: average unit value of economy k's imports of product j from economy k';

$UV_{k'kj}$: average unit value of economy k''s imports of product j from economy k.

The upper-suffix Z denotes one of the three intraindustry trade types, that is, one-way trade (OWT), horizontal intraindustry trade (HIIT), and vertical intraindustry trade (VIIT) as in table 1A.2.

For our analysis, we chose to identify horizontal IIT by using the range of relative export/import unit values of 1/1.25 (i.e., 0.8) to 1.25.

We used Japan's customs data provided by the Ministry of Finance

Table 1A.2   **Categorization of trade types**

Type	Degree of trade overlap	Disparity of unit value
One-Way Trade (OWT)	$\dfrac{\text{Min}(M_{kk'j}, M_{k'kj})}{\text{Max}(M_{kk'j}, M_{k'kj})} \leq 0.1$	Not applicable
Horizontal Intraindustry Trade (HIIT)	$\dfrac{\text{Min}(M_{kk'j}, M_{k'kj})}{\text{Max}(M_{kk'j}, M_{k'kj})} > 0.1$	$\dfrac{1}{1.25} \leq \dfrac{UV_{kk'j}}{UV_{k'kj}} \leq 1.25$
Vertical Intraindustry Trade (VIIT)	$\dfrac{\text{Min}(M_{kk'j}, M_{k'kj})}{\text{Max}(M_{kk'j}, M_{k'kj})} > 0.1$	$\dfrac{UV_{kk'j}}{UV_{k'kj}} < \dfrac{1}{1.25}$ or $1.25 < \dfrac{UV_{kk'j}}{UV_{k'kj}}$

(MOF). Japan's customs data are recorded at the nine-digit HS88 level and the data classified by HS88 are available from the year 1988. The nine-digit HS88 code has been changed several times for some items, and the HS code was revised in 1996. Using the code correspondence tables published by the Japan Tariff Association for code changes, we made adjustments to make the statistics consistent with the original HS88 code. In Japan's customs statistics, export data are recorded on a free on board (f.o.b.) basis, while import data are on a cost plus insurance and freight (c.i.f.) basis. We should note that our estimate of the VIIT share is biased upward because of this difference.

Outsourcing Measures

Following Feenstra and Hanson (1999) and other previous studies, we constructed outsourcing measures as follows:

For each industry i, we measure imported intermediate inputs as

$$(A1) \qquad \sum_j (\text{input purchases of good } j \text{ by industry } i)$$

$$\cdot \left[\frac{(\text{imports of good } j)}{(\text{consumption of good } j)} \right]$$

where consumption of good j is measured as (shipments + imports – exports). The *broad* measure of foreign outsourcing is obtained by dividing imported intermediate inputs by total expenditures on nonenergy intermediate inputs in each industry. The *narrow* measure of outsourcing is obtained by restricting attention to those inputs that are purchased from the same JIP industry as the good being produced. Using Japan's customs data, Hiromi Nosaka, Tomohiko Inui, Keiko Ito, and Kyoji Fukao compiled trade data at the basic industry classification of the I-O tables in 1990 prices as part of the JIP database project at the Economic and Social Research Institute, Cabinet Office, Government of Japan. The correspondence between the Fukao-Ito industry classification and the 1980-85-90 Japan Linked Input-Output standard classification for manufacturing industries is presented in table 1A.3. The correspondence between the JIP classification and the Fukao-Ito classification for manufacturing industries is presented in table 1A.4. When calculating the outsourcing measures, we first calculated the input coefficients by Fukao-Ito industry and aggregated the imported intermediate inputs in each Fukao-Ito industry into the corresponding JIP industry. As for the narrow outsourcing measure, we restricted the Fukao-Ito industry subscripts i and j in equation (A1) to be within the same JIP industry. We should note that we only took account of intermediate inputs from manufacturing industries.

Table 1A.3   Correspondence table: Fukao-Ito classification correspondence to 1980-85-90 Japan linked I-O standard classification (manufacturing)

Fukao-Ito Classification	Linked I-O	Fukao-Ito Classification	Linked I-O
57 Beef meat (bone meat), pork (born meat)	1111-010	98 Manufactured ice	1129-031
58 By-products of slaughtering and meat processing	1111-015	99 Feeds	1131-011
59 Processed meat products	1112-011	100 Organic fertilizers, n.e.c.	1131-021
60 Bottled or canned meat products	1112-021	101 Tobacco	1141-011
61 Animal oils and fats	1112-031	102 Raw silk	1511-011
62 Drinking milk	1112-041	103 Fiber yarns	1511-021
63 Dairy products	1112-042		1511-031
64 Frozen fish and shellfish	1113-011		1511-041
65 Salted, dried, or smoked seafood	1113-021		1511-099
66 Bottled or canned seafood	1113-031	104 Cotton and staple fiber fabrics	1512-011
67 Fish paste	1113-041	105 Silk and artificial silk fabrics	1512-021
68 Fish oil and meal	1113-051	106 Woolen fabrics, hemp fabrics, and	1512-031
69 Other processed seafoods	1113-099	other fabrics	1512-091
70 Milled rice	1114-011		1512-099
71 Other grain milling	1114-019	107 Knitting fabrics	1513-011
72 Wheat flour	1114-021	108 Yarn and fabric dyeing and	
73 Other grain milled products	1114-029	finishing (processing)	1514-011
74 Noodles	1115-011	109 Rope and nets	1519-011
75 Bread	1115-021	110 Fabricated textiles for medical use	1519-031
76 Confectionary	1115-022	111 Other fabricated textile products	1519-099
77 Bottled or canned vegetables and fruits	1116-011	112 Woven fabric apparel, knitted apparel	1521-011
78 Preserved agricultural foodstuffs	1116-021	113 Other wearing apparel and clothing accessories	1522-011
79 Refined sugar	1117-011	114 Carpets and floor mats, bedding,	
80 Other sugar and by-products of sugar	1117-019	other ready	1529-090
81 Starch	1117-021	115 Timber	1611-011
82 Dextrose, syrup, and isomerized sugar	1117-031	116 Plywood	1611-021
83 Vegetable oils, cooking oil	1117-040	117 Wooden chips	1611-031
84 Vegetable meal	1117-043	118 Wooden products for construction	1619-091
85 Crude salt	1117-051	119 Other wooden products, n.e.c.	1619-099
86 Salt	1117-052	120 Wooden furniture and fixtures, wooden fixtures	1711-010
87 Condiments and seasonings	1117-061	121 Metallic furniture and fixtures	1711-031
88 Prepared frozen foods	1119-011	122 Pulp, waste paper	1811-011
89 Retort foods	1119-021	123 Foreign paper and Japanese paper	1812-011
90 Dishes, sushi, lunchboxes, school lunch	1119-090	124 Paperboard	1813-011
91 Refined sake	1121-011	125 Corrugated cardboard	1813-021
92 Beer	1121-021	126 Coated paper and building (construction) paper	1813-022
93 Ethyl alcohol for liquor manufacturing	1121-031	127 Corrugated cardboard boxes, other paper	1821-010
94 Whiskey and brandy	1121-041	128 Other pulp, paper, and processed paper products	1829-090
95 Other liquors	1121-099	129 Newspapers	1911-011
96 Tea and roasted coffee	1129-011	130 Printing, plate making, and book binding	1911-021
97 Soft drinks	1129-021	131 Publishing	1911-031

(continued)

Table 1A.3 (continued)

Fukao-Ito Classification	Linked I-O	Fukao-Ito Classification	Linked I-O
132 Ammonia	2011-011	173 Gelatin and adhesives, other final	2079-011
133 Chemical fertilizer	2011-021	chemical products	2079-090
	2011-029	174 Gasoline	2111-011
134 Soda ash	2021-011	175 Jet fuel oils	2111-012
135 Caustic soda	2021-012	176 Kerosene	2111-013
136 Liquid chlorine	2021-013	177 Light oils	2111-014
137 Other industrial soda chemicals	2021-019	178 Heavy oil A	2111-015
138 Titanium oxide	2029-021	179 Heavy oils B and C	2111-016
139 Carbon black	2029-022	180 Naphtha	2111-017
140 Other inorganic pigments	2029-029	181 LPG (liquified petroleum gas)	2111-018
141 Compressed gas and liquified gas	2029-031	182 Other petroleum refinery products	2111-019
142 Other industrial inorganic	2029-099	183 Coke	2121-011
chemicals	2029-011	184 Other coal products	2121-019
143 Ethylene	2031-011	185 Paving materials	2121-021
144 Propylene	2031-012	186 Plastic films and sheets, plastic	
145 Other petrochemical basic		plates, pipe	2211-010
products	2031-019	187 Tires and inner tubes	2311-011
146 Pure benzene	2031-021	188 Other rubber products	2311-019
147 Pure toluene	2031-022	189 Rubber footwear	2319-011
148 Xylene	2031-023	190 Plastic footwear	2319-021
149 Other petrochemical aromatic		191 Leather footwear	2411-011
products	2031-029	192 Leather and fur skins	2412-011
150 Acetic acid	2032-011	193 Miscellaneous leather products	2412-021
151 Acetic acid vinyl monomer	2032-012	194 Sheet glass, safety glass, and	
152 Styrene monomer	2032-013	multilayered glass	2511-010
153 Synthetic rubber	2032-014	195 Glass processing materials, other	
154 Synthetic alcohol, ethylene		glass products	2519-090
dichloride	2032-019	196 Cement	2521-011
155 Methane derivatives	2039-021	197 Ready mixed concrete	2522-011
156 Oil and fat industrial chemicals	2039-031	198 Cement products	2523-011
157 Plasticizers	2039-041	199 Pottery, china, and earthenware for	
158 Synthetic dyes	2039-051	construction	2531-011
159 Other industrial organic chemicals	2039-099	200 Pottery, china, and earthenware for	
	2039-011	industry	2531-012
160 Thermosetting resins	2041-011	201 Pottery, china, and earthenware for	
161 Thermoplastic resin, polyethylene		home use	2531-012
(low density)	2041-091	202 Clay refactories	2599-011
162 High functionality resins	2041-092	203 Other structural clay products	2599-021
163 Other resins	2041-099	204 Carbon and graphite products	2599-031
164 Rayon, acetate	2051-011	205 Abrasive	2599-041
165 Synthetic fibers	2051-021	206 Miscellaneous ceramic, stone, and	2599-091
166 Medicaments	2061-011	clay products	2599-091
167 Soap and synthetic detergents,		207 Pig iron	2611-011
surface active	2071-010	208 Ferroalloys	2611-021
168 Cosmetics, toilet preparations,		209 Crude steel (converters), crude	
and dentrifrices	2071-021	steel (electric)	2611-031
169 Paints and varnishes	2072-011	210 Scrap iron	2612-011
170 Printing ink	2072-021	211 Steel, steel strip (ordinary steel),	
171 Photographic sensitive materials	2073-011	steel bar	2621-011
172 Agricultural chemicals	2074-011	212 Hot rolled steel (special steel)	2621-011

Table 1A.3 (continued)

Fukao-Ito Classification	Linked I-O	Fukao-Ito Classification	Linked I-O
213 Steel pipes and tubes (ordinary steel)	2622-011	251 Printing, bookbinding, and paper processing	3029-093
214 Steel pipes and tubes (special steel)	2622-012	252 Casting equipment	3029-094
215 Cold-finished steel	2623-011	253 Plastic processing machinery	3029-095
216 Coasted steel	2623-012	254 Semiconductor making equipment	3029-099
217 Forged steel	2631-011	255 Machinists' precision tools, metal	3019-021
218 Cast steel	2631-012	molds	3031-090
219 Case iron pipes and tubes	2631-021	256 Copy machine, electronic	
220 Case materials (iron)	2631-031	calculator, word	3111-010
221 Forged materials (iron)	2631-032	257 Vending machines	3112-011
222 Iron and steel shearing and slitting, other iron	2649-090	258 Amusement machinery	3112-012
223 Copper	2711-011	259 Other machinery for service industry	3112-019
224 Lead and zinc (inc. regenerated lead)	2711-021 2711-031	260 Electric audio equipment, magnetic tapes	3211-010
225 Aluminum (inc. regenerated lead)	2711-041	261 Radio and television sets	3211-021
226 Other nonferrous metals	2711-099	262 Household electric appliance	3211-099
227 Nonferrous metal scrap	2712-011	263 Electric computing equipment (main parts)	3311-010
228 Electric wires and cables, optical fiber cables	2721-010 2721-012	264 Wired communication equipment, radio	3321-010
229 Rolled and drawn copper and copper alloys	2722-011	265 Video recording and playback equipment	3331-010
230 Rolled and drawn aluminum	2722-021	266 Electric measuring instruments	3332-011
231 Nonferrous metal castings and forgings	2722-031	267 Semiconductor devices, integrated circuits	3341-010
232 Nuclear fuels	2722-041	268 Electron tubes	3359-011
233 Other nonferrous metal products	2722-099	269 Generators	3411-011
234 Metal products for construction	2811-011	270 Electric motors	3411-012
235 Metal products for architecture	2812-011	271 Relay switches and switchboards, transformers	3411-020
236 Other metal products, n.e.c.	2899-090	272 Electric lighting fixtures and apparatus	3421-011
237 Boilers, turbines, engines	3011-010	273 Electric bulbs	3421-031
238 Conveyors	3012-011	274 Batteries, wiring devices and supplies	3421-090
239 Refrigerators and air conditioning apparatus	3013-011	275 Passenger motor cars	3511-011
240 Pumps and compressors	3019-011	276 Trucks, buses and other cars, motor vehicles	3511-019
241 Other general industrial machinery and equipment	3019-090	277 Two-wheel motor vehicles	3531-011
242 Mining, civil engineering, and construction materials	3021-011	278 Internal combustion engines for motor vehicles	3541-021
243 Chemical machinery	3022-011	279 Steel ships	3611-011
244 Metal machine tools	3024-011	280 Ships except steel ships	3611-021
245 Metal processing machinery	3024-021	281 Internal combustion engines for vessels	3611-031
246 Agricultural machinery	3029-011	282 Repair of ships	3611-101
247 Textile machinery	3029-021	283 Rolling stock	3621-011
248 Food processing machinery	3029-031	284 Repair of rolling stock	3621-101
249 Sawmill, wood working, veneer, and plywood	3029-091		
250 Pulp, equipment, and paper machinery	3029-092		

(*continued*)

Table 1A.3   (continued)

Fukao-Ito Classification	Linked I-O	Fukao-Ito Classification	Linked I-O
285 Aircraft	3622-011	295 Medial instruments	3719-031
286 Repair of aircraft	3622-101	296 Toys, sporting, and athletic goods	3911-010
287 Bicycles	3629-011	297 Musical instruments, audio and	
288 Transport equipment for industrial		video recorders	3919-010
use	3629-091	298 Writing instruments and stationery	3919-031
289 Other transport equipment, n.e.c.	3629-099	299 Small personal adornments	3919-041
290 Camera	3711-011	300 "Tatami" (straw matting) and	
291 Other photographic and optical		straw products	3919-051
instruments	3711-099	301 Ordnance	3919-061
292 Watches and clocks	3712-011	302 Miscellaneous manufacturing	
293 Professional and scientific		products	3919-099
instruments	3719-011		
294 Analytical instruments, testing			
machine	3719-021		

Note: n.e.c. = not elsewhere classified.

Other Variables Used in the Industry-Level Econometric Analyses

IT Hardware (Million Yen, 1990 Prices)

We mainly used IT hardware stock data in the JIP database. For details on the JIP database, see Fukao, Inui, Kawai, and Miyagawa (2004). Tangible IT assets (hardware) include office machines, computers, computer peripherals, communications equipment, optical instruments, and medical instruments. As only data until 1998 are available in the JIP database, we extended the IT hardware stock until 2000 by using the annual growth rate of real IT hardware stock from 1998 to 2000 in the JCER IT data.[19]

IT Software (Million Yen, 1990 Prices)

We constructed industry-level software stock data using the JIP database, the JCER IT data, and the software investment data underlying Motohashi (2002) and Jorgenson and Motohashi (2003).[20] The JCER data provide real software stock by two-digit industry but include only order-made software. In the JIP database, real software stock data that cover in-house software and general application software as well as order-made software are available until 1999. Therefore, we first divided the JIP software stock value at the macro level into each two-digit industry using the

19. We wish to thank Professor Tsutomu Miyagawa at Gakushuin University and Ms. Yukiko Ito at the Japan Center for Economic Research (JCER) for providing the JCER IT data.
20. We are also grateful to Dr. Kazuyuki Motohashi at the University of Tokyo for providing the data.

Table 1A.4   Correspondence table: JIP classification correspondence to Fukao-Ito classification (manufacturing)

JIP Industry	Fukao-Ito Classification									
11 Livestock products	57	58	59	60	61	62	63			
12 Processed marine products	64	65	66	67	68	69				
13 Rice polishing, flour milling	70	71	72	73						
14 Other foods	74	75	76	77	78	79	80	81	82	83
	84	85	86	87	88	89	90	99	100	
15 Beverages	91	92	93	94	95	96	97	98		
16 Tobacco	101									
17 Silk	102									
18 Spinning	103									
19 Fabrics and other textile products	104	105	106	107	108	109	110	111		
20 Apparel and accessories	112	113	114							
21 Lumber and wood products	115	116	117	118	119					
22 Furniture	120	121								
23 Pulp, paper, paper products	122	123	124	125	126	127	128			
24 Publishing and printing	129	130	131							
25 Leather and leather products	191	192	193							
26 Rubber products	187	188	189	190						
27 Basic chemicals	132	133	134	135	136	137	138	139	140	141
	142	143	144	145	146	147	148	149	150	151
	152	153	154	155	156	157	158	159	160	161
	162	163								
28 Chemical fibers	164	165								
29 Other chemicals	166	167	168	169	170	171	172	173		
30 Petroleum products	174	175	176	177	178	179	180	181	182	
31 Coal products	183	184	185							
32 Stone, clay, and glass products	194	195	196	197	198	199	200	201	202	203
	204	205	206							
33 Steel manufacturing	207	208	209	210						
34 Other steel	211	212	213	214	215	216	217	218	219	220
	221	222								
35 Nonferrous metals	223	224	225	226	227	228	229	230	231	232
	233									
36 Metal products	234	235	236							
37 General machinery equipment	237	238	239	240	241	242	243	244	245	246
	247	248	249	250	251	252	253	254	255	256
	257	258	259	278	281					
38 Electrical machinery	269	270	271							
39 Equipment and supplies for household use	260	261	262							
40 Miscellaneous electrical machinery	263	264	265	266	267	268	272	273	274	
41 Motor vehicles	275	276								
42 Ships	279	280	282							
43 Other transportation equipment	277	283	284	285	286	287	288	289		
44 Precision machinery and equipment	290	291	292	293	294	295				
45 Other manufacturing	186	296	297	298	299	300	301	302		

distribution ratios in the JCER IT data. Then, we further divided it into the JIP industry classification, using the distribution ratios of IT hardware by JIP industry. Because the JIP software stock data are available only until 1999, for the year 2000 we calculated the macro-level real software stock, using Motohashi's software investment data and software deflators.

Non-IT Physical Capital Stock (Million Yen, 1990 Prices)

Physical capital stock data including IT hardware stock by industry are available in the JIP database until 1998. We extended the data up to 2000 by using the investment data in METI's *Report on Industry Statistics,* which is based on the *Census of Manufacturers.* First, we aggregated the data on investment in fixed assets in the *Report on Industry Statistics* into the JIP-industry level and then deflated them using the gross domestic capital formation deflator (plant and equipment) in the *Annual Report on National Accounts* released by the Cabinet Office, Government of Japan. We assumed a depreciation rate of 10 percent and estimated the real physical capital stock for 1999 and 2000. Non-IT physical stock is defined as physical capital stock minus IT hardware stock.

Value Added (Million Yen, 1990 Prices)

We used value added data in the JIP database up to 1998. The data for 1999 and 2000 were constructed using the *SNA Input-Output Tables* released by the Cabinet Office, Government of Japan.

R&D Expenditure (Million Yen, 1990 Prices)

We used R&D expenditure data in the JIP database up to 1998. We extended the data up to 2000 using the *Report on the Survey of Research and Development,* Ministry of Public Management, Home Affairs, Posts and Telecommunications. The deflators were taken from the *Annual Report on the Promotion of Science and Technology,* Ministry of Education, Science, Sports and Culture.

VIIT (%)

The variable VIIT is defined as the share of vertical intraindustry trade in total trade values. For our definition of vertical intraindustry trade and data sources, see the second section of the appendix.

VIITworld/shipments (%)

This variable is calculated as (VIIT · [exports + imports]/2/domestic shipments). VIITworld takes account of Japan's trade with all countries in the world. Data on domestic shipments were taken from the JIP database up to 1998 and from the *SNA Input-Output Tables* for 1999 and 2000.

VIITasia9/shipments (%)

This variable is calculated in the same way as VIITworld/shipments. VIITasia9 takes account of Japan's trade with the following nine Asian countries: China, Korea, Taiwan, Hong Kong, Singapore, Indonesia, Malaysia, the Philippines, and Thailand.

VIITnon-asia9/shipments (%)

This variable is calculated in the same way as VIITworld/shipments. VIITnon-asia takes account of Japan's trade with all countries other than the nine Asian countries.

KL (Million Yen per Person, 1990 prices)

The capital-labor ratio was calculated using physical capital stock data and data on the number of workers taken from the JIP database for 1988–1998.

Wage (1990 = 1.0)

The labor-quality-adjusted wage index was taken from the JIP database for 1988–1998.

Rental Price (1990 = 1.0)

The rental price index of capital was taken from the JIP database for 1988–1998.

References

Berman, Eli, John Bound, and Zvi Griliches. 1994. Changes in the demand for skilled labor within U.S. manufacturing: Evidence from the Annual Survey of Manufacturers. *Quarterly Journal of Economics* 109:367–98.
Campa, Jose, and Linda S. Goldberg. 1997. The evolving external orientation of manufacturing: A profile of four countries. *Economic Policy Review* 3 (2): 53–81.
Davis, Donald R., and David E. Weinstein. 2003. Why countries trade: Insights from firm-level data. *Journal of the Japanese and International Economies* 17 (4): 432–47.
Falvey, Rodney E. 1981. Commercial policy and intra-industry trade. *Journal of International Economics* 11:495–511.
Feenstra, Robert C., and Gordon H. Hanson. 1996a. Foreign investment, outsourcing, and relative wages. In *The political economy of trade policy,* ed. Robert C. Feenstra, Gene M. Grossman, and Douglas A. Irwin, 89–127. Cambridge, MA: MIT Press.
———. 1996b. Globalization, outsourcing, and wage inequality. *American Economic Review* 86:240–45.
———. 1999. The impact of outsourcing and high-technology capital on wages:

Estimates for the United States, 1979–1990. *The Quarterly Journal of Economics* 114 (3): 907–40.

———. 2000. Aggregation bias in the factor content of trade: Evidence from U.S. manufacturing. *AEA Papers and Proceedings* 90 (2): 155–60.

———. 2001. Global production sharing and rising inequality: A survey of trade and wages. NBER Working Paper no. 8372. Cambridge, MA: National Bureau of Economic Research, July.

Fontagné, Lionel, Michael Freudenberg, and Nicholas Péridy. 1997. Trade patterns inside the single market. CEPII Working Paper no. 1997-07. Paris: Centre d'Etudes Prospectives et d'Informations Internationales, April.

Fukao, Kyoji, Tomohiko Inui, Hiroki Kawai, and Tsutomu Miyagawa. 2004. Sectoral productivity and economic growth in Japan, 1970–98: An empirical analysis based on the JIP database. In *Growth and productivity in East Asia.* Vol. 13 of NBER-EASE, ed. Takatoshi Ito and Andrew K. Rose, 177–220. Chicago: University of Chicago Press.

Fukao, Kyoji, Hikari Ishido, and Keiko Ito. 2003. Vertical intra-industry trade and foreign direct investment in East Asia. *Journal of the Japanese and International Economies* 17 (4): 468–506.

Genda, Yuji. 1998. Japan: Wage differentials and changes since the 1980s. In *Wage differentials: An international comparison,* ed. Toshiaki Tachibanaki, 35–71. London: Macmillan.

Godo, Yoshihisa. 2001. Estimation of average years of schooling by levels of education for Japan and the United States, 1890–1990. Foundation for Advanced Studies on International Development (FASID). Mimeograph.

Greenaway, David, Robert Hine, and Chris Milner. 1995. Vertical and horizontal intra-industry trade: A cross industry analysis for the United Kingdom. *Economic Journal* 105:1505–18.

Hijzen, Alexander, Holger Görg, and Robert C. Hine. 2003. International fragmentation and relative wages in the UK. IZA Discussion Paper Series no. 717. Bonn, Germany: Institute for the Study of Labor, February. http://www.iza.org.

Jorgenson, Dale W., Mun S. Ho, and Kevin J. Stiroh. 2002. Growth of U.S. industries and investments in information technology and higher education. In *Measuring capital in the new economy,* ed. Carol Corrado, John Haltiwanger, and Daniel Sichel. Chicago: University of Chicago Press, forthcoming.

Jorgenson, Dale W., and Kazuyuki Motohashi. 2003. Economic growth of Japan and the United States in the information age. RIETI Discussion Paper Series no. 03-E-015. Tokyo: Research Institute of Economy, Trade and Industry.

Katz, Lawrence F., and Ana L. Revenga. 1989. Changes in the structure of wages: The United States vs. Japan. *Journal of the Japanese and International Economies* 3:522–53.

Kimura, Fukunari. 2001. Fragmentation, internalization, and inter-firm linkages: Evidence from the micro data of Japanese manufacturing firms. In *Global production and trade in East Asia,* ed. Leonard K. Cheng and Henryk Kierzkoeski, 129–52. Norwell, MA: Kluwer Academic.

Ministry of International Trade and Industry, Government of Japan (MITI). 1999. *Tsutsho Hakusho.* MITI white paper on international trade. Tokyo: MITI.

Motohashi, Kazuyuki. 2002. IT investment and productivity growth in the Japanese economy and a comparison to the United States (in Japanese). RIETI Discussion Paper Series no. 02-J-018. Tokyo: Research Institute of Economy, Trade and Industry.

Pyo, Hak K., and Kwang-Hee Nam. 1999. A test of the convergence hypothesis by rates of return to capital: Evidence from OECD countries. CIRJE Discussion

Paper Series no. 99-CF-51. Tokyo: Center for International Research on the Japanese Economy, June.

Sachs, Jeffery D., and Howard J. Shatz. 1994. Trade and jobs in U.S. manufacturing. *Brookings Papers on Economic Activity,* Issue no. 19:1–84. Washington, DC: Brookings Institution.

Sakurai, Kojiro. 2000. *Gurobaru-ka to rodo shijo: Nihon no Seizogyo no Keisu* [Globalization and labor market: The case of Japanese manufacturing]. *Keizai Keiei Kenkyu* 21 (2).

———. 2004. How does trade affect the labor market? Evidence from Japanese manufacturing. *Japan and the World Economy* 10 (2): 139–61.

Comment   Chin Hee Hahn

Here is what I think this paper did. First, this paper starts out with some facts. It shows that, compared with the United States, Japan's economic growth until the 1990s was more dependent upon inputs accumulation, such as physical capital and labor quality growth. Also, it shows that the rate of return on capital has declined continuously for the past three decades and that, compared with the United States, the college wage premium increased only slightly.

Then, this paper raises the following question. Does the changing trade pattern reflect the changes in factor endowment conditions in such a way as to prevent the forces of diminishing returns to set in? This question is motivated by the presumption that if the Japanese economy adequately specialized in the physical and human capital–intensive products, especially during the 1990s when international division of labor with other East Asian countries expanded, the rate of return to physical capital, in particular, might not have declined continuously as observed.

To address this question empirically, this paper examines both interindustry and intraindustry trade and relates them to the changes in factor intensities. First, this paper performs factor content analysis and finds out that during the 1990s Japan increased net exports of physical capital stock and nonproduction labor but decreased net exports of production labor, which is consistent with the Heckscher-Ohlin theory. That is, the authors find that in terms of interindustry trade, the changes in the trade pattern during the 1990s reflects deepening of physical and human capital. Then the authors move on to examine whether international division of labor with other East Asian countries or vertical intraindustry trade (VIIT) can explain capital deepening and skill upgrading. They do not find any significant relationship between VIIT and the capital-labor ratio. As for

Chin Hee Hahn is a research fellow of the Korea Development Institute.

the skill upgrading, they get mixed results, which is sensitive to the definition of skilled labor.

The conclusion of the paper is that Japan is not adequately specializing in the export of capital-intensive goods so that trade did not play a large role in offsetting excess supply of capital.

Let me make several comments on this paper. My first comment is on the way the conclusion is drawn out. In fact, this paper carries out two types of analyses: factor content analysis and factor intensity regressions. However, with regard to the question of whether the changes in trade pattern adequately reflect the changes in factor endowments, these two analyses produces different answers. The factor content analysis shows that the changes in the trade pattern are consistent with capital deepening, for example. To the contrary, the factor intensity regressions show that the industry capital-labor ratio is not explained by VIIT. Because these two analyses give us two different pictures on the role of trade, the issue becomes a quantitative one. In other words, the issue becomes whether the factor content increase in the net export of capital during the 1990s was or was not sufficient enough to fully accommodate the aggregate capital deepening. However, the authors avoid this issue by providing a decomposition analysis, which suggests that aggregate capital deepening is largely attributable to within-industry effect. Based on this result, the authors seem to take the results on VIIT more seriously than the results by factor content analysis to reach their conclusion. Insofar as the decomposition analysis is sensitive to the level of aggregation, it doesn't seem to be clear enough whether we can draw out a clear conclusion relying on the capital-labor ratio regressions. That is, how much weight to put on the results from factor content analysis to evaluate the role of trade seems to be an unresolved issue. Recognizing this, the conclusion of the paper is only suggestive rather than conclusive.

My second comment is that the authors seem to rely too heavily on trade in order to explain the decline in rate of return to capital. Although the decline in the returns to capital could well be attributable to the inadequate changes in capital-intensive exports, it could be also attributable to the decline in the rate of total factor productivity improvement, especially during the 1990s. Table 1.1 of this paper clearly shows that the decline in the total factor productivity (TFP) growth rate is exactly what happened during the 1990s. Given this possibility, an entirely different interpretation of the results is not impossible. The story could go as follows. The factor content analysis suggests that the trade pattern changed, reflecting rapid capital deepening and skill upgrading. Although the decomposition exercise shows that capital deepening is largely attributable to within effect, this result could suffer from the industry aggregation problem and uncontrolled macroeconomic conditions. Thus, even though the VIIT did not contribute significantly to the capital deepening and skill upgrading, changes in trade patterns by and large played the role of offsetting the excess supply of capital. Given the decline in the TFP growth rate during the 1990s, the rate of return to capital would have declined further if it were not for the changes in trade patterns.

Comment   Ji Chou

The paper utilizes Japanese economic data to analyze vertical intraindustry trade (VIIT) and the division of labor in East Asia comprehensively and rigorously. The paper covers aspects from macroeconomics, industrial level to firm level, and the paper analyzes the argument step by step and includes notes for the possible drawback of compiled data.

The paper achieves the research goal with some interesting issues left. First, the finding that VIIT instead of outsourcing has a strong and positive relationship with skilled workers' share contrasts cases in the United States (Feenstra and Hanson 1996a,b, 1999) and the United Kingdom (Hijzen, Görg, and Hine 2003), but the finding is similar to another Japanese study (Sakurai 2000).

Because VIIT is goods differentiated by quality, while outsourcing is the import of intermediate inputs, high quality products could be critical components, rare materials, and highly value added final products. The industry, whose outsourcing measure is high in Japan as shown in table 1C.1 is not necessarily a technology-intensive industry. Therefore, the demand for skilled workers might not be high.

Second, the between effect is negative in the decomposition of capital-labor ratio growth as shown in figure 2.5 and figure 2.6 of the text. The authors accused it of the decline in private investment. But the decline of private investment might be caused by the decline of export demand rather than domestic demand. Because the between effect reflects the reallocation of capital among industries, the negative between effect might imply that the price in Japan cannot reflect market change promptly. This argument corresponds to the authors' last statement in their conclusion: "VIIT patterns might not be determined by the price of capital, but by other factors."

Third, the regression in the study seems to use the pooling estimation; the panel data approach may provide more information about the time and cross-section aspect.

Fourth, the authors use single-country data to analyze the VIIT and the division of labor in East Asia. Although the analysis catches most pictures of the Asian trade structure, the contribution of the NICs' foreign direct

Ji Chou is director of the Center for Economic Forecasting of the Chung Hua Institution for Economic Research.

Table 1C.1   **Vertical intraindustry trade and high narrow outsourcing in Japan**

High vertical intraindustry trade	High narrow outsourcing
Publishing and printing	Livestock products
Other chemicals	Processed marine products
Metal products	Lumber and wood products
Electrical machinery	Pulp, paper, and paper products
Other electrical machinery	Leather and leather products
Precision machinery and equipment	Basic chemicals
	Petroleum products
	Steel manufacturing
	Nonferrous metals
	Other electrical machinery
	Other transportation equipment
	Precision machinery and equipment

investment (FDI) to Association of Southeast Asian Nations (ASEAN) and China could be overlooked.

References

Feenstra, Robert C., and Gordon H. Hanson. 1996a. Foreign investment, outsourcing, and relative wages. In *The political economy of trade policy,* ed. Robert C. Feenstra, Gene M. Grossman, and Douglas A. Irwin, 89–127. Cambridge, MA: MIT Press.
———. 1996b. Globalization, outsourcing, and wage inequality. *American Economic Review* 86:240–45.
———. 1999. The impact of outsourcing and high-technology capital on wages: Estimates for the United States, 1979–1990. *The Quarterly Journal of Economics* 114 (3): 907–40.
Hijzen, Alexander, Holger Görg, and Robert C. Hine. 2003. International fragmentation and relative wages in the UK. IZA Discussion Paper Series no. 717. Bonn, Germany: Institute for the Study of Labor, February. http://www.iza.org.
Sakurai, Kojiro. 2000. *Gurobaru-ka to rodo shijo: Nihon no Seizogyo no Keisu* [Globalization and labor market: The case of Japanese manufacturing]. *Keizai Keiei Kenkyu* 21 (2).

2

Exporting and Performance of Plants
Evidence from Korean Manufacturing

Chin Hee Hahn

2.1 Introduction

It has been a widely accepted view that international trade and international openness play a key role in enhancing the growth rates of output and income. As a prime example, the past economic successes of Korea and several other East Asian countries have often been attributed, to a large extent, to the export-oriented development strategy. The World Bank (1993) points to the export-promotion development strategy as the hallmark of the East Asian miracle countries. Also, Krueger (1995) argues that the most salient distinguishing characteristic between the success of East Asian countries and the stalled growth of Latin American countries is the openness of the international trading regime, that is, outward-oriented trade strategy of the former versus import substitution development strategy of the latter. Even in recent years, many developing countries, including Korea, promote exports based on the belief that exporting activity per se is valuable, bringing additional economic benefits. There is little disagreement on the static gains from trade in the form of improved resource allocation and economic well-being. However, the dynamic relationship between increased trade and long-run output and productivity growth is less well understood.

This study examines the relationship between exporting and productivity using plant-level panel data on the Korean manufacturing sector dur-

Chin Hee Hahn is a research fellow of the Korea Development Institute.

The author would like to thank James Harrigan, Kyoji Fukao, editors, other seminar participants at the fourteenth NBER–East Asia Seminar on Economics, and two anonymous referees for helpful comments and suggestions. The author also appreciates excellent research assistance by Yonghun Jung.

ing the period of 1990 to 1998. The two key questions to be addressed are whether exporting improves productivity and whether more productive plants export. To consider the possibility that the benefits of exporting accrue through channels other than productivity, other measures of plant performance, such as shipment and employment, are also considered in the analysis.

There are numerous studies supporting that exporters are better than nonexporters in terms of various performance measures. That is, exporting plants are more productive, larger, more capital intensive, more technologically sophisticated, and pay higher wages compared with those plants producing for domestic markets only.[1] While these studies provided an important stepping stone toward understanding the exporting-performance nexus, they do not by themselves suggest that exporting activities bring medium- to long-run technological and other benefits over and above the static gains from trade. That is, exporters might be better than nonexporters before they start exporting due to factors other than exporting activity itself. Thus, in order to understand the role of international openness or, more narrowly, the role of exporting in the growth of productivity and output, it is necessary to understand the causal relationship between exporting and performance measures including productivity.

There are broadly two strands of theoretical explanations for the positive cross-sectional correlation between exporting and productivity. One explanation is that more productive plants self-select into the export market. In this case, causality runs from productivity to exporting. The usual argument is based on the existence of sunk entry costs associated with export market participation (Bernard and Jensen 1999a). In order to sell goods abroad, producers might have to incur additional costs, such as transport costs, modification costs to meet foreign tastes and regulations, and setup costs to establish a distribution network. With these costs present, only productive producers can expect to recoup entry costs after entering the foreign market.[2] An alternative explanation of the positive cross-sectional correlation between exporting and productivity is that exporting activity serves as a vehicle for diffusion of disembodied technology or knowledge across countries and, hence, improves productivity. By exporting, exporters learn from knowledgeable buyers who provide them with blueprints and give them technical assistance.[3] This explanation is often referred to as "learning effect." If these mechanisms are at work, then the

1. These studies include Aw and Hwang (1995), Aw and Batra (1998), Chen and Tang (1987), Haddad (1993), Handoussa, Nishimizu, and Page (1986), Tybout and Westbrook (1995), Aw, Chen, and Roberts (2001), Aw, Chung, and Roberts (2000), Bernard and Jensen (1995), and Bernard and Wagner (1997).
2. The existence of sunk costs is not an essential feature to explain self-selection. See Clerides, Lach, and Tybout (1998).
3. This explanation has long been provided by many trade economists. See Grossman and Helpman (1991), Ben-David and Loewy (1998), and Feeny (1999) for recent exposition.

positive correlation between exporting and productivity might reflect causation running from exporting to productivity.[4]

Several empirical studies provide evidence on the causal relationship between exporting and productivity. Most studies report that exporters are more productive than nonexporters before they start exporting, suggesting that the cross-sectional correlation between exporting and productivity partly reflects a self-selection effect. For example, Clerides, Lach, and Tybout (1998) find some evidence in favor of selection effect using plant-level panel data from Colombia, Mexico, and Morocco. Similar results are reported by Aw, Chung, and Roberts (2000) and Aw, Chen, and Roberts (2001) for Taiwan and Bernard and Jensen (1999b) for the United States. However, evidence in favor of learning effect is scarce. Although Bernard and Jensen (1999b) report that new entrants into the export market experience some productivity improvement at around the time of entry, these productivity gains are very short-lived.

Similar study exists for Korea. Aw, Chung, and Roberts (2000) report that they could not find any strong evidence that supports the learning-by-doing hypothesis or the self-selection hypothesis using plant-level data on the Korean manufacturing sector for three years spread over a five-year interval: 1983, 1988, and 1993. Their evidence on Korea differs from other countries in that even the self-selection hypothesis is not supported, although the lack of strong evidence of learning by doing may be consistent with findings in other countries. Aw, Chung, and Roberts provide two explanations for the absence of productivity-based self-selection in Korea. The first one is that while long-run expected profitability is an indicator by which the decision to export is eventually guided, plant productivity may not be a good indicator of plant profitability due to heterogeneity across producers on the demand side of the market, particularly in the case of Korea. The second explanation is that the Korean government's investment subsidies tied to exporting activity rendered plant productivity a less useful guide on the decision to export.

These explanations might or might not be close to reality in Korea. However, their rejection of the self-selection hypothesis as well as learning by doing in Korea seems somewhat problematic. As Aw, Chung, and Roberts (2000) show, there exists a strong and robust cross-sectional correlation between exporting and productivity even in Korea's case. That is, they show that exporters have higher productivity than nonexporters and that those differences are large and statistically significant. Then, the su-

---

4. Of course, as Tybout (2001) summarizes, there are other mechanisms whereby exporting may improve productivity. One is exploitation of economies of scale by exporting. However, after surveying the empirical evidence, Tybout (2001) concludes that productivity growth due to scale efficiency effects is likely to be very small. Another mechanism is enhanced incentive to innovate and eliminate waste by exporting. However, Tybout (2001) points out that the theoretically implied direction of change in efficiency critically depends upon model specifics.

perior productivity of exporters to those of nonexporters must have developed before or after export-market participation. In other words, the strong and robust cross-sectional correlation between exporting and productivity is at odds with the rejection of both self-selection and learning. Thus, there is a need to reexamine the relationship between exporting and productivity.

In this study, we use annual plant-level panel data from 1990 to 1998. Using the annual data has an advantage in that dynamic aspects of the exporting-productivity relationship can be more closely examined. In particular, the availability of an export variable at annual frequency allows us to pay more careful attention to the exporting history of a plant in the analysis. We follow two methodologies employed by Bernard and Jensen (1999a) and Bernard and Jensen (1999b). Both studies use a dummy variable regression approach and compare performance measures of plant groups before and after export-market entry. We prefer, however, the methodology used in the latter study, as it better utilizes available information on the exporting history of plants in grouping plants.[5] Nevertheless, we report empirical results by both methodologies.

This study sheds light on several policy issues. There are many studies documenting that international trade openness is one of the key factors explaining cross-country variations in long-run economic growth. For example, Sachs and Warner (1995) provide empirical evidence that openness and growth are positively related. Hall and Jones (1999) show that openness and institutional quality are the most important factors determining the long-run total factor productivity level, which accounts for most of the cross-country variations in the long-run output level. If we take these empirical findings seriously, then we need to understand exactly how openness improves a country's long-run output level and growth rate. In order to fully utilize the opportunity that openness provides, then the channels through which openness enhances aggregate productivity and output should be more clearly understood. For example, if openness enhances aggregate productivity not only through intrafirm technological learning but also through cross-firm and cross-industry resource reallocation, then openness per se might not be a cure-all. That is, greater openness accompanied by policies improving resource reallocation will be more effective than policies enhancing openness alone in order to exploit the potential benefits that openness provides.

Also, this study provides some empirical evidence that is necessary to evaluate and guide various measures to promote export. For example, if export-market entry mostly reflects a self-selection process—that is, good firms become exporters—then policies that intervene in the process are likely to bring about less-desirable outcomes than policies that do not in-

---

5. Details of the methodologies will be described in the following.

tervene. With regard to the learning effect, if there are no postentry rewards from exporting, then policies designed to increase the number of exporters become footloose and waste resources, as those firms and their workers will not receive any extra benefits. On the other hand, if exporting activity per se involves technological learning, then appropriate policy intervention might be to reduce barriers to export-market participation, such as export assistance, information programs, joint marketing efforts, and trade credits (Bernard and Jensen 1999a).

This paper is organized as follows. In the following section, some basic statistics on exporting plants are provided. Also, we examine cross-sectional correlation between exporting and various performance measures, including plant total factor productivity. In section 2.3 and section 2.4, we examine the existence of selection and learning effects using two different methodologies. In section 2.3, we report empirical results based on methodologies by Bernard and Jensen (1999a). In section 2.4, we follow methodologies by Bernard and Jensen (1999b), which allows us to utilize the advantages provided by the annual data set and to pay particular attention to the exporting history of plants. Section 2.5 summarizes the results and concludes.

2.2   Basic Statistics and Exporter Performance

2.2.1   Data

We briefly describe the data and provide some basic statistics on exporting plants. The data used in this study is the unpublished plant-level data underlying the Annual Report on Mining and Manufacturing Survey. The data covers all plants with five or more employees in 580 manufacturing industries at the KSIC (Korean Standard Industrial Classification) five-digit level. It is unbalanced panel data with about 69,000 to 97,000 plants for each year during the 1990–1998 period.[6] For each year, plant-level exports as well as other variables on production structures are available. Exports in this data set include direct exports and shipments to other exporters and wholesalers but do not include shipments for further processing. Following the convention in the literature, we define exporters in a given year as plants that reported a positive amount of exports. Accordingly, nonexporters in a given year are those plants with zero exports.[7]

---

6. Unfortunately, the plant-level data is not publicly available. The Korea Development Institute has been allowed access to the data set under the condition that no information on individual plants or firms are revealed in the analysis. We appreciate the Korea Statistical Office for allowing us to use the data set. Although the surveys exist after 1998, these could not be used due to incomplete information on the plant identity variable.

7. All the values of the export variable are either zero or positive. There are no missing or negative values.

2.2.2 Exporters and Export Intensity

Table 2.1 shows the number of exporting plants and average exports as a percentage of shipments (export intensity) during the 1990–1998 period. During the sample period, the exporting plants accounted for between 11.0 and 15.3 percent of all manufacturing plants. The share of exporting plants rose slightly between 1990 and 1992 but has since declined steadily until 1996. However, with the outbreak of the financial crisis in 1997, the share of exporting plants rose somewhat noticeably to reach 14.8 percent in 1998. The rise in the share of exporting plants since 1997 can be attributed mostly to the closing of nonexporting plants, rather than an increase in the number of exporting plants. The increase in the number of exporters since 1997 was only modest. These changes are broadly consistent with the huge depreciation of the Korean won and the severe contraction in domestic demand associated with the crisis.

Consistent with the high export dependency of the economy, the share of exports in shipments at the plant level is quite high in Korea. During the sample period, the unweighted average export ratio (exports-shipments) is between 43.6 and 54.8. The average export ratio steadily declines from 1990 to 1996 but rises with the onset of the crisis. The average export ratio

Table 2.1   Number of exporters and export intensity

Year	Total number of plants	Nonexporters	Exporters	Exports/shipments ratio (%) Unweighted	Weighted	Export growth (%)
1990	69,690 (100)	58,392 (85.0)	10,298 (15.0)	54.8	37.3	9.4
1991	72,213 (100)	61,189 (84.7)	11,024 (15.3)	54.3	37.3	13.9
1992	74,679 (100)	63,241 (84.7)	11,438 (15.3)	51.7	36.3	14.7
1993	88,864 (100)	77,514 (87.2)	11,350 (12.8)	49.9	36.0	12.5
1994	91,372 (100)	80,319 (87.9)	11,053 (12.1)	47.2	35.9	17.7
1995	96,202 (100)	85,138 (88.5)	11,064 (11.5)	44.8	37.2	26.7
1996	97,141 (100)	86,502 (89.0)	10,639 (11.0)	43.6	35.3	8.3
1997	92,138 (100)	80,963 (87.9)	11,175 (12.1)	44.2	38.0	27.5
1998	79,544 (100)	67,767 (85.2)	11,777 (14.8)	44.7	48.7	40.4

Notes: Export data in the final column are in current won from the Bank of Korea. Numbers in parentheses are *t*-statistics.

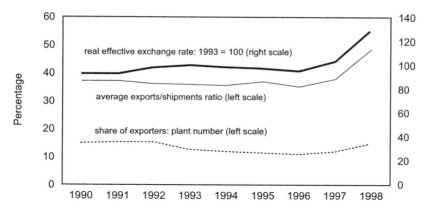

Fig. 2.1   Movements of share of exporters and export intensity

weighted by shipment is generally lower than the unweighted average export ratio, suggesting that smaller exporting plants have a higher export ratio.

One interesting point to note is that the rise in weighted export share is much more dramatic than in unweighted export share during the 1997–1998 period when there was a large depreciation in the won. Combined with the fact that new entries in the export market since 1997 were only modest, this suggests that the export boom during that period was mainly driven by the increase in export shipments of large firms who had been previously exporting. The fact that a huge favorable exchange rate shock triggered a large increase in exports of previous exporters and an only mild increase of new entries in the export market is consistent with the presence of sunk entry costs in the export market (see figure 2.1).

2.2.3   Performance of Exporters versus Nonexporters

It is a well-established fact that exporters are better than nonexporters by various performance standards. As a point of departure, we examine whether the same pattern holds in our data set for the period covered in this study. Table 2.2 compares various plant attributes between exporters and nonexporters for three selected years. In terms of number of workers and shipments, exporters are, on average, much larger in size than nonexporters. The difference in shipments is more substantial than the difference in the number of workers. So the average labor productivity of exporters, measured by production and value added per worker, are higher than that of nonexporters. Compared with the value added per worker differential, the difference in production per worker between exporters and nonexporters is more pronounced. This might reflect the more intermediate-intensive production structure of exporters relative to nonexporters.[8]

---

8. I am indebted to James Harrigan for pointing out this feature of the data.

Table 2.2   Performance characteristics of exporters vs. nonexporters

	1990		1994		1998	
	Exporters	Nonexporters	Exporters	Nonexporters	Exporters	Nonexporters
Employment (person)	153.6	24.5	119.4	20.0	95.1	17.8
Shipments (million won)	11,505.5	957.0	17,637.1	1,260.3	25,896.8	1,773.8
Production per worker (million won)	50.5	26.8	92.4	47.0	155.0	74.2
Value added per worker (million won)	16.5	11.3	31.0	20.4	51.3	29.6
TFP	0.005	−0.046	0.183	0.138	0.329	0.209
Capital per worker (million won)	16.8	11.9	36.0	21.9	64.6	36.7
Nonproduction worker/total employment (%)	24.9	17.1	27.5	17.5	29.6	19.2
Average wage (million won)	5.7	5.1	10.3	9.2	13.7	11.5
Average production wage (million won)	5.5	5.1	10.0	9.2	13.1	11.4
Average nonproduction wage (million won)	6.8	5.3	11.6	9.4	15.6	12.4
R&D/shipments (%)			1.2	0.6	1.4	0.6

Although exporters have a higher capital-labor ratio and higher share of nonproduction workers in employment than nonexporters, these differences in inputs do not fully account for the differences in labor productivity. As a consequence, levels of total factor productivity (TFP) of exporting plants are, on average, higher than those plants producing for domestic markets only.[9] Some of the differences in the TFP levels may be attributed to the differences in research and development (R&D) intensity. Controlling for the size of shipments, exporters spent about twice as much on R&D as nonexporters. From the worker's point of view, exporters had more desirable attributes than nonexporters. The average wage of exporters is higher than that of nonexporters. Although the wage of both production and nonproduction workers are higher for exporters compared to nonexporters, the differential in the wage of nonproduction workers is more pronounced.

Table 2.3 shows the average percentage difference in various performance measures between exporters and nonexporters for three years, which is estimated from the following regressions:

$$\ln Y_i = \alpha + \beta \text{EXPORT}_i + \gamma \text{INDUSTRY}_i + \delta \text{REGION}_i + \lambda \ln \text{SIZE}_i + \varepsilon_i,$$

where EXPORT_i is a dummy variable for exporters, INDUSTRY_i and REGION_i are dummy variables for the five-digit KSIC industry and plant location, and SIZE_i denotes plant size measured by number of employees. The three columns in table 2.3 show the estimated coefficients of exporter dummy variable without any control variables, with controls of industry and region, and with additional control of plant size.

The regression confirms that exporters outperform nonexporters in terms of various performance characteristics for all years, even after controlling for industry, region, and plant size. Also, all coefficients on the export dummy variable are highly significant. Controlling industry and region has little effect on the magnitude of the export premium. However, controlling for plant size greatly reduced the coefficients of the export dummy variable, which suggests that to a large extent the desirable characteristics of the exporters are attributable to their larger size. Nevertheless, the estimated export premium remained highly significant.

Controlling for industry and region, exporters employed more workers by about 100 percent. Controlling for industry, region, and size, the shipments of exporters were larger by about 50 percent, production per worker by about 50 percent, and value added per worker by about 20 to 30 percent. Although exporters have a higher capital-labor ratio and a higher share of nonproduction workers, they also have a higher TFP level. The TFP levels of exporters are, on average, 2.5 to 7.5 percent higher than nonexporters, with industry, region, and size controlled. Average wage is between 8 and

---

9. The TFP index is based on the multilateral chained index number approach. For details, see appendix.

Table 2.3   Exporter premia (%)

	Estimated exporter premia		
	No control	Industry and region controlled	Industry, region, and size controlled
1990			
Employment (person)	123.4	117.2	n.a.
Shipments (million won)	186.4	186.6	47.9
Production per worker (million won)	64.0	70.2	48.3
Value added per worker (million won)	30.2	35.1	21.7
TFP	5.1	5.9	2.5
Capital per worker (million won)	32.0	39.3	31.3
Nonproduction worker/total employment (%)	15.6	26.6	24.8
Average wage (million won)	11.8	16.3	8.1
Average production wage (million won)	7.1	12.3	6.7
Average nonproduction wage (million won)	25.7	27.0	8.4
1994			
Employment (person)	112.9	108.6	n.a.
Shipments (million won)	179.3	175.4	47.4
Production per worker (million won)	67.0	67.3	47.6
Value added per worker (million won)	33.9	34.3	23.5
TFP	4.5	4.5	3.8
Capital per worker (million won)	55.1	51.4	34.5
Nonproduction worker/total employment (%)	17.8	24.2	22.5
Average wage (million won)	12.5	15.0	9.7
Average production wage (million won)	8.6	11.7	8.4
Average nonproduction wage (million won)	22.6	23.0	8.8
R&D/shipments (%)	−54.7	−54.9	−6.4
1998			
Employment (person)	102.2	93.6	n.a.
Shipments (million won)	181.3	166.3	54.4
Production per worker (million won)	79.3	72.9	54.7
Value added per worker (million won)	48.4	43.9	32.5
TFP	12.0	10.2	7.5
Capital per worker (million won)	57.3	46.6	32.9
Nonproduction worker/total employment (%)	15.6	22.1	24.4
Average wage (million won)	19.1	17.9	12.5
Average production wage (million won)	14.8	14.1	10.5
Average nonproduction wage (million won)	25.5	23.6	12.0
R&D/shipments (%)	−48.2	−45.6	−7.4

Notes: n.a. = not applicable. All coefficients are significant at the 1 percent level.

13 percent higher for exporting plants compared to plants producing for domestic markets only.

The findings in the preceding cross-sectional analysis suggest that a significant TFP and other performance gaps do exist between exporters and nonexporters. As discussed earlier, however, these findings should not be interpreted as suggesting that exporting per se makes plants or firms better. We now turn to the issue of whether these performance gaps developed before or after exporting.

2.3   Selection and Learning: Methodology by Bernard and Jensen (1999a)

In this section, we follow Bernard and Jensen (1999a) and examine whether good plants export and/or whether exporting improves performance. In order to examine the existence of self-selection effect, we compare various plant characteristics between exporters and nonexporters before exporting. As in Bernard and Jensen (1999a), we divide our sample into two distinct subperiods—1990–1994 and 1995–1998. We select all plants that did not export in any of the first years and compare initial levels and growth rates of performance measures for exporters and nonexporters in the final year. For example, we compare various performance measures in 1990 for exporters and nonexporters in 1994.

In 1997 and 1998, export growth increased significantly with the huge depreciation of the won. If the huge depreciation in Korea's currency induced previously unproductive plants to enter the export market, then it will work against finding self-selection effects even if it really existed. Also, if nonexporting plants that stopped operations in 1998 following the severe contraction in domestic demand were located at the lower end of the productivity distribution, this factor will also work against finding the self-selection effect. Thus, the self-selection effect is more likely to be observable in the first subperiod if it exists.

The ex ante levels of performance measures of exporters compared with nonexporters are obtained as the coefficient on export dummy variable from the following regressions:

$$(1) \quad \ln Y_{i0} = \alpha + \beta \text{EXPORT}_{iT} + \gamma \text{INDUSTRY}_i + \delta \text{REGION}_i$$
$$+ \lambda \ln \text{SIZE}_{i0} + \varepsilon_i,$$

where $\ln Y_{i0}$ is logarithm of plant performance measures at the initial year of the period and EXPORT_{iT} is an export dummy variable at the final year of the period. Table 2.4 shows the estimated export premia expressed in percentages for 1990 and 1995.

Table 2.4 shows that exporters have on average more workers and larger shipments than nonexporters before exporting, regardless of the period examined. This result holds whether we control for industry, region, and plant size. Although inclusion of the plant-size variable reduces the size of the estimated exporter premia, they are still statistically significant. A similar conclusion holds for labor productivity measures, such as production per worker and value added per worker, as well as for capital-labor ratio and share of nonproduction workers. However, average wages of exporters are not significantly higher than those of nonexporters. Although wage

Table 2.4   **Ex ante export premia for future exporters: 1990–1994, 1995–1998 (%)**

	Ex ante export premia		
	No control	Industry and region controlled	Industry, region, and size controlled
1990			
Employment (person)	52.9	47.9	n.a.
	(16.2)	(16.2)	
Shipments (million won)	78.0	71.5	15.8
	(15.4)	(16.2)	(5.7)
Production per worker (million won)	25.7	24.1	16.4
	(7.6)	(8.7)	(6.0)
Value added per worker (million won)	17.3	15.8	11.1
	(6.6)	(6.6)	(4.6)
TFP	1.6	2.4	0.6
	(1.1)	(1.8)	(0.5)
Capital per worker (million won)	16.5	15.2	14.6
	(3.2)	(3.4)	(3.2)
Nonproduction worker/total employment (%)	14.6	15.6	13.5
	(5.1)	(6.2)	(5.3)
Average wage (million won)	5.4	4.1	1.3
	(3.1)	(2.6)	(0.8)
Average production wage (million won)	3.2	2.5	1.0
	(1.8)	(1.5)	(0.6)
Average nonproduction wage (million won)	11.1	9.5	0.5
	(5.5)	(4.8)	(0.3)
1995			
Employment (person)	43.3	43.0	n.a.
	(19.9)	(21.4)	
Shipments (million won)	72.2	69.2	18.4
	(20.9)	(22.7)	(9.6)
Production per worker (million won)	30.0	27.2	19.5
	(13.0)	(14.2)	(10.3)
Value added per worker (million won)	16.4	13.9	9.8
	(9.2)	(8.6)	(6.1)
TFP	0.9	−0.0	−0.9
	(0.9)	(−0.0)	(−0.9)
Capital per worker (million won)	33.8	29.9	25.3
	(9.1)	(9.5)	(8.0)
Nonproduction worker/total employment (%)	13.7	16.9	15.9
	(7.0)	(9.8)	(9.1)
Average wage (million won)	3.7	3.3	1.0
	(3.1)	(3.1)	(0.9)
Average nonproduction wage (million won)	2.2	2.1	0.8
	(1.7)	(1.9)	(0.7)
Average production wage (million won)	7.5	6.5	0.0
	(5.5)	(4.8)	(0.0)
R&D/shipments (%)	−25.5	−25.0	0.8
	(−2.1)	(−1.9)	(0.1)

Notes: n.a. = not applicable. Numbers in parentheses are *t*-statistics.

level measures of exporters are estimated to be higher than those of non-exporters without controlling for plant size, the coefficient on export dummy variable loses significance or becomes substantially smaller when the plant-size variable is included.

In table 2.4, ex ante TFP levels of exporters are estimated to be no higher than nonexporters, on average. The coefficient on the export dummy variable is not significantly different from zero in any of the regressions at the conventional significance level. In the regression with all control variables included for 1995–1998 period, the exporters' TFP premium is even negative although insignificant.[10]

In order to see whether future exporters experienced faster growth in various performance measures, we ran the following regressions:

$$(2) \quad \Delta \ln Y_{iT-1} = \alpha + \beta EXPORT_{iT} + \gamma INDUSTRY_i + \delta REGION_i$$
$$+ \lambda \ln SIZE_{i0} + \varepsilon_i$$

where $\Delta \ln Y_{iT-1}$ is the annual average growth rate of performance measures, such as TFP, shipments, and employment, between year 0 and $T - 1$. The estimated growth rate premia of exporters, which are the coefficients on the export dummy variable, are reported in table 2.5.

For both subperiods, the growth rates of employment and shipments were estimated to be higher for future exporters. With industry, region, and initial plant size controlled, the growth rate premia of exporters are 5.1 to 6.2 percent per year for employment and 6.0 to 8.3 percent per year for shipments, depending on the period. We could not find any strong evidence suggesting that TFP growth rates are higher in plants that will export in the future. Although TFP growth rate premia were positive in the later period, it became insignificant when controlling for plant size.

Let us summarize the preceding results, which are based on methodologies by Bernard and Jensen (1999a). Overall, exporters already have many of the desirable characteristics before they start exporting. Compared with nonexporters, exporters are larger, more capital intensive, have higher labor productivity, and hire proportionately more nonproduction workers several years before they start exporting. Also, future exporters experience higher growth rates of employment and shipments than nonexporters before they start exporting. However, we could not find significant ex ante differences in levels and growth rates of TFP between future exporters and nonexporters.

Now we examine whether exporting improves performance over various

---

10. One interesting point to note here is that the TFP premia of exporters are generally lower in the 1995–1998 period compared with those in the 1990–1994 period, although they are all insignificant. As discussed earlier, this may be due to the disappearance of low-productivity nonexporters from the sample and entries of previously unproductive producers into the export market during the crisis period.

Table 2.5   **Ex ante growth rate premia of future exporters: 1990–1994,**
                1995–1998 (%)

	Estimated ex ante growth rate premia		
	No control	Industry and region controlled	Industry, region, and size controlled
1990–1993 growth rates			
Employment (person)	2.8	2.6	5.1
	(4.8)	(4.5)	(8.9)
Shipments (million won)	3.6	3.8	6.0
	(3.6)	(3.8)	(6.1)
Production per worker (million won)	1.0	1.3	1.1
	(1.1)	(1.5)	(1.3)
Value added per worker (million won)	−1.0	−0.6	−0.5
	(−1.1)	(−0.7)	(−0.6)
TFP	0.2	−0.0	0.3
	(0.3)	(−0.1)	(0.5)
Capital per worker (million won)	1.5	0.5	−1.8
	(1.0)	(0.3)	(−1.2)
Nonproduction worker/total employment (%)	−0.1	0.1	−0.5
	(−0.1)	(0.2)	(−0.5)
Average wage (million won)	0.3	0.4	0.5
	(0.6)	(0.7)	(0.9)
Average production wage (million won)	−0.1	−0.1	−0.0
	(−0.1)	(−0.1)	(−0.0)
Average nonproduction wage (million won)	1.1	1.2	1.6
	(1.4)	(1.6)	(2.1)
1995–1997 growth rates			
Employment (person)	3.6	3.2	6.2
	(6.6)	(5.9)	(11.7)
Shipments (million won)	5.9	5.7	8.3
	(6.4)	(6.0)	(8.8)
Production per worker (million won)	2.1	2.2	1.8
	(2.5)	(2.6)	(2.2)
Value added per worker (million won)	1.6	1.7	1.2
	(1.9)	(2.0)	(1.3)
TFP	1.5	0.9	0.8
	(2.9)	(1.9)	(1.5)
Capital per worker (million won)	−0.2	−0.1	−2.1
	(−0.2)	(−0.1)	(−1.7)
Nonproduction worker/total employment (%)	0.2	0.2	−0.1
	(0.3)	(0.3)	(−0.1)
Average wage (million won)	1.5	1.3	1.1
	(2.6)	(2.2)	(1.8)
Average nonproduction wage (million won)	1.4	1.1	0.9
	(2.2)	(1.8)	(1.5)
Average production wage (million won)	0.9	0.8	1.0
	(1.2)	(1.0)	(1.3)
R&D/shipments (%)	−3.6	−3.3	−8.8
	(−0.4)	(−0.3)	(−0.8)

Note: See table 2.4 note.

Table 2.6   **TFP growth rate premium of current exporters over various time horizons**

	Subsequent annual TFP growth rate premium	
	No control	Industry, region, and size controlled
Short-run		
1990–1998	4.4	−0.9
	(7.2)	(−1.3)
Medium-run		
1990–1994	1.9	−0.6
	(2.3)	(−0.6)
1994–1998	5.0	2.1
	(8.2)	(2.9)
Long-run		
1990–1998	3.2	0.9
	(5.8)	(1.3)

Notes: Short-run premium is estimated from the pooled time series cross-sectional data. Medium- and long-run premia are estimated from cross-sectional data. Numbers in parentheses are *t*-statistics.

time horizons, following the methodologies by Bernard and Jensen (1999a). The performance measure we are most interested in is the TFP, because, if knowledge or technology spillovers do exist associated with exporting activity, they will show up primarily in TFP. Also, the question of whether there are extra TFP gains from exporting has been at the center of the debate on the benefits of exporting. As additional performance measures, we consider shipments and employment. The reason is that if there are benefits of exporting in the form of improved resource allocation, then they are likely to be captured, to a large extent, by changes in these two variables.[11]

To see whether current exporters perform better subsequently than nonexporters, we ran the following regressions:

$$(3) \quad \Delta \ln Y_{iT} = \alpha + \beta EXPORT_{i0} + \gamma INDUSTRY_i + \delta REGION_i + \lambda \ln SIZE_{i0} + \varepsilon_{iT}$$

where $\Delta \ln Y_{iT}$ is the average annual growth rate of various performance measures of plants for a time interval of length T. We vary the length of the time interval to examine short-run, medium-run, and long-run performances of current exporters relative to nonexporters. The short-run performance is estimated from the pooled time series and cross-sectional data with T equal to one. Medium- or long-run performance of exporters are estimated from the cross-sectional data.

Table 2.6 reports TFP growth rates of exporters relative to nonexporters, which are the coefficients on the export dummy variable in regression (3),

---

11. From here on, we confine our discussion to these three performance measures—TFP, shipments, and employment.

over various time horizons. In the short run, without any control variables, the TFP growth rates of exporters are significantly higher than nonexporters during the 1990–1998 period. However, when industry, region, and size of plants are controlled for, the coefficient on the export dummy variable becomes negative although insignificant. In the medium run, the results are mixed. In the earlier period, the coefficient on the export dummy went from positive to negative, although insignificant, with the inclusion of control variables. Meanwhile, in the later period, it was significantly positive regardless of the inclusion of control variables. However, the significantly positive export dummy variable in the later period might have been heavily influenced by the export boom during the 1997–1998 period. In the long run, the export dummy variable lost significance with the inclusion of control variables.

In table 2.7, we report growth rates of shipments of exporters relative to nonexporters. When controlling variables are not included in the regressions, the shipment growth rates of exporters are estimated to be significantly lower than nonexporters over various time horizons. When industry, region, and size of plants are controlled, however, the coefficients were reduced substantially in absolute magnitude or became insignificant. In the case of employment growth rates of exporters relative to nonexporters, which is reported in table 2.8, the coefficients on past export dummy variables are negative over various time horizons. However, when industry, region, and size of plants are controlled, they all became significantly positive.

Overall, we could not find any clear evidence of TFP improvement from exporting following the methodologies by Bernard and Jensen (1999a). Benefits of exporting are confined to faster employment growth. Subse-

Table 2.7   **Shipments growth rate premium of current exporters over various time horizons**

	Subsequent annual shipments growth rate premium	
	No control	Industry, region, and size controlled
Short-run		
1990–1998	−7.4	−3.5
	(−30.7)	(−12.7)
Medium-run		
1990–1994	−5.7	−2.2
	(−20.0)	(−6.4)
1994–1998	−2.0	0.3
	(−6.6)	(0.9)
Long-run		
1990–1998	−2.7	−0.1
	(−11.7)	(−0.5)

Note: See table 2.6 note.

Table 2.8   **Employment growth rate premium of current exporters over various time horizons**

	Subsequent annual employment growth rate premium	
	No control	Industry, region, and size controlled
Short-run		
1990–1998	–3.0	5.1
	(–22.6)	(33.9)
Medium-run		
1990–1994	–2.7	1.7
	(–15.5)	(8.5)
1994–1998	–2.4	2.2
	(–12.7)	(10.7)
Long-run		
1990–1998	–2.2	1.3
	(–15.0)	(7.5)

Note: See table 2.6 note.

quent growth rates of shipments of current exporters are no faster than that of nonexporters. These results are very similar to what Bernard and Jensen (1999a) found for the United States.

2.4   Selection and Learning: Methodology by Bernard and Jensen (1999b)

In the preceding analysis, which is based on methodologies by Bernard and Jensen (1999a), we could not find any strong evidence supporting the learning-by-exporting or self-selection hypothesis. Then is it justifiable to conclude that the decision to export, for example, is not based on TFP in Korea? The answer seems to be negative because the methodology previously employed does not follow the exporting history of plants closely enough. For example, in table 2.4, we selected plants that did not export during the 1990–1993 period and compared the TFP levels between exporters and nonexporters in 1994. However, the exporting history of those selected plants might vary after 1994. For example, among the plants classified as nonexporters in 1994, there might be productive plants that have entered the export market after 1994. Also, there might exist unproductive plants classified as exporters in 1994 that exited the export market after 1994.[12] With this phenomenon present, it will be hard to find TFP-based self-selection even if it exists in reality.

Now, with the exporting history of plants available at an annual fre-

12. At the same time, there are plants that switch exporting status more than twice since 1994. Without further analysis, it is hard to predict the effect of the presence of these plants in the sample.

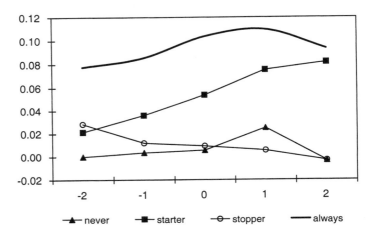

Fig. 2.2   Relative levels of TFP by plant group: Before and after

quency during our sample period, we can perform a more focused analysis. Following Bernard and Jensen (1999b), we take the entire exporting history of plants into account and classify them into the following five categories. There are plants that exported during the entire sample period, which are grouped as "always." Similarly, the "never" group consists of plants that never exported. The "starter" group represents plants that become exporters during the sample period and remain in the export market. Those that drop out of the export market and do not reenter are grouped as "stopper." The "other" plants are those that switched exporting status more than twice during the sample period.[13]

Then we examined a five-year window centered on the switching years for starter and stopper, in comparison with always, never, and other. The regressions are of the following form:

$$(4)\quad \ln Y_{it} = \sum_{g \in G} \sum_{k \in K} \beta_{gk} D_{gi} D_{ki} + \gamma \text{INDUSTRY}_i + \delta \text{REGION}_i + \theta \text{YEAR}_t + \varepsilon_{it}$$

where $\ln Y_{it}$ logs of various performance measures, G is the set of five plant groups defined as in the preceding, and K is the set of locations in the five-year window so that $K = \{-2, -1, 0, 1, 2\}$. D_g and D_k are dummy variables denoting plant group and location in the five-year window, respectively. Thus, the coefficient β_{gk} denotes mean values of each plant group g at each location k, controlling for industry, region, and year effects. Figure 2.2

13. Before grouping plants, we selected only those plants that operated either in export markets or domestic markets during the sample period. Thus, plants that ceased operating entirely or began operating during our sample period, for example, are excluded from the following analysis. This procedure, however, enables us to focus on the transition between domestic and export markets.

Table 2.9   **Relative TFP levels before and after exporting (or stopping exporting)**

Plant location	Plant group				
	Never	Stopper	Starter	Always	Other
−2	0.0	2.8	2.1	7.8***	3.0***
	(0.0)	(1.5)	(1.2)	(8.4)	(5.2)
−1	0.4	1.2	3.6**	8.5***	3.2
	(0.2)	(0.8)	(2.2)	(4.1)	(1.7)
0	0.6	0.9	5.4***	10.4***	4.1**
	(0.3)	(0.5)	(2.9)	(5.1)	(2.1)
1	2.5	0.6	7.5***	11.0***	5.8***
	(1.4)	(0.3)	(3.9)	(5.5)	(3.1)
2	−0.3	−0.3	8.2***	9.3***	4.1**
	(−0.2)	(−0.1)	(4.0)	(4.6)	(2.2)

***Coefficient is significantly different from Never (−2) at the 1 percent level.
**Coefficient is significantly different from Never (−2) at the 5 percent level.

shows movements of the total factor productivity level of the five plant groups, expressed as the difference from the never (−2), and table 2.9 shows corresponding coefficients and standard errors.

Figure 2.2 shows that there exists some learning effect associated with exporting. Plants that start exporting widen the TFP gap with those that never exported and close the gap with those that always exported after entering the exporting market. However, the learning effect is very short lived and pronounced immediately after entry into the export market. If the learning effect from exporting is long lived, then we can expect the following. First, the productivity gap between never and always will widen over time. Second, starter will not close the TFP gap with always, because the "always" group will enjoy first-mover advantage over the starter in improving the TFP level. However, neither of these phenomenon is observed in the figure.[14] Also, a large part of the TFP gap between starter group and always group disappears two years after they start exporting. In short, we find some evidence in favor of the learning-by-exporting hypothesis in the Korean manufacturing sector although the learning effect is rather short lived.

Figure 2.2 also confirms the existence of self-selection in the entry into and exit from the export market. Plants that start exporting have somewhat higher TFP levels compared to those that never export several years before they enter the export market. Table 2.9 shows that the TFP gap between those two groups are statistically significant one year before starting to ex-

14. Starters begin to improve relative TFP level even before they start exporting. However, as Bernard and Jensen (1999a) discuss, it is not easy to explain this phenomenon in a theoretically compelling way.

port. Also, those plants that drop out of the export market exhibit persistently lower and deteriorating TFP compared with always during the pre-exit period.

In order to see whether the benefits of exporting are realized in channels other than TFP improvement, we ran regression (4) with logs of shipments and employment as dependent variables, respectively. The results are reported in figure 2.3 and figure 2.4. Again, the estimated coefficients and their

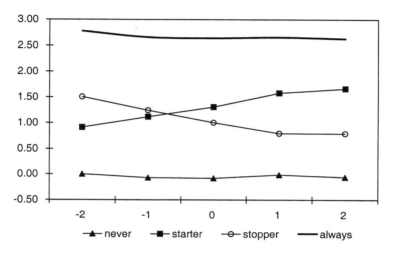

Fig. 2.3   Relative levels of shipments by plant group: Before and after

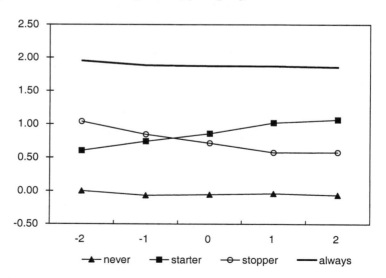

Fig. 2.4   Relative levels of employment by plant group: Before and after

standard errors are shown in table 2.10 and table 2.11. Similar to the case of TFP, plants that start exporting increase both shipments and employment at around the time of entry into the export market, relative to those plants that always export or never export. Also, the gaps in the levels of shipments and employment between always and never are fairly stable over time in terms of percentages, suggesting that the increase in shipments and employment by exporting does not last forever. When compared with relative TFP movements in figure 2.2, one noticeable feature in figure 2.3 and figure 2.4 is that the magnitudes of change in shipments and employment of starters relative to always and never are not very large within the five-year window. That is, exporting-related adjustments in shipments and employ-

Table 2.10 **Relative shipments levels before and after exporting (or stopping exporting)**

Plant location	Plant group				
	Never	Stopper	Starter	Always	Other
−2	0.0	150.6***	91.4***	277.6***	123.6***
	(0.0)	(20.9)	(13.5)	(77.7)	(54.7)
−1	−7.0	124.5***	112.0***	265.8***	116.9***
	(−0.9)	(20.1)	(17.7)	(32.7)	(15.3)
0	−8.1	100.6***	130.8***	264.1***	116.3***
	(−1.1)	(13.5)	(18.3)	(33.0)	(15.5)
1	−1.0	79.8***	158.0***	265.5***	122.7***
	(−0.1)	(10.3)	(20.9)	(33.9)	(16.7)
2	−5.8	79.3***	166.4***	262.9***	119.5***
	(−0.8)	(10.0)	(21.0)	(33.1)	(16.1)

***Coefficient is significantly different from Never (−2) at the 1 percent level.

Table 2.11 **Relative employment levels before and after exporting (or stopping exporting)**

Plant location	Plant group				
	Never	Stopper	Starter	Always	Other
−2	0.0	103.7***	60.4***	195.2***	82.5***
	(0.0)	(19.7)	(12.2)	(74.8)	(50.0)
−1	−6.9	84.4***	74.3***	188.3***	76.0***
	(−1.3)	(18.7)	(16.1)	(31.8)	(13.6)
0	−5.6	71.6***	85.7***	187.4***	78.1***
	(−1.0)	(13.2)	(16.4)	(32.1)	(14.3)
1	−4.0	57.6***	101.9***	187.3***	80.0***
	(−0.8)	(10.2)	(18.5)	(32.7)	(14.9)
2	−6.4	57.9***	106.7***	185.8***	78.1***
	(−1.2)	(10.0)	(18.4)	(32.1)	(14.4)

***Coefficient is significantly different from Never (−2) at the 1 percent level.

ment may take a much longer time, compared with TFP levels. While the reasons for the slower adjustment of shipments and employment are not clearly understood, this may suggest that it takes a long time for the gains in allocation efficiency from exporting to materialize. The TFP-based selection and learning effects and similar effects based on shipments and employment, as shown in figures 2.2 to figure 2.4 and tables 2.9 to table 2.11, was robust with the exclusion of the crisis period of 1997 to 1998, when export growth increased significantly with the depreciation in the exchange rate.[15]

2.5 Summary and Concluding Remarks

This study examines the relationship between exporting and various performance measures including TFP, using annual plant-level panel data on the Korean manufacturing sector during the period of 1990 to 1998. The two key questions examined are whether exporting improves productivity (learning) and/or whether more productive plants export (self-selection). Following the methodologies from Bernard and Jensen (1999b), this study provides some evidence modestly supporting both self-selection and learning-by-exporting effects. Also, the selection and learning effects are more pronounced at around the time of entry into and exit from the export market. Thus, positive and robust cross-sectional correlation between exporting and TFP is accounted for by both selection and learning effects. Although the results are somewhat sensitive to the methodologies employed, they are in contrast with Aw, Chung, and Roberts (2000) who do not find any strong evidence of self-selection or learning in Korea. Similar effects are observed when shipments or employment are considered as performance measures. Overall, this study suggests that the benefits from exporting have been realized not only through resource reallocation channel but also through the TFP channel in Korea.

Although the different conclusions derived in this study from Aw, Chung, and Roberts (2000) might well be due to the different time periods covered in the analysis, it may also arise from the differences in the data set and methodologies employed. The annual panel data set and methodologies employed in this study allow us to follow more closely the exporting history of plants and to observe important changes that occur at around the time of entry into and exit from the export market.

If foreign markets provide opportunities to improve aggregate TFP both through the intraplant TFP channel and also through the resource reallocation channel, as suggested by this study, then openness by itself may not be sufficient to fully exploit the potential benefits that openness provides. That is, greater openness accompanied by policies improving resource reallocation will be more effective than policies enhancing openness alone.

---

15. It is possible that the export boom during the crisis period biased the results toward finding learning effects if it caused disproportionate output expansion of new exporters.

Finally, it might be too hasty to jump to the conclusion, based on the short-lived nature of learning effect, that the export market does not play a significant role in a sustained increase in aggregate productivity. Suppose there is a continual entry and exit of producers in and out of the export market, which is documented in many other studies, and that each new cohort of entrants starts from higher TFP levels than its preceding cohorts. Under these circumstances, exporting may provide an opportunity for the continuous improvement of aggregate TFP, although the learning-by-exporting opportunity may be short lived from the viewpoint of individual producers.

Appendix

Measurement of Plant Total Factor Productivity

Plant TFP is estimated using the chained-multilateral index number approach as developed in Good (1985) and Good, Nadiri, and Sickles (1999). It uses a separate reference point for each cross section of observations and then chain-links the reference points together over time. The reference point for a given time period is constructed as a hypothetical firm with input shares that equal the arithmetic mean input shares and input levels that equal the geometric mean of the inputs over all cross-sectional observations. Thus, the output, inputs, and productivity level of each firm in each year is measured relative to the hypothetical firm at the base time period. This approach allows us to make transitive comparisons of productivity levels among observations in a panel data set.[16]

Specifically, the productivity index for firm i at time t in our study is measured in the following way:

$$\ln \text{TFP}_{it} = (\ln Y_{it} - \overline{\ln Y_t}) + \sum_{\tau=2}^{t} (\overline{\ln Y_\tau} - \overline{\ln Y_{\tau-1}})$$

$$- \left\{ \sum_{n=1}^{N} \frac{1}{2}(S_{nit} + \overline{S_{nt}})(\ln X_{nit} - \overline{\ln X_{nt}}) + \sum_{\tau=2}^{t}\sum_{n=1}^{N} \frac{1}{2}(\overline{S_{n\tau}} + \overline{S_{n\tau-1}})(\overline{\ln X_{n\tau}} - \overline{\ln X_{n\tau-1}}) \right\},$$

where Y, X, S, and TFP denote output, input, input share, TFP level, respectively, and symbols with an upper bar are corresponding measures for

---

16. Good, Nadiri, and Sickles (1999) summarize the usefulness of chaining multilateral productivity indices succinctly. While the chaining approach of the Tornqvist-Theil index, the discrete Divisia, is useful in time series applications where input shares might change over time, it has severe limitations in cross-section or panel data where there is no obvious way of sequencing the observations. To the contrary, the hypothetical firm approach allows us to make transitive comparisons among cross-sectional data, while it has an undesirable property of sample dependency. The desirable properties of both the chaining approach and hypothetical firm approach can be incorporated into a single index by the chained-multilateral index number approach.

hypothetical firms. The subscripts τ and n are indices for time and inputs, respectively. In our study, the year 1990 is the base time period.

As a measure of output, we used the gross output (production) of each plant in the survey deflated by the producer price index at the disaggregated level.[17] As a measure of capital stock, we used the average of the beginning and end of the year book value capital stock in the survey deflated by the capital goods deflator. As a measure of labor input, we used the number of workers, which includes paid employees (production and nonproduction workers), working proprietors, and unpaid family workers. Here, we allowed for the quality differential between production workers and all the other types of workers. The labor quality index of the latter was calculated as the ratio of average nonproduction workers' and production workers' wages of each plant, averaged again over the entire plants in a year. As a measure of intermediate input, we used the "major production cost" plus the "other production cost" in the survey. Major production cost covers costs arising from materials and parts, fuel, electricity, water, manufactured goods outsourced and maintenance. The other production cost covers outsourced services, such as advertising, transportation, communication, and insurance. The estimated intermediate input was deflated by the intermediate input price index.

We assumed constant returns to scale so that the sum of factor elasticity equals one. Labor and intermediate input elasticity for each plant are measured as average cost shares within the same plant-size class in the five-digit industry in a given year. Thus, the factor elasticity of plants is allowed to vary across industries and size classes and over time. Here, plants are grouped into three size classes according to the number of employees: 5–50, 51–300, and over 300.

References

Aw, B. Y., and G. Batra. 1998. Technology, exports, and firm efficiency in Taiwanese manufacturing. *Economics of Innovation and New Technology* 7 (1): 93–113.
Aw, B. Y., X. Chen, and M. J. Roberts. 2001. Firm-level evidence on productivity differentials: Turnover and exports in Taiwanese manufacturing. *Journal of Development Economics* 66 (1): 51–86.

17. Using the price index normalized to 1 at base period implies that we measure real outputs of plants at base year as the current values of production. We use industry-level price indexes rather than aggregate-level price indexes to control for price changes over time, which might differ across industries, in measuring real outputs of plants. Alternatively, if the aggregate price index, such as the gross domestic product (GDP) deflator, were used for all industries, this procedure will attribute any changes over time in relative prices among industries to changes in real outputs.

Aw, B. Y., S. Chung, and M. J. Roberts. 2000. Productivity and turnover in the export market: Micro-level evidence from the Republic of Korea and Taiwan (China). *The World Bank Economic Review* 14 (1): 65–90.

Aw, B. Y., and A. Hwang. 1995. Productivity and the export market: A firm-level analysis. *Journal of Development Economics* 47 (2): 313–32.

Ben-David, D., and M. Loewy. 1998. Free trade, growth, and convergence. *Journal of Economic Growth* 3:143–70.

Bernard, A. B., and J. B. Jensen. 1995. Exporter, jobs, and wages in U.S. manufacturing: 1976–1987. *Brookings Papers on Economic Activity, Microeconomics:* 67–112.

————. 1999a. Exceptional exporter performance: Cause, effect, or both? *Journal of International Economics* 47:1–25.

————. 1999b. Exporting and productivity. NBER Working Paper no. 7135. Cambridge, MA: National Bureau of Economic Research, May.

Bernard, A. B., and J. Wagner. 1997. Exports and success in German manufacturing. *Weltwirtschaftliches Archiv* 133 (1): 134–57.

Chen, T. J., and D. P. Tang. 1987. Comparing technical efficiency between import-substituting and export-oriented foreign firms in a developing country. *Journal of Development Economics* 26 (2): 277–89.

Clerides, S. K., S. Lach, and J. R. Tybout. 1998. Is learning by exporting important? Micro-dynamic evidence from Colombia, Mexico, and Morocco. *Quarterly Journal of Economics* 113:903–47.

Feeny, J. 1999. International risk sharing, learning by doing, and growth. *Journal of Development Economics* 58 (2): 297–318.

Good, David H. 1985. *The effect of deregulation on the productive efficiency and cost structure of the airline industry.* Ph.D. diss., University of Pennsylvania.

Good, David H., M. Ishaq Nadiri, and Robin Sickles. 1999. Index number and factor demand approaches to the estimation of productivity. In *Handbook of applied econometrics.* Vol. 2, *Microeconometrics,* ed. H. Pesaran and P. Schmidt, 14–80. Oxford, UK: Blackwell.

Grossman, G., and E. Helpman. 1991. *Innovation and growth in the world economy.* Cambridge, MA: MIT Press.

Haddad, M. 1993. How trade liberalization affected productivity in Morocco. Policy Research Working Paper no. 1096. Washington, DC: World Bank, Development Research Group.

Hall, R., and C. I. Jones. 1999. Why do some countries produce so much more output per worker than others? *Quarterly Journal of Economics* 114:83–116.

Handoussa, J., M. Nishimizu, and J. Page. 1986. Productivity change in Egyptian public sector industries after the 'opening.' *Journal of Development Economics* 20 (1): 53–74.

Krueger, Anne O. Policy lessons from development experience since the Second World War. In *Handbook of development economics.* Vol. 3B, ed. J. R. Behrman and T. N. Srinivasan, 2497–2550. Amsterdam: North-Holland.

Sachs, Jeffrey, and A. Warner. 1995. Economic reform and the process of global integration. *Brookings Papers on Economic Activity,* Issue no. 1:1–95. Washington, DC: Brookings Institution.

Tybout, J. R. 2001. Plant- and firm-level evidence on 'new' trade theories. NBER Working Paper no. 8418. Cambridge, MA: National Bureau of Economic Research, August.

Tybout, J. R., and M. D. Westbrook. 1995. Trade liberalization and dimensions of efficiency change in Mexican manufacturing industries. *Journal of International Economics* 31:53–78.

World Bank. 1993. *The East Asian miracle: Economic growth and public policy.* New York: Oxford University Press.

Comment   Kyoji Fukao

Using plant-level data, the author examines links between productivity and exporting and found evidence for the existence of both a self-selection mechanism (relatively productive firms tend to become exporters later) and learning-by-exporting effects. Compared with a preceding study on this issue by Aw, Chung, and Roberts (2000), which used data for 1983, 1988, and 1993 and, incidentally, did not find any significant evidence for self-selection or learning by exporting, this paper takes greater account of the dynamic aspects of the export-productivity nexus by using annual data for 1990–1998. The empirical analysis is carefully conducted, and I found the paper very instructive.

I have four comments.

My first comment relates to the drawbacks of using plant-level data for this type of analysis. It is true that, generally, total factor productivity (TFP) calculations at the plant level are more reliable than those at the firm level. For example, because firms usually produce a broad range of products, it is difficult to find an appropriate price index to deflate their nominal output. However, in the case of productivity comparisons between exporters and nonexporters, plant-level data is problematic. The reason is that exporting firms may have to incur fixed costs to penetrate foreign markets—a major part of which is probably incurred at the firm level rather than at the plant level. For instance, a firm's sales activities abroad are likely to be paid for by the head office.

Suppose that, because of this fixed cost, the domestic price of a certain product is lower than the export price. Then the TFP level of exporting plants will be estimated to be higher than that of nonexporting plants even when their actual productivity is identical. Probably one solution to this problem is to add firm dummies to the explanatory variables in the regression.

My second comment is on the effects of trade protection. Some of Korea's manufacturing industries are protected by tariff barriers. We will observe relatively high tariff rates and domestic prices for industries that are not competitive and do not export. Therefore, the estimated TFP of non-exporting plants might be biased upward. If we use industry dummies at

Kyoji Fukao is a professor at the Institute of Economic Research, Hitotsubashi University, and a fellow of the Research Institute of Economy, Trade and Industry (RIETI).

the disaggregated industry level, this bias will be small. So I would like to know more about the industry dummies used in the econometric analysis.

My third comment is on sample size. At the end of section 2.3, the author compares TFP of two groups of plants. The first group consists of plants that started exporting in 1994 and continuously exported thereafter, while the second group consists of plants that never exported during the sample period. Using this comparison, the author finds a significant ex ante TFP premium in 1990 for future exporters. This result is very interesting. But I am afraid that by defining new exporters and nonexporters in a very rigorous way like this, the sample size might become very small. I would like to know how many observations the author has in the first group (new exporters).

My final comment is that a brief overview of Korean trade and TFP growth would have been helpful. In the paper, the descriptive analysis is relatively limited, leaving questions such as in what industries are import tariffs high? What industries show a revealed comparative advantage? How does the Korean government subsidize private investments that are related to exporting activities? In what industries has TFP growth been high? If the author provided overviews of these issues, non-Korean readers would be better able to understand the results of the paper.

Reference

Aw, B. Y., S. Chung, and M. J. Roberts. 2000. Productivity and turnover in the export market: Micro-level evidence from the Republic of Korea and Taiwan (China). *The World Bank Economic Review* 14 (1): 65–90.

Comment   James Harrigan

The paper by Chin Hee Hahn is part of a growing literature on plant-level characteristics and participation in the international economy. As many other researchers have found in other countries and time periods, Hahn finds that exporting plants in Korea during the 1990s were better in many dimensions. In particular, in tables 2.2 and 2.3 Hahn finds that for three years (1990, 1994, and 1998), exporters are larger and more skill-, capital-, and intermediates-intensive. He also finds that labor productivity and total factor productivity (TFP) are higher for exporting plants; for example, in 1994, TFP was about 4 percent higher for exporting rather than nonexporting plants.

James Harrigan is a senior economist at the Federal Reserve Bank of New York, and a research associate of the National Bureau of Economic Research.

It is worth pausing to think about what it means for one plant to be better than another. Economists should usually focus on aggregate welfare, which depends inter alia on optimal resource allocation. Good resource allocation will generally require a mix of skill- and capital-intensive activities, as well as a mix of production for domestic consumption and for export, so correlations between these attributes have no obvious welfare implications. Productivity is a different story: greater TFP is always and everywhere a good thing, so it is reasonable to regard high-TFP plants as better than low TFP plants. This is not the case for labor productivity (variations that might reflect just variations in usage of other inputs), so I will focus for the rest of this comment on Hahn's results on TFP alone.

Because of the centrality of TFP, it is also worth pausing to consider measurement issues. In principle, TFP is a purely physical concept: for two plants producing *identical* output, we say that plant A has TFP 10 percent higher than plant B if, given identical inputs, plant A can produce 10 percent more output than plant B. In practice, two plants almost never produce exactly the same thing, and even if they did, economists rarely have data on physical outputs. As a consequence, calculations such as those done by Hahn use value data as a proxy for output. The problem is that values can vary due to variations in prices, conflating profitability, and productivity. At a minimum this implies random measurement error, but it might be worse: for example, an inefficient monopoly plant might have higher measured TFP than an efficient plant selling in a competitive market. The conclusion is that cross-plant TFP comparisons should be regarded with some skepticism.

Hahn is interested in explaining the cross-sectional correlations between TFP and exporting observed in tables 2.2 and 2.3. He considers two possibilities: high-TFP plants become exporters, or exporters have faster TFP growth. These are important hypotheses to distinguish, as any reasonable case for export promotion policies hinges on the relevance of the exporting-causes-productivity hypothesis. Quite surprisingly, tables 2.4–2.9 offer no support for *either* hypothesis: future exporters have TFP levels or growth rates no higher than future nonexporters (tables 2.4, 2.5, and 2.6), nor do exporters have faster TFP growth than nonexporters (table 2.7). As Hahn observes in his remarks about an earlier paper on Korean plant-level data that found the same thing, this result is very hard to explain: if exporters have higher TFP (as shown in tables 2.2 and 2.3), that advantage must have appeared at some point.

The obvious solution to the puzzle, though Hahn does not mention it explicitly, is that plants that started exporting before 1990 drive the positive cross-sectional correlation between TFP and exporting. This is indirectly confirmed by the results of table 2.10, which are illustrated in figure 2.2: plants that export throughout the period have substantially higher productivity than everyone else does.

International R&D Deployment and Locational Advantage
A Case Study of Taiwan

Meng-chun Liu and Shin-Horng Chen

3.1 Introduction

Recent decades have witnessed the upsurge of East Asia as a major manufacturing base within the developing world, initially as a result of the catching-up of Asian newly industrialized countries (NICs) and, more recently, as a result of the emergence of newly developing economies within the region, mainland China in particular. This has much to do with both indigenous innovation and the relocation of the value chain activities of multinational corporations (MNCs). Lall (2003) elaborates on these two points, arguing that the performance of economies such as Taiwan and Korea may be attributed more to the former, while other less-advanced economies within the region may be gaining more momentum from the latter.

There has, however, been a growing trend for countries in East Asia to seek to attract the R&D facilities of MNCs. On the one hand, not all foreign direct investment (FDI) has equal value because many of the MNCs' subsidiaries are as footloose as branch plants, which can of course lead to the so-called branch plant syndrome (Firn 1975). By contrast, the MNCs' subsidiaries with strong R&D mandates as well as strategic geographical or product range responsibilities tend to adhere more to the host economy and are hence considered to be highly desirable in terms of their effects on local wealth generation. There is, on the other hand, a matching trend within the process of globalization, which has MNCs consolidating the R&D activities of their subsidiaries on a global scale (Petrella 1989; OECD

Meng-chun Liu is deputy director of the International Division of the Chung-Hua Institution for Economic Research. Shin-Horng Chen is director of the International Division of the Chung-Hua Institution for Economic Research.

1997; Patel and Pavitt 1998; Guellec et al. 2001; Kaufmann and Tödtling 2001).

More importantly, the outreach of the MNCs' R&D activities was initially geared to the developed countries, but this has more recently focused on the developing world (Reddy 2000). In particular, countries such as India (Reddy 2000) and China (Xue and Wang 2001; Chen, Shih, and Kao 2002; Walsh 2003) have been documented as less advanced but nevertheless high-profile host countries for MNCs' offshore R&D facilities. The literature on R&D internationalization has proliferated over the past decade, focusing mainly on issues such as the current trends (OECD 1997; Patel and Pavitt 1998; Cantwell and Santangelo 1999; Gerybadze and Reger 1999; Voelker and Stead 1999; Patel and Pavitt 2000; Kumar 2001; Guellec, van Pottelsberghe de la Potterie 2001), organizational evolution (Zedtwitz 2002; Zedtwitz and Gassmann 2002) and the MNCs' motives (De Meyer 1993; Paoli and Guercini 1997; Cantwell and Santangelo 1999; Gerybadze and Reger 1999; Zander 1999). More recent research has addressed the locational aspect of the MNCs' R&D facilities, especially within a host country (Cantwell and Mudambi 2000; Cantwell and Iammarino 2000; Frost and Zhou 2000). However, the relevant literature remains largely based on the experiences of the developed countries.

Furthermore, less attention has been paid to research issues concerning the deepening of foreign corporate R&D activities in host countries, especially for those that are less advanced. Foreign corporate R&D deepening has been recognized as a means for host countries to anchor foreign-owned firms (Kearns and Ruane 2001). This is particularly important for a less-advanced country aiming to enhance the commitment of MNCs to its domestic economy even as its comparative advantage shifts. Moreover, the deepening of foreign corporate R&D in the domestic regions is useful in terms of capitalizing on the agglomeration effect of corporate R&D activities (Carrincazeaux, Lung, and Rallet 2001). Nonetheless, the substantial body of the site-selection literature has focused mainly on the geography of new R&D facilities and investment by MNCs while completely disregarding the fact that this may involve a cumulative process of expansion, contraction, and adaptation of firms' existing facilities in host-country locations (Frost and Zhou 2000).

Set against the preceding background, this paper aims to contribute to the current understanding of R&D internationalization by exploring factors underlying R&D activities in less-advanced economies, with Taiwan standing out as a prime example. The authors are aware that countries such as China and India have drawn considerable attention with regard to this issue (for example, Reddy 2000; Xue and Wang 2001; Chen, Shih, and Kao 2002; Walsh 2003), but on the one hand, little systematic evidence has yet been produced on this issue, while on the other hand, their unique attributes, such as huge market potential, may undermine the applicability of the experiences of these two countries to other less-advanced economies. By contrast, Taiwan, like the majority of the less-advanced economies, has a small domestic market; hence our empirical analyses will focus on the industrial and/or microaspect of the issues concerned. In particular, our studies aim to identify industrial conditions in a less-advanced country that may lead to the deepening of the offshore R&D activities of MNCs. While the determinants of foreign R&D have been explored within the current research using aggregate macro-level country-specific data, the role played by industrial conditions in a less-advanced host country remains largely unexplored to date.

Our empirical work draws on the Statistics on Overseas Chinese and Foreign Investment, a Taiwanese government database concerning foreign corporations' business operation activities in Taiwan, which enables us to utilize the aggregate industrial-level and time series data to examine the issues concerned. The paper is organized as follows. The next section begins with an examination of the literature on R&D internationalization in order to highlight factors that may be considered as locational advantages for a less-advanced host country in attracting MNCs' offshore R&D. We borrow the concept of locational advantage from Dunning's well-known eclectic paradigm and emphasize the significance of first-tier supplier advantage in a Taiwanese context. In the third section, we take advantage of an official database to reveal the patterns of foreign corporate R&D in Taiwan, followed in the subsequent section by a description of the research strategy employed in the paper, in terms of the model specifications and data source. The empirical results are presented and discussed in the penultimate section, followed in the final section by some general conclusions drawn from this study.

3.2   Locational Advantage of R&D Internationalization

In the studies on R&D globalization, the bottom line appears to be that although not yet truly globalized, R&D is undergoing a process of globalization (Howells 1992) and that its progress varies across sectors and economies (Casson and Singh 1993; Dunning 1994). Although more recent literature (OECD 1997; Patel and Pavitt, 1998; Guellec, van Pottelsberghe de la Potterie 2001; Cantwell and Santangelo 1999; Gerybadze and Reger 1999) has also confirmed that this is an escalating trend, despite this trend, the globalization of R&D has largely been considered as a developed country-centric phenomenon.

Reddy (2000), among others, has revealed a rising trend in terms of the R&D operations of MNCs in the developing world. The factors underlying this trend, as highlighted by Reddy, can be summarized as follows. In specific terms, MNCs are themselves facing an increasing need to monitor and learn the new global trends and, hence, to engage in multisourcing of technology inputs, partly because of rising R&D costs, the increasing demand for R&D personnel, and a shortage of R&D personnel in the industrialized countries. Conversely, some, if not a great many, of the less-advanced economies are able to provide an abundant supply of R&D personnel or skills, especially with regard to the so-called noncore R&D areas. This match of supply and demand has been facilitated by factors such as improved information and communication technologies, the flexibility of new technologies that allows delinking of manufacturing and R&D, and the comparative advantages of the less-advanced host countries.

For our empirical work, we propose a concept framework for further analysis that is essentially based on Dunning's (1993) eclectic paradigm, with a strong flavor of the evolutionary approach to technology (Nelson and Winter 1982; Frost and Zhou 2000). According to Dunning (1993), where firms possess advantages of ownership and internalization and host countries enjoy locational advantages, international production may take place. In our view, Dunning's paradigm may be useful for analyzing the offshore R&D activities of MNCs if one interprets ownership, internalization, and locational advantages in the context of R&D, with these advantages being related mainly to the technological routines and trajectories of the firms and the host countries (Dosi 1982). In short, what a firm and an economy can do, or is about to do, is linked strongly to their routines and previous bases.

In our opinion, the ownership advantages of MNCs generally lie in their core technology and world-class brand names. Their core technologies allow them to set the agenda, at an international level, and influence the way in which technology will progress, while their world-class brand names enable them to gain direct access to customers and marketplaces, which in turn facilitate their initiation of concepts for product development and the means of further exploiting market potential elsewhere.

The internalization advantages of MNCs may include systems integration capabilities, product planning capabilities, market access advantages, and information and communication networks. In particular, with systems integration capabilities and information and communication networks at their disposal, they may be able to deploy core and noncore R&D across boundaries, while maintaining control over the profits generated during the whole process. Likewise, the possession of product planning capabilities and market access advantages means that MNCs have control over the two ends of the "smiling curve" and, hence, have the final say in the benefits derived from the entire value chain they face.

With regard to Taiwan as a location for offshore R&D by MNCs, we have to refer to the way in which economic development has evolved on the island, as it is well known as a typical example of the export-oriented industrialization paradigm. Although this goes hand in hand with the process of migration from labor-intensive sectors towards high-technology and capital-intensive industries, Taiwan's major sectors are characterized by their vertical disintegration and the pursuit of "original equipment manufacturer" or "original design manufacturer" (OEM/ODM) contracts for brand marketers, without direct access to the final market. In terms of R&D, local firms may, in general, lack systems integration capabilities and the ability to take the initiative in product and technology development; however, some of the industrial players may be positioned as first-tier suppliers possessing innovation capabilities in certain areas and industrial segments, which could be considered as Taiwan's main locational advantage in offshore R&D. A notable example at issue is Intel, which has recently set up an R&D and innovation center in Taiwan dedicated to product innovation in wireless local area networks (WLANs) partly because Taiwan has been the major global supplier of WLAN sets. Other examples involving Sony and Hewlett Packard (HP) seem to follow the same logic. This is particularly feasible for a sector such as information technology (IT) because Taiwanese IT firms have evolved from pure manufacturers toward integrated service providers, giving rise to intensified interdependence between the network flagships and their Taiwanese subcontractors (Chen 2002). That said, even in an industry such as footwear, we can find the collocation of Nike's main offshore R&D center and its main supplier, Pao Cheng Industrial Corporation, in Taichung.

In order to elaborate on this point within an economy such as that of Taiwan, industrial clusters coevolve with the international industrial structure of the sectors concerned. In addition, whether these industrial clusters are sustainable depends heavily on the extent of localization that may involve at least two things: first, the presence of indigenous firms with substantial innovation capabilities and, second, the ability to "anchor" the network flagships. With regard to the latter, we mean more than the local operations or investments of the network flagships because they can be as footloose as branch plants, as compared to performance plants. Instead, we mean something like international linkages that are so enduring as to enable those indigenous firms to leverage for industrial upgrading.

Moreover, the trend toward globalization involves a process of increased disintegration, certainly of production, but even of innovative capabilities around the globe (Feenstra 1998), with the result that some, if not many, of the indigenous firms and/or industrial clusters in the less-advanced economies are nowadays able to shoulder important functions that used to be undertaken by their counterparts in the developed world. For one thing, outsourcing has become a widely adopted practice in quite a number of industries as a means of ensuring that brand marketers remain cost competitive. As a result, many network flagships have become hollowing-out corporations, focusing their operations on the two ends of the smiling curve, namely the R&D and marketing functions (Chen and Ku 2000; Kotabe 1996; Swamidass and Kotabe 1993; Venkatesan 1992), leading to a certain degree of delinking of R&D and manufacturing for the sector concerned; typical examples at issue include Ericsson in the handset industry and IBM in the personal computer (PC) industry. Within this process, the brand marketers are increasingly linked up with other firms that may not even be in the same neighborhood.

In addition, in many cases, innovation involves technical systems that are inherently large, comprising a set of jointly-consumed interdependent products (Windrum 1999). Because of network effects and product compatibility, successful innovations for technical systems entail intensive interfaces between multiple actors with different knowledge and skills bases, termed as "innovation networks." By implication, not only does such an innovation often result from the collective efforts of interrelated firms, but it also demonstrates that the value chain does not need to be completely internalized within individual firms. Therefore, in many cases, industrial competition takes place between rival technological and production networks that contain a multiplicity of differentiated firms, rather than between vertically integrated oligopolists.

In a sense, the evolutionary approach to technology (Nelson and Winter 1982) is a constructive building block underlying the concept of international linkages. The essence of this approach, in short, is that what a firm or an economy can do, or is about to do, is linked strongly to their routines and previous bases. In technological terms, a firm can be considered as a producer, repository, and user of knowledge, producing or acquiring knowledge and putting it to the most efficient use. Each firm's competitive advantage lies in its stock of knowledge, and because firms possess idiosyncratic knowledge, they are likely to be heterogeneous. Product innovation involves an assortment of knowledge related to various stages of the value chain. Knowledge applied to manufacturing, marketing, and customer services is complementary to the knowledge used in product innovation. Vertical integration of the innovation function in the value chain is only justified, however, if internalization is the best way to acquire the relevant knowledge, and this is not often the case. Because product innovations address the needs of customers, the knowledge most valuable to product innovation is that obtained from interacting with customers, in other words, marketing. Therefore, product innovation combined with marketing may be the optimal mix of services offered by a firm, which may involve interactions between firms and their customers and suppliers.

Relevant studies on this issue highlight some additional motives for MNCs' offshore R&D. A substantial part of the literature jointly suggests that the locational decisions of MNCs' offshore R&D are generally determined by the following four major factors. First, MNCs need to be close to their clients for the purpose of offshore R&D. The host country's industrial advantages can therefore be regarded as a driving force to anchor the offshore R&D of MNCs. In this regard, the accumulated production experiences and capabilities of a host country may serve as an important local condition in attracting MNCs' R&D facilities. For example, Fors and Zejan (1996) suggested that MNCs' offshore R&D is, to a large extent, found in locations where overseas production is taking place. Such expatriated R&D investment generally supports the local use of production technology and products, which are designed or created outside the home country.

Second, MNCs may undertake offshore R&D in order to access new foreign technologies for the development of new products and production processes. Due to the dynamics of technology, some R&D-oriented firms, those based in Asia and Europe, for example, have set up labs in the United States to take advantage of centers of excellence (Dambrine 1998; Voelker and Stead 1999). Fors and Zejan (1996) argue that MNCs tend to locate their R&D in the host regions that are relatively specialized, technologically, in the firms' own areas as a means of gaining access to foreign centers of excellence and taking advantage of localized knowledge spillovers. Similarly, Niosi (1999) indicated that learning is a critical element in the new trend of international R&D, which often entails locating closely to major innovation centers in order to broaden the scope of the parent's technological portfolio.

Third, it is regarded as becoming increasingly important for MNCs to relocate their R&D overseas in order to hire foreign R&D labor. Having examined locational choices for overseas R&D investment by MNCs based in the United States and Japan, Kumar (2001) argued that a country with an abundant R&D labor force will enjoy a locational advantage in attracting MNCs' R&D investment.

Fourth, the locational choice of MNCs' overseas R&D can be motivated by the ability to serve local markets. In an examination of determinants of foreign affiliates' R&D investment in sixteen Organization for Economic Cooperation and Development (OECD) countries, Gao (2000) highlighted the market size of host countries as a critical factor. Besides stressing the significance of foreign market size, Kumar (2001) summarized three locational advantages of host countries in driving foreign R&D investment; these were a large domestic market, an abundance of low-cost R&D manpower, and the overall scale of national technological effort. From an alternative perspective, Westney (1992) identified four research mandates for the offshore R&D of MNCs in terms of technology activity; these were technology transfer, product modification, new product development, and basic research. Each of these research mandates had its own types of linkages with the host economy. Foreign R&D sites can be similarly classified into two categories, namely, a home-base augmenting site and a home-base exploiting site (Kuemmerle 1997). A mandate for basic research, as in a home-base augmenting site, will require close linkages with local basic research centers, such as universities and research institutions. In contrast, for a home-base exploiting site, a mandate for local product modification will require close linkages to consumers.

The foregoing studies have relied mainly upon case studies, questionnaire surveys, or aggregate country data to examine the determinants of locational choices for MNCs' offshore R&D, and most of these studies were based on the experiences of the advanced countries. In light of this, we are motivated to apply industry-level data to examine the determinants of MNCs' R&D activities overseas in a newly industrialized economy, such as that of Taiwan.

3.3   Foreign Corporations' R&D in Taiwan

Many of the East Asian economies, including Taiwan, have orchestrated programs to attract foreign-owned R&D units, jumping on the bandwagon of promoting their local economies as international innovation hubs. This gives rise to an important question concerning what factors may drive MNCs' offshore facilities to become engaged in R&D activities. In a sense, foreign affiliates engaging in R&D activities may involve an evolutionary process of upgrading their strategic mandates. Ferdows (1997) described the path of MNCs' foreign plants to higher strategic roles. Foreign affiliates that are upgrading their mandates may have started from a lowly position, which could even be an offshore factory with the purpose of accessing low-cost production resources, a server factory for the purpose of proximity to market, or an outpost factory for the purpose of collecting information. They may, in due course, be upgraded to a higher position, which may be a source factory for low-cost production, and that will result in them having greater authority over procurement or, perhaps, a contributor factory for the purpose not only of serving specific national or regional markets but also for product or process engineering and the development and choice of suppliers. Finally, foreign affiliates promote their mandates to the position of a leading factory for the purpose of creating new processes, products, and technologies for the entire firm. This upgrading process of foreign affiliates' mandates spotlights the importance of a few intangible benefits in technology sourcing, namely learning from foreign clients, local suppliers, competitors, and foreign research centers and attracting talent globally, as opposed to tangible assets, namely reducing direct and indirect costs, capital costs, taxes, logistical costs, and jumping tariff and nontariff barriers.

Although it is well-documented that FDI has played an important role in Taiwan's economic development, it is seldom realized that, to some degree, some of the MNCs in Taiwan have also invested in R&D. From the data set provided by the Investment Commission at the Ministry of Economic Affairs (MOEA), we can calculate that Taiwan's estimated average R&D intensity for foreign-owned subsidiaries, over the periods 1987–

1991, 1992–1996, and 1997–2000, was 1.22 percent, 1.48 percent and 2.49 percent, respectively; this perhaps indicates that Taiwan's mandate has significantly improved in terms of MNCs' regional or global innovation networks. The last figure becomes more significant if we take into account the fact that Taiwan's total R&D expenditure accounted for just 2.30 percent of the island's gross domestic product (GDP) in 2002 (see table 3.1).

Having said that, it would be misleading to play down the significance of Taiwan's domestic R&D capacity. Besides its R&D intensity being as high as 2.30 percent in 2002, in terms of the U.S. patents granted, Taiwan ranks fourth in the world in 2001, with electrical and electronic machinery, equipment, and supplies as a product field outnumbering all other fields and registering an increase from 2,013 to 7,644 over the second half of the 1990s. This may imply that Taiwan's IT sector has moved from foreign technology to indigenous innovation (Wu, Lin, and Lin 2002). It is such an innovation capacity that enables Taiwan to leverage international R&D networks.

As table 3.2 shows, the survey for the whole period from 1987 to 2000 reveals that the electrical and electronic machinery industry registers the

Table 3.1   R&D intensity of foreign corporations and capital inflow in Taiwan's manufacturing sector

	1987–1991	1992–1996	1997–2000
R&D intensity ratio (%)	1.22	1.48	2.49
Capital inflow (US$1,000)	5,737,184	5,026,103	7,593,008

Source: Investment Commission, MOEA, Republic of China (ROC), *Statistics on Overseas Chinese and Foreign Investment.*

Table 3.2   R&D intensities and capital inflow of foreign corporations at industry level, 1987–2000

Manufacturing industry	R&D intensity	Capital inflow distribution
Electrical and electronic machinery	2.72	47.72
Primary metal and metal products	2.47	9.73
Machinery	1.47	11.23
Leather and related products	1.18	0.97
Pulp, paper, and allied products	0.97	0.61
Chemicals and chemical products	0.87	16.20
Rubber and plastic products	0.46	2.49
Textile and apparel	0.32	2.46
Food and beverages	0.26	5.92
Nonmetallic mineral products	0.24	2.23
Lumber, wood products, and furniture	0.17	0.43
Mean/Total	1.80	100.0

Source: Investment Commission, MOEA, ROC, *Statistics on Overseas Chinese and Foreign Investment.*

highest R&D intensity of foreign corporations, followed by the primary metal and metal products and machinery industries. By contrast, both the food and beverages and lumber, wood products, and furniture industries are the industries with the lowest R&D intensity of foreign corporations in Taiwan. Not surprisingly, these industries with high foreign R&D activities tend to fall in the category of the so-called high-tech industries, while the traditional industries registered a relatively lower level of foreign R&D intensity.

It should be noted that the Pearson correlation ratio shown in table 3.2 reaches a level of 0.724, pointing to a high and positive correlation between foreign corporate R&D intensity and the distribution of capital inflow within the manufacturing industry. Similarly, data on OECD members reveals a positive correlation between the share, on an international scale, of foreign affiliates' manufacturing turnover and that of manufacturing R&D (Guellec and Pattinson 2002). This may mean, on the one hand, that the former is a necessary condition for the latter, while on the other hand, in a Taiwanese context, this may suggest that an industry characterized by higher foreign R&D investment has become a major FDI target in recent decades. Those industries with high R&D intensity, such as Taiwanese IT firms in the electrical and electronic machinery and machinery sectors, have evolved from pure manufacturers toward integrated service providers and that these are indeed Taiwan's primary export industries.

3.4   Research Strategy

We draw on an official data bank for our empirical work and employ a regression technique to explore the factors determining the R&D intensity of foreign affiliates in Taiwan. This section discusses the research strategy and the key features of the empirical studies.

3.4.1   The Model

The principal aim of our empirical enquiry is to explore features that characterize foreign affiliates with a higher R&D intensity. The dependent variable is therefore denoted as Rdr, the R&D intensity of foreign corporations at industry level. Rdr_i is measured as the logarithm of the ratio of foreign corporations' total R&D expenditure performed to total sales in industry i. In this way, the total R&D expenditure of foreign subsidiaries is normalized by their sales to control for the size effect. In terms of explanatory variables, the study follows Varsakelis (2001) to incorporate the local procurement ratio in both materials (LOCMR) and capital goods (RAT1), along with export orientation (EXR), into the regression equation of foreign corporations' R&D intensity (RDR). We also examine the impact of R&D labor force (LRDP) and local industrial R&D capabilities (IRDR) on foreign corporate R&D activities. The definitions and measurements of the explanatory variables in the empirical model are described as follows:

KLR

Capital labor ratio (KLR) is measured by the ratio of the book value of fixed capital stock to total labor expenditure. We attempt to examine whether KLR has a statistically significant coefficient in the R&D intensity equation. This variable characterizes the attributes of the production technologies employed by foreign affiliates. Ramstetter (1999) compared foreign multinationals and indigenous firms in Asian manufacturing industries and found that MNCs generally adopt relatively high capital-intensive production technologies, which may suggest MNCs' endowments of firm-specific assets. However, a high KLR may, to some extent, indicate the homogeneity of products. An industry with high KLR provides high homogenous products with lower product differentiation. For this reason, we presume that a foreign firm associated with high capital intensity has a low incentive to undertake R&D investment in the host countries.

LOCMR

LOCMR is a local content ratio, measured by the share of the value of local materials to the value of purchased materials. The variable is designed to examine the locational advantage of a host country in terms of industrial capability. As argued by Reddy (2000), one of the main factors determining R&D investment by MNCs in the less-advanced economies is the capability of local industry to produce advanced manufactured products. This will be helpful for MNCs to exploit their innovation assets and enhance their market competitiveness. The LOCMR may reflect the local dependency of foreign affiliates, in terms of supply chains, underlining the industrial capabilities of the host countries. Thus, the coefficient of the variable is presumed to be statistically significant and positive in the model.

In addition, LOCMRS, a square term of LOCMR, is used in this model to take into account a possible nonlinear influence on RDR. That is, the increasing marginal R&D investment to foreign affiliates' local content can be confirmed when the possible coefficient for LOCMRS in this model is positive. By contrast, there is a decreasing marginal R&D investment in foreign affiliates' local content if the possible coefficient for LOCMRS is negative.

RAT1

This is the local capital investment ratio, measured by the ratio of local capital purchased to sales, by controlling the size effect. Similar to LOCMR, in this paper RAT1 is intended to examine whether the industrial capability of a host country can be a locational advantage in leveraging R&D investment by foreign affiliates. A host countries' effective industrial infrastructure, in terms of vertical industrial linkage, may attract foreign affiliates to undertake R&D activities in order to effectively interact with the local suppliers of capital goods for innovation. In addition, this research compares the effects of RAT1 with RAT2, which is the imported capital investment content, measured by the ratio of imported capital purchased to sales, on foreign corporate R&D intensity. We presume that the coefficient of RAT1 is positive in equation (1) and higher than that of RAT2.

EXPR

Export propensity (EXPR) is measured by the logarithm of the ratio of exports to sales. It is well documented that the market size of a host country plays an important role as a locational advantage in attracting foreign R&D to serve the local market and/or customize products for the local market. However, in some cases, foreign affiliates may function simply as an export outpost for their parent companies (Kumar 2001). This may be particularly true for an economy such as Taiwan, given its small market size. It is therefore possible that the R&D operations of MNCs' subsidiaries in Taiwan may be capitalizing on Taiwan's locational advantage in order to serve the international market. Thus, we presume that the coefficient of EXPR in the equation is statistically positive and significant.

It can, in fact, be argued that there exists a significant linkage between foreign corporations' decisions on local procurement and their product markets in terms of exports and imports. In the case of tariff-jumping FDI, foreign affiliates tend to utilize imported material and components in the production of goods to serve the host-country markets. In particular, Chen and Wang (1994) revealed that the United States's and Japanese MNCs in Taiwan producing electronic goods for export were inclined to utilize imports of materials and components; hence, there was a significantly negative relationship between MNCs' local content and their export orientation. Accordingly, this study aims to determine the interactive effect on MNCs' R&D investment from their foreign affiliates' local content and product exports; this is done by including a cross term, combining EXPR with LOCMR in the model. We consider that MNCs' affiliates with a high mandate may play the role of nexus, linking the host country's industries to their global production. Furthermore, foreign affiliates with a greater R&D commitment for new process technologies and products in the host countries may shoulder a higher strategic role in terms of local sourcing.

LRDP

Local industrial R&D capabilities (LRDP) is measured by the logarithm of numbers of R&D employees for each industry. This variable is a proxy

Table 3.3   **Definitions of variables used in the statistical analysis**

Variable	Definition	Impact on RDR
RDR	R&D intensity of foreign subsidiaries	
KL	Capital to labor ratio	+
RAT2	Imported capital content ratio	+
RAT1	Local capital content ratio	+
EXPR	Export ratio	+
LOCMR	Local material content ratio	+
EXPR*LOCMR	Cross term of EXPER and LOCMR	?
LRDP	Availability of R&D labor force	+

for the availability of R&D labor in the local industries. As shown in many studies, sourcing available R&D labor may motivate MNCs to relocate their R&D operations abroad (Kumar 2001). Thus, we presume that the coefficient of LRDP in the R&D intensity equation to be positive.

In order to examine the determinants of foreign corporate R&D intensity, industry-specific attributes are also taken into consideration in this study, with a summary of the variable definitions being provided in table 3.3. It should be noted, however, that this model does not consider certain omitted variables, including Taiwanese corporations' R&D investment and coordination costs of cross-border R&D, which are emphasized in many studies, such as Cantwell and Iammarino (2000) and Fischer and Behrman (1979). Taking the attribute of pooling data into account, we need to specify the fixed effects and random effects models. In addition, in the estimation of the regression models, we consider the influence of ten manufacturing industries but exclude the leather sector because of too many missing observations.

Based on the preceding discussion, the study derives a set of regressions for industry i, with the equation being:

$$(1) \quad \mathrm{Rdr}_{it} = a_0 + a_1 \mathrm{EXPR}_{it} + a_2 \mathrm{LOCMR}_{it} + a_3 \mathrm{EXPR}^*_{it} \mathrm{LOCMR}_{it}$$
$$+ a_4 \mathrm{RAT1}_{it} + a_5 \mathrm{RAT2}_{it} + a_6 \mathrm{KL} + a_7 \mathrm{LRDP}_{it},$$

where LOCMR_{it} is the ratio of local material expenditure to total material expenditure in percentage terms; EXPR_{it} denotes the proportion of exports to total sales in percentage terms; $\mathrm{LOCMR}^*_{it}\mathrm{EXPR}_{it}$ refers to the cross term of LOCMR_{it} and EXPR_{it}; KLR_{it} is the ratio of capital stock to total labor costs; RAT1 and RAT2 denote respective local capital investment ratio and imported capital investment ratio; and LRDP_{it} denotes the total R&D labor force in industry i in year t. All the variables are taken in terms of the derivative of the natural logarithm in the empirical models, while other specific industry attributes are reflected in the fixed effects or random effects model.

Within the literature, equation (2) is known as the fixed effects model if the intercept differs across individual groups (here the ten industries) and each individual intercept does not vary over time. Thus, equation (1) can be rewritten as

$$(2) \quad Rdr_{it} = a_0 + a_1 EXPR_{it} + a_2 LOCMR_{it} + a_3 EXPR^*_{it} LOCMR_{it}$$
$$+ a_4 RAT1_{it} + a_5 RAT2_{it} + a_6 KL + a_7 LRDP_{it} + \sum \lambda_i IND_i$$
$$+ \varepsilon_{it}.$$

In other settings, we may view each individual specific constant term as randomly distributed across individual groups. It follows, therefore, that equation (1) can be reformulated as the following equation:

$$(3) \quad Rdr_{it} = a_{0i} + a_1 EXPR_{it} + a_2 LOCMR_{it} + a_3 EXPR^*_{it} LOCMR_{it}$$
$$+ a_4 RAT1_{it} + a_5 RAT2_{it} + a_6 KL + a_7 LRDP_{it} + \varepsilon_{it}$$

where a_{0i} is the intercept with random disturbance characterizing the ith observation and can be expressed as $a_{0i} = a_0 + u_i$, $i = 1, 2, \ldots, 10$, and u_i is a random error term with a mean value of zero and variance of σ_u^2.

3.4.2   The Data

The data were collected from two sources over a period of fourteen years. The industry-level data set used in this study is provided by the Investment Commission, MOEA, Taiwan, and contains information on production and R&D by foreign affiliates in the manufacturing sector. Industry-specific R&D data is taken from the National Science Council. After missing values were deleted, the available industrial data over the period 1987–2000 was pooled together to provide our sample. Table 3.4 presents a summary of the descriptive statistics of these variables from 137 available observations.

Table 3.4   **Summary of statistics**

Variable	Mean	Standard deviation	Minimum	Maximum	No. of observations
RDR	−5.409	1.451	−11.614	−0.938	137
EXPR	−1.404	0.860	−4.765	−0.007	137
LOCMR	−0.784	0.518	−4.184	−0.007	137
LOCMRS	0.882	1.912	0.000	17.507	137
LOCMR*EXPR	1.019	0.808	0.006	5.359	137
LRATIO	−5.134	0.862	−8.164	−3.549	137
KL	1.401	0.904	−5.888	4.031	137
RAT1	−3.504	1.256	−8.662	−0.566	137
RAT2	−4.200	1.348	−10.094	−0.946	134

Source: Calculated from Investment Commission, MOEA, ROC, *Statistics on Overseas Chinese and Foreign Investment.*

Note: All variables are taken in terms of natural logarithm.

Table 3.5   **Correlation analysis**

	EXPR	LOCMR	LOCMRS	LOIM	RAT1	RAT2	LRDP
LOCMR	−0.185						
LOCMRS	0.168	−0.930					
LOCMR*EXPR	−0.667	−0.401	0.251				
RAT1	0.194	0.035	−0.016	−0.209			
RAT2	0.134	0.112	−0.121	−0.149	0.351		
LRDP	0.115	0.063	−0.102	−0.186	0.247	0.142	
KL	−0.119	−0.038	0.015	0.090	0.170	0.065	0.140

Source: Calculated by the authors.

Table 3.5 presents the correlation coefficients for all the variables used in our empirical model, with the statistics showing that where the correlation coefficient is over 0.5, high correlations exist between EXPR*LOCMR and EXPR, and LOCMR and LOCMRS; however, all the other correlation coefficients are rather small, suggesting that no serious problem of multicollinearity exists within our empirical model.

3.5   Empirical Results

This section presents and discusses the empirical results, which are summarized in table 3.6. The general specification in columns (1) to (4) of table 3.6 include export dependence, local input content and their cross-terms, while columns (5) to (8) also take capital labor ratio into account. Based on the ordinary least squares (OLS) residuals, Lagrange multiplier test statistics for chi-square were undertaken for each regression equation; the statistics for each equation are significant at the 5 percent level. It is therefore necessary for us to apply the Hausman test to each equation in order to examine the statistical robustness of the fixed and random effects models. The chi-square values of equations (1), (2), (3), and (6) in table 3.6 are statistically significant, suggesting that these models favor the fixed effects model as opposed to the random effects model.[1] We go on to examine the effect of time trend, referred to as YEAR, on the R&D intensity of foreign affiliates in table 3.7. The coefficients of time trend on each equation are positive but insignificant; thus, the following discussion is based mainly on table 3.6. The overall results suggest that six of the explanatory variables, EXPR, LOCMR, LOCMRS, EXPR*LOCMR, RAT1, and LRDP are significant (all at the 5 percent level) in some, if not all, of the equations.

Foreign-owned subsidiaries with higher R&D intensity are found to be

---

1. After taking into account the effect of period on the regression models, we measure the Hausman chi-square static for each equation in table 3A.1, which suggests that these models favor the two-way random model as opposed to the two-way fixed model. Generally, in terms of empirical outcome, the differences between table 3.6 and table 3A.1 are only minor.

Table 3.6   Regression results of foreign affiliates' R&D intensity at industry level in the one-way model

Variable	Fixed effect (1)	Fixed effect (2)	Fixed effect (3)	Random effect (4)	Random effect (5)	Fixed effect (6)	Random effect (7)	Random effect (8)
EXPR	1.336	0.941	1.014	0.915	1.021	1.318	0.889	0.927
	(3.898)**	(2.499)**	(2.785)**	(2.997)**	(2.989)**	(3.876)**	(2.436)**	(2.655)**
LOCMR	2.638	2.292	2.058	2.091	2.040	2.590	2.153	1.890
	(2.837)**	(2.347)**	(2.173)**	(2.313)**	(2.216)**	(2.807)**	(2.231)**	(2.029)**
LOCMRS	0.511	0.456	0.395	0.371	0.371	0.505	0.428	0.362
	(2.612)**	(2.230)**	(1.988)*	(1.949)	(1.924)*	(2.603)**	(2.115)**	(1.850)*
EXPR*LOCMR	1.015	0.859	0.827	0.860	0.882	1.018	0.828	0.779
	(2.860)**	(2.375)**	(2.311)**	(2.584)**	(2.550)**	(2.895)**	(2.328)**	(2.229)**
RAT1		0.257	0.238	0.303	0.268		0.270	0.261
		(2.332)**	(2.324)**	(3.296)**	(2.755)**		(2.503)**	(2.624)**
RAT2		0.098					0.090	
		(1.200)					(1.102)	
LRDP				0.498	0.476			
				(4.248)**	(2.807)**			
KL					−0.231	−0.209	−0.173	−0.200
					(−2.016)**	(−1.763)	(−1.481)	(−1.732)
Constant				−6.137	−5.693		−2.221	−2.612
				(−6.216)**	(−4.376)**		(−2.501)**	(−3.333)**
LM test χ2 (1) =	115.15**	79.38**	82.42**	15.63**	10.23**	117.20**	66.82**	73.40**
Hausman test	χ2(4) = 42.99**	χ2(6) = 58.16**	χ2(5) = 26.02**	χ2(6) = 9.18	χ2(7) = 3.43	χ2(5) = 66.17**	χ2(7) = 2.82	χ2(6) = 4.39
Observations	137	134	137	137	137	137	134	137

**Significant at the 5 percent level.

Table 3.7   Regression results of foreign affiliates' R&D intensity at industry level in the one-way model

Variable	Fixed effect (1)	Fixed effect (2)	Fixed effect (3)	Random effect (4)	Random effect (5)	Fixed effect (6)	Random effect (7)	Random effect (8)
EXPR	1.364 (3.856)***	0.995 (2.630)***	1.060 (2.879)***	0.933 (2.949)***	1.066 (3.016)***	1.358 (3.873)***	0.971 (2.621)***	1.000 (2.810)***
LOCMR	2.667 (2.846)***	2.311 (2.372)***	2.083 (2.196)**	2.085 (2.280)**	2.065 (2.222)**	2.630 (2.831)***	2.218 (2.299)**	1.954 (2.092)**
LOCMRS	0.512 (2.607)***	0.444 (2.173)**	0.387 (1.945)*	0.374 (1.940)*	0.376 (1.927)*	0.506 (2.600)***	0.425 (2.099)**	0.360 (1.839)*
EXPR*LOCMR	1.027 (2.870)***	0.876 (2.426)***	0.843 (2.352)***	0.859 (2.541)***	0.897 (2.555)***	1.037 (2.922)***	0.864 (2.423)***	0.813 (2.316)**
RAT1		0.282 (2.520)***	0.259 (2.461)***	0.291 (2.985)***	0.259 (2.526)***		0.289 (2.624)***	0.279 (2.715)***
RAT2		0.119 (1.430)					0.112 (1.350)	
LRDP				0.497 (3.708)***	0.440 (2.108)**			
KL					-0.230 (-1.989)**	-0.214 (-1.793)*	-0.185 (-1.584)	-0.212 (-1.827)*
YEAR	0.009 (0.342)	0.032 (1.241)	0.022 (0.885)	-0.004 (-0.170)	-0.004 (-0.170)	0.012 (0.495)	0.035 (1.368)	0.027 (1.076)
Constant				-6.118 (-5.705)***	-5.442 (-3.500)***		-2.172 (-2.092)***	-2.616 (-3.116)***
LM test χ2 (1) =	114.86**	78.44**	79.54**	15.48**	10.24**	116.91**	62.82**	73.40**
Hausman test	χ2(4) = 42.00**	χ2(6) = 40.95**	χ2(5) = 24.63**	χ2(6) = 7.97	χ2(7) = 1.84	χ2(5) = 59.75**	χ2(7) = 1.46	χ2(6) = 4.39
Observations	137	134	137	137	137	137	134	137

**Significant at the 5 percent level.

characterized by a greater degree of localization in terms of their sourcing of both production materials and capital goods. To interpret this finding, we can refer to Westney's (1990) argument that if their ties with the local scientific and technical community are gaining strength (and probably, therefore, greater R&D intensity) MNCs' offshore R&D units are given higher hierarchical mandates. To put this another way, Reddy (2000) championed the concept of first-tier supplier advantage as a locational advantage for attracting MNCs' R&D units, which may imply that foreign-owned subsidiaries with a higher degree of localization may need to devote more effort to R&D in order to effectively interact with their local suppliers.

In addition, we find that where Taiwanese industrial sectors have a larger pool of R&D employees, their constituent foreign affiliates tend to be more R&D intensive. On the one hand, this seems to imply that the R&D efforts of foreign affiliates in Taiwan are driven by a local technology pool. On the other hand, assuming that a larger pool of R&D employees in a sector implies that its local firms are more technology aggressive, one can argue that indigenous R&D efforts serve as a complement to, rather than a substitute for, the R&D activities of foreign affiliates. In the following we categorize three main effects, namely the local industry capability effect, market linkage effect, and R&D labor resource effect, for further discussion.

3.5.1 Local Industrial Capability Effect

Columns (1) and (2) in table 3.6 includes the LOCMR and LOCMRS measures. The coefficient of LOCMR is positive and statistically significant, revealing that foreign affiliates in Taiwan using more local materials in their production have higher R&D investment. The significant and positive coefficient for LOCMRS reveals the increasing scale of foreign affiliates' R&D investments to their local procurement of materials and components.

Two aspects stand out from these empirical results. First, the results support our hypotheses, in the previous section, that a host country's excellence in production capabilities, in terms of the industry value chain, can be regarded as a locational advantage in leveraging foreign corporations to increase their R&D investment, even in a less-advanced host country. Therefore, MNCs may need to establish their offshore R&D centers close to their production partners for the purpose of time to market due to the severe global competition. Second, the extent of local sourcing in terms of both production materials and capital goods not only reflects the degree to which MNCs' offshore facilities are localized in the host country but also may prompt them to upgrade their local operations in R&D terms.

Consistent with this, we also compare the effects of RAT1 and RAT2 on foreign corporate R&D intensity. From columns (2) and (6) in table 3.6, the coefficients of RAT1 are not only statistically significant and positive but also larger than those of RAT2, further demonstrating that local industrial infrastructure does matter in terms of driving foreign corporate R&D in a host country.

3.5.2   Market Linkage Effect

While much of the literature on R&D internationalization emphasizes the importance of market access for MNCs' offshore R&D, for an economy with small domestic market size, such as that of Taiwan, the market linkage effect may mean more to this issue and hence may be regarded as a location-specific advantage for such a host country in leveraging foreign R&D investment. For all specifications we find that those foreign-owned firms in Taiwan with a higher export propensity tend to be more R&D intensive. As an economy characterized by international competitiveness and export orientation, Taiwan may be able to act as a host for some MNCs in order to capitalize on its comparative advantages to serve the international market. Indeed, in a questionnaire survey undertaken for a separate study (Liu, Chen, and Lin 2002), R&D performers of foreign affiliates were asked to identify their highest-level R&D activities in Taiwan. The results showed that the level appeared to be, predominantly, the modification and development of products for the international market. Without denying the importance of market access to R&D internationalization, the evidence gleaned from that study suggests that given accumulated comparative advantage in production and the industrial value chain, host countries can still attract foreign R&D investment by playing the role of a hub for access to the international markets, even without large domestic market size.

It is interesting to note that the coefficient of the cross term EXPR*LOCMR is positive at the 5 percent level of statistical significance, indicating that there exists an important interaction effect between foreign affiliates' export propensity and local content ratio in enhancing foreign affiliates' incentives to undertake local R&D. The coefficient of the cross term EXPR*LOCMR is significantly positive, indicating that in Taiwan, foreign-owned firms with higher export propensity tend to be more R&D intensive in order to utilize more local materials and components. As is widely known, quite a substantial part of the manufacturing industry in Taiwan is internationally competitive and export oriented, with local players in many of the subsectors enjoying first-tier supplier status. By analogy, their MNC counterparts in Taiwan may have to act in the same way in order to exploit Taiwan's advantages. This may also indicate that as foreign affiliates in a host economy, such as that of Taiwan, begin to increase their R&D investment, there is a shift in their role, as they take on the role of nexus linking the local production capacity to their global production network.

The empirical results discussed previously are quite in line with the evolutionary process of foreign affiliates in upgrading their strategic roles within their parents' global production networks as described by Ferdows (1997). In our view, foreign affiliates' R&D investment in the host countries may go hand in hand with their rising mandate within their parents' global networks. From the perspective of Ferdows (1997), foreign affiliates can enjoy greater authority over procurement, production planning, process change, outbound logistics, product customization, and redesign decisions, as their mandates are upgraded from an offshore factory, or a server factory, to a source or contributor factory. By analogy, foreign affiliates may increase their R&D investment and raise their local procurement and exports simultaneously. This empirical outcome is also consistent with Jarillo and Martinez (1990), who examined the different roles played by MNCs' subsidiaries in Spain. They found that subsidiaries tended to receive stronger mandates from their headquarters if they engaged in geographical localization in terms of R&D, purchasing, manufacturing, and marketing in the host countries, while also aggressively integrating themselves into their groups (headquarters plus other subsidiaries). Thus, it is reasonable to argue that foreign affiliates with a higher R&D intensity may reflect the upgrading of their mandates in the business groups in terms of their localization and integration strategies.

3.5.3   R&D Labor Resource Effect

Finally, turning to the explanatory variable, LRDP, the estimated parameter has the expected positive sign in the regression model and is significant at the 5 percent level in the random effects models. It therefore follows that the local R&D labor pool at industry level is positively and significantly related to the corresponding foreign affiliates' R&D intensity, confirming our hypothesis that MNCs tend to locate their overseas R&D investment to countries with abundant R&D resources. This result is also consistent with much of the research emphasizing the escalating importance of supply-side forces in driving R&D internationalization. By implication, it can be argued that a host country needs to demonstrate its technological strengths in certain industrial segments in order to attract offshore R&D by MNCs.

3.6   Conclusions

Within the overall process of globalization, international economic development has much to do with the relocation of the value chain of MNCs and indigenous innovation. These two factors are, however, interrelated. Given the footloose nature of MNCs' cross-border operations, it is deemed increasingly important for a host country to attract MNCs' facilities with strategic mandates, such as R&D. Therefore, R&D internationalization has become a trend that is no longer confined to the developed world, as the less-advanced economies are becoming increasingly involved in this process. This gives rise to an important question as to what locational advantage a country may have and may be able to develop in order to attract MNCs' R&D activities.

In studying this issue, Taiwan appears to provide an interesting case. Although within this issue, such high-profile countries as China and India each have a large domestic market and a large pool of R&D labor, this is obviously not the case in Taiwan. In addition, Taiwan is not an economy characterized by technological leadership, which would be a distinct advantage in attracting technology-seeking FDI. However, despite these drawbacks, the Taiwanese case is more meaningful to many countries, including both developed and developing countries; indeed, this paper goes a step further than the previous research by exploring the issue at industry level, which appears to be more insightful.

Our empirical results show that in Taiwan, foreign affiliates with higher R&D intensity tend to be more export oriented and localized in terms of their sourcing of materials and capital goods. Of interest is the finding that such foreign affiliates also tend to be more R&D intensive. To interpret this finding, we can refer to Westney's (1990) argument that MNCs' offshore R&D units are given higher hierarchical mandates if their ties with the local scientific and technological community are gaining strength (and probably, therefore, greater R&D intensity). In fact, foreign affiliates tend to increase their R&D investment and have greater authority over material and component procurement, functioning as key suppliers and serving a specific regional market as they upgrade their strategic roles toward becoming a so-called leading factory.

Reddy (2000) championed the concept of first-tier supplier advantage as a locational advantage for attracting MNCs' R&D units, which may imply that foreign-owned subsidiaries with a higher degree of localization may need to devote more effort to R&D in order to effectively interact with their local suppliers. Moreover, we also find that foreign affiliates with a higher export propensity tend to be not only more R&D intensive but also that the effects of their export propensity has a positive interaction with the effects of the local sourcing of materials. This may have something to do with the heritage of Taiwan's economic development, which is widely known as being based upon export-oriented industrialization. In specific terms, some Taiwanese industries have successfully penetrated the international market, giving rise to a sound industrial infrastructure and capability. As a result, their foreign affiliate counterparts may be driven to invest more in R&D in order to capitalize on the Taiwanese comparative advantage, particularly if they are more reliant on local materials.

We are able to prove with statistical robustness that those sectors with a larger pool of R&D labor tend to attract more foreign affiliates' R&D activities. While some of our results are consistent with the previous findings, others may need to be interpreted in the context of the Taiwanese economy.

For example, the size of the local R&D labor force may reflect Taiwan's technological strengths in certain industrial sectors, which may in turn attract MNCs' to invest in R&D in Taiwan. This is in line with the so-called technology-related motive, namely, tapping into foreign science and technology resources.

Throughout the paper, there has been a focus on the concept of an evolutionary approach to technology in interpreting Taiwan's inward R&D internationalization. Without denying the possibility of leapfrogging development, we would like to emphasize the significance of a cumulative process of expansion to the efforts of less-advanced economies to anchor MNCs' offshore R&D. As Ernst (2000) puts it, an ideal location for knowledge-intensive activities is characterized by three conditions, attractive lead markets, a highly developed production structure, and excellent research environments, but not all of the criteria can be met at the same time by many locations in the less-advanced economies. The experiences of Taiwan seem to suggest that even without world-leading R&D centers of excellence, a less-advanced economy can still build up a competitive production base as a starting point to take part in global production networks, and, in due course, this accumulated production capability can become an incentive for foreign affiliates to invest in R&D.

Appendix

Table 3A.1 Regression results of foreign affiliates' R&D intensity at industry level in the two-way effects model

Variable	Random effect (1)	Random effect (2)	Random effect (3)	Random effect (4)	Random effect (5)	Random effect (6)	Random effect (7)	Random effect (8)
EXPR	1.299	0.938	0.974	1.014	1.058	1.287	1.041	0.034
	(3.708)**	(2.607)**	(2.780)**	(3.018)**	(3.012)**	(3.685)**	(2.725)**	(2.848)**
LOCMR	2.627	2.021	1.947	2.166	2.101	2.573	2.133	2.012
	(2.752)**	(2.097)**	(2.064)**	(2.316)**	(2.237)**	(2.705)**	(2.182)**	(2.120)**
LOCMRS	0.507	0.374	0.355	0.390	0.379	0.497	0.399	0.371
	(2.522)**	(1.835)*	(1.783)*	(1.979)**	(1.917)	(2.479)**	(1.931)**	(1.851)
EXPR*LOCMR	0.967	0.811	0.778	0.893	0.912	0.975	0.885	0.839
	(2.668)**	(2.293)**	(2.206)**	(2.559)**	(2.584)**	(2.703)**	(2.452)**	(2.351)**
RAT1		0.338	0.334	0.319	0.300		0.311	0.314
	(1.980)**	(3.085)**	(3.226)**	(3.154)**	(2.930)**		(2.754)**	(2.973)**
RAT2		0.174				0.167		
						(1.878)		
LRDP				0.484	0.481			
				(3.220)**	(2.693)**			
KL					−0.216	−0.184	−0.161	−0.190
					(−1.820)	(−1.489)	(−1.317)	(1.575)
Constant	−3.005	−1.822	−2.516	−5.839	−5.581	−2.807	−1.579	−2.261
	(−3.941)**	(−2.299)**	(−3.432)**	(−4.747)**	(−3.988)**	(−3.625)**	(−1.674)*	(−2.752)**
LM test $\chi^2(1)=$	119.11**	79.78**	82.93**	16.16**	10.93**	121.32**	67.01**	73.73**
Hausman test	$\chi^2(4) = 4.57$	$\chi^2(6) = 6.15$	$\chi^2(5) = 5.08$	$\chi^2(6) = 4.43$	$\chi^2(7) = 4.13$	$\chi^2(5) = 4.39$	$\chi^2(7) = 4.17$	$\chi^2(6) = 4.32$
Observations	137	134	137	137	137	137	134	137

**Significant at the 5 percent level.

References

Cantwell, J., and S. Iammarino. 2000. Multinational corporations and the location of technological innovation in the UK regions. *Regional Studies* 34 (4): 317–32.

Cantwell, J., and R. Mudambi. 2000. The location of MNE R&D activity: The role of investment incentives. Special issue, *Management International Review* 40 (1): 127–48.

Cantwell, J., and G. D. Santangelo. 1999. The frontier of international technology networks: Sourcing abroad the most highly tacit capabilities. *Information Economics and Policy* 11:101–23.

Carrincazeaux, C., Y. Lung, and A. Rallet. 2001. Proximity and localization of corporate R&D activities. *Research Policy* 30:777–89.

Casson, M., and S. Singh. 1993. Corporate research and development strategies: The influence of firm, industry and country factors on the decentralization of R&D. *R&D Management* 23 (2): 91–107.

Chen, S. H. 2002. Global production networks and information technology: The case of Taiwan. *Industry and Innovation* 9 (3): 247–64.

Chen, S. H., H. T. Shih, and C. Kao. 2002. *The trend of Taiwan-based firms' R&D activities in China and its impacts on Taiwan's industrial innovation* [in Chinese]. Final report to the Department of Industrial Technology, Ministry of Economic Affairs. Taipei: Chung-Hua Institution for Economic Research.

Chen, T. J., and W. J. Wang. 1994. Localization of the U.S. and Japanese electronics multinationals in Taiwan. In *Industrial structure and antitrust laws* [in Chinese], ed. W. W. Chu, 231–57. Taipei: Academia Sinica.

Chen, T. J., and Y. H. Ku. 2000. Foreign direct investment and restructuring: The case of Taiwan's textile industry. In *The role of foreign direct investment in East Asian economic development,* ed. T. Ito and A. O. Krueger, 319–45. London: University of Chicago Press.

Dambrine, C. 1998. Globalization of research and development: A business viewpoint. Paper presented at OECD Working Group on Innovation and Technology Policy conference, Facilitating International Technology Cooperation. 13–14 August, Seoul, Korea.

De Meyer, A. 1993. Internationalizing R&D improves a firm's technical learning. *Research Technology Management* 36 (4): 42–49.

Dosi, G. 1982. Technological paradigms and technological trajectories. *Research Policy* 11:147–62.

Dunning, J. H. 1993. *The globalization of business.* London: Routledge.

———. 1994. Multinational enterprises and the globalization of innovatory capacity. *Research Policy* 23:67–88.

Ernst, D. 2000. Global production networks and the changing geography of innovation systems: Implications for developing countries. East-West Center Economics Series Working Paper no. 9. Honolulu: East-West Center.

Feenstra, R. 1998. Integration of trade and disintegration of production in the global economy. *Journal of Economic Perspectives* 12 (4): 31–35.

Ferdows, K. 1997. Making the most of foreign factories. *Harvard Business Review,* March–April, 73–88.

Firn, J. 1975. External control and regional development: The case of Scotland. *Environment and Planning A* 7:393–414.

Fischer, W. A., and J. N. Behrman. 1979. The coordination of foreign R&D activities by transnational corporations. *Journal of International Business Studies* 10 (3): 28–35.

Fors, G., and M. Zejan. 1996. Overseas R&D by multinationals in foreign centers of excellence. Economic Research Institute Working Paper no. 111. Stockholm: Economic Research Institute, Stockholm School of Economics.

Frost, T., and C. Zhou. 2000. The geography of foreign R&D within a host country: An evolutionary perspective on location-technology selection by multinationals. *International Studies of Management* 30 (2): 10–43.

Gao, T. 2000. Multinational activity and country characteristics in OECD countries. Manuscript, 1–31.

Gerybadze, A., and G. Reger. 1999. Globalization of R&D: Recent changes in management of innovation in transnational corporations. *Research Policy* 28 (2–3): 251–74.

Guellec, D., and B. Pattinson. 2002. Innovation surveys: Lessons from OECD countries' experience. *STI Review* 27:77–101.

Guellec, D., and B. van Pottelsberghe de la Potterie. 2001. The internationalization of technology analyzed with patent data. *Research Policy* 30:1253–66.

Howells, J. 1992. Going global: The use of ICT networks in research and development. CURDS Working Paper no. 6. Newcastle, UK: Centre for Urban and Regional Development Studies, Newcastle University.

Jarillo, J. C., and J. I. Martinez. 1990. Different roles for subsidiaries: The case of multinational corporations in Spain. *Strategic Management Journal* 11 (7): 501–12.

Kaufmann, A., and F. Tödtling. 2001. Science-industry interaction in the process of innovation: The importance of boundary-crossing between systems. *Research Policy* 30:791–804.

Kearns, A., and F. Ruane. 2001. The tangible contribution of R&D-spending by foreign-owned plants to a host region: A plant level study of the Irish manufacturing sector (1980–1996). *Research Policy* 30:227–44.

Kotabe, M. 1996. Emerging role of technology licensing in the development of global product strategy: Conceptual framework and research propositions. *Journal of Marketing* 60:73–88.

Kuemmerle, W. 1997. Building effective R&D capabilities abroad. *Harvard Business Review,* March–April, 61–70.

Kumar, N. 2001. Determinants of location of overseas R&D activity of multinational enterprises: The case of US and Japanese corporations. *Research Policy* 30:159–74.

Lall, S. 2003. Industrial success and failure in a globalizing world. QEH Working Paper Series no. 102. Oxford, UK: Queen Elizabeth House, University of Oxford.

Liu, M.-C., S. H. Chen, and Y. J. Lin. 2002. *The evolution of industrial technology policies and its impacts on the economic, industrial, and technological co-opetition across the Taiwan Strait (1st year)* [in Chinese]. Final report to the Department of Industrial Technology, Ministry of Economic Affairs. Taipei: Chung-Hua Institution for Economic Research.

Nelson, R., and S. Winter. 1982. *An evolutionary theory of technology change.* Cambridge, MA: Harvard University Press, Belknap.

Niosi, J. 1999. The internationalization of industrial R&D from technology transfer to the learning organization. *Research Policy* 28:107–17.

Organization for Economic Cooperation and Development (OECD). 1997. *Patents and innovation in the international context.* Paris: OECD.

Paoli, M., and S. Guercini. 1997. R&D internationalisation in the strategic behaviour of the firm. SPRU Steep Discussion Paper no. 39. Brighton, UK: Science and Technology Policy Research, University of Sussex.

Patel, P., and K. Pavitt. 1998. National systems of innovation under strain: The internationalization of corporate R&D. SPRU Electronic Working Paper Series. 22:1–27.
———. 2000. Globalization of technology amongst the world's largest firms: Patterns and trends. Paper presented at conference, The Measurement of Industrial Technological Competitiveness in the Knowledge-Based Economy. 23–24 August, Taipei, Taiwan.
Petrella, R. 1989. Globalization of technological innovation. *Technology Analysis & Strategic Management* 1 (4): 393–407.
Ramstetter, E. D. 1999. Comparisons of foreign multinationals and local firms in Asian manufacturing over time. *Asian Economic Journal* 13 (2): 163–203.
Reddy, P. 2000. *Globalization of corporate R&D: Implications for innovation systems in host countries.* London: Routledge.
Swamidass, P. M., and M. Kotabe. 1993. Component sourcing strategies of multinationals: An empirical study of European and Japanese multinationals. *Journal of International Business Studies* 24 (1): 81–99.
Varsakelis, N. C. 2001. The impact of patent protection, economy openness and national culture on R&D investment: A cross-country empirical investigation. *Research-Policy* 30 (7): 1059–68.
Venkatesan, R. 1992. Strategic sourcing: To make or not to make. *Harvard Business Review,* November–December, 98–107.
Voelker, R., and R. Stead. 1999. New technologies and international locational choice for research and development units: Evidence from Europe. *Technology Analysis and Strategic Management* 11 (2): 199–209.
Walsh, K. 2003. *Foreign high-tech R&D in China: Risks, rewards, and implications for U.S.-China relations.* Washington, DC: Henry L. Stimson Center.
Westney, E. D. 1990. Internal and external linkages in the MNC: The case of R&D subsidiaries in Japan. In *Managing the global firm,* ed. C. Bartlett, Y. Doz, and G. Hedlund, 279–300. London: Routledge.
———. 1992. Organizational change and the internationalization of R&D. In *Transforming organization,* ed. T. A. Kochan and M. Useem, 245–60. New York: Oxford University Press.
Windrum, P. 1999. *The MERIT report on innovation networks in E-commerce.* Report prepared for the DGXII of the European Commission, SEIN Project. http://www.meritbbs.unimaas.nl/staff/windrum.html.
Wu, R. I., X. W. Lin, and H. Y. Lin. 2002. Moving from foreign technology to indigenous innovation—The case of Chinese Taipei. Paper presented at OECD-IPS workshop, Promoting Knowledge-Based Economies in Asia. 21–22 November, Singapore.
Xue, L., and S. Wang. 2001. Globalization of R&D by multinational corporations in China: An empirical analysis. Paper presented at Sino-U.S. conference, Technological Innovation. 24–26 April, Beijing.
Zander, I. 1999. How do you mean 'global'? An empirical investigation of innovation networks in the multinational corporation. *Research Policy* 28:195–214.
Zedtwitz, M. 2002. Organizational learning through post-project reviews R&D. *R&D Management* 32 (3): 255–68.
Zedtwitz, M., and O. Gassmann. 2002. Market versus technology drive in R&D internationalization: Four different patterns of managing research and development. *Research Policy* 31:569–88.

Comment   Thomas J. Prusa

This paper offers a new perspective on two important and related questions. First, why do firms engage in foreign direct investment (FDI)? And second, what exactly is transferred from parent to affiliate when FDI occurs? Liu and Chen persuasively argue that at least part of the answer to both questions is R&D.

In Dunning's electic paradigm the combination of firm-specific ownership and internalization advantages and host-country locational advantages are the necessary elements for FDI to occur. One unfortunate implication of the Dunning paradigm is that any given parent-affiliate relationship may be shorter lived than either party anticipated. After all, if a host country's locational advantage pulled in the parent company's investment, what happens when a new country with even more attractive locational attributes emerges? If the costs to terminating the relationship are not too large, the parent company will likely move foreign production to the new location. As the authors explain, the potential transitory nature of FDI-driven relationships can create additional risks and costs to the host country. A host government may pursue, therefore, policies that raise the cost to parent companies moving their affiliate production to the new low-cost location. But it must do so in a way that benefits the parent company. The authors explain that the costs to terminating a FDI relationship will be higher if the affiliate offers the parent firm more than simply low production costs. Thus, host countries whose foreign affiliates engage in R&D in addition to offering low-cost production will be a particularly attractive FDI location.

The paper is largely an attempt to examine whether there is a connection between affiliate R&D intensity and FDI with an eye toward the more intractable question of whether affiliate-based R&D activity can deepen the ties between the parent and affiliate. Taiwan serves as the case study for the inquiry. The authors begin by documenting a temporal connection between the R&D intensity and capital inflow (table 3.1). The authors then perform a series of fixed and random effect estimations to determine what exogenous factors explain R&D intensity. The factors can be thought of as either locational characteristics, such as the size of the local R&D labor force and the local capital content ratio, or firm/industry characteristics, such as the export ratio or the capital-to-labor ratio. In either case, one would think that if these factors were found to be significant influences, the host government could encourage nontransitory FDI by either investing in local resources or by encouraging FDI in particular industries.

Thomas J. Prusa is a professor of economics at Rutgers University, and a research associate of the National Bureau of Economic Research.

The findings are nicely exposited and very sensible. They find that within Taiwan, foreign affiliates with higher R&D intensity tend to be more export oriented, are localized within Taiwan in terms of their sourcing of materials and capital goods, and belong to sectors with a larger pool of R&D labor.

I do have a few minor comments on the current effort and also a couple of suggestions for future research. With respect to the current paper, I think the paper would have benefited from a more concerted effort to flush out exactly how the theory of FDI relates to the empirical question. Despite this comment the current discussion is excellent; in fact, the discussion of locational advantages and R&D is superb. My wish, however, is that the authors expounded more on the direction of causality. In particular, the discussion seems to indicate that both local R&D advantages can attract FDI and also that FDI deepening can encourage R&D. My sense is that this is two-way causality is correct. However, the econometric specifications really don't account for the potential connection.

I would have also liked to see the authors discuss whether R&D intensity has varied between local firms and foreign affiliates. It seems possible that the growth in R&D intensity is driven by the dynamism and innovation of local Taiwanese firms. This local innovation and creativity could have pulled-in FDI. While it seems hard to believe that local R&D has kept up with affiliate R&D, it would be helpful to document the differences.

I would also have liked to see a more detailed discussion of the industry-level differences and trends. The authors present evidence that R&D intensity and capital inflow vary considerably across industry. One industry, electrical and electronic machinery, stands out as a outlier in both dimensions. Are the results being driven by this one industry? This is unlikely, but it would bolster the findings if the authors gave a sense of the sensitivity of their results to one or two outliers.

With respect to future research, I have two suggestions. First, I think the dynamics are far more complicated than the current analysis suggests. In the current paper the authors control for dynamics by including a time trend. While it is highly reassuring that the results are largely unaffected when this trend is included, this is only the first pass. The issue needs more exploration. For instance, are the current parameter results largely a result of time series variation or cross-section variation? The authors might also consider allowing the individual parameters to vary across time, say by splitting the sample into "early" and "recent" time periods. Second, the regressions capture only contemporaneous effects. My sense is that in practice the connection between FDI and R&D intensity involves significant lags. That is, decisions and investments made years ago will impact current R&D.

The Effects of Overseas Investment on Domestic Employment

Tain-Jy Chen and Ying-Hua Ku

4.1 Introduction

It has long been a concern of policymakers that foreign direct investment (FDI) may cause job losses at home; indeed, labor unions generally consider FDI to be the equivalent of job exporting. The logic is simple; as production lines are relocated overseas, gone with them are the workers that served the domestic lines. This reasoning is, of course, oversimplistic because there could never be any guarantees that the production lines that were relocated overseas would have been able to survive the competition had they remained at home. If these production lines were to be eliminated anyway, then their relocation does not result in any job losses.

Conversely, there is always the possibility that overseas investment might well enhance the overall competitiveness of the investing company and therefore boost job opportunities at home that would otherwise have been swept away by competition. Ku (1998), for example, found that FDI enabled Taiwanese enterprises to restructure themselves and therefore increase their tenacity. She showed that firms engaging in overseas production had a better chance of survival than those that were not.

Those who are concerned about the adverse effects of overseas investment on domestic employment basically assume that overseas production is a substitute for exports; hence, as exports fall, so does employment. This is a conventional argument along the lines of Mundell (1957), who showed very elegantly, in a 2×2 model, that capital movement is equivalent to trade. Products produced in overseas locations not only replace exports,

Tain-Jy Chen is president of the Chung-Hua Institution for Economic Research and a professor in the department of economics at National Taiwan University. Ying-Hua Ku is a research fellow at the Chung-Hua Institution for Economic Research.

they may also in fact be reimported back home to substitute the products that were previously produced to serve the home market (Liu and Lin 2001). There are, however, counterarguments to Mundell's perfect substitution theory. Markusen (1983), for example, demonstrated the theoretical possibility that FDI and trade are complementary rather than substitutes; therefore, the relationship between FDI and job opportunities at home is indeed an empirical question.

Brainard and Riker (1997a,b) directly estimated the substitution elasticities between employment in parent companies and their foreign affiliates, as well as those between different affiliates, and found a very low degree of substitution between parent and affiliate employment, although there was a high degree of substitution between affiliates in developing countries. They also found that the relationship between employment in industrialized country affiliates and in developing countries was complementary rather than substituting.

Slaughter (1995) had earlier found a similar low degree of substitution between parent and affiliate employment when only production workers were considered. He noted that the employment of production workers did not seem to be systematically related to relative wages between the parent and the affiliate. This suggests that overseas employment corresponds only weakly to the wage gap between home and host countries, although it may correspond strongly to the wage gap between different overseas locations. Hatzius (1997) and Döhrn (1997) found similar results for Sweden with overseas employment of Swedish multinational firms responding to wages in actual and potential host countries but not to wages in Sweden. Blomström and Kokko (2000) also discovered that Swedish multinationals react to domestic policies rather than wages in determining whether to keep production at home.

This evidence suggests that overseas production and domestic production is closely related but not necessarily substitutable. In fact, there must be a division of labor between the parent and affiliates as FDI is an action taken to enhance the competitiveness of a company. To the extent that FDI reduces the costs of the parent's operations, it also helps the parent to expand its level of output, which, in turn, increases employment at home. Blomström, Fors, and Lipsey (1997), for example, found that overseas investment in developing countries by U.S. firms did have the effect of replacing domestic employment, but the same investment in developed countries did not; the replacement effect was, however, limited to production workers.

Findings that the employment effect from FDI may differ across labor groups are important, for this implies that FDI has important consequences for income distribution. For example, the examination of Swedish firms by Blomström, Fors, and Lipsey (1997) found that FDI contributes to growth in employment of unskilled labor at home because Swedish multinationals were investing abroad to acquire skilled workers to engage in R&D and other skill-intensive activities. Lipsey's (1994) study of U.S. multinationals also found that overseas affiliates allow the parent to employ more managerial and technical staff at the same level of domestic production. Feenstra (1996) showed that FDI in Mexico by U.S. firms increased the demand at home for skilled workers vis-à-vis unskilled workers, thus raising the relative wage of skilled workers and worsening income distribution for the investing country, whereas the reverse occurred in Mexico.

There is an indirect, but nevertheless very important, linkage between FDI and domestic employment, that is, the effect of FDI on domestic investment. If FDI outflows are accompanied by an equal reduction in the amount of domestic investment, then FDI may still reduce job opportunities at home even if overseas production is complementary to domestic production; Feldstein (1994) seems to suggest such a one-to-one substitution effect. Stevens and Lipsey (1992) also found a negative relationship between FDI and domestic investment, although not as clear as one-to-one replacement, however, Bayoumi and Lipworth's (1998) study of the case in Japan found no displacement effect on domestic investment from FDI. Again, the actual relationship is therefore an empirical question.

The purpose of this paper is therefore to examine the relationship between FDI and domestic employment at firm level, using Taiwan's manufacturing industry as an example. We find that overseas production leads to an increase in the domestic employment of managerial and technical workers but may also reduce the employment available to unskilled workers. Overseas production partially replaces inputs to domestic production, resulting in a decline in labor demand at a given output level; however, at the same time, overseas production reduces the costs of domestic production, leading to an expansion in output. These input-replacement and output-expansion effects combine to produce a net effect that is positive in most cases, although the net effect differs with different labor groups and the geographical location of overseas investment.

4.2 An Overview of Taiwan's FDI and Manufacturing Employment

Taiwanese firms made only sporadic outward investment before 1980. Beginning in the mid-1980s, Taiwanese firms started making more substantial foreign investment, driven by rising wages and rising value of Taiwanese currency, NT. Between 1987 and 1990, Southeast Asia and the United States were the major destinations of Taiwan's foreign investment. In the early 1990s, China emerged in the FDI map and eventually became the most popular destination for Taiwanese investors. In the second half of the 1990s, China took up almost a half of Taiwan's total amount of outward investment (see table 4.1). The manufacturing sector accounted for

Table 4.1   Taiwan's outward investment by location (US$1,000)

	Asia (excluding China)	America	Europe	China	Others	Total
1952–1990	1,077,710	1,844,332	115,171	0	39,298	3,076,511
1991	929,819	658,958	60,289	174,158	6,964	1,830,188
1992	369,929	449,096	45,933	246,992	22,301	1,134,251
1993	663,514	740,110	255,913	3,168,411	1,398	4,829,346
1994	559,471	988,336	22,209	962,209	46,748	2,578,973
1995	467,743	787,105	59,868	1,092,713	42,162	2,449,591
1996	661,717	1,442,953	11,875	1,229,241	48,859	3,394,645
1997	818,743	1,915,948	58,508	4,334,313	100,627	7,228,139
1998	580,819	2,637,021	33,828	2,034,621	44,634	5,330,923
1999	836,378	2,267,710	60,982	1,252,780	103,943	4,521,793
2000	851,065	3,946,021	62,225	2,607,142	217,751	7,684,204
2001	814,981	3,460,902	45,594	2,784,147	70,177	7,175,801
2002	528,054	2,475,575	123,416	6,723,058	243,001	10,093,104
Total	9,159,943	23,614,067	955,811	26,609,785	987,863	61,327,469

Source: Statistics on Overseas Chinese & Foreign Investment, Outward Investment, and Indirect Mainland Investment (various issues), Investment Commission, Ministry of Economic Affairs.

the majority of overseas investment, dominating the service and agriculture sectors. In the manufacturing sector, FDI is most active in the electronics, chemical, and textile industries. FDI appears to have important consequences on domestic employment.

Manufacturing employment in Taiwan reached a peak in 1987 when 2.821 million people were working in the manufacturing sector; thereafter, there was a general decline in manufacturing employment until it hit a trough in 1994, when 2.422 million people were working in the sector. It then started to recover through the mid- to late-1990s, with 2.655 million people being employed in the manufacturing sector by 2000 (see figure 4.1).

The available employment data suggests that the period 1987–1994 was a time when Taiwan's industry underwent dramatic restructuring. While there were losses of 399,000 manufacturing jobs throughout that period, there was nevertheless an increase in employment in the service sector of around 1.385 million, more than enough to offset these losses. Thus, unemployment rates remained at low levels throughout the 1990s.

It is also worth noting that 1987 was around the time when Taiwanese firms began to embark on the course of FDI, with more than US$43 billion being invested overseas from 1987 to 2000. Between 1987 and 1992, FDI was concentrated in Southeast Asia where Malaysia, Thailand, and Indonesia took the lion's share of Taiwan's overseas investment; however, from 1992 onward, the focus for FDI shifted to China. After the 1997 Asian financial crisis, FDI in Southeast Asia came to a virtual standstill

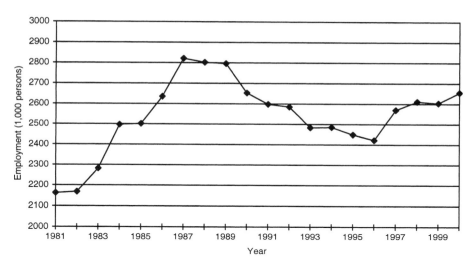

Fig. 4.1   Manufacturing employment, 1981–2000

whereas FDI in China continued to surge. In 2001, the global recession saw Taiwan's unemployment rate reaching an unprecedented 4 percent; thus, there were heightened fears that FDI may have led to rising unemployment at home.

Beneath the surface of a relatively stable employment situation in the 1990s, there was a rather dramatic transformation taking place in the industrial structure. Among twenty-two two-digit industries in the manufacturing sector, twelve had increased their employment levels whereas the remaining ten had seen their employment levels falling. The most rapid increase in employment occurred in the electronics industry in which 145,748 new jobs had been generated between 1991 and 2000, representing a 24.3 percent increase on the 1990 level. It was probably no coincidence that the electronics industry was also the industry that was most active in undertaking outward investment. In contrast, employment in the apparel industry recorded the largest number of job losses, at 54,104, representing a loss of more than one-third of its initial 1991 employment level. However, FDI from the apparel industry was also substantial; thus, the relationship between FDI and domestic employment is unclear, to say the least. In the following section, we will examine this relationship in more detail.

4.3   The Statistics on FDI and Employment

In this section, we present the employment data revealed by Taiwan's Census of Manufacturers and relate this to FDI. The census data are collected at plant level but are then aggregated into firm-level data; all of the following statistics are reported at firm level because it is considered that FDI is decided at firm level rather than at plant level. Changes in employment between 1993 and 2000 are studied, with 1993 having been chosen as the starting year because this was the first time that a comprehensive set of FDI statistics was collected in the census; 2000 is chosen as the terminal year because this was the most recent census year. A total of 75,101 firms are included in the 1993 census, of which 49,260 had survived until 2000, while the remaining 25,841 had exited the market during the period under study. Between 1993 and 2000, 27,585 new firms had entered the market, with these new entries during this eight-year period representing 36.7 percent of the stock of firms in the initial year, and the exiting firms representing 34.4 percent of the stock, a characteristically high turnover rate for Taiwan's industry (Aw, Chen, and Roberts 2001). All firms that have shown up in either the 1993 census or the 2000 census come to a total of 102,686, which forms our sample for comparison.

We classify all sample firms into two categories, the FDI group and the non-FDI group. The FDI group includes all firms that have undertaken overseas investment, and the non-FDI group includes those that have not undertaken any such investment. Although there are some missing data, the census does cover the majority of manufacturing firms. The total employment figures in the sample were 2,155,672 persons for 1993, and 2,291,396 for 2000, representing 89.8 percent and 92.9 percent, respectively, of the total employment estimated by the statistics authorities during the two census years.

We tabulate the turnover of sample firms in table 4.2, which shows that there were 4,283 firms in the FDI group and 98,403 firms in the non-FDI group. Although, in terms of the number of firms, the FDI group accounted for just 4.3 percent of the manufacturing sector (ignoring the

Table 4.2   **FDI and domestic employment, 1993–2000 (persons, %)**

Firm group	No. of firms	1993		2000	
		Employment	%	Employment	%
FDI firms	4,283	608,501	28.23	689,769	30.10
Survivors	2,843	558,243	25.90	625,013	27.28
Exited	900	50,258	2.33	n.a.	n.a.
New entrants	540	n.a.	n.a.	64,756	2.83
Non-FDI firms	98,403	1,547,171	71.77	1,601,627	69.90
Survivors	46,417	1,119,060	51.91	1,055,421	46.06
Exited	24,941	428,111	19.86	n.a.	n.a.
New entrants	27,045	n.a.	n.a.	546,206	23.84
Total	102,686	2,155,672	100.00	2,291,396	100.00

Source: Authors' calculation from *Census of Manufacturers,* 1993 and 2000.
Note: n.a. = not available.

missing data), it nevertheless accounted for 28.23 percent of total employment within the sector, which suggests that firms engaging in overseas investment are relatively large in size.

Out of the 4,283 firms in the FDI group, 3,743 firms were already in existence in 1993; the remainder was made up of new firms that entered during the period under study. From the initial 1993 cohort, 2,843 had survived the competition and remained active within the industry in 2000, representing a 76.0 percent survival rate.

Meanwhile, out of the 98,403 firms in the non-FDI group, 71,358 firms were already in existence in 1993, and 46,417 firms had survived up until 2000, representing a 65.0 percent survival rate. Simple statistics suggest that those firms that were engaged in overseas investment had a higher survival rate, supporting the findings of Ku (1998), which, in a study of Taiwan's electronics industry, showed that FDI did indeed increase the probability of survival.

Within our sample, the FDI group accounted for 28.23 percent of all manufacturing sector employment in 1993, but by 2000, this figure had risen to 30.10 percent. If we count only those firms that were in existence in 1993, the employment share in 2000 was 27.28 percent, representing only a slight fall on the 1993 proportion despite the fact that a quarter of them had been eliminated in the interim period. In contrast, the non-FDI group accounted for 71.77 percent of all manufacturing sector employment in 1993 and 69.90 percent in 2000. However, if new entrants are excluded, the surviving firms in the non-FDI group account for only 46.06 percent of employment in 2000. Simple statistics again suggest that FDI enabled investing firms to maintain more jobs at home.

It is worth noting that firms that exited the manufacturing industry during the period under study eliminated 478,369 jobs, or 22.2 percent of the total employment in 1993. These losses were more than offset by the 610,962 jobs created by new entrants coming into the industry during the eight-year period. Total employment provided by those firms that survived the period is virtually unchanged; however, employment per firm increased by 12.0 percent in the FDI group in contrast to the 5.7 percent decline in the non-FDI group.

4.4   The Effect of Investment Location

As demonstrated by Lipsey (1994) and Blomström, Fors, and Lipsey (1997), the employment effect of FDI may differ by investment location; thus, we should also examine the data on Taiwan to see whether geographical location matters. Taiwanese FDI had been concentrated in China since the early 1990s; however, there is one perspective that argues that investment in China is potentially more harmful to domestic employment than FDI in other regions. The reason for this, so the argument goes, is because

Table 4.3   Employment effect, by FDI location

Investment location	No. of firms	1993	Average employment	2000	Average employment	1993–2000 change (%)
China	1,048	122,179	116.58	112,710	107.55	–7.75
China and others	630	284,876	452.18	333,269	529.00	16.99
Other than China	692	101,698	146.96	135,752	196.17	33.49
Unknown	473	49,490	104.63	43,282	91.51	–12.54
Total	2,843	558,243	196.36	625,013	219.84	11.96

Source: Authors' calculation from *Census of Manufacturers,* 1993 and 2000.

of the cultural proximity and similarity in labor skills, with production in China being likely to duplicate what had previously been done in Taiwan and therefore exerting a strong substitution effect on domestic employment.

In order to examine the location effect, we classify those firms undertaking overseas investment into four subgroups according to the location of their investment. The first subgroup contains firms undertaking investment in China only, the second subgroup contains firms investing in China plus other regions, the third subgroup contains firms investing in regions other than China, and the fourth subgroup contains firms with unknown FDI locations. Table 4.3 provides details of the level of employment for the four respective subgroups in 1993 and 2000.

As the table shows, of the 2,843 firms that undertook overseas investment and survived the 1993–2000 period, 1,048 had invested only in China, 630 had invested in China and somewhere else, 692 had invested only outside of China, and the remainder had invested in unknown regions. Those investing only in China were apparently smaller in size as their average employment was only 116.58 in 1993, substantially lower than the average employment level for the entire FDI group; furthermore, the average employment of this subgroup declined again, to 107.55 employees, in 2000. In contrast, the subgroup investing only outside of China registered the highest growth rate in employment of all the subgroups, at 33.49 percent, while firms that invested in China and other regions saw their employment rise by 16.99 percent.

This seems to suggest that investing only in China undermines the investor's capacity to maintain jobs at home; however, this conclusion is somewhat premature as there are other factors that may affect domestic employment after an enterprise invests abroad. Two obvious factors are firm size and industry. It is well established within the literature that firm size is positively correlated to the ability to invest abroad (Caves 1971, 1996). Large firms may therefore be more capable of undergoing internal restructuring after they have invested abroad and therefore are more capable of maintaining jobs at home (Chen and Ku 2000).

Table 4.4   **Change in employment, 1993–2000 (ANOVA)**

Investment location	Industry			Size			Sample
	Low growth	High growth	F-statistics	Small	Large	F-statistics	
China	0.017	0.812	3.27*	0.044	4.238	27.43**	1,048
China and others	0.235	1.524	8.52**	0.628	1.669	27.15**	692
Other than China	0.183	0.532	4.59**	0.241	1.239	2.92*	630
Unknown	0.226	0.716		0.458	0.525		473
F-statistics	1.36	1.01		2.61**	1.19		2,843

**Significant at the 5 percent level
*Significant at the 10 percent level.

Industry is also an important factor because a high-growth industry provides more opportunities for firms to diversify after they have invested
abroad. In order to test the size and industry effects, we make a two-way
classification of firms according to their size and industry affiliations; firms
that employ more than 300 persons are classified as large firms; the rest are
small firms. Industries that have grown by more than 30 percent in output
between 1993 and 2000 are considered to be high-growth industries; otherwise they are low-growth industries; the demarcation line of 30 percent
is the average growth rate in entire manufacturing output for the period under study.

We apply analysis of variance (ANOVA) to determine how much FDI
location matters when controlling for industry and size and vice versa; the
results are shown in table 4.4, which indicates that when controlling for investment location, employment growth is significantly affected by both industry and size. Firms in the high-growth industries show a significantly
higher employment growth rate than those in the low-growth industries,
while large firms show a significantly higher employment growth rate than
small firms.

When both industry and firm size are controlled for, investment location
becomes inconsequential, except for the small-firm group where those investing in China only registered the lowest employment growth rate, as
compared to those investing outside of China. This seems to suggest that
job displacement, if there is any, may affect small firms that choose to invest solely in China.

4.5   Estimating the Effects of FDI on Employment

In this section, we estimate the statistical effects of FDI on employment,
using a production function to portray the relationship between domestic
and overseas operations. We basically treat overseas operation and domestic operation as joint production that can be portrayed by an appro-

priate production function. The output from overseas production may serve as an intermediate input to domestic production, thereby reducing the cost of domestic production; by so doing, this reduces the demand for domestic primary inputs, including labor. The output from overseas production may also add to the burden of domestic operations if it requires managerial and technical support from the headquarters. Here, we treat the output from both overseas and domestic operations as two joint outputs from centrally managed production aimed at minimizing overall costs.

We employ the generalized Leontief production function developed by Diewert (1971) and Hall (1973) to portray a cross-border operation yielding two distinctive outputs Y_1 and Y_2, where Y_1 is the output from domestic operations and Y_2 is that from foreign operations. There are three kinds of labor inputs to production, namely managerial workers, technical workers, and blue-collar workers. Labor is finely classified because we are concerned about the effects of FDI on different kinds of labor, given the complexity of the international division of labor. Three kinds of workers constitute a composite labor input underlying which is a subproduction function. The relationship between this composite labor input and capital is a Leontief relationship; therefore, the demand for labor can be solely determined by output levels and wages, irrespective of capital input. We can therefore depict the cost function of the composite labor as follows:

$$
\begin{aligned}
C(Y_1, Y_2, W_1, W_2, W_3) = {} & \beta_1 Y_1 W_1 + \beta_2 Y_1 W_2 + \beta_3 Y_1 W_3 + \beta_4 Y_2 W_1 + \beta_5 Y_2 W_2 \\
& + \beta_6 Y_2 W_3 + 2\beta_7 W_1 \sqrt{Y_1 Y_2} + 2\beta_8 W_2 \sqrt{Y_1 Y_2} \\
& + 2\beta_9 W_3 \sqrt{Y_1 Y_2} + 2\beta_{10} Y_1 \sqrt{W_1 W_2} + 2\beta_{11} Y_1 \sqrt{W_1 W_3} \\
& + 2\beta_{12} Y_1 \sqrt{W_2 W_3} + 2\beta_{13} Y_2 \sqrt{W_1 W_2} \\
& + 2\beta_{14} Y_2 \sqrt{W_2 W_3} + 2\beta_{15} Y_2 \sqrt{W_1 W_3} \\
& + 4\beta_{16} \sqrt{Y_1 Y_2 W_1 W_2} + 4\beta_{17} \sqrt{Y_1 Y_2 W_2 W_3} \\
& + 4\beta_{18} \sqrt{Y_1 Y_2 W_1 W_3},
\end{aligned}
$$

where C is the total cost of labor and W_1, W_2, and W_3 are the respective unit costs of managerial workers, technical workers, and blue-collar workers. Note that outputs Y_1, Y_2 are measured by value added in NT dollar terms. The sample covers firms from various industries, and value added is the only meaningful measuring unit common to all industries.

Although the generalized Leontief production function restricts the production technology to be constant returns to scale, it does allow the elasticity of substitution (or complementarity) between three kinds of labor to be flexible. The interrelationship between different kinds of labor in production is the focus of our study.

Using Shephard's lemma, we may derive the labor demand equation for each kind of worker:

$$(1) \quad L_1 = \frac{\partial C}{\partial W_1} = \beta_1 Y_1 + \beta_4 Y_2 + 2\beta_7 \sqrt{Y_1 Y_2} + \beta_{10} Y_1 \sqrt{\frac{W_2}{W_1}} + \beta_{11} Y_1 \sqrt{\frac{W_3}{W_1}}$$

$$+ \beta_{13} Y_2 \sqrt{\frac{W_2}{W_1}} + \beta_{15} Y_2 \sqrt{\frac{W_3}{W_1}} + 2\beta_{16} \sqrt{\frac{Y_1 Y_2 W_2}{W_1}}$$

$$+ 2\beta_{18} \sqrt{\frac{Y_1 Y_2 W_3}{W_1}}$$

$$L_2 = \frac{\partial C}{\partial W_2} = \beta_2 Y_1 + \beta_5 Y_2 + 2\beta_8 \sqrt{Y_1 Y_2} + \beta_{10} Y_1 \sqrt{\frac{W_1}{W_2}} + \beta_{12} Y_1 \sqrt{\frac{W_3}{W_2}}$$

$$+ \beta_{13} Y_2 \sqrt{\frac{W_1}{W_2}} + \beta_{14} Y_2 \sqrt{\frac{W_3}{W_2}} + 2\beta_{16} \sqrt{\frac{Y_1 Y_2 W_1}{W_2}}$$

$$+ 2\beta_{17} \sqrt{\frac{Y_1 Y_2 W_3}{W_2}}$$

$$L_3 = \frac{\partial C}{\partial W_3} = \beta_3 Y_1 + \beta_6 Y_2 + 2\beta_9 \sqrt{Y_1 Y_2} + \beta_{11} Y_1 \sqrt{\frac{W_1}{W_3}} + \beta_{12} Y_1 \sqrt{\frac{W_2}{W_3}}$$

$$+ \beta_{14} Y_2 \sqrt{\frac{W_2}{W_3}} + \beta_{15} Y_2 \sqrt{\frac{W_1}{W_3}} + 2\beta_{17} \sqrt{\frac{Y_1 Y_2 W_2}{W_3}}$$

$$+ 2\beta_{18} \sqrt{\frac{Y_1 Y_2 W_1}{W_3}},$$

where L_1, L_2, and L_3 denote managerial, technical, and blue-collar workers, respectively.

We may use seemingly unrelated regressions to estimate equation (1), taking into consideration the fact that disturbance terms in the three single equations may be somehow correlated. In undertaking the regression, we should impose cross-equation restrictions on parameters to ensure that the same estimate is produced for any parameter that appears in more than one equation. From the parameter estimates, we can easily measure the effects of Y_1 and Y_2 on each kind of labor demand, as shown in equation (1).

In order to measure the quantity of labor, data was drawn from the latest survey on employment undertaken by Taiwan's Bureau of Labor Affairs (BOLA) in 1999. The survey classifies labor into nine categories, but these nine categories are far too many to handle and also contain many zeros; therefore, they are combined into three categories to suit our purposes: (a) supervisory (managers), administrative, and professional staff are classified as managerial workers; (b) engineers, technicians, and specialists are classified as technical workers; and (c) operators, laborers, and service workers are classified as blue-collar workers. The raw data drawn from the three small labor categories are converted into a large category, using the Divisia index, with each sample mean being normalized to unity. We thus obtained the measures for L_1 (managerial workers), L_2 (technical workers), and L_3 (blue-collar workers).

Wage rates W_1, W_2, W_3 are obtained by dividing the respective total wage bills by the measures of L_1, L_2, and L_3. The data for domestic output (Y_1) and overseas output (Y_2) are obtained from the 1999 *Survey on Overseas Investment by Manufacturing Firms* undertaken by the Ministry of Economic Affairs (MOEA). This survey also provides information on investment locations, but it only covers manufacturing firms that possess overseas affiliates. The BOLA and MOEA surveys are combined to yield 394 observations, all of which are firms engaged in FDI. We then randomly drew 140 non-FDI firms from the BOLA survey in order to supplement the observations using firms without overseas affiliates. The total of 140 was taken so as to make the ratio of FDI to non-FDI firms roughly 3:1. The combined sample of 534 firms form the basis of our regression analysis, but only 451 of them contain complete data for entry into the regression estimation. It is generally believed that Taiwanese firms underreported their actual amounts of investment in China. Our usage of output value rather than investment amount in regression analysis avoids the underestimation problem. There may also be firms that hide their investment altogether. Hopefully, our randomly chosen non-FDI sample does not contain many of such firms. Both the MOEA and the BOLA surveys covered firms of all sizes, so there is no selection bias problem associated with size. The regression results are shown in table 4.5.

From equation (1), we can derive the effects of domestic output (Y_1) and overseas output (Y_2) on labor demand. They are, respectively,

$$(2) \quad \frac{\partial L_1}{\partial Y_1} = \beta_1 + \beta_7\sqrt{\frac{Y_2}{Y_1}} + \beta_{10}\sqrt{\frac{W_2}{W_1}} + \beta_{11}\sqrt{\frac{W_3}{W_1}} + \beta_{16}\sqrt{\frac{Y_2 W_2}{Y_1 W_1}} + \beta_{18}\sqrt{\frac{Y_2 W_3}{Y_1 W_1}}$$

$$\frac{\partial L_2}{\partial Y_1} = \beta_2 + \beta_8\sqrt{\frac{Y_2}{Y_1}} + \beta_{10}\sqrt{\frac{W_1}{W_2}} + \beta_{12}\sqrt{\frac{W_3}{W_2}} + \beta_{16}\sqrt{\frac{Y_2 W_1}{Y_1 W_2}} + \beta_{17}\sqrt{\frac{Y_2 W_3}{Y_1 W_2}}$$

$$\frac{\partial L_3}{\partial Y_1} = \beta_3 + \beta_9\sqrt{\frac{Y_2}{Y_1}} + \beta_{11}\sqrt{\frac{W_1}{W_3}} + \beta_{12}\sqrt{\frac{W_2}{W_3}} + \beta_{17}\sqrt{\frac{Y_2 W_2}{Y_1 W_3}} + \beta_{18}\sqrt{\frac{Y_2 W_1}{Y_1 W_3}}$$

and

$$(3) \quad \frac{\partial L_1}{\partial Y_2} = \beta_4 + \beta_7\sqrt{\frac{Y_1}{Y_2}} + \beta_{13}\sqrt{\frac{W_2}{W_1}} + \beta_{15}\sqrt{\frac{W_3}{W_1}} + \beta_{16}\sqrt{\frac{Y_1 W_2}{Y_2 W_1}} + \beta_{18}\sqrt{\frac{Y_1 W_3}{Y_2 W_1}}$$

$$\frac{\partial L_2}{\partial Y_2} = \beta_5 + \beta_8\sqrt{\frac{Y_1}{Y_2}} + \beta_{13}\sqrt{\frac{W_1}{W_2}} + \beta_{14}\sqrt{\frac{W_3}{W_2}} + \beta_{16}\sqrt{\frac{Y_1 W_1}{Y_2 W_2}} + \beta_{17}\sqrt{\frac{Y_1 W_3}{Y_2 W_2}}$$

$$\frac{\partial L_3}{\partial Y_2} = \beta_6 + \beta_9\sqrt{\frac{Y_1}{Y_2}} + \beta_{14}\sqrt{\frac{W_2}{W_3}} + \beta_{15}\sqrt{\frac{W_1}{W_3}} + \beta_{17}\sqrt{\frac{Y_1 W_2}{Y_2 W_3}} + \beta_{18}\sqrt{\frac{Y_1 W_1}{Y_2 W_3}}.$$

Table 4.5   **Regression estimates of generalized Leontief production function**

Independent variables	Parameter estimates	t-statistic
Dependent variable: Managerial workers (L_1)		
Y_1	-1.639×10^{-2}	0.299
Y_2	0.391	3.110**
YY	-0.232	2.430**
$Y_1 W_{12}$	9.552×10^{-2}	1.348
$Y_1 W_{13}$	0.103	3.152**
$Y_2 W_{12}$	-0.449	3.068**
$Y_2 W_{13}$	-3.610×10^{-2}	0.992
YYW_{12}	0.363	3.016**
YYW_{13}	-5.645×10^{-2}	1.187
Dependent variable: Technical workers (L_2)		
Y_1	0.389	3.014**
Y_2	0.739	3.985**
YY	-0.748	3.997**
$Y_1 W_{21}$	9.552×10^{-2}	1.348
$Y_1 W_{23}$	-0.131	2.230**
$Y_2 W_{21}$	-0.449	3.068**
$Y_2 W_{23}$	-0.125	2.101**
YYW_{21}	0.363	3.016**
YYW_{23}	0.177	2.254**
Dependent variable: Blue-collar workers (L_3)		
Y_1	0.205	4.116**
Y_2	0.195	3.514**
YY	-0.160	-2.541**
$Y_1 W_{31}$	0.103	3.408**
$Y_1 W_{32}$	-0.131	-2.380**
$Y_2 W_{31}$	-3.610×10^{-2}	0.992
$Y_2 W_{32}$	-0.125	2.101**
YYW_{31}	-5.645×10^{-2}	1.187
YYW_{32}	0.177	2.254**

Notes: System weighted $R^2 = 0.5649$; degree of freedom: 1,335; $YY = (Y_1 Y_2)^{1/2}$; $Y_1 W_{12} = Y_1 W_1^{-1/2} W_2^{1/2}$; $Y_1 W_{13} = Y_1 W_1^{-1/2}$; $Y_2 W_{12} = Y_2 W_1^{-1/2} W_2^{1/2}$; $Y_2 W_{13} = Y_2 W_1^{-1/2} W_3^{1/2}$; $YYW_{12} = (Y_1 Y_2)^{1/2} W_1^{1/2}$; $YYW_{13} = (Y_1 Y_2)^{1/2} W_1^{-1/2} W_3^{1/2}$.
**Significant at the 5 percent level.

If we fit the parameter estimates into equations (2) and (3), we obtain the estimated effects of Y_1 and Y_2 on labor demand. The values of Y_1 and Y_2, and W_1, W_2, and W_3, are taken to be the sample means. We estimate these effects for firms investing in different locations as we did in the previous section. The results are shown in table 4.6.

It can be seen from table 4.6 that the demand for all kinds of labor increases with an increase in domestic output. For example, for those firms investing in China only, the demand for managerial workers increases by 0.1760 for each NT\$ billion (Taiwanese currency) increase in domestic output (as Y_1 is measured in NT\$ billions). Since the Divisia index for labor has been normalized, this figure implies that in comparison with the

Table 4.6   Effects of domestic and overseas production on employment

	Managerial		Technical		Blue-collar	
	Domestic production	Overseas production	Domestic production	Overseas production	Domestic production	Overseas production
Investing in China only (136)	0.1760	−0.0291	0.2988	−0.0413	0.1412	−0.0481
Investing in China and others (126)	0.1847	−0.0286	0.2831	−0.0387	0.1264	−0.0220
Investing outside China (113)	0.1762	−0.0307	0.3018	−0.0533	0.1559	−0.0845

Notes: Domestic and overseas production is estimated in NT$ billions. Number of samples in parentheses.

Table 4.7   Sample means, by FDI group (NT$ million)

FDI location	Domestic output	Overseas output	Overseas/Domestic ratio	No. of samples
China only	1,795.3	851.9	0.475	136
China and others	3,995.0	2,805.8	0.702	126
Other than China	5,591.1	1,633.8	0.292	113

sample mean, there is an increase of 17.60 percent in managerial workers. Similarly, for each NT$ billion increase in domestic output, the demand for technical workers increases by 29.88 percent, and the demand for blue-collar workers increases by 14.12 percent. The results indicate that by 1999, the expansion in domestic production had led to an expansion in all three kinds of labor, although technical personnel tended to benefit the most, followed by managerial staff, and then blue-collar workers the least. This pattern prevails across all investment locations, despite the fact that firm size differs significantly across different subgroups. This implies that the output effect on employment is mainly driven by the nature of technology that, as Taiwanese industry intensifies its technology content, tends to favor technical workers.

Table 4.7 lists the mean values of Y_1 and Y_2 for the different FDI subgroups. It can be seen that the subgroup of firms investing in China only is the smallest of the three groups in terms of domestic output, followed by the subgroup investing in China plus other regions, with the subgroup investing only outside of China being the largest. However, the subgroup investing in China and other regions also has the highest overseas production ratio, at 0.702, followed by the China only subgroup at 0.475, and then the outside China subgroup at 0.292.

Referring back to table 4.6 also shows that overseas production has exerted a uniformly negative effect on each kind of labor, which suggests that when holding domestic output constant, domestic employment for a firm engaging in overseas production will decline by between 2 percent and 8 percent. This implies that overseas production complements domestic production and therefore reduces the need for labor inputs at any given output level. However, we should not jump to the conclusion that overseas production reduces domestic employment, because such a complementary relationship also cuts down the cost of domestic production, thus enhancing the competitiveness of the company as a whole, which, in turn, may lead to an expansion in domestic output. In other words, overseas production exerts a substitution effect that reduces the demand for labor at any given domestic output as well as an output effect that expands domestic production. The net result has to take both effects into account; thus, it is the output effect to which we now turn.

We take the *Census of Manufacturers* data and choose the firms that have survived throughout the period under study to explore the effects of FDI on domestic output. A simple regression is employed to estimate this effect:

$$(4) \quad LY99 = \alpha_0 + \alpha_1 LY93 + \alpha_2 DFI_1 + \alpha_3 DFI_2 + \alpha_4 DFI_3 + \alpha_5 DFI_4$$
$$+ \alpha_6 IND$$

where the variables are as follows:

$LY99$:   logarithm of domestic output in 1999
$LY93$:   logarithm of domestic output in 1993
DFI_1:   dummy variable for firms investing in China only
DFI_2:   dummy variable for firms investing in China and other regions
DFI_3:   dummy variable for firms investing only outside China
DFI_4:   dummy variable for firms investing in unknown regions
IND: dummy variable for high-growth industries

In equation (4), we use the output in the base year (i.e., 1993) to project the output in the future year, 1999. Thus the coefficient α_1 reflects the average growth rate between 1993 and 1999. The dummy variables, DFI_1–DFI_4, capture the extra growth attributable to overseas investments, and the dummy variable, IND, captures the extra growth attributable to industry affiliation. Included in the regression analysis were a total of 50,164 firms that survived the 1993–1999 period. The results are reported in table 4.8, which shows that the coefficients for dummy variables, DFI_1–DFI_4, were all positive and statistically significant. This suggests that foreign investment does indeed contribute to extra growth in output after controlling for the industry effect.

Compared to non-FDI firms, firms investing only in China recorded extra growth of 18 percent over the 1993–1999 period, those firms that invested in China and other regions gained an extra 51.7 percent, and those whose investment was only outside of China achieved 46.4 percent growth.

Table 4.8   **Effect of FDI on domestic output**

Dependent variable: $LY99$	Parameter estimates	t-statistic
Intercept	1.217	44.562**
$LY93$	0.869	303.763**
Investing in China only (DFI$_1$)	0.180	5.573**
Investing in China and others (DFI$_2$)	0.517	9.288**
Investing outside China (DFI$_3$)	0.464	13.071**
Unknown FDI regions (DFI$_4$)	0.424	10.530**
High-growth industry (IND)	0.198	21.388**

Notes: $R^2 = 0.6818$; F-statistic $= 17,915.45$; degrees of freedom: 50,158.
**Significant at the 5 percent level.

Table 4.9   **Overall effect of FDI on domestic employment**

	Managerial workers	Technical workers	Blue-collar workers
Investing in China only	0.0402	0.0717	0.0277
Investing in China and others	0.1185	0.1933	0.0755
Investing outside of China	0.0833	0.1415	–0.0237

The gains may be different, but other things being equal, FDI has indeed expanded their domestic output.

We can therefore estimate the output effect of FDI on domestic production using these estimates; that is, our aim is to estimate the additional domestic output that is attributable to FDI.

Taking the estimate of α in equation (4), this would be $\Delta Y_1 = Y_1 \cdot \alpha/(1 + \alpha)$, where α corresponds to the location of investment. This output effect is to be added to the substitution effect to come up with the net effect of overseas production on domestic labor demand; thus, the total effect of FDI on domestic labor L_i is

$$(5) \qquad \Delta L_i = \frac{\partial L_i}{\partial Y_1} \Delta Y_1 + \frac{\partial L_i}{\partial Y_2} \Delta Y_2,$$

where the first term reflects the output effect and the second term reflects the substitution effect.

Inserting the relevant parameter estimates into equation (5), using the relations established in equation (4), we obtain the estimates at the sample means for total employment effect arising from FDI. These are shown in table 4.9.

It can be seen from table 4.9 that the total employment effects on FDI are positive for all kinds of labor and for all investment locations, with the exception of those investments undertaken outside of China. For the subgroup investing only outside of China, domestic employment of blue-collar workers is adversely affected by FDI (a decline of 2.37 percent). The table also shows that technical workers are the biggest winners from FDI; regardless of the investment locations, the greatest increase is in the domestic employment of technical workers. We interpret this outcome as reflecting the fact that domestic production in recent years has been restructured towards more technology-intensive methods. Managerial workers also gain substantially from FDI but not as much as their technical counterparts. Blue-collar workers gain the least, and they may occasionally even lose. Capital outflow favoring technical workers was also found in Feenstra (1996), while Blomström, Fors, and Lipsey (1997) found that it favored managerial staff. In short, FDI may well affect different labor groups in different ways, but the overall effect is more likely to be positive than negative. The group that is most likely to feel any negative effects is the blue-collar group of workers.

It is noticeable that firms simultaneously investing in China and other regions create the greatest proportion of new jobs at home. We take this subgroup of firms to be truly in pursuit of globalization, since globalization leads to an expansion of domestic production. This also manifests itself in the largest parameter estimate for DFI_2 among all DFIs. Those investing only in China do not create as much demand for technical and managerial workers at home because production in China is characterized by a low technology requirement and simple production arrangements.

Going back to table 4.3 in which domestic employment is shown to decline for firms investing only in China, we may conclude that FDI, per se, is not to blame for the plight of labor; it is instead the fact that these investors belong to low-growth (or even declining) industries, as well as being small in size, that account for their inability to maintain their employment levels at home. In addition to the industry effect, the fact that the China-only group did not generate as much output-expansion effect as the other investment groups also contributes to their below-par performance. Although China production enhances the competitiveness of domestic production, just like other overseas production, it also takes market opportunities away from Taiwan because Chinese and Taiwanese suppliers are often viewed by foreign buyers (particularly in the Western markets) as close substitutes.

4.6 Conclusions

In this paper we study the effects of FDI on domestic employment by examining the data of Taiwan's manufacturing industry. In terms of growth in their number of employees, those firms investing abroad have outperformed those firms that have not undertaken such investment. Moreover, firms that have invested abroad have a higher probability of survival than the have nots; survival means maintaining some jobs at home.

Treating domestic production and overseas production as two distinct but interrelated outputs from a joint production function, we may estimate the effects of overseas production on domestic production and, thereafter, the consequences for domestic employment. Our study of Taiwanese manufacturing data indicates that overseas production reduces the demand for labor in domestic operations at any given domestic output. This implies that through joint production, overseas production reduces the input requirements at home to yield a given domestic output. In other words, overseas production substitutes for primary inputs in the domestic production process.

From a presumption of cost-minimization, this implies that overseas production complements domestic production to reduce the overall costs of cross-border operations, thereby enhancing the competitiveness of a company; this is to be achieved through a division of labor between the headquarters and the affiliates. Such enhanced competitiveness, in turn, helps firms to expand their domestic output, which leads to an increase in the demand for labor. Therefore, the total effect of FDI on domestic employment is a combination of output-expansion effect and input-substitution effect. Our estimates show that, in most cases, the output-expansion effect more than offsets the input-substitution effect to yield a net positive effect on domestic employment; however, the magnitude of employment effect arising from FDI differs across different labor groups.

In the case of Taiwan, technical workers tend to benefit most from FDI, followed by managerial workers, with blue-collar workers benefiting the least; indeed, they may even be adversely affected. This implies that after overseas investment has taken place, a reconfiguration of the division of labor within a firm will tend to shift domestic production toward technology- and management-intensive operations.

Different investment locations exert slightly different impacts on domestic employment mainly because of the differences in output-expansion effect. Those firms that invest only in China contribute the least to the expansion of domestic output, followed by firms that invest only outside of China, while FDI covering both China and other regions is most conducive to domestic output expansion.

References

Aw, B.-Y., X. Chen, and M. Roberts. 2001. Firm-level evidence of productivity differentials and turnover in Taiwanese manufacturing. *Journal of Development Economics* 66 (1): 51–86.
Bayoumi, T., and G. Lipworth. 1998. Japanese foreign direct investment and regional trade. *Journal of Asian Economics* 9 (4): 581–607.

Blomström, M., G. Fors, and R. Lipsey. 1997. Foreign direct investment and employment: Home country experience in the United States and Sweden. *Economic Journal* 107 (445): 1787–97.

Blomström, M., and A. Kokko. 2000. Outward investment, employment and wages in Swedish multinationals. *Oxford Review of Economic Policy* 16 (3): 76–89.

Brainard, S., and D. Riker. 1997a. Are US multinationals exporting US jobs? NBER Working Paper no. 5958. Cambridge, MA: National Bureau of Economic Research, March.

————. 1997b. US multinationals and competition from low-wage countries. NBER Working Paper no. 5959. Cambridge, MA: National Bureau of Economic Research, March.

Caves, R. 1971. International corporations: The industrial economics of foreign investment. *Economica* 38:1–27.

————. 1996. *Multinational enterprises and economic analysis.* Cambridge, MA: Cambridge University Press.

Chen, T. J., and Y.-H. Ku. 2000. Foreign direct investment and industrial restructuring: The case of Taiwan's textile industry. In *The role of foreign direct investment in East Asian economic development,* ed. I. Takatoshi and A. Krueger, 319–48. Chicago: University of Chicago Press.

Diewert, W. E. 1971. An application of the Shephard duality theorem: A generalized Leontief production function. *Journal of Political Economy* 79 (3): 481–507.

Döhrn, R. 1997. *Bestimmungsgründe von umfang und entwicklung der Auslandsaktivitäten deutscher unternehmen* [Determinants of the scope and development of overseas activities of German enterprises]. *Lecture notes.* Essen; RWI Institute.

Feenstra, R. 1996. Foreign investment, outsourcing and relative wages. In *Political economy of trade policy: Essays in honor of Jagdish Bhagwati,* ed. R. Feenstra and G. Douglas, 89–127. Cambridge, MA: MIT Press.

Feldstein, M. 1994. The effects of outbound foreign direct investment on the domestic capital stock. NBER Working Paper no. 4668. Cambridge, MA: National Bureau of Economic Research, March.

Hall, R. 1973. The specification of technology with several kinds of output. *Journal of Political Economy* 81 (4): 878–92.

Hatzius, J. 1997. Domestic jobs and foreign wages: Labour demand in Swedish multinationals. CEP Discussion Paper no. 337. London: Centre for Economic Performance.

Ku, Y.-H. 1998. Foreign direct investment and domestic restructuring: The case of Taiwan's electronic industry. *Taiwan Economic Review* 26 (4): 459–86.

Lipsey, R. 1994. Outward direct investment and the US economy. NBER Working Paper no. 4691. Cambridge, MA: National Bureau of Economic Research, March.

Liu, B.-J., and H.-L. Lin. 2001. Reverse imports and outward investment. *Taiwan Economic Review* 29 (4): 479–510.

Markusen, J. 1983. Factor movements and commodity trade as complements. *Journal of International Economics* 14 (3–4): 341–56.

Mundell, R. 1957. International trade and factor mobility. *American Economic Review* 47:321–35.

Slaughter, M. 1995. Multinational corporations, outsourcing and American wage diversion. NBER Working Paper no. 5253. Cambridge, MA: National Bureau of Economic Research, September.

Stevens, V., and R. Lipsey. 1992. Interactions between domestic and foreign investment. *Journal of International Money and Finance* 11 (1): 40–62.

Comment   Keiko Ito

This paper is very well written and organized and presents very interesting findings. It conducts rigorous quantitative analyses based on a couple of large sets of microdata and investigates the relationship between outward foreign direct investment (FDI) and domestic employment at the firm level. The authors argue that overseas production substitutes for the domestic production of primary inputs, which reduces the demand for labor in domestic operations; on the other hand, overseas production also lowers the costs of cross-border operations, which enhances companies' overall competitiveness and, in turn, helps them to expand domestic output. On the whole, therefore, FDI has a net positive effect on domestic employment. Because there are very few studies on this issue, particularly at such a microlevel, for middle-developed countries like Taiwan, this is a highly commendable paper.

The study makes an important contribution in the following respects. First, it deals with a very interesting and important topic. The effect of outward FDI on domestic labor demand is an issue of major concern in many developed countries, where people are worried about job losses as many production processes are shifted to low-wage countries. Although a large number of studies have been conducted for the United States and European countries, very few have looked at Asian countries to examine this topic. The second contribution of this paper is that it analyzes firm-level data. The authors use three sets of microdata—from the Manufacturing Census, the employment survey by Taiwan's Bureau of Labor Affairs, and the Survey on Overseas Investment by Manufacturing Firms by the Ministry of Economic Affairs—and combine the latter two data sets for their analysis. Third, the authors compile and analyze simple statistics and also conduct an econometric analysis of the data based on the generalized Leontief cost function framework. Both the simple analysis of the statistics in itself and their econometric investigation, which makes it possible to estimate the various effects of FDI on domestic labor demand quantitatively, provide valuable insights. Although we should note that their econometric analysis may include substantial errors and biases, it is certainly the last point that is the most important contribution of this paper. I will discuss the details of the econometric method later.

First, however, I would like to turn to specific comments. Table 4.1 shows that almost half of Taiwan's total outward FDI goes to China, based on which the authors focus on China as the main destination for FDI in the analysis that follows. In the following analyses, they divide sample firms according to the location of their FDI into four categories: China only, China

Keiko Ito is a lecturer of economics at Senshu University.

and others, other than China, and unknown. We should note, however, that, according to table 4.1, the United States is another large recipient of Taiwanese FDI, also accounting for almost a half of Taiwan's total FDI. Taiwan's FDI in the United States is conducted probably for the purpose of establishing a sales base, while FDI in China is for production. This difference may have a crucial influence on the estimated effects of FDI on the domestic demand for labor. In addition, the fact that the United States is such a large recipient of Taiwanese FDI implies that many firms in the "China and others" category would have undertaken investment in China and the United States. These firms are likely to produce in China and sell their products in the United States. The results throughout the paper might suggest that firms with both production and sales bases overseas (i.e., FDI covering both China and other regions) are most likely to experience an expansion of domestic output and employment.

Next, table 4.2 suggests that firms engaging in FDI have a higher survival rate than those that do not. We should point out that non-FDI firms are much smaller than FDI firms. Because larger firms are more likely to survive, the higher survival rate of FDI firms might be attributable to the difference in size of non-FDI firms and FDI-firms. In addition, I am not sure how the authors treat firms that were not undertaking FDI as of 1993 but were doing so as of 2000. These firms should have been in the "non-FDI firms" cohort in 1993 and entered the "FDI firms" cohort in 2000. In that case, are they treated as exited non-FDI firms and as new entrants among FDI firms? If the authors treat these firms like this, the exit rate for non-FDI firms may be exaggerated. It should be made clear whether non-FDI firms may only seem to have exited business, while in fact they only moved from one category to another.

Finally I would like to comment on the econometric analysis employed in this study. This study estimates labor demand functions derived from the generalized Leontief cost function, while most related previous studies employ the translog cost function approach. Probably because capital stock data at the firm level are not available, the authors assume that the elasticity of substitution between capital and composite labor is zero and therefore estimate the generalized Leontief function without capital input. However, I think that the strong assumption on the substitution between capital and labor may induce serious errors and derive biased estimates of cost parameters between subgroups in the labor force. According to Hamermesh's (1986) literature survey, previous empirical investigations conclude that the separability of labor from capital is not supported by the data and suggest that it is necessary to include the quantity or price of capital services. We should also note that the estimation may include further errors or biases due to the exclusion of factor inputs for overseas production. Given the unavailability of capital stock (or capital price) data and overseas factor inputs (or factor price) data at the firm level, there might be no choice but to exclude these inputs. However, we have to be careful in interpreting the estimated effects of domestic and overseas production on employment. The most consistent finding in previous studies on labor demand is that physical capital substitutes more easily for production workers (unskilled labor) than for nonproduction workers (skilled labor; Hamermesh 1986). Moreover, most previous studies found that the demand elasticity for nonproduction workers is lower than that for production workers (Hamermesh 1986). Given the decreasing trend in the price of capital in Taiwan, we may infer that the demand for blue-collar workers will decrease much more than the demand for managerial or technical workers when the capital input data are included in the analysis. Furthermore, if the wage level of blue-collar workers in Taiwan rose above that in China, the domestic demand for blue-collar workers among firms investing in China would be further reduced. It is certainly very difficult to include the price of overseas factor inputs due to data constraints. However, even when capital stock data are not available, it might still be possible to calculate or estimate the price of capital at the firm level, for example, by obtaining data on interest payments, the amount of debt, and so on, if these are available. Alternatively, the authors could estimate the price of capital at the industry level and use this for their cost function analysis, assuming that the price of capital is the same for all firms within an industry.

However, these are minor criticisms and suggestions for further expansion of a study that, overall, is solid and shows very interesting results. The authors were able to show that overseas production in most cases had a net positive effect on domestic labor demand and that technical workers were the biggest winners from FDI, while blue-collar workers gained the least. This implies that domestic production in Taiwan is tending to shift toward technology- and management-intensive operations. The observation that the shift in skilled-labor occurs in a middle-developed country like Taiwan will attract a lot of attention. However, we should be aware of possible errors or biases as a result of the exclusion of capital and overseas factor inputs, and I hope that the authors will get a chance to include these factor inputs in future studies.

Reference

Hamermesh, Daniel S. 1986. The demand for labor in the long run. In *Handbook of labor economics.* Vol. 1, ed. O. Ashenfelter and R. Layard, 429–71. Amsterdam: Elsevier Science.

Comment   Francis T. Lui

The paper by Tain-Jy Chen and Ying-Hua Ku raises an interesting empirical question that does not have an unambiguous theoretical answer. Does foreign direct investment (FDI) made by the home country cause job losses at home? Theoretically, there are two opposite forces at work. Overseas production substitutes exports. Reduction in exports lowers employment at home. On the other hand, a firm that makes overseas investment tends to be better able to use resources efficiently. This helps the firm to survive the competition at home and enables it to continue to hire workers. If the efficiency gain is big enough, the firm may even expand itself and increase employment.

The question of which force is stronger has important policy implications. Labor unions may believe that FDI hurts workers at home, and therefore they lobby against it. This question is also more general than it appears to be. Analytically it is similar to another policy question. Countries that contemplate importing labor from outside may face the same opposition. A firm using its money to hire imported workers in the home country is in a similar situation compared to another that sends money to other countries in the form of FDI. Importing labor also has two opposite effects. First, some local workers are displaced. Second, importing cheaper or more-efficient workers makes the firm more competitive at home. The chance for its migration to other countries decreases. Thus, there is also a job creation effect. The answer to whether labor should be imported is again an empirical issue.

The paper has set an example for policy research that is based on solid empirical findings and rigorous methodology. It assumes that the production function is generalized Leontief. By making use of the Shephard's lemma and estimating the cost function, the paper shows that a firm's employment of different types of workers is a function of their respective wage rates, its output at home and at the foreign country. It is found that an increase in the firm's output at the foreign country reduces employment of all types of workers at home, provided that output at home is held constant. It is also shown that overseas investment raises output at home, which in turn increases employment. According to the paper's estimates, the net effect of overseas investment on home employment is positive. The methodology is nicely developed, and the results are reasonable.

If overseas investment actually raises home employment, why do labor unions object to it? A plausible answer is that competition from abroad

Francis T. Lui is a professor of economics and director of the Center for Economic Development at the Hong Kong University of Science and Technology.

could lower the wage rates of workers at home. It would be useful if the authors could estimate the effect on wage rates.

The paper documents that there has been substantial restructuring of the Taiwanese economy during the sample period. From 1991 to 2000, the electronics industry has employed 145,748 more people, but the apparel industry has lost 54,104 jobs. Moreover, manufacturing has 400,000 fewer jobs, but the service sector has gained 1.4 million jobs in the period from 1987 to 1994. When economic restructuring takes place, the unemployment rate usually rises because people leaving an industry need time to generate offers from other industries. One would suspect that economic restructuring should be one of the factors that affect unemployment during the sample period. In a study on the effect of imported workers on employment in Hong Kong, we have found that it is essential to include restructuring as a control variable (Kwan, Lian, and Lui 1995). The latter can conveniently be measured by an index proposed by Lilien (1982), which tells us how extensive are the movements of workers from one sector to another. Our results indicate that economic restructuring significantly changes the unemployment rate, but the number of imported workers has little or no effect at all. To reduce the possibility of specification bias due to the omission of an important variable, the authors may want to address this issue in their future research.

Because globalization and fragmentation will likely continue, overseas investment will grow. The findings of this paper will become more and more relevant and important in the future.

References

Kwan, Yum-Keung, Y. Joseph Lian, and Francis T. Lui. 1995. Hong Kong's unemployment and imported labour. Hong Kong University of Science & Technology. Mimeograph.
Lilien, David M. 1982. Sectoral shifts and cyclical unemployment. *Journal of Political Economy* 90 (4): 777–93.

5

The Trade and Investment Effects of Preferential Trading Arrangements

Philippa Dee and Jyothi Gali

The number of preferential trading arrangements (PTAs) has grown dramatically over the last decade or so. By the end of March 2002, there were 250 agreements in force that had been notified to the World Trade Organization (WTO), compared with 40 in 1990 (WTO 2002).

The coverage of preferential trading arrangements has also tended to expand over time. The preferential liberalization of tariffs and other measures governing merchandise trade remains important in many agreements. But they increasingly cover a range of other issues—services, investment, competition policy, government procurement, e-commerce, labor, and environmental standards.

This paper examines, both theoretically and empirically, the effects of the trade and nontrade provisions of PTAs on the trade and foreign direct investment (FDI) flows of member and nonmember countries.

5.1 Theoretical Review

The first wave of PTAs in the 1950s to 1970s were generally limited in scope, with preferential liberalization of merchandise trade playing a central role (the European Union [EU] was an important early exception). In part, this was because general tariff levels were higher to start with.

The static analysis of first-wave PTAs challenged the presumption that

Philippa Dee is visiting fellow at the Asia-Pacific School of Economics and Government at Australian National University and formerly an assistant commissioner at the Australian Productivity Commission. Jyothi Gali is a senior research economist at the Australian Productivity Commission.

The views are those of the authors and do not necessarily reflect those of any institution with which they have been affiliated.

these were a step in the right direction.[1] It concluded that although PTAs eased one economic distortion, namely, the average tariff on imports in general, they exacerbated another, namely, the geographical disparity in import tariffs. This was a classic situation of second best, with no clear presumption in favor of gains to either PTA members or the world as a whole. The answer "depends," and the devil is in the detail. The analysis is summarized in the appendix, using a diagrammatic exposition similar to that first developed by Johnson (1960).

The literature also recognized that if the answer depends, then the question is an empirical one. Various analysts examined the trade effects of various PTAs, trying to determine whether they have encouraged imports in general—trade creation—more than they have pushed the geographic source of imports in the wrong direction—trade diversion. There is a degree of apparent consensus (summarized later) about which PTAs have been beneficial and which have been harmful to members. There have also been recent generalizations that PTAs are relatively benign.

Interest in PTAs revived early in the 1980s as the United States reacted first to EU expansionism and the loss of EU markets and then to the uncertain prospects for launching the Uruguay Round, by selecting partners for bilateral and regional trade arrangements. The second-wave agreements were predominantly *free trade agreements,* where members retained their own external tariffs, as opposed to *customs unions,* which adopt a common external tariff. Hence rules of origin became important to prevent trade deflection, whereby imports would enter through the country with the lowest external tariff. The second wave of PTAs also saw the inclusion of nontariff barriers and other nontraditional areas, such as dispute resolution and competition policy. However, the sectoral focus remained on goods markets.

With the second wave, the focus of theoretical work shifted to the dynamic question of whether PTAs were "building blocks" or "stumbling blocks" to multilateral free trade. Bhagwati, Krishna, and Panagariya (1999) identified two distinct approaches. First, suppose a PTA expands its membership. Will that reduce or increase welfare? If expansion increases welfare, then PTAs are seen as building blocks. Second, will a PTA expand its membership? And if so, is there an incentive for expansion to eventually cover the entire world, with nondiscriminatory free trade for all, or will it stop short? This approach uses political economy considerations.

Some partial answers to these questions were provided by Krugman (1993), Deardorff and Stern (1994), Baldwin, (1996), Levy (1997), and

1. The seminal work is Viner (1950). Other early contributions came from Gehrels (1957), Lipsey (1957, 1958), Johnson (1960), Mundell (1964), Corden (1972), and Riezman (1979). Comprehensive surveys of the literature are available in Baldwin and Venables (1995), Pomfret (1997), Bhagwati, Krishna, and Panagariya (1999), and Panagariya (2000), among others. Two recent policy-oriented reviews are by the WTO (1995) and the World Bank (2000).

Krishna (1998). The most recent, comprehensive analyses by Zissimos and Vines (2000) and Andriamananjara (2002) acknowledge that joining a PTA is the best safe-haven strategy when other countries are doing so. But they find that because PTA membership confers a terms of trade gain to members at the expense of nonmembers, at least some members will be better off limiting PTA membership than allowing expansion to cover the world as a whole.[2] Any redesign of the WTO rules disciplining the formation of PTAs would need to recognize that reality.

During the 1990s the number of PTAs expanded dramatically. In addition to new preferential initiatives by the EU and the United States, the third wave now includes players such as Japan. Until 2002 Japan was one of only four WTO members not to participate in any PTA (although it was a member of nondiscriminatory Asia-Pacific Economic Cooperation [APEC]). Its first agreement, the Japan-Singapore Economic Agreement for a New Age Partnership, typifies many new age agreements. The provisions governing merchandise trade are very limited. Both countries already have zero or very low tariffs on imports of nonagricultural products, and trade in agricultural products between them is minimal, but because of the sensitivity of the trade in cut flowers and goldfish, agricultural and fishery products (along with some petrochemical and petroleum goods) have been excluded from the bilateral agreement altogether. Instead, the agreement focuses on new age issues—especially e-commerce and services. Other such agreements include FDI, competition policy, government procurement, labor, and environmental standards.

Despite the evolution of third-wave or new age agreements, there has been little literature dealing with the effects of preferential nontariff provisions. Two exceptions are Pomfret (1997, chapter 10) and Ethier (1998a,b, 1999, 2001), who deal primarily with effects on investment.

Pomfret (1997) does not discuss in detail the economic welfare effects of discriminatory provisions governing foreign direct investment, but his discussion of the welfare effects of preferential nontariff barriers to trade is suggestive. Pomfret (1997) notes that the critical distinction is whether nontariff barriers are rent generating—allowing a markup of price over cost—or whether they are cost escalating—increasing the real resource costs of doing business.

The analogy with preferential liberalization of *investment provisions* is as follows:

- If investment barriers are of the sort to generate rents, then preferential liberalization will generate gains from investment creation as production is moved from a high-cost domestically-owned producer to a

---

2. These are further developments of the arguments about the negative externalities from terms of trade changes developed by Bond and Syropoulos (1996) and Bagwell and Staiger (1998, 1999), among others.

lower-cost member's affiliate. But it will also generate losses from investment diversion as production is moved from a low-cost nonmember affiliate (located somewhere in the world) to a higher-cost member affiliate.

- If investment barriers are of the sort to escalate costs, then preferential liberalization will unambiguously save real resources and increase welfare, irrespective of whether the partner is the least-cost location (see also Baldwin 1994).

Thus the welfare implications of preferentially liberalizing investment provisions are more positive than they were for preferential tariff liberalization because of the possibility of saving real resources. But the potential for losses from investment diversion also remains.

In a series of papers, Ethier (1998a,b, 1999, 2001) develops variants of a model in which investment responds in "beachhead" fashion to the preferential *trade provisions* of PTAs.

This model is an explicit attempt to capture some of the salient features of third-wave PTAs. Many third-wave agreements are between small and larger countries. The small countries want to reform their internal economies so that they can be accepted as members of the global trading system. The sign of successful reform is whether these countries attract FDI. The small countries use (often asymmetrical) trade concessions to large countries as a way of signaling a credible commitment to reform.

There is no presumption in Ethier's (1998b) framework that the investment they attract comes from the large PTA partner. The aim of these small reforming countries is often to divert investment from nonmember countries. Ethier (2001) also examines in detail the incentives for the larger country to accede to such an arrangement, even in preference to pursuing further multilateral reform. Finally, he shows that a world equilibrium in which small countries compete for investment in this fashion is beneficial because it internalizes an externality associated with agglomeration economies.

Ethier's (1998a,b, 1999, 2001) positive outlook on PTA formation comes from this benign view of competition for investment, rather than from the characteristics of PTAs per se. As he acknowledges, his model of PTA formation is consistent with massive amounts of investment diversion to take advantage of trade beachheads and subsequent trade diversion from those beachhead positions. But in his model, there is sufficient symmetry between countries for this trade and investment diversion to have no adverse welfare consequences—every country is the lowest-cost source of imports and the best host for FDI. With more diversity, this massive diversion is no longer benign.

Ethier's (1998a,b, 1999, 2001) positive view also depends on the competition for investment occurring through reform, which is seen as a good thing. If it were to occur through the competitive granting of investment incentives, or if reform involved inappropriate concessions forced by a larger hegemon (as Bhagwati [1999] fears), the competition for investment may itself be less benign.

At first sight, the focus of third-wave agreements on nontariff issues may suggest that traditional concerns about trade diversion are outmoded. But the theoretical literature suggests otherwise. Investment barriers can be used as a protective device, and preferential liberalization of investment provisions can generate investment diversion, with adverse consequences, as well as beneficial investment creation. Even where investment is attracted in beachhead fashion in response to trade liberalization provisions, both the investment and subsequent trade from the beachhead position may be diversionary. Thus the nontariff focus of third-wave agreements cannot shake the first-wave concerns about the adverse second-best effects of preferential liberalization.

The second section of this paper summarizes the trade and nontrade provisions included in a number of recent PTAs. The third section empirically estimates the effects of recent trade and nontrade provisions on bilateral trade and investment flows. The fourth section recapitulates the key findings.

5.2   Breadth of Coverage of PTAs

Figure 5.1 shows the discernible upward trend in the breadth of coverage of PTAs over recent times. On the vertical axis is an index measure of

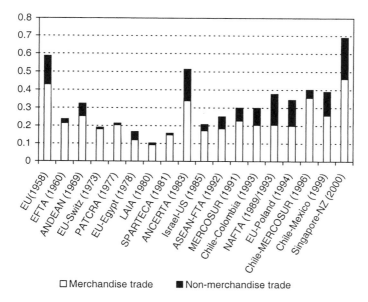

Fig. 5.1   Member Liberalization Index (MLI) for selected PTAs, index score ranges between zero and one
Source: Adams et al. (2003).

breadth of coverage, with provisions governing merchandise and nonmer-chandise trade scored separately. The Member Liberalization Index (MLI) is described in detail in Adams et al. (2003). On the horizontal axis is the date of establishment. Coverage has clearly tended to increase in the more recently established or expanded PTAs, and this has generally been be-cause of an expansion in the coverage of nonmerchandise trade issues.

The index includes provisions covering the following:

- Agricultural products—including domestic support measures, tariff quotas, sanitary and phytosanitary measures, tax exceptions, export incentives, and technical barriers to trade, among others
- Industrial products—including coverage and restrictiveness of rules of origin, safeguards, antidumping, coverage and timing of tariff pref-erences, among others
- Services—including provisions governing market access and national treatment in services
- General measures—general national treatment provisions, invest-ment rules, domestic competition policy, government procurement, intellectual property rights, and general provisions covering the tem-porary and permanent movement of people

These provisions are classified into two subindexes for quantitative anal-ysis. The merchandise MLI includes the provisions covering agriculture and industrial products—an index of traditional provisions. The nonmer-chandise MLI, covering third-wave issues, includes the services provisions, plus the general measures covering all trade.

The coverage varies from one PTA to another. Some involve only a few products or sectors, while others stretch well beyond the traditional tariff elimination. Note that the scores are based on how the language of the agreements is written, not on whether or how the provisions are used. A high index for nonmerchandise trade indicates that a PTA is more liberal to members in its services trade, investment, and related provisions. This index takes a high value for Singapore-New Zealand (NZ), followed by Closer Economic Relations (CER) (between Australia and New Zealand), the North American Free Trade Agreement (NAFTA) and the EU.

The provisions indexed in the MLI are treated as additive to and in-dependent of each other. In reality some provisions might interact to strengthen or weaken other provisions. For example, the time schedule for preferential tariff liberalization is closely related to the restrictiveness of rules of origin. The impact of interaction effects among the provisions in various PTAs is potentially an empirical question, but interaction effects have not been allowed for specifically in the construction of this index nor in the subsequent econometric analysis. For this reason, the econometrics may understate (where interaction effects reinforce) or overstate (where in-teraction effects cancel) the overall effects of PTAs.

The estimated relationship between these provisions and the level of trade (or investment) provides an indication of whether provisions included in PTAs have any effect collectively on trade (or investment) flows with member or nonmember countries. Because PTAs are by definition exclusive and discriminatory against nonmembers, trade and nontrade provisions that are favorable to the intra-PTA trade (or investment) may become barriers to nonmember countries.

5.3   Empirical Analyses

The key empirical task is to disentangle the effects of PTA formation or expansion from all other influences on trade and investment flows. There are two main approaches available in the literature.

First, ex ante studies have used counterfactual analyses based on partial or general equilibrium models. These models assume a certain model structure, with specific functional forms and parameter values to represent the countries in a base year prior to the formation of the PTA. Those models with a sufficiently tight theoretical structure can also be used to draw direct inferences about welfare. The model is then subjected to the preferential removal of tariffs alone, and the welfare effects are calculated. Surveys of assessments of PTAs using general equilibrium models can be found in De Rosa (1998) and Robinson and Thierfelder (2002). Scollay and Gilbert (2000) survey computable general equilibrium (CGE) assessments of APEC. Most of these studies find that PTAs create additional trade for both members and nonmembers. Most also find that PTAs improve welfare, at least among member countries.

However, these CGE analyses suffer from a number of theoretical and practical difficulties. Some (in particular, many of those covered by the Robinson and Thierfelder [2002] survey) assume fixed terms of trade. As noted by Panagariya and Duttagupta (2002), this is inconsistent with one of their other key assumptions, namely, product differentiation at the national level. Deardorff and Stern (1994) note how the assumption of national product differentiation can itself leave an "idiosyncratic stamp" on examinations of PTAs, in particular helping to explain Krugman's (1993) finding of welfare losses in a world of three trading blocs, a result that does not appear to carry over to empirical CGE analyses. But in addition, the assumption of fixed terms of trade rules out one of the key effects of PTAs, namely, terms of trade changes.

Further, the CGE studies typically use a very simple characterization of PTAs. Most assume comprehensive across-the-board elimination of tariffs (and sometimes nontariff barriers) among members, although most real-world PTAs have complex patterns of exemptions. In addition, the studies typically ignore many of the potentially trade-restrictive nontariff measures, such as rules of origin or local content requirements, that typically accompany the merchandise trade measures. Finally, they typically ignore provisions affecting nonmerchandise trade (although a notable exception is Hertel, Walmsley, and Itakura 2001).

This is not to deny that particular CGE models, when used with appropriate assumptions (such as variable terms of trade), can give valuable insights into the possible effects of important tariff provisions of PTAs. But conclusions drawn from *surveys* of CGE studies should be treated cautiously. And the results from CGE studies should not be generalized to draw conclusions about the effects of nonmerchandise trade provisions of PTAs.

By contrast, ex post studies of PTAs measure their trade creation and trade diversion effects by using econometric methods to establish a link between actual PTA formation and actual trade outcomes, controlling for the effects of all other influences. Because welfare is unobservable, these econometric studies cannot establish welfare effects directly. And as noted in the appendix, the link between trade outcomes and welfare is weak. But the studies do examine *actual* PTAs, in all their complexity, including nonmerchandise trade provisions. The present study is an ex post evaluation of the effects of PTAs.

5.3.1   Gravity Model

The gravity model is the key ex post econometric technique used to examine the determinants of bilateral trade flows. It is a model of trade flows based on an analogy with the law of gravity in physics. Trade between two countries is positively related to their size and inversely related to the distance between them. A number of other explanatory variables are added to this model to analyze various bilateral trade policy issues. In the augmented gravity model, trade between two countries is determined by supply conditions at the origin, demand conditions at the destination, and various stimulating or restraining forces. This specification has recently been shown to be consistent with a number of theoretical models of international trade.[3]

The standard way of assessing the impact of PTAs is to add PTA-specific binary dummy variables to the augmented gravity model to capture effects not captured through normal bilateral trade determinants. Studies adding PTA-specific dummy variables to capture the trade creation and diversion effects of PTAs date back to the 1970s. Aitken (1973) initially added one

3. The gravity model can be derived theoretically as a reduced form from a general equilibrium model of international trade in goods. Baier and Bergstrand (2001) derived it from a model of monopolistic competition. Feenstra, Markusen, and Rose (2001) derived it from a reciprocal dumping model of trade with homogeneous goods. Deardorff (1998) derived it from a model with perfectly competitive markets. Evenett and Keller (2002) showed empirically that the monopolistic-competition-based theory of trade fits the trade flows among industrialized countries well. Anderson and van Wincoop (2003) nevertheless showed that many empirical implementations have strayed from the theoretically derived reduced form.

dummy variable to his gravity model to capture the intrabloc effect of a PTA—"a gross trade effect" of Balassa (1967). Bayoumi and Eichengreen (1995) and Frankel (1997) added two dummy variables for each PTA to capture the separate effects on intrabloc and extrabloc trade. The first dummy variable takes a value of one when the two countries are members of the same PTA. The second dummy variable is one if either country in a particular pair belongs to the PTA. If a positive coefficient on the first dummy exceeds a negative coefficient on the second, then trade creation may be said to outweigh trade diversion.

Soloaga and Winters (2001) added three dummy variables for each PTA to distinguish an intrabloc effect, an extrabloc effect on imports, and an extrabloc effect on exports (see figure 5.2). The second and third dummy variables in their study measure the extent of import diversion and export diversion, respectively. They argued that both are needed because bloc members' imports and exports could follow different patterns after the formation of a PTA.

The current analysis also uses three dummy variables for each PTA. But instead of taking simple zero-one values, irrespective of the scope or coverage of the PTA provisions, the dummies take the value of the MLI index (or subindex) whenever the PTA is in force.

Because the gravity model is estimated using panel data, the PTA-specific dummy variables are introduced in one of two ways. Firstly, *dynamic* PTA-specific indexes are defined to take a nonzero value only for the years in which a PTA between the two countries is in force and to take a value of zero otherwise. These indexes capture the effect of the formation,

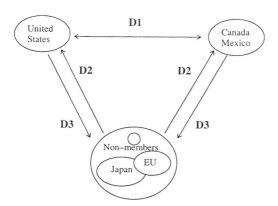

Fig. 5.2   Use of PTA-specific dummy variables in a gravity model—the example of NAFTA

Notes: D1 captures the effects of NAFTA on intrabloc trade. D2 captures the effects of NAFTA on members' imports from nonmembers—import diversion if the coefficient is negative. D3 captures the effects of NAFTA on members' exports to nonmembers—export diversion if the coefficient is negative.

expansion, and contraction of a PTA on trade and investment only after it occurs. In contrast, *antimonde* PTA-specific indexes take a nonzero value for all the years in the sample, irrespective of when the PTA was formed. These antimonde indexes are used as the panel analogue to the nondynamic indexes of previous cross-sectional gravity model studies. They have the same disadvantage as these studies of allowing the formation, expansion, and contraction of a PTA to affect trade and investment before the event.

5.3.2   Model Specification

Effects on Trade

The panel data includes information on all potential trading partners, even when a country has no exports to some partners in some years. Because the nature of trade relations in many countries in the World Trade Flows (1997, 2000) database is such that each country trades with a relatively small number of partners, the dependent variable contains a significant number of zero observations as well as many positive observations.[4] As a result, a Tobit estimation procedure is used to appropriately account for the censored nature of the dependent variable—the natural log of exports between country i and country j in year t.[5] Adams et al. (2003) describe the data sources in detail. The panel has a relatively long time dimension, covering 1970–1997 for the estimation of trade effects (1988–1997 for the estimation of investment effects). While this risks the problem of subsample instability, it has the advantage that it helps to overcome the problem of nuisance parameters in the estimation of fixed effects in a Tobit context (Greene 2002).

The gravity model estimated here allows for *product differentiation* at the country level. Much of the recent literature on PTAs has focused on imperfectly competitive behavior. Recognizing this is important for two reasons:

- Some economic integration has occurred among economies with almost similar structures and large volumes of intraindustry trade.
- There is a positive interaction between market structure and the gains from integration, often called the procompetitive effects of PTAs, which the new age agreements aim to capture.

4. For the full sample trade model, the number of observations is 116 countries × 115 partners × 28 years = 373,520, with about 44 percent having zero values.
5. There are a variety of alternate approaches to this problem. The zero values can be simply omitted as in the case of Frankel (1997), which leads to the possibility of selectivity bias. Arbitrarily small numbers can be used in place of zeros. Eichengreen and Irwin (1995) expressed the dependent variable as $Ln (1 + Y_{ij})$. Clark and Tavares (2000) and Soloaga and Winters (2001) used a Tobit specification for their cross-sectional gravity model.

The product differentiation model of Helpman and Krugman (1985) and Helpman (1987) is integrated into the current gravity model specification. In their models, one of the two goods is differentiated and the other is homogenous. The bilateral trade of each country is the sum of interindustry and intraindustry trade flows, with the latter being trade in the differentiated product.

The corresponding reduced form of gravity model for trade is

$$
\text{(1)} \quad \text{Ln } Y^*_{ijt} = a + \alpha_i + \gamma_j + \lambda_t + \beta_1 \text{Ln SGDP}_{ijt} + \beta_2 \text{Ln RLFA}_{ijt}
$$

$$
+ \beta_3 \text{Ln Similar}_{ijt} + \beta_4 \text{Ln Dis}_{ij} + \beta_5 \text{Ln RER}_{ijt} + \beta_6 \text{Ln TAR}_{ijt}
$$

$$
+ \beta_7 \text{Lin}_{ij} + \beta_8 \text{Bor}_{ij} + \beta_9 \text{Col}_{ij} + \beta_{10} \text{Cur}_{ij} + \beta_{11} \text{Is}_i + \beta_{12} \text{Is}_j
$$

$$
+ \beta_{13} \text{lock}_i + \beta_{14} \text{lock}_j + \beta_{15} 3\text{wave}_{ij} + \sum_{ij} \text{MRTA}_{ij}
$$

$$
+ \sum_{-j} \text{MRTA}_{i-j} + \sum_{-i} \text{MRTA}_{j-i} + \text{Ln } \varepsilon_{ijt}
$$

where

Ln	is natural logarithmic transformation;
Y^*_{ijt}	is the value of exports from country i to j in year t; using exports as a dependent variable rather than total bilateral trade allows the identification of export and import diversion separately;
α_i	is unobserved specific effects in exporting country i;
γ_j	is unobserved specific effects in importing country j;
λ_t	is unobserved specific effects in time period t;
SGDP_{ijt}	is the sum of bilateral gross domestic products (GDPs) of i and j in year t;
RLFA_{ijt}	is the absolute differences in GDP per capita of i and j in year t;
Similar_{ijt}	is similarity in country size between i and j in year t in terms of aggregate GDP;
Dis_{ij}	is distance between the two largest or capital cities of countries i and j;
RER_{ijt}	is the bilateral real exchange rate between i and j in year t;
Tar_{ijt}	is an average tariff rate in importing country j on goods from country i in year t;
Lin_{ij}	is a measure of linguistic similarity between i and j;
Bor_{ij}	is a dummy that takes a value 1 if i and j share a land border and 0 otherwise;
Col_{ij}	is a dummy that takes a value 1 if i and j have colonial linkages and 0 otherwise;
Cur_{ij}	is a dummy that takes a value 1 if i and j have the same currency and 0 otherwise;
Is_i	is a dummy that takes a value 1 when i is island nations and 0 otherwise;

Lock$_i$ is a dummy that takes a value 1 when i is a landlocked nation and 0 otherwise;

3wave$_{ij}$ is an index capturing the third wave provisions of a PTA, that takes a value of the nonmerchandise MLI index if the i and j are participants of a specific PTA in the sample and 0 otherwise; it also has a time dimension when defined in dynamic rather than antimonde form;

MRTA$_{ij}$ is an index capturing the merchandise trade provisions of a PTA, that takes the value of the merchandise MLI if both countries i and j belong to the same PTA and 0 otherwise; it also has a time dimension when defined in dynamic rather than antimonde form;

MRTA$_{i-j}$ is an index that takes the value of the merchandise MLI when the importing country j belongs to that particular PTA and 0 otherwise; it also has a time dimension when defined in dynamic rather than antimonde form;

MRTA$_{j-i}$ is an index that takes the value of the merchandise MLI when the exporting country i belongs to that particular PTA and 0 otherwise; it also has time dimension when defined in dynamic rather than antimonde form; and

ε_{ijt} is an error term.

From an econometric point of view, the α_i, γ_j and λ_t specific effects are treated as fixed unknown parameters. The use of three separate fixed effects is advocated by Matyas (1997, 1998) and avoids the omitted variable bias identified by Haveman and Hummels (1998) and Anderson and van Wincoop (2003).

The expected relationship of the observed explanatory variables with bilateral exports is discussed in detail in Adams et al. (2003). In a model of product differentiation, countries similar in size will trade more, and the trade will be of an intraindustry nature. The index of size similarity (Similar) captures this effect. By contrast, traditional trade theory says that countries with dissimilar levels of per capita GDP will trade more than the countries with similar levels. The absolute difference in the per capita GDP between exporting and importing countries (RLFA) is included as an explanatory variable in the gravity model as a way of distinguishing the traditional from the differentiated product approaches.[6]

The preceding gravity model specification includes the real exchange rate (RER) as a relevant price variable in order to control for fluctuations in relative prices among trading partners.

The average bilateral tariff rate (Tar) is expected to show a negative rela-

6. The specification based on product differentiation in the preceding also differs from traditional gravity model specifications by including the sum of importing and exporting country GDPs, rather than including each separately. This small loss of generality means that the product differentiation version does not encompass the traditional model fully.

tionship with trade. The PTA-specific indexes capture the extent of traditional and new age provisions of a PTA but not the size of the tariff preferences thereby created. Because the bilateral tariff variable includes preferential tariffs,[7] the overall measured effect of PTAs on trade will be split between the tariff variable and the PTA-specific indexes in specifications where both occur. To test whether the coefficients of the PTA-specific indexes are sensitive to the inclusion of the tariff variable, the gravity model is estimated initially without the tariff variable. It is then reestimated with the tariff variable for that subset of countries and time periods for which bilateral tariff data are available.

Effects on Investment

The product differentiation specification also provides a rationale for applying the gravity model to investment flows (Egger 2001).

The raw FDI data for this analysis are sourced from the United Nations Conference on Trade and Development (UNCTAD) and the Organization for Economic Cooperation and Development (OECD) for the period between 1988 and 1997 for about seventy-seven countries (see Adams et al. 2003). As there are some deficiencies in this data, the qualitative aspects of the analytical results rather than the precise magnitude of the investment estimates are of main interest.

The dependent variable in the gravity model is the natural logarithm of the stock of outward investment from home country to host country. The stock of outward investment is used as the dependent variable, rather than outflows, for two reasons. First, more outward stock than outflow data are available in the source documents. For many countries in the late 1980s and for some Latin American countries in early 1990s, the bilateral FDI flow data are not fully reported in the UNCTAD investment directories. Second, statistical tests suggested that a gravity model based on the stock of outward investment was preferred to a model based on outflows.

Apart from the more limited number of years and countries analyzed, the investment model is similar to the trade model. In particular, the key bilateral determinants are the same for trade and investment (see also Egger 2001), although the sign and magnitude of the impact of some of these explanatory variables differs.

For each PTA, three merchandise MLIs and three indexes of third-wave provisions are included in the investment gravity model to test how the investment to members, and to and from nonmembers, responds to the traditional and third-wave provisions embedded in each PTA. Three merchandise MLIs and only one (intrabloc) nonmerchandise MLI were included in the trade gravity model. Because of model convergence prob-

7. The bilateral tariff data are applied rates obtained from UNCTAD's Trade Analysis and Information System (TRAINS) database. As such they incorporate tariff preferences.

lems, the effects of new age provisions on exports to nonmembers and imports from nonmembers could not be analyzed separately in the trade model.

Two additional variables are added to the investment model because in addition to the investment provisions of PTAs, countries also negotiate bilateral investment treaties (BITs). About 191 PTAs were in force in 2000, with only a few covering investment provisions, while 1,941 BITs were in place then. The specification controls for whether an investment treaty is either signed or enacted between a pair of countries.

There are clearly some interdependencies between the trade equation and the investment equation, but in the absence of the remaining elements of the balance of payments, there is an insufficiently tight link to warrant seemingly unrelated regression or some other systems-estimation technique. Similarly, there are no obvious cross-equation restrictions that would improve the efficiency of estimation. One option would have been to include trade flows in the investment equation and investment flows in the trade equation, but this would have created a severe simultaneity problem. In the current PTA context, it was felt that including trade PTA dummies in the investment equation and vice versa was a minimalist approach to capturing the interdependencies.

The expected effects of traditional and new age provisions on investment are not straightforward.

If trade liberalization makes exporting from the home country relatively more attractive than FDI as a way to serve the regional market, then the trade provisions of a PTA could cause a reduction in intrabloc investment. But the trade provisions could also enable transnational corporations to operate vertically in a PTA area, stimulating intra-FDI flows among the relevant partners. The structure and motivation of investment will determine the net impact of trade provisions of PTAs on intra-PTA investment. So too will the structure and motivation of intrabloc trade (Markusen 1983).

According to Ethier (1998b, 2001), the inflows of FDI from nonmember countries into the PTA region are likely to go up in response to the trade provisions of PTAs, as nonmembers establish beachhead positions in one PTA member country in order to serve the market of the others. Alternatively, if multinationals are initially operating in member countries to serve the protected local market (the tariff jumping motivation for investment), then these multinationals may rationalize their network of affiliates after the formation of the PTA, and, as a result, some member countries could lose investment to nonmember countries.

Thus, the response of investment to the merchandise trade provisions of a PTA is an empirical question. The various possibilities can be tested in the following way.

If investment responds in beachhead fashion to the trade provisions of PTAs and in turn stimulates intrabloc trade, this can be identified by the combination of a positive and significant effect of trade provisions on intrabloc trade and a positive and significant effect of trade provisions on investment from nonmember countries.

Alternatively, a reversal of tariff-jumping investment can be identified by a positive and significant effect of trade provisions on investment to nonmember countries.

Investment may also respond to the nontrade provisions of PTAs. If, as a result, production is moved from a high-cost domestically owned producer to a lower-cost member's affiliate, this investment creation is likely to benefit members of the PTA. But if production is moved from a low-cost nonmember affiliate to a higher-cost member affiliate, this investment diversion may not benefit members.

Measures of net investment creation or diversion can be obtained by summing the significant coefficients of the three separate nonmerchandise MLI variables in parallel fashion to the trade equation. One further qualification to the welfare implications of investment is that if the initial nontrade restrictions are of the sort to raise costs rather than generate rents, then any investment relocation in response to their preferential removal will unambiguously benefit members.

5.3.3   New Evidence on Trade Creation and Diversion

The observable effects—normal bilateral trade determinants and trade provisions of PTAs—and unobservable country- and time-specific effects all significantly influence the bilateral trade flows. The signs and significance of the coefficients on the observable effects are generally as expected (see table 5.1). Interestingly, they support both traditional and product differentiation theories of trade because similarity in size and differences in income per head are both associated with higher bilateral exports. In the preferred specification with dynamic PTA variables and fixed effects, the coefficient on the sum of GDPs is about 2, as expected.

The new estimates of trade creation and diversion tend to be different from past estimates for most PTAs. Past estimates showed most PTAs to be trade creating in net terms. By contrast, the results here suggest most PTAs do not create additional trade, either for members or for nonmembers of the agreement. The net trade effects of preferential agreements found in this study are compared with past estimates in table 5.2, which shows whether the net effects are positive or negative.

Nearly all PTAs are found to have caused net trade diversion in the new assessment. The PTAs found to have inconclusive effects in past analysis drifted either way in the new assessment, but the Southern Common Market (MERCOSUR) was found here to have caused net trade diversion.[8]

---

8. The assessment of net trade effects is based on the marginal effects of PTAs reported in Adams et al. (2003), rather than the raw maximum likelihood Tobit estimates in table 5.1, for the preferred specification with dynamic PTA variables and fixed effects. Although the marginal effects and raw Tobit estimates are not equal (as explained in Adams et al. 2003), in practice the assessment of the direction of net trade effects is the same, whichever is used.

Table 5.1   Gravity model of trade: Econometric results from full sample

	Dynamic PTA indexes		Antimonde PTA indexes	
Variable name	Without fixed	With fixed[a]	Without fixed	With fixed[a,b]
Ln sum of exporting and importing countries GDP (SUM)	2.841***	2.008***	2.185***	2.066***
Similarity in exporting and importing country's GDPs	1.245***	0.637***	0.965***	0.665***
Ln of absolute differences in per capita GDPs of exporting and importing country	0.361***	0.310***	0.217***	0.251***
Ln distance	−1.729***	−2.193***	−2.292***	−2.306***
Ln bilateral real exchange rate	0.162***	0.054***	0.023**	0.049***
Linguistic similarity	0.000***	0.000***	0.000***	0.000***
Colonial	1.167***	1.759***	1.628***	1.575***
Border	−0.088	−0.571***	−0.529***	−0.626***
Currency union	1.201***	3.136***	1.148***	3.025***
Exporting country is an island	0.684***	−2.250***	0.670***	0.289
Importing country is an island	1.070***	−3.369***	1.163***	−3.268***
Exporting country is landlocked	−2.292***	−3.456***	−1.869***	−0.648*
Importing country is landlocked	−2.052***	3.276***	−1.929***	4.515***
Third-wave provisions of PTAs	20.074***	13.899***	−10.760***	−8.748***
Andean1	3.135*	4.544***	3.871***	2.774***
Andean2	2.496***	−0.600	11.257***	
Andean3	−0.943***	−3.088***	13.716***	
APEC1[c]	−2.081***	−2.727***	−0.052	0.091*
APEC2[c]	−0.240***	0.583***	2.118***	−0.666***
APEC3[c]	1.245***	0.486***	4.404***	1.941***
EFTA1	−6.252***	−7.023***	−1.972	−0.690
EFTA2	12.322***	0.252	9.111***	
EFTA3	17.195***	3.141***	15.189***	
EC/EU1	−16.129***	−16.022***	8.763***	9.608***
EC/EU2	5.344***	−1.209***	−8.208***	10.632***
EC/EU3	6.343***	−0.486*	−7.920***	18.188***
GCC1[c]	−0.400	−1.782***	−0.135	−0.341*
GCC2[c]	−0.498***	0.139*	0.950***	0.855***
GCC3[c]	−2.098***	−0.600***	0.118***	2.379***
LAFTA/LAIA1	30.591***	17.419***	28.057***	26.432***
LAFTA/LAIA2	−20.659***	−6.517***	−22.841***	
LAFTA/LAIA3	−5.267***	−0.635	−32.910***	
MERCOSUR1	−6.894**	−9.376***	0.800	1.075
MERCOSUR2	1.451***	1.929***	−5.002***	
MERCOSUR3	2.917***	−1.306***	23.916***	
NAFTA1	−17.152***	−14.970***	−2.072	−0.966
NAFTA2	5.195***	1.166**	7.310***	
NAFTA3	−2.720***	−0.790	−1.938***	
SPARTECA1	42.499***	35.093***	31.956***	31.573***
SPARTECA2	−9.865***	−0.402	−12.250***	
SPARTECA3	−13.312***	0.557	−18.496***	
CER1	−28.857***	−24.283***	−16.504***	−17.251***
CER2	3.329***	−2.229***	2.285***	
CER3	8.040***	−2.073***	7.650***	
EU-Switzerland1	−24.872***	−32.320***	−28.599***	−27.680***

Table 5.1   (continued)

Variable name	Dynamic PTA indexes		Antimonde PTA indexes	
	Without fixed	With fixed[a]	Without fixed	With fixed[a,b]
EU-Switzerland2	9.457***	5.339***	25.975***	
EU-Switzerland3	11.542***	5.076***	26.380***	
Chile-Colombia1	−17.149**	−14.407**	4.525*	3.281
Chile-Colombia2	2.234***	4.116***	−4.483***	
Chile-Colombia3	−0.251	2.237***	3.093***	
Chile-Mexico1			−4.187*	−4.096***
Chile-Mexico2			−4.933***	
Chile-Mexico3			1.400***	
US-Israel1	15.060***	10.984***	14.783***	14.185***
US-Israel2	−5.774***	−2.725***	1.888***	
US-Israel3	1.112**	−1.435**	9.056***	
Australia-PNG1	0.669	−6.200**	−10.816***	−10.797***
Australia-PNG2	0.784*	−1.202*	2.390***	
Australia-PNG3	1.487***	−0.946	−2.706***	
Singapore-New Zealand1			2.186*	1.802*
Singapore-New Zealand2			4.390***	
Singapore-New Zealand3			3.587***	
Chile-MERCOSUR1	−7.199**	−11.064***	−3.888***	−4.124***
Chile-MERCOSUR2	2.632***	2.136***	11.792***	
Chile-MERCOSUR3	0.328	1.145***	1.603***	
EU-Egypt1	−4.724	−8.702***	0.622	−0.055
EU-Egypt2	−12.498***	3.048***	3.582***	
EU-Egypt3	−15.582***	4.185***	−2.505***	
EU-Poland1	−19.307***	−27.309***	−9.699***	−11.991***
EU-Poland2	−4.386***	−0.834***	13.716***	
EU-Poland3	−2.186***	−0.741**	21.851***	
AFTA1	−3.783	−9.232***	−5.953***	−5.597***
AFTA2	7.170***	4.191***	0.492*	
AFTA3	7.375***	4.826***	−2.095***	
Constant	−12.101	−2.067***	−1.962***	−1.910***
LR χ^2 (chi2)	307,352.95	422,218.2	351,561.7	424,106.7
Log likelihood	−686,398.4	−629,010.8	−664,294.0	−628,021.5
σ (standard deviation of the error term)	4.407	3.547	4.036	3.542

Source: Authors' estimates.

Notes: Dependent variable = Ln exports; time period = 1970–1997; unbalanced panel; Tobit maximum likelihood estimates.

[a]To save space the fixed effect coefficients associated with exporting country, importing country, and time are not reported here.

[b]In the antimonde specification, some PTA indexes are dropped because of high multicollinearity between the country-fixed effects and the PTA indexes.

[c]While a Member Liberalization Index has not been calculated for APEC (a nonpreferential arrangement) or for the Gulf Cooperative Council (a preferential one), their possible effects on the trade flows of their members have been controlled for through a set of three conventional zero-one dummy variables.

***Significant at the 1 percent level.

**Significant at the 5 percent level.

*Significant at the 10 percent level.

Table 5.2   **New evidence on PTAs as causing net trade creation or diversion**

Past estimates			New estimates	
Net trade creation	Inconclusive	Net trade diversion	Net trade creation	Net trade diversion
Andean	LAIA	NAFTA	Andean	AFTA
CER	MERCOSUR		LAFTA/LAIA	EFTA
AFTA			United States-Israel	EC/EU
EEC/EU?			SPARTECA	MERCOSUR
EFTA?				NAFTA
				CER
				EU-Switzerland
				Chile-Colombia
				Australia-PNG
				Chile-MERCOSUR
				EU-Egypt
				EU-Poland

Sources: Past estimates assessment based on the findings from a majority of the following studies: Bayoumi and Eichengreen (1995), Frankel, Stein, and Wei (1995), Boisso and Ferrantino (1997), Frankel (1997), Fink and Primo Braga (1999), Krueger (1999b), Li (2000), Clark and Tavares (2000), Freund (2000), Gilbert, Scollay, and Bora (2001), and Soloaga and Winters (2001); table 5.1 source.

Overall, the main PTAs—NAFTA, the European Community (EC/ EU), MERCOSUR, and CER—as well as many bilateral agreements not considered previously, are found here to have created negative net trade effects. However, there is a qualification to this finding. In agreements with a small number of members, the intra-PTA effect is estimated imprecisely, with a large standard error, while the extra-PTA effect can be estimated more accurately.[9] Thus, the findings for those PTAs, such as CER, with a small number of members are less robust than those for larger PTAs. In addition, the measures of distance used in this study are unlikely to capture fully the ways in which changes in trading patterns and reductions in transport costs have raised the attractiveness of extrabloc as opposed to intrabloc trade for CER members over time.

As noted, the net trade effect criterion has limitations in assessing the effects on economic welfare. Nonetheless the new evidence suggests negative net trade effects for many PTAs, controlling for other factors.

A number of factors have contributed to the more negative findings in this study. These are now considered in turn.

All the past gravity model studies surveyed here estimated the PTA effects using PTA dummies defined in antimonde form.[10] The comparable

9. For example, the intra-CER dummy has positive values only for $14 \times 15 = 210$ observations and zero for remaining observations.
10. A more recent study with panel data and dynamic dummies is by Fukao, Okubo, and Stern (2003).

dynamic and antimonde estimates in this analysis are reported in table 5.1. They show that when PTA dummies are defined in antimonde form, the net trade effects are mainly positive, in contrast to the negative effects obtained for dynamic PTA variables.

In essence, when dummies are defined in dynamic form, the test for significance of their coefficients is a statistical test for whether the trade effects they capture are stronger after the formation or expansion of the PTA than before. In the past, this question has been assessed, at best, only by reference to the point estimates from various cross sections. Defining PTA dummies in dynamic form provides a more stringent statistical test of whether it was PTA formation, rather than some other set of factors specific to the bilateral country pair, accounting for the observed trade effects. The power of the test is further strengthened by the fact that individual country- and time-specific effects are controlled for separately, through the fixed effects. The more stringent test of the before and after effects of PTAs is the major factor accounting for the more negative findings of this study.

The differences are more prominent for the EC/EU and MERCOSUR agreements, where membership dynamics play an important role in their trade creation and diversion effects. For example, a significant negative intra-EU effect is found when using dynamic PTA specific indexes, compared to a significant positive effect found using antimonde indexes. The dynamic dummies account for individual countries switching from the European Free Trade Agreement (EFTA) to the EU.

Another reason for the more negative findings in this study is the use of panel analysis, which allows unobservable heterogeneity to be controlled for. Without allowing for country-specific effects, the coefficients on both the PTA variables and the other explanatory variables tend to be upward biased as are the test statistics for the significance of these variables. The likelihood-ratio test confirms the joint significance of the fixed effects.[11] This suggests that inferences based on past gravity model estimates without fixed effects suffer from omitted variable bias. Controlling for unobservable heterogeneity is another reason for the more negative findings in this study.[12]

A model with the average bilateral tariff variable as an additional determinant of trade is estimated on a restricted data set,[13] and the results are shown in table 5.3. The average tariff rate in the importing country has a

11. The calculated test statistic of 114,775.3 clearly rejects the null hypothesis, as is expected given the individual significance of most of the country- and time-specific fixed effects in the model.
' 12. The findings here are also more negative than those in a recent panel study by Clarete, Edmonds, and Wallack (2003). However, their study uses antimonde dummies and fails to control for unobserved country- and time-specific heterogeneity. It also controls for fewer observable factors than here.
13. The data set is restricted because of the lack of bilateral tariff data for a number of countries and for a number of years.

Table 5.3   **Gravity model of trade: Results from limited sample with tariff variable included**

Variable name	Dynamic PTA specific variables—fixed effects[a]		Antimonde PTA specific variables—fixed effects[a,b]	
	Without tariff	With tariff	Without tariff	With tariff
Ln sum of exporting and importing countries GDP (SUM)	2.063***	2.036***	2.838***	2.869***
Similarity in exporting and importing country's GDPs	0.562***	0.542***	1.534***	1.557***
Ln of absolute differences in per capita GDPs of exporting and importing country	−0.154***	−0.086***	−0.100***	−0.031
Ln distance	−1.404***	−1.393***	−1.458***	−1.469***
Ln bilateral real exchange rate	0.494***	0.513***	0.448***	0.454***
Ln tariff		−0.134***		−0.142***
Linguistic similarity	0.000***	0.000***	0.000***	0.000***
Colonial	1.141***	1.087***	1.170***	1.113***
Border	−0.099	−0.052	−0.138	−0.079
Currency union	0.230	0.425	0.203	0.421
Exporting country is an island	−0.718***	−0.746***	−0.472***	−0.492***
Importing country is an island	1.177***	1.338***	4.027***	4.380***
Exporting country is landlocked	−1.402***	−1.315***	−1.251***	−1.166***
Importing country is landlocked	−0.236	−0.300	0.421**	0.429**
Third-wave provisions of PTAs	1.222	1.748	−1.328	−2.067
Andean1	5.702***	5.545***	5.123***	5.123***
Andean2	−8.696***	−8.485***	2.428**	3.014***
Andean3	−1.503***	−1.461***	9.368***	9.130***
APEC1[c]	0.929***	1.032***	0.931***	1.029***
APEC2[c]	−0.839***	−0.817***	−6.988***	−7.133***
APEC3[c]	3.062***	2.994***	3.500***	3.414***
EFTA1	0.203	0.796	3.117	2.963
EFTA2	12.657***	14.513***		
EFTA3	11.631***	11.115***	8.552***	8.364***
EU1	−3.231***		3.626***	5.341***
EU2	5.184***	6.189***	1.118**	2.207***
EU3	−0.572	−0.289	−5.442***	−5.031***
GCC1[c]	2.348	2.406	2.210	2.217
GCC2[c]	−0.537	0.173		−1.452
GCC3[c]	−0.186**	−0.267***	0.051	−0.026
LAIA1	16.159***	16.046***	17.917***	17.605***
LAIA2	23.259***	24.735***		
LAIA3	15.478***	14.820***	−16.838***	−16.752***
MERCOSUR1	−1.432	−1.132	3.227	3.169
MERCOSUR2	−8.512***	−8.380***		
MERCOSUR3	1.793***	1.969***	18.830***	18.874***
NAFTA1	−2.800	−2.692	2.551	3.315
NAFTA2	13.591***	14.416***	29.870***	31.170***
NAFTA3	−8.453***	−8.562***	−8.137***	−8.385***
SPARTECA1	17.033***	18.523***	17.702***	19.271***
SPARTECA3	−11.930***	−12.128***	−14.163***	−14.880***
CER1	−8.356**	−8.976	−6.959**	−7.056**

Table 5.3 (continued)

Variable name	Dynamic PTA specific variables—fixed effects[a]		Antimonde PTA specific variables—fixed effects[a,b]	
	Without tariff	With tariff	Without tariff	With tariff
CER2	4.704***	5.267**	9.138***	9.382***
CER3	8.616***	8.523***	7.378***	7.396***
EU-Switzerland1	−15.405***	−14.934***	−15.718***	−15.541***
EU-Switzerland3	17.254***	16.723***	21.229***	20.401***
Chile-Colombia1	0.079	0.416	−1.304	−0.673
Chile-Colombia2	3.275***	3.013***	−18.101***	−18.457***
Chile-Colombia3	−0.705	−0.545	4.641***	4.742***
Chile-Mexico1			−4.612	−4.405
Chile-Mexico2			49.545***	50.383***
Chile-Mexico3			4.116***	4.243***
US-Israel1	7.763	10.386*	10.255*	13.218**
US-Israel3	11.120***	10.649***	10.811***	10.341***
Australia-PNG1	−1.166	−2.097	−3.080	−5.104
Australia-PNG3	−1.492*	−1.382	−3.609***	−3.157***
Singapore-NZ1			−0.235	1.892
Singapore-NZ3			1.307***	1.455***
Chile-MERCOSUR1	−3.654*	−3.440	−3.682***	−3.478***
Chile-MERCOSUR2	1.403***	1.321***	−4.953***	−4.780***
Chile-MERCOSUR3	−1.171**	−1.148**	−2.080**	−2.222**
EU-Egypt1	5.573	5.454	5.688***	4.870*
EU-Egypt3	0.682	0.144	0.336	0.006
EU-Poland1	2.517	1.837	−3.763**	−4.049**
EU-Poland2	−1.457***	−0.600*		
EU-Poland3	2.099***	1.956***	10.075***	9.820***
AFTA1	−9.693***	−8.204*	−9.629***	−8.946***
AFTA2	−0.484	0.354		
AFTA3	3.060***	2.827***	0.572	0.222
LR χ^2 (chi2)	32,088.3	28,186.5	33,800.9	29,892.8
Log likelihood	−77,034.8	−71,010.6	−76,178.6	−70,157.4
σ (standard deviation of the error term)	2.859	2.855	2.776	2.766

Source: Authors' estimates.

Notes: Dependent variable = Ln exports; time period = 1998–1997; unbalanced panel; Tobit maximum likelihood estimates.

[a]To save space, the fixed effect coefficients associated with exporting country, importing country, and time are not reported here.

[b]In the antimonde specification, some PTA indexes are dropped because of high multicollinearity between country-fixed effects and PTA indexes.

[c]While a Member Liberalization Index has not been calculated for APEC (a nonpreferential arrangement) or for the Gulf Cooperative Council (a preferential one), their possible effects on the trade flows of their members have been controlled for through a set of three conventional zero-one dummy variables.

***Significant at the 1 percent level.

**Significant at the 5 percent level.

*Significant at the 10 percent level.

significant and negative effect on its imports, as expected. The PTA-specific indexes also show a significant effect. This is because they capture not only the existence of tariff preferences (as also captured in the tariff variable) but also the effects of nontariff measures affecting merchandise trade, such as rules of origin.

The coefficients on the PTA-specific indexes are generally not sensitive to the inclusion or exclusion of the tariff variable. So the inclusion of a tariff variable makes little difference to the main findings of this study. But in some cases, negative intrabloc trade effects in the full sample become positive in the smaller sample. And perhaps not surprisingly, while the comparative advantage motivation for trade showed as significant in the full sample (with a positive and significant coefficient on the difference in per capita GDP), this is not the case in the restricted sample. These differences also show that what constitutes "normal" trade is conditioned by how many countries and years are in the sample—those studies with restricted time and country coverage, particularly where it is restricted to high-income developed countries, are likely to have results biased accordingly.

The nonmerchandise provisions show a positive (complementary) relationship with trade when PTA indexes are defined dynamically. Thus favorable investment and services trade provisions in PTAs can enhance merchandise trade between member countries once the agreement is in operation.

In summary, the main result is that PTAs are not as relatively benign as previous studies have indicated. After controlling for country- and time-specific effects and the degree of liberalization of merchandise trade provisions in an unrestricted sample and testing explicitly for whether the trade effects are significantly different after PTA formation than before, most PTAs were estimated to have negative trade creation. Other recent empirical assessments have shown a more optimistic outlook for trade in preferential agreements by ignoring these analytical issues.

One potential puzzle is that the intrabloc effect is found to be negative for apparently more comprehensive and liberal PTAs—EU, CER, NAFTA, MERCOSUR and some of the recent bilateral agreements. One possible reason is that total elimination of tariffs among members, as required by the General Agreement on Tariffs and Trade (GATT) Article XXIV, may not be optimal for members. For example, Frankel, Stein, and Wei (1995) found that a 22 percent reduction in tariffs below multilateral tariff levels may instead be optimal. However, this finding is driven by welfare effects, not by trade volume effects.

A more likely explanation is that, although the merchandise MLI used in this study has attempted to capture the potentially trade-restrictive effects of the nontariff merchandise trade provisions embodied in PTAs, it has not always captured them adequately. For example, as noted earlier, the merchandise MLI has treated the trade restrictive effects of rules of origin as being additive to and independent from the other provisions of PTAs. In reality, not only are rules of origin restrictive, they are also likely to neutralize or even reverse the trade effects of other provisions that are apparently quite liberal.[14]

The way in which rules of origin can operate in practice to counter the effects of other provisions that are apparently quite liberal can be seen most clearly in the case of NAFTA. There, the rules of origin are relatively complex—the specification of requirements for minimum change in tariff heading vary product by product and take up several hundred pages. Further, they are strictly enforced. The domestic content rules applied in the EU are also relatively complex. Even if the tariffs on each product are eliminated entirely (an apparently quite liberal provision), the complex rules of origin governing the sourcing of inputs to qualify for the tariff concession on output can undo the liberal effect of the tariff concession on output. This is not recognized in the MLI, which treats tariff provisions and rules of origin additively, not interactively. Thus, the MLI may overstate the effective amount of liberalization in agreements with complex rules of origin, explaining why it was that the *apparently* more comprehensive and liberalized PTAs were found to have a negative intrabloc effect, relative to average trade patterns in the sample.

Sensitivity Analysis

The preceding model specification differs from standard specifications in several respects. One is the inclusion of the sum of importing and exporting country GDPs, rather than each country's GDP separately. As noted, this comes from a model of product differentiation originating with Helpman and Krugman (1985) and Helpman (1987). But in the original model, the dependent variable was total bilateral trade—the sum of exports in both directions—rather than bilateral exports. This paper has followed Egger (2001) and others by using bilateral exports as the dependent variable to allow a more refined examination of the trade diversion issue. And the resulting estimate of the coefficient on the sum of GDPs is very similar to that of Egger (2001). But the question arises whether the results are sensitive to this treatment of GDPs, especially given the redefinition of the dependent variable. To test this, the preceding model was reestimated with (the log of) GDPs of importing and exporting country entered separately. The coefficient on the exporting country's GDP was 1.118, and the coefficient on the importing country's GDP was 0.766, with the sum being close to the result in table 5.1. In all other respects, the results were similar to those shown in table 5.1. The results are available on request from the authors.

---

14. For analyses of the welfare effects of rules of origin, see Duttagupta and Panagariya (2003), Krueger (1999a), Ju and Krishna (1998), and Krishna and Krueger (1995).

The specification also differs from some others by using triple-indexed fixed effects, controlling separately for importing country, exporting country, and time-related unobservable effects. This is in contrast to specifications that use a single country-pair fixed effect as well as a time effect. As noted, the triple-indexed approach was advocated by Matyas (1997, 1998) for econometric reasons. It is also the approach needed to control for the misspecifications identified by Haveman and Hummels (1998) and Anderson and van Wincoop (2003). Haveman and Hummels note that total exports are likely to be a better measure of "economic mass" than GDP. Gravity models are likely to be misspecified when bilateral exports grow faster than GDP simply because total exports grow faster than GDP, not because of some PTA effect. The extent to which total exports grow faster than GDP is an individual country effect, not a country-pair effect. Similarly, Anderson and van Wincoop (2003) note that in the correct theoretical specification, bilateral trade flows should depend on three measures of trade barriers—the bilateral trade barrier between the two countries and each country's resistance to trade with all regions. Again, the two latter resistance effects are country effects, not country-pair effects.

It was not possible to test the sensitivity of the preceding Tobit specification to the inclusion of a country-pair fixed effects because there were too many country-pair groups, preventing estimation. The approach also risks overspecification, with the country-pair effects duplicating much of the work of the PTA dummies.

A final piece of sensitivity analysis is the inclusion of a lagged dependent variable. Appropriate econometric estimation of such a specification in a Tobit context with fixed effects is unlikely to have been possible on a data set of this size. In many other contexts, ordinary least squares (OLS) would be an acceptable alternative to Tobit estimation in practice, with the results not differing greatly between the two estimation methods. Were this the case here, it would have been possible to test sensitivity to the inclusion of a lagged dependent variable in an OLS context. However, Tobit estimation matters greatly here, as would be expected with 44 percent of the observations on the dependent variable being zero. The OLS estimation of the original triple indexed specification on the full sample (with zero export values replaced by small positive numbers) led to results with a coefficient on the sum of GDPs being unreasonably low, at 0.555, and similar downward bias in other coefficients, including those on distance, currency union, and the PTA dummies. Thus the results of further sensitivity analysis on the OLS specification were judged unreliable. For what it is worth, adding a lagged dependent variable produced short-run coefficients even lower than the already low OLS estimates, while the value of the coefficient on the lagged dependent variable itself implied long-run coefficients somewhat higher than the OLS estimates. In all other respects, the results were unchanged.

5.3.4 New Evidence on Investment Creation and Diversion

The observable effects—normal bilateral investment determinants and traditional and third-wave provisions of PTAs—and unobservable country- and time-specific effects all significantly influence the bilateral stock of outward investment (see table 5.4).[15]

The signs of coefficients on the normal bilateral investment determinants are generally as expected. Larger absolute differences in per capita GDP are associated with outward FDI being lower than otherwise. Because absolute differences in per capita GDP also boost bilateral exports, the results lend some support to the idea that trade and FDI are substitutes when trade is motivated by differences in factor endowments (Markusen 1983). Only if investment treaties are enacted between countries do they have a significant positive effect on outward investment. When they are signed but not enacted, they tend to suppress outward investment. The presence of a currency union has no significant effect on outward FDI, although it had a significant and positive effect on bilateral exports.

PTAs have been categorized in table 5.5 according to whether investment responds in either tariff-jumping or beachhead fashion to the trade provisions or whether it responds instead primarily to the nonmerchandise trade provisions. A single PTA can fall into more than one category.

Only the South Pacific Regional Trade and Economic Cooperation Agreement (SPARTECA) and Andean agreements showed weak evidence of investment behavior responding in beachhead fashion to the trade provisions of the agreement. SPARTECA is a nonreciprocal agreement between Australia, New Zealand, and selected South Pacific Island countries with few nontrade provisions and with trade provisions only for selected products. But the nonreciprocal tariff preferences may have allowed the Pacific island countries to attract investment, not only from Australia and New Zealand, but also from other countries, to gain preferential access to the CER market.

Empirical evidence is weak for Ethier's more general view that PTA members can attract investment from nonmember countries, once other observable and unobservable factors are controlled for. In four agreements the trade provisions appear to have encouraged inward FDI from third parties—the Andean Pact, SPARTECA, ASEAN Free Trade Agreement (AFTA) and NAFTA—but in no case was the effect significant, and only in the first two agreements was the effect also associated with an increase in intrabloc trade (defining beachhead investment). In three agreements, it was the nontrade provisions that encouraged inward FDI from third parties—NAFTA, EU, and SPARTECA—but only in the first case was the effect significant. Thus when a PTA had a significant effect on inward FDI

---

15. The results in table 5.4 differ slightly from those in earlier versions of this paper.

Table 5.4   **Gravity model of investment**

	Dynamic PTA indexes	
Variable name[c]	Without fixed[b]	With fixed[a,b]
Ln sum of exporting and importing countries GDP (SUM)	1.496***	1.152***
Similarity in exporting and importing country's GDPs	0.086	−0.058
Ln of absolute differences in per capita GDPs of exporting and importing country	−0.487**	−0.603***
Ln distance	−0.682***	−0.572***
Ln bilateral real exchange rate	0.335**	−0.242*
Ln tariff	0.013	0.001
Linguistic similarity	0.000***	0.000***
Colonial	1.601***	1.285***
Border	0.615**	0.595**
Currency union	−0.716	−1.162
Home country is an island	−3.577***	−3.212***
Host country is an island	−1.004***	−1.174***
Home country is landlocked	−2.842***	−3.122***
Host country is landlocked	0.396	0.583**
Investment treaties signed	−1.525***	−1.782***
Investment treaties enacted	1.029**	1.055**
M-ANDEAN1	−4.664	−6.121
M-ANDEAN2	0.410	
M-ANDEAN3	0.557	
M-APEC1[d]	−0.117	−0.179
M-APEC2[d]	−0.555**	−0.259
M-APEC3[d]	−1.339***	−2.255***
M-EFTA1	3.090	1.433
M-EFTA2	1.139	
M-EFTA3	1.837*	
M-EU1	0.537	1.662
M-EU2	−0.559	−2.172
M-EU3	0.111	
M-NAFTA2	2.277	
M-NAFTA3	2.995	
M-SPARTECA1	11.279	10.430
M-SPARTECA2	3.309	
M-SPARTECA3	−8.729***	
M-CER1	−1.720	−0.026
M-CER2	−2.385	
M-CER3	10.641***	
M-US-Israel2	−6.742**	
M-US-Israel3	−5.725	
F-ANDEAN1	1.234	5.590
F-ANDEAN2	−11.326**	−10.022**
F-ANDEAN3	−8.575	−19.530*
F-APEC1[d]	0.095	0.003
F-APEC2[d]	0.813***	0.976***
F-APEC3[d]	0.553*	1.820***
F-EFTA1	14.308	−12.698
F-EFTA2	−16.474	−39.673***
F-EFTA3	138.905***	170.216***
F-EU1	1.812	2.471
F-EU2	2.136	0.795

Table 5.4   (continued)

Variable name[c]	Dynamic PTA indexes	
	Without fixed[b]	With fixed[a,b]
F-EU3	12.840***	17.634***
F-NAFTA1	−9.503*	−5.457
F-NAFTA2	5.802***	3.147*
F-NAFTA3	13.650***	10.317***
F-SPARTECA2	126.591	148.125
F-CER1	−0.647	3.999
F-CER2	1.617	−2.509
F-CER3	31.455***	23.847***
F-United States-Israel1	6.865	−8.098
F-United States-Israel2	−0.754	8.118
F-United States-Israel3	21.867*	54.425***
LR χ^2 (chi2)	1,113.8	1,444.7
Log likelihood	−2,192.9	−2,027.5
σ (standard deviation of the error term)	1.875	1.609

Source: Authors' estimates.

Notes: Dependent variable = Ln stock of outward investment; time period = 1988–1997; unbalanced panel; Tobit maximum likelihood estimates.

[a]To save space, the fixed effect coefficients associated with home country, host country, and time are not reported here.

[b]Some PTA indexes are dropped because of high multicollinearity among explanatory variables.

[c]"M" before each PTA name denotes index of traditional merchandise trade provisions, and "F" before each PTA name denotes index of new age provisions.

[d]While a Member Liberalization Index has not been calculated for APEC (a nonpreferential arrangement), its possible effects on the trade flows of its members has been controlled for through a set of three conventional zero-one dummy variables.

***Significant at the 1 percent level.

**Significant at the 5 percent level.

*Significant at the 10 percent level.

Table 5.5   **Main drivers of investment in PTAs**

No measurable impact	Tariff-jumping effects of trade provision	Beachhead effects of trade provisions	Nontrade provisions
MERCOSUR[a]	EFTA	SPARTECA[b]	Andean
AFTA[a]	CER	Andean[b]	EFTA
			EU
			NAFTA
			CER
			United States-Israel

Source: Table 5.4.

[a]PTA indexes for these agreements were dropped because of high multicollinearity among the explanatory variables.

[b]Only weak evidence for this characterization because the coefficients are not significant.

from third parties, it was in response to the nontrade rather than the trade provisions. It appears that Ethier's beachhead investment is not an important phenomenon empirically.

The EFTA and CER agreements showed evidence of investment behavior consistent with an unwinding of tariff-jumping behavior. But both of these agreements also showed significant evidence of investment responding to the nontrade provisions of the agreement. A total of five of the nine PTAs examined for investment effects showed significant evidence of investment responding to the nontrade provisions of the agreements.

While table 5.5 indicates investment responses to the traditional and third-wave provisions of PTAs, it does not indicate whether PTAs caused investment creation or investment diversion per se. A summary of the signs of the significant coefficients is reported in table 5.6.

As noted, the trade provisions of PTAs did not result in a significant increase in investment from nonmembers in any PTA. Trade provisions caused a reduction in outward investment (investment diversion) in SPARTECA but an increase in outward investment in EFTA and CER consistent with the unwinding of tariff-jumping investment.

The new age provisions in various PTAs have had a more widespread impact on investment than the trade provisions. The NAFTA agreement was estimated to have reduced investment among members. All other agreements considered had no significant effects on investment among members.

While NAFTA attracted investment from nonmembers, particularly into Mexico, the new age provisions in the Andean Pact and EFTA were unable to attract investment from nonmembers. For EFTA, the loss of membership to EU made it a less attractive place for foreign direct investment. This is similar to the findings of Baldwin, Forslid, and Haaland (1995), who found that EC caused a diversion of third-country capital

Table 5.6   **New evidence on investment creation and diversion**

Trade provisions			Third-wave provisions	
Extra-PTA (inward)	Extra-PTA (outward)	Intra-PTA	Extra-PTA (inward)	Extra-PTA (outward)
United States-Israel(–)	EFTA(+)	NAFTA(–)	Andean(–)	Andean(–)
	CER(+)		EFTA(–)	EFTA(+)
	SPARTECA(–)		NAFTA(+)	EU(+)
				NAFTA(+)
				CER(+)
				United States-Israel(+)

Source: Table 5.4, significant coefficients.
Note: Positive (+) symbol denotes investment creation, and negative (–) symbol denotes investment diversion.

from EFTA to the EU. The Andean Pact was similarly affected by the loss of Peru, although the findings for Latin American countries are also affected by incompleteness of the FDI outstock data.

The sum of significant coefficients on the indexes of third-wave provisions for each PTA can provide an indicative measure of the impact of these new age provisions on net investment creation (see table 5.7). Of the nine PTAs examined for investment effects, five showed positive net investment effects. Only the Andean Pact caused net investment diversion. This agreement apparently caused a reduction in both inward and outward investment with third parties, without succeeding in causing a significant boost in intrabloc investment. As noted, this result may in part reflect incompleteness in the FDI outstock data for Latin America.

The North American Free Trade Agreement, EU, EFTA, CER, and the US-Israel agreement caused net investment creation, not because they stimulated investment among members, but primarily because they appear to have stimulated outward investment from member to nonmember countries. This is consistent with some of the nontrade provisions of these agreements being nonpreferential in nature. It is also consistent with some of these regions being major sources of FDI, but this suggests that the estimated effects may well reflect the influence of causal factors not controlled for in the analysis that make these countries net capital exporters, rather than the effects of PTA formation and expansion per se. One example is financial deregulation and the growth of superannuation funds that have encouraged Australia to become a much more important capital exporter recently (Battellino 2002).

The South Pacific Regional Trade and Economic Cooperation Agreement had no significant impact on net investment creation, while the effects of MERCOSUR and AFTA on investment could not be distinguished because of problems of multicollinearity.

Though the investment results appear to be more positive than the results reported for trade, there are number of qualifications that need to be considered. Winters (1997) argued that new FDI from any source could go

Table 5.7   Net impact of PTAs' third-wave provisions on investment

Net investment creation	Net investment diversion	No measurable impact
EFTA	Andean	MERCOSUR[a]
EU		AFTA[a]
NAFTA		SPARTECA
CER		
United States-Israel		

Source: Table 5.4, fixed effects estimates, significant coefficients.
[a]PTA indexes for these agreements were dropped because of high multicollinearity among the explanatory variables.

into the production of goods for trade diversion and thus worsen the PTA's welfare overall. In similar tone, McLaren (2002) argued that

> A regional trade regime can plausibly be interpreted as a coordination failure, in which the anticipation that the world will break into regional trade blocs induces sunk private sector investments that then lead to a demand for regionalism. Under this argument, regionalism can be Pareto-worsening even though once sunk investments have been made it is, *ex post,* a relatively efficient compromise: hence, regionalism is "insidious," the damage it does to efficiency is hidden in the distortion of *ex ante* investments. (McLaren 2002, 572)

The gravity model estimates provide indications of the positive net investment effects of PTAs but do not consider whether the resulting investment contributes to trade diversion.

Further, as noted before, a finding of net investment creation is a weak indicator of whether the welfare gains from investment creation outweigh the costs of investment diversion. Investment diversion may dominate creation in welfare terms, even if it does not in "volume of investment" terms. On the other hand, if the nontrade provisions reduce restrictions that raise costs, member countries can gain in welfare terms, despite investment diversion. But in either case, members could well gain even more from multilateral liberalization of nontrade restrictions.

5.4   Summary

Theoretical work has always highlighted that while the merchandise trade provisions of PTAs can boost trade among members, this is often at the expense of nonmembers. So whether it benefits a country to join a PTA depends on the cost structures in partner countries, compared with the cost structures in third parties. If a preferential trade arrangement diverts a country's imports from a low-cost third party to a higher-cost preferential trade partner, it can be made worse off. Conversely, the opportunity for benefits is greater where the PTA partner is at world-best competitiveness and where liberalization under the PTA encourages imports from that source.

The new empirical work outlined in this paper suggests that of the eighteen recent PTAs examined in detail, twelve have diverted more trade from nonmembers than they have created among members. What is more, some of the apparently quite liberal PTAs—including EU, NAFTA and MERCOSUR—have failed to create significant additional trade among members (relative to the average trade changes registered among countries in the sample).

Part of the reason for this more negative finding than in previous studies is the rigorous statistical test that has been applied to ascertain whether intrabloc trade is significantly greater after bloc formation (or expansion) than before. In the past, this was assessed, at best, only by reference to the point estimates from various cross sections. But the finding is also consistent with the observation that many of the provisions needed in preferential arrangements to underpin and enforce their preferential nature—such as rules of origin—are in practice quite trade restricting.

While the increasing focus of PTAs on nontrade provisions may suggest that conventional concerns about trade diversion are outmoded, some theoretical literature suggests this conclusion would be premature.

On the one hand, in an increasingly integrated world economy, even minor *trade* concessions can have a significant impact on *investment* flows. And if investment is attracted into one PTA partner in order to serve the markets of the others, then the trade from such beachhead positions can constitute traditional trade diversion.

On the other, the *nontrade* provisions of PTAs, particularly those related to investment and services, can also have a significant impact on *investment* flows. But the preferential nature of the PTA provisions may mean that investment is diverted from a low-cost to a higher-cost host country, and such investment diversion can also be harmful.

The empirical work in this paper finds little evidence of beachhead investment, or an unwinding of tariff-jumping investment, in response to the trade provisions of PTAs. Only for SPARTECA and the Andean Pact, for example, is there (weak) evidence of FDI responding in beachhead fashion to trade provisions. And only for EFTA and CER is there some evidence of an unwinding of tariff-jumping investment.

There is evidence that FDI responds significantly to the nontrade provisions of PTAs. And in five of the nine PTAs examined for investment effects, the nontrade provisions led to net investment creation.

Although it is a weak test, this suggests that on balance, the nontrade provisions of these PTAs have created an efficient geographic distribution of FDI. This is consistent with the fact that at least some of the nontrade provisions (e.g., commitments to more strongly enforce intellectual property rights) are not strongly preferential in their nature.

Further, the theoretical literature has stressed that if the nontrade barriers are of the sort to raise the real resource costs of doing business, rather than simply to create rents that raise prices above costs, then preferential liberalization will be beneficial, even in the absence of net investment creation.

However, the trade that may be generated from the new FDI positions may still be diverted in the wrong direction in response to the trade provisions of PTAs and may therefore contribute to the net trade diversion also found here.

Thus the results of this paper suggest that there may be economic gains from the nontrade provisions of third-wave PTAs, but they also suggest that there are still economic costs associated with the preferential nature of the trade provisions. And these costs could be magnified in a world of increasing capital mobility.

Thus the findings of this research on the effects of the nontrade provisions of PTAs are more positive than those on the trade provisions. This suggests there could be real benefits if countries could use regional negotiations to persuade trading partners to make progress in reforming such things as investment, services, competition policy, and government procurement, especially if this is done on a nonpreferential basis.

Appendix

The Static Welfare Effects of PTAs

In figure 5A.1, S_a and D_a are the domestic supply and demand curves in country A. S_b is the supply curve of imports from the PTA partner country, showing that any quantity can be supplied from there at the price P_b. S_w is the supply curve of imports from the rest of the world, showing that any quantity can be supplied from there at price P_w. P_a^* is the initial, tariff-inflated price in country A, with the tariff t equal to $P_a^* - P_w$. Initially all imports $Q_c - Q_p$ come from the rest of the world, as with the same tariff t placed on imports from B, the local price in country A would exceed P_a^*. The tariff revenue on the imports from the rest of the world is $AEJF$. The quantity produced domestically is Q_p, and domestic consumption is Q_c.

Now suppose that country A eliminates its tariff on imports from B but

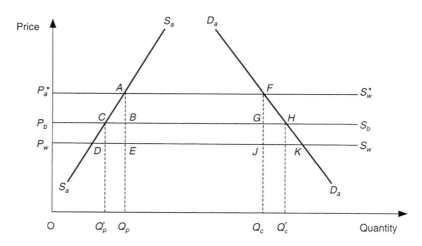

Fig. 5A.1   An illustration of trade creation and diversion effects of a PTA

retains it on imports from the rest of the world. With imports now available from B at P_b, the import quantity expands to $Q'_c - Q'_p$, with country B rather than the rest of the world becoming the source. Tariff revenue shrinks to zero. Domestic production shrinks to Q'_p, and domestic consumption expands to Q'_c.

The net effect of PTA formation on economic well-being in country A is given by $ABC + FGH - BEJG$. The first effect, the gain of $ABC + FGH$, is the net benefit to consumers and the net resource saving in production from having domestic production shrink from Q_p to Q'_p and consumption expand from Q_c to Q'_c. This is the trade creation gain from shifting high-cost domestic production to a lower-cost partner.[16] The second effect, the loss of $BEJG$, is that portion of the tariff revenue lost by shifting imports from the rest of the world to the higher-cost partner that is not recouped in lower domestic prices to consumers. It is the welfare loss from trade diversion and arises essentially because forgone domestic tariff revenue accrues instead as profit to producers in the partner country. The effect on country A is ambiguous a priori. Strictly speaking, only if the partner country is already at world-best production cost is a welfare gain to country A assured. But then A's economic motive for preferential rather than nondiscriminatory trade liberalization is unclear.

What about the welfare effects on the country receiving the preferential tariff concession and the effects on the rest of the world? Both face a change in demand for their product from country A, but because of the assumption of constant costs, there is no induced change in unit costs that can flow on to benefit domestic consumers or drive an improvement in resource allocation in those countries.[17] Thus, the effect on country A, the country granting the tariff preference, is the same as the welfare effect on the PTA and the world as a whole. This highlights one of the key weaknesses of the simple analysis—its assumption of constant costs of production in the partner country and in the rest of the world.

The simple analysis is nevertheless useful for outlining the nature of empirical tests for trade creation and trade diversion. Typically, these tests measure the amount by which the volume (or more often, the value) of trade increases with partner countries—$Q'_c - Q'_p$ in the preceding example—and compare it with the amount by which trade with the rest of the world is reduced—$Q_c - Q_p$ in the preceding example. If the net effect is positive, it is still only a weak test of whether the gains from trade creation outweigh the costs of trade diversion. It establishes that there is some pos-

---

16. Viner's (1950) original analysis omitted the consumption gain FGH. Johnson (1960) was the first to include it as part of the gains from trade creation, thereby ending unproductive debates about the possibility of welfare-increasing trade diversion (Gehrels 1957; Lipsey 1957; Michaely 1976).

17. If there is a preexisting distortion in the exporting sector of the exporting country, then an expansion of that sector could worsen the allocation of resources.

itive width to the triangles *ABC* and *FGH*, but it does not establish that their areas exceed that of *BEJG*. This also depends on the reduction in costs per unit of newly created trade and the increase in costs per unit of diverted trade. What can be concluded in this model is that if the empirical tests establish net trade creation in a volume or value sense, then the PTA may still have generated welfare losses, but if the empirical tests establish net trade diversion, then the PTA cannot have created welfare gains.

The assumption of constant costs in the partner country and in the rest of the world is consistent with perfect competition in those two markets. There has been a great deal of analysis examining the welfare effects of allowing unit production costs to vary in those two markets (see Panagariya [2000] for a summary), although the analysis has not always been explicit about the nature or source of the less-than-perfect competition in those markets.

The easiest way to see the dramatic effects that less-than-perfect competition can have is to imagine in figure 5A.1 that the producers in country *B* form a cartel and price up to the world price plus external tariff after they are granted the tariff preference. Their price would remain at P_a^*, the losses to country *A* from trade diversion would expand to *AEJF*, and the gains to *A* from trade creation would disappear completely! On the other hand, country *B* would now have a net gain in rent of *ABGF* that was previously tariff revenue accruing to *A*. The net loss to the PTA and the world as a whole would be *BEGJ*. Thus, less-than-perfect competition can preserve the losses from trade diversion but destroy the gains from trade creation.

One of the most general treatments of less-than-perfect competition is by Mundell (1964). He draws the following conclusions on the effects of a customs union, assuming that all goods are gross substitutes and initial tariffs are low:

> (1) The discriminatory tariff reduction by a member country improves the terms of trade of the partner country with respect to both the tariff reducing country and the rest of the world, but the terms of trade of the tariff-reducing country might rise or fall with respect to third countries.
> (2) The degree of improvement in the terms of trade of the partner country is likely to be larger the greater is the member's tariff reduction; this establishes the presumption that a member's gain from a free-trade area will be larger the higher are initial tariffs of partner countries. (Mundell 1964, 8)

A key to this result is the revenue transfer effect that can arise with less-than-perfect competition. It is also the basis for Panagariya's (1999) conclusion, for example, that the United States is likely to gain, but that Mexico could lose, from NAFTA.

References

Adams, R., P. Dee, J. Gali, and G. McGuire. 2003. The trade and investment effects of preferential trading arrangements—Old and new evidence. Productivity Commission Staff Working Paper. Canberra, Australia: Australian Government, Productivity Commission, May.

Aitken, N. 1973. The effect of the EEC and EFTA on European trade: A temporal cross-section analysis. *American Economic Review* 63 (5): 881–92.

Anderson, J., and E. van Wincoop. 2003. Gravity with gravitas: A solution to the border puzzle. *American Economic Review* 93 (1): 170–92.

Andriamananjara, S. 2002. On the size and number of preferential trading arrangements. *Journal of International Trade and Economic Development* 11 (3): 279–95.

Bagwell, K., and R. Staiger. 1998. Will preferential arrangements undermine the multilateral trading system? *Economic Journal* 108 (449): 1162–82.

———. 1999. An economic theory of the GATT. *American Economic Review* 89 (1): 215–48.

Baier, S. L., and J. H. Bergstrand. 2001. The growth of world trade: Tariffs, transport costs and income similarity. *Journal of International Economics* 53 (1): 1–27.

Balassa, B. 1967. Trade creation and trade diversion in the European common market. *Economic Journal* 77 (1): 1–21.

Baldwin, R. 1994. Towards an integrated Europe. London: Centre for Economic Policy Research.

———. 1996. A domino theory of regionalism. In *Expanding European regionalism: The EU's new members,* ed. R. E. Baldwin, P. Haapranta, and J. Kiander, 25–48. Cambridge, UK: Cambridge University Press.

Baldwin, R. E., R. Forslid, and J. Haaland. 1995. Investment creation and investment diversion: Simulation analysis of the single market program. CEPR Discussion Paper no. 1308. London: Centre for Economic Policy Research.

Baldwin, R. E., and A. J. Venables. 1995. Regional economic integration. In *Handbook of international economics.* Vol. 3, ed. G. Grossman and K. Rogoff, 1597–1644. Amsterdam: Elsevier.

Battellino, R. 2002. Australia as a capital exporter. Paper presented at conference, The Impact of an Australian–US Free Trade Agreement: Foreign Policy Challenges and Economic Opportunities. 29–30 August, Canberra, Australia.

Bayoumi, T., and B. Eichengreen. 1995. Is regionalism simply a diversion? Evidence from the evolution of the EC and EFTA. CEPR Discussion Paper no. 1294. London: Centre for Economic Policy Research.

Bhagwati, J. 1999. Regionalism and multilateralism: An overview. In *Trading blocs: Alternative approaches to analyzing preferential trade agreements,* ed. J. Bhagwati, P. Krishna, and A. Panagariya, 3–32. Cambridge, MA: MIT Press.

Bhagwati, J., P. Krishna, and A. Panagariya. 1999. *Trading blocs: Alternative approaches to analyzing preferential trade agreements.* Cambridge, MA: MIT Press.

Boisso, D., and M. Ferrantino. 1997. Economic distance, cultural distance, and openness in international trade: Empirical puzzles. *Journal of Economic Integration* 12 (4): 456–84.

Bond, E., and C. Syropoulos. 1996. The size of trading blocs, market power and world welfare effects. *Journal of International Economics* 40 (3–4): 411–37.

Clarete, R., C. Edmonds, and J. Wallack. 2003. Asian regionalism and its effects on trade in the 1980s and 1990s. *Journal of Asian Economics* 14 (1): 91–129.

Clark, X., and J. Tavares. 2000. A quantitative approach using the gravity equation.

Development Discussion Paper no. 748. Cambridge, MA: Harvard Institute for International Development, Harvard University.

Corden, M. 1972. Economies of scale and customs union theory. *Journal of Political Economy* 80 (3): 465–75.

Deardorff, A. V., and R. Stern. 1994. Multilateral trade negotiations and preferential trading arrangements. In *Analytical and negotiating issues in the global trading system,* ed. A. V. Deardorff and R. Stern, 53–85. Ann Arbor: University of Michigan Press.

Deardorff, A. V. 1998. Determinants of bilateral trade flows: Does gravity work in a neoclassical world. In *The regionalization of the world economy,* ed. J. A. Frankel, 23–28. Chicago: University of Chicago Press.

De Rosa, D. A. 1998. Regional integration arrangements: Static economic theory, quantitative findings and policy guidelines. World Bank. Mimeograph. http://www.worldbank.org/research/projects/regional.htm.

Duttagupta, R., and A. Panagariya. 2003. Free trade areas and rules of origin: Economics and politics. IMF Working Paper no. WP/03/229. Washington, DC: International Monetary Fund.

Egger, P. 2001. European exports and outward foreign direct investment: A dynamic panel data approach. *Weltwirtschaftliches Archiv* 137 (3): 427–49.

Eichengreen, B., and D. A. Irwin. 1995. Trade blocs, currency blocs and the reorientation of world trade in the 1930s. *Journal of International Economics* 38 (1–2): 1–24.

Ethier, W. 1998a. The new regionalism. *Economic Journal* 108 (449): 1149–61.

———. 1998b. Regionalism in a multilateral world. *Journal of Political Economy* 106 (6): 1214–45.

———. 1999. Multilateral roads to regionalism. In *International trade policy and the Pacific Rim,* ed. J. Piggott and A. Woodland, 131–52. New York: St. Martin's.

———. 2001. The new regionalism in the Americas: A theoretical framework. *North American Journal of Economics and Finance* 12 (2): 159–72.

Evenett, S. J., and W. Keller. 1998. On theories explaining the success of the gravity equation. *Journal of Political Economy* 110 (2): 281–316.

Feenstra, R. C., J. R. Markusen, and A. K. Rose. 2001. Using the gravity equation to differentiate among alternative theories of trade. *Canadian Journal of Economics* 34 (2): 430–47.

Fink, C., and C. A. Primo Braga. 1999. How stronger protection of intellectual property rights affects international trade flows. World Bank Working Paper no. 2051. Washington, DC: World Bank. http://www.worldbank.org/html/dec/Publications/Workpapers/wps2000series/wps2051/wps2051.pdf.

Frankel, J. 1997. *Regional trading blocs in the world economic system.* Washington, DC: Institute for International Economics.

Frankel, J., E. Stein, and S. Wei. 1995. Trading blocs and the Americas: The natural, the unnatural, and the super-natural. *Journal of Development Economics* 47 (1): 61–95.

Freund, C. 2000. Different paths to free trade: The gains from regionalism. *Quarterly Journal of Economics* 115 (4): 1317–41.

Fukao, K., T. Okubo, and R. M. Stern. 2003. An econometric analysis of trade diversion under NAFTA. *North American Journal of Economics and Finance* 14: 3–24.

Gehrels, F. 1957. Customs union from a single-country viewpoint. *Review of Economic Studies* 24 (1): 61–64.

Gilbert, J., R. Scollay, and B. Bora. 2001. Assessing regional trading arrangements in the Asia-Pacific. Policy Issues in International Trade and Commodities Study Series no. 15. Geneva: United Nations Conference on Trade and Development.

Greene, W. 2002. The behaviour of fixed effects estimator in non-linear models. New York University, Department of Economics, Stern School of Business. Mimeograph.

Haveman, J., and D. Hummels. 1998. Trade creation and trade diversion: New empirical results. *Journal of Transnational Management Development* 3 (2): 47–72.

Helpman, E. 1987. Imperfect competition and international trade: Evidence from fourteen industrial countries. *Journal of the Japanese and International Economies* 1 (1): 62–81.

Helpman, E., and P. Krugman. 1985. *Market structure and international trade.* Cambridge, MA: MIT Press.

Hertel, T., T. Walmsley, and K. Itakura. 2001. Dynamic effects of the "new age" free trade agreement between Japan and Singapore. *Journal of Economic Integration* 16 (4): 446–84.

Johnson, H. 1960. The economic theory of customs union. *Pakistan Economic Journal* 10 (1): 14–32.

Ju, J., and K. Krishna. 1998. Firm behaviour and market access in a free trade area with rules of origin. NBER Working Paper no. 6857. Cambridge, MA: National Bureau of Economic Research, December.

Krishna, K., and A. O. Krueger. 1995. Implementing free trade areas: Rules of origin and hidden protection. NBER Working Paper no. 4983. Cambridge, MA: National Bureau of Economic Research.

Krishna, P. 1998. Regionalism and multilateralism: A political economy approach. *Quarterly Journal of Economics* 113 (1): 227–51.

Krueger, A. 1999a. Free trade agreements as protectionist devices: Rules of origin. In *Trade theory and econometrics: Essays in honour of John S. Chipman,* ed. R. M. James, C. M. James, and R. Raymond, 91–102. New York: Routledge.

———. 1999b. Trade creation and trade diversion under NAFTA. NBER Working Paper no. 7429. Cambridge, MA: National Bureau of Economic Research, December.

Krugman, P. 1993. Regionalism versus multilateralism: Analytical notes. In *New dimensions in regional integration,* ed. J. de Melo and A. Panagariya, 58–79. Cambridge, UK: Cambridge University Press.

Levy, P. 1997. A political-economic analysis of free-trade agreements. *American Economic Review* 87 (4): 506–19.

Li, Q. 2000. Institutional rules of regional trade blocs and their impact on international trade. In *The political consequences of regional trade blocks,* ed. R. Switky and B. Kerremans, 85–118. London: Ashgate.

Lipsey, R. 1957. Mr. Gehrels on customs unions. *Review of Economic Studies* 24 (2): 211–14.

———. 1958. *The theory of customs unions: A general equilibrium analysis.* PhD diss., University of London.

Markusen, J. R. 1983. Factor movements and commodity trade as complements. *Journal of International Economics* 14 (3–4): 341–56.

Matyas, L. 1997. Proper econometric specification of the gravity model. *World Economy* 21 (3): 363–68.

———. 1998. The gravity model: Some econometric consideration. *World Economy* 20 (3): 397–401.

McLaren, J. 2002. A theory of insidious regionalism. *Quarterly Journal of Economics* 117 (2): 571–608.

Michaely, M. 1976. The assumptions of Jacob Viner's theory of customs unions. *Journal of International Economics* 6 (1): 75–93.

Mundell, R. 1964. Tariff preferences and the terms of trade. *Manchester School of Economic and Social Studies* 32:1–13.

Panagariya, A. 1999. The regionalism debate: An overview. *World Economy* 22 (4): 477–511.

———. 2000. Preferential trade liberalization: The traditional theory and new developments. *Journal of Economic Literature* 38 (2): 287–331.

Panagariya, A., and R. Duttagupta. 2002. The "gains" from preferential trade liberalisation in the CGE models: Where do they come from? University of Maryland. Mimeograph. http://www.bsos.umd.edu/econ/panagariya/apecon/techpaper.htm.

Pomfret, R. 1997. The economics of regional trading arrangements. Oxford, UK: Clarendon Press.

Riezman, R. 1979. A 3 × 3 model of customs unions. *Journal of International Economics* 9 (3): 341–54.

Robinson, S., and K. Thierfelder. 2002. Trade liberalisation and regional integration: The search for large numbers. *Australian Journal of Agricultural and Resource Economics* 46 (4): 585–604.

Scollay, R., and J. Gilbert. 2000. Measuring the gains from APEC trade liberalisation: An overview of CGE assessments. *World Economy* 23 (3): 175–97.

Soloaga, I., and L. A. Winters. 2001. Regionalism in the nineties: What effect on trade? *North American Journal of Economics and Finance* 12 (1): 1–29.

Viner, J. 1950. *The customs union issue.* New York: Carnegie Endowment for International Peace.

Winters, L. 1997. Assessing regional integration arrangements. Washington, DC: World Bank, Development Research Group.

World Bank. 2000. *Trade blocs.* Washington, DC: World Bank.

World Trade Flows (WTF). 1997. *World trade flows database 1970–1992.* Cambridge, MA: National Bureau of Economic Research.

———. 2000. *World trade flows 1980–1997* database. Davis: Institute of Governmental Affairs, University of California.

World Trade Organization (WTO). 1995. *Regional trading arrangements and the world trading system.* Geneva: WTO.

———. 2002. Work of the Committee on Regional Trade Agreements. http://www.wto.org/english/tratop_e/region_e/regcom_e.htm.

Zissimos, B., and D. Vines. 2000. Is the WTO's Article XXIV a free trade barrier? CSGR Working Paper no. 49/00. Warwick, UK: Centre for the Study of Globalisation and Regionalisation, University of Warwick.

Comment   Bih Jane Liu

The number of preferential trading arrangements (PTAs) has grown dramatically over the last decade or so. How PTAs affect the trade and investment among member countries and between member and nonmember countries thus becomes a very important issue nowadays. This paper, focus-

Bih Jane Liu is professor of economics at National Taiwan University.

ing on this important issue, is very comprehensive and well written. It not only surveys the related theoretical and empirical literature thoroughly, but it also has done a great job in collecting the data and doing the econometric analysis. By using a gravity model to examine eighteen PTAs over the period of 1970–1997, this paper shows that most of the PTAs, including the European Union (EU), the North American Free Trade Agreement (NAFTA), and the Southern Common Market (MERCOSUR), have diverted more trade from nonmember countries than they have created among member countries. In addition, it shows that for most of the agreements where nontrade provisions have affected foreign direct investment (FDI), the PTAs effects have been investment creation rather than diversion.

Although I agree with most of the points that the authors made in this paper, as a discussant I would like to raise some questions.

The first question is related to model specification. This paper uses PTA variables and many country-specific variables to capture the trade relationship among countries. Thus the usual problem of omitted-variable bias in gravity models could be avoided to a certain degree. However, the complicated heterogeneity relationship among member countries and between member and nonmember countries still could not be completely captured by these two kinds of variables, for example, if there are three countries, A, B, and C, in the same trading bloc. A and B are natural partners, but A and C are not. Apparently, the trade creation and diversion effects between A and B would be different from that between A and C. In this case the PTA variables could not be used to differentiate the different trade effect between A and B and A and C. The question then is whether the features of heterogeneity can be captured by the variables such as GDP, real exchange rate, distance, country dummies, linguistic similarity, and so on? To me, the answer seems unclear. Moreover, to derive trade creation or trade diversion effects, the inclusion of PTA dummies in the gravity equation may not be sufficient. This is because PTA dummies reveal little about cost of production across different countries. Some variables related to wage or cost of production and/or the cross terms of these variables with PTA dummies may be needed to understand whether trade from lower-cost PTA members can be created and whether trade is diverted from lower-cost PTA nonmembers to higher-cost PTA members after a trading bloc is formed.

The second question has something to do with the endogeneity problem. We all know that GDP, GDP per capita, and the real exchange rate are endogenous variables that should be determined simultaneously with exports (the dependent variable) within the model. However, in this paper these endogenous variables are used as the right-hand-side variables in the gravity equation (1). As a result, the error term in equation (1) will be correlated with them, and hence the estimators will be biased. To avoid the endogeneity problem, I would suggest that the authors use lag variables or to run simultaneous equations.

This paper utilizes the panel data for the period of 1970–1997 to examine eighteen PTAs. While it achieves maximum degree of freedom, I am wondering whether the results thus obtained will suffer from subsample instability and heteroskedasticity. This is because the relationship between exports and country-specific factors may vary across different trading blocs. A sensitivity analysis may serve to make sure that the results are robust even for subsamples or subperiod samples.

Past studies showed that most PTAs are trade creating in net terms. By contrast, the results from this paper suggest that most PTAs do not create additional trade, either for members or for nonmembers of the agreements. I suspect that it has something to do with the induced investment effect. If PTAs have significant investment creation effect as shown in this paper, then this new investment may be either a substitute for or a complement of trade and will hence affect trade flows indirectly. In the case where investment creation does substitute for intraregional trade, we may observe negative trade creation as shown in this paper. To show whether negative trade effect is indeed caused by investment, I would suggest that the authors run trade and investment equations simultaneously with each variable appearing in the other equation. By doing so, we are able to better understand the interrelationship between trade and investment under PTAs.

One last point is that the wave of globalization together with a reduction in transport costs and an improvement in communication and technologies all make outward direct investment and foreign outsourcing become more prevalent in the 1990s. This in turn changes the nature of international trade from trade in final goods to trade in intermediate inputs. Because the empirical data in this paper cover the time period from 1970 through 1997, how this change in trade structure should be taken into account in the study of the impacts of PTAs will also deserve special attention.

Comment   Erlinda Medalla

First of all, let me say that I really enjoyed reading Philippa Dee and Jyothi Gali's paper. The primary reason I chose to discuss this paper is because I wanted to get reacquainted with the topic and get on track with the literature. And on this, the paper does an excellent job.

The paper is very provocative.

I cannot fault the logic (how arguments are developed).

Erlinda Medalla is a senior research fellow of the Philippine Institute for Development Studies.

But to me, there are some jarring notes and conclusions. And I admit there is still a lot I don't completely understand.

My comments come from these two reactions I had, which could be interrelated. Conclusions jar in my mind because I probably did not completely understand the matter.

Hopefully, my comments will help the paper become more understandable to people less technical in orientation and to people who have not done work and are not familiar with the intricacies of the topic.

The Member Liberalization Index

I am not clear on how is it actually estimated. My understanding is that it reflects the coverage of the provisions of the preferential trading arrangement (PTA) (whether or not they are used).

The paper mentions that a high index indicates that the PTA is more liberal to members in the particular area covered by the provisions of the PTA. In nonmerchandise trade, if this is among the provisions of the PTA and its share in total trade is x percent, then I take it that this is the value it takes. (If this is close enough, then my subsequent reading and understanding of the analysis would not be too erroneous.) Nonetheless, I think the authors need to explain this further.

The Gravity Model

I appreciate the distinction made between ex ante CGE analysis and the ex post technique of the gravity model. I think both have merits.

The merit of the gravity model, as mentioned, is that it is ex post and examines actual PTA. The shortcoming is that it only looks at links between the PTA formation and trade outcomes.

My own bias is that simply looking at trade outcomes is very limiting. Judging the benefits merely based on trade effects (whether trade creating or trade diverting) is not enough. As the paper says, there is weak linkage between trade and welfare. And this is precisely what we want to look at when we want to assess if a PTA is beneficial or not.

This is one of the jarring notes I was referring to earlier. Looking at trade diversion and trade creation is based mainly on a static model explained in the appendix. It is not only static, it is also just a (very) partial analysis.

When domestic production contracts because of the PTA, the gain is not only the reduction in the former deadweight loss. The additional gain is the resources this releases (maybe not all because of sunk costs) to relatively more profitable activities. The resulting less-distorted relative prices (as, in effect, the relative prices facing producers with the higher tariff for all trading partners result in higher relative domestic prices of importables) with PTA would mean a better resource allocation, at least from the point of view of the individual member country.

Nonetheless, it is always good to look at a number of approaches but keep in mind their particular limitations.

The Specifications of the Model

It was a bit difficult to figure out. I had to read it several times to understand why it is that the dependent variable is exports from country i to j. Was there another specification that uses imports of country i from country j? If not, I thought the authors also wanted to measure import diversion? Or are they all mixed together (y is really either export or import). Then I figure that we are dealing with a comprehensive set of data, such that a bilateral export to one is bilateral imports of another? It would help if there is more explanation of this at the outset.

In the explanatory variables, why use the sum of GDP and then the absolute difference rather than use directly separate GDPs of the partner countries? Connected to this, should there be an overall activity level variable, for example, world GDP (or GDP of the ROW)?

The three dummy variables used for each PTA have not been easy to follow and visualize because of the large sample of countries. The first dummy is easier to understand. It takes on the value of the MLI for exports where the bilateral flow is between countries with a PTA, say for exports from Australia to New Zealand, with Closer Economic Relations (CER). Hence, CER1 is the corresponding MLI. In addition, I understand CER2 and CER3 are zero. (Am I right?) For exports involving two countries outside this particular PTA (say exports from Thailand to the Philippines, not members of CER), the three dummies are zero (all CER dummies are zero), but if they have their own PTA (e.g., AFTA), there needs to be an additional three dummies, the first of which will be MLI (AFTA1 dummy value is MLI). Furthermore, for exports from Australia (of CER) to, say, Thailand (of AFTA), then AFTA2 is MLI related to AFTA. And finally, for exports from Thailand to Australia, CER3 is MLI related to CER. (Did I understand it correctly?) This is really complicated, and I congratulate the effort there must have been in dealing with such a huge amount of observations involving numerous variables.

I needed to understand this clearly in order to understand the meaning of the coefficients of the three dummies and why they capture intrabloc trade and import and export diversion, which brings me to my next comment. What is the impact of using MLI rather than zeroes and ones? And in separating exports and imports, does this not introduce an upward bias on trade diversion? (Because standard deviation for the sum adds up.) In the first place, is this the interpretation, simply summing up the coefficients to get the net trade effects? I deduced this from the explanation in the case of Frankel (1997), who uses only two dummies. Is my interpretation correct?

The paper made, toward the end, a qualification on the results about the intra-PTA effect having large standard error, compared to the extra-PTA effect, which is estimated more accurately. Doesn't this pose a serious limitation? How robust will the estimate be on the net?

Finally, the paper later mentioned (when discussing investments) that because of model convergence problems, the effects of new age provisions on exports to and imports from nonmembers could not be analyzed separately. Does the author have some a priori notions about the direction of effects?

On Investments

I have similar misgivings on this as in the previous analysis on trade outcomes.

Instead of exports, it uses stock of outward investment. Isn't flow the more appropriate variable? (I thought flow is easier to measure than stock.) Accepting this, why outward, not inward, FDI? I would think that for a member country, this is what is important to find out. Again, I may just be missing something here. They are just two sides of the same coin. But using inward FDI would have had more intuitive appeal. It would help if the authors explain why (even in a footnote), as it was not readily obvious to me and possibly to other readers as well (especially nontechnical ones who I think this paper is important to reach).

I tend to share Ethier's (2001) arguments that there is likely "beachhead" response from nonmember countries on FDI. I also agree that some investments could be lost from tariff-jumping-motivated investments. However, in this age of reduced trade barriers, how much of these are left?

Finally, whether there is investment diversion or not, I think the receiving country would always gain (although there may be a reduction in global welfare).

On the whole, I would like to congratulate the authors for such an excellent paper. I learned a lot from it, and it has inspired me to study it more. It was well thought out and well written.

References

Ethier, W. 2001. The new regionalism in the Americas: A theoretical framework. *North American Journal of Economics and Finance* 12 (2): 159–72.
Frankel, J. 1997. *Regional trading blocs in the world economic system.* Washington, DC: Institute for International Economics.

The Formation of International Production and Distribution Networks in East Asia

Mitsuyo Ando and Fukunari Kimura

6.1 Introduction

In our half-a-century experience in development studies, we learn that accomplishing long-sustained growth and continuous poverty reduction is not an easy task at all. In this regard, it is worth noting that the East Asian region has continued to serve as the world's growth center for decades. It is thus natural for researchers to investigate secrets of the East Asian performance and seek its relevance to less-developed countries (LCDs) in other parts of the world. In the study on the "East Asian Miracle" conducted in the early 1990s, the World Bank (1993) emphasized the existence of well-managed macroeconomic fundamentals and wisely designed microeconomic policies. On the top of it, the East Asian economies obtained another virtue in the last decade, that is, the formation of international production/distribution networks.

The international production/distribution networks consist of vertical production chains extended across the countries in the region as well as distribution networks throughout the world. The major players are corporate firms belonging to the machinery industries, including general machinery, electrical machinery, transport equipment, and precision machinery though some firms in other industries, such as textiles and garment, also develop the

Mitsuyo Ando is assistant professor of economics at Hitotsubashi University, and Fukunari Kimura is professor of economics at Keio University.

We thank all the conference participants for useful comments and great encouragement. The MITI (METI) database was prepared and analyzed in cooperation with the Applied Research Institute, Inc. and the Research and Statistics Department, the Minister's Secretariat, the Ministry of International Trade and Industry (currently the Ministry of Economy, Trade, and Industry), and the Government of Japan. The opinions expressed in this paper, though, are those of the authors.

networks. While the formation of similar production networks is observed between the United States and Mexico and between Germany and Hungary/ Czech Republic, the networks in East Asia are distinctive at least at this moment in time in the following characteristics: first, they have already become a substantial component of each country's economy in the region. Each country's manufacturing activities and international trade cannot be discussed without the networks anymore. Second, the networks involve a large number of countries at different income levels. Cross-country differences in factor prices and other location advantages seem to be effectively utilized in the formation of vertical production chains. Third, the networks include both intrafirm and arm's-length relationships, partially across different firm nationalities. Multinational enterprises (MNEs) as well as indigenous firms in each country are forming sophisticated interfirm relationships.

The formation of international production and distribution networks in East Asia was initiated by drastic changes in development strategies of each country. In the mid-1980s and the early 1990s, the East Asian developing economies started applying new development strategies in which the benefit from hosting foreign direct investment (FDI) is aggressively explored. The new development strategies do emphasize the utilization of market forces, but they are not simple laissez-faire policies; rather, they pursue new roles of government involvement in the process of development. East Asia is presenting a model of new development strategies in the globalization era.

The development of international production and distribution networks in East Asia has also provided substantial impact on our academic thought on trade and FDI patterns. The traditional comparative advantage theory still has a certain explanatory power in the interpretation of across-industry location choices, based on international differences in technological level and factor prices. The enhanced importance of the trade in intermediate goods as well as the industrial clustering, however, has stimulated the development of new theoretical thoughts in international trade theory, particularly in the literature of fragmentation theory and agglomeration theory. In addition, the sophisticated pattern of intrafirm corporate structure and interfirm relationship developed in East Asia has inspired research to incorporate the analysis of corporate behavior into international trade theory beyond the traditional approach of trade and FDI.

The purpose of this paper is to prove the importance of international production and distribution networks in East Asia and confirm their distinctive characteristics. Although it is difficult to directly observe the detailed mechanics of the networks with comprehensive statistics, there exist various side-evidences as well as theoretical discussions reinforcing the argument. The next section briefly reviews drastic changes in policy framework, which is a necessary condition for the formational of international production and distribution networks, observed in the Southeast Asian countries and China in the latter half of the 1980s and the early 1990s. Section 6.3 sketches the current status of theoretical thoughts explaining the mechanics of international production and distribution networks. Then, the paper turns to statistical analysis on the characteristics of the networks in East Asia. Section 6.4 presents overall trade patterns of major East Asian countries and argues the significance of trade in machinery goods, particularly machinery parts and components, on both the export and import sides. Section 6.5 utilizes the microdata of Japanese corporate firms and takes a closer look at the nature of networks in East Asia through the pattern of FDI. Section 6.6 quantifies the magnitude of economic activities of Japanese firms in different channels of transactions in terms of value added contents, based on the firm nationality approach proposed by Baldwin and Kimura (1998). Section 6.7 discusses policy implication of the networks, particularly in the context of formulating free trade agreements (FTAs), and the last section concludes the paper.

6.2   Drastic Changes in Development Strategies

Why has an extensive international production and distribution network been formulated in East Asia and not in other regions such as Latin America? One of the crucial factors is the set of policies implemented by the East Asian developing economies from the mid-1980s and the early 1990s.[1]

Most of the East Asian economies have traditionally applied a dual-track approach, that is, an approach trying to foster both import-substituting industries and export-oriented industries at the same time. There was, however, an important difference between forerunners (i.e., Japan, Korea, and Taiwan) and latecomers (i.e., the Southeast Asian countries and China); the latter actively utilized incoming FDI not only in export-oriented industries but also in some major import-substituting industries, such as automobiles, domestic electric appliances, pharmaceuticals, food processing, and others.

While the latecomer countries have maintained the dual-track approach throughout their path of industrialization, they have changed the weights between import-substituting industries and export-oriented industries over time. From the 1970s to the mid-1980s, these countries introduced selective FDI primarily in import-substituting industries. At that time, potentially competing domestic industries were insulated by policies that limit the activities of foreign companies only in geographically segregated places such as export-processing zones though FDI for export promotion was indeed invited. From the mid-1980s in Malaysia and Thailand and

---

1. Kimura (2003) discusses new development strategies applied by the East Asian economies more in detail. Pangestu (2003) provides the summarized information on evolution in industrial policies in East Asia in the 1950s–1990s as well as policies and measures for promoting exports in Asia.

from the early 1990s in the Philippines, Indonesia, and China, however, they began to switch their FDI hosting policy from a selective-acceptance policy to a basically accept-everybody policy. They started trying to host as many foreign companies as possible and formulate industrial clusters while still keeping trade protection for import-substituting industries.

The dual-trade approach requires a complicated policy package. What a country has to do to invite export-oriented foreign companies is simple though difficult to carry out; it must provide the world's-best or second-best location advantages for incoming investors. Trade protection, of course, negatively affects location advantages. So as to partially neutralize negative effects of import-substituting industry protection, the Southeast Asian countries have introduced a duty-drawback system, that is, the system of refunds of duties and indirect taxes on imported inputs in export production. Besides, various types of FDI facilitation measures are crucial to attract foreign companies. In particular, aggressive policy of inviting foreign small and medium enterprises (SMEs) effectively works in the formation of industrial clusters. These countries have concentrated their public resources on the development of economic infrastructure, including roads, ports, electricity and water supply, telecommunications, and industrial estate services. At the same time, they have improved the services of FDI-hosting agencies, ending up with yielding considerable facilitation.

It does not mean that these countries give up fostering local indigenous firms. Instead of hastily providing protection for immature local entrepreneurs, they set a short-term priority on quickly building up a critical mass of agglomeration and hooking their economies up to international production and distribution networks by aggressively inviting foreign companies. The focus of local industry promotion is shifted to enhancing capability to penetrate into vertical production chains. Although inefficient import-substituting industries being left have to be cleaned up, new development strategies with aggressively utilizing incoming FDI bear fruit in the Southeast Asian countries and China. This sets a sharp contrast with LDCs in other parts of the world.

6.3   Supporting Economic Logic

What sort of economic logic explains the mechanics of international production and distribution networks? In the discussion on the international division of labor, the theory of comparative advantage based on the relative cost of production in autarky is still valid in a number of circumstances; technological gap and factor price differences explain location patterns of industries to some extent. In interpreting the mechanics of international production and distribution networks, however, at least three new lines of thought must be incorporated into our analytical framework.

The first line of thought is the fragmentation theory. It is a powerful tool when we analyze patterns of vertical FDI going to LDCs to formulate vertical production links or cross-border production sharing systems.[2] The traditional international trade theory primarily explains industry-wise location patterns. The patterns often observed in East Asia besides industry-wise location patterns, however, are the production-process-wise location patterns. A typical example of production-process-wise location patterns is found in semiconductor-related electronics industry. This industry as a whole is obviously capital-intensive or human capital-intensive, but its production activities are finely segmented and located in various places. The fragmentation theory neatly presents the logic behind such a location pattern.

Deardorff (2001b, 121) defines fragmentation as "the splitting of a production process into two or more steps that can be undertaken in different locations but that lead to the same final product." Suppose that there is initially a big factory located in Japan taking care of all the production activities from upstream to downstream. If we carefully look at individual production blocks, however, we may find that some production blocks require close attention by technicians while others are purely labor-intensive. If we can separately locate each of the production blocks in an appropriate place, for instance, in Japan, Malaysia, and China, considering vertical production chains, we may save the total production cost, compared to the cost with production blocs put altogether in one place. Because the East Asian countries still have substantial differentials in labor costs, the concept of fragmentation across different cones formalized by Deardorff (2001a) seems to be particularly useful in understanding the nature of vertical production chains.

Fragmentation becomes economical when the cost of service links (SL) connecting production blocks (PB) is low enough. The SL cost includes transport costs, telecommunication costs, and various coordination costs between PBs. SL cost heavily depends on the nature of technology in each industry. Globalization, however, reduces SL cost in general and enables firms in many industries to fragment their PBs further to reduce the total production cost. Because SL cost tends to carry strong external economies of scale, the concentration of fragmented PBs is often observed. The forces of fragmentation and agglomeration sometimes work in the opposite direction, but globalization actually accelerates both at the same time, which results in a situation where some countries significantly enjoy the fruit of globalization while others do not.[3]

The second line of thought is the agglomeration theory. This is an extension of international trade theory with external economies of scale

2. As for the fragmentation theory, see Jones and Kierzkowski (1990), Arndt and Kierzkowski (2001), Deardorff (2001b), and Cheng and Kierzkowski (2001).

3. Where to locate fragmented production blocs also depends on the nature of the products. For instance, when parts and components are considerably standardized and the delivery timing is not too delicate, firms try to find suppliers of the cheapest products in the world. On the other hand, when parts and components are highly customized, and closer communication with suppliers is important, they would like to form industrial clusters.

while introducing the concept of "space" from city planning and other academic fields.[4] Although the microfoundation of spatial agglomeration has not been fully explored, the importance of agglomeration or industry clusters as a source of location advantage is increasingly recognized in both theoretical and empirical literature. Economies of scale or agglomeration effects do not necessarily depend on the initial condition under autarky; in an extreme case, a country may start having agglomeration purely by chance. In this sense, the source of gains of trade in the "new" international trade theory is logically different from those in the traditional theory of comparative advantage, and such nature of the "new" theory addresses the possibility of the new role of government. Among the factors that generate location advantages for MNEs to invest, agglomeration is one of the crucial elements, particularly in LDCs. Governments in East Asia are obviously conscious of the potential role of government in formulating agglomeration or industrial clusters.

The third line of thought is the internalization theory of corporate firms. A firm typically does not conduct everything from upstream to downstream. It sets its upstream-side boundary by purchasing materials or parts from other firms and determines its downstream-side boundary by selling their products to other firms or consumers. Such a boundary setting decision is here called an "internalization decision." In addition, a firm cuts its internalized activities into thin slices and places these slices at appropriate places. This is called a "location decision." A firm makes an internalization decision and a location decision at the same time, considering its own firm-specific assets such as technology and managerial know-how. Internalization may have different dimensions. For example, an internalization decision would be made across different functional activities such as financial management, personnel management, research and development (R&D) activities, parts procurement, sales activities, and others.

In East Asia, particularly in China, various kinds of internalization patterns with innovative interfirm relationships emerge in the effort of concentrating on core competences. Original equipment manufacturing (OEM) contracts, electronics manufacturing service (EMS) firms, and contractual/ordinary processing are such examples. Such sophistication is particularly salient in machinery industries. Technological progress in the line of developing "modules" accelerates the formation of sophisticated interfirm relationship. The international trade theory has not yet fully digested elements of ownership advantages and internalization advantages that Dunning's ownership, location, and internalization (OLI) theory presents.[5] However, the importance of internalization choices cannot be neg-

4. As for the agglomeration theory, see Krugman (1991, 1995) and Fujita, Krugman, and Venables (1999).
5. As for the OLI theory, see Dunning (1993). Kimura (2000, 2001) analyzes the microdata of Japanese manufacturing firms and claims that corporate structure and interfirm relationship are jointly chosen with the location of activities.

lected when the international division of labor is at issue. Fragmentation theory and agglomeration theory must be combined with the internalization theory of corporate firms.

6.4   Recent Trade Flows in East Asia

Now let us review the trade pattern of East Asia. It is a well-known fact that the East Asian economies have rapidly developed intraregional trade relationships since the early 1980s. The Ministry of Economy, Trade and Industry (METI; 2003) presents some basic figures. Intraregional trade of East Asia grew from US$104.3 billion in 1981 to US$333.1 billion in 1991 and then US$702.8 billion in 2001; that is, it increased by 3.2 times in 1981–1991 and 2.1 times in 1991–2001. Trade intensity indices among the East Asian economies also had an upward trend, suggesting the development of increasingly closer economic relationships.

Fukao, Ishido, and Ito (2003) decompose bilateral trade flows into one-way trade, vertical intraindustry trade (VIIT), and horizontal intraindustry trade (HIIT) and compare the trade pattern of East Asia with the one of Europe. They find that international trade in East Asia has still a substantial amount of one-way trade, but the share of VIIT rapidly increases. Ando (2004), on the other hand, decomposes overall trade flows in machinery industries for each East Asian economy into one-way trade, VIIT, and HIIT, based on international trade data at the Harmonized System (HS) six-digit level, in the 1990s. The results clearly present relative declines in one-way trade and drastic increases in VIIT for machinery trade, particularly for machinery parts and components trade, suggesting the development of vertical international production chains in the 1990s in East Asia.

In addition to these findings, we would like to claim that one of the most important changes in the trade pattern of the region is an explosive increase in trade in machinery goods, particularly trade in machinery parts and components for both exports and imports. Table 6.1 shows the values and shares of exports and imports of machinery goods and machinery parts and components[6] in major East Asian economies[7] in 1996 and 2000.[8]

---

6. See table 6A.1 for a definition of parts and components in our study.

7. Due to the lack of data available from the United Nation's (UN) data sources, table 6.1 and figure 6.1 do not include Taiwan, which has also played an important role in developing the networks in East Asia.

8. Although table 6.1 shows only machinery shares in 1996 and 2000, a comparison with the shares at the beginning of the 1990s makes clearer the trend of increase in machinery trade and machinery parts and components in the 1990s; shares of machinery goods and machinery parts and components in total exports, for instance, are respectively 1.8 percent and 0.7 percent for Indonesia, 23.6 percent and 14.9 percent for Thailand, 37.2 percent and 23.5 percent for Malaysia, 42.3 percent and 15.5 percent for Korea, 52.6 percent and 22.6 percent for Singapore, and 76.2 percent and 26.8 percent for Japan in 1990, 18.8 percent and 6.7 percent for China in 1992, and 37.0 percent and 16.1 percent for Hong Kong in 1993. See Ando (2004) for further discussion.

Table 6.1   Importance of machinery trade in the East Asian economies

	Japan				Thailand			
	Exports		Imports		Exports		Imports	
	1996	2000	1996	2000	1996	2000	1996	2000
Value								
Total (US$1,000)	410,944,244	479,244,574	349,185,062	379,661,760	55,672,988	68,780,636	72,311,216	61,445,996
Share of:								
Machinery goods in total	74.9	74.9	28.1	32.0	40.3	45.6	50.4	47.1
Parts and components in total	35.4	36.2	12.1	16.1	21.7	28.7	30.3	34.0
Parts and components in machinery goods	47.3	48.3	43.1	50.2	54.0	62.8	60.1	72.2

	Korea				Philippines			
	Exports		Imports		Exports		Imports	
	1996	2000	1996	2000	1996	2000	1996	2000
Value								
Total (US$1,000)	129,696,331	172,264,221	150,320,064	160,477,507	20,537,617	38,072,479	34,697,094	33,802,416
Share of:								
Machinery goods in total	54.2	59.6	40.9	41.4	58.7	77.4	53.8	54.1
Parts and components in total	24.1	29.0	20.7	26.5	46.5	60.9	35.7	43.4
Parts and components in machinery goods	44.5	48.7	50.6	64.0	79.1	78.7	66.4	80.2

	Hong Kong				Indonesia			
Value								
Total (US$1,000)	180,914,323	202,683,171	201,282,410	214,039,820	49,811,786	62,117,778	42,923,875	33,509,943
Share of:								
Machinery goods in total	38.8	45.5	41.7	47.6	10.7	18.1	42.2	28.7
Parts and components in total	19.5	27.0	20.2	28.7	4.4	9.3	21.7	15.7
Parts and components in machinery goods	50.4	59.4	48.5	60.2	41.8	51.2	51.4	54.6

	Singapore				China			
Value								
Total (US$1,000)	122,882,738	137,803,198	131,337,708	134,544,130	151,046,318	249,201,432	138,831,036	225,091,657
Share of:								
Machinery goods in total	70.4	71.8	63.0	65.3	26.6	36.2	42.5	44.3
Parts and components in total	36.8	45.7	39.0	46.0	10.0	15.3	19.2	28.1
Parts and components in machinery goods	52.3	63.7	62.0	70.4	37.4	42.3	45.3	63.5

	Malaysia			
Value				
Total (US$1,000)	78,308,476	98,224,808	77,901,213	81,287,187
Share of:				
Machinery goods in total	57.3	64.4	62.7	66.0
Parts and components in total	33.7	41.9	42.4	52.5
Parts and components in machinery goods	58.9	65.0	67.7	79.5

Source: Authors' calculation; based on PC-TAS (UN Comtrade only for Hong Kong's exports).

Machineries are here defined as HS 84-92; that is, they include general machinery, electric machinery, transport equipment, and precision machinery. To capture the features of the trade patterns in East Asia more vividly, figure 6.1 summarizes the shares of machinery goods and machinery parts and components in total exports and imports for economies in East Asia as well as other regions, such as North and South America and Europe in

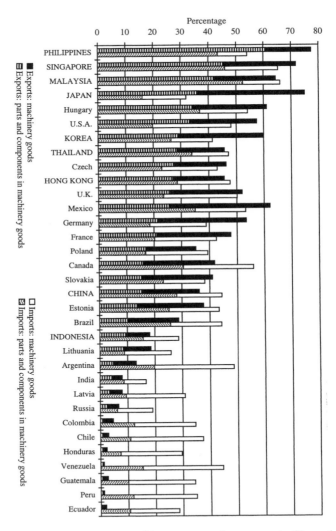

Fig. 6.1   Machinery goods and machinery parts and components: Shares in total exports and imports in 2000

Source: Authors' calculation, based on UN PC-TAS (UN COMTRADE for exports of Hong Kong and exports and imports for Russia and Slovakia.

2000. Note that figure 6.1 plots countries from the one with the highest share of machinery parts and components exports, aiming at addressing the relative significance of machinery parts and components trade among countries in various regions.

An astounding fact is that the shares of machineries in each East Asian country's total exports and imports are indeed very large. Except the cases of imports for Japan and China and exports and imports for Indonesia, the shares of machinery trade are as high as 40 percent or even higher, up to 77 percent, for both export and import sides. They imply how significant the machinery industries are in the East Asian economies. Furthermore, the shares of parts and components in machinery trade are also very high; they are 40 percent to 50 percent and even reach 80 percent in cases of the Southeast Asian countries, and the shares are further increasing even in the short period between 1996 and 2000. These suggest a large portion of back-and-forth transactions of intermediate goods in the international production and distribution networks in machinery industries, which are extended across a large number of countries at different income levels in the region.

In other regions, on the other hand, higher shares of machinery trade and those of machinery parts and components trade are observed only for some specific countries such as Mexico, the United States, Hungary, the Czech Republic, and Germany (figure 6.1). These suggest the existence of networks in machinery industries between the United States and Mexico and between Germany and some Central and Eastern European countries, but these networks are not extensively covering a number of countries. The fact that the shares of machinery exports and imports are indeed high but the share of machinery parts and components exports is not as high in Mexico would support the evidence where Mexico imports machinery parts and components from the United States, assembles them, and exports final goods back to the United States, rather than developing networks across neighboring countries.

Moreover, other countries, particularly the ones in Latin America, present much lower shares of machinery exports than countries in East Asia. At the same time, the shares of machinery exports are much lower than the shares of machinery imports in these countries. These suggest that, in these economies, machinery industries are not well developed yet, and their manufacturing activities are still of the import-substituting type.

Note that not all countries in East Asia are effectively connected with such networks at this moment. The Cambodia, Myanmar, Laos, and Vietnam (CMLV) countries have not been fully involved with the networks yet. These countries have substantially low wage levels but are not entirely successful in attracting labor-intensive production processes. This fact suggests that government policies to reduce service-link costs and encourage agglomeration are crucially important for a country to hook up to international production and distribution networks.

6.5   Evidence from the Microdata of Japanese Firms

Corporate firms in the forerunners of development in the region, Japan, Korea, and Taiwan, have had strong technological competitiveness in machinery manufacturing. Because machines are typically made of a large number of parts and components, the competitiveness in machines depends on both the quality and production cost of parts and components and the managerial ability of vertical production networks in which corporate firms in East Asia particularly have their strengths. When these firms became mature enough to compete in the international arena, and the Southeast Asian countries and China prepared for proper policy environment in the mid-1980s and the 1990s, the formation of international production and distribution networks was a natural consequence.

The networks consist of both intrafirm geographical extension and interfirm business relationships. Up to the 1980s, an important component of the Japanese economic system was the subcontracting system (*shitauke* in Japanese) or long-term relationships between large downstream assemblers and upstream SMEs.[9] However, the interfirm relationship of Japanese firms has drastically changed since Japanese firms started to actively conduct FDI in the mid-1980s.[10] It is often observed that both large assemblers and SMEs make FDIs together to form a certain size of agglomeration in Southeast Asia or China. Even in such cases, upstream-downstream relationships become more competitive, nonexclusive ones. With strict cost consideration, many Japanese firms are now open to extend their production chains to firms with other nationalities as far as the technological level meets.

Although it is very difficult to trace the nature of such corporate relationships by statistical figures, this section attempts to present some evidence of corporate firms' behavior to understand the mechanics of international production and distribution networks in East Asia by analyzing the firm-level microdata of Japanese corporate firms. Tables in this section are constructed from either of the two sets of microdata, both of which are conducted by the Ministry of International Trade and Industry (MITI), Government of Japan: (a) the fiscal year (F/Y) 1996 and F/Y 2001 Basic Survey of Business Structure and Activity and (b) the F/Y 1999 Survey (the twenty-seventh Basic Survey) of Overseas Business Activities of Japanese Companies. The first firm-level database provides detailed information on parent firms located in Japan and also the number, industry, and regional location of their foreign affiliates. In tables 6.2 to 6.5, constructed from this

9. As for the economic interpretation of the Japanese subcontracting system, see Kimura (2002).
10. At least in the latter half of the 1990s, we can statistically verify that intrafirm transactions of Japanese affiliates in East Asia are gradually substituted by arm's-length transactions. See Kimura and Ando (2004b) for further discussion.

database, foreign affiliates are defined as those with no less than 20 percent Japanese ownership. The second database presents information on the performance of foreign affiliates. In table 6.6, obtained from this database, foreign affiliates include both "affiliates abroad," with no less than 10 percent ownership by Japanese parent firms, and "affiliates of affiliates abroad" with no less than 50 percent ownership by "affiliates abroad" (both called "Japanese affiliates abroad" hereinafter). A more detailed explanation of these databases is given in appendix A.

Table 6.2 presents (a) the number of parent firms with foreign affiliates and the number of foreign affiliates; (b) the number of parent firms with affiliates in East Asia and the number of affiliates in East Asia; (c) the number of parent firms with affiliates in North America and the number of affiliates in North America; and (d) the number of parent firms with affiliates in Europe and the number of affiliates in Europe, by the industry of parent firms and by the industry of affiliates in 2000.[11] In 2000, 3,773 out of 27,655 firms located in Japan (in the data set) have a total of 18,943 foreign affiliates. Among them, 2,994 firms have 10,224 affiliates in East Asia. That is, as many as 80 percent of the Japanese firms going abroad have at least one affiliate in East Asia, and 54 percent of the foreign affiliates of Japanese firms are located in East Asia.

Japanese manufacturing parent firms, particularly machinery parent firms, are active investors in East Asia; close to 70 percent of the Japanese parent firms with affiliates in East Asia are in the manufacturing sector (industries 120 to 320) and half of them are in the machinery sector (290 to 320). The pattern observed for affiliates in East Asia by the industry of affiliates also reveals how dominant manufacturing activities are in East Asia, which is clearly different from the patterns for affiliates in North America or Europe. In East Asia, 60 percent of the affiliates in the region are manufacturing, regardless of the industries of their parent firms, while 38 percent of the affiliates in North America and 31 percent of the affiliates in Europe are.[12] The number of affiliates actually increased in the five years from 1995 to 2000, from 9,132 to 10,224 in East Asia, while the numbers decreased from 3,928 to 3,499 in North America and from 3,019 to 2,913 in Europe. Manufacturing activities are dominant and have been intensified in East Asia in terms of both Japanese parent firms and their affiliates.

Japanese SMEs with regular workers of less than 300 have greatly contributed to such expansion of manufacturing activities in East Asia by Japanese firms. Table 6.3 presents the number of Japanese parent firms with affiliates in East Asia, North America, and Europe in 2000 by the size of parent firms and by the number of affiliates. The table shows that more

---

11. See table 6A.2 for industry classification.
12. See Kimura and Ando (2003) for a comparative study between Latin America and East Asia, based on the microdata of Japanese corporate firms.

Table 6.2   Japanese parent firms and foreign affiliates by industry, 2000 F/Y

A. Parent firms with foreign affiliates

Industry	By industry of parent firm				By industry of affiliate	
	No. of parent firms	%	No. of affiliates	%	No. of affiliates	%
Manufacturing sector						
Nonmachinery sectors 120–280, 340	1,259	33.4	4,779	25.2	4,427	23.4
Machinery sectors						
290	378	10.0	1,821	9.6	961	5.1
300	489	13.0	2,608	13.8	2,014	10.7
310	283	7.5	1,526	8.1	1,168	6.2
320	96	2.5	426	2.2	292	1.5
Sub total	2,505	66.4	11,160	58.9	8,872	46.8
Nonmanufacturing sector						
480	864	22.9	6,460	34.1	5,790	30.6
Others	404	10.7	1,323	7.0	4,281	22.6
Subtotal	1,268	33.6	7,783	41.1	10,071	53.2
Total	3,773	100.0	18,943	100.0	18,943	100.0

B. Parent firms with affiliates in East Asia

Industry	By industry of parent firm				By industry of affiliate	
	No. of parent firms	%	No. of affiliates	%	No. of affiliates	%
Manufacturing sector						
Nonmachinery sectors 120–280, 340	1,038	34.7	2,910	28.5	3,198	31.3
Machinery sectors						
290	286	9.6	810	7.9	543	5.3
300	429	14.3	1,598	15.6	1,475	14.4
310	222	7.4	752	7.4	664	6.5
320	75	2.5	226	2.2	202	2.0
Subtotal	2,050	68.5	6,296	61.6	6,082	59.5
Nonmanufacturing sector						
480	697	23.3	3,350	32.8	2,627	25.7
Others	247	8.3	578	5.7	1,515	14.8
Subtotal	944	31.5	3,928	38.4	4,142	40.5
Total	2,994	100.0	10,224	100.0	10,224	100.0

C. Parent firms with affiliates in North America

Industry	By industry of parent firm				By industry of affiliate	
	No. of parent firms	%	No. of affiliates	%	No. of affiliates	%
Manufacturing sector						
Nonmachinery sectors 120–280, 340	460	28.9	843	24.1	592	16.9
Machinery sectors						
290	205	12.9	411	11.7	187	5.3
300	215	13.5	434	12.4	223	6.4
310	178	11.2	383	10.9	291	8.3
320	47	3.0	79	2.3	41	1.2
Subtotal	1,105	69.4	2,150	61.4	1,334	38.1
Nonmanufacturing sector						
480	340	21.4	1,085	31.0	1,179	33.7
Others	147	9.2	264	7.5	986	28.2
Subtotal	487	30.6	1,349	38.6	2,165	61.9
Total	1,592	100.0	3,499	100.0	3,499	100.0

D. Parent firms with affiliates in Europe

Industry	By industry of parent firm				By industry of affiliate	
	No. of parent firms	%	No. of affiliates	%	No. of affiliates	%
Manufacturing sector						
Nonmachinery sectors 120–280, 340	251	27.5	647	22.2	362	12.4
Machinery sectors						
290	130	14.2	468	16.1	157	5.4
300	148	16.2	436	15.0	214	7.3
310	87	9.5	256	8.8	132	4.5
320	34	3.7	89	3.1	36	1.2
Subtotal	650	71.1	1,896	65.1	901	30.9
Nonmanufacturing sector						
480	193	21.1	781	29.9	1,308	44.9
Others	71	7.8	146	5.0	704	24.2
Subtotal	264	28.9	1,017	34.9	2,012	69.1
Total	914	100.0	2,913	100.0	2,913	100.0

Source: MITI database.

Notes: Others includes industries "050," "540," and "other." Number of affiliates for the cases (A), (B), (C), and (D) are the (A) number of foreign affiliates, (B) number of affiliates in

Table 6.3 Foreign affiliate ownership patterns of Japanese parent firms, 2000 F/Y (number of parent firms)

Number of regular workers of parent firm	Number of affiliates											Total	%
	1	2	3	4	5	6	7	8	9	10	More		
In East Asia													
50 to 99	301	67	25	12	1	2	1				1	410	13.7
100 to 199	413	101	34	23	7	1	2		2			583	19.5
200 to 299	196	92	30	12	8	10	3	2	1		1	355	11.9
300 to 499	242	99	36	28	18	8	6	4	2		4	447	14.9
500 to 999	209	117	65	42	27	20	5	2	4	2	10	503	16.8
1,000 or more	136	107	77	54	55	45	27	38	16	19	122	696	23.2
Total	1,497	583	267	171	116	86	44	46	25	21	138	2,994	100.0
In North America													
50 to 99	90	13	2							1		106	6.7
100 to 199	185	14	2	1			1					203	12.8
200 to 299	129	18	2									149	9.4
300 to 499	183	30	10	2	1	2			1			229	14.4
500 to 999	210	58	20	6	3	1	1	2			2	303	19.0
1,000 or more	271	126	69	39	28	17	10	7	7	1	27	602	37.8
Total	1,068	259	105	48	32	20	12	9	8	2	29	1,592	100.0
In Europe													
50 to 99	26	2										29	3.2
100 to 199	58	8	2	1								69	7.5
200 to 299	43	11	2	1								56	6.1
300 to 499	84	21	8	3	1	3						120	13.1
500 to 999	113	24	16	4	2	2		1	1	1	3	167	18.3
1,000 or more	178	93	55	37	17	18	14	8	10	9	34	473	51.8
Total	502	159	83	46	20	23	14	9	11	10	37	914	100.0

Source: MITI database.

than 40 percent of the Japanese firms going to East Asia are SMEs, while the shares are much lower in North America and Europe. Furthermore, the fact that a considerable number of firms, including SMEs, have plural affiliates in East Asia also supports that Japanese SMEs are actively involved in manufacturing activities in the region. Such active FDI by Japanese SMEs in East Asia have contributed to forming a critical mass of industrial clusters.

As suggested by table 6.2, Japanese parent firms do not necessarily establish affiliates in their own industries where they have main activities.[13] In general, parent firms have various activities across industries and establish foreign affiliates in order to conduct a subset of those activities. Table 6.4 provides the detailed information on sector switching between parent firms and their affiliates in East Asia; panel A of table 6.4 includes all sized Japanese firms with affiliates and panel B of table 6.4 focuses on SMEs. The rows denote the industry of parent firms while the columns denote the industry of foreign affiliates. Thus, diagonal cells of the tables indicate the number of non-sector-switching affiliates while off-diagonal cells denote the number of sector-switching affiliates.

In East Asia, 75 percent of the affiliates owned by all sized manufacturing parent firms are in the manufacturing sector.[14] Among them, we observe many sector-switching manufacturing affiliates with manufacturing parent firms (in nondiagonal cells for industries 120 to 340 in both rows and columns), in particular, sector-switching machinery affiliates with manufacturing parent firms (in nondiagonal cells for industries 120 to 340 in rows and industries 290 to 320 in columns). In addition, even manufacturing SMEs have sector-switching manufacturing affiliates, particularly sector-switching machinery affiliates in East Asia, which is not often observed in North America or Europe. Such behavior is typical in manufacturing activities aimed at supplying intermediate goods for other firms or for their own affiliates. It implies that Japanese firms have played an important role in developing vertical production networks in the region.[15]

Moreover, manufacturing parent firms also have nonmanufacturing affiliates, particularly in the wholesale trade sector. Sector-switching nonmanufacturing affiliates with manufacturing parent firms (in cells for in-

---

13. A firm often has various activities at the same time. The industrial classification of a firm located in Japan is determined by the largest activities the concerned firm conducts in terms of the value of sales.

14. In the case of manufacturing SMEs, the share of manufacturing affiliates is much higher; as many as 87 percent of their affiliates are manufacturing.

15. As discussed in footnote 13, while parent firms have in general various activities across sectors, foreign affiliates often conduct a narrower range of activities. What we claim here is that foreign affiliates are more likely to be involved in activities to participate in the production and distribution networks in East Asia even if such activities are not the main activities of parent firms, and thus many cases of sector-switching machinery affiliates (with parent firms mainly involved in other sectors than machinery sectors) can be observed.

Table 6.4   Sector switching between parent firms and their affiliates in East Asia

A. Industries of Japanese parent firms and affiliates in East Asia, 2000 FIY (number of affiliates)

Industry of parent firm	\ Industry of affiliate in East Asia 050	120	130	140	150	160	170	180	190	200	210	220	230	240	250	260	270	280	290	300	310	320	340	480	540	Other	Total
050	2																									1	3
120		145	1							2														20	3	12	183
130		5	28							12														19	1	9	74
140				70	7			2															1	10	1	5	96
150					73	1			2															12	1	7	96
160						14	1	2																		1	18
170							25														1			8	1	1	36
180								45															1	5	1	4	56
190									63	3														9	1	5	81
200	1	9	2	43	4	2		1		520	3	15	3		4	4	4	7	1	8	7	3	6	174	5	41	867
210											2	4								1			10	9	4	6	36
220										7		184	6		1		2			8			5	33	1	9	254
230										1		3	89					1					3	15	5	12	128
240														6												1	7
250	2									4					87	1	1	7	1	3	4	4		21	12	12	159
260	3														1	51	3	10	2	8	4			7		26	115
270	3									1		2			1		161	14	3	30	14		2	30	1	20	282
280	1	1				2			1			4	1		2		14	161	3	27	5	1		34		20	277
290		4								10		4			1	8	3	15	362	65	20	1	15	214	1	87	810
300				2	2		1		1	8		8			3	1	30	27	79	1009	25	14	9	304	13	62	1598
310							1					2			2	5	14		22	25	569	17	3	59	5	28	752
320										2		1			3		10	1	6	18	17	131	3	22	2	9	226
340																				14		6	66	48	6	5	145
480	9	115	11	83	157	13	8	14	9	174	11	60	22	3	70	47	32	63	39	266	34	22	56	1516	80	468	3350
540	1	3	1		12					3	2								12	3				12	100	54	205
Other		2	2		3	5				3					2		3	2	12	4	3			11	6	312	370
Total	22	284	43	208	258	38	37	63	80	709	17	313	121	11	179	113	222	303	543	1475	664	202	199	2627	256	1237	10224

(continued)

Table 6.4 (continued)

B. Industries of Japanese parent SMEs and affiliates in East Asia, 2000 FIY (number of affiliates)

Industry of parent firm	\	\	\	\	\	\	\	\	\	\	\	\	\	\	\	\	\	\	\	\	\	\	\	\	\	\	\
	050	120	130	140	150	160	170	180	190	200	210	220	230	240	250	260	270	280	290	300	310	320	340	480	540	Other	Total
050	2																										2
120		41								1														4		3	49
130			2																								2
140				29	2																			6			37
150				4	43				2															5	1		55
160						7	1																1				9
170						2	15																1	5			23
180								12											1					5			18
190									18										1				5	4	4		32
200										80	1	1			1		1	6	2			1		8	2	1	104
210											1													3			4
220										2		72	2				1	1	2	3	1	7		4			95
230													22											9	2		25
240														6													7
250															23			1	1				2				30
260																12		1	1		1			2			18
270																	58	1	1	2							65
280		2							1			4			1	1		72	4				7				91
290				1											1	1	1	8	109	10	4	4	7	14	3	7	179
300				1								5	3				2	5	1	232	3		5	40	3	6	303
310												1			2	1		1	3	3	45			10		1	61
320				1																		34	3	10			47
340																				1			24	18			41
480	1	22	1	18	57	4	3	5	8	23	3	24	9	2	8	2	14	17	14	40	10	10	18	401	17	43	774
540	1	1		1														1	3	3	3		1	4	9	7	31
Other										2										1	3			2	1	50	63
Total	4	66	3	56	102	13	19	17	31	108	5	117	33	10	37	15	78	114	140	301	65	56	69	545	35	126	2165

Source: MITI database.

dustries 120 to 340 in rows and industries 050, 480, and 540 and "others" in columns) make up 25 percent of the affiliates owned by all sized manufacturing parent firms and 13 percent of the affiliates owned by manufacturing SMEs, suggesting that another strategy in East Asia is to establish global production and distribution networks by internalizing wholesale trade activities. Note that these ratios are much smaller than in North America (49 percent for all sized firms and 48 percent for SMEs) and Europe (60 percent and 51 percent).

Before moving to the performance of Japanese affiliates abroad, let us formally analyze the characteristics of Japanese parent firms investing in East Asia. Panel A of table 6.5 reports the results of logit regression analysis for Japanese parent firms in all sectors and panel B of table 6.5 reports the results of Japanese manufacturing parent firms. The dependent variable for regression No. 1 in both tables is whether a firm has foreign affiliate(s) or not. Similarly, the dependent variable for regressions (3), (4), and (5) is whether a firm has affiliate(s) in East Asia or North America or Europe. The independent variables are the number of regular workers (in log), tangible assets per regular workers, foreign sales, research and development (R&D) expenditure, and advertisement expenditure.[16] For the whole samples, firms with foreign affiliates are likely to have large employment size, capital-intensive technology, large foreign sales, and large R&D expenditure. The coefficients for both the firms' size and R&D expenditure in the case of affiliates in East Asia are much smaller than those in the case of North America and Europe. It can be concluded that firms going to East Asia are relatively small as we have descriptively discussed, and thus less R&D-intensive, compared with firms going to North America or Europe.[17]

Table 6.6, in turn, focuses on the performance of Japanese affiliates in East Asia, North America, and Europe. The table presents (a) the destination of sales and (b) the origin of purchases by Japanese affiliates in East Asia. Most of the goods and services produced by Japanese affiliates in East Asia go to the local market, to Japan, or to other East Asian countries: 49.6 percent for local, 21.9 percent for Japan, and 21.2 percent for countries within the region except local and Japan.[18] By-origin purchases by Japanese affiliates in East Asia also show that they purchase most goods and services from the local market (41.1 percent) or import them from Japan (33.4 percent) or from other East Asian countries (20.7 percent). Japan's share in purchases is slightly higher than in sales, probably due to

16. Note that variables for foreign sales, R&D expenditure, and advertisement expenditure are in ratios to total sales.

17. Kimura and Ando (2004b) conduct a similar analysis on the characteristics of Japanese parent firms and statistically demonstrate that another feature of Japanese firms going to East Asia is that they are likely to more flexibly deinternalize their activities and to outsource some fragmented production processes, compared to those going to North America or Europe.

18. Contrary to popular opinion, sales to North America by Japanese affiliates in East Asia are small (3.4 percent). Sales to Europe are also small (2.6 percent).

Table 6.5   **Logit estimation: Japanese parent firms, 1995 F/Y**

	Dependent variables			
Variable	Foreign affiliates: with = 1; without = 0 (1)	Affiliates in East Asia: with = 1; without = 0 (2)	Affiliates in North America: with = 1; without = 0 (3)	Affiliates in Europe: with = 1; without = 0 (4)
A. Parent firms: All sectors				
Constant	−5.547***	−5.713***	−8.302***	−11.085***
	(−42.82)	(−42.77)	(−45.23)	(−40.40)
Number of regular workers (log)	0.694***	0.693***	0.960***	1.236***
	(31.00)	(30.22)	(32.91)	(30.83)
Tangible assets per regular workers	0.010***	0.003*	0.009***	0.007***
	(6.55)	(1.66)	(5.10)	(2.85)
Foreign sales: ratio to total sales	7.132***	5.146***	5.288***	5.564***
	(25.06)	(22.84)	(23.61)	(23.12)
R&D expenditure: ratio to total sales	9.565***	6.160***	12.479***	11.031***
	(8.50)	(6.02)	(10.06)	(8.51)
Advertisement expenditure: ratio to total sales	−0.122	−1.546	1.656	2.757*
	(−0.14)	(−1.19)	(1.42)	(1.92)
Log likelihood	−5,948.385	−5,425.176	−3,366.289	−1,823.668
No. of observations	13,623	13,623	13,623	13,623

Table 6.5 (continued)

Variable	Foreign affiliates: with = 1; without = 0 (1)	Affiliates in East Asia: with = 1; without = 0 (2)	Affiliates in North America: with = 1; without = 0 (3)	Affiliates in Europe: with = 1; without = 0 (4)
	(1')	(2')	(3')	(4')
B. Parent firms: Manufacturing sector				
Constant	−5.769***	−5.924***	−8.302***	−11.628***
	(−35.19)	(−35.63)	(−37.83)	(−33.81)
Number of regular workers (log)	0.775***	0.770***	1.078***	1.340***
	(26.97)	(26.74)	(28.72)	(26.60)
Tangible assets per regular workers	0.006***	0.000	0.010***	0.008***
	(2.93)	(0.09)	(4.61)	(2.77)
Foreign sales: ratio to total sales	6.200***	4.275***	4.899***	5.065***
	(20.10)	(17.61)	(19.35)	(18.26)
R&D expenditure: ratio to total sales	6.341***	3.469***	9.834***	9.265***
	(5.51)	(3.39)	(7.48)	(6.99)
Advertisement expenditure: ratio to total sales	0.846	−0.030	2.570	1.798
	(0.79)	(−0.03)	(1.60)	(1.56)
Log likelihood	−3,994.629	−3,715.727	−2,291.635	−1,275.963
No. of observations	8,577	8,577	8,577	8,577

Dependent variables

Source: MITI database.

Note: Numbers in parentheses are *t*-statistics.

***Significant at the 1 percent level.

*Significant at the 10 percent level.

Table 6.6   Intraregional production networks: Sales and purchases by Japanese affiliates in East Asia, 1998 F/Y

Industry	No. of affiliates	%	Total sales (million JPY)	Sales: Share in total sales (%)						Total purchases (million JPY)	Purchases: Share in total purchases (%)						
				%	Local	Japan	Third countries (total)	East Asia	North America	Europe		%	Local	Japan	Third countries (total)	East Asia	North America	Europe
Manufacturing sector																		
120 + 130	162	2.6	343,929	1.5	69.1	16.2	14.7	6.4	3.3	3.5	137,424	0.9	78.8	6.6	14.6	8.0	0.4	0.5
140 + 150	399	6.4	503,397	2.2	43.6	30.2	26.1	12.2	4.9	7.4	254,218	1.7	54.0	26.6	19.4	13.1	2.3	0.8
160	23	0.4	17,204	0.1	15.3	56.3	28.3	24.0	0.9	0.1	7,818	0.1	94.0	2.7	3.3	0.0	0.0	3.3
170	14	0.2	7,073	0.0	52.8	34.3	12.9	8.8	4.0	0.0	4,821	0.1	75.2	13.8	11.0	7.0	0.0	3.0
180	36	0.6	50,256	0.2	74.2	12.5	13.3	9.0	3.5	0.0	15,328	0.1	62.5	20.5	17.0	14.1	1.8	1.1
190	27	0.4	27,536	0.1	77.8	0.4	21.8	11.5	0.4	5.5	2,694	0.0	73.7	16.6	9.8	0.0	1.9	7.8
200	529	8.5	1,414,684	6.1	69.8	6.7	23.5	15.7	5.0	1.5	579,333	3.8	53.6	19.4	27.0	13.3	6.8	1.9
210	17	0.3	36,418	0.2	21.2	65.7	13.1	2.9	0.0	10.2	32,061	0.2	21.7	18.0	60.4	45.4	10.3	3.9
220	109	1.8	92,230	0.4	64.7	20.1	15.2	9.7	1.7	2.9	38,584	0.3	68.0	25.7	6.3	5.1	0.2	0.5
230	54	0.9	107,614	0.5	41.4	34.3	24.3	13.2	4.9	5.1	24,259	0.2	57.4	23.6	19.0	17.1	0.3	1.6
240	16	0.3	7,196	0.0	4.5	21.2	74.3	22.5	44.0	7.8	5,282	0.0	10.0	6.8	83.2	41.2	9.8	3.2
250	160	2.6	334,130	1.4	69.7	17.2	13.2	8.8	3.5	0.8	140,533	0.9	41.3	31.5	27.2	23.1	3.3	0.5
260	166	2.7	423,491	1.8	85.4	2.9	11.7	6.5	2.6	0.1	229,136	1.5	19.2	70.0	10.8	10.4	0.0	0.2
270	110	1.8	281,041	1.2	55.9	15.6	28.6	26.3	0.9	1.0	155,313	1.0	44.1	31.7	24.2	19.0	0.3	1.1
280	121	1.9	97,240	0.4	70.9	13.4	15.7	11.9	1.9	1.4	47,014	0.3	67.8	29.0	3.2	1.7	0.3	1.1
290	315	5.1	688,971	3.0	32.4	40.7	27.0	14.8	5.5	4.6	400,705	2.6	57.7	32.2	10.1	8.8	0.8	0.4
300	916	14.7	5,191,673	22.3	32.3	32.9	34.8	24.9	5.3	3.0	3,711,079	24.4	35.8	37.0	27.2	26.3	0.3	0.2
310	478	7.7	2,140,129	9.2	81.0	11.1	7.9	2.2	3.5	1.5	1,380,996	9.1	53.4	37.2	9.4	6.1	2.5	0.7
320	100	1.6	464,375	2.0	27.2	45.9	26.9	23.1	1.5	2.0	271,580	1.8	40.2	41.2	18.6	14.5	2.6	1.5
330 + 340	83	1.3	95,985	0.4	22.3	63.6	14.1	2.8	7.5	2.9	63,645	0.4	55.1	37.7	7.1	5.9	0.4	0.7
Nonmanufacturing sector																		
480	957	15.4	8,524,268	36.7	41.3	19.4	39.3	33.0	2.2	2.8	6,333,657	41.6	28.4	35.2	36.4	28.3	1.5	2.7
Others	1,421	22.9	2,386,309	10.3	77.7	11.2	11.1	8.0	1.5	1.2	1,387,281	9.1	72.7	19.5	7.8	5.5	1.1	0.6
Total	6,213	100.0	23,235,149	100.0	49.6	21.9	28.4	21.2	3.4	2.6	15,222,761	100.0	41.1	33.4	25.5	20.7	1.5	1.3

Source: MITI database.

Note: "Others" includes industries "050," "540," and "other."

the supply of complicated machinery parts and components from Japan.[19] These reveal that more than 90 percent of the sales and purchases by Japanese affiliates are among the East Asian countries, including Japan, and suggest the presence of active intraregional production networks in East Asia. In addition, a similar picture is observed for sales by U.S. affiliates in East Asia; besides the local market (56.2 percent), 17.1 percent of the goods produced by U.S. affiliates in East Asia goes to other East Asian countries.[20] This supports that active intraregional production networks have been developed not only by Japanese firms but also by other MNEs, such as U.S. firms and indigenous firms in the region.

In the case of North America and Europe, in contrast, sales to Japan are fairly small; 5.2 percent and 5.8 percent, respectively. In addition, more than half of the sales of the affiliates in the regions are from affiliates in the nonmanufacturing sector (59.2 percent for North America and 63.4 percent for Europe), particularly in wholesale trade sector (47.5 percent and 44.2 percent). This indicates that they aim to sell products in the local market or in countries nearby rather than forming vertical chains of production networks.

The empirical observation we have discussed may not directly prove the relevance of three lines of new theoretical thought. However, active FDI by Japanese SMEs, the existence of many sector-switching manufacturing affiliates, and intraregional trade by Japanese affiliates indeed imply how such logic works in developing international production and distribution networks in East Asia.

6.6   Evidence from the Firm Nationality Approach

The last section tried to capture the activities of Japanese firms in East Asia by analyzing affiliate holdings and by-destination sales and by-origin purchases. These statistical figures, however, do not directly indicate the magnitude of Japanese firms' activities in exporting from Japan and producing in East Asia and who is trading with whom. The amount of gross sales does not necessarily reflect the importance of each transaction because intermediate inputs embodied in traded commodities may be counted multiple times. One of the ways to quantify the importance of transactions is to introduce the concept of value added contents.

To quantify the whole Japanese firms' activities in different locations and embodied value added contents in international transactions, this section employs the firm nationality approach, which is first proposed by Baldwin and Kimura (1998) and Kimura and Baldwin (1998) in a two-

---

19. The share of purchases from North America is quite small.
20. Unfortunately, statistics for purchasing side are not available for U.S. affiliates in East Asia. See Kimura and Ando (2004a) and Lipsey (2004) for further discussion on the activities of U.S. firms in East Asia.

country setting and is extended to a three-country setting by Kimura (1998). The three-country setting considers three geographical territories, that is, Japan, Asia,[21] and the rest of the world (ROW) as well as three nationals, that is, Japanese, Asians, and foreigners (the national of ROW). "Japanese" consist of Japanese-owned firms located in Japan, households, and governments located in Japan and foreign affiliates of Japanese firms (FAJFs) located in Asia and ROW.[22] Asians and foreigners are defined in the symmetric way. Three nationals reside in three different locations, and thus nine blocks are drawn as in figure 6.2. Conceptually, transactions within a block and between blocks are illustrated as eighty-one (nine times nine) arrows in total. We can, however, fill out fourteen arrows of transactions because only statistical data from the Japanese side are readily available.

The numbers shown for fourteen arrows in figure 6.2 stand for the estimated Japanese value added contents of each transaction added at the starting point of the corresponding arrow in 2000. Table 6B.1 provides the summary table and the estimation method of each estimate. Additional explanation of the estimation method and data description is given in appendix B as well. Table 6.7 presents estimates of the value added contents embodied in sales by Japanese to Asians in Asia and to foreigners in ROW, estimated based on table 6B.1.

Although these figures are only rough estimates with a number of reservations on the data set, the value added account provides useful insights on the activities of Japanese MNEs, including intrafirm and arm's-length relationships. The following are the three major findings. First, activities of Japanese firms have gradually shifted from Japan to Asia. When we focus on Japanese firms who sell products to Asians in Asia, value added contents of "to produce in Japan and distributing through FAJF in Asia" and value added contents of "to produce in Asia and sell locally" increased from 1996 to 2000 (increase in the share by 2.1 percent), while the share of "to produce in Japan and export directly" decreased by 3.7 percent.[23] Also, when we compare value added contents of "to produce in Asia and sell locally" with "to produce in Japan and distribute through FAJF in Asia," the former becomes larger in 2000 though it was smaller in 1996. This implies that importance of local value added has enhanced vis-à-vis inputs from Japan.

Second, international production and distribution networks consist not only of Japanese firms but also of the mixture of firms of different nation-

21. Asia stands for Asian countries east of Pakistan in this section.
22. Note that "Japanese" in this definition is different from those on the residency basis or those in the sense of factor holders; we treat FAJF as controlled by Japanese and count all activities of FAJF as activities by Japanese.
23. The same analysis (figure 6.2 and table 6.7) was also conducted for 1996, but the results were omitted in the paper.

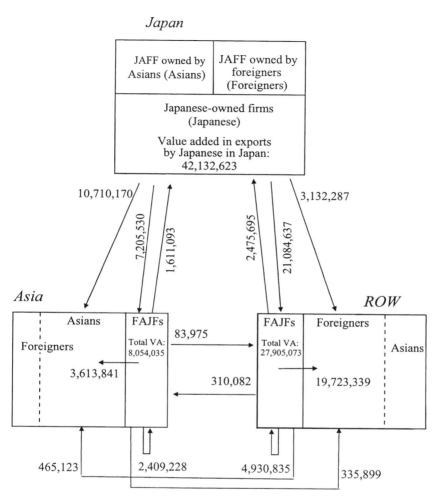

Fig. 6.2   Japanese value added embodied in sales to Asians and foreigners by Japanese: Three-country setting (2000)

Source: Table 6B.1.

Note: Unit = million JP yen.

alities. When value added in exports by Japanese in Japan to Asians (Asian firms) and foreigners (MNEs other than Japanese) in Asia is compared with that to Japanese (Japanese affiliates in Asia) in Asia, for instance, the former is larger than the latter. Thus, it is not true that the activities by Japanese firms are solely based on subcontracting relationships or intrafirm relationships between Japanese parent firms and Japanese affiliates in East Asia though such activities still consist of a significant portion;

Table 6.7   Major channels for Japanese firms to sell products abroad in 2000 (million JPY)

	VA contents	%
For Japanese firms to sell products to Asians in Asia (total of below):	18,373,691	100.
To produce in Japan and export directly	10,710,170	58.
To produce in Japan and distribute through FAJF in Asia	3,233,118	17.
To produce in Japan and distribute through FAJF in ROW	351,439	1.
To produce in Asia and sell locally	3,613,841	19.
To produce in ROW and export to Asia	465,123	2.
For Japanese firms to sell products to foreigners in ROW (total of below):	38,394,682	100.
To produce in Japan and export directly	3,132,287	8.
To produce in Japan and distribute through FAJF in ROW	14,902,647	38.
To produce in Japan and distribute through FAJF in Asia	300,511	0.
To produce in ROW and sell locally	19,723,339	51.
To produce in Asia and export to ROW	335,899	0.

Source: The above figures are estimated based on table 6B.1.

Note: Minor indirect channels such as "to produce in Japan and to distribute through FAJF in ROW and then through FAJF in Asia" are omitted.

rather, the activities do include transactions with indigenous firms and MNEs in Asia.[24]

In addition, when we again focus on Japanese firms who sell products to Asians in Asia, the channel for direct exports to Asia from Japan is still important as the share of "to produce in Japan and export directly" suggests: 58.3 percent in 2000. In direct exports from Japan to Asia, capital goods for "Asian" firms are certainly significant. Besides, intermediate inputs, particularly machinery parts and components, for "Asian" firms are also large; combined with the information on Japan's export in table 6.1, roughly one-third to half of them are machinery parts and components.

Third, the connection with North America or Europe is thin for both exports and imports. Among several channels for Japanese firms to sell products, the shares of "to produce in ROW and export to Asia" and "to produce in Asia and export to ROW" are pretty small. These low ratios imply weak connections with North America and Europe, confirming that contrary to popular opinion, sales to North America by Japanese affiliates in East Asia are small.

6.7   Current Policy Issues

We now observe proliferation of bilateral and regional preferential trade arrangements all over the world, and the wave of regionalism comes to

24. The transactions between Japanese firms in Japan and Japanese affiliates in ROW are indeed large, but the purpose is to sell Japanese products locally (in North America or Europe) rather than contributing to forming networks. This is consistent with the facts observed in section 6.5 that the large portion of affiliates in North America and Europe is in the wholesale trade sector and more than 40 percent of the total sales by affiliates in North America or Europe are from affiliates in the wholesale trade sector.

East Asian developing economies. It is sometimes claimed that the formal policy formation for regional economic integration is a bit delayed in East Asia, compared with other regions such as Latin America and Central and Eastern Europe. However, we would like to claim that the development of international production and distribution networks provides different economic backgrounds and different policy demands, and thus the implication of regionalism may also be different.

The dual-track approach has so far worked pretty well in East Asia. Figure 6.3 presents over-time changes in the customs-duty import ratios in East Asian developing countries. This is the ratio of total customs duty revenue of a country to the cost, insurance, and freight (c.i.f.)-based import value. It is immediately noticed that the ratios are much smaller than the average tariff figures that we usually discuss as an indicator for trade barriers. Moreover, the ratios present clear decreasing trends over time. These phenomena are partly due to unilateral tariff reduction for information technology (IT)-related products in the 1990s and also due to the effective usage of the duty-drawback system. In fact, MNEs in export-oriented industries are now paying a very small amount of tariffs in these countries.

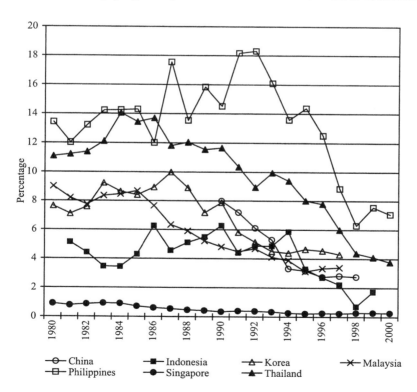

Fig. 6.3   Custom duties import ratios in East Asia
Sources: Drawn from Ando and Estevadeordal (2003).

Such a policy package has at least partially mitigated antiexport biases with trade protection for import-substituting industries and has allowed them to attract both import-substituting FDI and export-oriented FDI so far.

Further activation of the international production and distribution networks, however, requires new policy setting. First, fostering import-substituting industries was not, after all, very successful, with a few exceptions, and the cost of protection gradually becomes unbearable. Indeed, Southeast Asian countries and China still have high tariffs for a number of import-substituting industries. To substitute imports by domestic production, governments of these countries have long provided trade protection for domestic firms or incoming foreign companies. However, trade protection still cannot be removed because of the long-lasting poor competitiveness of these industries. The protection cost is borne by consumers and other industries, including export-oriented industries. It cannot be continued forever, and policymakers gradually recognize that it is now time to reorganize these industries in a more competitive environment. These industries include automobiles, domestic electric appliances, petrochemicals, and iron and steel.

Second, even if tariffs are properly removed, the business environment of East Asia is still far from borderless. Cross-border transaction costs are high for various reasons. Physical infrastructure in transportation and telecommunications is one of the important factors to improve the business environment. Trade facilitation in customs clearance and other bureaucratic procedures is another vital element. As a more abstract form of transaction costs, legal systems and economic institutions, such as standards, intellectual property rights protection, and dispute settlement facilities, are also crucial. To keep attracting FDI and encourage the formulation of agglomeration, policies beyond simple tariff removal become essential.

Third, the sophistication of networks and the development of agglomeration require extensive involvement of local indigenous firms. The focus of local industry promotion is not placed on infant industry protection for import substitution anymore. Rather, the issue is what the government can do in order to make local indigenous firms penetrate into international vertical production chains. Policymakers know that impatient performance requirements for foreign companies such as local contents requirement and technology transfer requirement have not worked very well. Government-financed technology development centers for local technicians have also borne lukewarm results in many cases. The governments should ultimately make an effort in enhancing human resources for both entrepreneurs and engineers, but human capital development takes time. The role of government is obviously important, but there is no easy policy to reach the goal.

These three issues are, in the authors' opinion, natural policy agenda in the formation of the international production and distribution networks, and we hope that policymakers in this region have clear minds in confronting these issues. The East Asian countries are now actively engaging the effort toward formulating regional trade arrangements. The contents of such arrangements are expected to reflect necessary policy reform in the East Asian countries.

6.8 Conclusion

This paper claimed the importance of international production and distribution networks in East Asia and tried to verify their distinctive characteristics in their significance in each economy, their extensiveness covering many countries in the region, and their sophistication weaving both intrafirm and arm's-length transactions. Although a lot of difficulties exist in capturing those characteristics with official statistical figures, the finely disaggregated international trade statistics proves that production-block-wise fragmented patterns of location choices have extensively been developed in East Asia. The microstructure of production and distribution networks is hard to observe directly, but microdata of Japanese parent firms and their foreign affiliates suggest the sophistication of networks that consist of both intrafirm and arm's-length transactions, including firms with various firm nationalities. We observe that the formation of international production and distribution networks has been backed up by drastic changes in development strategies fully utilizing the force of globalizing corporate activities. The mechanics of the networks seem to be well explained by new economic thought of fragmentation and agglomeration. The formation of the networks carries profound policy implication in reformulating development strategies and designing regional trade arrangements.

Appendix A

Data Sources for Section 6.5

The Basic Survey of Business Structure and Activity (*Kigyo Katsudo Kihon Chosa* in Japanese) is the MITI survey, first conducted for F/Y 1991, then for F/Y 1994, and annually since then. The Basic Survey has several attractive features. First, the samples in the survey are comprehensive, covering all firms with more than fifty workers, capital of more than thirty million yen, and establishments in mining, manufacturing, wholesale and retail trade, and restaurants. Foreign affiliates covered in the survey are those with no less than 20 percent Japanese ownership. Second, the ratios of questionnaire returns are high; the actual ratios are not disclosed but are about 90 to 95 percent. Statistics collected by the Government of Japan are legally classified into two categories: designated statistics (*shitei toukei*) and approved statistics (*shounin toukei*). The Basic Survey is the first type, and thus firms in the survey must return the questionnaires under the Statistics Law. Third, it provides firm-level data rather than the data on an establishment basis. Although establishment-level data are useful in analyzing production activities, firm-level data are much more appropriate to examine corporate activities as a whole (see table 6A.1).

The Survey of Overseas Business Activities of Japanese Companies, which is also conducted by MITI, has been conducted annually since F/Y 1970. Firms targeted by the survey are those with Japanese affiliates abroad of Japanese firms, except firms in finance, insurance, or real estate. The Survey of Overseas Business Activities is of the approved type so that the effective return ratios tend to be as low as 60 percent (in the case of the F/Y 1999 survey, the returned ratio is 56.0 percent). As explained in section 6.5, Japanese affiliates abroad include both "affiliates abroad" with no less than 10 percent ownership by Japanese parent firms and "affiliates of affiliates abroad" with more than 50 percent ownership by such "affiliates abroad," but the survey can distinguish the former and the latter if necessary.

The industry classification used in this paper is presented in table 6A.2. Because the industry classification of the Survey of Overseas Business Activities is different from that of the Basic Survey, the latter industry classification is matched with the former to make them comparable. Unfortunately, services sectors are not fully covered by both surveys.

Table 6A.1   Definition of machinery parts and components

HS classification

840140, 840290, 840390, 840490, 840590, 8406, 8407, 8408, 8409, 8410, 8411, 8412, 8413, 8414, 841520, 841590, 8416, 8417, 841891, 841899, 841990, 842123, 842129, 842131, 842191, 842199, 842290, 842390, 842490, 8431, 843290, 843390, 843490, 843590, 843680, 843691, 843699, 843790, 843890, 843991, 843999, 844090, 844190, 844240, 844250, 844390, 8448, 845090, 845190, 845240, 845290, 845390, 845490, 845590, 8466, 846791, 846792, 846799, 846890, 8473, 847490, 847590, 847690, 847790, 847890, 847990, 8480, 8481, 8482, 8483, 8484, 8485, 8503, 850490, 8505, 850690, 8507, 850890, 850990, 851090, 8511, 8512, 851390, 851490, 851590, 851690, 851790, 8518, 8522, 8529, 853090, 8531, 8532, 8533, 8534, 8535, 8536, 8537, 8538, 8539, 8540, 8541, 8542, 854390, 8544, 8545, 8546, 8547, 8548, 8607, 8706, 8707, 8708, 870990, 8714, 871690, 8803, 8805, 9001, 9002, 9003, 900590, 900691, 900699, 900791, 900792, 900890, 900990, 901090, 901190, 901290, 9013, 9014, 901590, 901790, 902490, 902590, 902690, 902790, 902890, 902990, 903090, 903190, 903290, 9033, 9110, 9111, 9112, 9113, 9114, 9209

Table 6A.2   **Industry classification**

Manufacturing sector	
120	Food processing
130	Beverages, tobacco, and animal feed
140	Textiles
150	Apparel
160	Wood and wood products
170	Furniture and fixtures
180	Pulp, paper, and paper products
190	Publishing and printing
200	Chemicals
210	Petroleum and coal products
220	Plastic products
230	Rubber products
240	Leather and leather products
250	Ceramics, clay, and stone products
260	Iron and steel
270	Nonferrous metal
280	Metal products
290	General machinery
300	Electric machinery
310	Transport equipment
320	Precision machinery
330	Arms
340	Other manufacturing
290 + 300 + 310 + 320	Machinery sector
Nonmanufacturing sector	
050	Mining
480	Wholesale trade
540	Retail trade
Other	Services and other

Appendix B

The Estimation Method and Data Sources for Section 6.6

The detailed estimation method is described in table 6B.1. Japanese value added in exports of Japanese-owned firms is calculated by subtracting the import component in the exports. The proportion of the import component in exports (8.504 percent) is obtained from Management and Coordination Agency (1999). Exports of Japanese-owned firms are calculated by subtracting exports of Japanese affiliates of foreign firms (JAFF) from exports of Japan. The data for exports of JAFF are available from METI (2002b). Assuming that the ratio of value added to sales is the same no matter where the sales destination is, we obtain the Japanese value added in ex-

Table 6B.1   Exports versus FDI by Japanese-owned firms (million JPY)

Row no.	Category	2000 Exports	2000 Value added (VA)	%
(1)	Japanese value added in exports of Japanese-owned firms in Japan	46,048,596	42,132,623	100.0
(1.1)	In exports to FAJFs (Japanese)	30,919,567	28,290,167	
(1.1a)	located in Asia	7,875,240	7,205,530	17.1
(1.1b)	located in ROW	23,044,326	21,084,637	50.0
(1.2)	In exports to Asians (non-Japanese)	11,705,616	10,710,170	
(1.2a)	located in Asia	11,705,616	10,710,170	25.4
(1.2b)	located in ROW	n.a.	n.a.	
(1.3)	In exports to foreigners (non-Japanese and Asian)	3,423,414	3,132,287	
(1.3a)	located in Asia	n.a.	n.a.	
(1.3b)	located in ROW	3,423,414	3,132,287	7.4
(2)	Value added by FAJFs in Asia	36,376,123	8,054,035	100.0
(2.1)	In goods and services sold to Japanese	18,537,086	4,104,295	
(2.1a)	located in Japan	7,276,515	1,611,093	20.0
(2.1b)	located in Asia (other FAJFs in Asia)	10,881,299	2,409,228	29.9
(2.1c)	located in ROW (other FAJFs in ROW)	379,272	83,975	1.0
(2.2)	In goods and services sold to Asians (non-Japanese)	16,321,948	3,613,841	
(2.2a)	located in Japan	n.a.	n.a.	
(2.2b)	located in Asia	16,321,948	3,613,841	44.9
(2.2c)	located in ROW	n.a.	n.a.	
(2.3)	In goods and services sold to foreigners (non-Japanese and Asian)	1,517,089	335,899	
(2.3a)	located in Japan	n.a.	n.a.	
(2.3b)	located in Asia	n.a.	n.a.	
(2.3c)	located in ROW	1,517,089	335,899	4.2
(3)	Value added by Japanese affiliates in ROW	92,638,856	27,905,073	100.0
(3.1)	In goods and services sold to Japanese	25,617,494	7,716,611	
(3.1a)	located in Japan	8,218,775	2,475,695	8.9
(3.1b)	located in Asia (other FAJFs in Asia)	1,029,405	310,082	1.1
(3.1c)	located in ROW (other FAJFs in ROW)	16,369,314	4,930,835	17.7
(3.2)	In goods and services sold to Asians (non-Japanese)	1,544,107	465,123	

Table 6B.1 (continued)

Row no.	Category	2000 Exports	Value added (VA)	%
(3.2a)	located in Japan	n.a.	n.a.	
(3.2b)	located in Asia	1,544,107	465,123	1.7
(3.2c)	located in ROW	n.a.	n.a.	
(3.3)	In goods and services sold to foreigners (non-Japanese and Asian)	65,477,255	19,723,339	
(3.3a)	located in Japan	n.a.	n.a.	
(3.3b)	located in Asia	n.a.	n.a.	
(3.3c)	located in ROW	65,477,255	19,723,339	70.7

Sources: METI (2001) for exports of Japan; METI (2002b) for exports of JAFF; METI (2002a) for sales and purchases of FAJF. Management and Coordination Agency (1999, pp. 406) for the import inducement coefficient of export in Japan for 1995: 0.08504.

Notes: n.a. = not available. FAJF: Foreign affiliates of Japanese firms that include "affiliates abroad" with no less than 10 percent ownership by Japanese parent firms and "affiliates of affiliates abroad" with more than 50 percent ownership by such "affiliates abroad"; JAFF: Japanese affiliates of foreign firms with foreign share of more than one-third; ROW: All countries other than Japan and Asia (region); Japanese: Households and governments in Japan + all firms located in Japan – JAFF + FAJF; Asians: Households and governments in Asia + Asian-owned firms located in Asia + affiliates of firms owned by Asians in Japan and ROW; Foreigners: Households and governments in ROW + foreign-owned firms located in ROW + affiliates of foreign firms in Japan and Asia.

Method of estimation, by row number:

(1) ([Japanese total exports] – [Exports by JAFF]) × (1 – 0.08504) = (1.1) + (1.2) + (1.3)

(1.1) (1.1a) + (1.1b) = (1.1)

(1.1a) ([Imports from Japan by FAJF in Asia] – [Imports from JAFF by FAJF in Asia (n.a.)]) × (1 – 0.08504)

(1.1b) ([Imports from Japan by FAJF in ROW] – [Imports from JAFF by FAJF in ROW (n.a.)]) × (1 – 0.08504)

(1.2) (1.2a) + (1.2b) = (1.2)

(1.2a) ([Japanese exports to Asia] – [Exports to Asia by JAFF (available only for exports to Asia)] × (1 – 0.08504) – (1.1a) – (1.3a)

(1.2b) [Japanese exports to p.c. nationals located in ROW (n.a.)] × (1 – 0.08504)

(1.3) (1.3a) + (1.3b) = (1.3)

(*continued*)

Table 6B.1 (continued)

(1.3a) [Japanese exports to foreigners located in Asia (n.a.)] × (1 − 0.08504)

(1.3b) ([Japanese exports to ROW] − [Exports to ROW by JAFF]) × (1 − 0.08504) − (1.1b) − (1.2b)

(2)   (Sales by FAJF in Asia) − (Purchases by FAJF in Asia) = (2.1) + (2.2) + (2.3)

(2.1) (2.1a) + (2.1b) + (2.1c) = (2.1)

(2.1a) (2) × (Ratio of sales to Japan by FAJF in Asia) − (2.2a) − (2.3a)

(2.1b) (2) × ([Ratio of local sales by FAJF in Asia] × [Ratio of sales to FAJF in local sales by FAJF in Asia (proxy: 0.4)])

(2.1c) (2) × ([Ratio of sales to ROW by FAJF in Asia] × [Ratio of sales to FAJF in ROW in sales to ROW by FAJF in Asia (proxy: 0.2)])

(2.2) (2.2a) + (2.2b) + (2.2c) = (2.2)

(2.2a) (Value added in goods and services sold to JAFF [owned by Asians] by FAJF in Asia [n.a.])

(2.2b) (2) × (Ratio of local sales by FAJF in Asia) × (Ratio of sales to Asians in local sales by FAJF in Asia [proxy: 0.6]) − (2.1b) − (2.3b)

(2.2c) (Value added in goods and services sold to Asians located in ROW by FAJF in Asia [n.a.])

(2.3) (2.3a) + (2.3b) + (2.3c) = (2.3)

(2.3a) (Value added in goods and services sold to JAFF [owned by foreigners] by FAJF in Asia [n.a.])

(2.3b) (Value added in goods and services sold to foreigners located in Asia by FAJF in Asia [n.a.])

(2.3c) (2) × (Ratio of sales to ROW by FAJF in Asia) × (Ratio of sales to foreigners in sales to ROW by FAJF in Asia [proxy: 0.8]) − (2.1c) − (2.2c)

(3) (Sales by FAJF in ROW) − (Purchases by FAJF in ROW) = (3.1) + (3.2) + (3.3)

(3.1) (3.1a) + (3.1b) + (3.1c) = (3.1)

(3.1a) (3) × (Ratio of sales to Japan by FAJF in ROW) − (3.2a) − (3.3a)

(3.1b) (3) × ([Ratio of sales to Asia by FAJF in ROW] × [Ratio of sales to FAJF in Asia in sales to Asia by FAJF in ROW (proxy: 0.4)])

(3.1c) (3) × ([Ratio of local sales by FAJF in ROW] × [Ratio of sales to FAJF in local sales by FAJF in ROW (proxy: 0.2)])

(3.2) (3.2a) + (3.2b) + (3.2c) = (3.2)

(3.2a) (Value added in goods and services sold to JAFF [owned by Asians] by FAJF in ROW [n.a.])

(3.2b) (3) × (Ratio of sales to Asia by FAJF in ROW) × (Ratio of sales to Asians in sales to Asia by FAJF in ROW [proxy: 0.6]) − (3.1b) − (3.3b)

(3.2c) (Value added in goods and services sold to Asians located in ROW by FAJF in ROW [n.a.])

(3.3) (3.3a) + (3.3b) + (3.3c) = (3.3)

(3.3a) (Value added in goods and services sold to JAFF [owned by foreigners] by FAJF in ROW [n.a.])

(3.3b) (Value added in goods and services sold to foreigners located in Asia by FAJF in ROW [n.a.])

(3.3c) (3) × ([Ratio of local sales by FAJF in ROW] × [Ratio of sales to foreigners in sales to ROW by FAJF in ROW (proxy: 0.8)]) − (3.1c) − (3.2c)

ports of Japanese-owned firms to FAJF in Asia (7,205,530 million Japanese (JP) yen), to FAJF in ROW (21,084,637 million JP yen), to Asians in Asia (10,710,170 million JP yen), and to foreigners in ROW (3,132,287 million JP yen). There is no information on exports to foreigners in Asia or exports to Asians in ROW.

Value added earned by FAJF in Asia (8,054,035 million JP yen) is calculated as sales minus purchases, which are available from METI (2002a). Assuming again that the ratio of value added to sales is the same no matter where the sales destination is, we obtain the value added by FAJF in goods and services sold to Japanese located in Japan (1,611,093 million JP yen), to Japanese located in Asia (2,409,228 million JP yen), to Japanese located in ROW (83,975 million JP yen), to Asians located in Asia (3,613,841 million JP yen), and to foreigners located in ROW (335,899 million JP yen). Data are not available for sales by FAJF to Asians in Japan and ROW or those to foreigners in Japan and ROW. Value added by FAJF in ROW in goods and services sold to various places is estimated in the same way.

The Ministry of Economy, Trade and Industry (2002b) defines Japanese affiliates of foreign firms as those with foreign share of more than one-third. Therefore, exports of JAFFs in the analysis are those by such affiliates. The Ministry of Economy, Trade and Industry (2002a) defines Japanese affiliates abroad as both "affiliates abroad" with no less than 10 percent ownership by Japanese parent firms and "affiliates of affiliates abroad" with more than 50 percent ownership by such "affiliates abroad" as mentioned previously. Thus, sales and purchases by FAJFs in the analysis are those by such affiliates. In METI (2002a), it is known that exports in sales and imports in purchases by FAJFs are overstated because FAJFs are sometimes reported as exports and imports when they are selling locally, but the ultimate destinations and origins are foreign countries. We therefore regard 30 percent of sales and purchases to and from Japan and ROW in manufacturing as local transactions. Moreover, there is no available information on the magnitude of transactions among FAJFs in METI (2002a). We therefore use 0.4 (0.6) as a proxy of the ratio of sales to FAJFs (Asians) in local sales by FAJFs in Asia, 0.2 (0.8) as a proxy of the ratio of sales to FAJFs (foreigners) in sales to ROW by FAJFs in Asia, 0.4 (0.6) as a proxy of the ratio of sales to FAJFs in Asia (Asians) in sales to Asia by FAJFs in ROW, and 0.2 (0.8) as a proxy of the ratio of sales to FAJFs (foreigners) in local sales by FAJFs in ROW.

Because both METI (2002a) and METI (2002b) are approved statistics, the returned ratios are not so high. As for METI (2002b), 1,935 out of 3,742 parent firms returned the questionnaires (the returned ratio is 51.7 percent). In the case of METI (2002a), 2,157 out of 3,430 parent firms returned the questionnaires (the returned ratio is 62.9 percent), and the number of Japanese affiliates abroad covered is 14,991.

References

Ando, Mitsuyo. 2004. Fragmentation and vertical intra-industry trade in East Asia. Paper presented at conference, 79th Annual Western Economic Association International. 30 June–3 July, Vancouver, Canada.

Ando, Mitsuyo, and Antoni Estevadeordal. 2003. Trade policy formation in Latin America and Asia-Pacific: A comparative analysis. Paper presented at the LAEBA panel at the FIEALC meeting, Globalization in Asia and Latin America: Trade, Investment and Finance. 24 September 2003, Osaka, Japan.

Arndt, Sven W., and Henryk Kierzkowski. 2001. *Fragmentation: New production patterns in the world economy.* Oxford, UK: Oxford University Press.

Baldwin, Robert E., and Fukunari Kimura. 1998. Measuring U.S. international goods and services transactions. In *Geography and ownership as bases for economic accounting,* ed. R. E. Baldwin, R. E. Lipsey, and J. D. Richardson, 9–36. Chicago: University of Chicago Press.

Cheng, Leonard K., and Henryk Kierzkowski. 2001. *Global production and trade in East Asia.* Boston: Kluwer Academic.

Deardorff, Alan V. 2001a. Fragmentation across cones. In *Fragmentation: New production patterns in the world economy,* ed. Sven W. Arndt and Henryk Kierzkowski, 35–51. Oxford, UK: Oxford University Press.

———. 2001b. Fragmentation in simple trade models. *North American Journal of Economics and Finance* 12:121–37.

Dunning, John H. 1993. *Multinational enterprises and the global economy.* Wokingham, UK: Addison-Wesley.

Fujita, Masahisa, Paul Krugman, and Anthony J. Venables. 1999. *The spatial economy: Cities, regions, and international trade.* Cambridge, MA: MIT Press.

Fukao, Kyoji, Hikari Ishido, and Keiko Ito. 2003. Vertical intra-industry trade and foreign direct investment in East Asia. RIETI Discussion Paper Series no. 03-E-001.

Jones, Ronald W., and Henryk Kierzkowski. 1990. The role of services in production and international trade: A theoretical framework. In *The political economy of international trade: Essays in honor of Robert E. Baldwin,* ed. Ronald W. Jones and Anne O. Krueger. Oxford, UK: Basil Blackwell.

Kimura, Fukunari. 1998. Japanese multinationals and regional integration in Asia. In *Asia & Europe: Beyond competing regionalism,* ed. Kiichiro Fukasaku, Fukunari Kimura, and Shujiro Urata, 111–33. Brighton, UK: Sussex Academic Press.

———. 2000. Location and internalization decisions: Sector switching in Japanese outward foreign direct investment. In *The role of foreign direct investment in East Asian economic development,* ed. Takatoshi Ho and Anne O. Krueger. Chicago: University of Chicago Press.

———. 2002. Subcontracting and the performance of small and medium firms in Japan. *Small Business Economics* 18:163–75.

———. 2003. Development strategies for economies under globalisation: Southeast Asia as a new development model. In *New Asian regionalism: Responses to globalisation and crises,* ed. Tran Van Hoa and Charles Harvie, 72–95. London: Palgrave.

Kimura, Fukunari, and Mitsuyo Ando. 2003. Fragmentation and agglomeration matter: Japanese multinationals in Latin America and East Asia. *North American Journal of Economics and Finance* 14 (3): 287–317.

———. 2004a. The economic analysis of international production/distribution networks in East Asia and Latin America: The implication of regional trade arrangements. *Business and Politics,* forthcoming.

———. 2004b. Two-dimensional fragmentation in East Asia: Conceptual framework and empirics, in "Outsourcing and fragmentation: Blessing or threat?" special issue, *International Review of Economics and Finance,* forthcoming.

Kimura, Fukunari, and Robert E. Baldwin. 1998. Application of a nationality-adjusted net sales and value added framework: The case of Japan. In *Geography and ownership as bases for economic accounting,* ed. R. E. Baldwin and J. D. Richardson, 49–80. Chicago: University of Chicago Press.

Krugman, Paul. 1991. Increasing returns and economic geography. *Journal of Political Economy* 99:183–99.

———. 1995. *Development, geography, and economic theory.* Cambridge, MA: MIT Press.

Lipsey, Robert E. 2004. *U.S. firms and East Asian development since 1990.* Paper presented at workshop of the World Bank Institute, Foreign Direct Investment and Economic Development: Lessons from East Asian Experience. 30 November and 1 December 2003, Bali, Indonesia.

Management and Coordination Agency. 1999. *1995 input-output tables: Explanatory report.* Tokyo: Management and Coordination Agency, Government of Japan.

The Ministry of Economy, Trade and Industry (METI). 2001. *White paper on international trade 2001* [in Japanese]. Tokyo: METI, Government of Japan.

———. 2002a. *The 31st survey of overseas business activities of Japanese companies* [in Japanese]. Tokyo: Printing Office, Ministry of Finance, Government of Japan.

———. 2002b. *The 35th survey of Japanese affiliates of foreign firms* [in Japanese]. Tokyo: Printing Office, Ministry of Finance, Government of Japan.

———. 2003. *White paper on international trade 2003* [in Japanese]. Tokyo: METI, Government of Japan.

Pangestu, Mari. 2003. In *Development, trade, and the WTO: A handbook,* ed. Bernard Hoekman, Philip English, and Aaditya Matto, 149–59. Washington, DC: World Bank.

World Bank. 1993. *The East Asian miracle: Economic growth and public policy.* Oxford, UK: Oxford University Press.

Comment   Meng-chun Liu

This paper, by Professors Ando and Kimura, which concentrates on Japan's machinery industries as a case study, intends to underline the international production and distribution networks comprising vertical production chains and distribution networks across East Asian countries in the organization of international trade.

This is an interesting paper that contains a careful statistical analysis. Generally speaking, from the perspective of production networks, the paper is motivated to explore the ways in which Japanese firms organize their international trade with neighboring East Asian countries. The paper be-

Meng-chun Liu is the deputy director of the International Division of the Chung Hua Institution for Economic Research.

gins with an introduction to policy backgrounds within East Asia and then goes on to provide theoretical ideas and empirical works relevant to cross-border production networks. It concludes by utilizing Baldwin and Kimura's "firm nationality approach" to measure the economic activities of Japanese firms in terms of their transaction channels.

Some interesting results are derived by their empirical work, yet we still look forward to the authors' clarifying some questions about this paper. First of all, the paper highlights an important research issue, particularly in the context of the global economy. We have indeed seen significant integration of the global economy in recent decades, brought about by expanding international trade and direct capital flows, with the increasing integration of global markets and the disintegration of the production process clearly going hand in hand. We may therefore regard the disintegration of production processes as the overseas expansion of production networks, with the manufacturing and service activities being performed both at home and abroad. Trade liberalization and the reduction in international transaction costs are two important factors driving the global integration process. Both international outsourcing and prolonged production "roundaboutness" are characteristic features of production networks, while international outsourcing plays a critical role in the process of international production networks, and the improvements in transaction efficiencies will generally enlarge international outsourcing.

This paper stresses that the production networks are organized by corporations' foreign direct investment (FDI) and "the mixture of firms of various nationalities." In other words, the paper recognizes that the formation of production networks relies on both FDI and international subcontracting relationships. Furthermore, cross-border production networks underline the phenomenon of prolonged production roundaboutness, and it seems that Japanese firms play a central role in arranging the international division of labor, which is both vertically integrated and producer driven (as opposed to the alternative form of production network that is horizontally integrated and buyer driven).

The role of multinationals and FDI in shaping international trade is well recognized in the literature. Drawing on the theories of the fragmentation, agglomeration, and internationalization of corporate firms, the authors suggest, theoretically, that firms' comparative advantages can still work in determining trade patterns. This is a good starting point from which to describe the formation of production networks and trade patterns across regional countries; however, the paper seems to link the empirical results to the theoretical background rather weakly.

Second, the products manufactured by the machinery industries are capital goods in nature, with the demand for such products being derived by the suppliers of downstream industries. That is, the trade in machinery and relevant components is heavily reliant upon the development of the importing countries' downstream industries. Moreover, the international transfer of production technologies is usually embodied in capital goods, comprising mainly machinery. Without a doubt, outward FDI from Japanese firms to East Asia, as well as the attendant technology transfers, can help to boost trading in machinery between Japan and its trading partners; however, this paper seems to ignore these important driving forces.

Third, table 6.1 in this paper provides data on the importance of trade in machinery in the East Asian economies. Taiwan was ranked as the fifteenth largest trading economy in the world in 2002, and it also has significant trade with Japan, especially in machinery. However, table 6.1 does not include Taiwan's machinery trade data. The authors are expected to take this into account.

Finally, in this paper, production agglomeration plays an important role in influencing trading patterns via the formation of production networks. Foreign direct investment is clearly dominant in many industrial clusters in East Asia, such as the Kelang Valley and Penang in Malaysia, and some of the early studies have argued that indigenous firms fail to achieve industrial linkage with FDI firms, thus weakening the industrial cluster, in terms of shaping its comparative advantages. One of the preconditions for successful development of clusters is therefore the participation of local indigenous firms in the production networks, which raises important policy implications. For example, in addition to the enhancement of human resources, which is mentioned in this paper, the government may need to consider how to promote entrepreneurship in the host developing countries.

Comment   Somkiat Tangkitvanich

The issue of production and distribution networks is important but has not received sufficient attention in trade literature in the past. The authors have identified key patterns that characterize the nature of the production and distribution networks in East Asia. Based on two sets of detailed survey data, they have shown, convincingly, that the production and distribution networks in East Asia are geographically extensive, sophisticated, and important to the understanding of trade patterns in the region. The readers, however, need to be aware that the data presented in this paper are based solely on surveys of Japanese multinational corporations (MNCs). As a result, any comparison of the characteristics of production and distribution networks in East Asia and that of other regions such as Latin America should be noted with care.

Somkiat Tangkitvanich is research director for Information Economy at the Thailand Development Research Institute.

In the paper, the extensiveness and the sophistication of the production and distribution networks are analyzed by using three theories: the fragmentation theory, the agglomeration theory, and the internalization theory of firms. As a policy researcher trying to understand the implications of the results, I am attracted to two issues that are not explicitly addressed by the paper. The first issue concerns the efficiency of the current production network in East Asia. This question arises because the formation of the network is driven not only by the comparative advantage of each production location but also by the host country's foreign direct investment (FDI) policy. As suggested in the paper, until recently, FDI policy in Southeast Asia was based on the "selective acceptance" principle. Because investments in many industries, particularly the machinery industries, involve high sunk costs and are thus subject to increasing returns, the extensiveness and sophistication of the current production and distribution networks identified by the authors may simply be an outcome of past investment policy that promotes inefficient capital-intensive industries.

My second point is related to the first one. The authors mentioned in passing at the end of the paper the implications of the production and distribution networks on regional trade arrangement. Suppose that the existing networks are a result of past misguided policy, can regional trade arrangements, currently mushrooming in the region, provide some remedies and how? Traditional pair-wise bilateral free trade agreements (FTAs) are unlikely to provide the necessary economic integration for an industry whose production networks involve more than two countries. For example, suppose that a product is first produced in country A, then slightly processed in country B without a substantial transformation, and then finally exported to country C. Even though C may have bilateral FTAs with A and B separately, neither FTAs would be beneficial because the product would be classified as originating from A. A regionwide FTA appears to be a far more superior solution, provided that the rules of origin are carefully designed. These two issues should be explored in future studies.

The Impacts of an East Asia Free Trade Agreement on Foreign Trade in East Asia

Shujiro Urata and Kozo Kiyota

7.1 Introduction

The world economy has been witnessing the surge in free trade area (FTA) since the early 1990s.[1] By December 2002, some 250 FTAs have been reported to the General Agreement on Tariffs and Trade/World Trade Organization (GATT/WTO), and of those 130 were reported after the establishment of the WTO in January 1995.[2] More than 170 FTAs are currently in force, and 70 additional FTAs are expected to be operational, although they are not yet reported. According to the WTO, by the end of 2005, if FTAs reportedly planned or already under negotiation are concluded, the total number of FTAs in force may approach 300. Among the regions of the world, East Asia was not active in establishing FTAs until recently. Indeed, until 2002, when the Japan-Singapore FTA was enacted, the Association of Southeast Asian Nations (ASEAN) Free Trade Area (AFTA) was the only major FTA in the region. Many East Asian econ-

Shujiro Urata is a professor of economics at Waseda University, and a research fellow at the Japan Center for Economic Research. Kozo Kiyota is an associate professor in the International Graduate School of Social Sciences at Yokohama National University.

The authors would like to thank Dukgeun Ahn, Philippa Dee, Kyoji Fukao, Takatoshi Ito, Erlinda Medalla, Andrew Rose, Robert M. Stern, and the seminar participants at the Fourteenth Annual East Asia Seminar on Economics for their helpful comments and suggestions on the earlier version of the paper. Any remaining errors are the authors' alone. Kozo Kiyota was a visiting scholar at the University of Michigan, Ann Arbor, when the present version of the paper was prepared and would like to thank the Kikawada Fellowship Program for providing financial support for this research.

1. FTA means Free Trade Agreements, Free Trade Area, or Free Trade Association.
2. Under the GATT/WTO, the term *regional trade agreements* (RTAs), which include FTAs and customs unions, are used to describe regionalization. But in this paper we use the term FTAs to mean RTAs, as many RTAs, especially those in East Asia, are FTAs. See the WTO website at http://www.wto.org for the information on RTAs.

omies started showing a strong interest in FTAs toward the end of the 1990s. Although East Asia has so far seen the creation of only a few FTAs, including AFTA and the Japan-Singapore FTA, it is likely to observe the establishment of many FTAs in the near future. Indeed, it may not be unrealistic to imagine the formation of the East Asia FTA, covering all East Asian countries and economies.

In light of strong interest in FTAs by East Asian economies, this paper attempts to examine the impact of the East Asia FTA on trade patterns in East Asia by using a multisector computable general equilibrium (CGE) model. Because FTA removes tariff and nontariff barriers on trade among members, the East Asia FTA is expected to have substantial impacts on the trade patterns of East Asian economies. An analysis of the impacts of an East Asia FTA is useful not only for researchers interested in trade issues but also for policymakers interested in responsible trade policies.

The structure of the paper is as follows. Section 7.2 reviews recent developments in FTAs in East Asia. Section 7.3 presents the model and the data used in the simulation analysis. One important objective of this section is to examine trade and protection patterns in East Asia to set the stage for the simulation analysis of the impact of an East Asia FTA on trade in East Asia. Section 7.4 discusses the results of the simulation. Section 7.5 concludes the paper.

7.2   Emergence of FTAs in East Asia

East Asia was not active in the formation of regional trade agreements, such as FTAs, until recently.[3] Indeed, the AFTA was the only major FTA until Japan and Singapore enacted the Japan-Singapore FTA (formally Japan-Singapore Economic Partnership Agreement) in November 2002. This section provides a brief discussion on the recent developments concerning FTAs in East Asia.

The ASEAN Free Trade Area was established in 1992 with six ASEAN member countries: Indonesia, Malaysia, the Philippines, Singapore, Thailand, and Brunei. New ASEAN members—Vietnam, Myanmar, Cambodia, and Laos—joined AFTA in the latter half of the 1990s, and AFTA currently has ten member countries. The main objective of AFTA is to develop competitive industries in ASEAN by promoting intra-ASEAN trade. Several factors contributed to the formation of AFTA. One is the realization of the need to capture export markets in the face of increasing FTAs in the world. Another factor is the emergence of China as a competitor for attracting foreign direct investment (FDI). The end of the cold war also had an impact on ASEAN, as it made ASEAN concentrate on economic development. Besides AFTA, ASEAN as a group as well as its members have

---

3. Urata (2002) discussed recent developments on FTAs in East Asia.

become active in FTA discussions with other countries. One of the FTAs involving ASEAN that has received the most attention recently is that with China, which will be discussed in the following. The ASEAN is also discussing the possibility of FTAs with Japan and Korea.

Compared to ASEAN countries in Southeast Asia, the countries in Northeast Asia including China, Japan, and Korea had not been active in FTAs until recently. Despite increasingly strong interest in FTAs by Northeast Asian countries, there is only one FTA (Japan-Singapore FTA) that has been enacted so far. Japan is currently negotiating an FTA with Mexico, and it has been studying possible FTAs with Korea, ASEAN, Thailand, Malaysia, and the Philippines. The importance of FTAs with East Asian countries for Japan and East Asia is understood by many Japanese, including policymakers and business people. However, the moves toward the formation of FTAs have been rather weak because of strong opposition from various groups such as noncompetitive farmers, who would suffer from trade liberalization of agricultural products.

Korea started having an interest in FTAs before Japan. In 1998, Korea disclosed a plan to start FTA negotiations with Chile, and it also set up a joint-study group at the private level on an FTA with Japan. Korea started negotiations with Chile in 1999, and Korea and Chile signed the agreement in October 2002 after difficult negotiations on liberalization of agricultural imports. Although the agreement was signed, it has not yet been ratified by the Korean National Assembly because of strong opposition from the farmers. Korea also started studying the possible FTA with ASEAN.

China's active FTA strategy has received a lot of attention. China joined the WTO in 2001 and established an access to the world market, and it started to pursue regional strategies by using FTAs. China signed a framework agreement on comprehensive economic cooperation with ASEAN in November 2002. The agreement, which was proposed strongly by China, includes not only trade liberalization but also cooperation in the areas of FDI and economic development. China and ASEAN started negotiations on FTA in January 2003 with a target for its conclusion by June 2004. China has offered various schemes attractive to ASEAN and particularly to its new members, such as economic cooperation for the new ASEAN members and advanced trade liberalization (early harvest) in agricultural products. In addition to ASEAN, China has proposed to Japan and Korea to establish a trilateral FTA including these three countries.

The idea of an FTA covering East Asian countries has emerged. At the Leaders' Summit meeting of ASEAN+3 (China, Japan, and Korea) in 1998, the leaders decided to set up the East Asia Vision Group to study long-term vision for economic cooperation. The group has presented the leaders with recommendations including the establishment of an East Asia FTA. Despite the recommendation from the East Asia Vision Group, the East Asia FTA has not yet become a concrete agenda at the Leaders' meeting.

One can think of various factors that have led to an emerging interest in FTAs among the countries in East Asia. Many countries consider FTAs as an effective way to penetrate the markets of the member countries. Some countries think FTAs would promote deregulation and structural reform to revitalize their economies. The financial crisis in East Asia increased the awareness of the need for regional cooperation such as FTAs to avoid another crisis and to promote regional economic growth. Rivalry in the region has been a factor contributing to an increased interest in FTAs. Specifically, both China and Japan, which are competing to become a "leader" in the region, are keen on using FTAs to strengthen the relationships with ASEAN and the Newly Industrializing Economies (NIEs). Indeed, in November 2002, Japan proposed an economic partnership framework to ASEAN one day after China agreed to start FTA negotiations with ASEAN. It should also be noted that ASEAN and the NIEs also consider FTAs as a means to maintain and increase their influential position in East Asia.

Currently, the establishment of a China-Japan-Korea FTA appears difficult not only because of the opposition groups against trade liberalization but also because of the differences in their views on past history and other noneconomic issues. Rather than a China-Japan-Korea FTA, the establishment of three ASEAN+1 FTAs, namely ASEAN-China, ASEAN-Japan, and ASEAN-Korea, may be more likely. Indeed, ASEAN may be interested in establishing three ASEAN+1 FTAs to keep their negotiating position before moving to the establishment of an East Asia FTA.

Considering that an FTA would contribute to economic growth of the countries involved and considering that FTAs are likely to increase in other parts of the world, it is hoped that East Asia would work hard to establish an East Asia FTA by overcoming the obstacles with active cooperation. With these observations in mind, we attempt to investigate the likely impacts of the East Asia FTA on East Asian economies in the following sections.

7.3   The Impacts of an East Asia FTA on East Asian Economies: A Simulation Analysis

7.3.1   The Model

This section investigates the economic impacts of an East Asia FTA on East Asian economies using the standard Global Trade Analysis Project model (GTAP model) developed by Hertel (1997).[4] This is a multisector,

---

4. The impacts of an East Asia FTA using a CGE model are also examined in Ballard and Cheong (1997) although they do not focus on the impacts on trade patterns. For more detail, see Ballard and Cheong (1997).

multicountry computable general equilibrium (CGE) model that has been widely used in a number of studies. The characteristics of the GTAP model are summarized as follows. The demand side of the standard GTAP model assumes that total national income is allocated using fixed value shares among three kinds of final demand—government, private household, and savings—which are derived from an aggregate utility function of the Cobb-Douglas form. The single representative household in each country maximizes a constant difference of elasticity expenditure (CDE) function. The CDE function is calibrated to different income and the price elasticity of demand, and calibrated elasticity is used to specify private household demand function.

On the production side, the standard GTAP model employs constant returns-to-scale technology and perfect competition. Production in each sector in each country is represented by a multilevel production function of a Leontief form that involves value added and intermediate inputs generated from the input-output tables. The demands for factors and intermediate inputs are represented by a nested constant elasticity of substitution (CES) function. Each firm uses a CES composite of domestically produced and imported intermediate goods and determines the optimal mix of imported and domestic goods given domestic and import prices. Imports are distinguished by country of origin (Armington assumption).[5]

Labor is mobile across industries but not across countries. Capital is mobile across industries and countries, and its accumulation is endogenously determined. Investments are assembled to be allocated across regions through a hypothetical global sector called the global bank in such a way that the global bank equates the change in the expected rates of return across countries. Transport margins are derived from equating supply and demand in another hypothetical global sector called the global transportation sector. Equilibrium satisfies the conditions in that demand equals supply for all goods and factors, and representative firms in each industry earn zero profit.

While a standard GTAP model is useful in analyzing the impact of trade policy, there are some limitations. First, the Armington assumption may be a problem because it assumes that every country has some market power and may therefore be able to influence its terms of trade. This assumption is not realistic for small countries such as those in East Asia. Second, the model assumes perfect competition, which may not be appropriate as some sectors may have an imperfectly competitive structure.[6] Third, the standard GTAP model assumes a static framework, which might cause some

5. For more details about the current standard GTAP model, see http://www.gtap.agecon.purdue.edu/products/models/current.asp.

6. There are some CGE models that include imperfect competition and scale economies. For instance, Brown, Kiyota, and Stern (2004) introduce monopolistic competition, which makes it possible to introduce intraindustry trade without the Armington assumption.

problems in analyzing the timing of establishment of an FTA.[7] Fourth, the standard GTAP model does not incorporate FDI partly because of the limited availability of bilateral FDI flow data at the sectoral level and difficulty in modeling an FDI mechanism. As such, the impacts of an FTA on FDI are not captured. Finally, the data do not capture some of the nontariff measures and most of the barriers in trade in services. Because of these limitations, the use of the GTAP model may underestimate the real impacts of an FTA.

7.3.2   The Data

The main data come from the GTAP Database Release 5 (GTAP-5), which contains sixty-six countries/regions and fifty-seven sectors for 1997.[8] The database provides production and consumption structures described in a social accounting matrix for each country. To facilitate the computation, the database is aggregated into twenty countries and twenty-one sectors.

In the GTAP-5, trade barriers, which include tariff and nontariff measures, are described as the differences between domestic market prices and world market prices. Thus, the tariff and nontariff measures cover import tariffs, export subsidies, and domestic supports (output subsidies, intermediate input subsidies, land-based payments, and capital-based payments).[9] However, the information on the barriers in service trade is still under development and does not cover many barriers.[10] Hence, this paper focuses on merchandise trade, that is, agricultural, mining, and manufacturing trade, in analyzing trade flows.

Trade Patterns of East Asian Economies

Table 7.1 summarizes the export and import compositions of East Asian economies in 1997 from GTAP-5. Three distinct features are observed in this table. First, the major exports of many East Asian economies are textiles and machinery, especially electric equipment. Second, the major imports of many East Asian economies are concentrated in electric equipment and general machinery. Third, the shares of imports for agriculture and food products and beverages are larger than the corresponding export shares for all the economies except Vietnam. However, we should also note that most East Asian economies show low compositional shares in trade

7. Ianchovichina and McDougall (2000) develop a dynamic GTAP model based on the standard GTAP model.
8. For the GTAP-5, see Dimaranan and McDougal (2002).
9. In GTAP-5, zero rates are reported for antidumping duties, price undertakings, and voluntary export restraints (VERs) due to the absence of up-to-date data (Dimaranan 2002, 16-A-11).
10. Because of the limited data availability, the number of sectors significantly decreases when we include the trade barriers in services in the CGE analysis. For a study that focuses on the trade barriers in services, see Brown and Stern (2001).

	NIEs						ASEAN				
Sector	China	Japan	Korea	Hong Kong	Singapore	Taiwan	Indonesia	Malaysia	The Philippines	Thailand	Vietnam
Exports											
Agriculture	2.5	0.1	0.2	0.0	0.5	0.4	3.8	0.8	2.0	1.7	10.9
Forestry	0.1	0.0	0.0	0.0	0.1	0.0	0.2	1.1	0.0	0.3	0.3
Fishing	0.3	0.0	0.3	0.1	0.1	0.2	0.5	0.1	0.4	0.4	0.5
Mining	2.2	0.0	0.0	0.0	0.0	0.1	23.4	5.0	1.2	0.3	17.1
Food products and beverages	3.6	0.6	1.7	2.9	1.8	1.4	7.4	6.6	5.6	13.0	13.7
Textiles	20.4	2.0	12.7	39.9	1.3	11.0	14.0	3.7	9.1	9.2	19.1
Pulp, paper, and paper products	2.7	0.8	1.7	4.1	1.5	2.9	15.3	6.0	2.5	2.8	4.2
Chemicals	8.2	9.9	13.6	4.9	15.5	10.8	11.2	9.2	3.1	11.2	3.3
Iron, steel, and metal products	6.3	6.8	9.7	3.3	3.1	8.9	3.1	2.9	3.3	3.6	1.0
Transportation machinery	2.2	21.7	13.7	0.1	1.4	3.7	0.8	1.1	1.2	1.8	0.3
Electronic equipment	14.6	25.0	29.1	21.4	59.1	35.9	7.3	52.6	58.0	31.7	3.6
General machinery	14.4	29.7	12.9	17.2	13.2	18.1	3.9	8.2	9.3	13.3	4.1
Other manufacturing	22.7	3.4	4.3	5.9	2.3	6.8	9.3	2.6	4.3	10.7	22.0
Total	100.0	100.0	100.0	100.0	100.0	100.0	100.0	100.0	100.0	100.0	100.0
Imports											
Agriculture	2.7	4.8	3.5	3.0	1.3	3.3	6.6	2.3	2.8	2.2	1.0
Forestry	0.5	1.2	0.6	0.3	0.0	0.2	0.1	0.1	0.3	0.3	0.0
Fishing	0.1	0.8	0.1	0.8	0.1	0.2	0.0	0.2	0.0	0.1	0.0
Mining	3.8	15.9	16.0	0.7	6.2	6.8	3.3	1.0	7.2	8.4	0.2
Food products and beverages	4.3	10.0	3.5	6.6	3.2	3.6	4.4	3.8	5.9	4.0	4.3
Textiles	10.8	7.1	4.2	13.6	2.7	3.1	4.5	2.2	4.1	2.7	13.5
Pulp, paper, and paper products	4.3	6.0	2.9	3.0	1.8	3.4	2.6	2.2	2.2	2.3	2.5
Chemicals	18.8	11.0	12.9	8.5	12.5	13.9	18.9	11.0	9.8	12.5	30.4
Iron, steel, and metal products	9.5	6.6	13.9	11.4	6.7	9.4	11.1	9.5	6.8	11.6	8.5
Transportation machinery	4.2	5.6	4.6	5.9	5.9	6.7	9.9	7.8	8.5	7.5	6.4
Electronic equipment	14.8	12.7	13.7	23.2	37.0	22.8	7.5	36.0	30.9	19.6	7.0
General machinery	21.8	11.8	19.8	15.9	18.8	22.4	26.9	20.7	18.3	24.2	19.5
Other manufacturing	4.3	6.6	4.2	7.2	3.9	4.0	4.1	3.2	3.3	4.4	6.6
Total	100.0	100.0	100.0	100.0	100.0	100.0	100.0	100.0	100.0	100.0	100.0

Sources: Dimaranan and McDougall (2002); GTAP website, http://www.gtap.agecon.purdue.edu/products/models/current.asp.

Notes: Values of exports are evaluated at domestic market prices (VXMD). Exports are the sum of all partner countries. Values of imports are evaluated at world prices (VIWS). Imports are the sum of partner countries. Total excludes the services sectors.

(exports and imports) for agriculture and food products and beverages except for Thailand and Vietnam for exports and Japan for imports.

Table 7.2 presents the intraindustry trade (IIT) patterns and revealed comparative advantage (RCA) for East Asian economies.[11] The IIT index takes the value between 0 and 100, and it increases with the extent of intraindustry trade. The RCA takes the value greater than or equal to zero. If RCA for an industry for a country takes the value greater than unity, it is interpreted that the country has a comparative advantage in that industry. Similarly, if it takes the value less than unity, then the industry has a comparative disadvantage.

There are three notable findings in this table. First, for many economies, pulp, chemicals, and electronic equipment tend to show large figures for the IIT index. Second, most of agriculture, forestry, fishing, mining, and food products and beverages do not register large IIT figures. Third, the largest RCA is likely to be observed in electric equipment. Specifically, electric equipment represents the largest RCA figures for Japan, Korea, Singapore, Taiwan, the Philippines, and Thailand. The large numbers also appear in textiles and fishing. It is interesting to note that transportation machinery takes values greater than unity only for Japan and Korea, while general machinery takes values greater than unity only for Japan and Taiwan.

These observations indicate that many East Asian economies have a comparative advantage in the production of electric equipment, and many economies appear to engage in vertical division of labor in electronic equipment production. Specifically, many East Asian economies' competitiveness comes from labor-intensive assembling operations in the production of electronic equipment, as they import electronic parts and components to assemble finished products and export them to foreign countries.

Table 7.3 presents the three types of regionalization measures in terms of trade for East Asian economies.[12] The absolute measure compares the scale of a particular intraregional trade relationship to world trade, while the relative measure compares it to its overall regional trade. The double-relative measure, which is commonly called the trade intensity index, shows the intensity or bias of the intraregional trade relationship by taking into account its importance in world trade. The value of unity for the double relative measure can be interpreted so that the intraregional trade relationship is neutral, while the relationship is more (or less) biased when the measure is greater (or less) than unity.

The computed absolute measures show that intraregional trade in East Asia and ASEAN amount to 11 and 1 percent of world trade, respectively.

11. For the formulas used to compute the IIT index and RCA index, see the appendix.
12. The definitions of the three measures are given in the appendix. See Petri (1993) and Urata (2001) for the discussion of the regionalization measures and their application to East Asian economies.

Table 7.2   Intraindustry trade (IIT) patterns and revealed comparative advantage of East Asian economies in 1997

Sector	China	Japan	Korea	Hong Kong	Singapore	Taiwan	Indonesia	Malaysia	The Philippines	Thailand	Vietnam
			NIEs						ASEAN		
Intraindustry trade (IIT) index											
Agriculture	34.5	4.2	6.3	0.9	32.9	14.1	40.6	21.2	26.9	38.6	17.6
Forestry	9.3	1.4	1.5	0.3	40.2	8.2	36.6	5.5	12.0	15.2	21.0
Fishing	24.5	7.4	23.5	4.9	24.9	13.3	5.7	14.7	11.0	13.6	19.9
Mining	13.5	0.7	0.5	0.2	0.9	1.5	10.8	14.7	2.3	2.8	2.7
Food products and beverages	36.5	14.0	32.8	23.5	51.0	39.6	40.7	43.8	48.0	36.9	43.9
Textiles	38.7	50.8	50.9	43.3	46.0	35.2	27.6	52.5	26.5	32.6	31.9
Pulp, paper, and paper products	65.6	26.5	35.8	52.8	60.0	60.4	22.5	42.8	69.1	61.8	49.2
Chemicals	56.9	73.0	54.4	21.1	56.2	46.9	63.1	78.8	28.8	69.5	13.9
Iron, steel, and metal products	60.3	56.7	51.7	15.7	42.8	51.9	43.8	48.0	47.8	42.2	14.4
Transportation machinery	42.1	32.6	40.7	1.4	21.9	55.0	13.7	22.0	16.0	21.4	4.9
Electronic equipment	53.2	55.8	57.8	30.8	65.8	52.1	62.3	66.0	67.8	69.3	22.9
General machinery	58.5	46.3	43.9	29.7	49.0	57.7	26.0	55.0	47.6	56.7	17.2
Other manufacturing	22.0	67.1	78.7	36.9	43.5	59.1	36.6	64.6	46.9	53.8	23.1
Revealed comparative advantage (RCA)											
Agriculture	0.88	0.03	0.06	0.01	0.15	0.13	1.28	0.27	0.50	0.51	3.71
Forestry	0.33	0.03	0.03	0.00	0.45	0.09	0.82	5.78	0.13	1.51	1.39
Fishing	1.63	0.13	1.51	0.47	0.48	1.08	2.73	0.61	1.59	2.12	2.95
Mining	0.37	0.01	0.01	0.00	0.01	0.01	3.81	0.81	0.14	0.05	2.84
Food products and beverages	0.68	0.12	0.31	0.30	0.30	0.26	1.36	1.18	0.76	2.19	2.56
Textiles	3.53	0.33	2.13	3.75	0.19	1.92	2.34	0.60	1.13	1.40	3.24
Pulp, paper, and paper products	0.64	0.17	0.38	0.52	0.30	0.67	3.45	1.33	0.41	0.58	0.98
Chemicals	0.67	0.77	1.07	0.22	1.10	0.88	0.88	0.71	0.18	0.81	0.26
Iron, steel, and metal products	0.86	0.88	1.28	0.24	0.37	1.22	0.41	0.38	0.33	0.43	0.13
Transportation machinery	0.20	1.91	1.23	0.01	0.12	0.35	0.07	0.10	0.08	0.14	0.02
Electronic equipment	1.17	1.91	2.26	0.94	4.14	2.90	0.57	4.00	3.33	2.26	0.28
General machinery	0.86	1.69	0.74	0.56	0.69	1.09	0.23	0.46	0.40	0.70	0.24
Other manufacturing	4.00	0.57	0.73	0.56	0.36	1.20	1.58	0.43	0.54	1.67	3.81

Sources: See table 7.1 sources.

Note: For definition of IIT index and RCA, see the appendix in the main text.

Table 7.3   Regionalization in trade for East Asian economies in 1997

Sector	East Asia Exports Absolute measure	Exports Relative measure	Imports Relative measure	Imports Double relative measure	ASEAN Exports Absolute measure	Exports Relative measure	Imports Relative measure	Imports Double relative measure
Total	0.11	0.44	0.50	2.02	0.01	0.21	0.20	3.17
Agriculture	0.04	0.56	0.19	2.53	0.01	0.19	0.13	3.81
Forestry	0.10	0.71	0.20	1.38	0.01	0.07	0.22	1.79
Fishing	0.18	0.84	0.52	2.37	0.02	0.22	0.54	6.52
Mining	0.05	0.81	0.19	2.87	0.01	0.13	0.14	2.67
Food products and beverages	0.07	0.58	0.33	2.72	0.01	0.15	0.24	3.37
Textiles	0.17	0.48	0.77	2.20	0.00	0.08	0.15	2.32
Pulp, paper, and paper products	0.07	0.55	0.45	1.72	0.01	0.11	0.26	2.83
Chemicals	0.10	0.56	0.49	3.32	0.02	0.31	0.25	3.78
Iron, steel, and metal products	0.12	0.63	0.47	2.68	0.01	0.30	0.10	4.81
Transportation machinery	0.04	0.18	0.32	2.54	0.00	0.24	0.04	4.26
Electronic equipment	0.22	0.42	0.68	1.61	0.05	0.23	0.32	5.73
General machinery	0.11	0.46	0.52	1.31	0.01	0.29	0.13	1.63
Other manufacturing	0.09	0.29	0.52	2.12	0.01	0.11	0.16	3.82

Sources: See table 7.1 sources.

Notes: East Asia is all of the countries listed in table 6.1 (or table 6.2), while ASEAN is Indonesia, Malaysia, the Philippines, Singapore, Thailand, and Vietnam. For a definition of each measure, see the appendix in the main text.

As to the relative measures, the share of intraregional exports in East Asia's exports was 44 percent, while the share of intraregional imports in East Asia's imports was larger, at 50 percent. These findings on the relative measures for exports and imports indicate that East Asia is an important source of imports rather than a destination of exports. The relative measures for exports and imports for ASEAN are 21 and 20 percent, respectively, significantly smaller compared with trade in East Asia. The ASEAN countries depend on non-ASEAN countries, particularly other East Asian countries, in their trade. The computed double-relative measures show that trade in both East Asia and ASEAN have strong intraregional bias. Intraregional bias is particularly strong for ASEAN trade, reflecting the presence of the AFTA, under which preferential treatment is given to intra-ASEAN trade.

The results for disaggregated-sector levels reveal several interesting developments. First, for electronic equipment, fishing, and textiles, intraregional trade in East Asia has a significant share in world trade, indicating that these products are actively traded in the region. Second, for electronic equipment and textiles, East Asia is an important source of imports rather than a destination of exports, reflecting the pattern of production and trade, in which parts and components are procured in East Asia to be assembled for the finished products in East Asia, which in turn are exported to outside the region. Third, high double-relative measures are observed for ASEAN trade vis-à-vis East Asia trade for all products except mining, indicating the influence of the AFTA on trade in a wide range of products.

Nominal and Effective Rate of Protection for East Asian Economies

In the GTAP database, trade barriers, which include tariff and nontariff measures, can be expressed as the difference in prices between domestic market prices and world market prices. We denote the difference as the nominal rate of protection (NRP). We also compute the effective rate of protection (ERP), which accounts for the protection on value added by taking into account the protection given not only to the product under study but also to intermediate inputs used for the product.[13]

Table 7.4 presents the calculated results of NRPs and ERPs from the GTAP database. There are three notable findings in this table. First, for China, Japan and Korea, the levels of protection on agriculture and food products and beverages are extremely high. The NRPs on food products and beverages are also high for these three countries and Taiwan. The results for China are somewhat surprising, as China exports substantial magnitudes of agricultural products, and food products and beverages.

Similarly, ERPs tend to be high for these industries in these countries with few exceptions, indicating that these industries are given substantial

---

13. The appendix explains the computational method of ERP.

Table 7.4   Nominal and effective rate of protection of East Asian economies in 1997

Sector	China	Japan	Korea	Hong Kong	Singapore	Taiwan	Indonesia	Malaysia	The Philippines	Thailand	Vietnam
			NIEs						ASEAN		
Nominal rate of protection (NRP) in 1997 (%)											
Agriculture	41.3	58.4	110.9	0.0	3.5	6.0	5.2	31.1	15.0	20.3	13.6
Forestry	2.6	0.2	2.0	0.0	0.0	0.4	1.1	0.0	0.5	1.5	3.3
Fishing	14.2	4.9	15.8	0.0	0.0	31.1	7.5	1.4	6.6	44.9	8.9
Mining	0.2	-1.4	3.9	0.0	0.0	4.9	2.8	1.1	1.0	0.3	3.2
Food products and beverages	37.4	50.0	37.7	0.0	4.6	26.1	14.8	14.8	18.7	37.2	36.5
Textiles	25.7	10.7	8.0	0.0	0.0	8.1	15.6	16.1	13.6	26.7	34.0
Pulp, paper, and paper products	11.7	2.2	5.3	0.0	0.0	2.9	6.2	9.1	11.4	12.6	19.1
Chemicals	12.6	2.3	7.0	0.0	0.0	3.7	7.1	8.6	6.4	15.3	16.1
Iron, steel, and metal products	9.7	1.0	4.9	0.0	0.0	4.0	8.1	6.1	8.1	11.9	8.1
Transportation machinery	18.9	0.0	4.6	0.0	0.0	13.2	25.4	19.7	10.3	31.5	36.9
Electronic equipment	11.9	0.0	8.0	0.0	0.0	2.9	8.1	0.8	3.1	8.8	9.7
General machinery	13.5	0.3	7.8	0.0	0.0	4.9	3.9	5.1	5.5	10.4	6.7
Other manufacturing	16.9	5.5	7.3	0.0	0.0	5.6	9.5	8.2	12.0	13.2	16.9
Effective rate of protection (ERP) in 1997 (%)											
Agriculture	51.6	84.2	154.2	0.0	4.3	-0.5	5.1	37.3	16.2	20.6	14.7
Forestry	0.6	-1.8	0.9	0.0	-0.1	0.3	0.5	-0.2	-0.2	1.3	3.1
Fishing	9.5	2.4	21.5	0.0	0.0	40.2	8.2	1.1	6.6	54.3	10.0
Mining	-5.4	-3.3	4.6	0.0	0.0	5.5	2.7	1.1	0.1	-0.1	3.6
Food products and beverages	60.5	104.7	-57.6	0.0	8.2	90.6	30.1	-15.4	29.2	71.2	133.9
Textiles	33.2	19.3	12.9	0.0	0.0	16.1	22.6	26.7	18.7	37.1	83.6
Pulp, paper, and paper products	10.6	3.5	7.7	0.0	0.0	4.5	12.0	19.6	24.1	15.4	60.8
Chemicals	22.2	3.8	9.4	0.0	0.0	5.6	11.6	-1.0	4.6	17.8	58.1
Iron, steel, and metal products	17.5	1.5	7.2	0.0	0.0	7.0	11.8	10.2	16.6	14.0	15.1
Transportation machinery	36.0	-1.1	4.8	0.0	0.0	30.9	35.7	27.8	18.5	37.9	156.8
Electronic equipment	14.7	-0.8	16.3	0.0	0.0	3.9	9.1	-2.4	1.4	9.2	19.8
General machinery	21.3	-0.1	11.7	0.0	0.0	8.7	1.7	6.5	6.2	11.2	19.9
Other manufacturing	24.6	10.8	11.2	0.0	0.0	11.5	10.6	12.4	18.8	15.2	34.0

Sources: See table 7.1 sources.

Note: For the definition of NRP and ERP, see the appendix in the main text.

protection from import competition. Two exceptions are agriculture in Taiwan and food products and beverages in Korea, for which negative ERPs are obtained. These negative results are due to the fact that NRPs given to intermediate goods for the production of agriculture (in the case of Taiwan) and food products and beverages (in the case of Korea) are higher than NRPs given to agriculture and food products and beverages. In other words, agriculture in Taiwan and food products and beverages in Korea suffer from negative discrimination imposed by their governments.

Second, a high level of protection is given in paper, chemicals, and machinery industries in ASEAN countries as well as China, and these industries tend to represent larger figures for ERP than for NRP. Such patterns of protection, that is, higher ERP than NRPs, are common in many countries and characterized as tariff escalation. Indeed, tariff escalation is regarded as rational patterns of tariff protection for the development of a particular industry, although the effectiveness of such a policy appears questionable. It is to be noted that high protection is observed for the transportation machinery industry in many ASEAN countries and China, reflecting the importance of the industry for these governments.

Third, there are virtually almost no trade barriers in Hong Kong and Singapore. Only agriculture and food products and beverages receive protection, although the level of protection given to these industries by these governments is substantially lower when compared to the cases for other East Asian economies.

7.4 Simulation Results

We conducted a simulation analysis to discern the impacts of an East Asia FTA by removing trade barriers among East Asian economies. In this section we examine the results. We begin with the results for GDP and economic welfare in terms of equivalent variation (EV) and then turn to the results on overall as well as sectoral outputs and trade.

Table 7.5 presents simulation results for GDP and EV for East Asian economies with a few selected countries. The results indicate that all FTA member economies obtain benefits from an East Asia FTA in terms of gross domestic product (GDP) and EV. The positive impacts are very large for the ASEAN countries. Among the ASEAN countries, Thailand gains substantially. Indeed, Thai GDP is estimated to increase as much as 16 percent from an East Asia FTA. The large gain for Thailand is attributable mainly to the high protection imposed on the Thai economy before an East Asia FTA. Vietnam and Indonesia also would gain substantially from an East Asia FTA.

By contrast to the gains accrued to the FTA members, nonmember countries experience negative impacts in the forms of declines in GDP and EV. These negative impacts are mainly attributable to the trade diversion

Table 7.5   Estimated effects of an East Asia FTA on real GDP and equivalent variation, for
                   selected countries/regions

	GDP (changes from base data, %)	Equivalent variation	
		Changes from base data (US$ million)	Changes divided by GDP in 1997 (%)
Australia/New Zealand	−0.23	−1,342	−0.29
China	1.27	5,485	0.64
Hong Kong	1.41	3,389	2.42
Japan	0.05	8,199	0.19
Korea	1.71	7,805	1.75
Taiwan	1.51	5,597	1.87
Indonesia	5.61	10,209	4.89
Malaysia	2.83	2,279	2.15
The Philippines	2.02	602	0.77
Singapore	2.26	2,944	3.69
Thailand	15.90	19,790	12.54
Vietnam	8.42	1,446	6.61
Other Asia	−0.31	−1,803	−0.34
United States	−0.06	−7,059	−0.09
EU	−0.01	−1,807	−0.02

Sources: See table 7.1 sources.
Note: Figures indicate the changes from base data.

effect from the East Asia FTA, by which nonmember countries' exports to
East Asia are substituted by member countries' exports as a result of preferential treatment given to trade between the members. It should be noted
that the negative impacts on the United States and the European Union
(EU) are quite small while they are somewhat substantial for Australia/
New Zealand and Other Asia. Relatively large negative impacts for Aus-
tralia/New Zealand and Other Asia stem from the fact that East Asia is a
very important region for their export destination. Because the results of
the simulation depend on the elasticity of substation between domestic and
imported products, we examine how sensitive our results are to the size of
elasticity by conducting a simulation with a 10 percent increase in the elasticity values. We found that the results are greater by approximately 10 percent, indicating the importance of the size of elasticities in determining the
impacts of FTA.[14]

The impacts of an East Asia FTA on the changes in real outputs and real
exports in agriculture and manufacturing sectors are presented in table
7.6. For Hong Kong, Singapore, Indonesia, Malaysia, the Philippines, and
Thailand, positive impacts on real outputs are observed in almost all industries. One major exceptional sector is transportation machinery, whose

14. The results are not given in the paper, but they are available on request from the authors.

Sector	China	Japan	Korea	Hong Kong	Singapore	Taiwan	Indonesia	Malaysia	The Philippines	Thailand	Vietnam
Changes in real outputs (%)											
Agriculture	4.5	-3.9	-11.9	0.3	4.7	1.6	1.3	0.4	2.0	5.2	0.4
Forestry	-0.2	-1.8	-3.6	1.7	-7.4	3.2	8.6	2.1	2.1	16.3	11.4
Fishing	0.9	-2.8	7.6	-2.6	7.8	-1.0	3.9	2.5	1.3	12.6	6.1
Mining	-0.2	-0.7	-2.1	3.8	4.1	-0.9	1.4	1.7	4.1	19.2	-8.3
Food products and beverages	1.6	-3.4	30.1	19.3	36.7	6.9	5.3	15.3	-1.3	23.5	8.9
Textiles	-0.2	-2.3	17.4	3.2	1.9	17.1	3.7	7.7	13.9	8.4	174.8
Pulp, paper, and paper products	-1.1	-0.4	1.9	3.3	3.7	1.6	8.9	4.3	0.8	16.1	16.9
Chemicals	-1.6	1.1	3.4	5.5	11.1	7.1	1.4	4.4	2.0	10.6	-2.0
Iron, steel, and metal products	-1.5	2.2	-1.4	4.7	7.7	0.0	2.9	1.4	6.7	20.1	-18.3
Transportation machinery	-16.2	5.2	1.0	-7.9	-14.3	-6.9	-47.8	-24.0	29.3	-11.0	-55.1
Electronic equipment	6.9	-0.7	-1.9	0.9	1.9	-2.5	17.4	5.7	8.9	29.2	-0.9
General machinery	-1.6	2.2	-4.8	7.4	5.5	1.7	22.8	7.4	12.7	26.8	-3.7
Other manufacturing	1.6	-0.5	0.9	8.1	5.0	2.5	7.3	1.2	5.8	18.1	12.9
Changes in real exports (%)											
Agriculture	194.5	41.8	451.7	19.4	43.6	28.3	2.6	27.8	118.2	-53.5	-14.7
Forestry	3.6	3.8	-1.3	11.3	-7.4	13.5	13.9	-2.9	15.6	25.1	-11.2
Fishing	28.7	33.3	21.4	0.6	14.9	2.2	11.3	28.6	36.5	17.9	11.8
Mining	4.2	-1.1	-11.5	-11.1	3.2	-1.2	-0.6	0.0	4.1	24.8	-22.0
Food products and beverages	78.9	88.5	462.1	136.3	78.2	131.8	52.0	40.3	27.7	74.0	71.0
Textiles	29.2	44.0	32.1	8.5	4.4	26.8	11.5	22.1	28.3	23.5	209.5
Pulp, paper, and paper products	6.7	19.0	15.3	12.5	6.7	6.9	11.3	9.3	6.5	19.6	56.5
Chemicals	10.1	8.6	10.5	19.5	12.5	16.6	1.2	12.5	9.7	14.5	16.2
Iron, steel, and metal products	11.6	15.5	6.5	17.0	10.2	6.1	9.0	12.0	18.3	36.4	-16.0
Transportation machinery	26.9	13.6	7.7	-25.1	-22.8	12.1	105.8	105.1	104.3	137.7	107.8
Electronic equipment	20.2	-1.2	0.2	1.2	2.0	-2.0	36.0	5.8	9.0	32.8	8.4
General machinery	11.2	5.7	-1.6	13.3	8.1	6.0	44.4	12.2	17.2	36.0	1.2
Other manufacturing	9.2	8.9	11.6	31.0	8.3	7.9	9.1	8.9	17.9	25.5	28.1

Source: Model simulation.

Note: The changes in real outputs and exports indicate the deviation from base data. Services are not reported as trade barriers in service sectors are not available, and it might underestimate the impacts of an East Asia FTA.

production declines for these economies except for the Philippines. Indeed, it should be noted that production of transportation machinery declines for all the economies except Japan and the Philippines. Unlike the case for many economies noted in the preceding, China, Japan, Korea, and Taiwan show sectoral variations in the direction of the changes in output.

Notable increases in output production are observed for the following sectors for the East Asian economies: agriculture (China, Singapore, and Thailand); food products and beverages (Korea, Hong Kong, Singapore, Malaysia, and Thailand); textiles (Korea, Taiwan, the Philippines, and Vietnam); electronic equipment (China, Indonesia, the Philippines, and Thailand); and general machinery (Indonesia, the Philippines, and Thailand). Some notable declines in output production are recorded as follows: agriculture (Japan and Korea); iron and steel (Vietnam); and transportation machinery (China, Singapore, Indonesia, Malaysia, Thailand, and Vietnam). These findings reveal the difficulty in establishing an East Asia FTA because of its negative impacts on the sectors with political influence in respective economies.

We have examined the impacts of an East Asia FTA on output at the sectoral level and found variations in its impacts among the sectors. It is of interest to examine if any systematic patterns exist in explaining the impact of an East Asia FTA among different sectors and economies. One would expect that the output of the sector that has a comparative advantage would increase more compared to that of the sectors with comparative disadvantage as a result of an FTA, because freer trade environment would give greater opportunities for output expansion for the sectors with comparative advantage. Along the similar line of the argument, one would expect that output of the protected sector would decline as a result of an FTA because of increased import competition. We examined these hypotheses by conducting regression analysis covering eleven economies and thirteen sectors. For the analysis, three different models are examined. The dependent variable, which is the same for the three models, is the rate of change in output, and explanatory variables are RCA, NRP, and ERP at base year, respectively. The results of the analysis support the first hypothesis, indicating that an FTA increases output of the sectors with comparative advantage (see table 7.7). However, they do not support the second hypothesis.

It is interesting to observe that exports increase for all the economies for almost all products with a few exceptions. Even exports of transportation machinery, whose production is shown to decline, are expected to increase for all of the economies except for Hong Kong and Singapore. These contrasting patterns of change in production and exports in transportation machinery reflect increased incentive given to exportation as a result of elimination of protection under the East Asia FTA. The sectors with substantial increases in exports include the following: agriculture (China, Japan, Korea, Singapore, and the Philippines); food products and beverages (all economies); textiles (Japan, Korea, and Vietnam); transportation

Table 7.7   **Relationship between protection, comparative advantage, and growth**

Dependent variable	Growth of outputs			Growth of exports		
Constant	4.433**	3.505*	0.640	−2.931	19.300***	36.810***
	(2.271)	(1.939)	(0.308)	(−0.577)	(3.093)	(4.784)
NRP	0.014			3.293***		
	(0.123)			(11.429)		
ERP		0.066			0.747***	
		(1.184)			(3.899)	
RCA			3.837***			−5.219
			(2.795)			(−1.028)
R^2	0.000	0.481	0.010	0.097	0.053	0.007
Adj. R^2	−0.007	0.477	0.003	0.090	0.046	0.000
N	143	143	143	143	143	143

Sources: NRP and ERP are from table 7.4. RCA is from table 7.2. The growth of outputs and exports are from table 7.6.
Note: *t*-statistics are in parentheses.
***Significant at the 1 percent level.
**Significant at the 5 percent level.
*Significant at the 10 percent level.

machinery (Indonesia, Malaysia, the Philippines, Thailand, and Vietnam); electronic equipment (China, Indonesia, and Thailand); and general machinery (Indonesia and Thailand). One should note that these values are the rate of change, as such a large value may be partly due to the low initial value before the formation of an East Asia FTA. A case in point is agriculture and food products and beverages for Japan, for which large rates of export growth are expected partly because of low export value before the formation of an East Asia FTA.

Following the discussions on the determinants of the change in output in the preceding, we examine the determinants of the change in exports using the same framework. One would expect the sectors with a comparative advantage and the sectors with low protection to increase as a result of an East Asia FTA. The results show that exports of the sectors with high protection increase as a result of an East Asia FTA. This unexpected result can be explained by a shift of incentives from domestic sales to export sales because of the removal of protection. As to the relationship between RCA and export expansion, we could not detect the expected relationship.

The impacts of an East Asia FTA on export change lead to the changes in the composition of exports, which are shown in tables 7.8 and 7.9. The figures for 1997 indicate the export composition in 1997 (obtained from table 7.1) and those under FTA indicate the export composition after the simulation. Italic figures indicate the percentage changes between compositions in 1997 and those in FTA.

The results show that the impacts of an East Asia FTA are not large enough to change the composition of each economy's exports and imports

Table 7.8 Export compositions of East Asian economies resulting from an East Asia FTA (percentage shares in total)

Sector	China 1997	China FTA	China Change	Japan 1997	Japan FTA	Japan Change	NIEs Korea 1997	NIEs Korea FTA	NIEs Korea Change	Hong Kong 1997	Hong Kong FTA	Hong Kong Change	Singapore 1997	Singapore FTA	Singapore Change	Taiwan 1997	Taiwan FTA	Taiwan Change
Nonmanufacturing	5.0	8.7	3.7	0.2	0.2	0.0	0.5	1.0	0.5	0.2	0.2	-0.0	0.7	1.0	0.3	0.6	0.7	0.1
Agriculture	2.5	6.5	4.0	0.1	0.1	0.0	0.2	0.7	0.5	0.0	0.0	0.0	0.5	0.8	0.3	0.4	0.5	0.1
Forestry	0.1	0.1	-0.0	0.0	0.0	-0.0	0.0	0.0	-0.0	0.0	0.0	-0.0	0.1	0.1	-0.0	0.0	0.0	0.0
Fishing	0.3	0.3	0.0	0.0	0.0	0.0	0.3	0.3	0.0	0.1	0.1	-0.0	0.1	0.1	0.0	0.2	0.2	-0.0
Mining	2.2	1.8	-0.3	0.0	0.0	-0.0	0.0	0.0	-0.0	0.0	0.0	0.0	0.0	0.0	-0.0	0.1	0.1	-0.0
Manufacturing	95.0	91.3	-3.7	99.8	99.8	-0.0	99.5	99.0	-0.5	99.8	99.8	0.0	99.3	99.0	-0.3	99.4	99.3	-0.1
Food products and beverages	3.6	5.5	1.9	0.6	1.1	0.5	1.7	6.8	5.1	2.9	6.1	3.2	1.8	3.1	1.3	1.4	2.9	1.6
Textiles	20.4	21.2	0.8	2.0	2.6	0.6	12.7	14.4	1.7	39.9	38.3	-1.6	1.3	1.3	-0.0	11.0	12.9	1.8
Pulp, paper, and paper products	2.7	2.4	-0.4	0.8	0.9	0.1	1.7	1.7	0.0	4.1	4.1	-0.0	1.5	1.5	0.0	2.9	2.8	-0.0
Chemicals	8.2	7.3	-0.9	9.9	9.9	0.0	13.6	13.1	-0.5	4.9	5.1	0.2	15.5	16.4	0.9	10.8	11.6	0.8
Iron, steel, and metal products	6.3	5.7	-0.6	6.8	7.2	0.5	9.7	9.1	-0.6	3.3	3.3	0.1	3.1	3.2	0.1	8.9	8.7	-0.2
Transportation machinery	2.2	2.2	0.0	21.7	22.8	1.1	13.7	13.0	-0.7	0.1	0.1	-0.0	1.4	1.1	-0.4	3.7	3.8	0.1
Electronic equipment	14.6	13.9	-0.7	25.0	22.8	-2.2	29.1	25.4	-3.8	21.4	18.9	-2.5	59.1	56.5	-2.6	35.9	32.1	-3.8
General machinery	14.4	13.0	-1.4	29.7	29.1	-0.7	12.9	11.2	-1.7	17.2	17.1	-0.1	13.2	13.5	0.3	18.1	17.7	-0.4
Other manufacturing	22.7	20.2	-2.5	3.4	3.4	0.0	4.3	4.2	-0.1	5.9	6.8	0.9	2.3	2.4	0.1	6.8	6.8	-0.0
Total	100.0	100.0		100.0	100.0		100.0	100.0		100.0	100.0		100.0	100.0				

	ASEAN Indonesia 1997	FTA	Change	Malaysia 1997	FTA	Change	The Philippines 1997	FTA	Change	Thailand 1997	FTA	Change	Vietnam 1997	FTA	Change
Nonmanufacturing	27.8	25.0	-2.8	7.1	6.8	-0.4	3.6	5.7	2.0	2.7	1.7	-1.0	28.8	17.1	-11.6
Agriculture	3.8	3.8	-0.0	0.8	1.0	0.2	2.0	4.1	2.1	1.7	0.8	-0.9	10.9	7.2	-3.7
Forestry	0.2	0.2	-0.0	1.1	1.0	-0.1	0.0	0.0	0.0	0.3	0.3	-0.0	0.3	0.2	-0.1
Fishing	0.5	0.5	-0.0	0.1	0.1	0.0	0.4	0.5	0.1	0.4	0.4	-0.1	0.5	0.4	-0.1
Mining	23.4	20.6	-2.8	5.0	4.6	-0.4	1.2	1.1	-0.1	0.3	0.3	-0.0	17.1	9.4	-7.7
Manufacturing	72.2	75.0	2.8	92.9	93.2	0.4	96.4	94.3	-2.0	97.3	98.3	1.0	71.2	82.9	11.6
Food products and beverages	7.4	10.3	2.9	6.6	8.3	1.7	5.6	6.4	0.8	13.0	18.8	5.8	13.7	17.2	3.4
Textiles	14.0	13.5	-0.5	3.7	4.0	0.3	9.1	9.8	0.6	9.2	8.3	-0.9	19.1	33.6	14.5
Pulp, paper, and paper products	15.3	15.1	-0.2	6.0	6.0	-0.0	2.5	2.3	-0.2	2.8	2.4	-0.4	4.2	4.5	0.3
Chemicals	11.2	10.0	-1.1	9.2	9.3	0.1	3.1	2.9	-0.2	11.2	9.5	-1.7	3.3	2.5	-0.8
Iron, steel, and metal products	3.1	3.0	-0.1	2.9	3.0	0.0	3.3	3.4	0.0	3.6	3.5	-0.1	1.0	0.6	-0.4
Transportation machinery	0.8	1.3	0.5	1.1	1.9	0.8	1.2	2.0	0.8	1.8	2.9	1.1	0.3	0.3	0.1
Electronic equipment	7.3	8.3	1.0	52.6	50.0	-2.6	58.0	54.0	-4.0	31.7	30.1	-1.6	3.6	2.5	-1.0
General machinery	3.9	4.7	0.8	8.2	8.3	0.1	9.3	9.3	-0.0	13.3	12.9	-0.3	4.1	2.8	-1.3
Other manufacturing	9.3	8.9	-0.4	2.6	2.5	-0.0	4.3	4.3	0.0	10.7	9.8	-0.9	22.0	18.8	-3.1
Total	100.0	100.0		100.0	100.0		100.0	100.0		100.0	100.0		100.0	100.0	

Sources: See table 7.1 sources.

Notes: The figures in 1997 indicate the export composition in 1997 (from table 7.1). The figures in FTA indicate the export composition resulting from FTA (model simulation). The changes indicate the difference between 1997 and FTA (percentage points). Nonmanufacturing does not include service sectors. Services are not reported as trade barriers in service sectors are not available, and it might underestimate the impacts of an East Asia FTA.

Table 7.9   Import compositions of East Asian economies resulting from an East Asia FTA (percentage shares in total)

Sector	China 1997	China FTA	China Change	Japan 1997	Japan FTA	Japan Change	NIEs Korea 1997	NIEs Korea FTA	NIEs Korea Change	Hong Kong 1997	Hong Kong FTA	Hong Kong Change	Singapore 1997	Singapore FTA	Singapore Change	Taiwan 1997	Taiwan FTA	Taiwan Change
Nonmanufacturing	7.0	6.1	−0.9	22.6	21.1	−1.5	20.3	22.8	2.5	4.7	4.7	−0.0	7.6	8.2	0.6	10.6	10.7	0.1
Agriculture	2.7	2.7	−0.0	4.8	4.9	0.2	3.5	7.6	4.0	3.0	2.9	−0.0	1.3	1.5	0.2	3.3	3.6	0.2
Forestry	0.5	0.4	−0.1	1.2	1.1	−0.1	0.6	0.6	−0.1	0.3	0.3	−0.0	0.0	0.0	0.0	0.2	0.2	−0.0
Fishing	0.1	0.1	0.0	0.8	0.7	−0.0	0.1	0.2	0.0	0.8	0.8	−0.0	0.1	0.1	−0.0	0.2	0.3	0.1
Mining	3.8	3.0	−0.8	15.9	14.4	−1.5	16.0	14.5	−1.5	0.7	0.8	0.0	6.2	6.5	0.4	6.8	6.6	−0.2
Manufacturing	93.0	93.9	0.9	77.4	78.9	1.5	79.7	77.2	−2.5	95.3	95.3	0.0	92.4	91.8	−0.6	89.4	89.3	−0.1
Food products and beverages	4.3	5.3	1.0	10.0	13.3	3.4	3.5	3.3	−0.2	6.6	6.6	−0.0	3.2	3.3	0.2	3.6	4.3	0.7
Textiles	10.8	13.9	3.0	7.1	8.2	1.0	4.2	4.7	0.4	13.6	13.9	0.4	2.7	2.8	0.0	3.1	3.8	0.7
Pulp, paper, and paper products	4.3	4.0	−0.4	6.0	5.7	−0.4	2.9	2.8	−0.1	3.0	3.0	0.0	1.8	1.9	0.0	3.4	3.3	−0.1
Chemicals	18.8	17.0	−1.8	11.0	10.3	−0.8	12.9	12.3	−0.6	8.5	8.5	−0.0	12.5	12.6	0.1	13.9	13.8	−0.1
Iron, steel, and metal products	9.5	8.6	−0.9	6.6	6.3	−0.3	13.9	13.1	−0.9	11.4	11.4	0.1	6.7	6.8	0.2	9.4	9.4	−0.1
Transportation machinery	4.2	6.5	2.3	5.6	5.4	−0.1	4.6	4.8	0.2	5.9	5.9	0.0	5.9	5.7	−0.2	6.7	7.7	1.0
Electronic equipment	14.8	13.5	−1.3	12.7	11.9	−0.8	13.7	12.8	−0.9	23.2	22.8	−0.4	37.0	36.1	−0.9	22.8	20.9	−1.9
General machinery	21.8	20.3	−1.4	11.8	11.1	−0.7	19.8	19.2	−0.6	15.9	15.7	−0.1	18.8	18.7	−0.1	22.4	21.9	−0.5
Other manufacturing	4.3	4.7	0.4	6.6	6.7	0.1	4.2	4.3	0.1	7.2	7.3	0.1	3.9	3.9	0.1	4.0	4.1	0.1
Total	100.0	100.0		100.0	100.0		100.0	100.0		100.0	100.0		100.0	100.0		100.0	100.0	

| | ASEAN | | | | | | | | | | | | | | |
| | Indonesia | | | Malaysia | | | The Philippines | | | Thailand | | | Vietnam | | |
	1997	FTA	Change	1997	FTA	Change	1997	FTA	Change	1997	FTA	Change	1997	FTA	Change
Nonmanufacturing	10.0	10.8	0.8	3.7	4.8	1.1	10.2	10.1	-0.1	11.0	10.1	-0.9	1.2	1.6	0.4
Agriculture	6.6	7.6	1.0	2.3	3.5	1.1	2.8	3.1	0.3	2.2	2.7	0.6	1.0	1.3	0.4
Forestry	0.1	0.1	-0.0	0.1	0.1	-0.0	0.3	0.3	-0.0	0.3	0.2	-0.0	0.0	0.0	0.0
Fishing	0.0	0.0	-0.0	0.2	0.2	-0.0	0.0	0.0	0.0	0.1	0.1	0.0	0.0	0.0	0.0
Mining	3.3	3.1	-0.2	1.0	1.0	-0.0	7.2	6.7	-0.5	8.4	7.0	-1.4	0.2	0.2	0.0
Manufacturing	90.0	89.2	-0.8	96.3	95.2	-1.1	89.8	89.9	0.1	89.0	89.9	0.9	98.8	98.4	-0.4
Food products and beverages	4.4	5.0	0.7	3.8	4.1	0.4	5.9	7.0	1.1	4.0	5.4	1.4	4.3	6.6	2.3
Textiles	4.5	5.2	0.7	2.2	2.6	0.3	4.1	4.5	0.5	2.7	3.6	0.8	13.5	20.7	7.2
Pulp, paper, and paper products	2.6	2.7	0.0	2.2	2.2	0.1	2.2	2.2	0.0	2.3	2.2	-0.2	2.5	2.8	0.2
Chemicals	18.9	18.5	-0.4	11.0	10.8	-0.2	9.8	9.6	-0.3	12.5	11.9	-0.6	30.4	25.8	-4.6
Iron, steel, and metal products	11.1	11.3	0.2	9.5	9.0	-0.4	6.8	6.8	0.0	11.6	10.7	-0.9	8.5	7.2	-1.3
Transportation machinery	9.9	9.6	-0.3	7.8	9.5	1.7	8.5	8.3	-0.2	7.5	11.0	3.5	6.4	5.8	-0.6
Electronic equipment	7.5	7.0	-0.5	36.0	33.8	-2.2	30.9	30.0	-0.8	19.6	18.4	-1.2	7.0	6.1	-0.9
General machinery	26.9	25.8	-1.1	20.7	19.8	-0.9	18.3	18.0	-0.3	24.2	22.3	-1.9	19.5	16.3	-3.2
Other manufacturing	4.1	4.1	-0.0	3.2	3.3	0.1	3.3	3.4	0.1	4.4	4.4	-0.1	6.6	7.1	0.5
Total	100.0	100.0		100.0	100.0		100.0	100.0		100.0	100.0		100.0	100.0	

Sources: See table 7.1 sources.

Notes: See table 7.8 notes.

substantially.[15] Specifically, the changes in exports with more than 5.0 percentage points are confirmed for only a few sectors, such as mining in Vietnam, food products and beverages in Korea and Thailand, and textiles in Vietnam. For other sectors and economies, the magnitudes of the changes are less than 5.0 percentage points, most of which are less than 1.0 percentage point.

An analysis of the impacts of an East Asia FTA on the intraindustry trade pattern is of interest. One would argue that an FTA may expand intraindustry trade because enlarged regional market resulting from the elimination of trade barriers gives greater trade opportunities for differentiated products. However, the results shown in table 7.10 do not support this argument, as more than half of the cases, specifically 73 cases out of 143 cases (eleven economies and thirteen sectors), show a minus sign, reflecting the decline in the intraindustry trade.

We now turn to the impacts of an East Asia FTA on regional trading patterns. Table 7.11 presents the regionalization indexes for East Asia and ASEAN countries. The results indicate that for overall trade all three regionalization measures increase for East Asia as a result of an East Asia FTA. These observations, which appear to reflect that the trade diversion effect is greater than the trade creation effect, indicate that the establishment of the FTA promotes regionalization. This result is consistent with our expectation because an FTA is a trade arrangement, which treats the members preferentially and nonmembers discriminatorily. Contrary to the case for East Asia as a whole, intraregional trade bias declines for ASEAN, although the absolute and relative measures of regionalization increase. This finding indicates that for ASEAN, extra-ASEAN trade expands faster than intra-ASEAN trade.

At the sector level, for almost all sectors absolute and relative measures increase as a result of an East Asia FTA. This means that the importance of intraregional trade in East Asia and AFTA countries increase with respect to world trade as well as their own trade. The rates of change are particularly high for agriculture, food products and beverages, and transportation machinery for East Asia. Unlike the patterns observed for the absolute and relative measures, the rates of change for the double-relative measure are not uniform. For East Asian trade, large increases in regional bias are observed for agriculture, pulp, paper and paper products, and general machinery, while a notable decline is observed for chemicals. For ASEAN countries many products show a decline in bias with notable exceptions for agriculture and general machinery. These results imply that an East Asia FTA promotes the regionalization within East Asia, and it

---

15. It should be added that an East Asia FTA does not change the patterns of RCA significantly, as can be expected from small changes in the compositions of exports. The RCA figures under an East Asia FTA are available from the authors on request.

Table 7.10   Changes in Intraindustry trade index

Sector	China 1997	FTA	Change	Japan 1997	FTA	Change	NIEs Korea 1997	FTA	Change	Hong Kong 1997	FTA	Change	Singapore 1997	FTA	Change	Taiwan 1997	FTA	Change
Intraindustry trade (IIT) index																		
Agriculture	34.5	17.8	-16.7	4.2	5.2	1.0	6.3	4.3	-2.0	0.9	1.1	0.2	32.9	55.4	22.5	14.1	13.8	-0.2
Forestry	9.3	9.7	0.3	1.4	1.5	0.0	1.5	1.6	0.0	0.3	0.3	-0.0	40.2	41.1	0.9	8.2	7.9	-0.3
Fishing	24.5	25.5	1.0	7.4	9.3	1.9	23.5	26.3	2.8	4.9	5.1	0.2	24.9	34.5	9.7	13.3	14.5	1.2
Mining	13.5	14.2	0.7	0.7	0.7	-0.0	0.5	0.4	-0.0	0.2	0.2	-0.0	0.9	0.9	-0.0	1.5	1.4	-0.0
Food products and beverages	36.5	33.4	-3.1	14.0	19.2	5.3	32.8	37.6	4.8	23.5	37.2	13.6	51.0	51.5	0.5	39.6	54.1	14.5
Textiles	38.7	40.8	2.1	50.8	56.3	5.5	50.9	49.4	-1.5	43.3	56.9	13.7	46.0	48.6	2.5	35.2	34.9	-0.2
Pulp, paper, and paper products	65.6	60.7	-4.9	26.5	29.6	3.1	35.8	34.1	-1.8	52.8	49.6	-3.2	60.0	59.1	-0.8	60.4	59.2	-1.2
Chemicals	56.9	48.7	-8.2	73.0	70.3	-2.7	54.4	52.9	-1.6	21.1	20.9	-0.3	56.2	53.9	-2.3	46.9	43.2	-3.7
Iron, steel, and metal products	60.3	56.7	-3.6	56.7	52.3	-4.4	51.7	51.8	0.0	15.7	17.4	1.7	42.8	43.6	0.7	51.9	49.0	-2.9
Transportation machinery	42.1	23.5	-18.5	32.6	31.0	-1.6	40.7	34.7	-6.1	1.4	1.0	-0.4	21.9	19.9	-2.0	55.0	42.2	-12.8
Electronic equipment	53.2	47.3	-5.9	55.8	57.6	1.7	57.8	56.5	-1.3	30.8	28.7	-2.2	65.8	67.5	1.7	52.1	52.2	0.2
General machinery	58.5	53.6	-4.9	46.3	45.5	-0.8	43.9	40.7	-3.2	29.7	27.4	-2.4	49.0	50.7	1.7	57.7	54.3	-3.5
Other manufacturing	22.0	23.1	1.1	67.1	65.0	-2.2	78.7	79.3	0.6	36.9	32.7	-4.2	43.5	46.2	2.7	59.1	56.9	-2.2

(continued)

Table 7.10   (continued)

	ASEAN Indonesia 1997	FTA	Change	Malaysia 1997	FTA	Change	The Philippines 1997	FTA	Change	Thailand 1997	FTA	Change	Vietnam 1997	FTA	Change
Intraindustry trade (IIT) index															
Agriculture	40.6	29.8	-10.8	21.2	41.6	20.4	26.9	24.1	-2.7	38.6	31.3	-7.3	17.6	20.8	3.1
Forestry	36.6	33.9	-2.7	5.5	5.6	0.1	12.0	12.6	0.6	15.2	16.2	1.0	21.0	21.7	0.7
Fishing	5.7	6.1	0.4	14.7	30.8	16.1	11.0	8.7	-2.3	13.6	32.3	18.7	19.9	25.3	5.4
Mining	10.8	11.5	0.7	14.7	14.5	-0.2	2.3	2.3	0.0	2.8	3.0	0.2	2.7	4.3	1.5
Food products and beverages	40.7	38.6	-2.1	43.8	41.3	-2.6	48.0	42.3	-5.7	36.9	32.4	-4.5	43.9	27.8	-16.1
Textiles	27.6	24.8	-2.8	52.5	54.6	2.2	26.5	21.3	-5.2	32.6	30.9	-1.6	31.9	31.1	-0.9
Pulp, paper, and paper products	22.5	23.0	0.5	42.8	43.7	0.9	69.1	64.3	-4.8	61.8	62.9	1.1	49.2	44.9	-4.3
Chemicals	63.1	61.7	-1.4	78.8	72.5	-6.3	28.8	30.4	1.6	69.5	64.6	-4.9	13.9	13.9	0.1
Iron, steel, and metal products	43.8	42.8	-1.0	48.0	50.1	2.0	47.8	49.9	2.1	42.2	44.3	2.1	14.4	11.4	-3.0
Transportation machinery	13.7	2.7	-11.0	22.0	11.7	-10.3	16.0	20.0	4.1	21.4	9.9	-11.5	4.9	4.4	-0.5
Electronic equipment	62.3	61.7	-0.6	66.0	66.7	0.7	67.8	66.7	-1.1	69.3	64.0	-5.3	22.9	23.2	0.3
General machinery	26.0	30.9	4.9	55.0	56.9	1.9	47.6	50.3	2.7	56.7	61.8	5.0	17.2	20.5	3.3
Other manufacturing	36.6	36.8	0.2	64.6	63.9	-0.7	46.9	40.7	-6.2	53.8	54.0	0.1	23.1	26.7	3.7

Sources: See table 7.1 sources.

Notes: The figures in 1997 indicate the IIT index in 1997 (from table 7.2). The figures in FTA indicate the IIT index under FTA. The changes indicate the difference between 1997 and FTA. Services are not reported as trade barriers in service sectors are not available, and it might underestimate the impacts of an East Asia FTA.

Table 7.11   Regionalization in trade for East Asian economies resulting from an East Asia FTA

	East Asia				ASEAN			
Sector	Exports		Imports		Exports		Imports	
	Absolute measure	Relative measure		Double relative measure	Absolute measure	Relative measure		Double relative measure

A. Regionalization in 1997 (from Table 3)

Sector	East Asia Exports Absolute measure	East Asia Exports Relative measure	East Asia Imports Relative measure	East Asia Imports Double relative measure	ASEAN Exports Absolute measure	ASEAN Exports Relative measure	ASEAN Imports Relative measure	ASEAN Imports Double relative measure
Total	0.11	0.44	0.50	2.02	0.01	0.21	0.20	3.17
Agriculture	0.04	0.56	0.19	2.53	0.01	0.19	0.13	3.81
Forestry	0.10	0.71	0.20	1.38	0.01	0.07	0.22	1.79
Fishing	0.18	0.84	0.52	2.37	0.02	0.22	0.54	6.52
Mining	0.05	0.81	0.19	2.87	0.01	0.13	0.14	2.67
Food products and beverages	0.07	0.58	0.33	2.72	0.01	0.15	0.24	3.37
Textiles	0.17	0.48	0.77	2.20	0.00	0.08	0.15	2.32
Pulp, paper and paper products	0.07	0.55	0.45	1.72	0.01	0.11	0.26	2.83
Chemicals	0.10	0.56	0.49	3.32	0.02	0.31	0.25	3.78
Iron, steel and metal products	0.12	0.63	0.47	2.68	0.01	0.30	0.10	4.81
Transportation machinery	0.04	0.18	0.32	2.54	0.00	0.24	0.04	4.26
Electronic equipment	0.22	0.42	0.68	1.61	0.05	0.23	0.32	5.73
General machinery	0.11	0.46	0.52	1.31	0.01	0.29	0.13	1.63
Other manufacturing	0.09	0.29	0.52	2.12	0.01	0.11	0.16	3.82

(continued)

Table 7.11 (continued)

Sector	East Asia			ASEAN		
	Exports		Imports	Exports		Imports
	Absolute measure	Relative measure	Double relative measure	Absolute measure	Relative measure	Double relative measure
B. Regionalization resulting from an East Asia FTA						
Total	0.14	0.53	2.17	0.02	0.22	3.09
Agriculture	0.13	0.85	3.06	0.01	0.36	5.55
Forestry	0.11	0.72	1.38	0.01	0.07	1.78
Fishing	0.23	0.87	2.30	0.02	0.25	6.43
Mining	0.06	0.82	2.84	0.01	0.14	2.65
Food products and beverages	0.18	0.80	2.93	0.02	0.16	2.97
Textiles	0.24	0.57	2.11	0.01	0.08	1.92
Pulp, paper and paper products	0.09	0.61	3.42	0.01	0.12	3.69
Chemicals	0.12	0.62	2.72	0.02	0.33	4.75
Iron, steel and metal products	0.14	0.68	2.58	0.01	0.33	4.34
Transportation machinery	0.08	0.36	2.64	0.00	0.20	3.97
Electronic equipment	0.24	0.45	1.34	0.05	0.24	1.63
General machinery	0.14	0.52	2.23	0.01	0.32	3.95
Other manufacturing	0.12	0.37	1.91	0.01	0.13	3.04

	Changes from 1997 (A) to FTA (B)							
Total	0.03	0.08	0.10	0.15	0.00	0.01	0.02	−0.09
Agriculture	0.09	0.29	0.27	0.52	0.01	0.17	0.08	1.73
Forestry	0.00	0.01	0.00	0.00	0.00	0.00	0.00	−0.01
Fishing	0.04	0.04	0.07	−0.07	0.01	0.03	0.07	−0.10
Mining	0.00	0.01	0.00	−0.03	0.00	0.01	0.00	−0.02
Food products and beverages	0.11	0.22	0.32	0.22	0.01	0.01	0.09	−0.40
Textiles	0.07	0.10	0.11	−0.09	0.00	0.00	0.00	−0.40
Pulp, paper and paper products	0.02	0.06	0.06	1.70	0.00	0.01	0.02	0.87
Chemicals	0.02	0.05	0.06	−0.60	0.00	0.02	0.02	0.97
Iron, steel and metal products	0.02	0.06	0.06	−0.10	0.00	0.03	0.02	−0.47
Transportation machinery	0.05	0.18	0.28	0.10	0.00	−0.03	0.00	−0.28
Electronic equipment	0.02	0.03	0.03	−0.27	0.00	0.01	0.02	−4.10
General machinery	0.02	0.06	0.07	0.92	0.00	0.03	0.02	2.32
Other manufacturing	0.03	0.08	0.11	−0.20	0.00	0.02	0.03	−0.77

Source: Model simulation.

Notes: For the definition of variables, see the appendix in the main text. Services are not reported as trade barriers in service sectors are not available, and it might underestimate the impacts of an East Asia FTA.

encourages ASEAN countries to have closer relationships with other East Asian economies.

7.5 Conclusions

In light of increasingly strong interest in FTAs and an East Asia FTA among many East Asian economies, we investigated the economic impacts of an East Asia FTA on East Asian economies with a focus on trade patterns by conducting a simulation analysis utilizing a CGE model. We found that an East Asia FTA brings positive impacts to East Asian economies in terms of economic growth and economic welfare. As to its impacts on trade patterns for East Asian economies, the simulation results show relatively small impacts, but they reveal some interesting patterns. We found that the sectors with a comparative advantage increase output and those with strong protection increase exports. The former relationship is expected, but the latter finding is not consistent with the expectation.

One explanation for this unexpected result is that an FTA shifts an incentive from domestic sales to export sales for protected sectors. Although exports of many sectors would increase as a result of an East Asia FTA, output production of some sectors is likely to decline. These potentially impacted sectors oppose an East Asia FTA. To overcome such opposition and to establish an East Asia FTA, financial and technical assistance should be given to potentially impacted workers to ameliorate the costs of adjustment. An East Asia FTA is found to promote regionalization in trade in East Asia, partly at the cost of exports from outside the region. Indeed, it has negative impacts in terms of economic growth and welfare on nonmembers. These findings argue strongly for the need to pursue worldwide trade liberalization under the WTO. Indeed, the formation of an East Asia FTA has to be regarded as a step toward multilateral liberalization.

We have examined the impacts of an East Asia FTA on trade patterns in East Asia by using a CGE model. Our results present useful information on the likely impacts of such an FTA. However, we do realize some shortcomings. First, there are some features of FTAs that could not be incorporated satisfactorily in our model, and we need to devise ways to incorporate them more satisfactorily. They include rules of origin, FDI, technology transfer associated with FDI, international labor mobility, and others. Besides the issues related to the simulation model, which is constructed at the sector level, we also realize the need to investigate the likely impacts of FTAs at the firm level to discern the detailed impacts of FTAs. As the availability of firm-level data has become better in recent years, researchers should analyze the impacts of trade liberalization on firms' trading behavior to draw some implications on the impacts of FTAs. Finally, we strongly hope that our results will be used for policy discussions on an East Asia FTA.

Appendix

Definitions of Variables

Regionalization Index

We use three types of regionalization index. The first index is called absolute measure and is defined as

$$A = \frac{x_{jk}}{\sum_k \sum_j x_{jk}},$$

where j and k indicate home and partner countries, respectively. x_{jk} represents exports from country j to country k, respectively. Therefore, absolute measure captures the export share of country j to country k relative to world total exports.

The second index is called relative measure, which is defined as

$$B = \frac{A}{\dfrac{\sum_k x_{jk}}{\sum_k \sum_j x_{jk}}} = \frac{x_{jk}}{\sum_k x_{jk}}.$$

The relative measure indicates the export share of country j to country k relative to country j's total exports.

The third index is called double-relative measure. Double-relative measure is the export share of country j to country k divided by home and partner export shares so that we could partly control both home and partner's scale.

$$C = \frac{A}{\left(\dfrac{\sum_k x_{jk}}{\sum_k \sum_j x_{jk}}\right)\left(\dfrac{\sum_j x_{jk}}{\sum_k \sum_j x_{jk}}\right)} = \frac{x_{jk} \times \sum_k \sum_j x_{jk}}{\sum_j x_{jk} \times \sum_k x_{jk}}$$

The value of exports is evaluated at the domestic market price while value of imports is evaluated at the world price.

Intraindustry Trade (IIT) Index

The intraindustry index is defined as

$$\text{IIT}_{ij} = \left(1 - \frac{\sum_k |x_{ijk} - m_{ijk}|}{\sum_k (x_{ijk} + m_{ijk})}\right) \times 100,$$

where i, j, and k indicate industry, home country, and partner country, respectively. x_{ijk} and m_{ijk} represent exports and imports of industry i in country j to country k, respectively. The IIT index takes a value between 0 and

100. The larger the index, the larger the intraindustry trade will be. The value of exports is evaluated at the domestic market price while the value of imports is evaluated at the world price.

Note that the definition of the IIT index in the GTAP model is different from that of a Grubel-Lloyd type IIT index. The former is differentiated across countries in the same industry. The latter is differentiated across subindustries (or detailed level of industries) in the same industry.

Revealed Comparative Advantage (RCA)

RCA is defined as

$$RCA_{ij} = \frac{\dfrac{x_{ij}}{\sum_i x_{ij}}}{\dfrac{\sum_j x_{ij}}{\sum_j \sum_i x_{ij}}},$$

where i and j indicate industry and home country, respectively. x_{ij} represents exports of industry i in country j to the world and evaluated at domestic market price. Therefore, $RCA_{ij} > 1$ means that industry i in country j has comparative advantage (compared with world average) while $RCA_{ij} < 1$ means i in country j has comparative disadvantage.

Nominal Rate of Protection (NRP)

The rate of protection in imports is defined as

$$t_{ij} = \frac{(m_{ij}^M - m_{ij}^W)}{m_{ij}^W},$$

where i and j indicate industry and home country. m_{ij}^M and m_{ij}^W are the values of imports evaluated at the domestic market price and at the world price, respectively. Hence, the rate of protection in imports includes both tariff barriers and nontariff measures.

Effective Rate of Protection (ERP)

We define ERP as follows:

$$ERP_{ij} = \frac{t_{ij} - \sum_z t_{mj} a_{izj}}{1 - \sum_z a_{izj}},$$

where i, z, and j indicate final goods industry, intermediate goods industry, and home country, respectively. a_{izj} indicates the input coefficient from industry z to i in country j obtained from the input-output table in the GTAP database. t_{ij} is the NRP defined as in the preceding. The rate of protection in this analysis, therefore, includes both tariff and nontariff barriers.

References

Ballard, Charles L., and Inkyo Cheong. 1997. The effects of economic integration in the Pacific Rim: A computational general equilibrium analysis. *Journal of Asian Economics* 8 (4): 505–24.

Brown, Drusilla K., Kozo Kiyota, and Robert M. Stern. 2004. Computational analysis of the U.S. bilateral free trade agreements with Central America, Australia, and Morocco. RSIE Discussion Paper no. 507. Ann Arbor: Research Seminar in International Economics, University of Michigan.

Brown, Drusilla K., and Robert M. Stern. 2001. Measurement and modeling of the economic effects of trade and investment barriers in services. *Review of International Economics* 9 (2): 262–86.

Dimaranan, Betina V. 2002. Construction of the protection data base. In *Global trade, assistance, and production: The GTAP 5 data base,* ed. Betina V. Dimaranan and Robert A. McDougall, 16-A-1–16-A-12. West Lafayette, IN: Center for Global Trade Analysis, Department of Agricultural Economics, Purdue University.

Dimaranan, Betina V., and Robert A. McDougall, eds. 2002. *The GTAP 5 data base.* West Lafayette, IN: Center for Global Trade Analysis, Department of Agricultural Economics, Purdue University.

Hertel, Thomas W., ed. 1997. *Global trade analysis: Modeling and applications.* Cambridge, UK: Cambridge University Press.

Ianchovichina, Elena, and Robert McDougall. 2000. Theoretical structure of dynamic GTAP. GTAP Technical Paper no. 17. West Lafayette, IN: Center for Global Trade Analysis, Department of Agricultural Economics, Purdue University.

Petri, Peter A. 1993. The East Asian trading bloc: An analytical history. In *Regionalism and rivalry: Japan and the United States in Pacific Asia,* ed. Jeffrey A. Frankel and Miles Kahler, 21–48. Chicago: University of Chicago Press.

Urata, Shujiro. 2001. Emergence of an FDI-trade nexus and economic growth in East Asia. In *Rethinking the East Asian miracle,* ed. Joseph Stiglitz and Shahid Yusuf, 409–60. New York: Oxford University Press.

———. 2002. A shift from market-led to institution-led regional economic integration in East Asia. Paper presented at the RIETI international conference, Asian Economic Integration. 22–23 April, Tokyo, Japan.

Comment   Dukgeun Ahn

This article addressed very timely one of the most contemporary trade issues for East Asian countries. As explained by authors, the East Asian countries not conventionally enthusiastic about regional trading arrangements have recently been eager to establish divergent forms of FTAs. The very first free trade arrangement (FTA) in East Asia already entered into force between Japan and Singapore. Japan is now working on a FTA with Mexico. Korea is also about to ratify its first FTA with Chile and will soon

Dukgeun Ahn is director of the WTO and Trade Strategy Center at the Korea Development Institute (KDI) School of Public Policy and Management.

begin an FTA negotiation with Singapore. After signing a framework agreement on comprehensive economic cooperation with the Association of Southeast Asian Nations (ASEAN), China has been undertaking FTA negotiations to conclude by June 2004. It is also expected that Korea and Japan formally start FTA negotiation at least by early next year. Policymakers as well as academics discuss even the prospect of a trilateral FTA, including Korea, Japan, and China, or comprehensive economic cooperation encompassing the entire ASEAN+3 (China, Japan, and Korea). All these developments would substantially change trade politics in the world trading system. In that regard, the analysis in this article made an important contribution by attempting empirical assessment on economic effects of an East Asia FTA.

Using a simulation analysis, the authors conjectured that gross domestic product (GDP) growth and equivalent variation (EV) would increase although the magnitudes of increases might not be significant for most East Asian countries. They also found that trade structures and composition of East Asian countries would not be substantially affected by an East Asian FTA, while regionalization among them would tend to be intensified. In addition, they concluded that the expected growth in exports would be larger in sectors with stronger protection. These interesting assessments may be qualified by incorporating some of subsequent factors.

First, the simulation model employed by the authors basically depicts the world in 2010, in which they anticipated, inter alia, the abolition of the Multifiber Agreement (MFA) and incorporation of the North American Free Trade Agreement (NAFTA), Japan-Singapore Economic Partnership Agreement (JSEPA), and the ASEAN Free Trade Area (AFTA). Considering various major FTA negotiations in the East Asian region, the simulation model may be extended to incorporate more FTAs, for example, between China-ASEAN, Japan-Mexico and Korea-Chile, which are all plausibly envisioned to be in force by 2010.

Second, the simulation model may reflect one of the most common features of the recent FTA arrangements—that parties to FTAs typically make concessions and commitments beyond the scope of the WTO. The FTAs negotiated after the inception of the WTO normally include "WTO plus" commitments in various areas, such as investment, trade in service—particularly, movement of natural persons, trade facilitation, trade remedy system, intellectual property protection, and a range of economic cooperative measures. When this commonality is reflected in the model, the positive effect of an East Asia FTA would be sizably augmented.

Third, despite impressive data management for statistical testing and meticulous empirical modeling by the authors, the empirical results show some abnormal assessment for certain variables. For example, in table 7.11, real exports for the Korean "food products and beverage" and agricultural sectors appear to grow most—by 15.8 percent and 15.5 percent, respectively—among all industry sectors of East Asian countries when an East

Asia FTA is established. This result does not comply with most economic forecasts or explanation. It would require more compelling economic explanations or recalibration of some data.

Fourth, the authors concluded that the expected growth in exports would be larger with an East Asia FTA as the existing protection level was higher. They also explained that this result was caused by incentive shifts for producers to export rather than sell in domestic markets as a result of removal of protection. This rationale, however, does not explain why the removal of protection is necessarily linked to increased export. In other words, removal of high tariffs for agricultural sectors in Japan would not suddenly create incentives or ways for Japanese farmers to export more when they face more fierce competition in domestic markets. Maybe a more compelling explanation for this relationship is the reciprocal nature of protection levels. Normally, when one country maintains high protective measures for particular sectors, its trading partners are more likely to have similar protection in those industry sectors. Because FTA negotiations are conducted mostly on the basis of reciprocity, dismantling those protective measures in one country would be more likely to induce or be accompanied by equivalent elimination of protection. In that sense, there may be a possibility to promote more trade in more protected sectors, albeit no guarantee for increased exports.

Last, the empirical finding that FTA benefits are compromised with the existence of adjustment costs representing friction of labor mobility reinforces the importance of the trade adjustment assistance (TAA) program in terms of trade policy. The United States has somewhat extensive experience of using TAA programs to facilitate labor adjustment when substantial trade liberalization demands unbearable industry restructuring, at least in the short term. The Trade Act of 2002 to accommodate Doha Round negotiation again stipulates elaborated TAA programs. Although the TAA programs implemented by the U.S. government have not been particularly successful, trade policy measures in line with the TAA programs would be necessary for East Asian countries to address convoluted policy coordination and properly realign conflicting economic interests.

Comment   Erlinda Medalla

Let me start by congratulating the authors for the insightful paper. The paper is well focused, and they presented substantial key findings without inducing information overflow.

I have already indicated in my comments to the earlier paper about my

Erlinda Medalla is a senior research fellow of the Philippine Institute for Development Studies.

preference for using the computable general equilibrium (CGE) approach to analyze the impact of regional trade agreements (RTAs).

I wish, however, that there was more explanation about the exact model used, so the reader, especially those unfamiliar with the Global Trade Analysis Project (GTAP) model, would have a greater understanding of how it works. Perhaps there should be an appendix that provides the equations used and the list of parameters and assumptions employed. Perhaps, in the paper itself, there could be a diagram illustrating the framework and the workings of the model. The part on the description of the model (section 7.3.1) could certainly do with a bit more elaboration.

Despite the limitations of the CGE approach, which the earlier paper alluded to and that the authors also point out, I think it is still one of the best methods of assessing the impact of RTAs, especially RTAs that are still being formulated.

Of course, considering that in the new age partnership, the other elements (outside-goods trade liberalization) are probably equally (if not more) important, one wishes for more than what presently the model could do. And indeed, in their conclusion, they point to the need for designing new ways to incorporate these other elements more satisfactorily.

Having pointed out these limitations, the only other things to watch out for are the data used, the assumptions used, and the interpretation of the results.

I have no questions about the data used. My questions are more on the assumptions.

On the Simulation Scenarios

In constructing the standard scenario, the paper projected growth in factors of production from 1997 to 2010, among other things (which built-in key agreements made). The inherent assumption is that these would be the same regardless of the formation of the RTA. Supposedly, the growth rates of these factors would be what would be without the formation of the RTA being assessed (the East Asia FTA). The paper presents the basis for the estimates of the growth in population in skilled-unskilled labor. But what about capital? How was the standard scenario estimated? This was not made clear in the paper.

The GTAP model would then supposedly simulate the standard scenario on GNP, allocation among countries, and so on—the works. In the process, are identities maintained? Equilibrium conditions are, of course, supposed to be maintained. But what happens to accounting identities and initial conditions? For example, does the system go back to the initial trade balance for individual countries or maybe just the global balance, with exchange rate as the balancing factor? Is the exchange rate endogenous?

In this regard, the paper mentioned some of the endogenous variables.

What are the exogenous variables, are there any, and why are they exogenous?

How about the elasticities used? Where do they come from and what are they based on? If assumptions are used, was there sensitivity analysis made covering a range of assumptions? Are results sensitive to changes? I think a paragraph (or even just a footnote) on this would help.

On the Interpretation and Presentation of Results

One of the problems most people have about CGEs is that it is like a magic box. Put something in and results come out as if by magic. (This is why an explanation of the model, probably a diagram, would be useful.)

I obtained a lot of insights from the results of the models and the variables looked at. However, I think the paper could do with more elaboration of these results, especially in terms of where these results are coming from. What is the major factor contributing to the changes? Indeed, what drives the model? Providing more explanation would help demystify the CGE approach.

The Effects of Financial Crises on International Trade

Zihui Ma and Leonard K. Cheng

8.1 Introduction

The world suffered three major financial crises in the last ten years, namely, the European Monetary System (EMS) crisis in 1992–1993, the Mexican crisis in 1994–1995 (which spread to a number of South American countries), and the Asian crisis in 1997–1998. Economists usually believe these crises were the results of weak economic fundamentals, for examples, declining foreign reserve, increasing foreign debt, capital account and current account deficits, fiscal deficit, and so on.

Obviously, a current account deficit can be a very important factor because, other things being equal, it increases foreign debt, decreases foreign reserves, and weakens confidence in the exchange rate of the domestic currency. Almost all countries that suffered financial crises had faced rising current account deficits before the crises occurred. So such deficits are widely regarded as an important factor of financial crises.

International trade links play an important role in the so-called contagious effect, that is, a crisis in one country causes a new crisis in another country with relatively good fundamentals. Glick and Rose (1999) provided some analysis of the relationship between trade and contagion, while

Zihui Ma is lecturer of international economics at Renmin University of China. Leonard K. Cheng is professor and department head of economics at the Hong Kong University of Science and Technology.

We thank Chin Hee Hahn, Kozo Kiyota, Andrew Rose and other seminar participants at the Fourteenth NBER-East Asia Seminar on Economics for helpful comments and suggestions. The work described in this paper was substantially supported by a grant from the Research Grant Council of the Hong Kong Special Administrative Region, China (Project no. HKUST6212/00H).

Forbes (2001) went further to construct some statistics measuring the importance of trade linkages in transmitting crises.

Because most economists agree that international trade is one of the important factors in explaining financial crises, it seems natural and logical to ask the reverse question: what are the effects of financial crises on international trade? Surprisingly, little research on this subject has been done. Perhaps the reason is that the answer appears to be obvious. Conventional wisdom would predict that a financial crisis, by bringing about a recession in the macroeconomy, would lead to a drop in imports. Exports, however, may rise because of both a decline in domestic demand and a devaluation of the domestic currency. A weakening or collapse of the financial system, in particular the banking system, however, might weaken the country's export capability. So the aggregate effects of a financial crisis on the macroeconomy are unclear. This paper tries to ascertain whether the ambiguity can be resolved empirically.

We divide all the past financial crises into two types: banking crises and currency crises. These two different types of crises had different attributes and different effects on international trade. This paper begins by analyzing theoretically the effects of banking and currency crises on international trade. Then it uses bilateral trade data, macroeconomic data, and geographic data to test the theoretical predictions. Overall, the empirical results provide support for the theoretical predictions.

This paper contributes to the literature in two ways. First, it provides a theoretical framework for understanding the impact of financial crises on international trade and the channels of crises transmission through trade. Second, it estimates the effects of banking crises and currency crises on imports and exports. The estimated results can be used to predict the impact of financial crises on trade, thus providing useful information for risk management to policymakers.

The remainder of the paper is organized as follows. Section 8.2 reviews previous works on the relationship between international trade and financial crisis. Sections 8.3 and 8.4 analyze the effects of banking crises and of currency crises on trade, respectively. Section 8.5 describes the data and methods used to estimate the effects of these crises. Section 8.6 reports the results of empirical estimation and statistical testing. Section 8.7 concludes.

8.2   Literature Review: Trade and Financial Crises

Economists pay attention to the role played by trade in financial crises for two reasons. First, trade imbalance has been shown to be one of the important factors that trigger financial crises. Current deficits may decrease foreign reserves. As Krugman (1979) pointed out, a currency crisis is more likely to happen in an economy that does not have enough foreign reserves.

Second, financial crises may be transmitted through trade linkages from an affected country to others despite the latter's relatively good fundamentals. In explaining such contagion effects, economists have tried to identify the channels through which contagion was spread. As trade is the most obvious economic linkage between countries, much research has been devoted to this connection. While the importance of trade imbalance in triggering crises is widely accepted, there is no agreement on the importance of trade in transmitting financial crises.

Eichengreen and Rose (1999) used a binary-probit model to test whether bilateral trade linkages transmitted crises between industrial countries between 1959 and 1993. They found that the probability of a financial crisis occurring in a country increased significantly if the country had high bilateral trade linkages with countries in crises. They concluded that trade was an important factor. Glick and Rose (1999) conducted a similar analysis with more countries between 1971 and 1997 and obtained a similar result. Forbes (2000) used a company's stock market data to study the importance of trade in financial crises transmission, and his result also showed that trade played an important role.

However, other papers have provided different answers to the problem. For instance, Baig and Goldfajn (1998) thought that trade linkage was unimportant in the East Asian Crisis because the direct bilateral trade volumes between these economies were very small. Masson (1998), analyzing the Mexican crisis and the Asian crisis, obtained similar results.

All the papers that analyzed the relationship between trade and financial crises ignored the reverse question: how did financial crises affect international trade? We argue that the effects of financial crises on trade are a precondition for discussing whether trade transmits crises. If financial crises do not affect countries' imports and exports at all, how can financial crises be transmitted through the trade channel? So before we analyze the importance of trade in transmitting financial crises, we need to clarify the effects of financial crises on international trade. As pointed out previously, little work has been done on this topic to date. It seems there is a belief that financial crises only affect countries' imports and exports through changes in the exchange rates. Because the effects of exchange rates have already been thoroughly analyzed before, it may seem that there is no need to study the question. However, this view may not be correct.

A devaluation of a national currency will increase the volume of exports and reduce the volume of imports. Classic international trade theory shows that a devaluation improves the trade balance if the Marshall-Lerner condition is satisfied. Because in a financial crisis a country usually experienced a devaluation of its national currency, the same analysis would apply, that is, the affected countries' imports will decrease, but their exports will increase after the crises.

Furthermore, financial crises (including currency crises, banking crises, or both) could also affect trade through channels besides the exchange rate. Calvo and Reinhart (1999) pointed out that financial crises usually caused capital account reversal (sudden stop) and triggered an economic recession. Mendoza (2001) showed that in an economy with imperfect credit markets these sudden stops could be an equilibrium outcome. The economic recession reduces not only domestic demand but also total output and export capability, whereas capital outflow forces the country to increase export. Thus, whether exports increase or decrease after financial crises is unclear without further analysis.

Before we analyze how financial crises affect the crisis countries' imports and exports, let us first define financial crises. Eichengreen and Bordo (2002) have provided definitions of currency crises and banking crises:

> For an episode to qualify as a currency crisis, we must observe a forced change in parity, abandonment of a pegged exchange rate, or an international rescue. For an episode to qualify as a banking crisis, we must observe either bank runs, widespread bank failures and suspension of convertibility of deposits into currency such that the latter circulates at a premium relative to deposits (a banking panic), or significant banking sector problems (including but not limited to bank failures) resulting in the erosion of most or all of banking system collateral that are resolved by a fiscally-underwritten bank restructuring. (15–16)

The above definitions are adopted in this paper. In the next two sections, we analyze the effects of banking crises and currency crises on the macroeconomy and trade.

8.3   Impact of Banking Crises

A classical framework of bank runs was developed by Diamond and Dybvig (1983). Let us recapitulate the key elements of their model. Agents are endowed with goods that can be invested in a long-term project or stored without costs. The long-term project is profitable but illiquid, that is, if investors do not liquidate the project before it matures, its return is greater than the initial investment; however, if the project is liquidated before it matures, the fire-sale return is less than the initial investment. Each agent can be impatient or patient with fixed probabilities, but there is no aggregate uncertainty, that is, the total number of impatient agents is fixed and known by all agents. At the beginning, agents do not know their own types but must decide if they will invest in the project. After they have invested (or have decided not to invest), but before the project matures, each agent realizes his or her own type. Impatient agents must consume immediately, whereas patient agents do not consume anything until the project matures. Agents' types are private information, so even if each agent knows his or her own type, other people do not know.

On the one hand, if an agent does not invest in the project but turns out to be patient, then the agent has missed a profitable investment opportunity. On the other hand, if the agent invests in the project but turns out to be impatient, the agent will have suffered a loss. In this case, the agent has to liquidate the long-term investment before it matures.

Agents can improve their utilities by pooling risk through the creation of a bank. All agents deposit their goods in the bank. Depending on the number of impatient agents, the bank sets aside a part of deposits as reserves and invests the rest in the project. When agents realize their types, impatient agents withdraw their deposits from the bank's reserves and patient agents wait for the project to mature. After the project matures, the bank distributes the return of the project to patient agents. By way of pooling risk through the bank, impatient agents do not suffer fire-sale losses, and patient agents can enjoy the benefits of the project.

However, there is a problem because agents' types are private information. Patient agents can pretend to be impatient and withdraw their deposits before the project matures. Normally, they have no incentive to do so because withdrawing early decreases their utilities. However, patient agents may wish to withdraw their deposits if there is panic. When that happens, the bank's reserves will not be enough to meet the agents' demand. The bank has to liquidate the long-term project before it matures, but it cannot meet the withdrawal if all patient agents try to withdraw because the fire-sale return of the project is less than the initial investment. The result is a bank run, and some agents get nothing back.

The preceding is the classical framework of bank runs. It does not analyze the effect of bank runs on imports and exports. We extend this model to feature international trade by making four additional assumptions.

1. We assume that agents belong to two categories: local agents and foreign agents. Local agents are endowed with local goods, and foreign agents are endowed with foreign goods. Both foreign and local agents may be patient or impatient with the same probability. Both local and foreign goods can be bought and sold in the international market.

2. The long-term project needs both foreign and local goods as inputs, and it produces local goods. As the aggregate investment increases, the investment demand for local and foreign goods also increases. For simplicity, we assume that foreign agents' deposits are less than the investment demand for the foreign goods. So the bank always has to export some local goods for the sake of importing foreign goods.

3. Foreign agents only consume foreign goods, and local agents consume both local and foreign goods. The returns that agents receive from the bank are local goods, so they need to exchange a part or all of the return for foreign goods in the international market.

4. There are overlapping generations. When the project matures, a new

generation of agents appears. Like the previous generation, they deposit their goods in the bank, and the bank invests deposits in a new long-term project. We assume that the number of local agents is fixed, but the number of foreign agents depends on the experience of the previous generation. If no bank run occurs in the previous generation, the number of new foreign agents will be the same. Otherwise, the number of new foreign agents will decrease, that is, capital inflow decreases after a bank run.

We can analyze the impact of banking crises on imports and exports under the preceding assumptions. If a bank run occurs before the project matures, all agents withdraw their deposits. Due to the illiquidity of the project, only some of them can get their deposits back. On the average, agents suffer losses. All foreign agents (without a bank run, only impatient foreign agents) leave the economy bringing with them the withdrawal. After the banking crisis, capital inflow decreases. So banking crises affect international trade through three channels.

1. *Income channel.* If a bank run occurs, the bank has to liquidate the long-term investment before it matures, and all depositors suffer some losses. With a lower income, local agents' demand for foreign goods goes down. Through this channel, both imports and exports decrease during and after banking crises.

2. *Foreign capital flow channel.* In the absence of bank runs, patient foreign agents withdraw after the project matures, but the withdrawal would be offset by an inflow of new investment made by the next generation of foreign agents. However, a bank run causes them to withdraw early and also reduces new foreign investment in the future. So banking crises can stimulate exports during crises but reduce them after crises.

3. *Investment demand channel.* As aggregate investment decreases, the input demand for foreign goods drops. So banking crises have negative longer-term effects on imports through this channel. On the other hand, as foreign investment decreases, the economy must export more local goods to import foreign goods as investment input. As a result, banking crises will simulate exports after crises.

The real world is more complicated than that highlighted in the preceding theoretical framework. For instance, developed countries usually may be able to defend their banking systems when banking crises occurred, so net capital outflow might not happen. As a second example, some less-developed countries (e.g., some African countries) are unsuccessful in attracting a lot of foreign capital, so the impact of capital flow would be insignificant during banking crises. As a third example, several Latin American countries (e.g., Mexico, Brazil, and Venezuela) stopped repaying foreign debt during debt crises in the 1980s, so the amount of net foreign capital outflow would be less than that suggested by the theoretical analysis.

8.4   Impact of Currency Crises

Currency crises often occur due to one of two reasons: runaway fiscal deficits or external shocks. We analyze them in turn. As Krugman (1979) pointed out, if a government cannot control its budget deficit, it has to finance the deficit by printing money, thus triggering currency depreciation. The currency crises in Brazil, Mexico, and Argentina would be a case in point.

An external shock (it may be a currency crisis in another country) may cause the demand for local products to decrease in the international market. If the economy's exchange rate remains unchanged, it must experience a price deflation, which is often a painful process because cutting prices is difficult, and cutting the civil servants' salary may be particularly challenging. During a price deflation, firms usually suffer losses while unemployment rises. To minimize the social costs, the government may choose to give up the fixed exchange rate regime. A case in point would be the experience of Thailand, Malaysia, Taiwan, and Singapore before and during the Asian financial crisis. These economies faced competition in their export market from China, and the devaluation of the Japanese yen in 1996 worsened their trade position further. They discovered that their cost structures were too high to support their currencies, so they had to give up the fixed exchange rates despite their relatively good fundamentals. The Thai government gave up its fixed exchange rate in July 1997, triggering the Asian financial crisis. Even though Hong Kong's currency board was maintained, it paid a heavy price in the form of price deflation and fiscal deficit.

During a currency crisis, the exchange rate would be more uncertain. Importers and exporters are exposed to greater exchange rate risk and may choose to reduce their business to reduce their exposure. As a result, currency crises may have negative impacts on imports and exports in the short term.

In the longer term, the market equilibrium is gradually restored. However, imports and exports may not return to the original level because a currency crisis can produce persistent impact on imports and exports through three channels.

1. *Income channel.* This channel exists if a crisis is triggered by external shocks. As the demand for local products declines, the consumer's income falls. So both imports and exports decline.

2. *Substitution effect channel.* This channel exists if a crisis triggered by

external shocks. As the relative price of local products decreases, consumers tend to increase their consumption of local product and decrease their demand for foreign goods, so both imports and exports decrease.

3. *Wealth channel.* Regardless of whether a currency devaluation is caused by a fiscal deficit or an external shock, consumers always suffer wealth losses due to money holdings, forcing consumers to decrease their consumption. As consumers' demand for foreign goods decreases, imports decrease; as their demand for local product decreases, other things being equal, the economy is able to export more.

If a devaluation is expected, consumers can reduce losses by reducing their money holdings. They can exchange domestic currency for foreign currency before the devaluation and then reverse the process after the devaluation. If the cash-in-advance constraint holds, their consumption would decrease during the devaluation as they reduce their money holding in anticipation of the devaluation. As a result, imports decrease and, if the price elasticity of demand for exports is larger than unity, the value of exports increases in the short term. After the devaluation, however, consumptions may return to the original level. So expected devaluations will have only short-term impact on imports and exports.

However, according to Eichengreen and Bordo (2002), currency crisis often occurred when governments abandoned their fixed exchange rates suddenly. The Mexico crisis was a good example. Before the abandonment of its fixed exchange rate, the interest rate of the peso was relatively low, and the market did not predict the devaluation. As Kaminsky and Reinhart (1999, 484) have pointed out, "For currency crises, [real, our own] interest rates bounce around in the range of 0 to 2 percentage points per month below the average during periods of tranquility." In short, most currency crises were unexpected, and thus the impact on imports and exports through the wealth channel would be larger than if the crises were expected.

8.5   Data, Crises, and Estimation Model

Having analyzed in theory the effects of banking crises and currency crises on foreign trade, let us use real-world data to test the preceding theoretical predictions.

The data include bilateral the export value from 1981 to 1998 as contained in the World Trade database; gross domestic product (GDP), population, and exchange rate data between 1979 and 1998 as contained in the International Financial Statistics database; distances, common land border, the number of the landlocked countries, and the number of the island countries as contained in Frankel and Rose's (2002) database. Eichengreen and Bordo (2002) have provided a list of financial crises found in the ma-

Table 8.1   **Country list and crisis frequency (1980–1998)**

	Banking crisis frequency	Currency crisis frequency		Banking crisis frequency	Currency crisis frequency
Argentina	4	6	Japan	1	0
Australia	1	2	Korea Republic	2	3
Austria	0	0	Malaysia	2	2
Bangladesh	1	2	Mexico	2	6
Belgium-Lux	0	1	The Netherlands	0	1
Brazil	2	3	New Zealand	1	3
Canada	0	2	Nigeria	1	6
Chile	1	2	Norway	1	1
China	0	4	Pakistan	0	5
Colombia	1	0	Paraguay	1	3
Costa Rica	1	1	Peru	1	4
Denmark	1	2	The Philippines	2	5
Ecuador	1	5	Portugal	0	1
Egypt	2	1	Singapore	1	1
Finland	1	3	South Africa	1	7
France	1	1	Spain	0	3
Germany	0	0	Sri Lanka	1	0
Greece	0	2	Sweden	1	1
Hong Kong	2	0	Switzerland	0	0
Iceland	0	2	Thailand	3	2
India	1	2	Turkey	3	4
Indonesia	3	4	United Kingdom	0	2
Ireland	0	2	Uruguay	1	3
Israel	0	0	United States	1	1
Italy	1	2	Venezuela	2	4
Jamaica	0	4	Zimbabwe	1	7

jor economies (see table 8.1). We use the same list in our analysis because the included countries are sufficiently representative.

We show the frequency of currency crises and banking crises in figures 8.1 and 8.2, respectively. There were 128 currency crises between 1980 and 1998. As shown in figure 8.1, the number of currency crises peaked in 1982, 1986, and 1992, with more than ten crises each year. In 1982, the debt crisis occurred in many Latin American countries, and five Latin American countries had currency crises. In addition, six other countries experienced currency crises due to the high U.S. interest rate. In 1986, there were thirteen currency crises in both developed and developing countries, spreading over Asia, Africa, Europe, North and South America. In 1992, many European countries quit EMS under speculative attacks. In 1997 and 1998, several Asian countries that had stable exchange rates for a long time, such as Malaysia and Korea, experienced currency crises, even though the frequency of currency crises was not significantly higher than the average level.

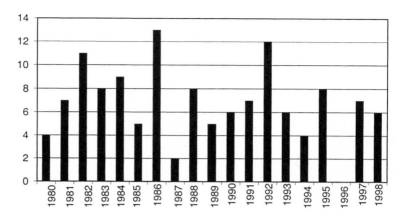

Fig. 8.1   Histogram of currency crises: 1980–1998

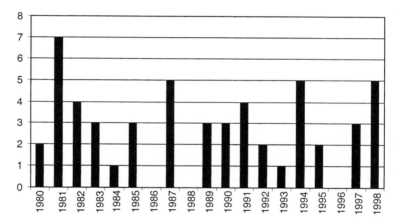

Fig. 8.2   Histogram of banking crises: 1980–1998

According to Eichengreen and Bordo's (2002) definition, currency crises do not always manifest themselves as currency devaluations. For instance, the Swedish krona did not depreciate in 1992, but Sweden's central bank had to rely on an international rescue effort to defend its currency. Therefore, we regard that as a currency crisis. In contrast, while the Hong Kong dollar was attacked in 1997 and 1998, there was neither devaluation nor international rescue. Therefore, we do not classify that as a currency crisis. We classify currency crises that ended with devaluations as "successful" currency crises and the others as "unsuccessful" currency crises. According to these definitions, 113 currency crises were successful, and 15 were unsuccessful.

There were fifty-three banking crises between 1980 and 1998. From figure 8.2 we can see that in 1981, 1987, 1994, and 1998, there were more than five crises each year. These peaks of banking crises were close to the peaks of currency crises.

If a banking crisis and a currency crisis occur in a country in the same year, we regard that as a "twin crisis." There were five twin crises during 1980–1998. This definition is not perfect because it ignores some cases in which that banking crisis and currency crisis occurred closely but in subsequent calendar years.

We use bilateral trade data to test the theoretical predictions because we would like to isolate external effects that vary across countries. For example, if a country and its main trading partner fall into financial crises at the same time, the country's exports and imports are affected by both internal and external shocks. However, we would not be able to include the external shock as explanatory variable if we use their aggregated (across countries) trade data. The use of bilateral trade data allows us to include the importing and exporting countries' crisis dummies as explanatory variables, thus avoiding biases caused by inappropriate use of dummies in analyzing aggregate trade data.

The gravity model is widely used to estimate bilateral trade value. The basic idea is that trade between any pair of countries is positively related to their economic sizes but inversely related to the distance between them. Some other factors, such as common land border, can also affect bilateral trade value. This methodology has proven to be successful in explaining variations in bilateral trade. We extend the gravity model by including crisis variables. The regression equation to be adopted is as follows:

$$\log(export_{t,i,e}) = \lambda \cdot \log(export_{t-1,i,e}) + \theta_1 X_{t,i,e} + \theta_2 Y_{t-1,i,e} + \theta_3 Y_{t-2,i,e}$$
$$+ \theta_4 C_t + \theta_5 C_{t-1} + \theta_6 C_{t-2} + C + \gamma \cdot t + \varepsilon_{t,i,e}$$

where $export_{t,i,e}$ is exports from country e to country i at time t. As trade relationships take time to build and to break, we allow for the underlying continuity of trade over time by including $\log(export_{t-1,i,e})$ as an explanatory variable. $X_{t,i,e}$ is a set of macroeconomic variables that affect trade between country i and e at time t. Based on the gravity equation framework, X is taken to include the following variables: igdp, the log of GDP of the importing country; egdp, the log of GDP of the exporting country; ipop, the log of the population of importing country; epop, the log of the population of exporting country; dis, the log of the distance between importing and exporting countries; comland, a common land border dummy equal to 1 if the trading countries have a common land border and 0 otherwise; nland, the number of trading countries being landlocked (i.e., 0, 1 or 2); nisland, the number of trading countries being islands countries (i.e., 0, 1, or 2); C is constant term; $idev_t = \log iex_t - \log iex_{t-1}$, the rate of devaluation of the importing country's currency relative to the U.S. dollar, where iex_t is the exchange rate (measured in domestic currency/U.S. dollar) of the importing country's currency at time t; $edev_t = \log eex_t - \log eex_{t-1}$, the rate of devaluation of the exporting country's currency relative to the U.S. dollar.

Since a currency devaluation has both short-term and longer-term effects, the explanatory variables $Y_{t-1,i,e}$ and $Y_{t-2,i,e}$ include the first and second lag of the devaluation variables, namely, lagidev, lagedev, lag2idev, and lag2edev.

To capture the possibility of time trends, we also include time t as an explanatory variable.

C_t, C_{t-1}, and C_{t-2} are crisis dummy variables and their first and second lags. C_t includes bi_t, be_t, ci_t, and ce_t, the banking crisis dummies of the importing and exporting countries and the currency crisis dummies of the importing and exporting countries, respectively.

$bi_t = 0$ if country i does not fall into a banking crisis at time t;
  1 otherwise.
$ce_t = 0$ if country i does not fall into a currency crisis at time t;
  1 otherwise.

We analyze how financial crises affected foreign trade over a period of three consecutive years. The effects on trade during the crisis years are regarded as "short term" and the effects on trade one and two years after crises are regarded as "longer term." We do not consider lags in excess of two years because the major crises were not more than three years apart. For example, the EMS crisis (1992–1993), the Mexican crisis (1994–1995), and the Asian crisis (1997–1998). Furthermore, as these three clusters of crises were no more than two years apart, lags in excess of two years would run into an identification problem whether an observed effect was caused by the current or previous crisis.

8.6   Estimation Results and Statistical Tests

The economic structure of the world economy has changed greatly as it continues to evolve. As a result, the characteristics of the financial crises in different periods varied not only because the affected countries were different but also because economic linkages at different points in time were different. For instance, in the 1980s, the international financial market was less developed and there was relatively little international borrowing by the private sector. At that time, most financial crises occurred in Latin American and African countries, where much borrowing was by governments. In the 1990s, the financial crises also hit the developed countries and East Asian countries. In the latter case international borrowing of short-term money was an important cause of the crises, as there was a rapid expansion of international lending to the private sector of Asia's "emerging economies."

The factors thought to be crucial in causing financial crises in different periods were different. In the 1980s the Latin American crisis countries were unable to control their fiscal deficits and current account deficits. Their economic fundamentals were regarded as very weak before the crises broke out. Krugman's (1979) first-generation currency crisis model has been widely used to explain this kind of crisis. Then came the crises in the early 1990s that were explained by second-generation models pioneered by Obstfeld (1996). These models highlight the inconsistency in macroeconomic policy objectives and issues of credibility and commitment. Finally, third-generation models featuring financial fragility, self-fulfilling prophecy, and "contagion" have been developed to explain the occurrence of currency crisis despite strong macroeconomic performance and absence of fiscal deficits.

The affected countries' responses to crises were also different at different times. For instance, during the Latin America debt crisis in the 1980s, the governments of many indebted countries decided to suspend the repayment of their foreign debts, but during the Asian financial crisis in 1997–1998, only Malaysia attempted to control capital outflow.

Because the financial crises exhibited different properties during the 1980s and 1990s, we divide our sample into two subsamples (1982–1990 and 1991–1998), estimate regression equations separately for each period, and compare the effects of financial crises in different periods. Before we proceed, let us test whether the impact of financial crises on trade were the same before and after 1990. The null hypothesis is

$$H_0 \colon [\theta_4 \quad \theta_5 \quad \theta_6]'_{year<=1990} = [\theta_4 \quad \theta_5 \quad \theta_6]'_{year>=1991},$$

where $[\theta_4 \quad \theta_5 \quad \theta_6]'$ are the coefficients of current, lag, and second-lag crisis dummies. The value of the F-statistics, $F[12,41545]$ is 6.32. That is to say, H_0 is rejected, suggesting that there were structural differences before and after 1990.

8.6.1   Gravity Model with Lagged Dependent Variables and Rates of Devaluation

Before we examine the impact of financial crises, let us check the behavior of the gravity model with a lagged dependent variable and rates of devaluation, that is,

$$\log(export_{t,i,e}) = \lambda \cdot \log(export_{t-1,i,e}) + \theta_1 X_{t,i,e} + \theta_2 Y_{t-1,i,e} + \theta_3 Y_{t-2,i,e}$$
$$+ C + \gamma \cdot t + \varepsilon_{t,i,e},$$

where $X_{t,i,e}$ includes igdp, egdp, ipop, epop, dis, comland, nland, and nisland. The devaluation variables are either omitted or included.

The estimation results when the devaluation variables are omitted are reported in the first two columns of table 8.2. The model's fit is relatively good. In both periods, R^2 is greater than 0.93. Most coefficients are signif-

Table 8.2   **Gravity equation without crisis dummies**

	1982–1990	1991–1998	1982–1990	1991–1998
Lag export	0.87089	0.86802	0.86957	0.86896
	(0.00323)***	(0.00318)***	(0.00323)***	(0.00319)***
igdp	0.13928	0.11356	0.13255	0.11274
	(0.00532)***	(0.00478)***	(0.00532)***	(0.00481)***
egdp	0.14958	0.13325	0.15153	0.13073
	(0.00576)***	(0.00518)***	(0.00584)***	(0.00523)***
ipop	−0.02198	−0.00774	−0.01444	−0.00794
	(0.00432)**	(0.00365)**	(0.00434)***	(0.00371)**
epop	−.03737	−0.00831	−0.03899	−.00613
	(0.00443)***	(0.00368)**	(0.00446)***	(0.00374)***
idev			−0.18552	−0.07608
			(0.01417)***	(0.02107)***
edev			−0.04551	−0.05185
			(0.01411)***	(0.02113)***
lagidev			−0.06591	−0.03792
			(0.01708)***	(0.01838)**
lagedev			0.06308	0.06076
			(0.01700)***	(0.01840)***
lag2idev			0.19746	0.09049
			(0.02029)***	(0.01316)***
lag2edev			−0.02290	−0.04737
			(0.02011)	(0.01311)***
dis	−0.13329	−0.11617	−0.12433	−0.11599
	(0.00764)***	(0.00703)***	(0.00765)***	(0.00703)***
comland	0.04533	0.11118	0.08437	0.10838
	(0.03067)	(0.02800)***	(0.03081)***	(0.02813)***
nland	−0.00637	−0.09191	−0.01318	−0.09007
	(0.01469)	(0.01320)***	(0.01469)	(0.01320)***
nisland	0.05365	0.03890	0.04458	0.03878
	(0.00959)***	(0.00870)***	(0.00968)***	(0.00874)***
year	0.01406	−0.01277	0.01496	−0.01265
	(0.00202)***	(0.00201)***	(0.00202)***	(0.00206)***
Observations	21,500	20,084	21,500	20,084
R^2	0.9317	0.9468	0.9326	0.947

***Significant at the 1 percent level.
**Significant at the 5 percent level.

icant, and their signs are consistent with theoretical predictions of the gravity model. An unstable result is time trend: it was significantly positive during 1982–1990 but significantly negative during 1991–1998. Because the volume of trade for all countries is expressed in U.S. dollars, the changing value of the U.S. dollar over time may provide some clues. The value of the U.S. consumers' price index (CPI) increased by 41.5 percent during 1982–1990 but by 22.6 percent in 1991–1998. So even if the time trend of the real value of exports was the same, the time trend of exports measured in current U.S. dollars could be different.

Other differences between the two periods include the coefficients of ipop, epop, comland, and nland. Although the signs of the coefficients for these population variables in both periods are negative, the absolute values decreased significantly in the 1990s. The absolute values of the coefficients of comland and nland in 1991–1998 were higher than those in 1982–1990.

Next, we add the rates of devaluation and their lags, idev, edev, lagidev, lagedev, lag2idev, and lag2edev, as explanatory variables. The results are reported in the last two columns of table 8.2.

The signs of all the newly added explanatory variables are identical in both periods. To understand the effects of devaluation, we draw impulse response functions in figures 8.3 and 8.4 by considering devaluations of 50 percent, or equivalently by setting idev and edev equal to 0.4055.

In figures 8.3 and 8.4, either in the 1980s or in the 1990s, devaluations

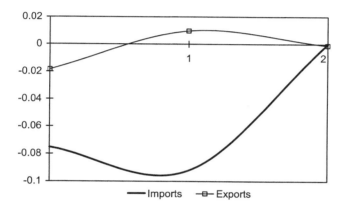

Fig. 8.3 **Impulse response functions induced by devaluation: 1982–1990**

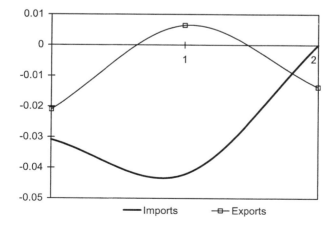

Fig. 8.4 **Impulse response functions induced by devaluation: 1991–1998**

had negative impact on imports. However, the impact was short term. Except for the effects on GDP, imports almost fully recovered in the second year after the devaluation. In contrast, the impact of devaluations on exports was somewhat more complicated. In the year of devaluation, exports decreased, but a year later, exports rebounded significantly, only to decrease again in the second year after the devaluation.

The results are consistent with the theoretical predictions. If a devaluation is expected to occur, then consumers reduce their cash holdings to avoid loss, decreasing consumption, decreasing imports, and increasing exports in the short term. After the devaluation, consumption rebounds so imports and exports return to the original level. The decrease in exports in the devaluation year may be due to the low price elasticity of exports in the short term, but the result that the longer-term exports are less than the original level is hard to explain because it would be questionable whether the price elasticity of demand for exports would remain less than unity two years after devaluation.

8.6.2   Adding Crisis Dummies

Now let us add financial crisis dummies to the regression equation. First, we include the banking crisis dummy and the currency crisis dummy separately. The results are reported in table 8.3.

The first two columns of table 8.3 show that the impact of banking crises was unclear between 1982 and 1990. The short-term effects on imports and exports were insignificant, and the longer-term effects were negative but not always significant. The results for 1991–1998 were more significant. Imports decreased significantly in all three years. Exports increased in the crisis years but fell back in the first year after banking crisis.

Impulse response functions induced by the banking crisis dummy are presented in figures 8.5 and 8.6. We focus on the results for 1991–1998 in figure 8.6. The impact on imports not only was negative but also tended to decrease further.

The last two columns of table 8.3 show the effects of currency crises, and the impulse response functions induced by the currency crisis dummies are shown in figures 8.7 and 8.8. From the table and figures, we find that the effects on imports in the two periods were very similar. In both periods, imports decreased in all three years. However, the effects on exports in the two periods were somewhat different. In 1982–1990, there was a significant negative impact of currency crises on exports in the short term (i.e., the coefficients of ce_t and $lagce_{t-1}$ were significantly negative), and the negative impact was mitigated but not reversed in the second year after crises. In stark contrast, the effects of currency crises on exports in 1991–1998 were significantly positive in all three years.

When all crisis dummies are included as explanatory variables, the results are reported in table 8.4. The results for banking crises are very simi-

	1982–1990	1991–1998	1982–1990	1991–1998
Table 8.3	**Estimation results with separate crisis dummies**			

	1982–1990	1991–1998	1982–1990	1991–1998
Lag export	0.86976	0.86851	0.86849	0.86890
	(0.00323)***	(0.00318)***	(0.00323)***	(0.00319)***
igdp	0.13149	0.11327	0.12863	0.10831
	(0.00533)***	(0.00480)***	(0.00538)***	(0.00484)***
egdp	0.15080	0.13190	0.15098	0.13325
	(0.00585)***	(0.00522)***	(0.00586)***	(0.00526)***
ipop	−0.01478	−0.00371	−0.01154	−0.00109
	(0.00434)***	(0.00376)	(0.00436)***	(0.00383)
epop	0.03950	−0.00734	−0.03819	−0.01016
	(0.00446)***	(0.00378)*	(0.00447)***	(0.00386)***
idev	−0.18671	−0.06225	−0.16387	−0.07087
	(0.01426)***	(0.02115)***	(0.01501)***	(0.02141)***
edev	−0.04301	−0.06271	−0.03050	−0.05268
	(0.01421)***	(0.02124)***	(0.01494)**	(0.02147)***
lagidev	−0.05899	−0.01953	−0.05678	−0.02099
	(0.01718)***	(0.01871)	(0.01830)***	(0.01927)
lagedev	0.06568	0.05136	0.07026	0.05198
	(0.01711)***	(0.01877)***	(0.01825)***	(0.01928)***
lag2idev	0.19066	0.08434	0.19057	0.09188
	(0.02039)***	(0.01346)***	(0.02114)***	(0.01374)***
lag2edev	−0.02843	−0.03143	−0.03533	−0.05060
	(0.02021)	(0.01344)**	(0.02099)*	(0.01367)***
bi	0.01191	−0.12165		
	(0.02405)	(0.02079)***		
be	−0.02214	0.10471		
	(0.02382)	(0.02077)***		
lagbi	−0.07878	−0.08646		
	(0.02238)***	(0.02183)***		
lagbe	−0.02052	−0.01553		
	(0.02231)	(0.02208)		
lag2bi	−0.02929	−0.04187		
	(0.02294)	(0.02201)*		
lag2be	−0.04835	−0.06378		
	(0.02293)**	(0.02227)***		
ci			−0.09436	−0.07649
			(0.01609)***	(0.01446)***
ce			−0.07407	0.03537
			(0.01617)***	(0.01441)**
lagci			−0.07638	−0.08108
			(0.01583)***	(0.01498)***
lagce			−0.04656	0.04742
			(0.01595)***	(0.01496)***
lag2ci			−0.00918	−0.03020
			(0.01551)	(0.01512)**
lag2ce			0.03137	0.02885
			(0.01558)**	(0.01521)*
dis	−0.12227	−0.11668	−0.12028	−0.11711
	(0.00512)***	(0.00702)***	(0.00766)***	(0.00704)***

(*continued*)

Table 8.3   (continued)

	1982–1990	1991–1998	1982–1990	1991–1998
comland	0.08925	0.10719	0.08780	0.10574
	(0.03083)***	(0.02808)***	(0.03076)***	(0.02811)***
nland	–0.01821	–0.08939	–0.00716	–0.09212
	(0.01477)	(0.01317)***	(0.01468)	(0.01318)***
nisland	0.04177	0.04011	0.04648	0.03844
	(0.00971)***	(0.00874)***	(0.00967)***	(0.00874)***
year	0.01378	–0.01328	0.01224	–0.01330
	(0.00204)***	(0.00206)***	(0.00204)**	(0.00207)***
Observations	21,500	20,084	21,500	20,084
R^2	0.9327	0.9473	0.9329	0.9472

***Significant at the 1 percent level.
**Significant at the 5 percent level.
*Significant at the 10 percent level.

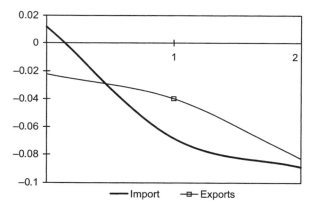

Fig. 8.5   Impulse response functions induced by banking crisis (without currency crisis dummies): 1982–1990

lar to those obtained previously when currency crisis dummies were omitted (table 8.3). In 1982–1990, the effects of banking crises were insignificant except for the coefficient of lagbi$_t$. Figure 8.9 shows impulse response functions induced by the banking crisis dummies. In 1991–1998, imports decreased and exports increased significantly in the short term, and both imports and exports decreased in the longer term. Comparing the impulse response functions in figure 8.10 with figure 8.6, we find that after controlling for the effects of currency crises, the accumulated impact of banking crises in the second year after crises was negative.

    The results for currency crises are similar to those obtained previously when banking crisis dummies were omitted. In both periods, imports de-

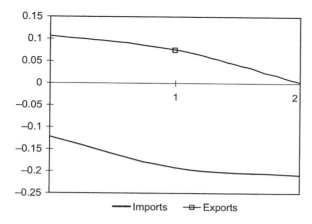

Fig. 8.6   Impulse response functions induced by banking crisis (without currency
crisis dummies): 1991–1998

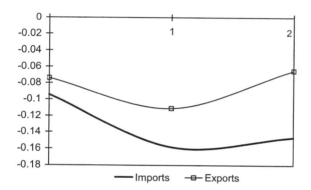

Fig. 8.7   Impulse response functions induced by currency crisis (without banking
crisis dummies): 1982–1990

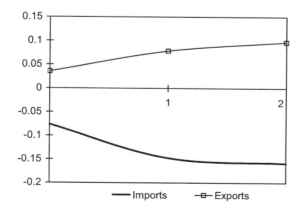

Fig. 8.8   Impulse response functions induced by currency crisis (without banking
crisis dummies): 1991–1998

Table 8.4   **Estimation results with both kinds of crisis**

	1982–1990	1991–1998
Lag export	0.86863	0.86844
	(0.00323)***	(0.00318)***
igdp	0.12788	0.10963
	(0.00538)***	(0.00485)***
egdp	0.15057	0.13468
	(0.00587)***	(0.00527)***
ipop	−0.01186	0.0060652
	(0.00436)***	(0.00384)
epop	−0.03861	−0.01081
	(0.00447)***	(0.00387)***
idev	−0.16730	−0.06468
	(0.01516)***	(0.02145)***
edev	−0.02874	−0.05658
	(0.01509)*	(0.02153)***
lagidev	−0.04889	−0.01034
	(0.01846)***	(0.01951)
lagedev	0.07141	0.04303
	(0.01842)***	(0.01955)**
lag2idev	0.18519	0.08749
	(0.02121)***	(0.01396)***
lag2edev	−0.03832	−0.03564
	(0.02106)*	(0.01392)***
bi	0.00727	−0.09415
	(0.02414)	(0.02212)***
be	−0.02139	0.09248
	(0.02391)	(0.02210)***
lagbi	−0.07255	−0.05597
	(0.02267)***	(0.02255)**
lagbe	−0.01203	−0.03449
	(0.02259)	(0.02286)
lag2bi	−0.00815	−0.02217
	(0.02318)	(0.02234)
lag2be	−0.03053	−0.07947
	(0.02319)	(0.02261)***
ci	−0.08686	−0.04932
	(0.01632)***	(0.01553)***
ce	−0.07142	0.01902
	(0.01641)***	(0.01548)
lagci	−0.07985	−0.06788
	(0.01599)***	(0.01535)***
lagce	−0.04558	0.05128
	(0.01611)***	(0.01535)***
lag2ci	−0.01080	−0.03417
	(0.01560)	(0.01528)***
lag2ce	0.02943	0.04003
	(0.01568)*	(0.01538)***
dis	−0.11827	−0.11733
	(0.00770)***	(0.00704)***
comland	0.09122	0.10606
	(0.03078)***	(0.02808)***
nland	−0.01102	−0.09101
	(0.01477)	(0.01317)***

Table 8.4   (continued)

	1982–1990	1991–1998
nisland	0.04454	0.03987
	(0.00971)***	(0.00875)***
year	0.01150	−0.01366
	(0.00205)***	(0.00207)***
Observations	21,500	20.084
R^2	0.9329	0.9474

***Significant at the 1 percent level.
**Significant at the 5 percent level.
*Significant at the 10 percent level.

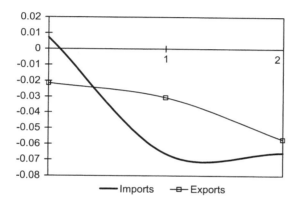

Fig. 8.9   Impulse response functions induced by banking crisis (with currency crisis dummies): 1982–1990

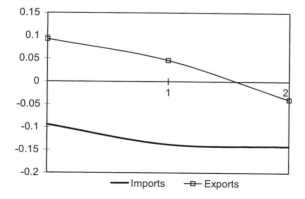

Fig. 8.10   Impulse response functions induced by banking crisis (with currency crisis dummies): 1991–1998

creased in all three years. The impact of currency crises on exports was significant except that during the crisis years in 1982–1990. The impulse response functions for the currency crisis dummy during the two periods are given in figures 8.11 and 8.12, respectively. In 1982–1990, exports decreased in the short term and remained below the original level despite a subsequent recovery. In 1991–1998, the short-term effect on exports was insignificant, and exports exceeded the original level beginning in the first year after currency crises. After controlling the effects of banking crises, the impact of currency crises on exports was insignificant during the crisis years. So the significantly positive coefficient of ce_t in table 8.3 seems to be the result of omitting the banking crisis dummies.

We summarize the theoretical predictions and empirical results about

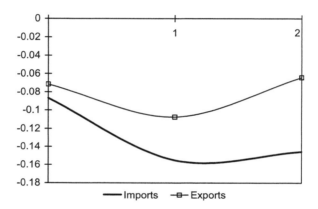

Fig. 8.11   **Impulse response functions induced by currency crisis (with banking crisis dummies): 1982–1990**

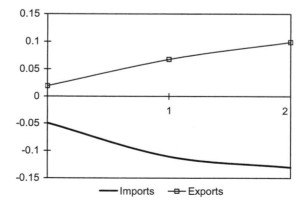

Fig. 8.12   **Impulse response functions induced by currency crisis (with banking crisis dummies): 1991–1998**

the impact of banking crises and currency crises in tables 8.5 and 8.6, respectively. Because the model includes GDP and devaluation as explanatory variables, the effects of the crisis dummies capture the effects of crises through channels other than economic recession or currency devaluation. Theoretical analysis predicts that exports increase during banking crises due to foreign outflow, and in the longer term, changes in exports depend on the aggregate effect through the foreign capital flow channel and the investment demand channel; imports would decrease due to reduction in investment demand.

In 1982–1990, the empirical results for banking crises do not support the theoretical predictions. In particular, there was no increase in exports during banking crises. Perhaps the theoretical predictions were inappropriate for this period because many developing countries stopped repaying foreign debts when they struggled with the financial crises. Furthermore, the amount of foreign capital flow into less-developed economies was relatively modest.

The empirical results for 1991–1998 were broadly consistent with theoretical predictions. The negative longer-term effect of banking crises on imports is as predicted. Although the theories predict the short-term effect on

Table 8.5   **The effects of banking crisis on trade**

| | Theoretical prediction | | | | Empirical results | |
	Income channel	Foreign capital flow channel	Investment demand channel	Aggregate effects (except income channel)	1982–1990	1991–1998
Imports (short)	−			?	?	−
Imports (longer)	−		−	−	?	−
Exports (short)	−	+		+	?	+
Exports (longer)	−	−	+	?	?	−

Notes: Dash = negative; plus sign = positive; question mark = unclear or insignificant.

Table 8.6   **The effects of currency crisis on trade**

| | Theoretical prediction | | | | | Empirical results | |
	Market chaos channel	Income channel	Substitution effect channel	Wealth channel	Aggregate effects (except income channel)	1982–1990	1991–1998
Imports (short)	−				−	−	−
Imports (longer)	−	−	−	−	−	−	−
Exports (short)	−				−	−	?
Exports (longer)	−	−	+	?	−[a]	+	

Notes: See table 8.5 notes.
[a]The accumulated effect was negative but tended to increase.

imports to be insignificant, the empirical negative impact on imports during crisis years may be due to the use of annual data (as opposed to quarterly or monthly data), which might have been influenced by the longer-term effects. The positive impact on exports in the short term is consistent with the theoretical prediction about the effect of capital outflow. The results that exports decreased in the longer term (the second year after crisis) implies that the negative effect via the capital flow channel overwhelmed the positive effect through the investment demand channel.

Theoretical analysis predicts that currency crises had negative impact on imports both in the short term (due to market chaos) and the longer term (due to wealth loss plus substitution effect if crisis was triggered by external shocks). The short-term effect on exports are negative, but the longer-term effect was ambiguous because the positive effect via the wealth channel ran counter to the negative effect via the substitution effect if the crisis was triggered by external shocks.

Comparing the empirical results of currency crises with the theoretical predictions, we discover three phenomena. First, consistent with theoretical predictions, the impact of currency crises on imports were negative in both the short term and the longer term. Second, the short-term effect via the market chaos channel in 1991–1998 was weaker than that in 1982–1990, so exports decreased significantly in crisis years in 1982–1990 but did not change significantly in 1991–1998. Third, in 1982–1990, exports after the crisis recovered but still remained below the original level. We are not certain whether it was due to a weakening of the short-term effect or if the longer-term effect had kicked in. In contrast, in 1991–1998, exports increased significantly after currency crises, implying that the impact via the wealth channel overwhelmed the impact through the substitution effect channel. Generally, the empirical results in both periods are broadly consistent with theoretical predictions.

8.6.3   Twin Crises, Successful and Unsuccessful Crises

Let us check for the effects of twin crises by adding a twin crisis dummy, $tc_t = bi_t \times ci_t$, and its first and second lags. Clearly $tci_t = 1$ if and only if both bi_t and ci_t are equal to 1.

The estimation results are listed in table 8.7. Most coefficients of the twin crisis dummy variables are insignificant even though the values of the coefficients are not small in relative terms.

As we pointed out previously, currency crises may be "successful" or "unsuccessful." Because currency devaluations did not occur in unsuccessful currency crises, their impact could be different from that of successful crises. We separate the currency crisis dummies into two more refined groups of variables: sc stands for a successful currency crisis (i.e., both currency crisis and devaluation happen); fc stands for an unsuccessful currency crisis (i.e., a currency crisis without devaluation). The results

Table 8.7   **Estimation results with twin crisis dummies**

	1982–1990	1991–1998
Lag export	0.86877	0.86833
	(0.00323)***	(0.00319)***
igdp	0.12765	0.10960
	(0.00539)***	(0.00486)***
egdp	0.15061	0.13460
	(0.00588)***	(0.00528)***
ipop	−0.01171	0.00089734
	(0.00436)**	(0.00386)
epop	−0.03865	−0.01044
	(0.00447)***	(0.00389)***
idev	−0.15667	−0.06641
	(0.01608)***	(0.02161)***
edev	−0.02151	−0.05560
	(0.01599)	(0.02235)**
lagidev	−0.06552	−0.01134
	(0.02035)***	(0.01960)
lagedev	0.06187	0.04110
	(0.02025)***	(0.01991)**
lag2idev	0.19037	0.08756
	(0.02133)***	(0.01407)***
lag2edev	−0.03601	−0.03680
	(0.02118)*	(0.01405)***
bi	0.01752	−0.08838
	(0.02575)	(0.03191)***
be	−0.00993	0.10311
	(0.02551)	(0.01825)***
lagbi	−0.08615	−0.06949
	(0.02356)***	(0.03000)**
lagbe	−0.02074	−0.03919
	(0.02350)	(0.03070)
lag2bi	0.00052686	−0.02985
	(0.02373)	(0.02743)
lag2be	−0.03660	−0.09457
	(0.02376)	(0.02784)***
ci	−0.08610	−0.04906
	(0.01643)***	(0.01673)***
ce	−0.06722	0.02059
	(0.01653)***	(0.01613)
lagci	−0.08321	−0.07232
	(0.01607)***	(0.01629)***
lagce	−0.04637	0.04860
	(0.01620)***	(0.01631)***
lag2ci	−0.00878	−0.03609
	(0.01570)	(0.01617)**
lag2ce	0.02657	0.03514
	(0.01578)*	(0.01628)**
tci	−0.07250	−0.01222
	(0.07379)	(0.04424)
(continued)		

Table 8.7   (continued)

	1982–1990	1991–1998
tce	–0.08419	–0.02618
	(0.07263)	(0.04281)
lagtci	0.17891	0.03273
	(0.09067)**	(0.04514)
lagtce	0.10041	0.01055
	(0.08874)	(0.04540)
lag2tci	–0.13564	0.02193
	(0.11350)	(0.04579)
lag2tce	0.16103	0.04215
	(0.12235)	(0.04627)
dis	–0.11825	–0.11755
	(0.00770)***	(0.00705)***
comland	0.09047	0.10623
	(0.03078)***	(0.02808)***
nland	–0.01042	–0.09064
	(0.01478)	(0.01321)***
nisland	0.04481	0.04019
	(0.00971)***	(0.00878)***
year	0.01148	–0.01389
	(0.00207)***	(0.00210)***
Observations	21,500	20,084
R^2	0.933	0.9474

***Significant at the 5 percent level.
**Significant at the 5 percent level.
*Significant at the 10 percent level.

are reported in table 8.8. Because most currency crises were successful, it is not surprising that the coefficients of sc are close to those of c in table 8.4. We find that the longer-term effects of unsuccessful currency crises were unclear: almost all coefficients of lagfc and lag2fc are insignificant. However, the short-term effects of unsuccessful crises in the two periods were different. In 1982–1990, imports did not change significantly, but exports decreased significantly after an unsuccessful currency crisis. However, in 1991–1998, an unsuccessful currency had negative effects on imports but positive effects on exports. Most of the other coefficients were not affected by the separation into two different currency crisis variables.

8.6.4   How Large are the Effects on Trade?

Because the variables are expressed in logarithmic terms, we can compute the size of the effects from the regression results contained in tables 8.5 and 8.6 and by using the impulse response functions in figures 8.9, 8.10, 8.11, and 8.12. In 1991–1998, a country's imports on average would decline by about 9.7 percent during the year in which a banking crisis occurred, by

Table 8.8   **Estimation results with both "successful" and "unsuccessful" currency crisis dummies**

	1982–1990	1991–1998
Lag export	0.86855	0.86796
	(0.00324)***	(0.00320)***
igdp	0.12621	0.11027
	(0.00547)***	(0.00488)***
egdp	0.15203	0.13519
	(0.00598)***	(0.00530)***
ipop	−0.01021	0.00029741
	(0.00443)**	(0.00385)
epop	−0.03987	−0.01036
	(0.00456)***	(0.00388)***
idev	−0.16159	−0.06904
	(0.01536)***	(0.02209)***
edev	−0.02700	−0.04247
	(0.01528)*	(0.02218)*
lagidev	−0.04797	−0.00798
	(0.01872)**	(0.01975)
lagedev	0.07718	0.03514
	(0.01865)***	(0.01978)*
lag2idev	0.18412	0.08705
	(0.02152)***	(0.01400)***
lag2edev	−0.05234	−0.03529
	(0.02136)**	(0.01395)**
bi	0.00495	−0.09108
	(0.02417)	(0.02233)***
be	−0.02285	0.08417
	(0.02395)	(0.02231)***
lagbi	−0.07791	−0.05444
	(0.02281)***	(0.02268)**
lagbe	−0.00509	−0.04039
	(0.02274)	(0.02298)*
lag2bi	−0.00653	−0.02153
	(0.02327)	(0.02238)
lag2be	−0.03390	−0.08059
	(0.02329)	(0.02265)***
sci	−0.10246	−0.04392
	(0.01748)***	(0.01641)***
sce	−0.06925	0.00505
	(0.01757)***	(0.01636)
lagsci	−0.08581	−0.06681
	(0.01741)***	(0.01585)***
lagsce	−0.05739	0.05068
	(0.01751)***	(0.01586)***
lag2sci	−0.01370	−0.03521
	(0.01704)	(0.01570)**
lag2sce	0.05255	0.04344
	(0.01709)***	(0.01580)***

(*continued*)

Table 8.8   (continued)

	1982–1990	1991–1998
fci	0.01289	−0.08822
	(0.04149)	(0.04050)**
fce	−0.10889	0.11401
	(0.04199)***	(0.04028)***
lagfci	−0.05894	−0.06386
	(0.03678)	(0.06416)
lagfce	0.01192	−0.00087749
	(0.03759)	(0.06417)
lag2fci	0.01488	−0.00998
	(0.03678)	(0.06430)
lag2fce	−0.08725	−0.00735
	(0.03752)**	(0.06431)
dis	−0.011826	−0.11804
	(0.00770)***	(0.00705)***
comland	0.09110	0.10594
	(0.03077)***	(0.02808)***
nland	−0.01006	−0.09101
	(0.01485)	(0.01318)***
nisland	0.04415	0.04004
	(0.00971)***	(0.00876)***
year	0.01141	−0.01402
	(0.00206)***	(0.00214)***
Observations	21,500	20,084
R^2	0.933	0.9474

***Significant at the 1 percent level.
**Significant at the 5 percent level.
*Significant at the 10 percent level.

13 percent in the first year after crises, by 14.5 percent in the subsequent year; exports would increase by about 8.8 percent during the crisis year, by 5 percent in the first year after crisis, but would decrease by 2 percent in the second year after crisis. The country's imports would drop by about 4.3 percent during the year in which a successful currency crisis occurred, by 9.7 percent and 12.4 percent in the subsequent two years, respectively; exports would increase by about 0.5 percent (insignificant) during the crisis year, by about 5 percent and 9 percent in the two subsequent years after crises, respectively. The results show that the impact of financial crises on international trade was very strong.

8.7   Conclusions and Directions for Further Research

We have analyzed how financial crises affected international trade in the last two decades, an important question largely ignored by the literature. Our theoretical analysis predicts that imports will decrease during and after a banking crisis, whereas exports will rise during but fall after the crisis. Theoretical analysis predicts imports and exports will fall during currency crises, but the effect after the crisis depends on the source of external shocks. By estimating a model of bilateral trade between fifty countries over a period of nineteen years with real-world data, we have found that the empirical results are generally consistent with the theoretical predictions, especially in 1991–1998. The empirical results also show that after currency crises exports increased more significantly in 1991–1998 than in 1982–1990. That may be a clue of "contagious crisis" in the last decade.

This paper has focused on the value of trade, but an alternative measure would be the volume of trade. In addition, the impact of financial crises on different tradable goods may be different. It would be interesting to explore whether the relationships between trade and financial crisis varied systematically across different products. For instance, products that enjoyed a comparative advantage versus those that suffered a comparative disadvantage. Another possible direction for future research is the effects of economic structures and government policies on trade. We found that the impact of financial crises was different between the 1980s and 1990s. Whether and how much of this difference was attributable to differences in economic structures and government policies seems to be a worthwhile topic to explore.

References

Baig, Taimur, and Ilan Goldfajn. 1998. Financial market contagion in the Asian crisis. International Monetary Fund Working Paper no. WP/98/155. Washington, DC: IMF, November.

Calvo, Guillermo A., and Carmen M. Reinhart. 1999. When capital inflows come to a sudden stop: Consequences and policy options. Working Paper, June.

Diamond, Douglas W., and Philip H. Dybvig. 1983. Bank runs, deposit insurance, and liquidity. *Journal of Political Economy* 91:401–19.

Eichengreen, Barry, and Michael D. Bordo. 2002. Crises now and then: What lessons from the last era of financial globalization? NBER Working Paper no. 8716. Cambridge, MA: National Bureau of Economic Research.

Eichengreen, Barry, and Andrew K. Rose. 1999. Contagious currency crises: Channels of conveyance. In *Changes in exchange rates in rapidly developing countries: Theory, practice, and policy issues,* ed. Takatoshi Ito and Anne O. Krueger, 29–50. Chicago: University of Chicago Press.

Eichengreen, Barry, Andrew K. Rose, and Charles Wyplosz. 1996. Contagious currency crises. NBER Working Paper no. 5681. Cambridge, MA: National Bureau of Economic Research, July.

Frankel, Jeffrey, and Andrew K. Rose. 2002. An estimate of the effect of currency unions on trade and income. *Quarterly Journal of Economics* 117 (2): 437–66.

Forbes, Kristin. 2000. The Asian flu and Russian virus: Firm level evidence on how crises are transmitted internationally. NBER Working Paper no. 7807. Cambridge, MA: National Bureau of Economic Research, July.

————. 2001. Are trade linkages important determinants of country vulnerability to crises? NBER Working Paper no. 8194. Cambridge, MA: National Bureau of Economic Research, March.
Glick, Reuven, and Andrew K. Rose. 1999. Contagion and trade: Why are currency crises regional? *Journal of International Money and Finance* 18:603–17.
Kaminsky, Graciela L., and Carmen M. Reinhart. 1999. The twin crises: The causes of banking and balance-of-payments problems. *American Economic Review* 89:473–500.
Krugman, Paul. 1979. A model of balance of payments crises. *Journal of Money, Credit and Banking* 11:311–25.
Masson, Paul. 1998. Contagion: Monsoonal effects, spillovers, and jumps between multiple equilibria. International Monetary Fund Working Paper no. WP/98/142. Washington, DC: IMF, September.
Mendoza, Enrique G. 2001. Credit, prices, and crashes: Business cycles with a sudden stop. NBER Working Paper no. 8338. Cambridge, MA: National Bureau of Economic Research, June.
Obstfeld, Maurice. 1996. Models of currency crises with self-fulfilling features. *European Economic Review* 40:1037–47.

Comment   Chin Hee Hahn

It has been recognized in the previous literature that financial crises have a "contagious effect." While the focus of several preceding studies was on whether trade linkage plays a role in transmitting crises across countries, this paper examines more closely how financial crises affect exports and imports. Insofar as understanding the effects of financial crises on trade flows is complementary to understanding the role of trade in transmitting crises, this paper raises a very important question. To address this question, this paper provides an outline of the theoretical framework as well as an empirical analysis. I think this paper is a serious attempt to add to the literature on the effects and transmission of financial crises.

Nevertheless, the specification of the regressions doesn't seem to allow us to interpret the empirical results clearly. Because the basic regression model includes gross domestic product (GDP) and devaluation variables, the estimated coefficients on crisis dummy variables and, hence, the impulse responses of trade flows to crises would capture the effect of crises on trade that is not captured by changes in the GDP or the exchange rate. However, financial crises are likely to affect trade mostly by affecting the GDP or the exchange rate. The theoretical framework in this paper also suggests that this is likely to be the case. Then, what interpretation we can give to the coefficients on crisis variables and, hence, to the impulse responses, seems to be somewhat unclear. For example, if there is less foreign

Chin Hee Hahn is a research fellow of the Korea Development Institute.

capital inflow after a banking crisis to finance domestic investment projects, then it is likely to affect the GDP or the exchange rate or both, at least in the short term. Then, the estimated effect of a banking crisis on trade, controlling for the GDP and changes in the exchange rate, is likely to capture those effects of the banking crisis that is not associated with changes in the GDP or the exchange rate. At least, the theoretical framework in this paper does not tell us clearly what these effects are. Viewed from this perspective, the estimated magnitudes of the effects of crises on trade flows seem to be very large. For example, a banking crisis reduces imports by about 12 percent during the crisis year, and by about 20 percent cumulatively during the three-year period after the crisis, with these effects not associated with changes in the GDP or the exchange rate.

Comment   Kozo Kiyota

This paper examines the impacts of banking and financial crises on international trade both theoretically and empirically. Hypotheses drawn from the theoretical analyses are in table 8C.1. The aggregated effects of a banking crisis on exports (except income channel) are positive in the short term while those on imports are negative in the long term. On the other hand, all aggregated impacts of currency crises on international trade except long-term exports are negative.

To test these hypotheses, the authors estimated a gravity model with banking and currency crises dummies, using data for fifty countries from 1982 to 1998. As table 8C.1 shows, the empirical analysis generally supports the theoretical prediction. The short-run impacts of currency crises on exports are positive for the period 1982–1990. On the other hand, for the period 1991–1998, currency crises had negative impacts on imports in the short and long terms. In addition, the analysis confirmed that banking crises had negative impacts on imports in the short term but positive impacts on exports in the long term. The authors also examined the scale of these impacts on international trade using an impulse-response function and found that these impacts were significantly strong.

The question addressed in this paper is one of the most important issues in analyzing the impacts of financial crises. The paper has three important findings. First, the channels and impacts of banking crises on international trade are different from those of currency crises. Second, the impacts of the crises are different between the short and long terms. Finally, the impacts of crises are different between the 1980s and the 1990s. This is an excellent

Kozo Kiyota is associate professor in the faculty of business administration at Yokohama National University.

Table 8C.1 The effects of banking and currency crises on trade: Theoretical prediction and empirical results

	The effects of banking crises on trade					
	Theoretical prediction				Empirical results	
	Income channel	Foreign capital flow channel	Investment demand channel	Aggregate effects (except income channel)	1982–1990	1991–1998
Imports						
Short term	−			?	?	−
Long term	−			−	?	−[a]
Exports						
Short term	−	+		+	?	+[a]
Long term	−	−	+	?	?	−

	The effects of currency crises on trade						
	Theoretical prediction					Empirical results	
	Market chaos channel	Income channel	Substitution effect channel	Wealth channel	Aggregate effects (except income channel)	1982–1990	1991–1998
Imports							
Short term		−			−	−[a]	−[a]
Long term	−		−	−	−	−[a]	−[a]
Exports							
Short term		−			−	−[a]	−[a]
Long term	−		−	+	?	−	+

Sources: Tables 8.5 and 8.6.
Notes: Dash = negative; plus sign = positive; question mark = unclear or insignificant.
[a]Empirical results support theoretical prediction.

paper with important policy implications. However, there is some room for improvement, which is summarized as follows.

1. In the currency crises model, the different impacts between short and long terms are not very clear. For instance, why does the income channel work only for the long term in a currency crisis while it works for both the short and long term in a banking crisis? Because the different impacts between the short and long terms is one of the important findings of this paper, further explanation of the difference would be helpful.

2. The authors investigate the effects of twin crises. However, they offer no explanation about the interaction between banking and currency crises in their theoretical analysis. Therefore, the expected impacts of twin crises are not clear. The empirical analysis employs a dummy variable that is defined as the cross term of banking and financial crises dummies. This is also

difficult to interpret because the cross term can reflect several combinations of the impacts (for instance, positive signs are obtained whenever the impacts of two crises are the same despite each coefficient of crises being positive or negative). Similarly, the authors do not provide any explanation about the expected impacts of "successful" and "unsuccessful" crises. This, in turn, implies that it is hard to interpret the estimation results. The authors could therefore provide some discussion of the expected effects of twin crises and "successful" and "unsuccessful" crises in their theoretical section.

3. The authors should provide more information about their empirical methodology. It is not clear whether their regression analysis employed a panel-data method such as a random-effect model. Further, the authors should present such basic indicators as the mean, variance, and correlation matrix of the variables. Such information could help to determine if some of the insignificant results might be caused by an inappropriate estimation method, specification error, or multicollinearity of independent variables.

4. This paper uses annual data in the empirical analysis. However, banking and currency crises may occur rapidly. Therefore, annual data might not capture some of the important impacts on international trade. If data are available, quarterly or monthly data would be more appropriate to capture the impacts of the crises.

5. The authors found that the impact of financial crises was different between the 1980s and 1990s. This is an interesting finding. More useful information could be obtained if the authors reported table 8.1 separately for the 1980s and the 1990s. That is, were the same countries affected in both the 1980s and the 1990s, or did countries face changes after 1990? Simple modification of table 8.1 might provide much helpful information.

6. There are several extensions of the research that could be pursued, including the impacts of financial crises on comparative advantage, intraregional trade, intraindustry trade, and intrafirm trade. Among these topics, the effects of banking and financial crises on intraregional trade could be an especially interesting topic. Because financial crises tend to be regional (Glick and Rose 1999), such analysis might also reveal the different impacts between banking and financial crises.

Reference

Glick, Reuven, and Andrew K. Rose. 1999. Contagion and trade: Why are currency crises regional? *Journal of International Money and Finance* 18:603–17.

WTO Dispute Settlements in East Asia

Dukgeun Ahn

9.1 Introduction

On January 13, 1995 when few experts could fully understand the newly established dispute settlement mechanism under the WTO, Singapore submitted the consultation request for a dispute settlement against Malaysia concerning import prohibitions on polyethylene and polypropylene.[1] It was the very beginning of the WTO dispute settlement system that is the essence of the current world trading system.[2] This case was subsequently resolved with a mutually agreed solution and so notified on July 19, 1995.

This birth history of the WTO dispute settlement showed the interesting fact that it was East Asian members that opened Pandora's box for the new era in the world trading system. Since then, East Asian members have actively participated in utilizing and augmenting the WTO dispute settlement system. These experiences and lessons thereof are briefly discussed in the following.

Dukgeun Ahn is director of the World Trade Organization (WTO) and Trade Strategy Center at the Korea Development Institute (KDI) School of Public Policy and Management.

I am grateful to participants at the fourteenth annual NBER–East Asia Seminar on Economics, especially John Whalley, Da-Nien Liu, Tain-Jy Chen, Takatoshi Ito, and Andrew Rose for their insightful comments on the earlier draft. I am also grateful to two anonymous referees for useful comments and Hyunjeong Kim for her research assistance.

1. WTO, *Malaysia—Prohibition of Imports of Polyethylene and Polypropylene* (WT/DS1/1).

2. During the very first month of the WTO, only two consultation requests were submitted to the WTO DSB. The other case was *US—Standards for Reformulated and Conventional Gasoline* (DS2) that resulted in the first panel/Appellate Body proceedings.

9.2   General Agreement on Tariffs and Trade (GATT) Dispute Settlements in East Asia

9.2.1   GATT/WTO Accession

Among East Asian members, China was, in fact, one of the drafting members of the GATT and joined the GATT in 1948. Then Indonesia joined the GATT, not by accepting the Protocol of Provisional Application, but instead by succeeding contracting party status under Article XXVI:5(c) in 1950.[3]

Japan acceded to GATT on September 1955 and, at the time of accession, fourteen contracting parties invoked Article XXXV. Subsequently, thirty-three contracting parties invoked Article XXXV by succession in respect to Japan when they became liberated from Belgium, France, and the United Kingdom. Three other contracting parties also invoked Article XXXV when they later joined the GATT. All these Article XXXV invocations were later gradually disinvoked to normalize the GATT relationship with Japan (WTO 1995, 1034–36). After the Tokyo Round negotiation, Japan accepted all nine new agreements, often termed as "Side Codes." (See table 9.1.)

The Korean government first sought to join the GATT in 1950, when it eagerly tried to be recognized as an independent state in the international community after liberation from Japan. At that time, the Korean government delegation sent to Torquay, England finished the GATT accession negotiation and signed the relevant documents.[4] This first attempt, however, failed when the Korean government could not complete the requisite domestic ratification procedures due to the Korean War during 1950 to 1953.[5] The Korean government resumed its effort to accede to the GATT in 1965 when it vigorously pursued export promotion as the primary element of economic development policies. After extensive internal discussion on potential economic benefits and costs, the Korean government finally submitted its accession application to the GATT secretariat on May 20, 1966 and conducted the tariff negotiations with twelve contracting parties from September to December 2, 1966.[6] Korea officially acceded to the GATT in 1967, in accordance with Article XXXIII of the GATT.[7] On the other hand, Korea invoked Article XXXV for nonapplication of GATT with respect to

3. Malaysia, Singapore, Hong Kong, and Macao also acceded to the GATT under Article XXVI:5(c). See WTO (1995, 1145–46).
4. See GATT (1952) *Basic Instruments and Selected Documents* (hereinafter *BISD*), vol. 2, 33–34. At that meeting, Austria, Peru, the Philippines, and Turkey also finished the accession negotiation. While Austria, Peru, and Turkey formally became contracting parties in 1951, the Philippines formally joined the GATT on December 27, 1979.
5. See Tae-Hyuk Hahm (1994, at 5).
6. The Working Party for Korea's accession included fourteen contracting parties. See Hahm (1994, 23).
7. See GATT (1968, 60), Korea—Accession under Article XXXIII: Decision of 2 March 1967, *BISD*, no. 15.

Table 9.1   **GATT/WTO Accession for East Asian members: As of August 2003**

Country	GATT/WTO Accession date	GPA[a]	TCA[b]	ITA[c]	BT[d]
China	Dec. 11, 2001	N	Observer	Y	N
Taiwan	Jan. 1, 2002	Negotiating Accession	Y	Y	N
Hong Kong, China	April 23, 1986	Jan. 1, 1997	N	Y	Y
Indonesia	Feb. 24, 1950	N	Observer	Y	Y
Japan	Sep. 10, 1955	Jan. 1, 1996	Y	Y	Y
Korea	April 14, 1967	Jan. 1, 1997	Observer	Y	Y
Macao, China	Jan. 11, 1991	N	Y	Y	N
Malaysia	Oct. 24, 1957	N	N	Y	Y
The Philippines	Dec. 27, 1979	N	N	Y	Y
Singapore	Aug. 20, 1973	Jan. 1, 1996	Observer	Y	Y
Thailand	Nov. 20, 1982	N	N	Y	Y

[a]Plurilateral Agreement on Government Procurement.
[b]Plurilateral Agreement on Trade in Civil Aircraft (WT/L/434, dated November 26, 2001).
[c]Ministerial Declaration on Trade in Information Technology Products.
[d]Basic Telecommunication Negotiations (annexed to the fourth protocol of the General Agreement on Trade in Services).

Cuba,[8] Czechoslovakia,[9] Poland,[10] and Yugoslavia.[11] These Article XXXV invocations were all simultaneously withdrawn in September 1971.[12]

Korea began its formal participation as a contracting party at the Tokyo Round of the multilateral trade negotiation, although it was merely as a minor player (Kim, forthcoming). Subsequently, Korea joined the four Side Codes: Subsidies Code,[13] Standards Code,[14] Customs Valuation Code,[15] and Antidumping Code.[16] Korea had never joined the sectoral agreements

8. See GATT, L/2783 (1967).
9. See GATT, L/2783 (1967).
10. See GATT, L/2874 (1967).
11. See GATT, L/2783 (1967).
12. See GATT, L/3580 (1971). See also WTO (1995, 1034–36). On the other hand, it is noted that fifty contracting parties invoked Article XXXV in respect to Japan at its accession in 1955. See GATT, L/2783 (1967).
13. This is the agreement on Interpretation and Application of Articles VI, XVI, and XXIII. In Korea, it was signed on June 10, 1980 and entered into force on July 10, 1980 as Treaty no. 709. See Ministry of Foreign Affairs, *Compilation of Multilateral Treaties,* vol. 5 (in Korean).
14. This is the Agreement on Technical Barriers to Trade. In Korea, it was signed on September 3, 1980 and entered into force on October 2, 1980 as Treaty no. 715. See Ministry of Foreign Affairs.
15. This is the Agreement on Implementation of Article VII. The Customs Valuation Code entered into force on January 1, 1981, while the other three codes entered into force on January 1, 1980. See GATT (1982, 40), *BISD,* no. 28. In Korea, it was entered into force on January 6, 1981 as Treaty no. 729. See Ministry of Foreign Affairs.
16. This is the Agreement on Implementation of Article VI. Korea accepted the Antidumping Code on February 24, 1986, and the code entered into force for Korea on March 26, 1986 as Treaty no. 877. See GATT (1987, 207), *BISD,* no. 33. See also Ministry of Foreign Affairs, *Compilation of Multilateral Treaties,* vol. 8 (in Korean).

on bovine meat, dairy products, and civil aircraft nor the Agreement on Import Licensing Procedures as a plurilateral agreement. Korea joined the Agreement on Government Procurement during the Uruguay Round and implemented it only from January 1, 1997, while all other signatories except for Hong Kong applied it from January 1, 1996.[17]

China was one of twenty-three original GATT contracting parties and signed the Protocol of Provisional Application on April 21, 1947. Subsequently, China participated in the first two rounds of multilateral trade negotiation, the Geneva and Annecy Rounds. After the People's Republic of China (PRC) was founded on October 1, 1949, the Taiwan authorities withdrew from the GATT in the name of the Republic of China. This withdrawal came into effect on May 5, 1950. China tried to resume its GATT relations after it secured a seat at the United Nations (UN) in October 1971. In January 1984, the PRC became a member of the GATT Committee on Textiles and in November 1984, an observer to the GATT Council and other subsidiary meetings.

On July 10, 1986, the PRC officially applied to resume China's status as a contracting party and the Working Party on China's accession was established on March 4, 1987.[18] The Working Party included sixty-eight Members to be the biggest working party for GATT/WTO accession. Since then, China sent a delegation to the Uruguay Round negotiations and finally the head of the Chinese delegation signed the final documents of the Uruguay Round along with the other 125 member countries (Yang and Jin 2001). Therefore, the Uruguay Round agreements are supposed to apply to China once it becomes a formal member of the WTO. For bilateral negotiations concerning China's accession, thirty-seven members requested negotiations with China.[19] China finally finished its accession negotiations with all those members and signed the membership agreement on November 11, 2001.[20] Having completed the domestic ratification procedure for its WTO accession on August 25, 2000, China became a formal member on December 11, 2001, thirty days after the accession approval.

China committed, upon accession, to comply with the Trade-Related Investment Measures (TRIMs) Agreement, without recourse to the provisions of Article 5 of the TRIMs Agreement and to eliminate all subsidy

17. See WTO, Agreement on Government Procurement, Article XXIV:3. Hong Kong also had one more year for implementation to apply from January 1, 1997.

18. More technically, China's application for accession was not to reenter the GATT but to resume a contracting party status of the GATT. The chairman of the Working Party was Mr. P.-L. Girard from Switzerland. See GATT, C/M/207.

19. These countries include Argentina, Australia, Brazil, Canada, Chile, Colombia, Costa Rica, Cuba, Czechoslovakia, Ecuador, EC, Guatemala, Hungary, Iceland, India, Indonesia, Japan, Kirghizstan, Latvia, Malaysia, Mexico, New Zealand, Norway, Pakistan, Peru, the Philippines, Poland, Singapore, Slovakia, South Korea, Sri Lanka, Switzerland, Thailand, Turkey, Uruguay, the United States, and Venezuela.

20. The Chinese membership agreement runs to 1,500 pages and weighs 13 kilograms. See http://www.chil.wto-ministerial.org/english/thewto_e/minist_e/min01_e/min01_11nov_e.htm.

Table 9.2   **GATT disputes involving Thailand**

As complainant		
United States—Measures affecting the importation and internal sale of tobacco		DS44/R
As respondent		
Thailand—Restrictions on importation of and internal taxes on cigarettes	United States	BISD 37S/200

programs falling within the scope of Article 3 of the WTO Agreement on Subsidies and Countervailing Measures (SCM). In addition, China shall not maintain or introduce any export subsidies on agricultural products. Therefore, China did not get any special waiver period as a developing country. Moreover, the importing WTO member may use a methodology that is not based on a strict comparison with domestic prices or costs in China if the producers under investigation cannot clearly show that market economy conditions prevail in the industry, producing the like product with regard to manufacture, production, and sale of that product. Once China has established, under the national law of the importing WTO member, that it is a market economy, the preceding provision shall be terminated provided that the importing member's national law contains market economy criteria as of the date of accession. In any event, the provisions of nonmarket economy shall expire fifteen years after the date of accession.

In addition, China agreed to accept the so-called transitional product-specific safeguard mechanism against its products in cases where products of Chinese origin are being imported into the territory of any WTO member in such increased quantities or under such conditions as to cause or threaten to cause market disruption to the domestic producers of like or directly competitive products. The accession protocol of China defines that "market disruption shall exist whenever imports of an article, like or directly competitive with an article produced by the domestic industry, are increasing rapidly, either absolutely or relatively, so as to be a significant cause of material injury, or threat of material injury to the domestic industry."[21] In other words, this special safeguard mechanism effectively lowers the threshold for invoking safeguard actions from serious injury to material injury that is normally required for unfair trade cases such as antidumping or countervailing measures. This special safeguard mechanism shall be terminated twelve years after the date of accession.

9.2.2   Limited Experience Except for Japan

During the GATT period, formal trade dispute settlements were not frequently utilized by East Asian countries except for Japan. (See tables 9.2 and 9.3.) Thailand had disputes concerning tobacco with the United States

21. See WTO, WT/ACC/CHN/49, paragraph 16.4.

Table 9.3   GATT disputes involving Korea

As complainant			
EC—Article XIX action on imports into the U.K. of television sets from Korea	Settled		Cases under Article XXIII
As respondent			
Korea—Restrictions on imports of beef	Australia, New Zealand, United States	BISD 36S/202, 36S/234, 36S/268 (adopted on Nov. 7, 1989)	Cases under Article XXIII
Korea-Antidumping duties on imports of polyacetal resins from the United States	United States	BISD 40S/205 (adopted on April 27, 1993)	Case under the Tokyo Round anti-dumping code

as both a complainant and a respondent. Korea was challenged twice at the GATT dispute settlement system and brought a complaint against the European Community (EC). Other East Asian countries were not visible, at least in terms of the GATT dispute settlement system. It is partly because those countries acceded to the GATT relatively late and partly because their trade volumes were not significant during the GATT period.

Japan was, however, one of the most frequent targets for complaints in the GATT dispute settlement system.[22] While it brought twelve complaints on eleven distinct matters, mostly against the United States and the EC, Japan was challenged in twenty-eight cases on twenty-three distinct matters. Among twenty-eight cases challenged, thirteen cases went to a panel, and only six cases ended with substantive panel reports. Twelve complaints by Japan resulted in only two panel decisions. Under the GATT system, the EC and the United States were the major disputing parties. It is noted that whereas Japan stood against the EC in five cases as both complainant and respondent, the United States challenged Japan in twelve cases and was challenged by Japan in four cases. In terms of a subject matter, antidumping measures by trading partners were the primary target of Japan's complaints. To the contrary, import restrictive measures by Japan concerning agricultural, textile, and leather products were major issues disputed by other GATT contracting parties. (See tables 9.4 and 9.5.)

As indicated previously, Japan rarely used the GATT dispute settlement system as part of its trade diplomacy, while Japan was frequently targeted in dispute settlement cases (Jackson 1999). During the GATT regime, Japan was considered one of those countries that leaned toward pragmatism as opposed to other countries, among which was notably the United States, which favored legalism (Iwasawa 2000, supranote 26). Japan tried

22. The United States and the EC had been the two most frequently challenged countries under the GATT dispute settlement systems. The next frequent target was Japan. See Robert Hudec, *Enforcing International Trade Law,* 590–608 (1993).

Table 9.4   **GATT cases: Japan as a complainant**

Case name	Defendant	Date
Italian Import Restrictions—Consultations under Art. XXII.1	Italy	July 1960
United States—Suspension of Customs Liquidation (Zenith Case)— referred to a Working Party	United States	May 1977
United States—Tariff Measures on Light Truck Cab Chassis— consultations under Art. XXII.1 and XXIII.1	United States	May 1980
Austria—Quantitative Restrictions on Import of Japanese Video Tape Recorders—consultations under Art. XXII.1	Austria	Feb. 1981
EC—Import Restrictive Measures on Video Tape Recorders— consultation under Art. XXIII.1	EC	Dec. 1982
United States—Unilateral Measures on Imports of Certain Japanese Products—consultation under Art. XXIII.1	United States	April 1987
EC—Regulation on Imports of Parts and Components—dispute settlement under the Antidumping Agreement	EC	July 1988
EC—Regulation on Import of Parts and Components	EC	Aug. 1988
Korea—Imposition of Antidumping Duties on Imports of Polyacetal[a]	Korea	Sept. 1991
EC—Treatment of Antidumping Duties as a Cost in Refund Proceedings	EC	April 1992
EC—Antidumping Proceedings in the European Community on Audio Tapes and Cassettes Originating in Japan	EC	May 1992
United States—Provisional Antidumping Measures against Imports of Certain Steel Flat Products—consultations under the Antidumping Agreement	United States	June 1993

Source: Yuji Iwasawa (2000, 486–88).

Notes: Twelve cases on eleven distinct matters; two cases (in italics) went to a panel.

[a]This case does not seem to reach to the formal dispute settlement procedure as there is no official case number attached to this case. The Committee on Antidumping Practices simply noted that it was "informed of requests by Japan for bilateral consultations under Article 15:2 with Korea on anti-dumping duties on polyacetal resins." BISD 38S/85 (1992).

to resolve a dispute with mutual agreement rather than actually litigate merits of cases through the dispute settlement system. Whereas a sizable number of cases were filed against Japan under the GATT dispute settlement system, Japan seldom brought a dispute to the GATT until the late 1980s. Moreover, Japan continued its efforts to settle the dispute amicably by agreement between the parties even after a case was referred to a panel. Thus, among twenty-eight cases brought against Japan in the GATT, only six cases ended with a substantive report by the panel. Only two out of the twelve cases Japan brought to the GATT dispute settlement system concluded with panel decisions.

Japan was not very eager to bring a dispute to the GATT so as to assert its rights under the GATT. Japan generally tried to avoid having recourse to more confrontational panel procedures. It was not until 1988 that Japan requested the establishment of a panel for the first time, thirty-three years after its accession to the GATT. But after the *EC—Regulation on Import of Parts and Components* case ended with favorable decisions to Japan, the

Table 9.5   GATT cases: Japan as a defendant

Case name	Complainant	Date
Uruguayan Recourse to Art. XXIII[a]	Uruguay	Nov. 1961
Japan-Tariff Treatment of Sea Water Magnesite—consultations under Art. XXII.1	United States	Jan. 1964
Japan—Restrictions on Imports of Beef and Veal—consultation under Art. XXII.1	Australia	Nov. 1974
Japan—Measures on Import of Thrown Silk Yarn	United States	July 1978
Japanese Measures on Imports of Leather	United States	July 1978
Japan's Measures on Imports of Leather	Canada	Oct. 1979
Japan—Restraints on Imports of Manufactured Tobacco from United States	United States	Nov. 1979
Japan—Measures on Imports of Leather	India	April 1980
Japanese Measures on Edible Fats—consultation under Art. XXII.1	New Zealand	Oct. 1980
Japan—Certification Procedures for Metal Softball Bats—Dispute under the Standard Agreement	United States	Sept. 1982
Panel on Japanese Measures on Imports of Leather	United States	Jan. 1983
Japan—Nullification and Impairment of Benefits and Impediment to the Attainment of GATT Objectives	EC	April 1983
Japan—Measures Affecting the World Market for Copper Ores and Concentrates—consultations under Art. XXII.2 and good offices of the Director-General	EC	March 1984
Japan—Single Tendering Procedures—consultations under the Government Procurement Agreement	United States	Nov. 1984
Japan—Quantitative Restrictions or Measures Having Equivalent Effect Applied on Imports of Various Product—consultations under Art. XXII.1	Chile	Nov. 1984
Japan—Quantitative Restrictions on Imports of Leather Footwear	United States	March 1985
Japan—Restrictions on Imports of Certain Agricultural Products	United States	July 1986
Japan—Restrictions on Imports of Herring, Pollack, and Surimi	United States	Oct. 1986
Japan—Customs Duties, Taxes, and Labeling Practices on Imported Wines and Alcoholic Beverages	EC	July 1986
Japan—Trade in Semiconductors	EC	Feb. 1987
Japan—Tariff on Imports of Spruce, Pine, Fir (SPF) Dimension Lumber	Canada	Nov. 1987
Japan—Restrictions on Imports of Beef and Citrus Products	United States	March 1988
Japan—Restrictions on Imports of Beef	Australia	April 1988
Japan—Restrictions on Imports of Beef	New Zealand	May 1988
Japan—Restrictions on Imports of Certain Agricultural Products	United States	Feb. 1991
Japan—Restrictions on Imports of Certain Agricultural Products	Australia	April 1991
Japan—Restrictions on Imports of Certain Agricultural Products	New Zealand	Aug. 1992
Japan—Measures Affecting Imports of Certain Telecommunications Equipment	EC	Oct. 1994

Notes: Twenty-eight cases on twenty-three distinct matters; thirteen cases (in italics) went to a panel; six cases (in bold) ended with substantive reports by panels.

[a]Uruguayan submissions were related to the fifteen contracting parties, namely, Austria, Belgium, Canada, Czechoslovakia, Denmark, Finland, France, Federal Republic of Germany, Italy, Japan, the Netherlands, Norway, Sweden, Switzerland, and the United States.

Japanese government changed its attitude and has pursued more rule-oriented trade policies since.[23]

9.3   WTO Dispute Settlements in East Asia

9.3.1   Overall Statistics

The Uruguay Round negotiation crucially augmented the GATT dispute settlement system,[24] rectifying several systemic problems by instituting, inter alia, a quasi-automatic adoption mechanism, an appellate procedure, and a single unified system.[25] As mostly concurred, the WTO dispute settlement system has been working very effectively in resolution of trade disputes and to become the core part of the WTO system. As of December 31, 2003, 305 cases have been brought to the WTO dispute settlement body. Among them, 76 panel and Appellate Body reports were adopted, while 43 cases were resolved with mutually agreed solutions, and 24 cases were settled or inactive.[26] One provisional empirical observation is that trade tends to increase with more trade disputes.[27] This fact deserves a more rigorous empirical analysis, especially in respect to the simultaneity problem. (See table 9.6.)

The yearly trend of WTO dispute cases filed up to the end of 2003 is shown in figure 9.1. As illustrated in figure 9.1, WTO dispute cases were rapidly increased during the first three years and then averaged around thirty cases per year. Dispute cases concerning East Asian countries, however, show the interesting feature that the role of East Asian countries as complainants have increased recently compared to that as respondents. It is also noted that WTO disputes among East Asian countries are still rare. Instead, their complaints are predominantly focused on the United States, while the United States is also the most frequent complainant against the East Asian countries.[28] To the contrary, the EC has hardly been the target

23. Regarding the historical importance of *EC—Regulation on Import of Parts and Components* case in Japan, see (Iwasawa, 477).

24. After the Tokyo round negotiation that established nine additional so-called Side Codes, the GATT dispute settlement system suffered particularly from forum shopping problems. See, generally, Jackson (1990).

25. For detailed discussion on the WTO dispute settlement system, see, generally, Jackson (1998), Palmeter and Mavroidis (1999), U. E. Petersmann (1997), Special Issue, *WTO Dispute Settlement System, Journal of International Economic Law*, vol. 1, no. 2 (1998); and Waincymer (2002).

26. See WTO, WT/DS/OV/19 (dated 6 February 2004). See also Leitner and Lester (2004).

27. Professor Andrew Rose found this result using standard bilateral gravity models of trade. His provisional finding includes that this result does not depend on which country files against which country. I am very grateful for his sharing of this interesting empirical result. More rigorous econometric studies on this point will be presented by us.

28. As of December 31, 2003, 18 out of the total 42 complaints by the East Asian countries were against the United States. On the other hand, 14 complaints were filed by the United States against the East Asian countries.

Members	Number of cases as a respondent	Number of cases as a complainant	Total
Table 9.6		Statistics on WTO disputes by parties (until December 31, 2003)	
East Asian members			
China		1	1
Taiwan		1	1
Hong Kong, China		1	1
Indonesia	4	2	6
Japan	13	11	24
Korea	12	10	22
Malaysia	1	1	2
The Philippines	4	4	8
Singapore		1	1
Thailand	1	10	11
Total	35	42	79
Notable others			
Argentina	15	9	24
Australia	9	7	16
Brazil	12	22	34
Canada	12	24	36
European Communities	59	63	122
India	15	15	29
Mexico	10	13	23
United States	81	76	157
Total by all members	305	333[a]	638

Source: See Leitner and Lester (2004, 171–72, note 31).

[a]The discrepancy between the numbers is due to the fact that, in some cases, there are multiple complainants against one respondent.

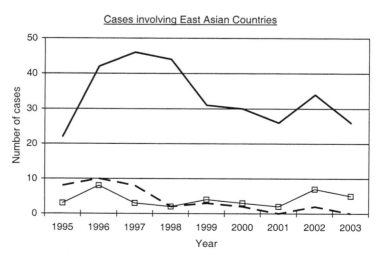

Fig. 9.1   Yearly trend of WTO dispute cases (until December 31, 2003)

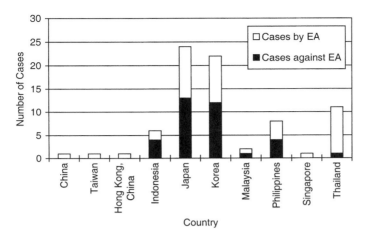

Fig. 9.2   WTO dispute cases for East Asian countries (until December 31, 2003)

for complaints by the East Asian countries, except for by Thailand, whereas it is the second most frequent complainant against them.[29] (See figure 9.2.)

9.3.2   Japan

Japan as Complainant

As a complainant, the primary disputing party for Japan has been the United States. Up to date, seven out of ten complaints are against the United States. In terms of subject matters, trade remedy measures, particularly antidumping measures by the United States, were the major issue to be disputed. One interesting observation is that Japan's challenges were mostly accompanied by the EC. Six out of eight cases reaching the panel procedure were complained jointly with the EC. Even the *US—Sunset Review* case (DS244) may be viewed as joint efforts with the EC following the *US—German Steel CVD* case (DS213). These joint complaints were not just against the United States but also Canada and Indonesia.

It is also noted that the automotive industry in Japan has actively utilized the WTO dispute settlement system to address WTO-inconsistent trade barriers in foreign markets. In that regard, it is noteworthy that three complaints against Brazil, Indonesia, and Canada are all concerned with measures related to the automobile industry. Considering the fact that the very first WTO complaint by Japan against the United States also dealt with the automobile industry, the WTO dispute settlement mechanism ap-

29. As of December 31, 2003, the EC was challenged by the East Asian countries in six cases, among which four cases were brought by Thailand.

Table 9.7   WTO disputes involving Japan

As complainant		
United States—Imposition of Import Duties on Automobiles from Japan under Sections 301 and 304 of the Trade Act of 1974	DS6	Mutually resolved
Brazil—Certain Automotive Investment Measures	DS51	In consultation
Indonesia—Certain Affecting the Automobile Industry	DS55	P/AB report
Indonesia—Certain Automotive Industry Measures	DS64	P/AB report
United States—Measure Affecting Government Procurement	DS95	Inactive
Canada—Certain Measures Affecting the Automotive Industry	DS139	P/AB report
United States—Antidumping Act of 1916	DS162	P/AB report
United States—Antidumping Measures on Certain Hot-Rolled Steel Products from Japan	DS184	P/AB report
United States—Continued Dumping and Subsidy Offset Act of 2000	DS217	P/AB report
United States—Sunset Review of Antidumping Duties on Corrosion-Resistant Carbon Steel Flat Products from Japan	DS244	P/AB report
United States—Definitive Safeguard Measures on Imports of Certain Steel Products	DS249	P/AB report
As respondent		
Japan—Taxes on Alcoholic Beverages	DS8/EC, DS10/Canada, DS11/US	P/AB report
Japan—Measures Affecting the Equipment of Telecommunications Equipment	DS15/EC	Inactive
Japan—Measures Concerning the Protection of Sound Recordings	DS28/US, DS42/EC	Mutually resolved
Japan—Measures Affecting Consumer Photographic Film and Paper	DS44/US	P/AB report
Japan—Measure Affecting Distribution Services	DS45/US	In consultation
Japan—Measures Affecting Imports of Pork	DS66/EC	In consultation
Japan—Procurement of a Navigation Satellite	DS73/EC	Mutually resolved
Japan—Measures Affecting Agricultural Products	DS76/US	P/AB report
Japan—Tariff Quotas and Subsidies Affecting Leather	DS147/EC	In consultation
Japan—Measures Affecting the Importation of Apples	DS245/US	P/AB report

Notes: "P/AB Report" means panel and Appellate Body reports were issued. "In AB" means the case is currently in the Appellate Body proceeding. Cases in italics indicate that panel reports were issued.

pears to play a crucial role for rectifying unfair competitive conditions regarding Japanese automotive industries. (See table 9.7.)

The very first complaint by Japan to the WTO Dispute Settlement Body (DSB), *US—Imposition of Import Duties on Automobiles from Japan under Sections 301 and 304 of the Trade Act of 1974* (DS6), indeed provided the Japanese government with profound confidence in the new system. Right after the WTO began its work in 1995, the United States threatened the unilateral retaliation on Japanese automobiles under Section 301.[30] In-

30. The legal justification of this Section 301 measure was, in fact, controversial. See Jackson, "US Threat to New World Trade Order," *Financial Times* (May 23, 1995, 17).

stead of undertaking "negotiations" as previously done, the Japanese government resorted to the WTO dispute settlement system by challenging the Section 301 measures.[31] The United States finally withdrew the Section 301 threat, and both parties notified the settlement of the dispute to the WTO on July 19, 1995 (Bhala 1998, 1066–68). The outcome of this case forcefully illustrated the effectiveness and usefulness of the WTO dispute settlement system as opposed to unilateralism.

Japan as Respondent

As a respondent, Japan has been challenged mostly by the EC and the United States. It is noted that whereas Japan has been challenged most by the EC, it has not raised so far any consultation request against the EC. Unlike other WTO members, especially the United States and the EC that have frequently utilized trade remedy measures to protect domestic industries, Japan rarely relied on those measures to constrain importation. Accordingly, Japan has never been challenged concerning application of trade remedy measures, which is, in fact, the most frequently disputed issue under the WTO dispute settlement system. Instead, the challenged area for Japan encompassed a range of issues from domestic tax system to distribution services and sanitary and phytosanitary (SPS) measures for agricultural products.

Interestingly, complaints against Japan were concentrated during the early WTO years, particularly 1995–1997. The last consultation request against Japan was submitted to the WTO on October 8, 1998 by the EC concerning the management of the tariff quotas for leather and the subsidies allegedly benefiting the leather industry and "Dowa" regions. The consultation for this case is technically pending yet. Since then, Japan has not been challenged by other WTO members. This may be explained by the fact that complaints against Japan under the WTO dispute settlement system have been concerning more systemic issues rather than case-specific actions, such as trade remedy measures, that are hardly used by the Japanese government. In other words, after somewhat intensive probing by other WTO members in the early WTO years, systemic or legal inconsistency of domestic policy measures or legal systems were mostly addressed and modified to comply with the WTO disciplines. There remain, therefore, few systemic problems to be addressed, at least in terms of the current WTO disciplines.

Among ten challenged cases, *Japan—Measures Affecting Consumer Photographic Film and Paper* (DS44, *Japan—Film*) deserves more explanation. This case is so far the only case in which the primary complaint is based on nonviolation claims (Durling and Lester 1999). Despite strenuous efforts by the United States to vindicate its claims, the panel ruled that the United States failed to demonstrate that, under GATT Article

---

31. See WTO, WT/DS6/1.

XXIII:1(b), the distribution measures nullify or impair benefits accruing to the United States.[32] This ultimate legal victory for Japan under the WTO dispute settlement system, after initiated by positive determination under the Section 301 proceeding, substantially strengthened the Japanese government's position concerning its domestic trade policies.[33] Typically, Japan has been vulnerable to blame for its convoluted nontariff barriers. But after this case, the Japanese government has become much more reluctant to accept its trading partners' loose allegations concerning unjustified or unreasonable nontariff barriers, at least those administered by the government.

Under the WTO system, Japan's dispute settlement has predominantly dealt with the United States. In terms of subject matters, antidumping measures, particularly by the United States, have been a major area for dispute settlement. On the other hand, the EC brought the most complaints regarding trade barriers in Japan. It is noted that Japan has not raised any complaints against the EC under the WTO system, although the EC was the most frequent target of Japan's complaints under the GATT system. It is also noteworthy that Japan is now one of the most active third parties for the WTO dispute settlement. As a third party, Japan has showed a strong interest in disputes concerning measures by the U.S. government.

9.3.3   Korea

Under the WTO system, the Korean government changed a dispute aversion attitude and has become considerably more active in asserting its rights through the dispute settlement mechanism.[34] Incidentally, since the middle 1990s, the trade balances with those major trading partners have been reversed and showed substantial deficits. For example, the trade deficit of Korea with respect to the United States began to occur from 1994 and remained throughout 1997, reaching $8.5 billion in 1997. This trend was again reversed in 1998 primarily due to the financial crisis that caused imports to plummet. Although there were some differences in the magnitude of the trade imbalances, the overall trends of trade balance were very much the same with respect to other major trading partners. The changes in such underlying economic circumstances would partly explain the more aggressive attitude of the Korean government toward formal dispute resolution.

Korea as Respondent

As of December 31, 2003, Korea was challenged by twelve complaints on nine distinct matters, as summarized in table 9.8. It is noted that complainants against Korea have so far been raised mostly by the United States

---

32. WTO, WT/DS44/R (adopted on April 22, 1998).
33. For comprehensive coverage of the relevant legal proceedings and documents concerning the *Japan—Film* case, see Durling (2001).
34. This part is substantially drawn from Ahn (2003).

Table 9.8   **WTO disputes involving Korea**

As complainant

United States—Imposition of Antidumping Duties on Imports of Color Television Receivers from Korea	DS89	In consultation
United States—Antidumping Duty on Dynamic Random Access Memory Semiconductors (DRAMS) of One Megabit or above from Korea	DS99	Mutually resolved
United States—Antidumping Measures on Stainless Steel Plate in Coils and Stainless Steel Sheet and Strip from Korea	DS179	P/AB report
United States—Definitive Safeguard Measures on Imports of Circular Welded Carbon Quality Line Pipe from Korea	DS202	P/AB report
Philippines—Antidumping Measures regarding Polypropylene Resins from Korea	DS215	In consultation
United States—Continued Dumping and Subsidy Offset Act of 2000	DS217	P/AB report
United States—Definitive Safeguard Measures on Imports of Certain Steel Products	DS251	P/AB report
United States—Countervailing Duty Investigation on Dynamic Random Access Memory Semiconductors (DRAMS) from Korea	DS296	In panel
EC—Countervailing Measures on Dynamic Random Access Memory Chips from Korea	DS299	In panel
EC—Measures Affecting Commercial Vessels	DS301	In panel

As respondent

Korea—Measures Concerning the Testing and Inspection of Agricultural Products	DS3, DS41/US	In consultation
Korea—Measures Concerning the Shelf Life of Products	DS5/US	Mutually resolved
Korea—Measures Concerning Bottled Water	DS20/Canada	Mutually resolved
Korea—Laws, Regulations, and Practices in the Telecommunications Procurement Sector	DS40/EC	Mutually resolved
Korea—Taxes on Alcoholic Beverages	DS75/EC, DS84/US	P/AB report
Korea—Definitive Safeguard Measure on Imports of Certain Dairy Products	DS98/EC	P/AB report
Korea—Measures Affecting Imports of Fresh, Chilled, and Frozen Beef	DS161/US, DS169/Australia	P/AB report
Korea—Measures Affecting Government Procurement	DS163/US	P/AB report
Korea—Measures Affecting Trade in Commercial Vessels	DS273/EC	In panel

Note: Cases in italics indicate that panel reports were issued.

and the EC. The only two other complaints were filed by Australia and Canada. Since the Korean government commenced the litigation of WTO cases in *Korea—Taxes on Alcoholic Beverages,* it seems predetermined to exhaust the full procedure of the dispute settlement system, at least if contested by other members.

Settlement by Consultation: Not Yet Ready to Litigate. Korea was a respondent in some of the very early cases in the WTO dispute settlement, which concerned somewhat unfamiliar obligations under the SPS and Technical Barriers to Trade (TBT) agreements. The United States made a consultation request against Korea on April 6, 1995 (DS3) and basically on the same matter again on May 24, 1996 (DS41).[35] Both cases were suspended because the United States did not take additional steps. On May 5, 1995, the United States made a consultation request regarding the regulation on the shelf life of products (DS5). This case was settled with a mutually acceptable solution.[36] The Canadian request for consultation regarding the Korean regulation on the shelf life and disinfection treatment of bottled water was also settled with a mutually satisfactory solution (DS20).[37] These four complaints were based on the SPS and TBT agreements in addition to the GATT and could be settled promptly.

On May 9, 1996, the EC requested consultations, alleging that the procurement practices for the Korean telecommunications sector were discriminatory against foreign suppliers and that the bilateral agreement with the United States was preferential (DS40). The parties also agreed on a mutually satisfactory solution during the consultation.[38]

The Korean government basically tried to settle the first five complaints, rather than actually litigate the cases. This is partly because the merits of the cases were relatively clear and partly because the economic stakes at issue were not substantial. In addition, the Korean government was not sufficiently prepared to handle the newly instituted WTO dispute settlement system in the procedural aspect and unfamiliar legal issues concerning the SPS and TBT agreements in the substantive aspect.

Full Litigation: Fight to the End. The very first case in which Korea experienced the whole WTO dispute settlement procedure was the *Korea—Taxes on Alcoholic Beverages* (*Korea—Soju*) case (DS75 and DS84). The EC and the United States contended that the Korean liquor taxes of 100 percent on whiskey and 35 percent on diluted *soju* were not consistent with the national treatment obligation under Article III of the GATT. Basically, this case was considered as a "revisited" *Japan—Taxes on Alcoholic Beverages* (*Japan—Shochu*) case (DS8, DS10, and DS11), in which the Japanese tax system to discriminate imported alcoholic beverages over *shochu* was found to be in violation of Article III of the GATT. As a legal strategy to

35. The second consultation request by the United States encompassed all amendments, revisions, and new measures adopted by the Korean government after the first consultation request. See WTO, WT/DS41/1, dated May 31, 1996.

36. See WTO, WT/DS5/5, dated July 31, 1995.

37. See WTO, WT/DS20/6, dated May 6, 1996.

38. See WTO, WT/DS40/2, dated October 29, 1997. Korea and the EC signed the Agreement on Telecommunications Procurement between the Republic of Korea and the European Community on October 29, 1997, and the agreement entered into force on November 1, 1997. Subsequently, Korea entered into a similar bilateral agreement for telecommunications equipment procurement with Canada. See Lie and Ahn (2003).

distinguish this case from the *Japan—Shochu* case, the Korean government tried to inject more antitrust law principles and experts in the panel proceeding because a large price gap between *soju* and whiskey might be deemed to represent a noncompetitive relationship of pertinent products in the antitrust law context.[39]

The panel and the appellate body held that the Korean taxes on *soju* and whiskey were discriminatory and the DSB adopted this ruling on February 17, 1999. The reasonable period for implementation was determined to be eleven months and two weeks, that is, from February 17, 1999 to January 31, 2000.[40] Subsequently, Korea amended the Liquor Tax Law and the Education Tax Law to impose flat rates of 72 percent in liquor tax and 30 percent in education tax that entered into force on January 1, 2000.[41] The DSB recommendation was successfully implemented a month earlier than the due date.

This case awakened the Korean public about the role and influence of the WTO dispute settlement system. The media and newspapers closely covered every step pertaining to this case, from the consultation request to the panel proceeding and the Appellate Body ruling. It was not just because this case was the first WTO dispute settlement proceeding for Korea but also because the popularity of the product concerned, *soju,* was probably incomparable to any other product in Korea. Despite objections by the general public as well as by *soju* manufacturers, the Korean government amended the tax laws to substantially increase liquor taxes on *soju,* instead of reducing the liquor tax on whiskey to the original level on *soju,* in order to eliminate the WTO-illegal tax gap while minimizing the potential adverse impact on public health and consequent social costs.[42] By experiencing the impact of the WTO dispute settlement decision, probably at the deepest and widest level of daily life, this case has played a crucial role in enhancing WTO awareness in Korea.

The first dispute settlement case under the Agreement on Safeguards also involved the Korean safeguard measure concerning dairy products (DS98).[43] On August 12, 1997, the EC requested consultations with Korea regarding the safeguard quotas that went into effect on March 7, 1997 and

39. For example, the Korean government tried to include antitrust law experts regardless of their nationality as panelists, but failed due to the objection by the complainants. See Kim (1999, 465–66). Except for this case, the Korean government as a respondent did not resort to the director general for the panel selection.

40. WTO, WT/DS75/16, WT/DS84/14, dated June 4, 1999.

41. WTO, WT/DS75/18, WT/DS84/16, dated January 17, 2000.

42. See, generally, Korea Institute of Public Finance (September 1999, 82–102). *Monthly Public Finance Forum* (in Korean).

43. The first complaint brought under the Agreement on Safeguards was *US—Safeguard Measure against Imports of Broom Corn Brooms.* See WTO, WT/DS78/1, dated May 1, 1997. This case was resolved without litigation although it remained technically pending. The actual panel decision concerning safeguard measures in the WTO system was issued for the first time in *Korea—Dairy Safeguards.* See WTO, WT/DS98/R, adopted January 12, 2000.

were to remain in force until February 28, 2001.[44] The panel and the Appellate Body held that the Korean safeguard measures were inconsistent with the obligations under the Agreement on Safeguards. The DSB adopted those rulings on January 12, 2000, and the reasonable implementation period was agreed to expire on May 20, 2000. Korea, through its administrative procedures, effectively lifted the safeguard measure on imports of the dairy products as of May 20, 2000.

Since its inception in 1987 to 1994, the Korea Trade Commission (KTC) had relied more on safeguard measures than on antidumping measures to address injury to domestic industries incurred by importation.[45] During 1987 to 1994, the KTC engaged in twenty-five safeguard and twelve antidumping investigations that resulted in sixteen safeguard and eight antidumping measures.[46] After this case, however, the KTC markedly abstained from using a safeguard measure whereas it substantially increased antidumping actions. For example, from 1997 to 2002, there were only four safeguard investigations but forty-six antidumping cases.[47] Accordingly, subsequent safeguard actions by the KTC appeared seriously disciplined by the WTO dispute settlement system. The safeguard mechanism in Korea was further elaborated with new laws and regulations on trade remedy actions.[48]

On the other hand, it was reported that the importation of dairy products at issue was reduced by about $70 million during the period in which the safeguard measure remained in force. This result, along with the outcome from *Argentina—Safeguard Measures on Imports of Footwear (Argentina—Footwear)*[49] case whose proceedings were conducted almost concomitantly, raised an important systemic issue for the WTO safeguard system. In the *Korea—Definitive Safeguard Measure on Imports of Certain Dairy Products* case, the termination of illegal safeguard measures pursuant to the DSB recommendation was undertaken only nine months prior to the original due date of the measures. In the *Argentina—Footwear* case, the implementation of the DSB recommendation by repealing the safeguard measure coincided with the original due date of the measure. Thus, the experience from these early safeguard cases raised imminent need for considering expeditious or accelerated dispute settlement procedures.

44. See WTO, G/SG/N/10/KOR/1, dated January 27, 1997 and G/SG/N/10/KOR/1/Supp.1, dated April 1, 1997.
45. On the other hand, the KTC has never even initiated a countervailing investigation to date. See Korea Trade Commission, *A History of 10 Years for the KTC,* in Korean (1997, 280–299).
46. Ibid.
47. See Korea Trade Commission, *Summary Report of Trade Remedy Action* (in Korean; February 2003, 1).
48. These are the Act on Investigation of Unfair Trade Practice and Trade Remedy Measures, Law 6417; and Implementing Regulation, Presidential Order no. 17222.
49. See WTO, WT/DS121/AB/R, adopted January 12, 2000. See also WTO, WT/DSB/M/75, dated March 7, 2000, at 2.

On February 1, 1999, the United States requested consultations with Korea in respect to a dual retail system for beef (*Korea–Beef II; DS161*). On April 13, 1999, Australia also requested consultations on the same basis (DS169). On January 10, 2001, the DSB adopted the panel and the Appellate Body reports that held that the Korean measures to be inconsistent with the WTO obligation. The parties to the dispute agreed that a reasonable implementation period would be eight months and thus expire on September 10, 2001.[50] The Korean government subsequently revised the 'Management Guideline for Imported Beef' to abolish the beef import system operated by the Livestock Products Marketing Organization.[51] In addition, on September 10, 2001, the Korean government eliminated the dual retail system for beef by entirely abolishing the Management Guideline for Imported Beef.[52] Thus, Korea considered that it had fully implemented the DSB's recommendation in this case.[53]

The only dispute settlement case concerning the Agreement on Government Procurement (GPA) to date is *Korea—Measures Affecting Government Procurement* (DS163).[54] On February 16, 1999, the United States requested consultations regarding certain procurement practices of the Korean Airport Construction Authority (KOACA). The panel ultimately ruled that the KOACA was not a covered entity under Korea's Appendix I of the GPA, even if the panel noted that the conduct of the Korean government with respect to the U.S. inquiries in the course of pertinent negotiation "[could], at best, be described as inadequate."[55] The United States did not make an appeal, and the panel report was adopted on June 19, 2000.[56] One of the important lessons from this case for the Korean government was about the discrepancy between its organizational mechanism for governmental offices that is based on decision-making structures and the WTO concession practice that is based on the institutional "entities" in the context of the GPA. The Government Organization Act of the Republic of Korea prescribes various government entities that actually constitute mere positions of certain level. Moreover, the Korean government has often established a special task force, group, or committee with specific mandates, whose legal foundations are obscure (Cho 2000, 152). This issue of how to determine the scope of covered entities in relation to a newly established

---

50. See WTO, WT/DS161, DS169/12, dated April 24, 2001.
51. See Ministry of Agriculture Notification 2000-82.
52. See Ministry of Agriculture Notification 2001-54.
53. See WTO, WT/DSB/M/110, dated October 22, 2001.
54. This case is the fourth complaint concerning government procurement. The first complaint, *Japan—Procurement of a Navigation Satellite* (DS73), was settled with a mutually satisfactory solution. The second and third complaints, *US—Measure Affecting Government Procurement* (DS88, DS95), were in respect to the same issue. The panel's authority lapsed as of February 11, 2000, when it was not requested to resume the proceeding after suspension of the works. See WTO, WT/DS88, DS95/6, dated February 14, 2000.
55. See WTO, WT/DS163/R, adopted on June 19, 2000, paragraph 7.80.
56. See WTO, WT/DS163/7, dated November 6, 2000.

governmental organ may require a more elaborate approach in the context of the GPA.

On October 24, 2000, the Committee of European Union Shipbuilders Associations filed a complaint under the trade barriers regulation (TBR) procedure concerning divergent financial arrangements for Korean shipbuilding industries. Although the commission was mindful of the extraordinary situation in Korea that was caused by the financial crisis in 1997, it found that parts of corporate restructuring programs and assistance through taxation for shipbuilding companies constituted prohibited subsidies within the meaning of the SCM.[57] On October 21, 2002, the EC made a formal request for a consultation with Korea under the WTO dispute settlement system on various corporate restructuring measures for the shipbuilding industry, alleging that they constituted prohibited subsidies under the SCM.[58]

This case was merely the beginning of much more controversial trade conflicts as regards corporate restructuring programs undertaken by the Korean government as parts of the IMF program to overcome the financial crisis. On July 25, 2002, the European Commission initiated a countervailing investigation on the Korean semiconductor producers, alleging that the governmental intervention in terms of debt-for-equity swaps and debt forgiveness for pertinent companies established illegal subsidies.[59] They concluded the countervailing proceeding with 35 percent of final duties. Apart from the EC's action against the Korean government, the U.S. authorities also initiated a countervailing investigation in November 2002 that ended up with a final determination for countervailing duties up to 57.73 percent.[60] The final duty was slightly reduced to 44.29 percent when the U.S. authorities corrected calculation mistakes.[61] These concomitant actions in the two major markets, if sustained in the final determinations, would risk the whole fate of the third largest semiconductor producer in the world. Furthermore, the legal validity of those actions would have significant implications for many other Korean industries that experienced similar restructuring programs in the course of the International Monetary Fund (IMF) program during the past few years. The Korean government brought complaints against both actions to the WTO DSB to vindicate the legitimacy of its systemic and structural measures adopted during the IMF program. The outcome of the WTO dispute settlement related to this dis-

57. See Commission Decision 2002/818/EC, OJ 2002 L 281/15.
58. See WTO, WT/DS273/1, dated October 24, 2002.
59. See WTO, G/SCM/N/93/EEC, dated March 12, 2003.
60. See U.S. Department of Commerce, *Preliminary Affirmative Countervailing Duty Determination: Dynamic Random Access Memory Semiconductors from the Republic of Korea,* http://ia.ita.doc.gov/download/drams-korea-draft-prelim-fr-notice.pdf.
61. See U.S. Department of Commerce, *Notice of Amended Final Affirmative Countervailing Duty Determination: Dynamic Random Access Memory Semiconductors from the Republic of Korea* (C-580-851).

pute would certainly be an interesting and important addition to the WTO jurisprudence.

Overall Comments. Considering the experience so far as a respondent in the WTO dispute settlement, the reaction by the Korean government appears to show a typical pattern of an average WTO member. For half of the complaints, Korea tried to settle the trade disputes without resorting to legal procedures. But, as it obtained more experience and the WTO jurisprudence became more sophisticated, Korea has become determined to take a more legalistic approach in dealing with complaints by other members.

When engaged in a WTO legal proceeding, Korea has been in full compliance with DSB recommendations. For all three cases in which Korea was found to be inconsistent with the WTO agreements, Korea fully implemented the DSB recommendations within the determined or agreed reasonable periods of time, even in politically loaded areas such as taxes and agriculture. It is also noted that Korea made appeals for all three cases in which the panels found some violations for its own measures. Last, it should also be noted that the areas challenged by other member countries are fairly diverse, ranging from SPS and TBT measures to government procurement, safeguard, domestic taxes, and retailing distribution systems. This is starkly contrasted with the cases in which Korea brought complaints, which concentrated mainly on antidumping measures. Overall, the dispute settlement experience of Korea as a respondent in such divergent areas under the auspice of the WTO has played a significant role in enhancing the public recognition of the importance of the multilateral trade norms in all aspects of economic activities and policy making.

Korea as Complainant

So far, the Korean complaints in the WTO dispute settlement system have focused primarily on the U.S. trade remedy measures, especially antidumping measures. Five out of the total nine complaints concerned antidumping matters, and seven complaints were against the United States. Only one case was against the Philippines, and the other was against the EC. Two cases concerned safeguard measures, and the other two concerned countervailing duties. In other words, the Korean complaints to the WTO dispute settlement system up to date can be simply summarized as exclusive concentration on trade remedy issues, predominantly caused by U.S. antidumping measures.

While Korea had been challenged in the WTO dispute settlement system from a very early period,[62] Korea appeared quite hesitant to bring com-

---

62. In 1995, three consultation requests were brought against Korea. The first two requests, *Korea—Measures Concerning the Testing and Inspection of Agricultural Products* (DS3) and *Korea—Measures Concerning the Shelf-Life of Products* (DS5), were made on April 6 and May 5, 1995.

plaints against other WTO member countries. It was not until July 1997 that Korea began to use the WTO dispute settlement system as a complainant. The first WTO case Korea brought to the DSB was in respect to the U.S. antidumping duties on Samsung color television receivers. On July 10, 1997, Korea requested a consultation, alleging that the United States had maintained an antidumping duty order for the past twelve years despite the cessation of exports as well as the absence of dumping. Subsequently, in response to the U.S. preliminary determination of December 19, 1997 to revoke the antidumping duty order, Korea withdrew its request for a panel. On August 27, 1998, the United States made a final determination to revoke the antidumping duty order that had been imposed on Samsung color television receivers since 1984. At the DSB meeting on September 22, 1998, Korea announced that it definitively withdrew the request for a panel because the imposition of antidumping duties had been revoked.[63]

For a similar case regarding antidumping duty orders on dynamic random access memory semiconductors (DRAMS), however, the United States did not readily revoke the orders and, on November 6, 1997, Korea requested the establishment of a panel. The DSB established a panel at its meeting on January 16, 1998. On March 19, 1998, the director general completed the panel composition, and Korea began its first panel proceeding as a complainant. The panel found the measures at issue to be in violation of Article 11.2 of the WTO Antidumping Agreement.[64] The United States did not make an appeal, and the DSB adopted the panel report on March 19, 1999.

Incidentally, this first win as a complainant in *US—DRAMS* came just eleven days after Korea lost its first WTO litigation as a respondent in *Korea—Soju*.[65] This somewhat fortunate timing of winning a WTO case contributed to alleviating the general concern and skepticism of the Korean public about the fairness and objectivity of the WTO dispute settlement system.

The two parties agreed on an implementation period of eight months, expiring on November 19, 1999. At the DSB meeting on January 27, 2000, the United States stated that it had implemented the DSB recommendations by amending the pertinent Department of Commerce (DOC) regulation, more specifically, by deleting the "not likely" standard and incorporating the "necessary" standard of the WTO Antidumping Agreement.

63. See WTO, WT/DS89/9, dated September 18, 1998.

64. See WTO panel report, *United States—Anti-Dumping Duty on Dynamic Random Access Memory Semiconductors (DRAMS) of One Megabit or Above from Korea (US—DRAMS)*, WT/DS99/R, adopted March 19, 1999.

65. The Appellate Body report for the *Korea—Soju* case was circulated on January 18, 1999, while the panel report for the *US—DRAMS* case was circulated on January 29, 1999. See WTO, *Korea—Soju*, WT/DS75, DS84/AB/R, adopted February 17, 1999.

The DOC, however, issued a revised Final Results of Redetermination in the third administrative review on November 4, 1999, concluding that, because a resumption of dumping was likely, it was necessary to leave the antidumping order in place. On April 6, 2000, Korea requested the referral of this matter to the original panel pursuant to Article 21.5 of the DSU and the EC reserved its third-party right. On September 19, 2000, Korea requested the panel to suspend its work and, on October 20, 2000, the parties notified the DSB of a mutually satisfactory solution to the matter, involving the revocation of the antidumping order at issue as the result of a five-year "sunset" review by the DOC.[66]

This case was the first case ever in which Korea won a favorable panel decision throughout the GATT/WTO system. Although it took one and a half more years for the United States to satisfactorily comply with the DSB recommendation after the adoption of the panel report, the sheer fact of winning a WTO dispute concerning chronic trade barriers of the major trading partners furnished the Korean government with confidence in the new WTO dispute settlement system. Unfortunately, however, the dismal implementation by the United States after the panel proceeding compromised confidence of a relatively new user concerning the effectiveness and fairness of the WTO dispute settlement system.[67] In any case, *US—DRAMS* clearly led the Korean government to adopt a more legal approach by utilizing the WTO dispute settlement system to address foreign trade barriers in subsequent cases. In other words, the experience and confidence gained from this case clearly led the Korean government to move to the direction of "aggressive legalism" in handling subsequent trade disputes.[68]

The *United States—Anti-Dumping Measures on Stainless Steel Plate in Coils and Stainless Steel Sheet and Strip from Korea* (*Korea—Stainless Steel*) case dealt with two separate antidumping actions by the U.S. authorities concerning stainless steel plate in coils (plate) and stainless steel sheet and strip in coils (sheet). For the antidumping case on plate, the DOC selected January 1 to December 31, 1997 as the period of investigation and issued the final dumping margin of 16.26 percent. The antidumping case for sheet covered April 1, 1997 through March 31, 1998 as the period of investigation and issued the final dumping margin of 58.79 percent for Taiwan and 12.12 percent for other Korean exporters, including POSCO. In this case, the panel was established on November 19, 1999 but actually composed on March 24, 2000.[69]

66. See WTO, WT/DS99/12, dated October 25, 2000.
67. For more positive assessment for Article 21.5 proceedings, see, generally, Kearns and Charnovitz (2002).
68. For the discussion of "aggressive legalism" by the Japanese government to deal with trade disputes, see Pekkanen (2001, 707–37).
69. It took 126 days to compose the panel, which is so far the longest period of time required for the panel appointment in cases involving Korea.

The underlying economic situation for this case is remarkably aberrational (Lane et al. 1999). The pertinent investigation periods included unprecedented fluctuation of exchange rates caused by the financial crisis. As illustrated in figure 9.3, the value of the Korean currency, won, precipitated to a half in a time span of just three months. The WTO panel found that the methodology adopted by the DOC to deal with such abnormity, including double currency conversion and the use of multiple averaging periods, were not consistent with the WTO obligations. Without the United States's appeal, the DSB adopted the panel report on February 1, 2001.

This case showed how vulnerable exporters might be in terms of antidumping actions as the exchange rates became abnormally fluctuating. Because dumping margin calculation permits various price adjustment to find ex-factory prices but no modification for volatile exchange rates except for averaging, unstable exchange rates can cause serious distortion in calculating dumping margins. This systemic problem may expose more exporters in developing countries that suffer from vacillating exchange rates to additional risks of being targeted by antidumping actions. Based on the Korean experience during the financial crisis, in which foreign exchange rates fluctuated at more than a normal or reasonable level, members may consider suspension of antidumping actions at least for a certain range of dumping margins that should reflect potential methodological errors. In

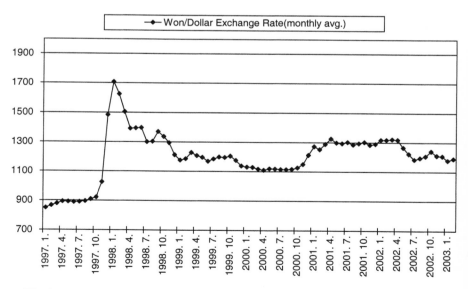

Fig. 9.3   Won/Dollar exchange rate trends

Sources: Bank of Korea, *Principal Economic Indicators* (March 2003). See also http://www .bok.or.kr.

other words, members may consider an increase of the current de minimis level for a period with exchange rate aberration.

On June 13, 2000, Korea made its fourth consultation request, again with the United States, in respect to the definitive safeguard measure imposed on imports of circular welded carbon quality line pipe. The definitive safeguard measure actually imposed by the president on February 11, 2000 was much more restrictive than that recommended by the International Trade Commission (ITC), disproportionately injuring the largest suppliers, that is, Korean exporters.[70] The exemption of Mexican and Canadian suppliers from the safeguard measure led them to become the largest and third-largest suppliers.

Korea considered that the U.S. procedures and determinations to impose the safeguard measure, as well as the measure itself, contravened various obligations under the Agreement on Safeguards and the GATT 1994. The panel concluded that the U.S. measure was imposed in a manner inconsistent with the WTO obligations. In the Appellate Body proceeding,[71] Korea's argument on the permissible extent of a safeguard measure was accepted, which seems one of the key findings for the WTO jurisprudence on safeguard.[72]

It is noted that this appellate proceeding was the first WTO dispute settlement litigation handled entirely by Korean government officials. It was a substantial development for Korea in terms of capacity building for utilizing the WTO dispute settlement system, particularly considering the previous cases in which foreign legal counsels played primary roles in WTO litigations. Moreover, when considering the fact that Korea is one of the WTO Members that did contribute to set the procedural practices to permit private counsel in a dispute settlement proceeding, the outcome of the *US—Line Pipe* appellate proceeding substantially enhanced self-confidence and capacity in terms of much needed legal expertise.

When both parties agreed on the reasonable period of time for implementation, with expiration on September 1, 2002, the arbitration under DSU Article 21.3 was suspended.[73] The U.S. government agreed to increase the in-quota volume of imports to 17,500 tons and lower the safeguard tariff to 11 percent, with the termination due of March 1, 2003.[74]

70. The imports above the first 9,000 short tons from each country would be subject to a 19 percent, 15 percent, and 11 percent duty for the first, second, and third year. See WTO panel report, *United States—Definitive Safeguard Measures on Imports of Circular Welded Carbon Quality Line Pipe from Korea (US—Line Pipe)*, WT/DS202/R, adopted March 8, 2002, paragraph 2.5.

71. See WTO Appellate Body report, *US—Line Pipe,* WT/DS202/AB/R, adopted March 8, 2002. The United States initially filed an appeal on November 6, 2001 (WT/DS202/7) but withdrew it for scheduling reasons on November 13 (WT/DS202/8). The appeal was refiled on November 19, 2001 (WT/DS202/9).

72. See, generally, Ahn (2001).

73. See WTO, WT/DS202/17, dated July 26, 2002.

74. See WTO, WT/DS202/18, dated July 31, 2002.

But, considering that the original due date of the safeguard measure that was set at February 24, 2003, the practical impact of the WTO dispute settlement system was to increase the in-quota volume from 9,000 to 17,500 tons only for the period of September 1, 2002 to February 24, 2003, while the latter measure remained until the end of February 2003. Thus, this case again illustrated the systemic problem in implementation of a safeguard dispute.

On December 15, 2000, Korea requested consultations with the Philippines concerning the dumping decision of the Tariff Commission of the Philippines on polypropylene resins. This antidumping order was actually the first antidumping measure by the Philippines against Korean exporters, as the first antidumping investigation against Korean electrolytic tinplates was dismissed for lack of merit.[75] The Tariff Commission of the Philippines imposed the provisional antidumping duties on polypropylene resins ranging from 4.20 percent to 40.53 percent and subsequently the final duties at slightly lowered levels.[76] Following the consultation on January 19, 2001 under the purview of the WTO dispute settlement system, the Philippines withdrew the antidumping order on November 8, 2001, and Korea did not pursue further action in the DSB.[77] This case is so far the only trade dispute for Korea elevated to the formal dispute settlement procedure as opposed to a developing country.

The fifth WTO complaint by Korea against the United States was also related to antidumping matters. On December 21, 2000, Korea, along with Australia, Brazil, Chile, EC, India, Indonesia, Japan, and Thailand, requested consultations with the United States concerning the amendment to the Tariff Act of 1930, titled Continued Dumping and Subsidy Offset Act of 2000 that is usually referred to as the Byrd Amendment. By distributing the antidumping and countervailing duties to domestic petitioners, the Byrd Amendment aimed to create more incentives to bring trade remedy actions. As the third-frequent target for antidumping and countervailing measures in the U.S. market, Korean exporters were very keen on the outcome of this case.[78]

The panel established by the requests from nine members was later merged with the panel requested by Canada and Mexico. The panel and the Appellate Body found that the Byrd Amendment was inconsistent with the Antidumping and SCM. Furthermore, the panel suggested that the United States bring the Byrd Amendment into conformity by repealing it. On

---

75. See WTO, G/ADP/N/65/PHL, dated September 21, 2000.
76. See WTO, G/ADP/N/72/PHL, dated March 6, 2001.
77. See WTO, G/ADP/N/85/PHL, dated February 22, 2002.
78. For antidumping measures, exporters from China and Japan are more frequent targets than those from Korea in the U.S. market. U.S. countervailing measures have targeted Italy, India, Korea, and France. See WTO, Statistics on Anti-dumping, http://www.wto.org/english/tratop_e/adp_e.htm and Statistics on Subsidies and Countervailing Measures http://www.wto.org/english/tratop_e/scm_e/scm_stattab8_e.htm.

April 2, 2003, the arbitrator was appointed to determine a reasonable period of implementation under DSU Article 21.3.

Ironically, a subsidiary company of a Korean manufacturer received a substantial "offset" disbursement under the Byrd Amendment. Zenith Electronics, owned by LG Electronics, received the disbursement of $24.3 million in 2001 and $9 million in 2002 from antidumping duties collected on Japanese television imports. The offset payment for Zenith Electronics in 2001 was indeed more than 10 percent of the total disbursement of $231.2 million in 2001.[79] In 2002, the total disbursement under the Byrd Amendment was increased to $329.8 million.[80]

On March 20, 2002, Korea requested consultation with the United States regarding the definitive safeguard measures on the imports of certain steel products and the related laws including Section 201 of the Trade Act of 1974 and Section 311 of the North American Free Trade Agreement (NAFTA) Implementation Act. The DSB established a single panel to include complaints by other members such as the EC, Japan, China, Switzerland, Norway, New Zealand, and Brazil.[81] In addition to most complainants that reserved third-party rights, Taiwan, Cuba, Malaysia, Mexico, Thailand, Turkey, and Venezuela also participated as third parties in the proceeding. On July 25, 2002, the director general composed the panel. Taiwan later decided to become a more active participant and made an independent consultation request with the United States on November 1, 2002.[82]

Concerning this U.S. Section 201 action, the Korean government made the first trade compensation request pursuant to Article 8 of the Agreement on Safeguards.[83] When the U.S. government did not agree on satisfactory compensatory arrangements, several WTO members, such as the EC,[84] Japan,[85] Norway,[86] China,[87] and Switzerland,[88] notified to the Coun-

---

79. See U.S. Customs and Border Protection, CDSOA FY2001 Disbursements Final, http://www.customs.ustreas.gov/xp/cgov/import/add_cvd. On the other hand, it is noted that only two ball bearing companies, Torrington and MPB (The Timken Company), received more offset payments in gross than Zenith Electronics in 2001. Their total disbursements amount to $62.8 million and $25 million, respectively. But the disbursement for Zenith Electronics is the second largest one in terms of individual claims, following a $34.7 million offset payment for Torrington in relation to ball bearings dumping from Japan.
80. See U.S. Customs and Border Protection, CDSOA FY2002 Disbursements Final, http://www.customs.ustreas.gov/xp/cgov/import/add_cvd/.
81. See WTO, WT/DS251/10, dated August 12, 2002.
82. See WTO, WT/DS274/1, dated November 11, 2002.
83. About 12 percent of trade remedy measures against Korean exports are safeguard actions. For example, as of December 31, 2002, Korean exporters are subject to ten safeguard measures and five investigations in India, the United States, Venezuela, China, Argentina, Canada, and EC. See the Korea Trade Investment Promotion Agency (KOTRA) Summary of Import Restrictions against Korean Exports 2002 (in Korean, December 2002).
84. See WTO, G/C/10, dated May 15, 2002.
85. See WTO, G/C/15, dated May 21, 2002.
86. See WTO, G/C/16, dated May 21, 2002.
87. See WTO, G/C/17, dated May 21, 2002.
88. See WTO, G/C/18, dated May 22, 2002.

cil for Trade in Goods of proposed suspension of concessions. Instead of proposing suspension of concessions, the Korean government notified the Council for Trade in Goods of the agreement that the ninety-day period set forth in Article 8.2 of the Agreement on Safeguards and Article XIX:3(a) of the GATT shall be considered to expire on March 19, 2005.[89] This agreement to postpone potential retaliation for about three years, however, practically wipes out all real impact on balancing trade interests, since the original safeguard measure is supposed to end on March 20, 2005.[90] In other words, the Korean government tried to avoid the possibility of actually exercising the suspension of concession against one of its major trading partners without the DSB authorization, while it still maintained a political gesture that it exercised a legal authority specifically enunciated under the Agreement on Safeguards.

On September 3, 2003, Korea brought a complaint regarding the EC's subsidy policy on shipbuilding industry. This complaint is basically in retaliation of the EC's challenge against the Korean government's role during the financial crisis in the shipbuilding industry.

Antidumping actions against Korea (from January 1, 1995 to June 30, 2002)

	Argentina	Australia	EC	India	South Africa	United States	Others	Total
AD initiation	9	11	21	18	13	19	54	145
AD measures	6	4	9	13	13	11	18	74

As described previously, Korea has had major problems regarding the U.S. antidumping practices. In some sense, its experience as a complainant in the WTO dispute settlement system almost exclusively against U.S. antidumping practices is puzzling because, during the period of January 1, 1995 to June 20, 2002, it was the EC that initiated the most antidumping investigations against exported products from Korea, and it was South Africa and India that actually imposed the most antidumping measures.[91] This fact seems to imply that the U.S. market still occupies an unbalanced economic importance in Korea.[92] Currently, Korea is actively engaged in pushing the agenda to revise the Antidumping Agreement in the Doha Development Agenda.[93]

89. See WTO, G/C/12, dated May 16, 2002. On the other hand, Australia, Brazil, and New Zealand extended the deadline for retaliation to March 20, 2005. See WTO, G/C/11, dated May 16, 2002 and G/C/13, 14, dated May 17, 2002.
90. See WTO, G/SG/N/10/USA/6, dated March 14, 2002.
91. See WTO, Statistics on Anti-dumping, http://www.wto.org/english/tratop_e/adp_e/adp_e.htm.
92. On the other hand, Japan, a country with a similar trade structure and attitude toward trade dispute settlement, has shown much diverse interest as a complainant concerning its target markets. See, generally, Iwasawa (2000).
93. For the Korean proposal regarding antidumping issues, see, for example, WTO, WT/GC/W/235/Rev.1, dated July 12, 1999; TN/RL/W/6, dated April 26, 2002; and TN/RL/W/10, dated June 28, 2002.

For three cases in which the entire dispute settlement procedure, including implementation, ended, the major problem Korea faced was the failure to ensure prompt and effective compliance by a respondent. The implementation for the *US—DRAMS* and *US—Line Pipe* cases was in fact not much more than the mere expiration of the original trade remedy measures. This result raises concern for effectiveness and fairness of the WTO dispute settlement system, especially when dealing with the WTO litigation demands' sizeable financial and human resources. In particular, the lack of legal systems to represent private parties' interest in line with Section 301 and TBR procedures would inevitably result in a less enthusiastic approach for resorting to the legal activism for many WTO members, including Korea, because government officials in charge of WTO disputes may not have an incentive to initiate all those costly procedures merely for "paper" winning.

9.3.4   Philippines

The Philippines' experience under the WTO dispute settlement system showed a typical pattern for developing-country members with comparative advantage in agricultural industry sectors. (See table 9.9.) Four complaints against its trading partners were all regarding import restrictive measures on agricultural products. In contrast, the Philippines were challenged twice concerning its own import barriers for industrial sectors, although it was also challenged once about import restriction on pork and poultry from the United States.

9.3.5   Thailand

Thailand is in some sense unique in the manner that they use the WTO dispute settlement system. Thailand is currently the most active developing-country complainant in the WTO. Whereas Thailand was challenged

Table 9.9   **WTO disputes involving the Philippines**

As complainant		
Brazil—*Measures Affecting Desiccated Coconut*	DS22	P/AB report
United States—Import Prohibition of Certain Shrimp and Shrimp Products	DS61	In consultation
Australia—Certain Measures Affecting the Importation of Fresh Fruit and Vegetables	DS270	In panel
Australia—Certain Measures Affecting the Importation of Fresh Pineapple	DS271	In consultation
As respondent		
Philippines—Measures Affecting Pork and Poultry	DS74, DS102/US	Mutually resolved
Philippines—Measures Affecting Trade and Investment in the Motor Vehicle Sector	DS195/US	In panel
Philippines—Antidumping Measures Regarding Polypropylene Resins from Korea	DS215/Korea	In consultation

Note: See table 9.7 note.

Table 9.10   WTO disputes involving Thailand

As complainant		
EC—Duties on Imports of Rice	DS17	Inactive
Hungary—Export Subsidies in Respect to Agricultural Products	DS35	Mutually resolved
Turkey—Restrictions on Imports of Textile and Clothing Products	DS47	In consultation
United States—Import Prohibition of Certain Shrimp and Shrimp Products	DS58	P/AB report
Colombia—Safeguard Measure on Imports of Plain Polyester Filaments from Thailand	DS181	Inactive
Egypt—Import Prohibition on Canned Tuna with Soybean Oil	DS205	In consultation
United States—Continued Dumping and Subsidy Offset Act of 2000	DS217	P/AB report
EC—Generalized System of Preferences	DS242	In consultation
EC—Export Subsidies on Sugar	DS283	In consultation
EC—Customs Classification of Frozen Boneless Chicken Cuts	DS286	In consultation
As respondent		
Thailand—Antidumping Duties on Angles, Shapes, and Sections of Iron or Nonalloy Steel and H-Beams from Poland	DS122/Poland	P/AB report

Note: See table 9.7 note.

only once so far by Poland concerning antidumping measures, it made ten consultation requests against other WTO members. The EC has been the most frequent target of Thailand's complaints. Other than the EC, Thailand's complaints were raised against various countries, including Colombia, Egypt, Hungary, Turkey, and the United States. It is noted that Thailand's complaints are often raised against other developing countries. In terms of subject matters, Thailand's dispute settlement experience also showed a typical pattern of developing countries by focusing mostly on foreign trade barriers on agricultural and textile products. (See table 9.10.)

9.3.6   Others

No WTO member has raised a formal complaint against China or Taiwan yet, although they joined the WTO more than a year and a half ago. (See table 9.11.) This does not mean that trade policy measures of both members are completely consistent with the WTO disciplines. In fact, as many members are concerned, these two members with substantial trade volumes may still maintain numerous potentially controversial measures or laws, especially considering the short experience on multilateral trade disciplines. Although it is true that both members have exerted strenuous efforts to bring their system into conformity with the WTO system, more dispute cases concerning both members seem unavoidable for the future WTO dispute settlement system. In particular, the Chinese government has been very active in using trade remedy measures to protect domestic

Table 9.11   **WTO disputes as complainants**

China		
United States—Definitive Safeguard Measures on Imports of Certain Steel Products	DS252	In AB
Taiwan		
United States—Definitive Safeguard Measures on Imports of Certain Steel Products	DS274	In consultation
Hong Kong, China		
Turkey—Restrictions on Imports of Textile and Clothing Products	DS29	In consultation
Indonesia		
Argentina—Safeguard Measures on Imports of Footwear	DS123	In consultation
United States—Continued Dumping and Subsidy Offset Act of 2000	DS217	P/AB report
Malaysia		
United States—Import Prohibition of Certain Shrimp and Shrimp Products	DS58	P/AB report
Singapore		
Malaysia—Prohibition of Imports of Polyethylene and Polypropylene	DS1	Inactive

Note: See table 9.7 note.

Table 9.12   **WTO disputes as respondents**

Indonesia		
Indonesia—Certain Measures Affecting the Automobile Industry	DS54, DS64/Japan DS55/EC, DS59/US	P/AB report
Malaysia		
Malaysia—Prohibition of Imports of Polyethylene and Polypropylene	DS1/Singapore	Inactive

Note: See table 9.7 note.

import markets.[94] Some of these measures may not be free from WTO challenges in the future. (See table 9.12.)

Another interesting question is whether and how China would deal with Taiwan in terms of the WTO dispute settlement system. In case Taiwan raises a complaint against China and seeks to proceed to panel and the Appellate Body proceedings, there is no mechanism to block such procedures under the WTO dispute settlement system.[95] It would bring about a

94. Up to the end of April 2003, the Chinese authority initiated twenty-one antidumping investigations. Among them, seventeen cases involved Korean products.

95. Under the GATT system, a respondent could block the proceeding by declining consensus for panel establishment. This was changed under the WTO dispute settlement system that mandates panel proceedings, if requested by a complainant, after a sixty-day consultation period. For more detailed accounts on the WTO dispute settlement proceedings, see, generally, Waincymer (2002).

diplomatically sensitive situation in which China and Taiwan stand against each other with equivalent status in an international forum, which may cause a very difficult political dilemma for these members. Because the WTO is the only international organization of which Taiwan is a full member, Taiwan may have strong incentives to use the WTO dispute settlement system to promote the image as a political entity that is on par with China (Kong 2002). It remains to be seen how these members will agree to address this problem.

9.4   East Asia in the WTO Dispute Settlement Understanding (DSU) Negotiation

The DSU review mandated by a 1994 Ministerial Decision started in the DSB in 1997. The deadline stipulated as January 1, 1999 was extended to July 31, 1999, but there was no agreement by then. In November 2001, at the Doha Ministerial Conference, member governments agreed to negotiate to improve and clarify the DSU and conclude the negotiation not later than May 2003.

East Asian members have actively participated in various areas of the Doha negotiations, including reforming the dispute settlement system. In addition to Japan, Korea, and Thailand, who have often resorted to the WTO dispute settlement system, China and Taiwan are also making substantial contributions by submitting their own proposals to the DSU negotiation.

Although they have shown different emphases on varying issues, their proposals invariably try to enhance efficiency and transparency of the dispute settlement mechanism, particularly with respect to the implementation phase of the current procedure. For example, Japan and Korea submitted elaborated proposals concerning Articles 21 and 22. The proposal by Japan includes a detailed provision for compliance panel procedures.[96] Korea proposed that the compliance panel proceed to determine the level of the nullification or impairment and, if the Appellate Body modified or reversed the legal findings and conclusions of the compliance panel, the Appellate Body determine the final level of the nullification or impairment.[97]

China suggested augmentation of special and differential treatment in the DSU to developing-country members, including the least-developed countries.[98] Claiming that China is a developing-country member, China proposed that developed-country members exercise due restraint in cases against developing-country members. In other words, developed-country

96. See WTO, TN/DS/W/32, dated January 22, 2003.
97. See WTO, TN/DS/W/35, dated January 22, 2003.
98. See WTO, TN/DS/W/57, dated May 19, 2003.

members shall not bring more than two cases to the WTO DSB against a particular developing-country member in one calendar year. Moreover, while time periods applicable under the DSU for dealing with disputes involving safeguard and antidumping measures shall be half of the normal time frame, the shortened time frame shall not apply to the defending party that is a developing-country member.

Taiwan made extensive proposals to improve third-party rights in the WTO dispute settlement procedures.[99] But Taiwan opposed some of the proposals made by other members such as the opening of meetings to the public, public access to submissions, and developing guideline procedures for the handling of amicus curiae submissions.[100]

Malaysia made an interesting proposal concerning litigation costs.[101] It proposed that in a dispute involving a developing-country member and a developed-country member as a complaining party and as a party complained against, respectively, and where that dispute does not end with a panel or the Appellate Body finding against the former, the panel or the Appellate Body award litigation costs to the developing-country member to the tune of US$500,000 or actual expenses, whichever is higher.[102] The litigation costs shall include lawyers' fees, charges and all other expenses for preparation of necessary documents[103] and participation in the consultations, panel, and Appellate Body proceedings. The litigation costs shall also include travel, hotel, per diem, and other expenses for a reasonable number of the capital-based officials. In fact, litigation costs to deal with WTO disputes have become one of the most serious practical obstacles to utilize the WTO dispute settlement mechanism. Since private attorneys were permitted to panel and Appellate Body proceedings in early WTO years, their roles have quickly become indispensable elements of WTO litigations, probably except for a handful of members. The legal expenses to procure such professional lawyers turned out, however, to be sometimes way beyond the scope of budgetary constraints of developing countries. These problems led some WTO members to establish the Advisory Centre on WTO Law on October 5, 2001. Currently, Hong Kong, the Philippines, and Thailand are signatories to the Centre. Thailand suggested that the

99. See WTO, TN/DS/W/36, dated January 22, 2003.
100. See WTO, TN/DS/W/25, dated November 27, 2002.
101. See WTO, TN/DS/W/47, dated February 11, 2003.
102. The expenses shall be calculated for each stage of dispute settlement proceedings, which include consultation, panel, and the Appellate Body proceedings as well as the proceedings under Articles 21.3(c), 21.5, 22.6, and 25 of the DSU. The original panel and the panel established pursuant to Article 21.5 of the DSU shall take into account the expenses relating to the consultations preceding those panel proceedings for award of litigation costs. The award of litigation costs is binding on the parties and not subject to appeal.
103. The documents include request for consultations, oral or written submissions, and all other documents necessary for preparation and participation in the dispute settlement proceedings. They shall also include oral or written advice rendered prior to, during, or after consultations, panel, or the Appellate Body proceedings relating to the dispute.

Appellate Body be composed of nine persons, three of whom serve on any one case.[104] Furthermore, it proposed a new panel composition process, including a Roster of Panel Chairs comprising individuals who may be appointed as chair of a panel by lot.[105]

At its meeting on July 24, 2003, the General Council of the WTO agreed to extend negotiations in the DSB special session that is reviewing DSU. The time frame was extended from May 31, 2003 to May 31, 2004. How many proposals to improve the DSU can actually be agreed upon by members by May 2004 remains to be seen.

9.5   National Complaining Procedures for Private Parties

The WTO dispute settlement system is primarily for member governments. In other words, private parties may not be able to bring complaints directly to the WTO dispute settlement system even if it is indeed private parties that are aggrieved by WTO inconsistent measures of other WTO members. Those private parties have to persuade their own governments to raise complaints on behalf of their economic interests. This mechanism does not, however, function properly, as the discretionary decision of member governments on whether to bring a WTO complaint often does not stand in line with private parties' requests. Since the WTO agreement is not normally directly applicable, the lack of systemic nexus between the WTO dispute settlement system and private parties causes fundamental problems in the WTO system. This problem becomes more and more serious as the scope of the WTO system tends to expand by encompassing intrinsically private legal issues such as investment and competition.

Currently, the most notable examples of linking private parties to the WTO dispute settlement system are the Section 301 mechanism of the United States and the Trade Barriers Regulation system of the EC. Even if the unilateral retaliation has been the focal point of the Section 301, the most important aspect of the Section 301 mechanism in terms of trade policy is the establishment of the systemic procedures under which private parties can force the government to act on their petitions. The EC initially introduced the so-called New Trade Policy Instrument by Regulation 2641/84,[106] but substantially modified it pursuant to the WTO Agreement and adopted the TBR system.[107] In both the United States and the EC, many WTO complaints have been indeed initiated by petitions under those systems.

104. See WTO, TN/DS/W/30, dated January 22, 2003.
105. See WTO, TN/DS/W/31, dated January 22, 2003.
106. See Council Regulation (EEC) no. 2641/84 of September 17, 1984.
107. See Council Regulation (EC) no. 3286/94 of December 22, 1994. For a thorough overview of the TBR, see Bronckers (1997).

Despite the rather long history and experience under the multilateral trade system, Japan and Korea have not yet prepared such mechanisms in domestic legal or institutional systems. Most other East Asian countries do not have such systems either. Interestingly, China prepared a TBR-like system that would allow private parties to raise complaints against foreign trade barriers under systemic procedures and, in turn, lead to formal WTO complaints by the Chinese government. The Provisional Regulations for Investigation on Foreign Trade Barriers enacted from November 1, 2002 stipulates that natural or legal persons representing domestic industries, as well as domestic industries or companies, can apply for investigations. The investigation procedure under this regulation may not exceed six months and may be extended to nine months in exceptional circumstances. Article 29 provides that the Ministry of Commerce (previously, the Ministry of Foreign Trade and Economic Cooperation [MOFTEC]) may take one of the following, if foreign trade barriers are found to be in violation of international agreements: (a) bilateral consultation, (b) multilateral dispute settlement, or (c) other necessary measures. Although the current provisions do not exclude unilateral retaliation by taking "other necessary measures," the overall structure of the system is much more focused in connecting the WTO dispute settlement system and aggrieved domestic private parties. This development should give important lessons for other WTO members in general and East Asian members in particular.

9.6   Conclusion

The WTO dispute settlement system has become the core of the world trading system. Various trade disputes arising from divergent interpretation of the WTO agreements and de facto discriminatory impact of the domestic trade policy measures have been rectified by the legal rulings of the WTO panels and Appellate Body. Yet, there is huge discrepancy among the WTO members, especially in East Asia, in the degree of utilizing the WTO dispute settlement system. Moreover, East Asian members have shown a strong tendency in settling the disputes rather than litigating the cases. This fact should not be construed to indicate that the WTO dispute settlement system has been malfunctioning to represent the legitimate WTO rights and interests in East Asia. To the contrary, it is shown that major economic sectors—industrial or agricultural—of East Asian members have been able to use the WTO dispute settlement system for securing a level playing field. The next question for these members may be how to establish the domestic system to properly represent their private economic interests in a more balanced manner and how to make the WTO dispute settlement system a benign instrument for the entire economy, not a captive tool by a particular segment of industries.

References

Ahn, Dukgeun. 2001. A critical analysis of interpretation and application of WTO Agreement on Safeguards (in Korean). *International Trade Law* 41:9–51.
———. 2003. Korea on the GATT/WTO Dispute Settlement System: Legal battles for economic development. *Journal of International Economic Law* 6:597–633.
Araki, Ichiro. 2004. Beyond aggressive legalism: Japan and the GATT/WTO Dispute. In *WTO and East Asia: New perspectives,* ed. Mitsuo Matsushita and Dukgeun Ahn, 149–75. London: Cameron May.
Bhala, Rai. 1998. *World trade law.* Charlottesville, VA: Lexis Law.
Bronckers, Marco. 1997. Enforcing WTO law through the EC Trade Barriers Regulation. *International Trade Law and Regulation* 76 (3): 76–83.
Durling, James P. 2001. *Anatomy of trade disputes.* London: Cameron.
Durling, James P., and Simon N. Lester. 1999. Original meanings and the film dispute: The drafting history, textual evolution, and application of the non-violation nullification or impairment remedy. *The George Washington Journal of International Law and Economics* 32 (2): 211–68.
General Agreement on Tariffs and Trade (GATT). 1952. *Basic instruments and selected documents.* Vol. 2. Geneva: GATT.
Hahm, Tae-Hyuk. 1994. Reflections on the GATT accession negotiations. Diplomatic Negotiation Case no. 94-1. Seoul: Institute of Foreign Affairs and National Security.
Hudec, Robert. 1993. *Enforcing international trade law: The evolution of the modern GATT legal system.* Salem, NH: Butterworth Legal Publishers.
Iwasawa, Yuji. 2000. WTO dispute settlement and Japan. In *New direction in international economic law,* ed. M. Bronckers and R. Quick, 473–90. London: Kluwer Law International.
Jackson, John H. 1998. *The World Trade Organization: Constitution and jurisprudence.* London: Royal Institute of International Affairs.
———. 1990. *Restructuring the GATT system.* London: Council on Foreign Relations Press.
———. 1999. Western view of Japanese international law practice for the maintenance of the international economic order. In *Japan and international law: Past, present and future,* ed. N. Ando, 205–20. London: Kluwer Law International.
Kearns, Jason, and Steve Charnovitz. 2003. Adjudicating compliance in the WTO: A review of DSU Article 21.5. *Journal of International Economic Law* 5:331–52.
Kim, Chulsu. Forthcoming. Korea in the multilateral trading system: From obscurity to prominence. In *The Kluwer companion to the WTO Agreement.* London: Kluwer Law International.
Kim, Hyun Chong. 1999. The WTO dispute settlement process: A primer. *Journal of International Economic Law* 2:457–76.
Kong, Qingjiang. 2002. Can the WTO dispute settlement mechanism resolve trade disputes between China and Taiwan? *Journal of International Economic Law* 5:747–58.
Lane, Timothy, Atish Ghosh, Javier Hamann, Steven Phillips, Marianne Schulze-Ghattas, and Tsidi Tsikata. 1999. IMF-supported programs in Indonesia, Korea and Thailand: A preliminary assessment. IMF Occasional Paper no. 178. Washington, DC: International Monetary Fund.
Leitner, Kara, and Simon Lester. 2004. WTO dispute settlement 1995–2003: A statistical analysis. *Journal of International Economic Law* 7:169–81.
Lie, Han-young, and Dukgeun Ahn. 2003. Legal issues of privatization in govern-

ment procurement agreements: Experience of Korea from bilateral and WTO agreements. *International Trade Law and Regulation* 9 (2): 54–62.

Palmeter, David, and Petros C. Mavroidis. 1999. *Dispute settlement in the World Trade Organization: Practice and procedure.* London: Kluwer Law International.

Pekkanen, Saadia M. 2001. Aggressive legalism: The rules of the WTO and Japan's emerging trade strategy. *World Economy* 24:707.

Petersmann, U. E. 1997. *The GATT/WTO dispute settlement system: International law, international organizations and dispute settlement.* London: Kluwer Law International.

Waincymer, Jeff. 2002. *WTO Litigation: Procedural aspects of formal dispute settlement.* London: Cameron.

World Trade Organization (WTO). 1995. *Analytical index: Guide to GATT law and practice.* Geneva: WTO.

Guohua, Yang, and Cheng Jin. 2001. The process of China's accession to the WTO. *Journal of International Economic Law* 4:297–328.

Comment   Da-Nien Liu

This is an interesting paper, providing much valuable information on World Trade Organization (WTO) dispute settlement cases in the East Asia economies and greatly increasing the understanding of the participation of East Asia economies in the WTO dispute settlement system. Professor Ahn has done a thoroughly professional job in analyzing these Dispute Settlement Body (DSB) cases; most of the cases referred to in this article concern Japan and Korea because, for other East Asian countries, including Taiwan, DSB is a relatively new trade policy mechanism. I believe that there are valuable lessons to be learned from the experiences of these two countries; therefore, my comments are largely devoted to raising additional considerations and to questioning the areas in which more work could be done in the future.

I have four comments, the first of which is related to the issue of Japan as a complainant and a third party, while the second refers to a DSB case on Taxes on Alcoholic Beverages in Korea (the *Korea-soju* case, DS75 and DS84). The third question is related to the national complaint procedures for private parties, while the final question is on the subject of future amendments to the DSU in the East Asia economies.

First of all, as mentioned in the paper, the attitude of the Japanese government changed after 1998, when more DSB cases were initiated, and it is also noteworthy that Japan is now one of the most active third parties in WTO dispute settlement cases, where it has shown a strong interest in those cases concerning measures by the U.S. government. Here it may be

Da-Nien Liu is the deputy director of the Taiwan WTO Center of the Chung Hua Institution for Economic Research.

more interesting to learn the overall strategy of Japan regarding its DSB participation. Why would Japan, with its abundant resources and considerable experience in dispute settlement cases, choose to be an active third party? In particular, why should any country that has a substantial interest in certain cases choose to be a third party rather than a party to the dispute? As we know, a third party in dispute settlement cases does not need to spend considerable time, effort, and money in bringing a complaint to the panel, and it can also attend the first meeting of the panel where it can present its own views (with the exception of confidential information hearings). Most important, if it stands alongside the plaintiff, which subsequently wins the suit, it can also enjoy the benefits of the case on a most-favored nation (MFN) basis (if the respondent complies with the recommendations or rulings of the DSB). For a new WTO member, such as Taiwan, being a third party in a case is an appropriate way of gaining experience, while spending relatively little as it learns to further integrate itself into the multilateral trading system.

Second, in section 9.3.3, Professor Ahn refers to the *Korea-soju* case noting that "by experiencing the impact of the WTO dispute settlement decisions, probably at the deepest and widest level of daily life, this case has played a crucial role in enhancing WTO awareness in Korea." After losing the case, Korea was forced to amend the Liquor Tax Law and the Education Tax Law, that is, to increase the tax rate on *soju* in order to comply with the recommendations and rulings of the DSB.

I believe that this is a very important issue because Taiwan was faced with a similarly difficult situation when it amended its regulations on tobacco and wine, leading to a significant increase in the tax rate on rice wine so as to comply with the national treatment principle of the WTO. Many people in Taiwan could not accept the result because they had enjoyed low tax rates on rice wine for decades, and many of these people continued to believe that rice wine was only for cooking, not for drinking. However, the United States did not accept this point, and, as a result, many people complained of the Taiwanese government's failure in its trade negotiations with the United States, leading to a fundamental misunderstanding and negative impression of the WTO. It would be interesting to see how a government can succeed in educating its people with regard to DSB outcomes and help to provide a better understanding of WTO principles. I believe that this is important, for both Korea and Taiwan, and I expect that Professor Ahn could provide the East Asian economies with the fine details of some Korean experiences.

The third point relates to the issue of national complaint procedures for private parties. The paper notes that China was the first country in East Asia to implement a trade barriers regulation (TBR)-like system that would allow private parties to raise complaints against foreign trade barriers under systemic procedures, which would in turn lead to formal WTO complaints by the government; this is the so-called Provisional Regulations for the Investigation on Foreign Trade Barriers, which was enacted on November 1, 2002. It is also very interesting to consider the motivation behind China's application of this system. My question relates to whether, if the government concerned rejects the application of a private enterprise to raise a complaint, the private enterprise in question will have the right to appeal the government's decision through some administrative or judicial procedure based on an allegation that the discretionary decision of the government concerned is at odds with the interests of private parties. I think that this is also a very important point in assessing the functionality of the system.

Finally, I suggest that the paper could add more on the role that East Asia can play in future DSB negotiations. Although the DSB failed to complete its negotiations for amendments to the DSU before the end of May 2003, as mandated by the Doha Ministerial Declaration, the chairman of the DSB did present many proposals at the end of May.[1]

The following issues are also of considerable importance: improvements to third party rights, clarification of the controversy between the compensation and retaliation amendment of the "reasonable period of time," improvements to the implementation of the recommendations and rulings of the DSB, remand procedures of panel reports, and special considerations for developing countries (special and differential [S&D] treatments). All of these issues could have an impact on the East Asia countries in their application of the DSB mechanism and should call for further study. In particular I feel that the issues of compensation and retaliation, and the special treatment of developing-country members, are of significant importance.

Comment   John Whalley

This is an extremely interesting paper that carefully documents World Trade Organization (WTO) dispute settlement cases primarily involving Japan, Korea, and Thailand since 1994 when, as part of the Uruguay Round decision and the relabeling of the General Agreement on Tariffs and Trade (GATT) as the WTO, major changes took place in dispute settlement procedures. These included consensus to reject over consensus to accept, time limits for various stages of proceedings, a permanent roster of panelists, and an appellate procedure. Prior to 1994, East Asian in-

---

1. See (JOB (03)/91/Rev.1).

John Whalley is a professor of economics and director of the Centre for the Study of International Economic Relations, Department of Economics, University of Western Ontario, and a research associate of the National Bureau of Economic Research.

volvement in GATT dispute settlement was extremely limited and primarily involved cases against Japan. Japan in those years used GATT dispute settlement little in attempting to deal with problems of access and repeated violations of their GATT rights in North American and European markets. Professor Ahn shows how three leading East Asian traders are now much more aggressively pursuing WTO dispute settlement than before but (as table 9.5 shows) still far less aggressively than major non-Asian WTO members.

Relatively little, to my knowledge, has been written on the East Asian experience with WTO dispute settlement, and so this is a welcome contribution. Also, in my opinion, economists have relatively little to say in general about mechanisms for the enforcement of international legal arrangements, because if one accepts the folk theorem sets of trigger strategies rather than agreed procedures for the resolution of disputes should support international agreements. Let me further say, in passing, that the WTO itself (which is now really more of a World Everything but Trade Organization (WTO; environment, IP, labor standards, etc.) or a World Time and Trade Organization (WTTO; with the inclusion of intertemporal intermediation services such as banking) poses myriad paradoxes for economists. Why is global policy bargaining only confined to trade policy (which it now of course is not since the WTO is really the World Bargaining Organization)? Why are there no side payments? Why is bargaining constrained by agreed prior rules, such as MFN, which seemingly forgo gains from bargaining? And many more. . . .

I will concentrate my remarks on three questions not posed directly by Professor Ahn but implicit in his discussion. Why such limited use of dispute settlement by East Asian economies prior to 1994? Why is there an elevation in use after? And is it really true, as he suggests, that the post-1994 system is an improvement?

Why such limited use of dispute settlement by East Asians prior to 1994? I believe there is no simple or single answer to this question; instead, numerous factors enter. The GATT as it evolved from 1947 through 1957 (Treaty of Rome) was de facto more of a bilateral European Union (EU) U.S. accommodation in which other parties participated through MFN guaranteeing each of the two major parties (the United States and the EU) access rights to agreements the other negotiated. The trading system never was and still is not an arrangement between entities of equal size. And given this, most early disputes were inevitably EU-United States. Add to this the enormous cultural differences as far as legal systems and transparency in policy are concerned between the Asia economies and the EU and the United States, and the strategic interest in both Japan and Korea in maintaining security arrangements with non-Asian partners at the expense of trade redress and, in my view, key factors are exposed.

Why the increase in use post-1994? Clearly the change in WTO arrangements play some role as panels are automatic, and panel rulings can no longer be blocked. But there is more. One factor is the changed role and profile of legal arrangements generally in East Asia; another is the wider and more active country participation in WTO process; and yet another is the weakening of security considerations.

Is the post-1994 WTO process for resolving disputes really an improvement? Most WTO scholars seem to think so. Panels are effectively automatic, and panel rulings cannot be blocked. But as the late Bob Hudec so often documented, the overload of WTO cases and resulting impacts on the quality of WTO jurisprudence are major sources of concern. Added to these is the clear proliferation in panels as time limits for one panel process attempting to resolve a dispute spawn new and more panels (as happened in the *Banana's* case). True, there are no longer the ten-year-old delays as in the *EU-US DISC* case in the 1970s, but if parties with power do not accept panel rulings as fair and balanced and time limits are used to force their legal acceptance, further political (and eventually new legal) conflict ensues (as has happened).

Where are the East Asians headed in all this? My own view is into major conflict. The terms of China's WTO accession (especially in services such as banking) are breathtaking and may not be able to be implemented by 2007, inviting WTO dispute process and retaliation. If the Multifiber Arrangement (MFA) is replaced in 2005 by some new set of trade restricting measures against apparel in the Organization for Economic Cooperation and Development (OECD)-fresh WTO, conflict might well ensue, and the East Asians will be at the heart of this. How they use and foster dispute settlement may be key to their trade interests.

10

The Growing Problem of Antidumping Protection

Thomas J. Prusa

10.1 Introduction

While the public's and press's imagination has tended to focus on hot-button issues such as agriculture, labor standards, and the environment, it is the dozens, if not hundreds, of other less publicly visible policies that will largely determine the success of the Doha Round of the World Trade Organization (WTO). Chief among these less celebrated policies is antidumping (AD).

Antidumping is a fairly inconspicuous trade policy—I have never seen a picture of a WTO protestor carrying a placard lamenting the spread of AD or, for that matter, praising the virtues of AD. Despite its somewhat low public profile, many studies have shown that AD imposes heavy costs on both implementing and affected countries. For instance, Gallaway, Blonigen, and Flynn (1999) estimate that only the Multifiber Arrangement imposes larger welfare costs on the U.S. economy than do antidumping and countervailing duty actions.[1] Messerlin (2001) estimates that AD protection and farm policies were about equally as costly for European Union

Thomas J. Prusa is professor of economics at Rutgers University and a research associate of the National Bureau of Economic Research.

Much of the analysis included in this paper was done while I was a visitor at the East-West Center. The Center's hospitality and research support is deeply appreciated. I would also like to thank WTO Rules Division, and Jorge Miranda in particular, for making the WTO AD Measures Database available. As always, all mistakes and errors are my responsibility.

1. Data limitations require Gallaway, Blonigen, and Flynn (1999) to combine antidumping and countervailing duty protection in their analysis. Given that there were more than twice as many antidumping cases as countervailing duty cases, there is little sense that the primary distortion is due to countervailing duties. Perhaps more important, it should be recognized that their analysis year (1991) was one in which relatively few AD measures were in force in the United States. For instance, in 1991 most steel products from most countries were covered by an orderly marketing arrangement (OMA) and were not part of the Gallaway, Blonigen, and

(EU) countries. In terms of trade volume, Staiger and Wolak (1994) and Prusa (2001) each find that trade from affected countries often falls by more than 50 percent after the imposition of AD duties.

If AD protection is so costly, why has it remained a back-burner topic? There are two interrelated explanations. The first is quite simple: until ten to fifteen years ago, the AD users club was fairly small, making it easy for countries seeking reform to believe that AD was essentially a nuisance and hence to give it lower priority in negotiations. The second reason is that the four traditional users of AD—Canada, the United States, the EU, and Australia—have believed and continue to believe that more would be lost than gained if AD were to be reformed (from a mercantilist point of view).

But these explanations are no longer supported by the facts. While AD supporters may not be surprised to hear that AD is poised to become the world's biggest trade impediment, they may be shocked when they hear its ascendancy is primarily due to the AD activity of *new* users. Twenty years ago the top four users accounted for 98 percent of AD actions; nowadays these traditional AD users account for only about 40 percent of the disputes. Said differently, even though AD activity among the traditional users has fallen by about 25 percent over the past decade, total worldwide AD activity is up over 15 percent. Over the past decade the number of countries with an AD statute has doubled, and over the past twenty years the number of countries actively using AD has quadrupled. Put another way, within a few years the list of countries *not* using AD will be shorter than the list of countries of using AD. The once exclusive AD club now includes members from all parts of the globe and from all income levels.

Although the United States, Australia, and the EU still file more cases than other countries do, it now seems inevitable they will be passed by countries such as India, Mexico, Brazil, and perhaps most remarkable of all, the People's Republic of China. Once I control for size, it becomes apparent that new users are filing at prodigious rates, five, ten, and even twenty times the rate as the traditional users. These filing trends imply that the traditional users' mercantilist rationale for AD is rapidly eroding.

While some of these issues have been discussed in the literature (Miranda, Torres, and Ruiz 1998; Prusa 2001; Zanardi 2004), there has been no discussion of what these evolving trends mean for Asia-Pacific countries, the traditional target of AD protection. Supporters of AD often make reference to "sanctuary markets," "foreign cartels," and "establishing level playing fields" in their rhetoric; their comments implicitly or explicitly allude to Japan, South Korea, and the People's Republic of China.[2]

During the 1980s the Asia-Pacific countries were the targets of 30–40 percent of traditional users' AD actions. Has the spread of AD protection

---

Flynn (1999) calculation. Given that the steel industry accounts for about 30 percent of all U.S. actions, their estimate is probably a lower bound of the impact of U.S. antidumping protection.

2. The standard arguments justifying the need for AD protection can be found in Mastel (1998) and Cohen, Blecker, and Whitney (2003).

changed this? Or do Asia-Pacific countries continue to bear a disproportionate share of AD protection? I find that the proliferation has done nothing to alter the pattern: over the past decade Asia-Pacific countries are subject to about 40 percent of both new and traditional user AD actions.

Interestingly, I do see differences in the industry composition of trade
complaints between new and traditional users. Traditional and new users
both tend to target industries where they are losing comparative advantage. Because this pattern varies across countries, however, AD complaints
differ across source countries. In other words, the pattern of AD use says
as much about the filing country as it does about the target countries. If
country A's steel industry is ailing, then country A targets South Korea's
steel companies. If country B's apparel sector is ailing, then country B targets South Korea's apparel companies. If country C's tire industry is ailing,
then country C targets South Korea's tire companies.

Interestingly, when one controls for general macroeconomic influences on
the quantity of AD disputes among nations, I find broadly similar patterns
for new users (in general), Asian countries (specifically), and the traditional
users. Exchange rate appreciations, weak gross domestic product (GDP)
growth, and strong import growth all stimulate AD activity. I find some support for the view that the exchange rate matters less for new users, which suggests that new users have an even weaker injury test than traditional users do.

These evolving trends mean that Asia-Pacific nations' position toward
AD reform is more complicated than in the past. On the one hand, they
have been, and continue to be, subject to huge numbers of AD measures.
Reforming AD rules is in their national interest. On the other hand, evidence is emerging that Asia-Pacific nations are learning the joys of discretionary protection. Reforming AD rules will present commercial challenges to many powerful industries. For many new users the political
calculus toward AD reform will soon shift (or in some cases, has already
shifted) toward maintaining current rules.

The rest of the paper proceeds as follows. In the next section I give a
quick primer on AD rules and protection; the discussion highlights the disconnect between the theoretical justification for and the actual practice of
AD protection. I then review the trends in AD measures and document the
growing set of countries using AD. In section 10.4 I focus on AD protection by and against Asia-Pacific countries. In section 10.5 I examine how
macroeconomic variables affect new and traditional user filing activity.
Section 10.6 concludes with a discussion of how Asia-Pacific countries
might pursue AD reform.

10.2 Antidumping Overview—The Yawning Gap Between Theory and Practice

Under General Agreement on Tariffs and Trade (GATT)/WTO rules,
antidumping law protects domestic industries from unfair import compe-

tition. Specifically, AD law allows a country to impose special duties on goods from a particular country or group of countries if two claims can be proven: (a) that the imported goods are being sold in the domestic market at "dumped" prices; and (b) that the imports in question are causing or threatening to cause "material injury" to domestic producers of the "like product."

Antidumping supporters argue that dumping violates principles of fair trade and as such must be condemned. To the man on the street this broad description makes AD sound fine and, if anything, sounds vaguely reminiscent of antitrust law. If nothing else, the rhetoric of "free but fair" trade is irresistible. After all, who is in favor of unfair trade?

10.2.1 The Question of Dumping

To most people, AD law sounds like it is rooted in solid economics—namely, the idea that policymakers should discourage anticompetitive practices. There has been more than a century of legal analysis of what constitutes anticompetitive behavior through application of antitrust laws. Unfortunately, the definition of "unfair" trade practices and the application of AD remedies has been allowed to develop a life of its own and bears no resemblance to established standards of anticompetitive behavior. The anticompetitive practice most relevant to our AD discussion here is predatory pricing. This is where a firm prices low with the intent of driving rivals out of business. The standard for judging whether a firm is pricing in such a manner is to examine whether a firm's price falls below its marginal cost. Because marginal cost is essentially unobservable, Areeda and Turner (1975) have alternatively suggested looking at whether price is below average variable cost, that is, excluding fixed costs.

In simplest terms, dumping is simply defined as the practice of a firm selling at a price in its export market that is below "fair" value. Application of this definition is not so simple as it involves a more precise definition of "fair." In practice, two main ways have evolved to calculate fair value: (a) The price charged by the exporting firm in its own market for the same product, or (b) the cost of the product constructed from firm-level accounting data.[3]

Both of these definitions are very weak in terms of identifying economic behavior that could be considered anticompetitive, that is, the criteria to judge whether predatory pricing is occurring. Under the first definition, a firm is dumping simply by price discriminating, that is, charging different

---

3. The cost-based definition of dumping was only codified into GATT AD rules during the Tokyo Round. This amendment was demanded by domestic industries (most notably steel) in order to make AD more protective. As Messerlin (1989), Clarida (1996), and Lindsey (1999) have reported, U.S. and EU AD disputes are now being dominated by cost-based allegations. Such trends have led one noted legal expert to claim that cost-based AD petitions have become "the dominant feature of US antidumping law" (Horlick 1989, 136).

prices in different markets. It is virtually impossible to find a market in which firms are not price discriminating in some way, and antitrust laws do not deem this practice as anticompetitive per se.[4] If countries do not worry about price discrimination by firms for different consumers in the domestic economy, why should we worry about it across national borders?

The second definition of "fair" value leads to an even more ridiculous criterion by antitrust standards. As mentioned, antitrust authorities do worry about pricing below marginal cost (or, in practice, average variable cost), as this has become the standard for believing that the firm is not maximizing short-run profits but instead pricing in a predatory fashion to drive out rivals. In fact, one can see that relaxing standards to prosecute any firm that prices below average *total* cost (including fixed costs) for antitrust violations is ridiculous. This would mean that one could prosecute any firm that is making a loss. Yet, when many countries' antidumping authorities determine "fair value" through "constructed cost" measures, they not only include fixed costs, but they also add on their own estimate for what should be a normal profit for the firm in the market. As a result, they take the ridiculous to another level and convict a foreign firm for not making enough economic profit from a country's consumers.

Given this discussion, it should come as little surprise that almost all dumping determinations are affirmative and that dumping margins are usually quite large. In the United States, for example, over the past twenty-five years about 98 percent of the dumping determinations have been affirmative, and over the past five years the average calculated margin has exceeded 50 percent. While I do not have complete data on dumping determinations for other countries (an ongoing project), my preliminary research indicates that similar extreme patterns hold for other countries.

While one could argue that AD cases are only brought against firms who have violated some reasonable business principles, the simple truth is that if one were to apply AD regulations to domestic markets, one would discover not only that any firm that loses money has dumped (by definition) but also that any firm that does not report double-digit profits has dumped. In fact, WTO rules allow a country to claim an import is being dumped even though the foreign firm charges not only higher prices abroad than it does at home but also higher prices than its domestic competitors. Lindsey and Ikenson (2002) show how a producer that sells widgets in the export market at prices 13.96 percent higher than in its home market nonetheless winds up with a dumping margin of 7.37 percent.

---

4. In other words, its mere existence is not enough to rule the behavior illegal. It must be shown that the practice is intended to harm competition. Viscusi, Kip, and Harrington (1995) conclude that the enforcement of the U.S. Robinson-Patman Act against price discrimination for cases where it was a potentially anticompetitive behavior actually led to anticompetitive results and conclude, "Fortunately, enforcement by the Federal Trade Commission has declined in recent years" (298).

Indeed, WTO-sanctioned methodology implies that not only have most domestic firms "dumped" during bad years (when they announce losses) but also that most firms (foreign or domestic) dump even in good years simply because they report single-digit profit margins. Bluntly stated, according to how the GATT/WTO has defined the term, most economic transactions involve "dumping."

10.2.2   The Question of Causality

Under WTO rules, affirmative AD determinations with resulting AD duties require a finding of not only dumping but also of material injury (or threat of injury) to the domestic firm due to import competition. Of course, saying that having a foreign competitor in the market place is injurious to a domestic firm is like saying that water is wet. Competition reduces current firms' profitability, which is an indication of efficient markets. The criterion of "material" injury only raises the bar slightly by ruling out trivially small competitors. For all intents and purposes, in AD injury analysis, correlation and causality are the same. Remember, the legal standard is "material injury," and material injury can be interpreted as loosely as local authorities choose. As a practical matter, if there has been any increase in imports over the same time period that virtually *any* measure of economic performance has declined, imports can be blamed. Whether similar correlations exists between dozens of other potential factors is usually beside the point. Moreover, such marketplace occurrences have no necessary correlation with anticompetitive practices.

10.2.3   What AD Is Not (Competition Policy) and What AD Is (Protectionism)

As the preceding discussion suggests, AD is not antitrust law. The term "unfair" has evolved to mean something completely different in the practice of AD protection than standard notions of "anticompetitive." As such, there is a very large disconnect between AD protection and the competition policy of developed countries. Any changes in the marketplace that lead to less favorable outcomes for the domestic firm are considered unfair so that AD laws are truly about protecting domestic firms' interests, not competition. This places us back into the familiar realm of "beggar-thy-neighbor" trade policies, with many of the well-known economic welfare consequences.[5]

If AD is not about making markets competitive, what is it? For all intents and purposes, AD is simply protectionism dressed up in a nice suit. In many ways, AD is an almost ideal instrument of modern protection. First, it is sanctioned by the WTO. As a consequence, targeted countries cannot

---

5. The problems with AD are worse than this discussion suggests. As discussed at length in Blonigen and Prusa (2003), one of the ironies is that the economic literature has shown that AD laws likely help facilitate anticompetitive behavior on the part of firms.

immediately retaliate to a dumping order by raising their own tariffs. Implementing countries can always claim they are just exercising their negotiated right to "level the playing field." AD law allows politicians to offer protection to politically preferred industries without blatantly violating their GATT/WTO obligations. Second, the legal standards are, at best, easily satisfied and murky and, at the worst, nonsensical. As a result, AD duties always have a significant probability of satisfying the legal rules. As a result, AD duties often are nothing more than veiled protectionism. Third, as shown by Staiger and Wolak (1994), even a case that is ultimately rejected can significantly reduce trade. During the course of the investigation (usually about a year) the foreign companies are guilty until proven innocent. As a result, duties are imposed long before the final determination is made. This means that in many cases the attempt to restrain foreign rival's with higher tariffs is effectively costless: the legal fees associated with the filing are more than paid for by the increased profits stemming from the investigation effect. Fourth, subject countries can appeal the AD determination to the WTO dispute settlement body, but this is rare and the appeal process is lengthy.[6] Moreover, during the entire review process the AD duties remain in force. And then, even if its appeal is ultimately successful, the affected party has to wait for the implementing country to alter its policy. The bottom line: even if the appeal eventually results in it the removal of the AD order, the AD action can have affected trade for five or more years.

All things considered, most people only understand the rhetoric surrounding AD and know little how AD is actually implemented. Of those in the know, all but AD's staunchest supporters recognize that AD has nothing to do with keeping trade fair. AD has nothing to do with moral right or wrong; it is simply another tool to improve the competitive position of the complainant against other companies. As Stiglitz (1997) argues, there is essentially no connection between national welfare considerations and AD protection.

10.3 Emerging Trends in Antidumping Use— The Emergence of New Users

In order to get a handle on how widespread AD is, I reviewed the semiannual reports submitted to the WTO by member countries.[7] By agreement, all WTO members are required to make a semiannual report on their use of trade remedies, including antidumping activity.[8] Using these reports

---

6. Durling (2003) documents that only a tiny fraction of AD measures even request WTO consultations. He also finds that the typical WTO AD appeal takes more than three years to final determination.

7. Reports are available at http://www.wto.org.

8. Zanardi (2004) also reports AD activity by non-WTO members such as Taiwan and Russia and the People's Republic of China prior to their membership. My statistics do not include these additional disputes. Overall the differences between Zanardi's aggregate statistics and mine are minor.

I compiled a database of all AD actions filed by WTO members between 1980 and June 2002. In this section I will review the long-run trends in AD use and discuss the rising use of AD by new users. In the next section I will focus specifically on use of AD by East Asia and South Asia countries.

10.3.1   AD—The 900 Pound Gorilla

To say that antidumping is now the most popular form of international trade protection is an understatement. In terms of the quantity of trade litigation, antidumping has lapped the field—several times over. Between 1995 and 2000, WTO members reported 61 safeguard investigations, 115 countervailing duty investigations, and 1,441 antidumping investigations. When one recognizes that countervailing duty has long been the *second* most commonly used trade statute the filing statistics are even more astounding. Countervailing duty law takes the silver medal, but it is a distant second.

The preeminence of antidumping is neither an entirely recent phenomenon nor simply a one-year anomaly. In the United States, for instance, over the past twenty-five years there have been more than twice as many antidumping disputes as countervailing duty allegations. In fact, there have been more disputes filed under the U.S. antidumping statute than under *all other* U.S. trade statutes put together. The same is true for the EU. Antidumping is simply the 900-pound gorilla of trade laws.

10.3.2   A Long-Run Perspective on AD

There has been a steady, long-run increase in AD activity. In figure 10.1 I depict the number of filings since 1980. In order to give a broader picture and also to smooth year-to-year fluctuations, I have aggregated the annual statistics into five-year intervals. I have also extrapolated the data for January 2000 through June 2002 to come up with an estimated figure for the 2000–2004 period. As shown, starting from a base of about 700 AD disputes in 1980–1984, AD activity grew to over 1,200 disputes in 1990–1994 to over 1,400 disputes in 2000–2004 (estimated). Said differently, the number of AD disputes has doubled since the end of the Tokyo Round, which implies AD has averaged an annual growth rate of about 3.5 percent.

Of course, one reason why we have witnessed such a growth in AD disputes is the growth in trade. That is, as trade increases it should not be surprising to see an increase in dumping allegations. It therefore makes sense to control for the value of imports. Filing intensity not only gives an alternative measure of the long-run growth in AD but also facilitates comparing AD activity across countries. That is, the United States and EU are the world's largest importers and, as a result, they might be expected to file more cases. A country like New Zealand, for instance, may file fewer cases, but relative to what it imports, those few cases might indicate a very active AD policy.

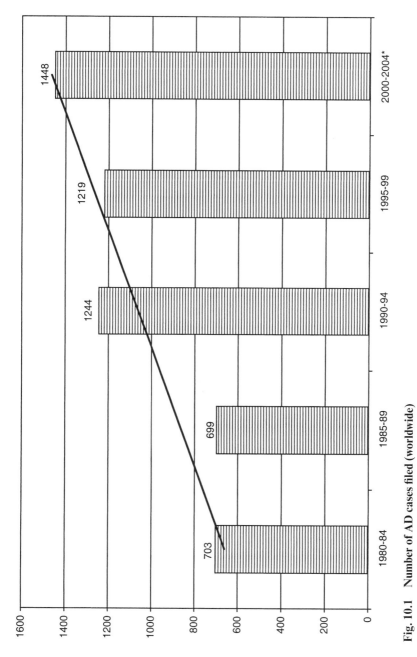

Fig. 10.1   Number of AD cases filed (worldwide)
Note: 2000–2004 total estimated using actual 2000–6.2002 filings.

I compute an "intensity" of AD metric by calculating the number of cases per real dollar of imports and normalize the intensity measure so that the intensity level (for the entire 1980–2002 period) of the world's heaviest AD user, the United States, is set to one.[9] Countries with intensity measures greater (less) than one file more (fewer) AD cases per dollar of imports than the United States.

In figure 10.2 depicts the intensity of AD filings since 1980. A couple of interesting lessons emerge. First, one's perspective on the long-run pattern of AD usage changes depending on whether I look at the raw numbers or intensity rate. Specifically, in figure 10.1 we saw that there has been a steady, long-run *increase* in AD activity; however, as shown in figure 10.2 the intensity of AD activity has experienced a steady, long-run *decrease*. Overall, the intensity of AD activity has steadily fallen about 2.4 to 1.5 over the past twenty years. In other words, even though the number of AD disputes has steadily increased, the volume of international trade has grown by an even faster rate. Figure 10.2 suggests that an important reason for the growth in AD is the growth in international trade. As it turns out, this is indeed a key lesson, but as I will discuss in the following, the lesson is somewhat subtler.

Second, as depicted in figure 10.2, on average, most other countries that file AD actions do so at about twice as intensively as the United States. In other words, even though the U.S. files more AD cases than any other country, when measured using the intensity index, the United States emerges as a fairly restrained user. The same is true for the EU (see table 10.1). In particular, the EU files a large number of cases, but its AD filing intensity puts it near the bottom of the list. By contrast, Australia and Canada, the other two traditional AD users, not only file a large number of cases but also have filing intensities that easily exceed that of the United States and EU. From the mercantilist perspective, these trends are a first indication that the EU and the United States have reason to be concerned by other countries' use of AD.

10.3.3   The Growth of New Users

Figure 10.2 does not incorporate the changing set of countries using AD protection over the sample period. Depending on the number and import intensity of new AD users, the preceding statistics might give a misleading impression of the trend in AD protection.

In table 10.2 I provide some information to help identify this trend. First, note the increase in the number of countries with AD statutes. Notice that early in the sample, only thirty-four nations/regions had an AD statute in their regulations governing international trade. Over time, more and more countries have codified their own AD statute. By 1990–1994, the number

9. Finger, Ng, and Wangchuk (2001) perform a similar calculation.

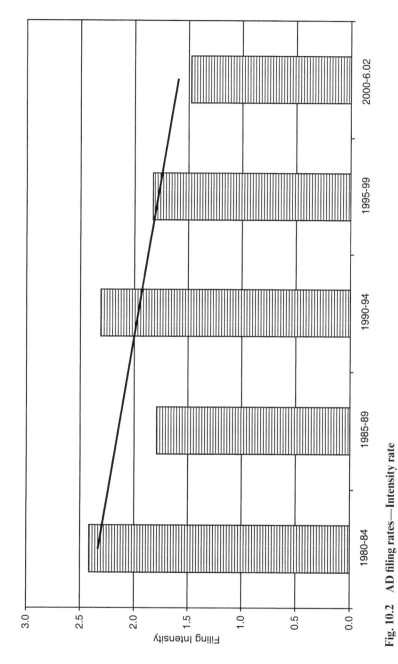

Fig. 10.2   AD filing rates—Intensity rate

Note: Filing intensity normalized so 1 = U.S. average for 1980–6.2002.

Table 10.1 AD filing patterns and success rates

Americas	No.	Intensity	% Aff.
United States	904	1.00	0.60
Canada	490	2.48	0.65
Argentina	235	16.79	0.69
Mexico	230	2.75	0.57
Brazil	165		0.52
Peru	37	12.19	0.65
Colombia	35	5.42	0.60
Venezuela	31	5.52	0.74
Chile	16	3.59	0.69
Trinidad-Tobago	10	18.06	0.90
Costa Rica	6	7.37	0.17
Uruguay	5	20.11	0.80
Jamaica	3		1.00
Panama	2	12.45	1.00
Nicaragua	2		1.00
Guatemala	1	5.72	1.00
Paraguay	1		1.00
Ecuador	1	3.28	1.00
El Salvador	0		
Honduras	0		
Bolivia	0		
Dominican Republic	0		
Cuba	0		
EU+			
European Community	663	0.84	0.66
Turkey	64	5.29	0.69
Finland	16	1.94	0.69
Sweden	15	0.97	
Austria	2	0.58	
Spain	1	0.65	
Cyprus	0		
Switzerland	0		
Norway	0		
East Europe-Central Asia			
Poland	35	4.99	0.29
Czechoslovakia	3		0.33
Bulgaria	1	3.97	1.00
Fm Yugoslavia	1		0.00
Fm German Dm Rp (East)	0		
Hungary	0		
Romania	0		
Fm USSR	0		
West Africa			
Cote D'Ivoire	0		

East Asia and Pacific	No.	Intensity	% Aff.
New Zealand	75	7.42	0.48
South Korea	74	0.89	0.64
Indonesia	43	10.34	0.60
The Philippines	22	2.16	0.55
Malaysia	22	0.75	0.73
Thailand	15	0.88	0.87
Taiwan	6	0.46	0.33
Japan	6	0.15	0.67
PR-China	6	0.61	0.83
Singapore	2	0.32	1.00
North Korea	0		
Papua N. Guinea	0		
Macao	0		
Vietnam	0		
Hong Kong	0		
Australia			
Australia	822	12.32	0.37
South Asia			
India	285	19.63	0.98
Nepal	0		
Sri Lanka	0		
Bangladesh	0		
Pakistan	0		
North Africa			
Egypt	33	8.24	0.91
Algeria	0		
Tunisia	0		
Mozambique	0		
Liby Arab Jm	0		
Middle East			
Israel	30		0.633
Bahrain	0		
Oman	0		
Jordan	0		
Qatar	0		
United Arab Em	0		
Iran	0		
Saudi Arabia	0		
East and Southern Africa			
South Africa	173	16.22	0.71
Malawi	0		
Kenya	0		
Zimbabwe	0		

Table 10.2   **Growth of AD law**

Time period	No. countries with AD statute[a]	No. countries filing AD actions	% cases filed by new users
1980–1984	34	8	1
1985–1989	38	10	11
1990–1994	45	24	36
1995–1999	61	32	61
2000–6.02	87	30	60

Sources: AD implementation dates, Zanardi (2004); filing rates, author's calculations.
[a]Count at beginning of period.

of countries with their own AD statute had grown to forty-five. As of mid-2002, eighty-seven countries had enacted their own AD statute.

Of course, just because a country has a statute does not necessarily imply that a country uses it. Japan, for instance, was one of the earliest adopters of AD protection but has rarely used it. But over the past two decades there has been a steady increase in the number of countries using AD. The number of countries initiating AD investigations has grown from eight (in 1980–1984) to twenty-four (in 1990–1994) to thirty (2000–June 2002).

Thus the four traditional AD users (the United States, EU, Canada, and Australia) have been joined by an expanding set of new users. And the new users have not been bashful about using AD (table 10.2). The share of AD cases accounted for by new users has soared from 1 percent (in 1980–1984) to 36 percent (in 1990–1994) to 60 percent (2000–June 2002).

Differentiating between new and traditional users, I depict the number of AD cases filed (see figure 10.3) and filing intensity (see figure 10.4). Several very important lessons can be gleaned. First, while overall AD disputes are on the rise (as seen in figure 10.1) the use of AD by traditional users has slightly fallen (or at best remained flat) over the sample period. Thus, the overall growth in AD activity is entirely driven by the embrace of AD protection by new users. New users have gone from filing a handful of complaints in 1980–1984 to filing hundreds of complaints *each* year in the last decade. Second, in terms of intensity of usage, new users are much more prolific in their use of AD than traditional users. While traditional users have an overall filing intensity of about 1–1.5, new users have an overall filing intensity of 3–4, more than twice the traditional users' rate. In other words, per dollar value of imports, new users file upwards of four times as many AD petitions as traditional users. Third, the role of new users is even starker when I examine the trend in filing intensity. The filing intensity for traditional users has steadily fallen over time to about 1 (i.e., the U.S. average for the entire sample). By contrast, the filing intensity of new users has grown sharply and has averaged well over 4 for the decade of

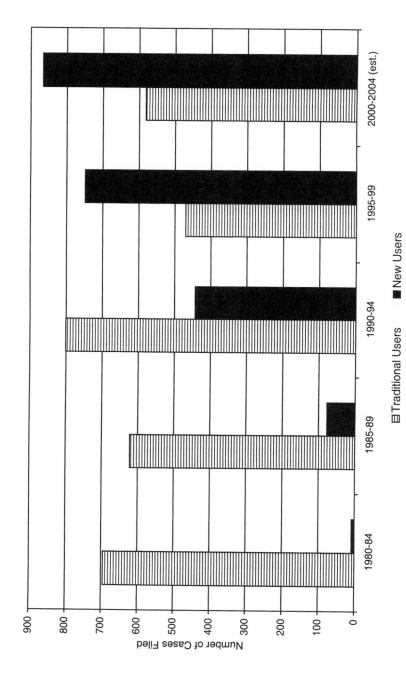

Fig. 10.3 Emergence of new users

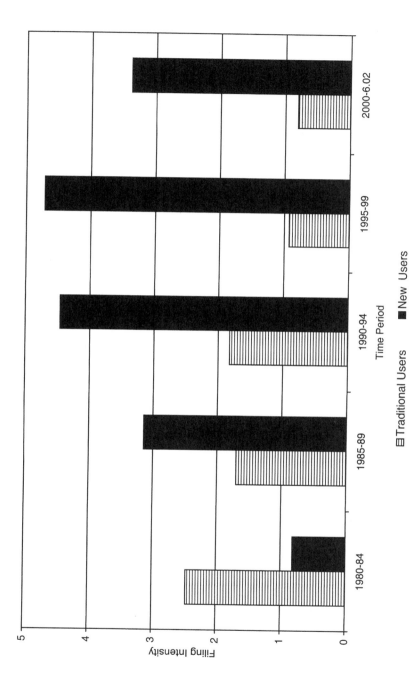

Fig. 10.4 Intensity rates, new vs. traditional users

Note: Filing intensity normalized so 1 = U.S. Average for 1980–6.2002.

the 1990s. The view that the growth in AD activity is simply a reflection of the growth in trade is not supported from this more detailed perspective. The filing intensity of new users, the source of the growth in number of AD disputes, has easily exceeded their import growth.

Table 10.1 sheds more light on these trends by looking at the individual country filing intensity. Argentina and South Africa have a filing intensity of almost 17; India's filing intensity is almost 20. In other words, if a given value of imports induces the two biggest traditional obstacles to AD reform (the United States and EU) to file about one case, the same imports would generate fifteen–twenty cases for some of the leading new users. Such statistics make it clear that new users have embraced AD in a way unfamiliar to traditional users.

In table 10.1 I also report the fraction of AD cases that ultimately result in some form of protection.[10] The two biggest traditional AD users—the United States and EU—each levy duties in about two-thirds of their cases. Most of the new users also report similar statistics. This is especially the case for those that use AD more heavily such as Argentina (69 percent of cases result in duties), Mexico (57 percent), Brazil (52 percent), and South Africa (71 percent). The big outliers are India (98 percent of cases result in duties) and Egypt (91 percent). Also worth noting is the People's Republic of China, with 83 percent of its cases resulting in duties. While the People's Republic of China only had a handful of cases during my sample, there has been a sharp increase in AD activity in the People's Republic of China in the last eighteen months. In addition, public statements by People's Republic of China officials seem to indicate a very aggressive attitude.

How should one interpret the prolific rate that new users have filed AD complaints? It seems to me there are several possibilities. Such trends could lead one to wonder that there is something unfair about the way AD law is currently written. Perhaps they might even lead to one to conclude (as I argued previously) that the AD system itself makes little economic sense and is simply thinly disguised protectionism.

Or, alternatively, if one is committed to the belief that AD simply levels the playing field and that AD rules as currently written are an acceptable way to promote fair trade, then one might conclude that for some reason exporters price particularly unfairly when selling to new users. This is a slightly uncomfortable position, as one must further explain why exporters who have been successful in many other markets must resort to unfair pricing when servicing the new users.

The most likely interpretation, especially by the traditional users such as the United States and EU, is that AD rules are correct but that new users are implementing the rules incorrectly. This final reading, however, is

---

10. Statistics on the size of dumping margins would also be a useful indicator of how AD use varies across countries. Unfortunately, such data is not generally available.

somewhat tenuous. To begin with, almost all of the new users have based their AD rules on either the U.S. or EU system. In most cases, the language of the rules is like language of the United States and EU; vague language and vast amounts of discretion characterize all countries' AD statutes. While there appears to some anecdotal evidence that some new users are even more casual in their dumping calculations, proving this assertion requires a careful case-by-case examination. In addition, the decided majority (about two-thirds) of WTO disputes involving AD actions have been aimed at actions of the traditional users, not new users. This suggests that AD use by traditional users has caused more rancor than AD use by new users. Moreover, new users have fared about the same as traditional users in these proceedings, each having about 50 percent of the claims accepted by the dispute panel (Durling 2003). At face value, it is not obvious that new users abuse AD rules to any greater degree than traditional users. Current AD rules are inherently flexible. The fact that the same set of facts leads India to find injury but might lead the United States to reject the case does not mean that India has violated the AD agreement. Finally, getting the new users to adopt different rules for their AD proceedings means that the traditional users will have to put AD rules on the agenda. While the United States reluctantly agreed to do so, its willingness to sincerely negotiate restraining AD is highly doubtful. Among many members of the U.S. Congress, for example, the current AD system is sacrosanct and even modest revisions to AD rules could jeopardize the whole agreement.[11]

10.4   AD and East Asian and South Asian Countries

10.4.1   General Trends—How Often Are They Targeted?

I now turn to the question of who has been subject to AD investigations. In table 10.3 I tabulate AD activity by region, where I have grouped according to the World Bank definitions with one exception. Given its long-standing use of AD, I pulled Australia from its standard World Bank region designation "East Asia and Pacific." Most of the other groupings are pretty self-explanatory: the "Americas" includes Canada, the United States, and countries in Latin and South America; "EU+" includes the EU, European Fair Trade Association (EFTA) countries, Turkey, and so on.

11. On November 7, 2001 the U.S. House of Representatives passed a resolution instructing the President to "preserve the ability of the United States to enforce rigorously its trade laws, including the antidumping and countervailing duty laws, and avoid agreements which lessen the effectiveness of domestic and international disciplines on unfair trade, especially dumping and subsidies" (http://www.thomas.loc.gov). Similarly, in May 2002 the Senate passed the Dayton-Craig amendment that would require that any Doha Round agreements to change the unfair trade provisions of the WTO be subject to a separate vote apart from the rest of the agreement.

Table 10.3   **No. AD actions (all users)**

	1980–1984	1985–1989	1990–1994	1995–1999	2000–6.02
	Against all countries/regions				
Initiating region					
Americas	332	368	645	479	350
East and Southern Africa	0	0	16	129	28
East Asia and Pacific	0	17	66	129	59
East Europe-Central Asia	0	0	24	12	4
Middle East	0	0	3	21	6
North Africa	0	0	0	24	9
EU+	133	132	215	193	88
South Asia	0	0	15	131	139
West Africa	0	0	0	0	0
Australia	238	182	260	101	41
Total	703	699	1,244	1,219	724
Percent by Asia-Pacific	0	2	7	21	27
Percent by Asia-Pacific (less India)	0	2	5	11	8
	Initiated by all countries/regions				
Affected region					
Americas	144	157	259	189	99
East and Southern Africa	4	6	15	24	21
East Asia and Pacific	205	256	461	524	337
East Europe-Central Asia	96	115	166	157	79
Middle East	6	9	11	17	20
North Africa	1	0	5	8	6
EU+	241	151	272	242	122
South Asia	3	3	48	51	34
West Africa	0	0	2	0	0
Australia	3	2	5	7	6
Total	703	699	1,244	1,219	724
Percent by Asia-Pacific	30	37	41	47	51
Percent by Asia-Pacific (less PRC)	26	34	29	34	36

Note: Countries classified into regions using World Bank system.

Let's begin by looking at table 10.3. In the top panel I tabulate by initiations by region against all countries. In the bottom panel I tabulate "affected" or "named" countries by region for cases filed by all countries. As one can see, the Americas are the leading users of AD followed by EU+ and Australia (top panel). Not coincidentally, these are the locations of the big four traditional users. Interestingly, the Americas and EU+ are also among the leading subjects of AD investigations (bottom panel).

At the bottom of table 10.3 I give the total cases against the Asia-Pacific and South Asia regions. Largely because of their exporting success, Asia-Pacific countries such as Japan, Taiwan, and South Korea have long been singled out in the rhetoric justifying AD protection. Mastel (1998) and Cohen, Blecker, and Whitney (2003) justify AD because it is the only policy available to remedy the anticompetitive effects of the (perceived) closed nature of Asian markets; or in their language, the anticompetitive effects of "sanctuary markets" and "foreign cartels."

As shown, a growing fraction of AD cases have been aimed against Asian markets, starting from 30 percent in the early 1980s and rising to about 50 percent in recent years. A big part of the increase is due to the integration of the People's Republic of China into the world trading system. In recent years about 20 percent of all AD cases target the People's Republic of China. Because the rules involving the People's Republic of China (and all nonmarket economies) differ from other Asia-Pacific countries, it makes sense if we break out the People's Republic of China cases. Once I drop the cases against the People's Republic of China, we see that the fraction of traditional user AD cases against Asia-Pacific countries has been fairly stable, averaging about one-third of the total.

The relatively stable pattern of use against Asia-Pacific countries begs the question of whether the pattern of filings is stable for both traditional and new users or whether traditional users activity against Asia-Pacific countries is declining and is being replaced by an upsurge in complaints by new users. To get at this issue, I tabulate AD filings breaking out new and traditional users (see table 10.4). The fraction of AD cases by traditional users against Asia-Pacific countries (less the People's Republic of China [PRC]) is even more stable than the overall trend. By contrast, the fraction of AD cases by new users against Asia-Pacific countries (less PRC) has grown fairly steadily over time, from 13 percent in 1980–1984 to 22 percent in 1990–1994 to 37 percent in 2000–June 2002. This is another indication that the proliferation of AD has adversely affected Asian countries.

10.4.2   General Trends—How Often Do They File Cases?

While the growth in AD activity against Asia-Pacific countries is notable, more impressive is the pattern of use by Asia-Pacific countries. As shown in table 10.3, Asia-Pacific countries accounted for *no* AD disputes in the early 1980s, and by the early 1990s they accounted for only 7 percent of all AD disputes. In recent years, however, use by Asia-Pacific countries has soared, and they now account for more than one-quarter of all disputes. It is important to point out, however, that India is by far the biggest source of AD activity in the Asia-Pacific region. In fact, India is quickly emerging as the leading user of AD in the entire world. If I drop cases initiated by India, the upward trend in AD activity by Asia-Pacific countries is still present but not nearly so stark: Asia-Pacific countries (less PRC) accounted for 0 percent of all AD activity in 1980–1984, 5 percent in 1990–1994, and 8 percent in 2000–June 2002.

In table 10.5 I detail AD activity focusing solely on the Asia-Pacific region. What is striking is the high percentage of cases within the region.

Table 10.4   **Number of AD actions (new and traditional users)**

	1980–1984	1985–1989	1990–1994	1995–1999	2000–6.02
Initiated by new users					
Affected region					
Americas	0	23	126	139	67
East and Southern Africa	0	0	4	12	9
East Asia and Pacific	1	14	149	299	212
East Europe-Central Asia	1	22	60	95	35
Middle East	0	0	1	7	16
North Africa	0	0	0	4	0
EU+	6	16	80	165	73
South Asia	0	1	19	22	16
West Africa	0	0	2	0	0
Australia	0	1	2	6	5
Total	8	77	443	749	433
New users					
% against Asia-Pacific	13	19	38	43	53
% against Asia-Pacific (less PRC)	13	17	22	28	37
Initiated by traditional users					
Affected region					
Americas	144	134	133	50	32
East and Southern Africa	4	6	11	12	12
East Asia and Pacific	204	242	312	225	125
East Europe-Central Asia	95	93	106	62	44
Middle East	6	9	10	10	4
North Africa	1	0	5	4	6
EU+	235	135	192	77	49
South Asia	3	2	29	29	18
West Africa	0	0	0	0	0
Australia	3	1	3	1	1
Total	695	622	801	470	291
Traditional users					
% against Asia-Pacific	30	39	43	54	49
% against Asia-Pacific (less PRC)	26	36	33	42	34
Total cases—% by new users	1	11	36	61	60

Note: Traditional users are United States, EU, Australia, and Canada.

Specifically, about two-thirds of the AD cases initiated by Asia-Pacific countries are aimed at other Asia-Pacific countries. This result is consistent with previous findings showing evidence of "club behavior" (Prusa and Skeath 2004); in effect, it appears that countries often aim AD protection against trading partners who are similar. At first glance, this result seems odd as it seems to suggest countries are more likely to unfairly dump in nearby markets or in markets where they have substantial economic ties. But as I will discuss in the following, what this result really re-

Table 10.5   **No. AD actions (Asia-Pacific focus)**

	1980–1984	1985–1989	1990–1994	1995–1999	2000–6.02
	Against Asia-Pacific only				
Initiating region					
Americas	89	131	221	181	150
East and Southern Africa	0	0	3	55	16
East Asia and Pacific	0	11	47	82	45
East Europe-Central Asia	0	0	0	5	0
Middle East	0	0	0	2	0
North Africa	0	0	0	8	4
EU+	15	49	106	128	43
South Asia	0	0	9	64	85
West Africa	0	0	0	0	0
Australia	104	68	123	50	28
Total	208	259	509	575	371
Percent Intra-Asia-Pacific	0	0	2	21	27
	Initiated by Asia-Pacific only				
Affected region					
Americas	0	0	10	18	13
East and Southern Africa	0	0	1	3	3
East Asia and Pacific	0	11	51	140	121
East Europe-Central Asia	0	0	2	40	7
Middle East	0	0	0	2	13
North Africa	0	0	0	0	0
EU+	0	5	12	49	31
South Asia	0	0	5	6	9
West Africa	0	0	0	0	0
Australia	0	1	0	2	1
Total	0	17	81	260	198
Percent Intra-Asia-Pacific		65	69	56	66

veals is that antidumping charges are driven by characteristics of the local economy.

10.4.3   Industry Pattern

The similarity in filing patterns by new and traditional users supports the notion that it is characteristic of the Asia-Pacific economies that drive AD protection. Perhaps new and traditional users alike feel Asia-Pacific home markets are closed, which allows their firms to price unfairly low in export markets. While I have no evidence directly contradicting this view, the position would be more credible if the same industries were subject to AD investigations.

To address this issue, I examined the use of AD by industry. In table 10.6 I report case initiations for the top industries (in the top panel of the table).

Table 10.6   Leading industries (ISIC, rev. 2): Percent of total cases

	All Others	Asia-Pacific
Initiating industries		
Iron and steel basic industries	23.0	12.2
Manufacture of basic industrial chemicals except fertilizers	10.9	23.4
Manufacture of synthetic resins, plastic materials and man-made fibres except glass	7.8	11.3
Manufacture of fabricated metal products except machinery and equipment, nec	5.3	0.9
Machinery and equipment except electrical, nec	3.1	2.2
Spinning, weaving and finishing textiles	2.8	8.1
Manufacture of pulp, paper and paperboard	2.4	5.4
Manufacture of glass and glass products	2.1	1.6
Manufacture of electrical industrial machinery and apparatus	2.1	0.0
Manufacture of textiles not elsewhere classified	1.9	1.4
Affected industries		
Iron and steel basic industries	27.5	13.6
Manufacture of basic industrial chemicals except fertilizers	13.5	11.0
Manufacture of synthetic resins, plastic materials and man-made fibres except glass	8.1	8.4
Manufacture of fabricated metal products except machinery and equipment, nec	4.0	5.9
Manufacture of pulp, paper and paperboard	3.7	1.5
Machinery and equipment except electrical, nec	3.2	2.8
Manufacture of drugs and medicines	2.4	2.4
Spinning, weaving and finishing textiles	2.4	4.8
Manufacture of electrical industrial machinery and apparatus	2.2	1.4
Manufacture of fertilizers and pesticides	2.2	0.6

I separate the filings by "Asia-Pacific" countries and by "All other" users. In the bottom panel I report affected industries.

The industries are ordered by use by "All other" countries. As seen, there are some similarities between the two lists, but more interesting are the differences. For instance, the steel industry accounts for a lot of AD disputes in most parts of the world. For instance, "Iron and steel basic industries" and "Manufacture of fabricated metal products" account for about 28 percent of AD filings (top panel of the table); these are predominately due to filings by the EU and the United States. However, the steel industry accounts for only 13 percent of Asia-Pacific filings. While this is a sizeable fraction, it is only half the "All others" total.

This suggests that it must be the Asia-Pacific steel mills that are the pre-eminent dumpers; but as shown in the bottom panel of the table, the steel industry accounts for far fewer Asia-Pacific disputes than for the other regions in the world. In other words, the steel industry outside the Asia-Pacific region uses AD to restrict trade from all sources. It does not solely target, or even disproportionately target, Asia-Pacific sources. This is evi-

Table 10.7   **AD Filings Against Asia-Pacific Countries; leading industries
(ISIC, Rev 2)**

	New Users		Traditional Users	
	Percent	Rank	Percent	Rank
Manufacture of basic industrial chemicals except fertilizers	14	1	9	2
Iron and steel basic industries	10	2	16	1
Manufacture of synthetic resins, plastic materials and man-made fibres except glass	8	3	8	3
Spinning, weaving and finishing textiles	7	4	4	6
Manufacture of textiles, nec	4	5	2	15
Manufacture of electrical apparatus and supplies, nec	4	6	2	10
Manufacture of drugs and medicines	4	7	2	20
Tire and tube industries	4	8	1	27
Manufacture of footwear, except vulcanized or moulded rubber or plastic footwear	3	9	1	34
Manufacture of motorcycles and bicycles	3	10	1	23
Manufacture of chemical products, nec	3	11	3	7
Manufacture of glass and glass products	3	12	3	8
Manufacture of fabricated metal products except machinery and equipment, nec	3	13	8	4

dence that AD often tells us more about the users than it does about the targets. The U.S. steel industry is often cited as an industry that has fallen behind their international competitors.[12]

The chemical industry is also an active user of AD. It is the leading industry among Asia-Pacific nations. The textiles industry (synthetic and natural) accounts for about 20 percent of Asia-Pacific AD disputes. By contrast, these industries are far less significant users for other nations.

In the bottom panel of table 10.6 I report industries targeted in AD actions. As was seen in the top panel, the industry breakdown differs between Asia-Pacific nations and others. To further analyze the cases against Asia-Pacific nations, in table 10.7 I report cases by new and traditional users. In this table I sort the list of top industries filed by new users. The industry most commonly investigated by new users is the chemical industry; it is the second most commonly investigated by traditional users. While the top three industries are the common across new and traditional users, after these three industries the two lists diverge substantially. The fifth most common industry among new users (Manufacture of textiles) is number fifteen among traditional users. The seventh most common industry among

---

12. The United States essentially made this claim in their 2001 petition for safeguard protection, arguing that they needed time to restructure and retool.

new users (manufacture of drugs and medicines) is number twenty among traditional users. The eighth most common industry among new users (tire and tube industries) is number twenty-seven among traditional users.

10.5   Macroeconomic Determinants of New and Traditional User Antidumping Activity

Knetter and Prusa (2003) provide an econometric analysis of the AD filing patterns of the four traditional users. They analyzed how macroeconomic factors in general, and fluctuations in real exchange rates in particular, can affect the determination of each of these criteria. I now extend that analysis and examine whether there is any difference in filing behavior between traditional and new users.

As explained in Knetter and Prusa (2003), a foreign firm's responses to a real exchange rate changes increases the likelihood that at least one of the AD criteria will be satisfied. At a theoretical level, real exchange rate changes can either increase or decrease filings, depending on which AD test is most responsive to pricing changes. They explain is that when the foreign currency weakens, the firm's costs (denominated in domestic currency units) fall. Therefore, normal response of foreign firms is to lower the domestic currency price of foreign goods. This would be expected to reduce the profits of domestic producers in the same industry by lowering their margins or market share.[13] They then note that in general this price response (in terms of its own home currency) implies that the foreign firm has increased the foreign currency price of shipments to the domestic market relative to other destinations but by less than the appreciation of the domestic currency. An increase in the foreign currency price of shipments to the domestic market obviously reduces the chance that the foreign firm is guilty of price-based dumping. Thus, with typical pricing-to-market behavior, a strong (weak) domestic currency will increase (decrease) the chance of injury and make it less (more) likely that the foreign firm is guilty of dumping pricing. If I presume that the incentive to file an AD case is positively related to the likelihood of affirmative decisions on the injury and dumping criteria, then in theory it is entirely possible that either exchange rate appreciations or depreciations can precipitate AD filings.

Empirically which effect is more important is also an open question. In particular, using a data set based on U.S. AD filings from 1982 to 1987, Feinberg (1989) finds that filings increase with a weaker dollar. By con-

---

13. Note that the dollar price of imported goods will fall relative to domestic goods with a real appreciation of the dollar provided the foreign firm does not completely offset the relative cost change with a markup change. The special case in which markups are adjusted to fully offset the effects of currency movements is known as "complete pricing-to-market" in the literature. The opposite case, in which exchange rate changes are fully passed through to foreign buyers, is known as "full pass-through."

trast, using a more comprehensive data set (more countries, longer time series), Knetter and Prusa (2003) find the opposite result: filings increase with a weaker domestic currency.

Fluctuations in economic activity, both in the importing country and the exporting country, might also affect filing decisions. Clearly, a slump in economic activity in the importing country makes it more likely domestic firms perform poorly, which may facilitate a finding of material injury. Also, a weak economy in the importing country might naturally lead foreign firms to reduce prices on shipments to the importing country. This could increase the likelihood of pricing below fair value. Thus I would expect that import country GDP will be negatively related to filings. It is less clear how export-country GDP is related to filings. One possibility is that a weak foreign economy increases the likelihood that foreign firms will cut prices to maintain overall levels of output. While such behavior might cause injury to domestic firms, it is not clear that it would trigger pricing below "fair value" in the price-based sense, as foreign firms would presumably be lowering prices to all markets (especially their own home market).

The World Bank's *World Development Indicators* provided real GDP data and imports for nearly every country involved in an AD dispute. In the empirical analysis I analyze the number of filings against individual countries. I therefore gathered bilateral real exchange rates between each of the filing countries and each country named in at least one AD case since 1980. The Economic Research Service of the U.S. Department of Agriculture was a convenient source for bilateral real exchange rates as they report exchange rates in a consistent fashion for virtually all countries in the world. The exchange rate is defined as foreign currency per unit of domestic currency so that an increase in the exchange rate reflects an appreciation of the filing country's currency.

Following Knetter and Prusa (2003), I estimate the panel data where I conjecture that the number of cases against an affected country by a filing country in each year is a function of the bilateral real exchange rate, filing country real GDP growth. In some specifications I also include the real value of imports from the affected country in order to investigate the extent to which AD filings are driven by import trends.

Because the number of filings is a nonnegative count variable, I will estimate the relationship between number of filings and macroeconomic factors using negative binomial regression, which is essentially a Poisson model with a more flexible error structure. Following Knetter and Prusa (2003), I normalize the real exchange rate variable by dividing each exchange rate series by its sample mean before taking logs. As discussed in Knetter and Prusa, countries generally analyze pricing behavior over the year prior to the filing of the case in order to assess dumping. By contrast, countries generally evaluate injury over a longer time horizon, often over the three years preceding the filing. As a result, I report results with a one-year lag on the real exchange rate and three-year lags on real GDP growth and imports.

I report "incidence rate ratios" associated with the parameter estimates. The incidence rate ratio (IRR) is the ratio of the counts predicted by the model when the variable of interest is one unit above its mean value and all other variables are at their means to the counts predicted when all variables are at their means. Thus, if the IRR for the real exchange rate is 1.50, then a one-unit increase in the real exchange rate (a 100 percent real appreciation given that I use the log of the real rate) would increase counts by 50 percent when all other variables are at their means. The t-statistics are reported for a test of the null hypothesis that the IRR $= 1$, which would imply no relationship between the dependent variable and the regressor.

In table 10.8 I present results using all observations on new and traditional user AD activity. The estimated impact for new users is just the base IRR, but for traditional users one needs to add the base IRR to the "traditional user" IRR. For example, in the model the IRR for the real exchange rate for traditional users is 1.65 (exp ln[1.12] + ln[1.47] = 1.65).

I first note that the results (for all model specifications) confirm the Knetter-Prusa (2003) findings—namely, that domestic currency appreciation unambiguously lead to an increase in AD filings. Second, I note that the exchange rate has a much smaller impact for new users (an IRR of 1.12 versus 1.65 for traditional users). This implies that the real exchange is particularly important for the injury determination for traditional users. One interpretation of this finding is that the injury standard is sufficiently weak

Table 10.8   **Negative binomial estimation of bilateral filings: Traditional versus new users**

Model	(1)	(2)	(3)	(4)
rxr (−1)	1.115	1.184	1.233	1.167
	(3.12)***	(3.17)***	(4.08)***	(2.90)***
rxr (−1) – traditional user	1.471	1.146	1.128	1.138
	(4.22)***	(1.27)	(1.15)	(1.20)
Growth imports			1.241	1.264
			(3.86)***	(4.09)***
Growth imports – traditional user			0.954	0.879
			(0.65)	(1.74)
Growth GDP		0.823		0.588
		(0.44)		(1.18)
Growth GDP – traditional user		0.964		1.377
		(0.08)		(0.70)
Observations	6,835	4,804	4,947	4,799

Note: Absolute value of z-statistics in parentheses.
***Significant at the 1 percent level.

for new users that there is no need for import competing industries can win their claim with little regard for the strength of the currency.

Domestic GDP growth is negatively related to filings, but the impact is not statistically significant. Once again, this finding confirms what Knetter and Prusa (2003) found. In contrast with the exchange rate, however, I do not find any significant difference between new and traditional users.

Finally, I also include specifications with the growth in imports over the prior three years. Here I find the import growth has about the same impact on AD filings by new users (an IRR of 1.23) but has almost no impact on filings by traditional users (an IRR of about 1.39).

In table 10.9 I compare the traditional users with just East Asian and South Asian countries. Qualitatively, the results are very much similar to those in table 10.8; specifically, the results indicate a real exchange rate appreciation stimulates AD activity. Interestingly, the magnitude of the impact for East Asian (South Asian) countries is smaller (larger) than for traditional users. For both regions, however, the difference is not statistically significant.

Finally, I again see that import growth stimulates AD disputes, especially for India (South Asia) and the impact is almost three times as large

Table 10.9   **Negative binomial estimation of bilateral filings: Traditional versus Asian users**

Model	(1)	(2)	(3)	(4)
rxr (−1)	1.358	1.356	1.392	1.327
	(3.35)***	(3.93)***	(3.68)***	(3.09)***
rxr (−1) – East Asia	0.857		0.841	0.879
	(0.77)		(0.87)	(0.64)
rxr (−1) – South Asia	1.344		1.112	0.986
	(0.96)		(0.36)	(0.05)
Growth imports			1.189	1.114
			(3.93)***	(2.37)**
Growth imports – East Asia			0.892	0.952
			(1.01)	(0.42)
Growth imports – South Asia			2.221	2.881
			(3.18)***	(3.47)***
Growth GDP	0.767	0.753		0.777
	(2.43)**	(2.52)**		(2.26)**
Growth GDP – East Asia	0.458			0.42
	(1.18)			(1.30)
Growth GDP – South Asia	1.636			0.131
	(0.37)			(1.36)
Observations	3,418	3,418	3,550	3,418

Note: Absolute value of z-statistics in parentheses.
***Significant at the 1 percent level.
**Significant at the 5 percent level.

as for traditional users. Such a large estimate could be interpreted in more than one way. On the one hand, it might simply reflect a huge increase in unfair trade activity. On the other hand, given the earlier discussion, it is more plausible to interpret this as a sign that AD protection often emerges as a country liberalizes its tariffs and quotas. In the case of India, for instance, during the 1990s tariffs fell by about one-half. The natural response for import-competing industries is to turn to AD to restore the previous level of protection.

10.6   Concluding Comments

Overall, the long-run trend in AD use is a serious concern for the world trading system. The data presented in this paper make it clear that AD has long been the leading administered trade barrier, and its growth over the past two decades now makes AD the standout. On average, AD filings have grown about 36 percent in each of the past two decades. What is perhaps the most troubling aspect of this growth is that most of the growth in AD activity over the past fifteen years has been due to use by countries who previously never even had an AD statute on their books. These new users have embraced AD enthusiastically, with filing rate fifteen–twenty times those of the traditional users.[14]

Asia-Pacific nations have been significantly affected by the proliferation of AD. They have been frequent targets of AD actions by traditional users, and the rhetoric justifying AD protection subtly and not so subtly alludes to U.S. and European fears about competing with Asian economies. Even if the People's Republic of China is excluded, Asia-Pacific economies have accounted for about one-third of all AD cases.

It is important to recognize, however, that it is the *proliferation* of AD that is the current driving force behind AD actions. As depicted in figure 10.5, the number of cases against Asia-Pacific nations by traditional users has declined over the past decade. So while the total number of AD disputes against Asia-Pacific has risen, the source of the trade restrictions is different. And hence, the explanations behind the disputes are different than it was a decade ago.

Now, the main reason for the most trade disputes involving Asia is new users. New users now account for about 60 percent of all cases against Asia-Pacific nations. Furthermore, more than half of these cases are initiated by other Asia-Pacific nations. In other words, many of the trade disputes are intraregional disputes.

Rather than viewing this as a problem, the intraregional nature of many

14. One piece of information that would be useful to know is how much trade has been affected by the increased number of AD investigations. Because the WTO reports provide almost no information on the products covered, that task will have to be delayed until a later date.

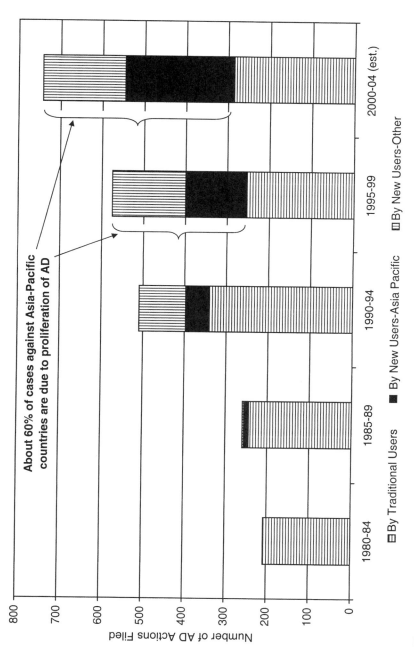

Fig. 10.5   AD actions against Asia-Pacific countries

of the disputes points to a potential solution to the AD problem. Namely, regional trade agreements might be the light at the end of the tunnel. Even under the most optimistic scenarios, significant AD reform within the WTO is unlikely. The entrenched positions of the United States and EU make such a scenario unlikely. On the other hand, we now have several examples of regional agreements that limit, or prohibit, AD use within the free trade area. The earliest example is the European Community/European Union who prohibits AD actions within the union. The Trans-Tasman pact prohibits antidumping disputes between Australia and New Zealand. The recent Chile-Canada Free Trade Agreement also prohibits antidumping disputes.

If Asia-Pacific nations want to curb antidumping it is likely that the only real prospect is via regional agreements. Once enough such agreements are signed, the WTO negotiations have much greater likelihood of succeeding.

References

Areeda, Phillip E., and David F. Turner. 1975. Predatory pricing and related practices under section 2 of the Sherman Act. *Harvard Law Review* 88:697–733.
Blonigen, Bruce A., and Thomas J. Prusa. 2003. Antidumping. In *Handbook of international trade,* ed. E. K. Choi and J. Harrigan, 456–76. Oxford, UK: Blackwell Publishers.
Clarida, Richard H. 1996. Dumping in theory, in policy, and in practice. In *Fair trade and harmonization,* ed. J. Bhagwati and R. Hudec. Cambridge: MIT Press.
Cohen, Stephen D., Robert A. Blecker, and Peter D. Whitney. 2003. *Fundamentals of U.S. foreign trade policy.* 2nd ed. Boulder, CO: Westview Press.
Durling, James P. 2003. Deference, but only when due: WTO review of antidumping measures. *Journal of International Economic Law* 6 (1): 125–53.
Feinberg, Robert M. 1989. Exchange rates and unfair trade. *Review of Economics and Statistics* 71 (4): 704–07.
Finger, J. Michael, Francis Ng, and Sonam Wangchuk. 2001. Antidumping as safeguard policy. World Bank Working Paper no. 2730. Washington, DC: World Bank, December.
Gallaway, Michael P., Bruce A. Blonigen, and Joseph E. Flynn. 1999. Welfare costs of US antidumping and countervailing duty laws. *Journal of International Economics* 49:211–44.
Horlick, Gary N. 1989. The United States antidumping system. In *Antidumping law and practice,* ed. J. H. Jackson and E. A. Vermulst, 99–166. Ann Arbor: University of Michigan Press.
Knetter, Michael M., and Thomas J. Prusa. 2003. Macroeconomic factors and antidumping filings: Evidence from four countries. *Journal of International Economics* 61:1–17.
Lindsey, Brink. 1999. The US antidumping law: Rhetoric versus reality. CATO Institute Center for Trade Policy Studies Working Paper no. 7. Washington, DC: CATO.
Lindsey, Brink, and Dan Ikenson. 2002. Antidumping 101: The devilish details of

'unfair trade' law. CATO Institute Center for Trade Policy Studies Working Paper no. 20. Washington, DC: CATO.

Mastel, Greg. 1998. *Antidumping laws and the U.S. economy.* Armonk, NY: M. E. Sharpe.

Messerlin, Patrick A. 1989. The EC antidumping regulations: A first economic appraisal 1980–85. *Weltwirtschaftliches Archiv* 125:563–87.

———. 2001. *Measuring the costs of protection in Europe.* Washington, DC: Institute for International Economics.

Miranda, Jorge, Raul A. Torres, and Mario Ruiz. 1998. The international use of antidumping: 1987–1997. *Journal of World Trade* 32:5–71.

Prusa, Thomas J. 2001. On the spread and impact of antidumping. *Canadian Journal of Economics* 34 (3): 591–611.

Prusa, Thomas J., and Susan Skeath. 2004. Modern commercial policy: Managed trade or retaliation? In *Handbook of international trade,* Vol. 2, *Economic and legal analysis of trade policy and institutions.* ed. E. K. Choi and J. Hartigan. Cambridge, MA: Blackwell.

Staiger, Robert W., and Frank A. Wolak. 1994. Measuring industry specific protection: Antidumping in the United States. *Brookings Papers on Economic Activity, Microeconomics:* 51–118.

Stiglitz, Joseph E. 1997. Dumping on free trade: The US import trade laws. *Southern Economic Journal* 64:402–24.

Viscusi, W. Kip, John Vernon, and Joseph E. Harrington, Jr. 1995. *Economics of regulation and antitrust.* 2nd ed. Cambridge, MA: MIT Press.

Zanardi, Maurizio. 2004. Antidumping: What are the numbers to discuss at Doha? *The World Economy* 27 (3): 403–33.

Comment   Takatoshi Ito

Dr. Prusa's paper shows the pattern and characteristics of antidumping (AD) filings since 1980. The paper is a great source for statistics on AD users and countries targeted by AD. Among many interesting findings in the paper, the following stands out. The number of AD cases has increased dramatically, but so was trade. A concept of AD intensity, defined as the number of AD filings divided by real imports and normalized against the U.S. average (1980–2002), is introduced for further analysis. Initially, the United States, the European Union (EU), Canada, and Australia (the traditional users) have dominated in filing AD cases, both in the raw number and in intensity. However, in recent years, a new set of countries has been using AD more aggressively. An increase in the AD intensity recently is due to an increase of the new users rather than an increase in the use of the traditional users. Among the new users, India filed a large number of cases, and its intensity is high, followed by New Zealand, Argentina, Turkey,

Takatoshi Ito is a professor at the Research Center for Advanced Science and Technology, University of Tokyo, and a research associate of the National Bureau of Economic Research.

Poland, South Africa, India, and Indonesia. As for the target countries, the East and Southeast Asian countries have been heavily targeted. Proliferation of AD in recent years is more due to new users than the traditional four. In terms of targets of the AD actions, two features are prominent. First, American countries and countries in the EU have been hitting each other with AD actions. Second, Asian countries have been targeted more than countries in any other region. In analysis of what explains AD actions, it is found that, among other obvious factors, the real exchange rate is particularly important in the determination of AD filing by traditional users.

My comments are centered on questions about whether the findings are surprising and whether any other interesting facts can be found from his rich statistics. Before answering these questions, I have to review the basics of the concept of dumping.

Dumping is an act to sell goods at an "unfairly" low price (that is, below normal value) for exports. Producers in a country where the exports were "dumped" have to prove that they suffer an "injury" resulting from dumping. However, the concept of dumping has been a source of controversy because "unfairly low prices" (or normal value) and "injury" are difficult to define in economic terms.

Dr. Prusa correctly points out AD has been a thinly veiled device for protectionism, because it is difficult to find a genuine case of "dumping" from the theoretical point of view. The definition of AD used in the real world is far from one that could be justifiable in economic theory. I fully agree with this argument. The AD can be applied in practice when the three conditions are met: (a) when the imported price (PM) to country U from exporting country K is "unfairly" low (below normal value), (b) when imports cause an "injury" to domestic industry of country U; and (c) when there is a causal link from (a) to (b).

The first condition is troublesome because mainstream economic theory typically does not offer a concept of "fair" price or normal value. How about the average price (AC) of the firm of country K? If the company is selling goods in country U at below-average price (that is, losing money), then the company is charged to be "dumping." But is selling goods at prices below AC necessarily an "unfair" act? Probably not. If the fixed cost, say assembly lines at home and a distribution network in country U, is already sunk, then companies have incentives to produce and sell at or above marginal costs (MC), and most economists think that PM > MC act to be "fair." Then how about a case where exporters are selling at lower prices than MC? Is a condition PM < MC unfair? However, MC is harder to calculate, especially when a product in question is one of the many products produced by the company. The third possible way, and in fact most common in practice, to define a fair price is to compare PM to domestic price of the same goods in the exporting country, K.[1] It is difficult to establish whether the domestic price is "normal" to begin with. Moreover, what if products sold domestically in country K are slightly different in specifications and durability from products sold in the export market in U?

If the exporting firm has a monopolistic power to discriminate the two markets in K and U, then prices they charge may be quite different as a natural result of profit maximization, depending on the price elasticities of demands in the two markets. It is quite possible that profit maximization with discriminating prices would make the prices in U lower than prices in K, with different design of products. But is it unfair? Probably not. So, there is little basis to prove the first condition of AD from the purely economic point of view. The definition is inherently political.

The difficulty also exists in the definition of "injury," the second condition for dumping. What is injury? Economic theory may arguably define injury as a situation where the sum of consumers' surpluses and producers' surpluses are reduced by a deliberate act of trading partners (companies or the government). If consumers' surpluses increase more than producers' profits due to cheaper imports being introduced, the nation's welfare most likely increases.[2] However, in practice, the injury is often measured by sales and profits of producers that compete against imports. First of all, the country would not be able to use AD if there is no import-competing firm. Most of the least-developed countries and small economies with limited range of products would not be able to use AD. Suppose that there are companies that produce goods that compete against imports. When the market share of domestic firms goes down sharply, while the market share of imports goes up sharply, then injury is easier to prove. Even if imports are increasing the market share, the expanding market may absorb the increase without decreasing the domestic firms' sales. In that case, injury is less likely to be proven legally. When the market is not expanding and an increase in imports is roughly matched by a decline in domestic production, the case for injury more likely holds up. Therefore, dumping is less likely to be brought up in the growing stage of the industry or product cycle

1. According to the WTO rule, "[T]he normal value is generally the price of the product at issue, I the ordinary course of trade, when destined for consumption in the exporting country market" (http://www.wto.org/english/thewto_e/whatis_e/eol/e/wto04/wto4_7.htm).

2. A proponent of the use of AD may argue that even if the gains by consumers may exceed the producers' losses in the short run, the foreign companies may increase the prices once the domestic firms become extinct. This is called predatory behavior, most likely a violation of antitrust (antimonopoly) law. This is a theoretical possibility, and many economists would agree that such a behavior should not be tolerated. However, it is very difficult to prove this has happened because often it is very difficult to hold on to monopoly power, unless it is based on patented technology or a brand name. Even patents become obsolete in competition for better technology and a brand name can be challenged in the long run.

but more likely in the mature market or declining stage of products in the importing country.

Let me next answer the question of whether findings in this paper are surprising. Based upon the practical interpretations of "unfair prices" and "injury" explained previously, what are the most likely countries that would bring up the case of AD. We expect that AD is used by large Organization for Economic Cooperation and Development (OECD) countries in the industries or products that have become rather stagnant. The traditional users identified by the author fit this description. Therefore, for that part, it is not surprising.

A surprise comes in the analysis of AD intensity, the number of AD filings adjusted for their real exports. Even a small country can be an intensive user of AD in these statistics. However, we would expect that AD users are more or less advanced in some industries so that they are threatened by imports to those industries from other less-developed countries. Some of the users, like New Zealand and Argentina, fit the description. However, other countries such as India, Egypt, South Africa, and Indonesia are less obvious from prior observations.

In the list of AD heavy users, measured either in number or in intensity, wealthier Asian countries—Japan, South Korea, and Taiwan—are conspicuously absent. This is more surprising than natural. These countries have high-income countries and have a wide range of industries, some of them are more or less matured. Let us explore reasons for the lack of AD use by wealthier East Asian countries. Exporters of these countries have traditionally been late comers compared to western firms and have been expanding their shares in other countries, not to mention in the domestic markets. The domestic economies were expanding rapidly in the high-speed growth, and these countries were in the position to chase the front-runner of the United States and EU in many industries from the 1980s to 1990s. From textiles to electronics, to steel, and to automobiles, East Asian firms have grown from domestic-only firms to global players. There was no need to complain about imports from abroad at the domestic market. This explanation may be sufficient for the 1960s and 1970s. But Japan has seen increases in imports of manufactured goods from other Asian countries since the early 1990s. Imports of color televisions have surpassed the domestic production in the late 1990s. However, AD has rarely been used by Japan.[3] I only list some of possible explanations of why Japan has been so restrained: first, the Japanese government, with power over industries, may be a model student of the General Agreement on Tariffs and Trade/World Trade Organization (GATT/WTO; maybe except for agricultural prod-

---

3. The most prominent case of protection from imports was Japan's attempt of using safeguard against three agricultural products from China in 2001. After China announced the use of retaliatory tariffs, the two countries settled the disputes without making them into a trade war.

ucts) not to use unjustifiable trade restrictions; second, Japan may have been afraid of retaliation by countries that absorb its exports, that is, Japan may lose more than gain when AD actions lead to a trade war; third, Japan may lack an institutional framework, such as U.S. trade representatives (USTR) and the ability of shrewd legal maneuvering to impose AD while avoiding being hit by retaliatory actions.

The fact that Asian countries have growth rapidly with increasing manufacturing exports made them vulnerable to AD actions against them. It has been shown in figure 10.5 that AD actions against Asia-Pacific countries were taken mostly by the traditional users of AD until 1994. After 1995, about 60 percent of cases against Asia-Pacific countries were taken by new users of AD. One of the reasons why AD actions by traditional users have declined may be that Japan and Korea have been invested directly in countries that have had trade disputes. For example, Japanese consumer electronics and automobile investments in North America have lessened trade conflicts between the two countries, although automobiles have not been products for AD actions. AD actions by new users against Asian countries are an interesting phenomenon. This suggests that less-developed countries have become users against imports from more-developed countries. For example, China took AD actions against Japan in seven products from 2000 to 2001. Indeed, this is a new pattern.

In summary, this is a very interesting paper analyzing AD actions with a large data set. Some results are expected by common sense observations based on political economy, while some other results are new. The observed patterns and regression results are rich enough that they may stimulate more work in this area.

Comment   Chong-Hyun Nam

This is an interesting and highly informative paper. Thomas Prusa carefully reviews the General Agreement on Tariffs and Trade/World Trade Organization (GATT/WTO) rules related to antidumping (AD), explaining how easily they can be abused for protectionist purposes. Prusa then investigates the trends and historical development of AD actions with utmost care and with special attention being given to Asia-Pacific countries.

Let me first say that I have little disagreement with what Prusa said in the paper. A good analytical work, however, often raises more questions than it answers. My comments are therefore largely devoted to raising questions with some considerations that the author may want to consider for further work or, perhaps, in other papers.

Chong-Hyun Nam is a professor of economics at Korea University.

My first question is concerned with the astonishingly rapid increase and widespread AD actions across countries, particularly for the past dozen years or so. More alarming is that the intensity of AD actions undertaken by the new users is incredibly high, as much as five, ten, even twenty times that of the United States. Why did it happen? How can one explain this? Prusa puts forth a good argument for that. That is, the new users tend to be mostly developing countries, including such countries as Argentina, Mexico, South Africa, and India, and they have long suffered from AD actions by the traditional users. The traditional users happen to be mostly advanced countries, including such countries as the United States, EU, Canada, and Australia. Prusa suggests that the new users have finally learned the important lesson from the traditional users that AD is not only profitable but also is a WTO-consistent way of restricting foreign imports.

I agree with Prusa's argument, but I may add a few more arguments to that. One is the possibility of the so-called predatory AD argument. I wonder if there is some truth in it, though I have no hard evidence for that. I recall that, when I served as a member of the tariff board for the Korean government some years ago, I heard this argument most frequently from Korean AD petitioners. This argument may not make much sense when it is used by advanced countries against imports from developing countries because imports from developing countries tend to be more or less highly competitive and more-standardized products.

This argument, however, may gain some steam if it is used by the new AD users against imports from advanced countries because imports from advanced countries are likely to include more high-tech oriented commodities for which they have some price discriminating power in international markets. It may be worth it, therefore, to explore this point further.

Another argument is that policy options available for developing countries to protect their domestic firms or industries have become rather thin in recent years. In the past, developing countries enjoyed flexibility in their use of trade and industrial policies under the GATT's rules of the so-called special and differential treatment. Through successive GATT/WTO rounds, however, their tariff and nontariff barriers have been substantially reduced or entirely eliminated, and at the same time, their industrial subsidy programs have gone through a rationalization process because they have been heavily countervailed by advanced countries. So many developing countries may have been driven to rely more on the modern (?) form of protection like AD actions than before, as was the case for advanced countries in the past.

My second question is why then has AD emerged as the most popular means of protection, much preferred to other means of protection, such as safeguard or countervailing duties (CVD)? This point is shown very well in figure 10.1 in the paper. Needless to say, this is because the threshold for the use of AD is much lower and less costly than the use of safeguard or

CVD. For instance, AD is basically dealing with individual firms for their private subsidies, whereas CVD is dealing with foreign governments for their public subsidies. On the other hand, the use of safeguard measures risks retaliation if adequate compensation is not being made to its trading partners. All of these would have helped to make AD a more preferred form of protection to the safeguard or CVD measures.

A natural question to ask is what we can do about the abuse of AD actions for protectionist purposes. An easy answer to this question is to make it harder to use the AD measure. Prusa seems to have a rather dim view on this possibility because neither the traditional AD users nor the new users would be interested in changing the current AD rules at the moment. That may be true. But the abuse of AD rules somehow needs to be brought under control, and that can be done only by the WTO, I suppose. Perhaps Asia-Pacific countries may play a major role in that direction. They may begin with easy things to agree upon to change the AD rules. For instance, they may try to have AD petitioners pay a penalty or bear part of lawyer expenses for any invalid charges they make. At the same time, the WTO needs to make more efforts to amend the current safeguard rules by relaxing the requirement for compensation so that it can become a main route for temporary import relief. Import restrictions would be, at least, more transparent and nondiscriminatory under this route.

There is one final comment. I would have liked it very much if the paper could have provided even a crude estimate about trade impacts of AD actions undertaken by the traditional users, or by the new users, or by both. That will help a great deal for us to understand the nature and economic costs involved with AD actions.

Tight Clothing
How the MFA Affects
Asian Apparel Exports

Carolyn L. Evans and James Harrigan

11.1 Introduction

Apparel is the archetypal labor-intensive footloose manufacturing industry. It is also very distorted by protection. This protection is unusually opaque, as world trade in textiles and apparel is heavily influenced by a complex system of bilateral quotas called the Multifiber Arrangement (MFA). Our goal in this paper is to improve our understanding of the extent and effects of the MFA, making use of a unique data set on product-level U.S. import quotas. We combine the quota data with very detailed data on trade flows, transport costs, and tariffs, and we focus on the East Asian exporters who have traditionally supplied the bulk of U.S. apparel imports. Our findings include the following:

- The MFA constrains exporters in East Asia, although many exports are not subject to binding quotas, especially those from China and Hong Kong.
- Trade liberalization during the 1990s helped East Asian exporters to expand their sales to the United States, but hurt them relative to their competitors in Mexico and Asia.

Carolyn L. Evans is an economist at the Board of Governors of the Federal Reserve System. James Harrigan is a senior economist at the Federal Reserve Bank of New York and a research associate of the National Bureau of Economic Research.

We thank our discussants, Leonard Cheng and Philippa Dee, the editors, and other conference participants for their comments. We thank Frederick Abernathy, John Dunlop, Donald Foote, Janice Hammond, and David Weil for help with the data. Christina Marsh provided excellent research assistance. The views expressed in this paper are those of the authors and do not necessarily reflect the position of the Federal Reserve Bank of New York or the Board of Governors of the Federal Reserve System.

- Technological change, which led to an increased demand for timely delivery, also hurt East Asia relative to Mexico and the Caribbean.
- The MFA raised import prices and transferred many billions of dollars in quota rents to holders of quota licenses in East Asia and elsewhere.

11.2   U.S. Trade Policy in Apparel

A variety of restrictions have long affected trade in textile and apparel products. As early as the 1950s, the United States adopted policies intended to limit the imports of such products. One of the broadest policies, however, became effective in 1974. The MFA established a system of quotas, negotiated bilaterally, that limited imports of textile and apparel products.

Recently, efforts have been made to liberalize trade in apparel. Participants in the Uruguay Round of trade talks under the WTO agreed to phase out the MFA beginning in 1995. The MFA was replaced by the Agreement on Textiles and Clothing (ATC), which put in place a system for gradual elimination of quantitative restrictions. The ATC incorporated a series of stages, with phaseouts occurring at the beginning of 1995, 1998, 2002, and 2005, at which time all remaining quotas will be eliminated. Remaining quotas are progressively enlarged, using agreed-to increasing growth rates. The agreement also established a special safeguard mechanism for protection against surges and a monitoring body to supervise implementation. The United States has participated in the MFA phaseout process. Note, however, that when the first stage of quota elimination began in 1995, the United States was one of only four World Trade Organization (WTO) members that still maintained import restrictions under the MFA.[1]

When the MFA first came into effect, China was not a member of the WTO, so it was not a part of the initial MFA phaseout process. However, upon accession to the WTO at the end of 2001, China became eligible for participation in the MFA quota elimination process. Thus, the United States generally implemented the first three stages of "integration" (i.e., into the MFA quota liberalization program) for China in the first part of 2002.[2] When it joined the WTO, China also agreed to a special safeguard on its textile and apparel exports. Under this safeguard mechanism, if a WTO member felt that textile and apparel imports from China threatened to "impede the orderly development of trade in these products," it could re-

1. According to the WTO, the other countries were Canada, the European Community (EC) and Norway. Many other WTO Members maintained the right to use the transitional safeguard mechanism in the ATC. Only nine members were deemed to have integrated 100 percent at the outset (WTO 2003). For example, see OTEXA (2003b).

2. See Federal Register (2001, 2002), WTO (2001), and United States International Trade Commission (2004).

quest that China limit its exports to that country, generally for no more than one year. If consultations did not lead to a different solution, China would agree to hold its exports of the given product "to a level no greater than 7.5 per cent (6 per cent for wool product categories) above the amount entered during the first 12 months of the most recent 14 months preceding the month in which the request for consultations was made" (WTO 2001, 46–47).[3] This safeguard mechanism will remain in place until December 31, 2008. As a result, although MFA quotas will generally be eliminated by January 1, 2005, their growth in imports from China could remain limited, depending on developments with regard to this special safeguard mechanism.

In addition to agreeing to eliminate quantitative restrictions, the United States agreed to reduce its tariffs on textile and apparel products. According to the Office of Textiles and Apparel (OTEXA, a division of the U.S. Commerce Department that administers the United States's MFA quotas), tariffs on textile and apparel products were slated to decline from a trade weighted average of 17.2 percent ad valorem in 1994 to a trade weighted average of 15.2 percent ad valorem in 2004. The majority of these reductions were to be phased in over the ten years (see OTEXA 1995).

Regional liberalization efforts have also affected the degree to which quantitative restrictions constrain trade. The main regional agreements affecting the period that we examine are the Caribbean Basin Initiative/Caribbean Basin Economic Recovery Act (CBI/CBERA) and the North American Free Trade Agreement (NAFTA).[4] The CBI/CBERA programs, initially enacted in the mid-1980s, provided preferential treatment for imports from twenty-four countries in that region.[5] While apparel products are generally not eligible for CBI/CBERA benefits, apparel assembled in the Caribbean Basin using U.S.-origin components receives preferential treatment in the form of easing of quotas and/or reduced duties. While

3. Note that at the end of 2003 the United States used this safeguard mechanism for imports from China of three categories of imports: knit fabric, cotton and man-made fiber brassieres, and cotton and man-made fiber dressing gowns.

4. The Andean Trade Preference Act (ATPA) was another program that provided benefits that, in some cases, applied to trade in apparel. The ATPA was signed into law on December 4, 1991 but excluded many apparel products. More specifically, ineligible products included, "textile and apparel items subject to textile agreements on the date that the ATPA took effect" (Shelburne and Chao 2002, 43). In 1996, of wearing apparel and accessories (Standard and Industrial Classification [SIC] 1987-based product group 238) imports from ATPA countries, $1.2 million of $6.8 million entered duty-free, and in 1997 $1.2 million out of $15 million entered duty-free. In 1995, ATPA countries also became eligible for 9802 benefits. Assembled apparel items ($185 million with 47 percent U.S.-content value) accounted for almost 95 percent of the value of U.S. imports from ATPA beneficiaries under Harmonized Tariff Schedule (HTS) item 9802.00.80 in 2001; the other industrial group with appreciable amounts was textile mill products ($10 million with 54 percent U.S.-content value). See Shelburne and Chao (2002).

5. Note that benefits were subject to the countries satisfying certain conditions.

these trade preferences clearly affected imports from this region, there were no major changes to the policy over the time period that we examine.

Prior to the enactment of NAFTA in 1994, Mexico did not receive trade preferences on apparel exports commensurate with those available to the CBI countries (Pregelj 2000). The enactment of NAFTA, however, significantly changed the relative position of CBI countries vis-à-vis Mexico. Many apparel articles not eligible for benefits under CBI/CBERA were scheduled for a gradual reduction in duties under NAFTA. Further, provisions for production-sharing arrangements with Mexico became more advantageous than those for production sharing with CBI countries. (This change in the relative position of Mexico versus the CBI countries can be seen in the change in tariff incidence by region between 1990 and 1998, as shown in figures 11.5 and 11.6.)

The differential effect of these preferential agreements on Mexico/CBI versus Asia should be kept in mind. However, there were generally no significant changes in the treatment of CBI countries over this time so that NAFTA is the more important element to consider. Further, in the section in which we discuss changes in patterns of imports from Asia versus Mexico/CBI, the tariff and quota data should capture the effects of the preferential agreements.

11.3 The Extent of Protection in Apparel

Given this elaborate structure of trade restrictions, it is not surprising that textiles and apparel have often been characterized as the "bad boy" of broader efforts to liberalize trade flows. For example, Michael Finger and Ann Harrison (1996, 48) write, "Although textiles and apparel account for less than 2 percent of total employment in the U.S. economy, protecting them against import competition accounts for 83 percent of the net cost to the U.S. economy of all import restrictions."

U.S. imports of apparel encounter both tariff and quota protection at the border. Data on tariff rates is fairly readily available. We utilize trade data on apparel imports, tariffs, and transport costs from CD-ROMS purchased from the U.S. Department of Commerce. These data are reported at the ten-digit Harmonized Tariff Schedule (HTS) level, which is the finest level of disaggregation available. Among other things, the data include information on import values, import quantities, tariffs, transport costs, and source country.

The data suggest a high level of protection in this sector, at least at the beginning of the 1990s. Figure 11.1 shows histograms, weighted by import values, of tariff rates across all sources of apparel imports. In 1990 and 1991, about half of U.S. imports paid tariffs of over 16 percent, and virtually none came in duty-free. There has been some liberalization since the early 1990s.

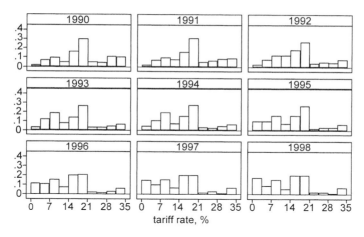

Fig. 11.1   Distribution of tariff rates, 1990–1998

Notes: The histogram is weighted by import values and includes values ≤ = 35 percent, 98.5 percent of data. This histogram illustrates the incidence of tariffs or quota fill rates weighted by the value of imports. The vertical axis measures the share of total imports, and the height of the bars gives the share of imports in a particular range of tariffs or quota fill rates.

However, by 1998, high tariffs were much less prevalent, and about 20 percent entered nearly duty-free (with tariffs of less than 2 percent).

Information on quota incidence is more difficult to obtain than data on tariffs. As a result, analysis evaluating the extent to which the quota system has restricted imports to the United States has been somewhat limited. Information on U.S. textile and apparel quotas is maintained by OTEXA within the U.S. Department of Commerce. Working with OTEXA, we have assembled a comprehensive product-level time series on the U.S. MFA program. Quota levels vary by product, year, and trading partner. We obtained records on all apparel quotas from 1990 to 1998. The Office of Textiles and Apparel uses their own import classification system to administer the MFA, which has no simple relationship to any other U.S. or international system of reporting trade data. The product categories are broken down by type of fiber (cotton, wool, silk, man-made, and other) and are fairly broad: categories include "dresses," "sweaters," "underwear," and so on. Using this data, we are able to examine the extent to which quotas have restricted imports of apparel and textile.

The most important indicator of a quota's restrictiveness is its "fill rate," defined as the percentage of a quota that is used. Fill rates that are much less than 100 percent suggest that the quota is not binding, while higher fill rates indicate that the quota indeed keeps imports below what they would otherwise be. Table 11A.1 summarizes quota incidence in 1991 and 1998 by commodity.

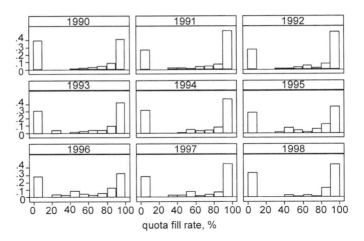

Fig. 11.2   Distribution of quota fill rates, 1990–1998

Notes: The histogram is weighted by import values. This histogram illustrates the incidence of tariffs or quota fill rates weighted by the value of imports. The vertical axis measures the share of total imports, and the height of the bars gives the share of imports in a particular range of tariffs or quota fill rates.

Figure 11.2 illustrates the incidence of quotas. It shows histograms of quota fill rates across all sources of apparel imports, weighted by import values, for each of the years in the sample. If we define a binding quota as one with a fill rate of 90 percent or above, the figure shows that about 40 percent of U.S. apparel imports came in under binding quotas throughout the 1990s.[6] One question of interest is whether the gradual liberalization under the WTO has affected the incidence of quotas. Many of the required changes in quota restrictions have been delayed until the very last phaseout period. In the case of the United States, nearly 50 percent of the planned phaseouts will not occur until the final tranche on January 1, 2005.[7] In fact, according to the 1998 review of the implementation of the agreement, a number of countries complained that a vast majority of liberalization in terms of the value of trade would indeed not occur until the final phases of the program (see WTO 1998). This slow progress on liberalization is reflected in the fact that there has been little change in the proportion of trade coming in under binding quotas during this period. Nevertheless, the fact that much of the trade is not affected by a binding quota suggests that even the current restrictions are not as onerous as might have been expected.

6. Industry experts define a quota as restrictive or "constraining" if it is filled to between 85 and 90 percent. Although this level is still below the maximum allowed export limit, complexities in the quota management system (including complex aggregates) can make it difficult to completely fill a quota (USITC 2002). The European Union (EU) defines quotas 95 percent filled as constraining. See USITC (2002).

7. See OTEXA (2003a). This is consistent with the liberalization requirements of the ATC.

Figures 11.1 and 11.2 cover all sources of U.S. apparel imports and are not necessarily indicative of the barriers facing East Asian exporters. Figure 11.3 shows the value of apparel imports from East Asia. China and Hong Kong are the largest exporters of both constrained and unconstrained imports, while the smaller exporters (Thailand, Singapore, Indonesia, and the Philippines) seem to have their exports very tightly capped by MFA quotas.

Table 11.1 shows the extent to which quotas have applied to U.S. imports, and it confirms the visual impression of figure 11.2: the share of U.S.

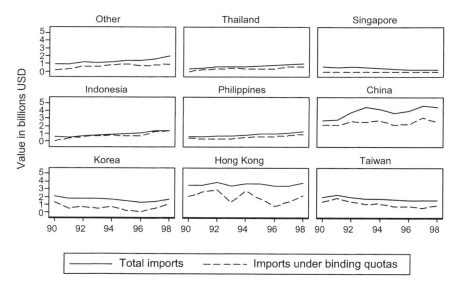

Fig. 11.3   U.S. apparel imports from East Asia, 1990–1998

Table 11.1   U.S. apparel imports from all sources, percent of total

	Unrestricted	Nonbinding quota	Binding quota
1990	39	20	41
1991	27	21	52
1992	27	22	51
1993	30	27	42
1994	30	23	47
1995	27	37	36
1996	27	41	32
1997	28	27	45
1998	33	23	44

Notes: Table reports the share of total imports subject to different levels of quotas. Unrestricted imports face no quota. A nonbinding quota is defined as having a fill rate between 0 and 90, and binding quotas have fill rates of at least 90 percent.

imports coming in under a binding quota did not change much during the 1990s. It is important to remember that the 1990s were a time of booming demand in the United States, so it may be that expanding quota limits simply kept pace with growing demand, leaving the equilibrium amount of quota-constrained trade roughly equal. Indeed, the import-weighted average binding quota grew by 10 percent per year over the period. Table 11.2 illustrates that there was substantial liberalization for the major East Asian exporters, with China and Hong Kong seeing their quota-constrained exports fall by more than 15 percentage points as a share of their total exports, while Taiwan's quota-constrained share fell by 25 percentage points. By contrast, Thailand, Indonesia, the Philippines, and Korea all found themselves more tightly constrained in 1998 than they were in 1991.

Figures 11.2 and 11.3 and tables 11.1 and 11.2 establish that the aggregate U.S. quota coverage didn't change much, while the big East Asian exporters saw some liberalization. How is this possible? The answer is Mexico and the Caribbean. Figure 11.4 shows that the 1990s saw a substantial shift in apparel import market share away from Asia and toward Mexico

Table 11.2	Quota incidence in East Asia: Percent of imports under binding quota		
		1991	1998
	Other	33	48
	Thailand	53	59
	Singapore	0	0
	Indonesia	81	99
	The Philippines	58	70
	China	74	57
	Korea	28	65
	Hong Kong	73	57
	Taiwan	83	58

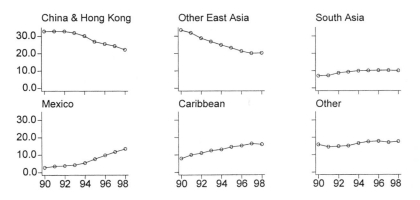

Fig. 11.4   Share of U.S. apparel imports, 1990–1998

and the Caribbean. This was at least partly due to tariff liberalization that favors these countries close to the United States, as seen in figures 11.5 and 11.6. However, as tariffs were liberalized for Mexico and the Caribbean, Mexico became more constrained by quotas, as illustrated in figures 11.7 and 11.8.

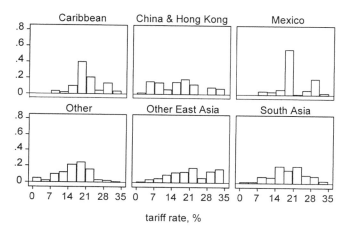

Fig. 11.5   Tariff incidence by region, 1991

Notes: The histogram is weighted by import values and includes values ≤ = 35 percent, 98.5 percent of data. This histogram illustrates the incidence of tariffs or quota fill rates weighted by the value of imports. The vertical axis measures the share of total imports, and the height of the bars gives the share of imports in a particular range of tariffs or quota fill rates.

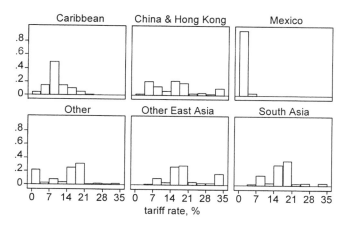

Fig. 11.6   Tariff incidence by region, 1998

Notes: The histogram is weighted by import values and includes values ≤ = 35 percent, 98.5 percent of data. This histogram illustrates the incidence of tariffs or quota fill rates weighted by the value of imports. The vertical axis measures the share of total imports, and the height of the bars gives the share of imports in a particular range of tariffs or quota fill rates.

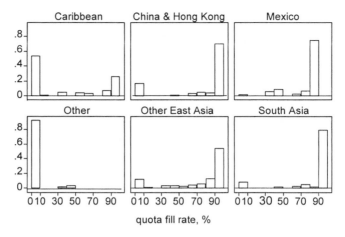

Fig. 11.7   Quota incidence by region, 1991

Notes: The histogram is weighted by import values. This histogram illustrates the incidence of tariffs or quota fill rates weighted by the value of imports. The vertical axis measures the share of total imports, and the height of the bars gives the share of imports in a particular range of tariffs or quota fill rates.

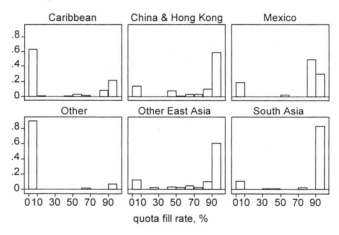

Fig. 11.8   Quota incidence by region, 1998

Notes: The histogram is weighted by import values. This histogram illustrates the incidence of tariffs or quota fill rates weighted by the value of imports. The vertical axis measures the share of total imports, and the height of the bars gives the share of imports in a particular range of tariffs or quota fill rates.

11.4   Trade and the Demand for Timeliness

Trade policy in the form of NAFTA and the CBI is certainly part of the reason for the market share shifts seen in figure 11.4. Another explanation, discussed in detail in Evans and Harrigan (2004), is that an increased demand for timeliness (by which we mean a short and reliable lag between order and delivery) has affected the pattern of trade. In apparel retailing, the demand for timely delivery comes from fluctuations in demand and varies by product category. To measure the demand for timeliness, we collected data from a major U.S. department store chain on the percentage of various apparel categories that are subject to "rapid replenishment," that is, which are reordered continuously throughout the selling season. This business strategy was almost unknown in 1990 but was in widespread use by the end of the decade (see Abernathy et al. 1999). Since rapid delivery is most profitable from nearby locations, our hypothesis is that imports of products where rapid replenishment is important have grown disproportionately from countries near the United States.

A possible substitute for proximity is airfreight: imports that are shipped by air from distant countries can arrive just as quickly as products shipped by sea or land from nearby countries. Air freight has gotten much cheaper over time (see Hummels 2001), but it remains far more expensive than other modes, suggesting that only products that have a high ratio of value to weight ("light" products) can profitably be shipped by air. If airfreight is a substitute for proximity, and if airfreight is only profitable for light products, then we should see that light products have increasingly been sourced from countries far from the United States.

To investigate this hypothesis, we estimated the following equation on a single long-time difference from 1991 to 1998:

$$(1) \qquad \Delta m_{ic} = \mu_i + \mu_c + \alpha\Delta\tau_{ic} + \beta_1 r_i d_c + \beta_2 v_{ic} d_c,$$

where the μs are product- and country-fixed effects and

Δm_{ic} = growth in imports in product i from country c.
$\Delta\tau_{ic}$ = change in ad valorem trade barriers.
$\quad r_i$ = percent of products in category i subject to rapid replenishment.
$\quad d_c$ = indicator equal to 1 for countries close to the United States (Mexico, Caribbean, Canada).
$\quad v_{ic}$ = value-to-weight ratio of product i from country c in last year of sample.
Larger values of v_{ic} correspond to lighter products.

The hypotheses are that $\beta_1 > 0$ and $\beta_2 < 0$ would support our hypothesis: products where replenishment is important and products that are heavy grew more rapidly from nearby countries. We test this hypothesis using only observations where quotas were not binding, and the results are given in table 11.3 (which is closely related to results in Evans and Harrigan 2004; see that paper for more details, data description, and sensitivity analysis). The proximity-replenishment effect β_1 is about one, with a t-statistic of 3. How big is this effect? Because the range of the replenishment variable is between 0 and 67 percent, an estimated β of 1.04 implies that high-replenishment products from nearby countries grew $1.04 \times 67 = 70$ percentage points faster than otherwise. This is a big effect: it is more than 2.5

Table 11.3   **Import growth 1991–1998**

Variable	Estimate
Proximity × replenishment	0.9968
	3.00
Proximity × (value/weight)	−0.132
	−2.42
Trade barriers	−1.259
	−7.60

Notes: All regressions include country and product fixed effects. Sample is observations not constrained by quotas ($N = 2{,}753$). *t*-statistics in italics. Dependent variable is bounded import growth between 1991 and 1998:

$$G_{ic} = 200 \cdot \frac{m_{ict} - m_{ic,t-1}}{(m_{ict} + m_{ic,t-1})}$$

times faster than the mean level of bounded growth and almost half again as fast as median growth. For products where replenishment is less important, with a replenishment percentage of 25 percent, the estimates still imply a big proximity effect, with imports growing 26 percentage points faster from nearby countries than more remote sources. The replenishment-proximity effect is also large relative to the effects of protection: the estimated parameters imply that, for high-replenishment products, proximity to the United States is equivalent to a 53 percentage point reduction in tariffs, while for goods with a replenishment percentage of 25 percent, proximity is equivalent to a 20 percentage point tariff reduction.

The effect of weight is also large. The standard deviation of the value-weight ratio is 230; multiplying this by the estimated β_2 means that imports of light products grew $-0.132 \times 230 = 30$ percentage points more slowly from nearby than from faraway countries.

11.5   The Effect of Protection on Import Prices

We have shown that both trade policy and geography have had an important effect on the pattern and volume of trade in apparel. We now turn to the effect of U.S. trade policy on the prices of apparel imports. With two or more competing exporters, a key parameter is the degree of substitutability in the importer's demand between the products of the different exporters. We consider a few simple cases here, as a guide to empirical work.

The simplest model that is relevant to the MFA is one where there are two exporters, only one of whom faces a binding quota and whose exports are perfect substitutes in the importer's demand. The situation is illustrated in figure 11.9.

The import demand curve facing two exporting countries A and B is given by $m(p)$. A has lower costs $c_A < c_B$, so that in the absence of trade re-

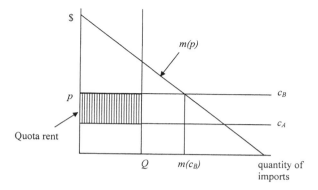

Fig. 11.9   Effects of a quota when imports are perfect substitutes

strictions all imports would be from A. However, a quota has been placed on imports from A, $m_A \leq Q$. As a result, the world price is determined by cost in B, $p = c_B$, with exporters in A earning a rent per unit equal to the cost difference.[8] The quota binds, with $m_A = Q$ and $m_B = m(c_B) - Q$.

An interesting thing about this little model is that it implies that, across a group of exporting countries, there need be no relationship between unit value and a binding quota: the two countries charge the same price even though one is bound by a quota and the other is not. Furthermore, any change in the level of the quota will have no effect on price, as long as $Q \leq m(c_B)$; beyond that point, B's market share goes to zero and any further quota relaxation leads to a fall in price as the equilibrium moves down the demand curve.

What if imports from A and B are imperfect substitutes? This case is illustrated in the two panels of figure 11.10. A relaxation of the quota constraint on A leads to lower prices on imports from A, which in turn shifts the demand curve facing exporters in B. Depending on the elasticities of demand in the two markets, and the elasticity of supply in B, relative prices of A and B exports can rise, fall, or stay the same. A useful benchmark is one where the own elasticity of demand is the same, while the cross elasticity is less than the own elasticity: in this case, the shift down in B's demand curve is less than the fall in the price facing A. This implies that the equilibrium price of imports from A will fall relative to the price of imports from B when the quota on A is relaxed. In the cross section, then, binding quotas will be associated with higher prices. Note, however, that the equilibrium price difference across exporters depends on many structural parameters of demand and supply that are impossible to estimate without a great deal of information.

---

8. Technical point: the importer is indifferent between buying from A or B at any price, so assume an infinitesimally lower price from A to close the model.

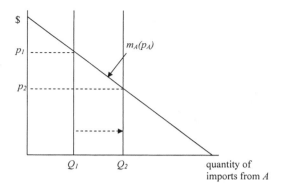

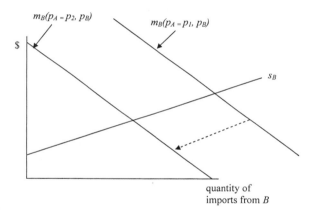

Fig. 11.10   Effects of a quota when imports are imperfect substitutes

What about nonbinding quotas? In most models unfilled quotas will have no effect, and the equilibrium is the same as one with no quotas at all.

This theoretical discussion suggests a simple reduced-form model for the effect of quotas on import prices:

$$(2) \qquad \ln p_{ict} = \alpha_i + \alpha_c + \alpha_t + \beta_1 \ln(1 + \tau_{ict}) + \beta_2 \ln(1 + \text{fillrate}_{ict})$$
$$+ \beta_3 \text{binding}_{ict} + \varepsilon_{ict}$$

In equation (2), the αs are product-, country-, and year-fixed effects. The slope coefficients β measure the effects of

(1) τ_{ict} (ad valorem trade barriers, including tariffs and transport costs);
(2) fillrate$_{ict}$ (the proportion of a quota that is used. By definition, the fill

rate for flow not subject to a quota is zero [since the implicit quota is infinite]); and (3) binding$_{ict}$ (a dummy variable equal to 1 if the quota is binding).

A drawback of equation (2) is that it imposes constant coefficients across products and years. Our data has enough cross-sectional variability to make year-by-year estimation feasible, so we also estimate

$$(3) \qquad \ln p_{ict} = \alpha_{it} + \alpha_{ct} + \beta_{1t} \ln(1 + \tau_{ict}) + \beta_{2t} \ln(1 + \text{fillrate}_{ict})$$
$$+ \beta_{3t} \text{binding}_{ict} + \varepsilon_{ict}$$

While equations (2) and (3) are nonstructural, theory does give some suggestions about the interpretation of the slope coefficients. β_1 summarizes how free on board (f.o.b.) import prices respond to ad valorem trade barriers and is expected to be negative to the extent that the United States has market power. If nonbinding quotas don't have any effect, β_2 is likely to be zero, given that the effect of binding quotas is measured by β_3.

A problem with estimating equations (2) and (3) is that we do not have true price data and must make do with unit values instead. Unit values are constructed from the raw data by dividing the value of shipments by the physical quantity of imports (usually measured by "dozens" in the case of apparel). Unit values in a given category can differ across exporters even if identical goods have identical prices everywhere, to the extent that the composition of exports within a category differs by source country. The theory of "quality upgrading" suggests that binding quotas induce higher unit values, in which case $\beta_3 > 0$ may measure quality differences rather than quota rents (see Feenstra, forthcoming, chap. 8).

Table 11.4 shows the results of estimating equations (2) and (3). We report both ordinary least squares (OLS) and weighted least squares (WLS) estimates, with the weights given by import values. We focus here on the WLS results.

The column headed "barriers" suggests that the United States does indeed have market power in apparel, with a significantly negative elasticity of import prices with respect to ad valorem barriers in most years. Interestingly, the effect seems to have declined over time, with an elasticity of –0.5 at the beginning of the sample and only –0.06 by 1998.

Binding quotas had a sizable impact on prices, with an overall effect of 6.3 percentage points. Between 1990 and 1996, the quota effect was on the order of 5–10 percentage points, an effect which jumped to 24 in the "Asia Crisis" year of 1997 before becoming slightly negative in the recovery year of 1998. This anomalous behavior may be due to the fact that two of the largest quota-constrained exporters, China and Hong Kong, did not devalue in 1997, while other countries did.

Controlling for whether a quota is binding, the fill rate has no effect, as

Table 11.4   Price effects

	OLS			Weighted LS		
	Barriers	Quota	Fill rate	Barriers	Quota	Fill rate
1990–198	−0.241	0.102	0.000	−0.016	0.063	−0.003
	−29.0	*5.1*	*0.0*	*−2.7*	*14.2*	*−1.9*
1990	−0.395	0.205		−0.504	0.108	
	−11.2	*3.1*		*−8.5*	*7.5*	
1991	−0.302	0.104		−0.212	0.053	
	−10.4	*2.0*		*−3.9*	*4.0*	
1992	−0.235	0.097		−0.390	0.054	
	−8.1	*1.8*		*−9.2*	*4.2*	
1993	−0.211	0.133		−0.343	0.065	
	−9.1	*2.4*		*−11.9*	*5.0*	
1994	−0.266	0.159		−0.179	0.096	
	−10.4	*3.0*		*−7.8*	*6.6*	
1995	−0.303	0.057		−0.182	0.076	
	−11.2	*1.1*		*−7.9*	*5.5*	
1996	−0.257	0.080		−0.062	0.088	
	−9.1	*1.5*		*−2.9*	*6.2*	
1997	−0.264	0.115		0.010	0.242	
	−9.6	*2.2*		*0.5*	*18.5*	
1998	−0.264	0.129		−0.060	−0.034	
	−10.6	*2.6*		*−2.8*	*−2.5*	

Notes: Dependent variable is log unit value of imports into the United States by exporter, product, and year. See text for definitions of regressors. All regressions include exporter and product fixed effects, and first row regressions include year fixed effects. For weighted least squares, the weights are import values. *t*-statistics in italics.

shown in the first row of table 11.4. For clarity in reporting, we excluded the fill rate as a regressor in the year-by-year regressions.[9]

Our results suggest that effect of quotas on prices is a step function: for fill rates between zero and 90 percent, the effect is zero, and for fill rates above 90 the effect is constant. This is the right specification only if quotas bind precisely when fill rates hit 90 percent but not before or after. To check this we estimated versions of equation (2) that included dummies for fill rates in the intervals [80,85], [85,90], [90,95), and [95,100]. The results suggests that quotas start to bind at fill rates of around 85 percent and that the price effect is constant between 85 percent and 100 percent.[10] However, the

9. This result is not surprising, but it does cast doubt on the results of Krishna and Tan (1998). They find a positive effect of fill rate on import prices but fail to control for whether the quota is binding.

10. In particular, the coefficient on the indicator for the [80,85] interval is insignificantly different from zero, while the other intervals are all significantly positive. In addition, an *F*-test fails to reject the hypothesis that the coefficients on the [85,90), [90,95), and [95,100] intervals are equal.

results from assuming that quotas bind at a fill rate of 85 percent are not materially different from the results reported in table 11.4.

What do these results imply about the level of quota rents? It is impossible to answer this question with any confidence, as our statistical model is nonstructural, but a back of the envelope calculation is instructive. Using the overall WLS binding quota effect of 6.3 percent and multiplying by the aggregate quantity of quota-constrained imports between 1990 and 1998 ($106.5 billion) gives an estimate of quota rents of $6.71 billion. This is almost surely a lower bound on the cost of the MFA for U.S. apparel consumers, as the elimination of quotas would likely reduce world prices.

11.6   Conclusions

The 1990s had both good and bad news for East Asian apparel exporters. Their overall exports to the United States increased, at least partly due to trade liberalization in the form of reduced tariffs and expanded quotas. But both discriminatory trade policy (NAFTA and the CBI) and technological change (which made proximity to the U.S. market more valuable) conspired against East Asia, leading to a loss of market share to Mexico and the Caribbean. As trade continues to liberalize, trade policy may cease to be an advantage for exporters near the U.S. market, but their geographical advantage will persist. This suggests that even when the MFA is finally phased out, trade patterns are unlikely to return to where they were before NAFTA and the CBI.

The MFA continued to substantially distort trade even after the founding of the WTO. We find that MFA quotas tightly constrained many East Asian exporters and led to substantially higher import prices in the United States. A rough calculation suggests that MFA quotas yielded many billions of dollars in quota rents to holders of quota licenses.

Appendix

Table 11A.1   Binding quota incidence and market share by commodity

Description	Commodity no.	Percent binding 1991	1998	Market share, 1998
M&B knit shirts, cotton	338	66	58	10.7
M&B cot. trousers/breeches/shorts	347	56	35	10.4
W&G cotton trousers/slacks/shorts	348	63	30	8.4
W&G knit shirts/blouses, cotton	339	48	60	7.4
M&B cotton shirts, not knit	340	71	54	6.4
W&G mmf. knit shirts and blouses	639	64	86	4.9
Other M&B mmf. coats	634	79	43	3.5
W&G mmf. coats	635	54	28	3.2
M&B mmf. trousers/breeches/shorts	647	69	64	3.1
M&B mmf. knit shirts	638	55	70	3
W&G cot. shirts/blouses, non-knit	341	47	71	2.6
Mmf. dresses	636	59	32	2.6
W&G mmf. slacks/breeches/shorts	648	66	62	2.3
Other mmf. apparel	659	38	22	2.3
Other cotton apparel	359	46	17	1.8
W&G not-knit mmf. shirts and blouses	641	60	43	1.8
W&G sweaters, wool	446	64	56	1.6
W&G mmf. sweaters	646	6	47	1.6
W&G wool coats	435	29	11	1.5
Mmf. skirts	642	30	40	1.4
Sweaters, other non-cot. veg. fibers	845	85	73	1.3
Cotton sweaters	345	49	68	1.2
M&B not-knit mmf. shirts	640	38	27	1.1
Cotton dresses	336	47	51	1
W&G not-knit silk shirts and blouses	741	0	0	1
Mmf. hosiery	632	48	0	0.9
W&G silk knit shirts and blouses	739	0	0	0.9
M&B suit-type coats, wool	433	5	6	0.8
Cotton hosiery	332	12	2	0.7
Wool knit shirts/blouses	438	3	61	0.7
M&B sweaters, wool	445	27	43	0.7
Trousers/breeches/shorts, silk and veg.	847	67	56	0.7
Cotton skirts	342	31	32	0.6
M&B wool trousers/breeches/shorts	447	19	8	0.6
W&G wool slacks/breeches/shorts	448	31	14	0.6
Non-knit shirts and blouses, silk and veg.	840	24	43	0.6
W&G cotton coats	335	46	26	0.5
W&G silk coats	735	0	0	0.4
Silk dresses	736	0	0	0.4
Knit shirts and blouses, silk and veg.	838	30	37	0.4
Other M&B coats, cotton	334	48	16	0.3
Wool skirts	442	31	12	0.3
M&B mmf. suit-type coats	633	19	10	0.3
M&B mmf. sweaters	645	3	17	0.3
M&B mmf. down-filled coats	653	58	71	0.3

Table 11A.1   (continued)

Description	Commodity no.	Percent binding 1991	Percent binding 1998	Market share, 1998
Silk skirts	742	0	0	0.3
W&G silk trousers/breeches/shorts	748	0	0	0.3
W&G coats, silk and veg. blends	835	69	37	0.3
Dresses, silk and veg. blends	836	0	62	0.3
Other M&B wool coats	434	3	2	0.2
Other wool apparel	459	22	19	0.2
W&G mmf. down-filled coats	654	64	77	0.2
Silk neckwear	758	0	0	0.2
Skirts, silk and veg. blends	842	5	9	0.2
M&B suit-type coats, cotton	333	33	1	0.1
Wool dresses	436	61	3	0.1
M&B silk knit shirts	738	0	0	0.1
M&B not-knit silk shirts	740	0	0	0.1
W&G silk sweaters	746	0	0	0.1
M&B silk trousers/breeches/shorts	747	0	0	0.1
Other silk apparel	759	0	0	0.1
M&B suit-type coats, silk and veg.	833	3	1	0.1
Sweaters, silk blends	846	5	2	0.1
Other silk and non-cot. veg. apparel	859	43	24	0.1
M&B down-filled coats	353	75	72	0
W&G down-filled coats	354	77	88	0
Wool hosiery	432	1	2	0
Wool shirts/blouses, not-knit	440	10	5	0
M&B suit-type silk coats	733	0	0	0
Other M&B silk coats	734	0	0	0
M&B silk sweaters	745	0	0	0
Hosiery, silk and veg. blends	832	1	2	0
Other M&B coats, silk and veg.	834	55	51	0
Neckwear, silk and veg. blends	858	0	0	0

Notes: Abbreviation M&B = men and boys; W&G = women and girls; Mmf. = man-made fiber.

References

Abernathy, Frederick H., John T. Dunlop, Janice H. Hammond, and David Weil. 1999. *A stitch in time: Lean retailing and the transformation of manufacturing—Lessons from the apparel and textile industries.* New York: Oxford University Press.

Evans, Carolyn L., and James Harrigan. 2004. Distance, time, and specialization: Lean retailing in general equilibrium. *American Economic Review* forthcoming.

Federal Register. 2001. Announcement of import limits for certain cotton, wool, manmade fiber, silk blend and other vegetable fiber textiles and textile products produced or manufactured in the People's Republic of China and amendment of export visa and certification requirements for textiles and textile products integrated into GATT 1994 in the first, second, and third stage. *Federal Register* 66 (249): 67,229–332.

———. 2002. Amendment of import limits for certain cotton, wool, man-made fiber, silk blend and other vegetable fiber textiles and textile products produced or manufactured in the People's Republic of China. *Federal Register* 67 (53): 12,525–538.

Feenstra, Robert C. Forthcoming. *Advanced international trade.* Princeton, NJ: Princeton University Press.

Finger, J. Michael, and Anne Harrison. 1996. Import protection for U.S. textiles and apparel: Viewed from the domestic perspective. In *The political economy of trade protection,* ed. Anne O. Krueger, 43–49. Chicago: University of Chicago Press.

Hummels, David. 2001. Time as a trade barrier. Purdue University. Unpublished Manuscript.

Krishna, Kala M., and Ling Hui Tan. 1998. *Rags and riches: Implementing apparel quotas under the multi-fibre arrangement.* Ann Arbor: University of Michigan Press.

Office of Textiles and Apparel (OTEXA). 1995. *Tariff (duty) rate reductions.* http://otexa.ita.doc.gov/duty.htm.

———. 2003a. *Integration.* http://otexa.ita.doc.gov/integ.htm.

———. 2003b. *United States final integration by phase.* http://otexa.ita.doc.gov/fedreg/FINAL_List.pdf.

Pregelj, Vladimir N. 2000. *IB95050: Caribbean Basin interim trade program: CBI/NAFTA parity.* CRS Issue Brief for Congress. Washington, DC: Congressional Research Service.

Shelburne, Robert C., and Elaine L. Chao. 2002. Trade and employment effects of the Andean Trade Preference Act. Bureau of International Labor Affairs Economic Discussion Paper no. 60. Washington, DC: U.S. Department of Labor.

United States International Trade Commission (USITC). 2002. *The economic effects of significant U.S. import restraints.* USITC Publication no. 3519. Washington, DC: USITC.

———. 2004. Textiles and apparel: Assessment of the competitiveness of certain foreign suppliers to the U.S. market. USITC Publication no. 3671. Washington, DC: USITC.

World Trade Organization Council for Trade in Goods (WTO-CFG). 1998. *Major review of the implementation of the agreement on textiles and clothing in the first stage of the integration process.* Geneva, Switzerland: WTO-CFG.

World Trade Organization (WTO). 2001. *Report of the Working Party on the accession of China.* Geneva, Switzerland: WTO.

———. 2003. *Textiles: Agreement, Textiles Monitoring Body (TMB), The agreement on textiles and clothing.* http://www.wto.org/english/tratop_e/texti_e/texintro_e.htm.

Comment   Leonard K. Cheng

This is an interesting empirical study of the effects of protectionist measures as represented by both tariffs and quotas on U.S. apparel imports,

Leonard K. Cheng is head of the department and professor of economics at Hong Kong University of Science and Technology.

with a particular focus on imports from East Asia. The tariffs reflect the results of nondiscriminatory global trade liberalization as well as discriminatory regional trade liberalization, whereas the quotas are those under the Multifiber Arrangement (MFA). Many researchers have talked about the MFA, a complex system of bilateral quotas, but few have taken the time and effort to examine what the "quota fill rates" (i.e., the extent to which quotas were actually binding) were like, how the fill rates evolved over time, and how the quotas with different fill rates affected the prices of U.S. apparel imports.

The paper's four main findings pertain to (a) the constraints of MFA quotas (as measured by their fill rates) faced by different apparel exporters; (b) the effects of discriminatory regional trade liberalization on exports from East Asia versus exports from Mexico and the Caribbean; (c) the impact of geographical distance; and (d) the impact of MFA quotas on free on board (f.o.b.) prices paid by the United States for its apparel imports. None of them is very surprising, but it is reassuring to obtain them from the empirical data and through hypothesis testing. I would like to congratulate the authors for their rich factual findings and interesting results from hypothesis testing.

One finding is that "China and Hong Kong are the largest exporters of both constrained and unconstrained imports, while the smaller exporters (Thailand, Singapore, Indonesia, and the Philippines) seem to have their exports very tightly capped by MFA quotas" (chap. 11 in this volume). Indeed, table 11.2 shows that the percentage of imports under binding quota in 1998 was 99 percent for Indonesia, markedly higher than that for the other East Asian exporters. (However, contrary to the preceding statement, the percentage for Singapore was zero!) Was it because the smaller exporters were given small quota growth rates than the bigger exporters? Or was it because the cost structures in 1998 of the formerly competitive exporters like Hong Kong made them uncompetitive? Was the initial quota of Indonesia small because it was a latecomer in the export of apparels so that the same quota growth rates like other exporters simply was not enough to exploit fully its cost advantage? It seems difficult to understand why China, presumably a low-cost production site, had only 57 percent of binding quotas in 1998. What were the reasons? Did it have anything to do with antidumping threats or shifts in commodity composition? It would be helpful if the authors could answer these questions.

The authors tested the relevance and importance of geographical distance as a determinant of exports of apparels that are subject to "rapid replenishment"—a form of just-in-time delivery in global supply chains. The variables used to explain the growth of imports of different products from different exporters included (a) product and country dummies, (b) change in ad valorem tariff rates, (c) distance dummy multiplied by the percentage of rapid replenishment products, and (d) distance dummy multiplied by the value-to-weight ratio. I am glad the authors are able to use the last variable to implement my earlier suggestion to consider the availability of air freight as a counterweight to geographical proximity for high value (per-unit weight) products. Besides having the right signs, the two coefficients for distance and the value-weight ratio are both statistically and economically significant.

In conducting the preceding test, the authors used only observations where quotas were not binding. That is a clever way to exclude quotas from their estimation equation. However, I suspect the reader would not be completely satisfied because the impact of quota constraints on exports remains unanswered. It would be great if the authors can find some ways to answer this question. For instance, can they use the estimation equation obtained in the preceding manner to predict the growth of U.S. imports of the excluded observations (which by definition are quota constrained) and then examine whether the prediction errors vary systematically with the degree of quota constraints or, better still, estimate the effects of quotas from the prediction errors?

The second hypothesis testing was about the determinants of f.o.b. prices received by different suppliers of apparel products to the United States. The determinants included were (a) product, country, and time dummies, (b) tariff rate, (c) quota fill rate, and (d) a dummy variable for binding quotas. Two models of demand and supply (namely, one for homogeneous products and the other for differentiated products) were developed to generate hypotheses about the effect of quotas on f.o.b. prices, exports by different suppliers, and their market shares. The adopted estimation equation seems to have rejected the model of homogeneous products, which predicts that "any change in the level of the quota will have no effect on price" (chap. 11 in this volume) so long as there are other suppliers besides the supplier with a quota constraint. However, the adopted estimation equation is indeed not inconsistent with the homogeneous products model if B's supply curve is upward sloping. Under this last condition, an increase in A's quota would lead to a decrease of the price of the homogeneous product supplied by both A and B. The authors perhaps should soften their conclusion in the case of homogeneous products that "any change in the level of the quota will have no effect on price" (chap. 11 in this volume).

The following are two minor issues to point out. First, the authors are aware that the coefficient of the binding quota dummy captures both the supply restriction effect of binding quotas and the quality upgrading effect brought about by such quotas. They should note that the quality upgrading effect may invalidate their conclusion that the estimated "quota rents of $6.71 billion . . . is almost surely a lower bound on the cost of the MFA for U.S. apparel consumers" (chap. 11 in this volume). Second, they interpret "rapid replenishment" as a technological change. I am not sure that is the most appropriate interpretation. I personally would prefer to interpret it as a change in demand or, more specifically, an increase in demand for fashion goods, that is, goods with a short shelf life.

To sum up, I enjoyed reading this very interesting and informative paper and have learned a lot from it. I commend the authors for their useful contribution to the literature on the MFA, global and regional trade liberalization, and location advantages.

Comment   Philippa Dee

I very much enjoyed the paper—empirical work is essential if we are to understand the trade effects and welfare consequences of nontariff measures such as the Multifiber Arrangement (MFA). My comments are of two types—technical comments and comments on the policy "bottom line."

The main technical point is on the role of rapid replenishment. Clearly this has been part of the revolution in textiles and clothing over the last decade. But the paper assumes in its functional form that rapid replenishment is only a factor in countries such as Mexico and the Caribbean, which are geographically close to the United States. But it is not clear that its role is so restricted. The chief executive officers (CEOs) of Hong Kong textile companies describe themselves as being, not in the textile and clothing business, but in the supply chain management business. The key to this is logistics, and logistics is only partly geography.

These Hong Kong–based CEOs also state that Mexico is competitive on a narrow range of goods that meet the U.S. rules of origin but that elsewhere it is not competitive. Why is this, when shipping delays clearly work in Mexico's favor? The minimum shipping times are three days from Mexico, compared with twelve days from Hong Kong and fifteen days from China, a definite advantage for Mexico in clothing, where a product cycle can last as little as forty-five days.

The answer lies in the ability of Hong Kong supply chain managers to cover the entire product chain, from design onward, and to shepherd a product from sample making to delivery in just three weeks. In doing so, they may divide the production and sourcing process into as many as ten or twelve stages across the whole Asian region, reconfiguring its architecture for each new order. And with this extent of value added, they find it a small cost to air freight the final product.

According to interviews, availability of MFA quotas no longer figures prominently in the production and sourcing decisions of these Hong Kong

Philippa Dee is visiting fellow at the Asia-Pacific School of Economics and Government at Australian National University and formerly an assistant commissioner at the Australian Productivity Commission.

CEOs (Spinanger and Verma 2003). Instead, the key factors are politics and stability in the host country; quality of transport infrastructure in the host country; quality of telecommunications infrastructure in the host country; policies (other than quotas) affecting international trade and investment; labor costs; policies affecting labor, health, and the environment; and lack of restrictions on capital and profits transactions. Prominent in this list are factors that affect the ability of the CEOs to meet the demands of rapid replenishment. Therefore, I would like to see the rapid replenishment variable applied to all countries in the sample, not just those that are geographically close to the United States. Distance also matters, but its effects are probably adequately controlled for by the country-fixed effects.

In the model of how quotas affect prices, it is good to see the use of both perfect competition and imperfect competition models. But it is not clear that rents from MFA quotas have always flowed to exporters, given the monopsony buying power of companies like Karstadt in Germany or Walmart in the United States. And if importers are sharing the rents, then quotas will have a price impact even in a perfectly competitive supply situation.

The effects of quotas on prices will be affected more generally by supply side factors in general equilibrium. These effects can be worked out in a structural model of the textile and clothing sector. Yang (1994) is an early example of such work.

The price effects are estimated econometrically using weighted least squares. A further technical point is whether import values are the right weights. The concern is similar to concerns about the use of import weights for tariff averaging. In both cases, the lowest weights can be given to situations where trade barriers are most tightly binding. In any event, the weighted least squares estimates are very volatile.

A policy bottom line of the paper is that the geographical advantage of Mexico will persist so that even when the MFA is phased out, trade patterns will not return to where they were before NAFTA. But the available evidence suggests this may not be the case. Even in the two years beyond 1998, where the paper's sample ends, the trade shares into the United States turned against Mexico and back to China and Hong Kong. The paper by Spinanger and Verma (2003) also gives several cogent examples of where the sourcing of textiles and clothing from China has changed quickly and dramatically in response to changing quotas elsewhere.

References

Spinanger, D., and S. Verma. 2003. The coming death of the ATC and China's WTO accession: Will push come to shove for Indian T&C exports. Kiel Institute for World Economics. Mimeograph.

Yang, Y. 1994. *Trade liberalisation and externalities: A general equilibrium assessment of the Uruguay Round.* PhD diss., Australian National University, Canberra, Australia.

Border Delays and
Trade Liberalization

Edgar Cudmore and John Whalley

12.1 Introduction

In a number of lower income and transitional economies it is common for there to be significant delays at the border when achieving customs clearance. This can be due to complex customs formalities, which sometimes are continually changing, capacity constraints given limited facilities, and/or corruption at the border. In some African economies, there are reported delays of three–six months to achieve customs clearance,[1] although this is perhaps extreme.

Our paper begins with the observation that if such delays are significant and the length of the delay is endogenously determined, then trade liberalization through tariff reductions that increase the length of the queue can be welfare worsening. Tariff reductions, as have occurred in recent years in the Commonwealth of Independent States (CIS), thus appear to be bad policy without first addressing customs clearance issues. We show this for small open-economy cases in a simple general equilibrium model where

Edgar Cudmore is a PhD candidate at the University of Western Ontario. John Whalley is professor of economics and codirector of the Centre for the Study of International Economic Relations, Department of Economics, University of Western Ontario, and a research associate of the National Bureau of Economic Research.

We are grateful to other conference participants and our two discussants for helpful comments. We acknowledge the Gorbachev Foundation for grant support, Natalia Tourdyeva, Ksenia Yudaeva, and Konstantin Kozlov at the Center for Economic and Social Research (CEFIR), Katrin Kuhlmann at the Office of the Special Trade Representative (STR), and Konstantine Loukine at the International Development Research Center (IDRC) for comments, data, and discussion.

1. See the recent WTO Trade Policy Review Mechanism (TPRM) Report on Togo (1999, 30).

there is a physical constraint on the volume of imports that can be admitted. We then analyze extensions where corruption occurs and, finally, where some imports are perishable. We apply our analysis to data on Russian trade for the late 1990s, with the results emphasizing the themes that not only is it best to deal with border and administrative delays first before engaging in trade liberalization but also that the quantitative orders of magnitudes for the costs involved can be large.

12.2   A Model of Trade with Border Delays

The role and significance of border delays for trade liberalization in a number of economies around the world is reflected in anecdotal evidence as to their importance for the trade of Russia and other former Soviet Union countries. Hare (2001, 484), in a recent piece on trade policy in CIS transition economies, says "It is often asserted that inadequate physical infrastructure—roads, railways, and the like—inhibits trade, though solid evidence for this is lacking. More often, the real barrier to trade is again institutional, taking the form of unreasonable customs delays at many borders in the transition economy region, accompanied by widespread demands for bribes to expedite the movement of goods."

The precise length of these delays and even how precisely they arise is unfortunately poorly documented in the literature, but their impact on trade is unquestionable. There is some suggestion in the literature that continual changes in customs legislation and uncertainty as to how they are to be implemented is a key factor. Equally, these delays are also thought to reflect the time taken for negotiations between officials and importers over valuation, which it is thought can fall dramatically through the use of negotiation intermediaries. Bribes seem to be involved in this process. These and other issues in the Russian case are discussed in Beilock (2002) and Wolf and Gurgen (2000). Delays in the range of weeks or months for clearance are often claimed in anecdotes, with six weeks being an approximate mean figure suggested to us for Russia in conversations, although this varies substantially with the port of entry and transportation mode.

12.2.1   A Simple Model

The purpose of our paper is to focus on the interactions between border delays and trade liberalization in light of their seeming importance in these cases. We formalize these interactions in a model of a simple pure exchange economy, which is small, and a taker of prices on world markets and engaged in trade. For expositional simplicity of structure, we assume for now there is no production and all goods are traded (these features can be changed in numerical application). The world prices for the N goods we take as given by the $\overline{\pi}_i^w$. Tariff rates t_i apply to imports ($t_i = 0$ for exports), and we assume the direction of trade is predetermined.[2]

In this economy, domestic prices depart from world prices on the import side both due to tariffs and per-unit queuing costs at the border $T^q(\pi)$. For simplicity, we assume these costs are the same for all goods and that units for goods are denominated in comparable physical terms (e.g., tons). Thus, if M goods are imported and $(N - M)$ exported and the direction of trade is unchanged,

$$(1) \qquad \pi_i^d = \pi_i^w(1 + t_i) + T^q(\pi) \quad (i = 1 \ldots M).$$

T^q is assumed to be indexed and so is homogeneous of degree one in π and is endogenously determined.

The economy has market demand functions, $\xi_i(\pi^d, R, Q)$, and nonnegative endowments, w_i, for each of the N goods, where π^d denotes the N-dimensional vector of domestic commodity prices. R defines tariff revenues, and Q represents the aggregate endogenously determined queuing costs (denominated in units of the good being imported). These demand functions are nonnegative, continuous, homogeneous of degree zero in π^d and satisfy Walras Law, that is, at all price vectors π^d

$$(2) \qquad \sum_{i=1}^{N} \pi_i^d [\xi_i(\pi^d, R, Q) - w_i] = 0.$$

Assuming there is a single representative consumer in this economy, their budget constraint is given by

$$(3) \qquad \sum_{i=1}^{N} \pi_i^d \xi_i(\pi^d, R, Q) = \sum_{i=1}^{N} \pi_i^d w_i + R - \sum_{i=1}^{M} T^q(\pi)(\xi_i - w_i).$$

For simplicity, border delays are assumed to reflect a constraint on the volume of imports that can be processed over the period of time covered by the model (e.g., one year). Thus, for now, we consider this to be a physical constraint rather than one reflecting corruption or other considerations. If C represents the administratively determined physical capacity constraint on imports, then

$$(4) \qquad \sum_{i=1}^{M} [\xi_i(\pi^d, R, Q) - w_i] \leq \overline{C},$$

where R denotes tariff revenues $\sum_{i=1}^{M} \overline{\pi}_i^w t(\xi_i - w_i)_i$, and $Q = \sum_{i=1}^{M} \pi T^q(\pi)(\xi_i - w_i)$ denotes the total queuing costs.

In this simple model, if the capacity constraint on imports is binding

---

2. This is a standard assumption in most theoretical trade models, although numerically the direction of trade can change when trade policies change. See Abrego, Riezman, and Whalley (2001) for a recent discussion of the likelihood of this assumption being false in comparisons between free trade, customs unions, and Nash equilibria.

then per-unit queuing costs $T^q(\pi^w)$ are determined in equilibrium along with domestic prices π^d, tariff revenues, and domestic demands ξ_i. The effect of tariff liberalization will be to lower tariff revenues and increase queuing costs. In the case where tariff rates are uniform across commodities, tariff reductions simply generate a corresponding increase in queuing costs. Because the latter use real resources, tariff reducing trade liberalization will typically be welfare worsening.

12.2.2   Model Extensions

This simple model can be extended in a number of ways that capture additional mechanisms through which border delays and trade liberalization can interact.

Corruption

One is the presence of corruption. This can be modeled simply in this framework as the ability of customs officials to extract a bribe for allowing passage of goods. We assume that there is a bound to the bribe, which for simplicity we take to be the ability of an official to send the importer to the back of the line in the event a bribe is not paid. If we assume that officials can only do this once, as otherwise they would reveal themselves as corrupt officials if they repeat the denial of clearance, this means that the bribe that can be extracted by the official is within epsilon of the queuing costs T^q. For simplicity, we take the bribe paid to equal T^q, which will now change relative to the no-corruption case.

The preceding discussion suggests that the queuing costs in the particular formulation outlined previously are halved, with bribes making up the remaining difference between world and domestic prices for imports. Thus, if B represents the bribe paid per-unit import

$$(5) \qquad \pi_i^d = \overline{\pi}_i^w(1 + t_i) + T^q + B$$

and by construction $B = T^q$.

This also means that in equation (4) the real resource loss from queuing is halved and exports increase, as fewer export earnings are needed to cover queuing costs. Corruption in this case is thus socially desirable as real resource costs are now partially replaced by a transfer of income to government officials.

Perishability

A further elaboration on the basic model can be used to show how differential impacts of queuing on different commodities can result. One way this can happen is if perishable commodities are more adversely affected by queuing than nonperishable commodities. Differential impacts of border delays across commodities are the end result with added distortionary costs.

We can capture this by defining a variable γ_i, which represents the fraction of goods shipped that actually arrive, where $\gamma_i \leq 1$, and $(1 - \gamma_i)$ is the perish rate for good i.[3] We can then make γ_i a function of the time spent queuing so as to capture the feature that perish rates increase with queuing time.

Thus, for each unit shipped and paid for, only γ_i units actually arrive; or,

$$(6) \qquad \pi_i^d = \frac{\pi_i^w(1 + t_i) + T^q}{\gamma_i}$$

and

$$(7) \qquad \gamma_i = 1 - \lambda T^q,$$

where λ is a constant, and so perish rates increase with queuing time.

With this formulation, differential impacts of queuing by commodity result and even uniform tariff liberalization now has differential impacts by good.

Other Extensions

Various other extensions to this basic model can also be made, which for space reasons we do not elaborate on in any detail. We can use a model with production rather than a simple pure exchange economy with endowments. We can also incorporate nontraded as well as traded goods. Both of these are standard in numerical general equilibrium models of actual economies (see Shoven and Whalley 1992), although neither changes the basic analytical structure in which queuing costs are endogenously determined.

We can also modify the model set out previously for cases in which different commodities incur different queuing costs per unit weight due to differing administrative procedures. This could arise with valuation procedures being more complex for, say, components for electronic products compared to basic commodities such as coal. This can be done by building in different factors of proportionality into the analysis for queuing costs for the various quantities imported. Again, the essential structure of the model remains unchanged.

12.3   Some Calculations Using Russian Data

Using this simple framework, we have made some calculations using Russian data to explore the possible quantitative orders of magnitude involved with analysis of trade liberalization that incorporate border delays. The delays reported in the Russian case appear to be lengthy and a major

---

3. Implicitly, the assumption here is that customs clearance only occurs for the nonperished goods (perished goods are disposed of before customs clearance occurs). Alternative formulation under which all goods are cleared for customs and only the nonperished portion is sold could also be used.

restraint on trade. These calculations thus serve to underline the point that if tariff reforms occur with no attention being paid first to administrative considerations and border delays, liberalization can be welfare worsening rather than welfare improving as is usually the case in conventional models rather than providing accurate point estimates of actual impacts. Importantly, they suggest that there are costs rather than benefits from trade liberalization in such cases, and they can be substantial.

To apply the model set out previously to the Russian case, we use constant elasticity of substitution (CES) demand functions and, in addition, specify the model so as to also include both a non-traded goods sector and two traded goods so that distortions between perishable and nonperishable imports can be analyzed. All model variants thus include four goods (an exportable, two importables, and a nontraded good).

We use the standard applied general equilibrium modeling approach of calibration to a base-case data set, followed by counterfactual equilibrium analysis (see Shoven and Whalley 1992). To make our calculations of the impacts of trade liberalization incorporating border delays, we have constructed a benchmark equilibrium data set for Russian trade, consumption, and endowments (taken to equal production) by averaging data for 1997, 1998, and 1999.[4] These are years during which there was substantial variation in Russian trade performance due to the 1998 financial crisis, and using averages in this way partially mitigates extremes in any one year's data. We use tariff data from World Bank sources for 1999,[5] which suggests an approximate average tariff rate across all imports of 10 percent. We assume an average border delay of three weeks in customs clearance (six weeks is the figure often claimed). This is the basis for an approximate estimate that with nondelay shipping times from Western Europe of three days and formal transportation cost in the range of 5 percent (see Hummels [1999] for a recent discussion of the size of transportation costs in trade), delay costs could be in the range of 30 percent of the value of imports. We use this estimate as the base-case value in our computations, making some modifications in the perishability case.

We use calibration methods and this data to determine both share and elasticity parameters in preferences. For the case of CES preferences, demands are given by

$$
(8) \qquad X_i = \frac{\alpha_i I}{(\pi_i^d)^\sigma \sum_{j=1}^{N} \alpha_j (\pi_j^d)^{1-\sigma}} \quad (i = 1 \ldots N),
$$

---

4. Data on trade and consumption are taken from the 2001 *World Development Indicators.* Data on production by industry (which we use to represent endowments) originates from Goskomstat sources, and we are thankful to Natalia Tourdyeva for providing it for us.

5. Data on tariff rates are taken from the 2001 *World Development Indicators,* published by the World Bank.

where α_i are CES shares, σ is the substitution elasticity, and income, I, is given by

$$(9) \qquad I = \sum_{i=1}^{N} \pi_i^d w_i - \sum_{i=1}^{M} T^q(\overline{\pi}_i^w)(\xi_i - w_i).$$

In this case, the import demand elasticity, η_i^m, for import good i is given by

$$(10) \qquad \eta_i^m = (-\sigma - S_i(1 - \sigma))\frac{X_i}{(X_i - W_i)} \quad (i = 1 \ldots N),$$

where S_i is the income expenditure share on good i.

These elasticities are not constant and so direct calibration is not possible. The convention in calibration literature is to use a literature estimate and choose σ so that the implied point estimate of the elasticity in the neighborhood of the benchmark equilibrium is literature consistent. If share parameters on imported goods are large, then negative values of σ can result from calibration if import demand elasticities in the neighborhood of one are used. This is common in general equilibrium trade models, as the majority of estimates in the literature are around one (see Erkel-Rousse and Mirza 2002). Not recognizing the significance of nontraded goods can result in this problem as expenditure shares on traded goods are smaller in models with nontraded goods than without them, and this is one reason for including them in the model.

Using GAMS (1996) solution software, we calibrate both the basic model and associated variants to the averaged 1997–1999 benchmark data set. We then evaluate the effects of tariff reform for each model variant by computing counterfactual equilibria that we also compare to the base case. We also use a model variant where no border delays are present, which we term the conventional case. In this event, gains from tariff liberalization occur.

We classify the trade data into importables and exportables based on the sign of net trade flows by commodity. We use equation (8) to calibrate model share parameters from data on consumption and prices, choosing units for goods in the model such that world prices are one. Equation (8) is used jointly in calibration with equation (9), which determines σ given shares, once import price elasticity values are assumed.[6] Our calibrations yield share and elasticity parameter estimates for the basic model variants for assumed values of import price elasticities lying between -1 and -2 (one is the most frequently used in empirical trade models) as set out in table 12.1.

Using models parameterized in this way, we have generated two sets of results that allow us to analyze the interactions between trade liberaliza-

---

6. We calibrate to the import price elasticity of the first import good, and, as share parameters on the two imports are similar, these two import price elasticities are very close.

Table 12.1   Calibrated basic model parameters from 1997–1999 Russian data

		Share parameters in preferences		
Assumed import price elasticity	σ generated by calibration	Imported goods	Exportables	Nontraded goods
–1.0	0.314	0.260 0.220	0.068	0.452
–1.5	0.676	0.276 0.234	0.064	0.426
–2.0	1.038	0.293 0.248	0.060	0.399

Table 12.2   Impacts of trade liberalization in Russia in the presence of border delays: Models calibrated to averaged 1997–1999 data

	Basic model with border delays	Extended model with corruption	Extended model with perishability
A. Import price elasticity = –1			
Welfare gain/loss as Hicksian EV as % of income	–0.130	–0.146	–0.134
Impacts on import volumes (% change)	0	0	–0.078 (perishable) 0.017 (nonperishable)
Impacts on export volumes (% change)	0.711	0.920	0.723
B. Import price elasticity = –1.5			
Welfare gain/loss as Hicksian EV as % of income	–0.248	–0.245	–0.253
Impacts on import volumes (% change)	0	0	–0.431 (perishable) 0.095 (nonperishable)
Impacts on export volumes (% change)	1.361	1.550	1.369
C. Import price elasticity = –2			
Welfare gain/loss as Hicksian EV as % of income	–0.343	–0.310	–0.347
Impacts on import volumes (% change)	0	0	–0.989 (perishable) 0.217 (nonperishable)
Impacts on export volumes (% change)	1.887	1.969	1.883

tion and border delays. In table 12.2, we show welfare and trade impacts of liberalization in the basic model with border delays and in two model extensions that incorporate corruption and perishability. These estimates are reported for the three values of assumed import price elasticities used in calibration in table 12.1.

Results in table 12.2 show negative welfare effects of trade liberalization measured in terms of the Hicksian equivalent variation as a percentage of income in all cases. These costs become larger as the assumed price elasticity rises as both substitution elasticities and share parameters change the evaluation of utility pre- and postliberalization changes. Larger impacts on queuing costs across these cases reflect the different share parameters generated by calibration. Costs are smaller in the with-corruption cases, for high elasticities and larger for smaller elasticities. The real resource costs from queuing in corruption cases are approximately one-half of those in no-corruption cases, and in that sense corruption is good in the model. But changes in queuing costs are comparable. Perishability raises costs slightly for all import price elasticity cases. Import volumes only change in the perishability cases. Here, because tariff reductions raise queuing costs and these increase proportionally more for perishable goods, imports of perishable goods fall and imports of nonperishable goods rise.

The second set of results in table 12.3 compares those from the basic model with border delays to those from a more conventional model with no border delays. To make this comparison, we use a case for a conventional tariff model where there are no queuing costs in the base case so that in this model relative price effects of tariff liberalization come into play as tariffs are eliminated and no queuing costs enter. In the comparable border delay model, the capacity constraint on imports remains. A tariff equal to the combined queuing plus tariff wedge in the base model is applied to the conventional model. We then consider a reduction in this tariff by 10 percentage points. In both of these cases, we use an import price elasticity of minus one in calibration. As table 12.3 indicates, the signs of welfare effects are reversed between models, and the absolute values of effects are different.

These simulation results thus clearly show how trade liberalization can be welfare worsening in the presence of border delays. Tariff reductions have little or no impact on domestic prices because of the capacity constraint on processing imports. More queuing results in added real resource costs, rather than generating revenues as is true with tariffs. The presence of corruption tends to weaken these effects as lowered tariffs now increase transfers to corrupt officials with smaller effects on aggregate incomes. Perishability considerations affect the costs of liberalization through more product loss, and added queuing results. And the differences relative to a conventional trade liberalization model are in sign.

This analysis and the simulations reported therefore point to the significant role that border delays can play in influencing the effects of trade liberalization. Without prior attention to administrative procedures and customs

Table 12.3	Comparing result of trade liberalization in Russia using a conventional model and one incorporating border delays, averaged 1997–1999 data	
	Conventional model (no border delays)	Basic model with border delays
Import price elasticity = −1		
Welfare gain/loss as Hicksian EV as % of income	0.044	−0.130
Impacts on import volumes (% change)	0.931	0
Impacts on export volumes (% change)	0.614	0.711

clearance, trade liberalization can become welfare worsening by increasing queuing costs. Trade liberalization in CIS states that does not first deal with administrative delays can thus be viewed as potentially counterproductive.

12.4   Directions for Future Work and Broader Policy Implications

While simple, it is worth emphasizing again that the preceding analysis can be potentially misleading if applied mechanically to trade policy reform where border delays operate and that our purpose is more to raise the issue of analytical process in the presence of border delays than to provide a precise forecast of impact.[7] In this concluding section we briefly indicate some of the difficulties with our simple treatment and, in the process, suggest possible directions for future work. Customs procedures, preshipment inspection, and other related issues have been part of World Trade Organizations (WTO) discussions for some time. Our analysis, in part, draws attention to some of the analytical issues with these issues by implicitly arguing that for trade liberalization in many countries around the world to be effective, it needs to be accompanied by administrative reforms.

There are several issues that our simple analytics raise, and more complex formulations can often lead to differing conclusions from the analysis. For instance, we treat $\bar{C}$ as a fixed physical constraint, but if there is instead a cost of processing function at the border, things can change. Liu's papers (1985, 1996), for instance, suggest that if the speed of processing at the border is under the control of customs officials, then more bribes may be able to be extracted than in our treatment of corruption. On the other hand, relaxing the rigid $\bar{C}$ constraint should also lower the costs of induced queuing. In some cases the outcome of trade liberalization may be ambiguous and likely depend on demand elasticities where speed is endogenous and bribes occur. When demands are inelastic, trade liberalization may increase processing costs due to longer delays by rent extracting officials, and vice versa when demands are elastic.

The evaluation of corruption as being welfare improving in this simple structure may also be misleading if induced corruption in the trade sector leads to spreading corruption elsewhere in the economy. Our simple analysis assumes only that bribes substitute for tariffs at no economic cost. If corruption is costly, liberalization need not be welfare worsening, and cases where imperfect substitutes are involved will also need to be considered.

The fixed production assumption in the model misses further issues. This assumption may lead to an underestimate of the welfare gains from tariff liberalization by ignoring production side effects and could equally overstate the gains from corruption. There are also no externalities from cor-

7. We are grateful to Francis Lui, Chong-Hyun Nam, and Andrew Rose for many of the observations and points in this section.

ruption present in the analysis and, hence, wider implications for the rule of law are not discussed.

At the end of the day, however, our analysis suggests that border delays and customs procedures (with associated links to processes of corruption) are perhaps more important for contemporary trade analysis than currently recognized and highlight the need to move beyond tariff-based discussions in numerical work on trade liberalization impacts. The specifics of such analyses will vary from case to case.

References

Abrego, L., R. Riezman, and J. Whalley. 2001. How reasonable are the assumptions used in theoretical models?: Computational evidence of the likelihood of trade pattern changes. NBER Working Paper no. 8169. Cambridge, MA: National Bureau of Economic Research, March.

Beilock, R. 2002. Will new roads help? Institutional barriers to international transport in eastern Europe and the CIS. University of Florida, Department of Food and Resource Economics. Mimeograph.

Erkel-Rousse, H., and D. Mirza. 2002. Import price elasticities: Reconciling the evidence. *Canadian Journal of Economics* 35 (2): 282–306.

Hare, P. G. 2001. Trade policy during the transition: Lessons from the 1990s. *The World Economy* 24 (4): 484.

Hummels, D. 1999. Have international trade costs declined? University of Chicago, Graduate School of Business. Mimeograph.

Lui, F. T. 1985. An equilibrium queuing model of bribery. *Journal of Political Economy* 93 (4): 760–81.

———. 1996. Three aspects of corruption. *Contemporary Economic Policy* 14 (3): 26–29.

Shoven, J. B., and J. Whalley. 1992. *Applying general equilibrium.* Cambridge, UK: Cambridge University Press.

Wolf, T., and E. Gurgen. 2000. Improving governance and fighting corruption in the Baltic and CIS countries: The role of the IMF. *Economic Issues* 26:1–17.

World Trade Organization (WTO). 1999. *Trade policy review: TOGO 1999.* Geneva, Switzerland: WTO.

Comment   Francis T. Lui

Cudmore and Whalley have constructed a model that reminds us of an interesting possibility in international trade. Trade liberalization, if not preceded by some institutional reforms, could result in welfare worsening. The

Francis T. Lui is a professor of economics and director of the Center for Economic Development at the Hong Kong University of Science and Technology.

institutional factor being studied here is the capacity constraint on the amount of goods that can be cleared at the customs at any period of time. Liberalization lowers prices and increases the quantity demanded for imported goods. Because of the capacity constraint, people will spend more real resources and waiting time for customs clearance. The loss in welfare can be partly mitigated if bribes, which are transfer payments, are used to shorten the waiting time for some people. If the goods have different degrees of perishability, a uniform reduction in tariffs could increase the costs of delays differentially.

The model constructed is that of general equilibrium. This has the advantage that the calibrated results for estimating the quantitative effects of various scenarios are more reliable. However, we can easily get the main theoretical results by simply using an extremely simple partial equilibrium model to tell the story.

In figure 12C.1, D represents the demand curve for the traded good and C^* is the capacity constraint at the customs. When the price is P_1, the real resource loss due to waiting, as is well known, is P_1ABF. If the price is P_2, real resource loss is P_2ABE. However, when corruption is possible, people can pay bribes to compete for the good rather than relying on waiting. The price mechanism is partially restored, and the real resource loss is obviously reduced.

The issue of perishability is similar to the question of differential time costs in the literature of queuing theory and bribery. When people waiting in line have different values of time, those who have higher values can pay greater bribes so that they can be served sooner. This again introduces an element of the pricing mechanism into the allocation process and improves

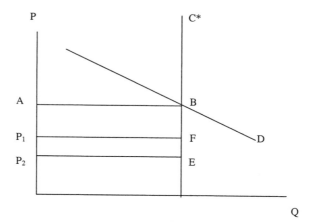

Fig. 12C.1   Partial equilibrium analysis of the Cudmore-Whalley model

welfare. Governments dealing with the problem that goods waiting at the customs are perishable can legalize bribery. This can be done by simply creating priority queues, where the waiting time depends on whether some fees have been paid. Trade liberalization of perishable goods should be accompanied by the introduction of priority queues.

The paper treats capacity constraint as exogenous. In the real world, this is often not the case. The quantity of goods that can be processed at the customs depends very much on how fast the officers want to work. A natural extension of the model is to ask how C^* responds to corruption and trade liberalization.

In Lui (1985), I show that corruption generally increases the speed of the service provided by the officers. Without corruption, they have little incentive to work hard. C^* is therefore small. The high waiting costs will discourage people from joining the queue. When officers can accept bribes, they want to attract more customers. This can be done by their working faster. C^* therefore increases. By doing so, officers can increase the total value of the bribes they can get.

The effect of trade liberalization on C^* is ambiguous. Assume that given any price level for a good, the capacity constraint C^* is always chosen in such a way that the officer can maximize the bribes he receives. The latter can be represented by the area of P_1ABF in the figure, when the price is P_1. Now let trade liberalization reduce the price to P_2. Will the optimal C^* increase or not? The answer generally depends on the elasticity of demand for the good. In the case of constant price elasticity, it can easily be shown that trade liberalization causes C^* to fall, provided that demand is inelastic. As a result, corrupt officers will slow down their service. However, when demand for the good is elastic, liberalization will lead to a higher value of C^* because the officers will work faster. Thus, introducing endogeneity to C^* can enrich the model's implications.

The welfare-improving property of corruption in this model is partly due to the static nature of the analysis. If corruption is possible, officers at the customs are in a position to receive bribe payments. This will induce rent-seeking activities through which people can compete for those officer positions. At equilibrium, the possible real resource saved by bribe transfers will be completely depleted by costly rent-seeking activities aimed at acquiring the officer positions. Thus, in the long run, there is no gain in welfare when corruption is allowed.

To summarize, the paper is stimulating. It can be extended in many ways.

Reference

Lui, Francis T. 1985. An equilibrium queuing model of bribery. *Journal of Political Economy* 93 (4): 760–81.

Comment   Chong-Hyun Nam

This is an excellent paper, one that greatly increases our understanding of the role of border delays and corruption in relation to trade liberalization. The message of the paper is very clear: any trade liberalization can become welfare worsening by increasing queuing costs. On the other hand, corruption can be welfare improving if queuing costs are replaced by income transferring bribes. The paper tries to prove these theses both by constructing a model and by applying the model to the Russian data.

I think the subject of the paper is very timely indeed, since a more broad issue of trade facilitation, which includes border delay problems, has become a hot topic for negotiation in recent years both at the Asia-Pacific Economic Cooperation (APEC) and at the World Trade Organization (WTO) levels.

Costs related to trade facilitation have long been thought an important factor that determines transaction costs in international trade, along with such traditional factors as tariff and nontariff barriers and transportation costs. Among these factors, however, tariff and nontariff barriers have been losing their significance as major impediments to trade through successive General Agreement on Tariffs and Trade/World Trade Organization (GATT/WTO) rounds, while transportation costs have also been decreasing over time due to technological innovations and increasing shipping capacities. As a result, the relative importance of trade facilitation or border delays has become much more conspicuous and, hence, deserves greater attention than before. This paper is focused on this issue.

I have three comments to make. The first one is about the capacity constraint on imports as given in equation (4) in the paper, which is presumably the main source of border delays. This capacity constraint may prove to be too strong an assumption, I suppose. This is because, with the capacity constraint, any import liberalization amounts to replacing import tariffs simply by some tariff-equivalent import quotas, leaving no change in import volumes. This capacity constraint assumption later on leads to empirical results that import liberalization has no impact at all on import volumes, as shown in table 12.2 in the paper. I have difficulty following the logic that import liberalization can increase queuing costs while it has no impact on import volumes.

I wonder, therefore, if there is a way either to relax the capacity constraint assumption or to replace the capacity constraint equation by some queuing costs equation that is expressed as a function of import volumes.

My second comment concerns the role of corruption. As expressed in equation (5) in the paper, a bribery variable enters into the equation where a bribe can successfully replace or substitute queuing costs with no eco-

Chong-Hyun Nam is a professor of economics at Korea University.

nomic costs as a bribe represents an income transfer from importers to officials. This leads to an automatic conclusion that corruption is welfare improving.

Well, I have some sympathy with this conclusion. Corruption can be quite effective sometimes in making officials work harder and for longer hours and thereby helps to expand the import capacity constraint or reduces queuing costs. We used to call such a bribe an express fee in Korea. Officials are collecting private taxes or getting paid for their extra services provided to the importers!

Corruption, however, can be welfare worsening, too. Above all, it is illegal and, hence, causes external diseconomies to the society. Even if there is no legality problem, it can entail social costs, as officials may sabotage their normal work duties in order to incite importers to bribe them. To put it differently, they may not like to move before they are getting bribed. In an extreme case, if there are markets developed for corruption and they are perfectly competitive, importers may end up wasting real resources for bribing as much as gains expected from the bribing, for example, by hiring expensive lobbyists or ex-government officials.

My final comment is about the assumption of fixed productions in the model, initially given as endowments so that they cannot change despite trade liberalization. This assumption, no doubt, would have contributed to an underestimation of welfare gains expected from trade liberalization, as shown in table 12.3 in the paper.

On balance, there are good reasons to believe that empirical results obtained in the paper represent a gross underestimation for potential welfare gains from trade liberalization and an overestimation for welfare gains expected from corruption. I am worried that such results may provide the wrong signals to Russian policymakers or the public that trade liberalization is only trivially important, whereas corruption is not all that bad. Do we need to send such a signal to Russia, which is already suffering from rampant corruption?

Contributors

Dukgeun Ahn
KDI School of Public Policy and
   Management
Chong-nyang-ri-dong, Dong-dae-mun-
   ku
Seoul 130-868, Korea

Mitsuyo Ando
Faculty of Economics
Hitotsubashi University
Naka 2-1, Kunitachi,
Tokyo 108-8601, Japan

Shin-Horng Chen
Chung-Hua Institution for Economic
   Research
75 Chang-Hsing Street
Taipei 106, Taiwan
Republic of China

Tain-Jy Chen
Chung-Hua Institution for Economic
   Research
75 Chang-Hsing Street
Taipei 106, Taiwan
Republic of China

Leonard K. Cheng
Department of Economics
School of Business and Management
Hong Kong University of Science and
   Technology
Clear Water Bay
Kowloon, Hong Kong

Ji Chou
Chung-Hua Institution for Economic
   Research
75 Chang-Hsing Street
Taipei 106, Taiwan
Republic of China

Edgar Cudmore
Department of Economics
The University of Western Ontario
London, Ontario, Canada N6A 5C2

Philippa Dee
Asia Pacific School of Economics and
   Government
Australian National University
Canberra Act 0200, Australia

Carolyn L. Evans
Board of Governors of the Federal
    Reserve System
20th Street and Constitution Avenue,
    NW
Washington, DC 20551

Kyoji Fukao
Institute of Economic Research
Hitotsubashi University
Naka 2-1, Kunitachi
Tokyo 186, Japan

Jyothi Gali
Australian Productivity Commission
Level 3 Nature Conservation House
Corner Emu Bank and Benjamin Way
Belconnen Act 2617, Australia

Chin Hee Hahn
Department of Industrial and
    Corporate Affairs
Korea Development Institute
207-41, Chongnyangri-Dong,
    Dongdaemun-Gu
Chongnyang, Seoul, Korea

James Harrigan
International Research Function
Federal Reserve Bank of New York
33 Liberty Street
New York, NY 10045

Keiko Ito
Faculty of Economics
Senshu University
2-1-1 Higashi-mita, Tama-ku
Kawasaki 214-8580, Japan

Takatoshi Ito
Graduate School of Economics
University of Tokyo
7-3-1 Hongo, Bunkyo-ku
Tokyo 113-0033, Japan

Fukunari Kimura
Faculty of Economics
Keio University
2-15-45 Mita, Minato-ku
Tokyo 108-8345, Japan

Kozo Kiyota
Faculty of Business Administration
Yokohama National University
79-4, Tokiwadai, Hodogaya-ku
Yokohama 240-8501, Japan

Ying-Hua Ku
Chung-Hua Institution for Economic
    Research
75 Chang-Hsing Street
Taipei 106, Taiwan
Republic of China

Bih Jane Liu
Department of Economics
National Taiwan University
21 Hsu-Chow Road
Taipei 100, Taiwan

Da-Nien Liu
Chung-Hua Institution for Economic
    Research
75 Chang-Hsing Street
Taipei 106, Taiwan
Republic of China

Meng-chun Liu
Chung-Hua Institution for Economic
    Research
75 Chang-Hsing Street
Taipei 106, Taiwan
Republic of China

Francis T. Lui
Center for Economic Development
Hong Kong University of Science and
    Technology
Clear Water Bay
Kowloon, Hong Kong

Zihui Ma
Department of Economics
Hong Kong University of Science and
    Technology
Clear Water Bay
Kowloon, Hong Kong

Erlinda Medalla
Philippine Institute for Development
  Studies
NEDA sa Makati Building
106 Amorsolo St., Legaspi Village
Makati, Philippines

Chong-Hyun Nam
Department of Economics
Korea University
1 Anam-Dong, Sungbuk-ku
Seoul 136-701, Korea

Thomas J. Prusa
Department of Economics
Rutgers University
New Jersey Hall
New Brunswick, NJ 08901-1248

Andrew K. Rose
Haas School of Business
  Administration
University of California
Berkeley, CA 94720-1900

Somkiat Tangkitvanich
Thailand Development Research
  Institute
565 Ramkhamaeng 39 (Thepleela 1)
Wangthonglang
Bangkok 10310, Thailand

Shujiro Urata
School of Social Sciences
Waseda University
1-6-1 Nishiwaseda
Shinjuku, Tokyo
169-8050, Japan

John Whalley
Department of Economics
University of Western Ontario
Social Science Centre
London, Ontario, Canada N6A 5C2

Author Index

Subject Index